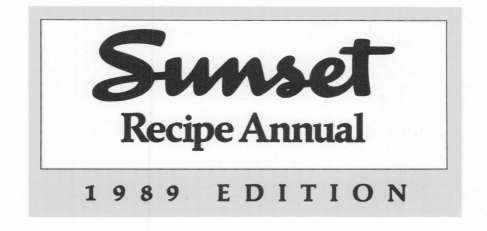

Sunset
Recipe Annual

1989 EDITION

Every Sunset Magazine recipe and
food article from 1988

By the Sunset Editors

Knife-and-Fork Tapas (page 142)

Lane Publishing Co. ■ Menlo Park, California

Our Tribute to 1988

Bob's Scrambled Eggs (page 297)

In this cook book, you'll discover—and rediscover—every food article and recipe that appeared in *Sunset Magazine* during 1988. If you've already enjoyed a taste of our first *Recipe Annual*, you know what culinary adventures await you in this sequel.

We're very proud of it. In 1988, as in other years, *Sunset Magazine* reported on a wide range of food subject matter—from new, simpler ice cream makers to yesterday's cast-iron Dutch ovens, and from exotic Burmese cuisine to easily carved holiday roasts. In these pages, you'll meet cooks who shared their favorite recipes with us, including a celebrated California chef and an immigrant from Russia. As always, there's plenty of sturdy everyday fare, too, as well as recipes for young cooks.

Of special note in 1988 was our report from China's kitchens, which presents marvelous home cooking that hasn't yet made its way to restaurants here. We invite you to partake of this unique cuisine, along with the many other superb recipes, menus, and ideas that you'll find in this book.

Cover: Refreshing tart-sweet berries combine with lemon and pistachios in Strawberry Lemon Crunch Cake (page 101). Design by Susan Bryant. Photography by Darrow M. Watt. Photo and food styling by Susan Massey-Weil.

Back cover: Sourdough treats include (from back left, clockwise) whole-grain bread, sesame loaf, double dill braid, oat-corn and blueberry-bran muffins, fennel biscuits, apricot bread, oat-wheat waffles, and chocolate-cherry cake. Recipes begin on page 112. Photography by Darrow M. Watt.

Sunset Magazine
    Editor: William R. Marken

Sunset Books
    Editor: Elizabeth L. Hogan

All material in this book originally appeared in the 1988 issues of *Sunset Magazine* and was created by the following editors, illustrators, and photographers:

Food and Entertaining Editor, Sunset Magazine
Jerry Anne Di Vecchio

Food Staff, Sunset Magazine
Linda Anusasananan
Sandra Bakko Cameron
Pamela J. Eimers
Paula Smith Freschet
Bernadette Hart
Elaine S. Johnson
Annabel Post
Betsy Ann Reynolds

Illustrations
David Broad (*Chefs of the West*)
Alice Harth (*Kitchen Cabinet*)

Photography
Glenn Christiansen
Peter Christiansen
Norman A. Plate
Darrow M. Watt
(*see page 320 for individual credits*)

This Annual was produced by Sunset Books.

Contributing Editors
Susan Warton
Helen Sweetland
Cornelia Fogle

Design
Williams & Ziller Design

Contents

A Letter from Sunset

Food and Entertaining Editor Jerry Anne Di Vecchio (second from right) and staff gather around photographer while shooting Nut Lace Cookies (page 284).

DEAR READER,

Welcome to *Sunset's* second *Recipe Annual*. As a sequel to last year's Annual, it gathers together every *Sunset Magazine* food story published in 1988.

A lavishly stocked cook book, this Annual also chronicles another year in *Sunset's* flavorful history. In May, we celebrated the 90th anniversary of our magazine. Named for the Southern Pacific's train, the *Sunset Limited*, the magazine was originally a promotional leaflet for the railroad. (In 1928, *Sunset* was purchased by Laurence W. Lane and has remained in the Lane family ever since.)

A glimpse through the year. From January to December of 1988, we published a banquet of features and recipes to enthrall and engage every appetite, interest, and cooking style.

As in every year, we combed not just the West but the whole world for good stories. In April, our 12-page report on China's home cooking takes readers inside a tiny Beijing kitchen, as well as to a country banquet in a five-generation-old farmhouse. Presented in our report are Mr. Zhu's Steamed Fish, the Xin Light Lunch, and other family specialties you won't find on Chinese restaurant menus.

Our editorial team spent 15 days in the People's Republic, the first reporters from any major American magazine to receive permission to visit private homes this extensively. The team traveled to Beijing, Shanghai, Guangzhou, and Chengdu, researching the four areas of China where regional cuisines have become the most famous in the West. From the more than 300 dishes that were sampled, the editors brought back their favorites for testing here to be sure of excellent results in Western kitchens. We're pleased to share this unique taste of today's China.

To celebrate *Sunset's* long involvement with the West, our May anniversary issue was full of regional specialties. Feast your eyes, along with your palate, on the blue potatoes, nopales, and other native foods displayed in our Chef's Salad of the Americas.

Another Western favorite, sourdough, was revisited that same month with a roundup of new research and recipes. To accompany your fresh, fragrant loaf, prepare garlicky garden escargots—the same issue tells how to cultivate and cook them. And while the *petits gris* graze in their box, you can relax nearby, quenching your thirst with a tall, fruity glass of *agua fresca*, from our August pages.

For those who prefer meat, potatoes, and pie, there was plenty of hearty fare in 1988, such as April's "Salute to Umatilla County" (Oregon). At your next family gathering, treat everyone to our fruit cobblers for a crowd; in June, there's an easy chart to follow. In September, we featured the robust results of a Dutch oven cookoff in Utah. October's pages tell how to build a better burger—the secret's in the relishes. And in November, peerless pioneer pies celebrate autumn's apple bounty.

Fish fanciers must try February's weeknight potluck soup supper. If you crave crab, read about "Leave well enough alone" dinner parties in March. Adventurous diners can savor hot or cold versions of borscht in the same month, November's pumpkin-filled ravioli, or December's easy-carve buffalo roast.

Along with the unexpected, *Sunset* occasionally treats readers to sprinklings of fantasy. Join us in a January toast of the new year with fizzy sparklers and bubblers. With the summer come Watermelon Whatevers: turn to July's pages to find out what these are. In December, we created a Christmas cooky masterpiece of Western nuts and caramel.

Other experiences not to miss from 1988 include cooking with rose petals, box picnics from your hotel or inn, Korean Olympic appetizers, sipping and tasting a wine-maker's lunch, the how's and why's of woodstove cooking, effortless ice cream, and festive buffets with Spanish tapas or Italian contorni.

A LOOK BEHIND THE SCENES

Visitors who tour *Sunset's* Menlo Park, California, headquarters often stop to observe as our food editors create, taste, evaluate, and revise recipes in the test kitchens.

Newly remodeled in 1988, the kitchens are actually a recipe laboratory, where testing and tasting continue until *Sunset's* high standards are achieved. Besides tasting wonderful, the dishes must be attractive, nutritious, and achievable with as few steps and in as little time as possible. Recipes don't reach publication until you can prepare them at home with standard equipment in a reasonable length of time (we make occasional exceptions if the reward is worthwhile). When ready, the food is photographed, as shown on the facing page, in our studio or on location.

NEW THIS YEAR—NUTRITIONAL ANALYSES

Traditionally fitness-conscious, Westerners today want to understand in detail the nutritional composition of foods they cook, eat, and serve to their families. Increasing numbers of *Sunset's* readers are now evaluating the quantities of sodium, fat, and sugar in their diets.

In 1988, we responded to these concerns by giving a nutritional analysis, based on current USDA data, for every recipe published (the same feature was introduced in *Sunset Books* several years earlier). The box at right further explains our nutritional data.

A YEAR TO KEEP RELIVING

We hope that you, your family, and friends will turn *Sunset's* 1988 collection of recipes into many memorable meals. Food articles are arranged by month, as they appeared originally in the magazine. For your convenience, at the back of the book, we've prepared three indexes: one for article titles, another for recipe titles, and the last for general subject matter. Enjoy the yearlong banquet!

Food and Entertaining Editor,
Sunset Magazine

TO USE OUR NUTRITION INFORMATION

Sunset recipes contain nutrition information based on the most current data available from the USDA for calorie count; grams of protein, carbohydrates, and total fat; and milligrams of cholesterol and sodium.

This analysis is usually given for a single serving, based on the largest number of servings listed for the recipe. Or it will be for a specific amount, such as per tablespoon (for sauces), or by a unit, as per cooky.

The nutrition analysis does not include optional ingredients or those for which no specific amount is stated (salt added to taste, for example). If an ingredient is listed with an alternative—such as unflavored yogurt or sour cream—the figures are calculated using the first choice. Likewise, if a range is given for the amount of an ingredient (such as ½ to 1 cup butter), values are figured on the first, lower amount.

Recipes using regular-strength chicken broth are based on the sodium content of salt-free homemade or canned broth. If you use canned salted chicken broth, the sodium content will be higher.

JANUARY

Fir Tree Bread (page 10)

Sparkling beverages offer
a festive welcome to the New Year in our January issue. Our
travels in Southeast Asia provide an intriguing sampling
of Nyonya cuisine, liberally spiced with tropical flavors.
To perk up midwinter menus, we suggest French-Canadian
meat pies, hot stir-fried salads featuring savoy, a trio of
quick-to-prepare fish entrées, a whimsical raisin-studded
yeast bread, and a new contender for the title of
"perfect chocolate chip cooky."

7

Sparklers & Bubblers: Festive Party Drinks

THE DELIGHTFUL TICKLE *of bubbles lends a festive air to these drinks for any age group, just right for New Year's Eve or other celebrations.*

The effervescing refreshments get their fizz from sparkling wine or carbonated water combined with fruit or vegetable juices; decorate each with its own edible ornament—fruit, onions, or preserved ginger.

This is a good place to use an inexpensive sparkling wine (sometimes called California champagne; usually $3 to $6 for 750 ml.). Choose the driest wines available; look for "brut"—less sweet than "dry."

Set out the makings for these drinks on a table. Have wine and water bottles on ice, glasses and ingredients ready. Guests mix their own drinks, following instruction cards that you place next to each setup or creating their own innovations.

BUBBLING MARY

- 2 cups cold tomato juice
- 1 teaspoon liquid hot pepper seasoning
- 2 tablespoons lime juice
- 24 pickled cocktail onions
- 1 medium-size lime, cut in 8 wedges
- 1 to 1½ bottles (750 ml. each) cold brut-style dry sparkling wine, or 3 to 4 small bottles (10 oz. each) cold sparkling mineral water

In a pitcher, mix together tomato juice, pepper seasoning, and lime juice; keep cold. On each of 8 thin wooden skewers, thread 3 onions; tuck loaded skewers into a tall glass. Put lime wedges in a dish.

To make each serving, place 1 onion swizzle stick in a champagne flute or wine glass (6- to 8-oz. size). Pour ¼ cup tomato juice mixture into each glass, then fill with sparkling wine or mineral water; squeeze and drop a lime wedge into glass and stir with swizzle. Makes 8 servings.

PER SERVING: 73 calories, .64 g protein, 5 g carbohydrates, .04 g fat, 0 mg cholesterol, 266 mg sodium

TROPICAL SPARKLERS

- 2 unpeeled, ⅓-inch-thick, round slices of pineapple; or 8 slices of lemon, lime, or tangerine
- 2 cups cold pineapple or tangerine juice, or lemonade or limeade
- 1 to 1½ bottles (750 ml. each) cold brut-style dry sparkling wine, or 3 to 4 small bottles (10 oz. each) cold sparkling mineral water

Cut each pineapple slice into 6 wedges; then cut a ½-inch slash in each piece. Arrange fruit in a small dish. Pour juice into a pitcher and keep cold.

For each serving, pour about ¼ cup juice into a champagne flute or wine glass (6- to 8-oz. size). Fill with sparkling wine or water. Set fruit on glass rim to match or complement juice. Makes 8 servings.

PER SERVING: 96 calories, .38 g protein, 10 g carbohydrates, .05 g fat, 0 mg cholesterol, 7 mg sodium

MULLED APPLE-GINGER SPARKLER

- 2 cups apple juice
- ½ cup preserved ginger in syrup, chopped (include syrup)
- 8 cinnamon sticks (2 to 3 in. long)
- 1½ to 2 bottles (750 ml. each) cold brut-style dry sparkling wine, or 4 to 5 small bottles (10 oz. each) cold sparkling mineral water

In a 1- to 2-quart pan, mix apple juice, ginger with syrup, and cinnamon. Bring to a boil over high heat. Boil, uncovered, stirring occasionally, until juice is reduced to 1 cup, about 30 minutes; watch closely and stir to prevent scorching. Remove from heat. Cool, cover, and chill until cold, at least 1 hour or until the next day. Pour into a small bowl; keep cold.

For each serving, spoon about 2 tablespoons apple-ginger syrup and 1 cinnamon stick into a champagne flute or wine glass (6- to 8-oz. size). Fill glass with cold sparkling wine or mineral water. Makes 8 servings.

PER SERVING: 179 calories, .19 g protein, 26 g carbohydrates, .09 g fat, 0 mg cholesterol, 21 mg sodium

SQUEEZE, DROP & FIZZ

- 1 medium-size orange or lemon; cut fruit in half, then in quarters (8 pieces total)
- 8 sugar cubes (½-in. size)
- 1½ to 2 bottles (750 ml. each) cold brut-style dry sparkling wine, or 4 to 5 small bottles (10 oz. each) cold sparkling mineral water

Put fruit pieces in a small dish. For each serving, put 1 sugar cube into a champagne flute or wine glass (6- to 8-oz. size). Squeeze juice from 1 citrus quarter over sugar cube, then drop fruit into the glass and fill with sparkling wine or mineral water. Take care not to overflow. Makes 8 servings.

PER SERVING: 97 calories, .36 g protein, 6 g carbohydrates, .05 g fat, 0 mg cholesterol, 6 mg sodium

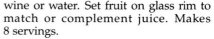

Four bubbly party drinks: inexpensive sparkling wine or mineral water tops off glasses of (left to right) spicy tomato juice with cocktail-onion swizzle, pineapple juice with fruit, apple-ginger syrup, and citrus juice with sugar cube.

Mixing his own frothy beverage, guest adds sparkling wine to glass with seasoned tomato juice. Pineapple juice (in pitcher) makes another spirited drink; decorate the glass with a fruit wedge.

Crusty Fir Tree Bread

WHIMSICALLY FORMED *to resemble a fir tree, this yeast bread is a shapely twist on Italian focaccia, which is baked in a thin, flat sheet. Like one popular version of focaccia, this dough is studded with raisins, drenched with olive oil, then sprinkled with salt and sugar, and baked. The result is a crisp, flavorful loaf you tear into chunks to eat.*

The bread is good hot or at room temperature; if you make it ahead, reheat to revive maximum flavor and texture.

FIR TREE BREAD

    1 **package active dry yeast**
    1 **cup warm water (110°)**
       About 6 tablespoons olive oil
    2 **tablespoons fresh rosemary**
       leaves, or 2 teaspoons dry
       rosemary leaves
    1 **teaspoon dry thyme leaves**
       About ¾ teaspoon salt
       About 2¾ cups all-purpose flour
    3 **tablespoons raisins**
    ½ **teaspoon sugar**
       About 5 fresh rosemary sprigs,
       each 4 to 6 inches long, optional
       Butter or margarine, optional

In a large bowl, mix yeast and water; let stand until yeast is softened, about 5 minutes. Stir in 3 tablespoons oil, rosemary leaves, thyme leaves, and ½ teaspoon salt. Add 2 cups flour.

To mix with a dough hook, stir until flour is moistened, then beat at high speed until dough is stretchy. Add about ¾ cup more flour, beating until dough begins to pull from bowl sides, about 4 minutes. Remove hook and cover bowl with plastic wrap.

To mix by hand or with an electric mixer, stir until flour is moist, then beat at high speed until dough is stretchy. Add ¾ cup more flour; stir with a heavy spoon until moistened. Scrape dough onto a lightly floured board and knead until smooth and elastic, about 5 minutes. Rinse, dry,

1 *Cut 5 slashes, each 2 inches long. To mold dough into tree shape, pull and twist at cuts; twists help tree retain form.*

2 *Poke raisins into puffy dough. Brush with olive oil, sprinkle with sugar and salt, then bake.*

and oil bowl; add dough and turn over so top is oiled. Cover with plastic wrap.

Let dough rise in a warm place until nearly double in volume, about 1 hour.

To expel air, knead with dough hook or on a lightly floured board. Shape dough into a ball and set in the middle of a greased 12- by 15-inch baking sheet. Pat dough out to make a 3- by 12-inch rectangle. With a razor blade or a sharp knife, cut 5 slashes, each about 2 inches long, in dough as shown in step 1 above. Pull cuts open, twisting dough strips several times, to create a triangular tree as wide and as tall as the baking sheet.

Cover lightly with plastic wrap and let rise in a warm place until puffy-looking, about 30 minutes.

With a finger, push raisins deep into the dough (step 2, above right). Brush dough generously with about half the remaining oil; it should pool into raisin-

filled depressions. Mix remaining salt with the sugar and sprinkle over the dough. Bake in a 375° oven until golden brown, about 30 minutes. Brush again with remaining oil; bake until richly browned, about 10 minutes longer. Using a spatula, gently slide bread from pan onto a platter to serve warm; garnish with rosemary sprigs. Or slip onto a rack to cool, then serve.

If made ahead, wrap cool bread airtight and freeze; thaw wrapped. To reheat, place unwrapped bread on baking sheet, loosely cover with foil, and bake in a 350° oven until warm, about 10 minutes.

Tear into chunks and eat plain or with butter. Makes 1 loaf, about 1 pound.

PER 2-OUNCE SERVING: 261 calories, 5 g protein, 36 g carbohydrates, 11 g fat, 0 mg cholesterol, 208 mg sodium

Tree-shaped loaf—flavored with olive oil and rosemary—has lots of good, crusty surface. Break off fragrant chunks to enjoy with soup.

Nyonya Cuisine—Both Chinese & Tropical

WHEN CHINESE TRADERS *ventured into Southeast Asia in the 15th century, many of them settled and married local women. The wives (or nyonya, as they were called in Malaysia and Indonesia) used native tropical seasonings to flavor ingredients familiar to Chinese palates. The result was a savory new cuisine called nyonya (or nonya), after the cooks.*

Here we introduce some classic nyonya dishes from Malaysia, Singapore, and Indonesia. The first menu is built on a hot-sour fish soup served buffet-style over noodles. Southeast Asian flavorings—tart tamarind, fragrant lemon grass, and astringent galangal—season the broth. Rice noodles are the Chinese contribution.

The second menu is a sampler. Here, you marinate and bake pork ribs in an aromatic paste of ground coriander, garlic, and ginger. Serve with stir-fried rice noodles—flavored with soy sauce, as a Chinese dish would be. The tropical influence is clearest in the soup and the vegetable mélange.

Look for the authentic ingredients—tamarind paste, dry galangal slices, fresh lemon grass, and dry rice noodles—in Asian markets; or use the alternatives.

LAKSA NOODLE BUFFET

**Fish Soup with
Rice Noodles & Condiments
Fresh Pineapple Spears
Iced Tea   Beer**

Boil noodles, coil and arrange on a platter, and prepare condiments up to several hours ahead. Cook the lean fish broth shortly before serving.

Set tart broth, noodles, and condiments on a table; guests assemble their own whole-meal soup in a large bowl.

FISH SOUP WITH RICE NOODLES & CONDIMENTS
(Laksa)

- 5 ounces (½ cup) unsalted tamarind paste (or ½ cup cider vinegar mixed with 1 tablespoon sugar)
- 1½ cups water (if using tamarind)
- 2 large onions, cut into small chunks
- 3 tablespoons salad oil
- 8 thin slices dry galangal (or fresh ginger), each slice about the size of a quarter

- 4 stalks fresh lemon grass, tough leaves trimmed off, stalks lightly crushed (or pared peel, yellow part only, from 4 small lemons)
- 8 cups regular-strength chicken broth
- 1 to 1½ teaspoons cayenne
- 4 pounds white-flesh fish fillets (such as rockfish), cut into 1-inch chunks, with bones removed
  Cooked rice noodles (recipe follows)
- 1 European cucumber, cut lengthwise into quarters, then thinly sliced crosswise
- 1 cup thinly sliced shallots
- 4 to 6 fresh red or green Fresno or jalapeño chilies (or 1 large red bell pepper), stemmed and seeded, cut into thin slivers
- 3 or 4 limes, cut into wedges
- ½ cup fresh mint leaves, cut into thin slivers

In a bowl, break tamarind into chunks; add water and let stand until pulp is soft, about 20 minutes. Rub paste off seeds.

Meanwhile, in a food processor or blender, whirl onions until puréed. In a 6- to 8-quart pan, combine oil, onions, galangal slices, and lemon grass. Cook, stirring, over medium heat, until onions are soft and no longer taste raw, about 10 minutes. Add broth and cayenne. Cover and bring to boiling over high heat.

Add fish, cover, and simmer until fish is opaque in thickest part, 3 to 5 minutes.

Pour tamarind liquid through a fine strainer into a bowl, pressing liquid from seeds and fibers. To broth, add liquid (or vinegar and sugar mixture) to taste. Remove from heat and ladle into a tureen.

Offer hot soup with noodles and condiments: cucumber, shallots, chilies, lime, and mint. To eat, place noodles in a bowl and pour soup over them; add a selection of condiments. Makes 8 servings.

PER SERVING: 553 calories, 49 g protein, 63 g carbohydrates, 11 g fat, 79 mg cholesterol, 202 mg sodium

Cooked rice noodles. In a 6- to 8-quart pan, bring 3 to 4 quarts water to boiling. Add 1 pound **dry rice noodles** (*mai fun* or rice sticks) or coiled dry vermicelli. Stir to loosen noodles and boil, uncovered, until noodles are barely tender to bite, 2 to 3 minutes for rice noodles or 4 to 5 minutes for vermicelli. Drain and place in a large bowl of cool water. When cool enough to handle, lift small handfuls of noodles out of water and loosely coil them; set on a platter. Cover and hold at room temperature up to 4 hours.

Up to a day ahead, marinate ribs and cut vegetables. The turmeric-seasoned vegetables can be prepared several hours in advance and served at room temperature. While the ribs bake, cook noodles and soup. If rice noodles are unavailable, serve plain hot rice instead. Offer dishes together. Serve chunks of fresh coconut for dessert.

SHRIMP & PINEAPPLE SOUP
(Lempah Udang Dan Nanas)

- 1 large onion, cut into 1-inch chunks
- ½ teaspoon ground turmeric
- ¾ to 1 teaspoon crushed dried hot red chilies
- 6 cups regular-strength chicken broth
- 2 stalks fresh lemon grass (or pared peel, yellow part only, from 2 small lemons)
- 4 cups fresh pineapple chunks, ¾-inch size (about half of a 3-lb. pineapple)
- 1 pound colossal shrimp (10 to 15 per lb.), shelled and deveined; leave shell on tails, if desired
- 6 to 8 tablespoons lemon juice
  Salt

In a blender or food processor, combine onion, turmeric, chilies, and ½ cup of the broth; whirl until smoothly puréed. Pour mixture into a 5- to 6-quart pan; add remaining 5½ cups broth. Trim off leafy parts of lemon grass; reserve for garnish or discard. Cut stalks into about 2-inch lengths and crush slightly. Add to broth. Bring to boiling. Reduce heat, cover, and simmer for 15 minutes. Add pineapple, cover, and simmer for 5 minutes. Add shrimp, cover, and simmer until opaque in thickest part (cut to test), 3 to 4 minutes. Add lemon juice and salt to taste. Pour into a tureen; garnish with lemon grass leaves, if desired. Makes 8 to 10 servings.

PER SERVING: 98 calories, 9 g protein, 11 g carbohydrates, 2 g fat, 56 mg cholesterol, 112 mg sodium

(Continued on next page)

Ladle tamarind-tart fish soup over coiled rice noodles; add condiments to season to taste. Choose from cucumber slices, hot chili slivers, shredded mint leaves, lime wedges, and sliced shallots.

STIR-FRIED RICE NOODLES
(Beehoon)

- 1 pound dry rice noodles (*mai fun* or rice sticks)
- ¼ cup salad oil
- 2 cloves garlic, pressed or minced
- ½ pound baby bok choy (or full-size bok choy, cut diagonally into 1½-in.-wide slices)
- 1 cup thinly sliced green onion
- ⅓ pound bean sprouts
- 3 to 4 tablespoons soy sauce
  Salt and pepper
  Fried shallots
  (recipe follows)
- 2 green onions, ends trimmed

In warm water to cover, soak rice noodles until soft, 20 to 30 minutes. Drain well.

Pour oil into a wok or 12- to 14-inch frying pan and place over high heat. Add garlic and bok choy; cook, stirring, for 1 minute. Add sliced green onion and bean sprouts; cook, stirring, for 1 minute. Reduce heat to medium. Add noodles, soy sauce, and salt and pepper to taste; cook, turning and gently stirring, until noodles are hot, 6 to 7 minutes. Pour onto platter. Sprinkle with 3 tablespoons fried shallots. Garnish with whole green onions. Makes 8 to 10 servings.

PER SERVING RICE NOODLES: 227 calories, 4 g protein, 44 g carbohydrates, 6 g fat, 0 mg cholesterol, 382 mg sodium

Fried shallots. Thinly slice ⅓ pound **shallots.** Pour about ¼ inch **salad oil** into a 10- to 12-inch frying pan over medium heat. When oil is hot, add shallots and cook, stirring, until crisp and golden, 6 to 8 minutes. Lift out with a slotted spoon; drain on paper towels. Makes about ⅓ cup.

PER TABLESPOON FRIED SHALLOTS: 46 calories, .74 g protein, 5 g carbohydrates, 3 g fat, 0 mg cholesterol, 4 mg sodium

TURMERIC SWEET-SOUR VEGETABLES
(Achar)

- 4 medium-size carrots, peeled and ends trimmed
- 1 small cauliflower (about 1 lb.)
- 1 small European cucumber, ends trimmed
- 1 large red bell pepper, stemmed and seeded
- 2 tablespoons salad oil
- 4 cloves garlic, minced
- 1 to 1½ teaspoons crushed dried hot red chilies
- 1 teaspoon ground turmeric
- ½ cup distilled white vinegar
- ½ cup water
- 3 tablespoons sugar
- 1 cup salted roasted peanuts, finely chopped
  Salt
  About 2 tablespoons fried shallots (recipe precedes)

Cut carrots into 2-inch lengths, then thinly slice to make ½- by 2-inch strips. Separate cauliflower into small flowerets (1-in. diameter). Cut cucumber into 2-inch lengths, then thinly slice lengthwise to make ½- by 2-inch strips; cut off and discard seeds. Cut red pepper into ¼- by 2-inch strips.

Pour oil into a 12- to 14-inch frying pan or wok and place over medium-low heat. Add garlic and chilies and cook, stirring, until garlic begins to turn golden. Add carrots and cauliflower; cook, stirring, for 3 minutes. Add cucumber, red pepper, and turmeric; cook, stirring, for 2 minutes. Add vinegar, water, and sugar and increase heat to high; cook, stirring, until liquid boils and vegetables are tender-crisp when pierced, 3 to 4 minutes. Stir in peanuts and salt to taste. Pour into a serving bowl. Sprinkle with shallots shortly before serving. Serve hot or at room temperature. Makes 8 to 10 servings.

PER SERVING: 157 calories, 5 g protein, 14 g carbohydrates, 11 g fat, 0 mg cholesterol, 77 mg sodium

CORIANDER SPARERIBS
(Tulang Babi Panggang Bumbu Ketumbar)

- 4 to 5 pounds pork spareribs
- ¼ cup sugar
- 3 tablespoons minced garlic
- 3 tablespoons lemon juice
- 2½ tablespoons ground coriander
- 1 teaspoon crushed dried hot chilies
- 1 teaspoon salt
- ⅓ cup water

Trim excess fat off ribs. Cut ribs apart between bones. In a 14- by 17-inch roasting pan, mix together sugar, garlic, lemon juice, coriander, chilies, salt, and water to make a paste. Add ribs, stirring gently to coat with seasoning paste. Cover and chill at least 4 hours or up to overnight.

Bake, covered, in a 400° oven until meat is almost tender when pierced, about 1 hour. Uncover and continue baking, stirring occasionally, until well browned, about 30 minutes. Lift out of pan. Serve hot. Makes 8 to 10 servings.

PER SERVING: 279 calories, 20 g protein, 6 g carbohydrates, 19 g fat, 96 mg cholesterol, 297 mg sodium

Nyonya sampler includes shrimp & pineapple soup, rice noodles, sweet-sour vegetables, and coriander spareribs.

Winter Salads with Savoy

FRILLY KALE LEAVES, *flushed with fuchsia or white, add welcome color to winter salads. Originally planted for its looks alone, ornamental kale is also sold as an edible green in many supermarkets. It's called salad savoy.*

The sturdy leaves hold up well in salads. Use the small tender leaves from the center raw, mixed with other greens, for a cool salad. Larger, tougher leaves are best wilted by a hot dressing, as in these salads. Brief heat softens the firm leaves slightly; overcooked, their color fades.

HOT APPLE & SAVOY SALAD

4 slices bacon, cut in ½-inch pieces
½ cup pecan or walnut halves
Salad oil
1 small onion, chopped
1 clove garlic, pressed or minced
1 tablespoon minced fresh ginger
2 teaspoons dry basil
1 large red or Golden Delicious apple, cored and thinly sliced
¼ cup wine vinegar
1 tablespoon sugar
About ¾ pound salad savoy, tough stems discarded and leaves washed, drained, and torn into bite-size pieces to make 2 quarts
Salt and pepper

Stir bacon in a 12-inch frying pan or 5- to 6-quart pan over medium-high heat until it is limp and begins to brown, 2 to 3 minutes. Add nuts and continue to cook, stirring, until bacon is crisp and nuts are lightly browned, 2 to 3 minutes more. With a slotted spoon, lift out bacon and nuts and place on paper towels to drain.

Add enough oil to pan to make ¼ cup. Add onion, garlic, ginger, and basil; cook, stirring, over medium heat until onion is limp, about 4 minutes. Add apple, vinegar, sugar, and salad savoy; cook, stirring, just until greens begin to wilt slightly, 1 to 2 minutes. Remove from heat and transfer to serving bowl. Sprinkle with nuts and bacon. Add salt and pepper to taste. Serve warm. Makes 4 servings.

PER SERVING: 316 calories, 5 g protein, 19 g carbohydrates, 26 g fat, 15 mg cholesterol, 181 mg sodium

SAVOY & SHRIMP SALAD

⅓ cup olive oil or salad oil
½ cup chopped shallots
2 tablespoons wine vinegar
1 tablespoon Dijon mustard
¾ pound salad savoy, tough stems discarded and leaves washed, drained, and torn into bite-size pieces to make 2 quarts
¼ pound tiny cooked shelled shrimp
1 cup cherry tomatoes, cut in halves
Salt and pepper

In a 12-inch frying pan or 5- to 6-quart pan, combine oil and shallots. Cook, stirring, over medium-high heat until shallots are limp, 2 to 3 minutes. Mix vinegar and mustard and add to pan. Add salad savoy and stir just until leaves begin to wilt, 1 to 2 minutes.

Remove from heat and add shrimp and tomatoes; mix. Pour into a large bowl. Add salt and pepper to taste. Serve warm. Makes 4 servings.

PER SERVING: 236 calories, 8 g protein, 10 g carbohydrates, 19 g fat, 55 mg cholesterol, 203 mg sodium

HOT CHICKEN & SAVOY SALAD

2 large oranges
2 tablespoons white wine vinegar
1 teaspoon minced fresh or crumbled dry rosemary
1 clove garlic, pressed or minced
¼ to ½ teaspoon crushed dried hot red chilies
⅓ cup salad oil
¼ cup thinly sliced green onion
¾ pound salad savoy, tough stems discarded and leaves washed, drained, and torn into bite-size pieces to make 2 quarts
1½ cups cooked chicken pieces, torn in shreds
Salt and pepper

Grate enough peel from oranges to make 1 teaspoon. Mix orange peel with vinegar, rosemary, garlic, and chilies; set aside. Cut peel and white membrane off oranges. Thinly slice oranges crosswise, then cut in half.

Showy kale is base for a handsome salad. Apples, seasoned with ginger, garlic, onion, and basil, dress the greens. Bacon and nuts garnish them.

In a 12-inch frying pan or 5- to 6-quart pan, combine oil and green onion. Cook, stirring, over medium-high heat until onion is limp, 2 to 3 minutes. Add vinegar mixture and salad savoy; cook, stirring, just until leaves begin to wilt slightly, 1 to 2 minutes.

Remove from heat. Place mixture in a large bowl. Arrange oranges and chicken pieces on greens; mix. Serve warm, adding salt and pepper to taste. Makes 4 servings.

PER SERVING: 336 calories, 18 g protein, 18 g carbohydrates, 23 g fat, 47 mg cholesterol, 68 mg sodium

French-Canadian Meat Pies

A FRENCH-CANADIAN *meat pie called tourtière has become traditional New Year's Day fare for family and friends of Cathleen Smith, of San Mateo, California.*

Mashed potatoes give moistness to a simple ground-meat filling enhanced by a light blend of herbs and spices. Another family favorite uses canned salmon and dill. Both pies make satisfying suppers.

TOURTIÈRE

1¼ **pounds ground lean boneless pork butt or shoulder**
1¼ **pounds ground veal**
1 **large onion, chopped**
1 **teaspoon *each* dry savory leaves and dry thyme leaves**
¼ **teaspoon *each* dry mustard and ground cinnamon**
⅛ **teaspoon ground cloves**
1 **tablespoon minced parsley**
1 **cup regular-strength beef broth**
2 **medium-size cooked russet potatoes (about ½ lb. each), peeled and mashed**
  Salt and pepper
  Tender pastry (recipe follows)

In a 12-inch frying pan or 5- to 6-quart pan over medium-high heat, combine pork, veal, and onion. Stir often until meat begins to brown and stick to bottom of pan, 18 to 20 minutes. Stir in savory, thyme, mustard, cinnamon, cloves, parsley, and broth. Reduce heat and simmer, uncovered, until most of liquid has evaporated, 15 to 20 minutes. Stir in mashed potatoes until blended thoroughly; season to taste with salt and pepper.

On a floured board, roll out 2 tender pastry pieces, each into an 11-inch round. Line each of 2 pie pans, 9-inch size, with a pastry round. Spoon meat mixture equally into pans. Roll out remaining 2 pastry pieces, each into a 10-inch round. Cover each pie with a round of pastry, then trim flush with pan rims and press edges with a fork to seal. Prick top in several places.

Bake and serve as directed, following. To store baked pies, wrap and freeze up to 1 month; thaw in the refrigerator, then reheat. Makes 2 pies; each serve 8.

PER SERVING: 413 calories, 18 g protein, 30 g carbohydrates, 24 g fat, 77 mg cholesterol, 155 mg sodium

Tender pastry. Stir together 4 cups **all-purpose flour**, ½ teaspoon **salt**, 2 teaspoons **sugar**. With your fingers, rub 1 cup **solid shortening** and ⅓ cup **butter**

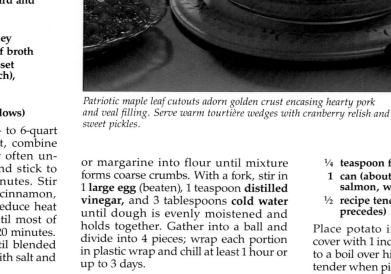

Patriotic maple leaf cutouts adorn golden crust encasing hearty pork and veal filling. Serve warm tourtière wedges with cranberry relish and sweet pickles.

or margarine into flour until mixture forms coarse crumbs. With a fork, stir in 1 **large egg** (beaten), 1 teaspoon **distilled vinegar,** and 3 tablespoons **cold water** until dough is evenly moistened and holds together. Gather into a ball and divide into 4 pieces; wrap each portion in plastic wrap and chill at least 1 hour or up to 3 days.

To bake pies. If desired, roll out remaining pastry scraps and cut into decorative shapes; lay on top of pies. Gently brush each pie top with 1 teaspoon milk. Bake on lowest rack of a 425° oven until tops are golden brown, 30 to 35 minutes. Serve hot. Or cool, then cover and chill until next day. To reheat pies, place in a 350° oven until hot in center, 25 to 35 minutes.

CANADIAN SALMON PIE

1 **medium-size russet potato (about ½ lb.), scrubbed**
2 **tablespoons butter or margarine**
1 **medium-size onion, chopped**
3 **tablespoons milk**
1½ **tablespoons minced fresh dill or ½ teaspoon dill weed**

¼ **teaspoon freshly ground pepper**
1 **can (about 15½ oz.) red or pink salmon, well drained**
½ **recipe tender pastry (recipe precedes)**

Place potato in a 1½- to 2-quart pan; cover with 1 inch water. Cover and bring to a boil over high heat; boil gently until tender when pierced, 20 minutes. Drain, let cool, peel, and coarsely shred.

In an 8- to 10-inch frying pan over medium-high heat, melt 2 tablespoons butter. Add onion and stir often until limp and golden, 7 to 8 minutes. Remove from heat; gently stir in potatoes, milk, dill, pepper, and salmon (keep chunks large).

On a lightly floured board, roll out half the pastry into an 11-inch round. Fit into a 9-inch pie pan. Fill with salmon mixture. Roll remaining dough into a 10-inch round. Cover pie with pastry, then trim flush with rim and press edge with tines of a fork to seal; prick top in several places. Bake and serve as directed, preceding. Makes 1 pie; serves 8.

PER SERVING: 389 calories, 14 g protein, 30 g carbohydrates, 24 g fat, 56 mg cholesterol, 386 mg sodium

Hurry-Up Dinners from Frozen Fish Fillets

AS INSURANCE *for evenings when time is short, a supply of lean, white fish fillets in the freezer can reassure the working cook. Used straight from the freezer, frozen fish can be quickly cooked to make low-calorie, high-protein entrées.*

Much fish sold frozen is now cleaned, filleted, and frozen right on the boat within a few hours of the catch, preserving its freshness. Frozen fish in our markets comes primarily from Alaska, the North Atlantic, and the Orient.

In stores, you'll see fillets frozen in blocks or individually (interleaved with sheets of plastic); packages weigh 10 to 24 ounces. Individual fillets often cost more per pound than blocks, but they can be separated without being thawed.

If you can see into the package, avoid fish with ice crystals and frozen or thawed liquid, indicating moisture lost from fish due to temperature fluctuations during handling. The fish should not have dark bruised spots, or a dry, cotton-like appearance. Frozen fish is usually lower priced and firmer textured than fresh fish.

Keep frozen fish cold on the way home, then place it in the freezer at once. Fish in prime condition can be stored, frozen, for one to three months. For best texture, cook it while it's still frozen.

White-flesh fish fillets most often sold frozen without added seasonings include sole, ocean perch, cod, haddock, halibut. They're interchangeable in these recipes.

BAKED RATATOUILLE & FISH

- 1 medium-size zucchini, sliced
- 1 small eggplant (¾ lb.), ends trimmed, cut into ½-inch chunks
- 1 *each* medium-size yellow and red bell peppers, stemmed, seeded, and cut into thin strips
- 1 tablespoon dry basil leaves
- 1 teaspoon dry oregano leaves
- 2 tablespoons olive oil
- 10 to 16 ounces individually frozen white-flesh fish fillets
- ¾ cup shredded havarti cheese, optional
  Salt and pepper

In a shallow 3-quart baking dish, combine zucchini, eggplant, bell peppers, basil, oregano, and olive oil. Cover and bake in a 425° oven for 40 minutes. Stir vegetables, then push to sides of dish; lay fish in center (in 2 layers, if needed). Cover, then bake until fish is opaque in center (cut to test), about 20 minutes. Sprinkle fish with cheese; bake, covered, just until cheese melts, 2 to 3 minutes. Add salt and pepper to taste. Serves 3 or 4.

PER SERVING: 141 calories, 12 g protein, 9 g carbohydrates, 7 g fat, 40 mg cholesterol, 56 mg sodium

LEAN FISH & PASTA CHOWDER

- 1 medium-size onion, sliced
- 1 large carrot, sliced
- ¼ cup minced parsley
- 1 teaspoon dry tarragon leaves
- ½ teaspoon ground pepper
- 2 tablespoons olive oil
- 2 bottles (8 oz. each) clam juice
- 1½ cups tomato juice
- ½ cup water
- ⅓ cup small seashell pasta
- 10 to 16 ounces frozen white-flesh fish fillets (frozen individually or as a block), thawed slightly and cut into 1-inch chunks

In a 4- to 5-quart pan over medium heat, cook onion, carrot, parsley, tarragon, and pepper in oil, stirring often, until onion is limp, about 10 minutes.

Stir in clam juice, tomato juice, water, and pasta. Bring to a boil over high heat, cover, and simmer for 5 minutes. Add fish and cook until it is opaque in center (cut to test), 3 to 5 minutes. Serves 4.

PER SERVING: 195 calories, 16 g protein, 18 g carbohydrates, 7 g fat, 50 mg cholesterol, 871 mg sodium

SIMMERED FISH & VEGETABLES WITH MUSTARD-HORSERADISH SAUCE

- 12 small thin-skinned potatoes (1½-in. diameter)
- ½ pound green beans, ends trimmed
- 1 bottle (8 oz.) clam juice
- 1 cup dry white wine
- 10 to 16 ounces individually frozen white-flesh fish fillets
- 1 tablespoon *each* cornstarch, water, and prepared horseradish, mixed
- ¼ cup coarsely ground Dijon mustard

Workday dinner of baked ratatouille and fish goes together quickly.

Place potatoes in a 2- to 3-quart pan with water to cover by 1 inch. Bring to a boil over high heat; cover and simmer for 10 minutes. Add beans and continue to simmer, covered, until both vegetables are tender when pierced, about 6 minutes.

Meanwhile, in a 10- to 12-inch frying pan over high heat, bring clam juice, wine, and fish to a simmer. Reduce heat, cover, and simmer until fish is opaque in center (cut to test), about 4 minutes.

Using a slotted spatula, transfer fish to a platter; keep warm. Boil fish liquid, uncovered, over high heat until reduced to 1 cup, 4 to 8 minutes. Whisk cornstarch mixture and mustard into liquid; stir until boiling. Pour into a bowl. Drain potatoes and beans; arrange alongside fish. Offer with sauce. Serves 3 or 4.

PER SERVING: 207 calories, 16 g protein, 35 g carbohydrates, .73 g fat, 45 mg cholesterol, 753 mg sodium

The Perfect Chocolate Chip Cooky

THE PERFECT COOKY *should have a slight crunch on the outside and be soft and very moist on the inside. It should be thick enough that you can feel your teeth sink into it. Its flavor should perfectly blend the sweetness of a buttery dough with the semisweetness of the chocolate. This is the standard Deryl Bear sets at his Hungry Bear Cookies stores in Corte Madera and Fresno, California.*

Before entering the professional cooky business, Mr. Bear experimented with batch after batch of cookies to find the secret to moist, chewy chocolate chip cookies.

His recipe proportions are much like those for traditional chocolate chip cookies, with a few exceptions. Brief baking at a high temperature forms a crust on the outside and maintains a chewy interior.

BEAR CHOCOLATE CHIP COOKIES

1 cup (8 oz.) cold unsalted butter, cut into chunks
1 cup firmly packed brown sugar
¾ cup granulated sugar
1 teaspoon salt, optional
2 large eggs
1½ teaspoons vanilla
2½ cups all-purpose flour
1¼ teaspoons baking soda
2 cups (8 oz.) walnuts, coarsely chopped
3 cups (18 oz.) semisweet chocolate baking chips

In a large bowl, beat butter, brown sugar, granulated sugar, and salt with an electric mixer until creamy and no butter flecks remain. Beat in eggs and vanilla until well blended. Add flour and baking soda; beat until well blended. With a spoon, stir in walnuts and chocolate chips.

With a small ice cream scoop or ¼-cup measure (fill cup about half-full), shape dough into 1½-inch-diameter balls (about 2½ tablespoons) and place close together on 10- by 15-inch baking pans. Cover and chill at least 6 hours or up to 4 days. (If time is short, you can omit chilling step, but cookies may not brown as rapidly.)

To bake, transfer cooky balls to 12- by 15-inch baking sheets, ungreased or lined with cooking parchment; space balls about 2½ inches apart. Flatten each ball to a ¾-inch-thick round; make sides go straight up and depress center of each cooky slightly. Let dough warm to room temperature, about 30 minutes.

Bake in a 400° oven until cookies are golden brown all around edges but center 1 inch is still pale, 8 to 10 minutes. (If you bake 2 pans in 1 oven, switch pan positions halfway through baking for more even browning.) Remove from oven and cool on pans until firm, about 5 minutes. Then transfer to racks. Serve cookies warm or cool.

If made more than 1 day ahead, cool, cover, and freeze in an airtight container. To reheat, place frozen cookies slightly apart on 12- by 15-inch baking sheets and bake in a 200° oven until warm, 12 to 15 minutes. Makes 3 to 3½ dozen. —*Deryl Bear, Fresno, Calif.*

PER COOKY: 233 calories, 3 g protein, 26 g carbohydrates, 14 g fat, 29 mg cholesterol, 36 mg sodium

Form cooky dough into 1½-inch-diameter balls and chill.

Flatten dough to ¾-inch thickness; make a slight depression in center.

Plump cookies fill cooky maker Deryl Bear's baking sheet. Inside a crisp shell is a soft interior that appears to have about equal parts of chocolate and cooky.

More January Recipes

OTHER JANUARY ARTICLES *suggest a savory snack based on pasta twists and Italian herb seasonings, a stylish way to prepare squab, and a tart for mushroom lovers.*

PASTA CRISPS

Fry curls of cooked pasta in oil, then flavor with Italian seasonings and cheese to make these addictive nibbles.

> 4 cups (10 oz.) dry pasta twists (multicolored or golden)
> Salad oil
> ½ cup grated parmesan cheese
> 1 teaspoon Italian herb mix (or ½ teaspoon crumbled dry basil leaves and ¼ teaspoon *each* crumbled dry oregano leaves and dry thyme leaves)
> ¼ teaspoon garlic powder
> Salt and cayenne

In a 5- to 6-quart pan, bring about 3 quarts water to boiling. Add pasta and boil, uncovered, until barely tender to bite, 6 to 8 minutes. Drain, rinse with cold water, drain well. Spread out in a single layer on a double thickness of paper towels; let stand until surface of pasta feels dry, 25 to 30 minutes. In a bowl, mix pasta with 2 tablespoons oil to coat.

Into a deep 3- to 4-quart pan, pour about 1 inch salad oil. Heat to 375° on a thermometer. Drop pasta, 1 piece at a time, into the oil (don't drop 1 piece on top of another or it will stick); add ½ to ¾ cup at a time. Cook, without stirring, until pasta is crisp and light gold, 3 to 5 minutes. Lift out with a slotted spoon and set on paper towels to drain. Repeat to cook the remaining pasta.

Place pasta in a large paper or plastic bag. Add cheese, Italian herbs, garlic powder, and salt and cayenne to taste. Shake well to coat pasta.

Serve or, if made ahead, let cool and store airtight up to 5 days. Makes 6 to 7 cups, about 12 to 14 snack servings.

PER ½ CUP: 174 calories, 4 g protein, 15 g carbohydrates, 11 g fat, 2 mg cholesterol, 55 mg sodium

SQUAB WITH LEMON SAUCE

Intensely flavored, dark-fleshed squab gains a refreshing contrast with this tangy lemon sauce. Marinated birds roasted quickly in a very hot oven acquire a rich color. When they are almost done, quickly cook the sauce to serve over them.

> 4 squab (12 to 16 oz. each)
> ¼ cup soy sauce
> ¼ cup dry sherry
> 2 tablespoons Oriental sesame oil or salad oil
> 2 teaspoons honey
> 1 teaspoon Chinese five spice (or ¼ teaspoon *each* ground cinnamon, ground cloves, ground ginger, and crushed anise seed)
> Lemon sauce (recipe follows)

Remove giblets and necks; reserve for other uses. With poultry shears or knife, cut along squab backbone to split open. Pull birds open, cracking bones slightly, so they will lie flat. Rinse birds, pat dry, and place in a large plastic bag set in a large bowl. Mix soy, sherry, oil, honey, and five spice. Pour mixture over squab. Cover and chill at least 1 hour or until the next day, turning birds occasionally.

Lay squab, skin side up, on a rack in a 12- by 15-inch broiler pan; reserve marinade. Bake, uncovered, in a 500° oven, brushing several times with reserved marinade, until the birds are browned and breast meat is pink at bone at wing joint (cut to test), about 20 minutes.

Transfer to 4 dinner plates and spoon lemon sauce over birds. Makes 4 servings.

PER SERVING: 1,056 calories, 58 g protein, 20 g carbohydrates, 81 g fat, 170 mg cholesterol, 1,109 mg sodium

Lemon sauce. Cut half of 1 large, thin-skinned **lemon** into thin slices; discard any seeds and end pieces. Ream remaining lemon half and another lemon to make ¼ cup juice.

Into an 8- to 10-inch frying pan over high heat, pour 1 teaspoon **salad oil.** Add 4 **fresh ginger** slices (each the size of a quarter) and stir-fry for 30 seconds. Add lemon slices, 1 cup **regular-strength chicken broth,** 3 tablespoons **sugar,** and the ¼ cup lemon juice. Bring to a boil, reduce heat, and simmer, uncovered, for 2 minutes.

Blend 1 tablespoon **cornstarch** with 2 tablespoons **water.** Pour into sauce and stir until sauce boils and thickens. Add ½ to 1 teaspoon **soy sauce** to taste. Discard ginger slices. Use sauce hot.

MUSHROOM TRIO TART

Three kinds of mushrooms, bound by a sherry-flavored custard, fill this luncheon or first-course tart. Offer with a salad.

> Pastry-lined 9- to 10-inch pie pan
> 1 cup (about 1 oz.) dry shiitake mushrooms
> Water
> ¼ cup (⅛ lb.) butter or margarine
> 4 cups (about ⅔ lb.) thinly sliced button mushrooms
> 1 small onion, chopped
> 1 package (3½ oz.) enoki mushrooms
> 1 large egg
> ½ cup half-and-half (light cream)
> ⅓ cup grated parmesan cheese
> 3 tablespoons dry sherry

Bake pastry in a 350° oven until light golden, 12 to 15 minutes. Set aside.

In a bowl, cover shiitake mushrooms with hot water; let stand until soft, 10 to 15 minutes. Lift from water; squeeze dry. Cut off and discard tough stems; slice caps into thin strips.

Melt butter in a 10- to 12-inch frying pan over medium heat. Add shiitake mushrooms, button mushrooms, and onion; stir often until liquid evaporates and mushrooms brown, about 20 minutes. Set aside about 10 of the best-looking button mushroom slices; spoon remainder into pastry. Cut coarse ends from enoki mushrooms. Arrange enoki in clusters, caps toward pastry rim, on sautéed mushrooms.

In a bowl, beat together egg, half-and-half, parmesan, and sherry; pour over mushrooms. Arrange reserved mushroom slices in center of enoki. Bake in a 350° oven until filling is set when gently shaken, about 20 minutes. Serve hot or at room temperature. Serves 6.

PER SERVING: 314 calories, 7 g protein, 22 g carbohydrates, 23 g fat, 77 mg cholesterol, 367 mg sodium

Sunset's Kitchen Cabinet®

Favorite recipes from our readers.

Slightly sweet, currant-flecked scones taste great for breakfast or a snack.

SWEET MARJORAM SCONES

About 1½ cups all-purpose flour
½ cup whole-wheat flour
½ teaspoon salt
½ teaspoon baking soda
1 teaspoon dry marjoram leaves
2 teaspoons baking powder
2 tablespoons sugar
¼ cup (⅛ lb.) butter or margarine, cut in chunks
½ cup currants
¾ cup buttermilk

In a food processor or large bowl, mix 1½ cups all-purpose flour, whole-wheat flour, salt, baking soda, marjoram, baking powder, and sugar until combined. Add butter; whirl or rub with your fingers until coarse crumbs form. Add currants; whirl or stir just until evenly distributed. Add buttermilk and whirl or stir just until evenly moistened.

Turn dough out onto a board lightly coated with all-purpose flour and knead 12 turns. On a greased 12- by 15-inch baking sheet, pat dough evenly into a round about 6½ inches in diameter. With a knife, score dough to mark 8 equal wedges.

Bake in a 425° oven until well browned, 25 to 30 minutes. Serves 4 to 8.—*Janet Moore, Beulah, Colo.*

PER SERVING: 209 calories, 5 g protein, 34 g carbohydrates, 6 g fat, 16 mg cholesterol, 379 mg sodium

---

Top bean chili in baked pancake with chilies, cheese, onions, salsa, avocado.

CHILI DUTCH BABY

⅓ cup butter or margarine
5 large eggs
½ cup yellow cornmeal
¾ cup all-purpose flour
1¼ cups milk
4⅔ cups thick homemade or purchased (40-oz. can) chili with beans
1 cup (4 oz.) shredded jack cheese
4 green onions, ends trimmed, sliced
1 can (4 oz.) diced green chilies
1 medium-size firm-ripe avocado, peeled, pitted, and sliced
Purchased green salsa

Place butter in a 10- to 12-inch cast-iron or other ovenproof frying pan. Heat in a 425° oven until butter melts, about 5 minutes. Remove from oven. Meanwhile, in a large bowl, whisk eggs, cornmeal, flour, and milk until smooth. Pour batter into hot pan. Spoon chili into center of batter, leaving a 1½-inch margin around chili.

Bake until pancake is well browned, about 30 minutes. Skim and discard fat from top of chili.

Cut pancake in wedges; offer cheese, green onions, chilies, avocado, and salsa to add to taste. Serves 6.—*J.L. Karsten, Kenai, Alaska.*

PER SERVING: 628 calories, 26 g protein, 51 g carbohydrates, 38 g fat, 311 mg cholesterol, 1,393 mg sodium

---

Oysters, crisp bacon pieces, and cheese fill toasted rolls; serve with watercress.

OPEN-FACE OYSTER SANDWICHES

4 small French rolls, each about 3 inches long
8 slices bacon
1 jar (10 oz.) small Pacific oysters, drained
8 thin slices cheddar cheese, about 3 ounces total
Watercress sprigs

Split each roll lengthwise and scoop out center, leaving ¾-inch rim; save centers for other uses. Place rolls on a 12- by 15-inch baking sheet and bake in a 375° oven until golden, 10 to 15 minutes; set aside on baking sheet.

In a 10- to 12-inch frying pan over medium-high heat, cook bacon (in 2 batches if needed), turning, until crisp. Lift from pan, drain on paper towels, and crumble. Discard all but 2 tablespoons fat from pan.

Cut oysters in 1-inch pieces; add to pan. Cook over medium heat until edges curl, about 2 minutes; stir often. Place an equal portion of oysters in each half-roll; sprinkle oysters with pan juices. Top each with a cheese slice, then sprinkle each with an equal amount of bacon. Bake in a 375° oven until cheese melts, about 5 minutes. Offer with watercress. Serves 4.—*Nancy Reed, Bremerton, Wash.*

PER SERVING: 377 calories, 18 g protein, 27 g carbohydrates, 21 g fat, 78 mg cholesterol, 692 mg sodium

PORK CHOPS WITH WALNUTS & WINE

- 4 **pork rib chops, each about ½ pound**
- 2 **tablespoons butter or margarine**
- ¾ **cup walnut halves or pieces**
- 1 **large onion, sliced**
- 1 **large clove garlic, minced**
- ⅓ **cup dry red wine or regular-strength beef broth**
- ½ **cup minced parsley**
    Salt and pepper

In a 10- to 12-inch frying pan over medium-high heat, brown chops in 1 tablespoon butter. Place chops in a 9- by 13-inch baking dish.

Add nuts and remaining butter to pan. Stir until nuts are golden, about 2 minutes. Lift out nuts; set aside. Add onion and garlic to pan. Cook until onion is limp, about 10 minutes; stir often. Add wine. Spoon mixture over pork; cover. Bake in 350° oven until meat is no longer pink in center at bone (cut to test), about 35 minutes.

Remove chops; keep warm. Pour onion and juices into frying pan with parsley. Boil over high heat until most of the liquid evaporates, about 4 minutes. Stir in nuts. Spoon sauce over chops. Add salt and pepper to taste. Makes 4 servings. —*Deborah Morgan, Albuquerque.*

PER SERVING: 674 calories, 33 g protein, 8 g carbohydrates, 57 g fat, 123 mg cholesterol, 129 mg sodium

Succulent pork chops bake with onions and red wine; toasted walnuts add crunch.

SICILIAN MUSHROOM SALAD

- 1 **large head butter lettuce, about 7 ounces**
- ⅓ **cup *each* olive oil and white wine vinegar**
- ¼ **cup drained capers**
- ⅔ **cup minced parsley**
- 2 **cloves garlic, minced**
- ⅓ **cup raisins**
- 1 **pound mushrooms, thinly sliced**
- 1 **large carrot, shredded lengthwise into long strips**
- ¼ **cup pine nuts**

Rinse lettuce, pat dry, wrap in paper towels; enclose in plastic bag. Chill at least 30 minutes or until next day.

In a bowl, mix oil, vinegar, capers, parsley, garlic, raisins, mushrooms, and carrot until coated. Cover and chill at least 30 minutes or up to 2 hours.

Meanwhile, place nuts in an 8- or 9-inch-wide pan. Bake in a 375° oven until golden, 5 to 7 minutes. Let cool. Arrange equal portions of butter lettuce on 6 salad plates. Top each serving with mushroom mixture, then sprinkle with equal portions of pine nuts. Makes 6 servings. —*Roxanne Chan, Albany, Calif.*

PER SERVING: 196 calories, 4 g protein, 14 g carbohydrates, 15 g fat, 0 mg cholesterol, 161 mg sodium

Slice mushrooms, shred carrot, marinate; then serve over butter lettuce leaves.

CITRUS CREAM & MERINGUE PIE

- 3 **large eggs, separated**
- 2 **teaspoons grated orange peel**
- ¼ **cup orange juice**
- ⅓ **cup lemon juice**
- ½ **cup all-purpose flour**
- 1¼ **cups sugar**
- 1¼ **cups milk**
- 1 **cup whipping cream, stiffly beaten**
    Oat crust (recipe follows)

In a small bowl, mix egg yolks, orange peel, and orange and lemon juices; set aside. In a 2- to 3-quart pan, mix flour and ¾ cup sugar; whisk in milk. Stir over medium heat until boiling. Whisk in yolk mixture; stir until bubbling. Cool; fold in cream. Pour into oat crust.

In a large bowl, beat egg whites until frothy. Beating on high speed, slowly add remaining sugar just until stiff peaks hold. Swirl over filling to pan edge. Bake in a 375° oven until golden, 8 to 10 minutes. Serves 8. —*Linda Williams, Irvine, Calif.*

PER SERVING: 539 calories, 8 g protein, 72 g carbohydrates, 25 g fat, 172 mg cholesterol, 179 mg sodium

Oat crust. In a 9-inch pie pan, evenly mix 1¼ cups **rolled oats,** ½ cup *each* firmly packed **brown sugar** and **butter** or margarine, and ¾ cup **all-purpose flour.** Press in pan. Bake in a 350° oven until golden, about 15 minutes. Let cool.

Waves of meringue cover lemon-and-orange cream filling in sweet oat crust.

EGGNOG IS THE PROGENY *of possets and syllabubs, those old-fashioned pick-me-ups that figure so prominently in antique novels in which spiritual heroines go into early declines.*

Those drinks, made with milk, sugar, spices, and wine, were probably first concocted as food for invalids, since they were stimulating, easily digestible, and had the added virtue of sweetness—a plus for languishing appetites. It was inevitable that they should become party beverages, deserting the pages of pharmacopoeia for the Bartender's Guide.

Traditional eggnog contains some spirit—usually brandy or rum—which, along with the eggs, cream, sugar, and milk, is supposed to ward off winter's chill.

But eggnog can be cooling, too—when converted into an ice cream. It would be hard to better Mick Hulbert's formula, made simple with store-bought nog.

For an off-season eggnog supply, you can freeze it in its cartons up to nine months. Thaw in the refrigerator and shake well before using.

M'S EGGNOG ICE CREAM

    2 cups whipping cream
    2 cups purchased eggnog
    ¾ cup sugar
    3 tablespoons light rum
    1 tablespoon vanilla
    1 teaspoon ground nutmeg

In a large bowl, stir together whipping cream, eggnog, sugar, rum, vanilla, and nutmeg.

Pour into an ice cream freezer container (use a 2-qt. size, or freeze in batches; if using an ice-and-salt maker, use 1 part salt to 8 parts ice). Freeze as manufacturer directs until dasher will no longer turn.

Serve ice cream softly frozen; for firmer consistency, repack with 1 part salt and 2 parts ice, or place container in the freezer until ice cream is firm, about 2 hours. To store, package airtight and freeze up to 1 month. Makes about 1½ quarts.

PER ½ CUP: 234 calories, 2 g protein, 20 g carbohydrates, 16 g fat, 69 mg cholesterol, 37 mg sodium

Mick Hulbert

Olympia, Wash.

IF YOU SEEK *a hearty side dish to accompany a ham steak or a grill of mixed sausages, look no further: Lamar Parker's Sweet Potatoes in Glazed Apples will do the job. What's more, any leftovers can be eaten warmed up for a toothsome midnight snack—a healthy alternative to pie.*

SWEET POTATOES IN GLAZED APPLES

    2 cups mashed cooked sweet
       potatoes (about 3 medium-size,
       1¾ lb. total)
       About 6 tablespoons melted butter
       or margarine
    ¼ teaspoon ground cinnamon
    ⅛ teaspoon ground nutmeg
       Salt
    8 large Granny Smith apples
       (about 4 lb. total)
    ¼ cup sugar
       Hot water
    ½ cup chopped pecans

Beat sweet potatoes with 2 tablespoons of the butter; stir in cinnamon and nutmeg. Season to taste with salt.

Cut out each apple core, leaving a cavity big enough to hold about ¼ cup of the potato mixture. Evenly stuff apples

"Eggnog figures prominently in antique novels in which spiritual heroines go into early declines."

with potato and arrange them in a 9- by 13-inch baking dish. Top evenly with the remaining butter and the sugar. Bake, uncovered, in a 325° oven, basting occasionally with juices. Cook until apples are tender when pierced, 50 to 60 minutes.

Serve warm or at room temperature. Stir 2 to 3 tablespoons hot water into pan juices to thin to desired consistency, then drizzle over apples and sprinkle with nuts. Makes 8 servings.

PER SERVING: 312 calories, 2 g protein, 49 g carbohydrates, 14 g fat, 23 mg cholesterol, 93 mg sodium

Lamar L. Parker

Tempe, Ariz.

MOST TERIYAKI CHICKEN *is grilled after marinating in a blend of soy sauce, sherry, and spices. William Haneline's Chula Vista Teriyaki Chicken simmers in its sauce of white wine and soy. Onion and red bell pepper lend additional flavor and texture, while chilies and garlic bring a touch of Szechwan.*

Two surprises top off the dish: raisins and cilantro. All these ingredients may seem incongruous in combination, but they blend into a sauce of deep, rather mysterious flavor.

CHULA VISTA TERIYAKI CHICKEN

- 1 tablespoon butter or margarine
- 1 tablespoon olive oil or salad oil
- 8 large chicken thighs (about 3 lb. total), skinned
- 1 medium-size onion, chopped
- 1 medium-size red bell pepper, stemmed, seeded, and chopped
- 2 cloves garlic, minced or pressed
- 2 small dried hot red chilies
- ¾ cup dry white wine
- ¼ cup soy sauce
- ½ cup raisins
  Fresh cilantro (coriander) sprigs

Melt butter with oil in a 10- to 12-inch frying pan over medium heat. Add chicken and brown on all sides (takes about 8 minutes); set chicken aside. Add to pan onion, bell pepper, and garlic; stir often until onion is limp, about 10 minutes. Push vegetables to the sides of the pan and lay chicken in center. Add chilies, wine, and soy; stir to blend.

Bring to a boil over high heat; cover, reduce heat, and simmer until meat is no longer pink at bone (cut to test), about 20 minutes.

With a slotted spoon, lift chicken and vegetables onto a platter and keep warm. Skim fat from pan juices and discard; stir in raisins. Bring to a boil over high heat; continue boiling until sauce is reduced to about ½ cup. Remove and discard chilies, if desired. Pour sauce over chicken and garnish with cilantro. Makes 4 servings.

PER SERVING: 368 calories, 40 g protein, 20 g carbohydrates, 14 g fat, 169 mg cholesterol, 1,231 mg sodium

Bill Haneline

Chula Vista, Calif.

JAMES ADAMS SENDS *this recipe from Lafayette, California, and not, as the ingredients suggest, from that other Lafayette—the one in Louisiana near Breaux Bridge, a shrine of Cajun cooking and home of a notable crayfish festival. Étouffée is an honored name in that part of the world. Derived from the French word for smothered, the name refers to a stew cooked (originally) in a covered pot.*

As with many Cajun dishes, you start with a roux of butter and flour and end by flirting with some hot seasoning.

"End by flirting with some hot pepper seasoning."

SHRIMP ÉTOUFFÉE

- ½ cup (¼ lb.) butter or margarine
- ¼ cup all-purpose flour
- 1 cup thinly sliced green onion
- 1 cup chopped yellow or white onion
- ½ cup chopped green bell pepper
- ½ cup chopped celery
- 2 cloves garlic, minced or pressed
- 1 bay leaf
- ¼ teaspoon dry thyme leaves
- ½ teaspoon dry basil leaves
- 1 can (8 oz.) tomato sauce
- 1 cup dry white wine
- 1 bottle (8 oz.) clam juice
- ½ cup water
- 1 tablespoon Worcestershire
- ½ teaspoon white pepper
- ¼ to ¾ teaspoon liquid hot pepper seasoning
- 1 tablespoon *each* grated lemon peel and lemon juice
- ¼ cup chopped parsley
- 1½ pounds tiny cooked shelled shrimp
- 4 to 6 cups hot cooked rice

Melt butter in a 4- to 5-quart pan over medium heat; stir in flour and cook until bubbly. Stir in green onion, chopped onion, green bell pepper, celery, garlic, bay leaf, thyme, and basil. Reduce heat to low and cook, uncovered, stirring often until vegetables are soft, 20 to 30 minutes.

Add the tomato sauce, wine, clam juice, water, Worcestershire, white pepper, and hot pepper seasoning to taste. Stirring, bring to a boil over high heat. Turn down heat and simmer, uncovered, stirring occasionally, until thickened and reduced to 4½ to 4¾ cups, about 45 minutes.

Stir in lemon peel, lemon juice, parsley, and shrimp. Simmer until shrimp are heated through. Serve with hot cooked rice. Makes 5 or 6 servings.

PER SERVING: 461 calories, 30 g protein, 46 g carbohydrates, 17 g fat, 266 mg cholesterol, 852 mg sodium

Lafayette, Calif.

January Menus

FOR OVERNIGHT GUESTS *who may join your family following festivities on New Year's Eve, we provide you with an expandable breakfast menu that requires little preparation and that can wait for people to rise and help themselves.*

Lunch and dinner menus feature Southwest elements. Laced with pine nuts and sausage drippings, a hot cabbage salad goes with a tortilla-wrapped sausage. For dinner, offer corn fritters to accompany roasted chicken and jalapeño jelly sauce.

NEW YEAR'S DAY BREAD & BUTTER BREAKFAST BUFFET

Spiced Apple Honey   Apricot Jam
Orange Marmalade Butter
Honeyed Peanut Butter
Assorted Breads   Gouda Cheese
Hard-cooked Eggs in the Shell
Tangerines & Bananas
Steaming Milk with Maple Syrup
Coffee

Since there's little to assemble and the menu easily expands for a larger group, a bread and butter buffet is a simple meal to provide for New Year's overnighters.

You choose from a variety of spreads, breads, cheese, and eggs. There's steaming maple syrup-flavored milk for the children, hot coffee for adults. If you like, instead of cream and sugar, add the sweetened milk to your coffee.

Since the spreads keep several weeks in the refrigerator, you can prepare them far in advance.

A day ahead, buy the breads, or have a supply in the freezer, ready to reheat. Choose from braided egg bread, croissants, brioche, panettone, English muffins, and dark rye, whole-wheat, or raisin bread; allow 2 or 3 pieces per person. You can also cook the eggs, 1 or 2 per person. For each serving, also buy 1 piece of fruit and about 2 ounces of cheese.

In the morning, brew the coffee and heat the milk, then keep both warm on a warming tray. Set foods on the buffet, with a toaster oven at hand so people can heat the bread, if desired.

Breakfast buffet of breads and spreads awaits late-morning risers. To round out the menu, add hard-cooked eggs and cheese.

SPICED APPLE HONEY

  1 **cup whipped honey**
  2 **tablespoons spiced apple butter**
 ½ **teaspoon ground nutmeg**
 ½ **teaspoon ground cinnamon**

In a bowl, mix honey, apple butter, nutmeg, and cinnamon. Serve, or cover and chill up to 1 month. Let warm to room temperature to serve. Makes 1 cup, 10 to 15 servings.

PER TABLESPOON: 53 calories, .05 g protein, 14 g carbohydrates, .03 g fat, 0 mg cholesterol, .85 mg sodium

ORANGE MARMALADE BUTTER

  1 **cup (½ lb.) butter or margarine, at room temperature**
 ½ **cup orange marmalade**

Beat butter and marmalade until well blended. Serve, or cover and chill up to 2 weeks. Serve at room temperature. Makes about 1½ cups, 10 to 15 servings.

PER TABLESPOON: 85 calories, .11 g protein, 5 g carbohydrates, 8 g fat, 21 mg cholesterol, 79 mg sodium

HONEYED PEANUT BUTTER

1 cup (½ lb.) lightly salted creamy or chunk-style peanut butter
½ cup (¼ lb.) butter or margarine, at room temperature
1 tablespoon honey

In a bowl, mix peanut butter, butter, and honey until blended. Serve, or cover and chill up to 2 weeks. Let warm to room temperature to serve. Makes 1½ cups, 10 to 15 servings.

PER TABLESPOON: 92 calories, 3 g protein, 2 g carbohydrates, 9 g fat, 10 mg cholesterol, 83 mg sodium

STEAMING MILK WITH MAPLE SYRUP

½ gallon (2 qt.) milk
¼ cup maple or maple-flavored syrup

In 3- to 4-quart pan, mix together milk and syrup. Warm over medium heat, stirring occasionally, until milk is hot and steaming, about 12 minutes. Do not boil.

To heat in a microwave oven, pour milk and syrup into a 2½- to 3-quart non-metal pitcher. Heat, uncovered, on full power (100 percent) until hot and steaming, about 7 minutes. Pour into mugs. Makes about 2 quarts, 10 to 15 servings.

PER SERVING: 93 calories, 4 g protein, 9 g carbohydrates, 4 g fat, 18 mg cholesterol, 64 mg sodium

---

TORTILLA SANDWICH SALAD LUNCH

Warm Cabbage Salad with Tortilla Sausage Sandwiches
Grapefruit Sparklers

Dollops of mustard, mayonnaise, and green salsa dress this Southwestern sausage sandwich. It goes with salad and grapefruit sparklers.

Heat tortillas in the oven as you brown the sausages and cook the salad. Then assemble sandwiches.

To make grapefruit sparklers, mix 1 part thawed frozen grapefruit juice concentrate with 4 parts sparkling water and serve over ice. If you like, add sliced fresh grapefruit to the drinks.

WARM CABBAGE SALAD WITH TORTILLA SAUSAGE SANDWICHES

6 cups shredded green cabbage
1 medium-size cucumber, peeled, halved, seeded, and sliced crosswise
1 medium-size firm-ripe tomato, cored, seeded, and chopped
½ cup *each* lightly packed chopped cilantro (coriander) and sliced green onion
5 Polish sausages (1¼ to 1¾ lb. total)
¼ cup pine nuts, optional
  Tortilla sausage sandwiches (recipe follows)
  About 2 tablespoons salad oil
4 cloves garlic, pressed or minced
  Lime dressing (recipe follows)
  Salt
  Lime wedges

In a bowl, mix cabbage, cucumber, tomato, cilantro, and green onion; set aside.

Chop 1 sausage; set aside. In a 10- to 12-inch frying pan, cook whole sausages, uncovered, over medium heat, turning occasionally, for 5 minutes. Add chopped sausage and continue to stir and turn, until both whole and chopped sausages are lightly browned, about 5 minutes longer. Add pine nuts and stir often until nuts are golden and whole sausages are hot in the center (cut to test), about 3 minutes longer.

Lift whole sausages from pan and keep warm for tortilla sandwiches. Add enough oil to pan drippings to make 3 tablespoons.

Add garlic to chopped sausage and drippings and stir over medium heat just until garlic is golden, about 1 minute. Add lime dressing; stir, freeing browned bits, until boiling.

Pour the hot liquid over cabbage mixture and mix gently; add salt to taste. Squeeze lime over individual salad portions and into sandwiches. Makes 4 large servings.

PER SERVING: 744 calories, 28 g protein, 28 g carbohydrates, 58 g fat, 119 mg cholesterol, 1,660 mg sodium

Tortilla sausage sandwiches. Stack 4 **flour tortillas** (6- to 7-in. size) and seal in foil. Heat in a 350° oven until warm, about 10 minutes. Or loosely enclose the flour tortillas in plastic wrap; heat in a microwave oven on full power (100 percent) until hot, about 1 minute.

To serve, wrap a warm tortilla around each warm Polish sausage (see preceding). If desired, offer **purchased green salsa, coarse-grain mustard,** and **mayonnaise** to spoon into tortilla.

Lime dressing. In a small bowl, stir together ¼ cup **lime juice,** 2 teaspoons **sugar,** and ¼ to ½ teaspoon **crushed dried hot red chilies.**

CHICKEN & FRITTERS DINNER

Roasted Chicken   Corn Fritters
Jalapeño Jelly Sauce
Watercress Salad
Baked Pears with Anise Seed
White Riesling or Orange Juice

A whole roasted chicken can be the focus of some of the easiest and most satisfying meals. All you do is pop the chicken in the oven until the skin is crisp and crackling and the meat succulent and moist.

You can buy a roasted chicken at the supermarket; but if you cook it at home, put the rinsed bird (giblets removed) breast up on a rack in a roasting pan and bake in a 375° oven until the meat at the thigh bone is no longer pink (cut to test). A 3½- to 4-pound chicken (enough for 4 servings) will be done in about 1 hour. If you don't baste the bird, the skin will have a crisper texture.

Cook the pears in the oven with the chicken, giving the chicken a 30-minute head start.

Rinse 4 cups watercress sprigs; wrap in paper towels, slip into a plastic bag, and chill while foods bake and you make the fritters. Serve the greens with a favorite dressing.

Serve the jalapeño jelly sauce with chicken and fritters.

(Continued on next page)

CORN FRITTERS

        Salad oil
    1   cup all-purpose flour
    2   large eggs, separated
    ⅔   cup milk
    1   package (10 oz.) frozen corn
        kernels, thawed
        Salt

In a wok or 3- to 4-quart deep pan, heat 1½ inches oil to 375° on a thermometer.

Meanwhile, whisk flour, egg yolks, and milk until smooth. Stir in corn; add salt to taste. In another bowl, whip egg whites just until soft, moist peaks form. Gently fold corn mixture into egg whites.

Spoon batter, 1½ to 2 tablespoons at a time, into hot oil, filling pan without crowding. Cook, turning with 2 spoons, until fritters are golden brown, 5 to 7 minutes. Adjust heat to maintain temperature at 375°. Lift out fritters with a slotted spoon and drain on paper towels. Keep warm (up to 20 minutes) while you cook remaining fritters. Add salt to taste. Makes about 2 dozen, 4 servings.

PER FRITTER: 61 calories, 2 g protein, 7 g carbohydrates, 3 g fat, 24 mg cholesterol, 10 mg sodium

JALAPEÑO JELLY SAUCE

    ½   cup mild or hot jalapeño jelly or
        hot pepper jelly
    ¼   cup distilled white vinegar
        Salt

In a 1- to 2-quart pan, melt jelly, uncovered, over medium heat, stirring often, until melted and smooth. Stir in vinegar. Add salt to taste. Let cool until just slightly viscous, about 8 minutes. Serve warm. Makes about ¾ cup, 4 servings.

PER TABLESPOON: 35 calories, .01 g protein, 9 g carbohydrates, .01 g fat, 0 mg cholesterol, 2 mg sodium

BAKED PEARS WITH ANISE SEED

    4   medium-size firm-ripe Comice or
        Anjou pears, peeled
    ¼   cup *each* hot water and firmly
        packed brown sugar
    2   tablespoons butter or margarine,
        melted
    ¼   teaspoon anise seed

Set pears upright in an 8- to 9-inch-diameter shallow baking pan (trim pear bottoms, if needed). Mix water, brown sugar, butter, and anise seed. Pour mixture over and around pears. Bake, uncovered, in a 375° oven until pears are tender when pierced, about 30 minutes; baste occasionally with pan juices. Serve warm with pan juices. Serves 4.

PER SERVING: 200 calories, .72 g protein, 38 g carbohydrates, 6 g fat, 16 mg cholesterol, 63 mg sodium

FEBRUARY

Blossom-Viewing Picnic (page 31)

Bright and sunny February
days inspire ideas for five spontaneous picnics. For casual
indoor entertaining, we suggest a potluck seafood soup
supper. Restaurateur Alice Waters shares a luncheon menu
with our readers. Other articles include whimsical,
flower-shaped Italian dinner rolls; jalapeño chilies in recipes
from soup to sorbet; and rolled gnocchi with a spinach
and pancetta filling. For your Valentine, we offer
chocolate-dipped macaroon hearts.

27

Seize-the-Day Picnics

FEBRUARY CAN BRING *the West some of its most dazzling weather—warm, bright days as grand as any spring will offer.*

But these memorable days arrive unexpectedly, amid late-winter flurries. Taking advantage of them requires a certain state of readiness.

To help you enjoy spontaneous outings this month, we propose impromptu picnics that get you on your way while the sun is shining. Our menus rely on foods you buy ready to serve, on purchased ready-to-eat foods you quickly combine, and on speedy alternatives to make.

Where to go? Every part of the West holds promise. Some locations can be counted on; others burst forth as sudden surprises.

But remember, as you're lured to some glorious picnic site, not to intrude on private property.

In California, the almond orchards that extend south down the Central Valley from Red Bluff and Chico spread a sudden pink canopy of bloom this month. When the sky is blue and the sun shining, a view of such an orchard, here or in similar climates elsewhere, is worth the trip: one good storm, and the fragile glory is lost until another year.

When nature takes it easy in the mountains, a sunny snowfield—at Shasta, Tahoe, Yosemite, or Mount Baldy, for example—can be a stimulating place to picnic and play.

In the milder Santa Ynez, Napa, and Sonoma valleys, hills greened by winter rains invite cycling and day-hikes.

And the Southwest's deserts are now at their most comfortable temperatures.

With their perpetual summer, San Diego's beaches are a February refuge almost as reliable as those of Hawaii. But, less predictably, beaches from the central California coast on up to Puget Sound can also be briefly bright and appealing.

To be ready to respond to outdoor temptation wherever it occurs, keep your picnic basket packed with napkins, cups, plates, spoons, forks, knives, a bottle opener, and a cloth to spread on a table or the ground.

*Each of the five picnics we suggest can go together quickly. Our menus include these codes: # means you buy it; * means you make it; #* means you can buy or make it; #/* means you combine purchased ready-to-eat components.*

The picnic planned for viewing blossoms has the most time-consuming cooking projects: roast duck and a pastry. Remember, you can instead buy Chinese roast duck (a roasted chicken from the deli will do in a pinch) and a bakery pastry. The onion mixture, savory butter, and salad dressing are quick to make.

Sandwiches for the bicycling picnic need marinated peppers, but you start with peppers in a jar.

For the snow picnic, nachos can be made with canned chili, or make the family's favorite and take a quart of it. Heat the chili at home or at the cabin.

creating pan bagnat, a salad-sandwich like those that are popular in Provence.

Stalks of fresh fennel have the crisp texture of celery, with a cooling taste you'll welcome after a good ride.

Fit perishable meats, cheeses, and greens into a small cooler to secure on one bicycle. On this Santa Ynez outing, a visit to one of the valley's fine wineries supplied one beverage and a pleasant detour. Be sure to bring plenty of mineral water for thirsty cyclists; they'll want some at rest stops, too.

PAN BAGNAT MAKINGS

For each sandwich, provide 1 **crusty roll** (about 6-in. size); about 1 ounce thinly sliced **dry salami,** corned beef, or cooked ham; about 1 ounce thinly sliced **Swiss cheese** or cheddar cheese; and 1 or 2 washed and crisped lettuce leaves. All these ingredients, except the bread, need to be carried in an insulated chest.

At the picnic, split the roll; fill with meat, cheese, and lettuce; then add **marinated roasted red peppers** (directions follow) with enough of the dressing to moisten the bread. Press shut and eat. Another option: bring thinly sliced **red onions** in a plastic bag to add to sandwiches. The peppers and onions don't need insulation to travel. Allow 2 sandwiches for a serving.

PER SANDWICH: 384 calories, 20 g protein, 32 g carbohydrates, 19 g fat, 50 mg cholesterol, 915 mg sodium

Marinated roasted red peppers. Empty 1 jar (7 oz.) **roasted red peppers** into a 1- to 2-cup leakproof container. Add ¼ cup **olive oil,** 2 tablespoons **red wine vinegar,** 1 tablespoon **minced parsley,** ¼ teaspoon **dry basil leaves,** ½ teaspoon **dry thyme leaves,** and **salt** and **pepper** to taste. Mix gently. If made ahead, cover and chill up to 2 days. Makes about 1 cup, enough for 3 sandwiches.

PER ¼ CUP: 130 calories, 0.4 g protein, 3 g carbohydrates, 14 g fat, 0 mg cholesterol, 2 mg sodium

Cyclists pause in view of Mission Santa Ynez for a picnic. Each makes their own French-style sandwich, pan bagnat, from shop-and-go delicatessan ingredients.

CYCLING PICNIC

Pan Bagnat Makings#/*
Fresh Fennel
Florentine Cookies#
Green Grapes   Tangerines
Plain or Flavored Mineral Water
Dry Chenin Blanc

Buy roasted red peppers and repack them in an oil-and-vinegar dressing; use to anoint made-at-the-site sandwiches of cold meats, cheeses, and crusty rolls,

Nachos in the snow at Yosemite features a bag lunch. Ladle hot chili into small bags of corn chips, add toppings, and eat from wrapper.

This picnic is especially easy to pack and easy to serve, and cleanup is a snap. Individual-size bags of corn chips become bowls to hold pleasant warm chili (homemade or canned) ladled from a thermos; other toppings include avocado dip, salsa, and cheese. The chips, in their bags, become hand-held, hand-warming nachos.

Raw vegetables are ready for munching as the troops ski in. Fresh and dried fruits, with purchased or homemade chocolate chip cookies, make dessert. And take a supply of extra juice, so snow players can carry off cartons for refreshment later on.

Use the snow as your cooler, pushing beverage bottles and cartons into this natural refrigerator.

NACHOS IN A BAG

3 cans (15 oz. each) chili con carne or 4 cups homemade
1 carton (8 oz.) refrigerated avocado dip
1 green onion, ends trimmed and thinly sliced (optional)
1 package (8 oz.) or 2 cups shredded cheddar cheese

Prepared salsa
12 bags (1¾ oz. each) corn chips or tortilla chips

Pour chili into a 1½- to 2-quart pan and stir over medium-low heat until hot, about 10 minutes. Transfer to a 1½-quart or larger wide-mouth thermos; hold in thermos no longer than 3 hours before serving.

Open avocado dip and sprinkle onion on dip; replace lid securely. Transport in an insulated bag along with cheese and salsa.

To eat, cut open bags of chips. Each diner adds chili, avocado dip, cheese, and salsa to his or her bag; eat directly from the bag. Makes 12 packets; allow 2 or 3 for each serving.

PER PACKET: 450 calories, 15 g protein, 42 g carbohydrates, 33 g fat, 38 mg cholesterol, 1,223 mg sodium

(Continued on next page)

Under flowering almond trees in the great Central Valley of California, two or four share a blossom-viewing picnic of roast duck, onion confit, wild miner's lettuce salad with mustard flowers, seasoned butter with black bread, and, of course, an almond tart.

A flowery site deserves a romantic menu, but the volatility of the season means the food must be gathered quickly. Buy a roast duck at a Chinese market, or roast your own, or buy a roast chicken. You can make the onion confit, prosciutto butter, and vinaigrette ahead and keep them ready to go.

As a pleasant dalliance, you might like to search for your salad in the greening countryside. Tender miner's lettuce is a delectable find; look for its dark green cup-shaped leaves in cool, moist soil with partial shade. Also gather a few of wild mustard's brilliant yellow flowers you'll likely see blooming now; their pungent bite is delicious in salad. These wild gleanings need to be rinsed thoroughly before using, so bring water; a plastic bag can serve as a bowl. If you want, bring along some butter lettuce greens as insurance; allow 1 to 2 cups for a serving.

An almond tart is our dessert proposal, as tribute to an almond-blossom view, but any pretty pastry that you buy is fine.

ROAST DUCK

Rinse a 4½- to 5-pound **duck** inside and out and pat dry; reserve neck and giblets for other uses. Prick duck all over (heavily in fattiest parts) with a fork. Rub with 2 tablespoons **lemon juice**, then lightly sprinkle with **salt** and **pepper**. If desired, quarter 1 medium-size **orange** and tuck into the body cavity (the fruit adds more fragrance than flavor).

Place duck, breast down, on a rack in an 11- by 13-inch baking pan. Roast in a 500° oven for 25 minutes. Turn breast up.

Continue to roast until breast is a light pink at the bone near the wing joint (cut to test) but no longer soft and wet-looking, 25 to 30 minutes longer; discard drippings. Seal hot duck loosely in foil or baking parchment, then wrap in several pretty towels and pack in an insulated chest; serve within 3 hours. Makes 2 to 4 servings.

PER SERVING: 691 calories, 39 g protein, 0.1 g carbohydrates, 58 g fat, 172 mg cholesterol, 121 mg sodium

ONION CONFIT

- 4 **medium-size onions, sliced**
- 8 **sprigs (each 2 in. long) fresh thyme or ¾ teaspoon dried thyme leaves**
- 3 **bay leaves**
- 6 **sprigs (each 2 in. long) fresh marjoram or ¾ teaspoon dried marjoram leaves**
- ¼ **cup olive oil or salad oil**
  Salt

In a 10- to 12-inch frying pan on medium-low heat, simmer onions, thyme, bay leaves, and marjoram in oil, covered, until onions are very soft and golden, about 1½ hours; stir occasionally. Add salt to taste. Let cool; serve at room temperature. If made ahead, cover and chill up to 3 days. Transport in an attractive jar. If picnic is for 2, leftovers hold well and don't require chilling until you get home. Serves 4.

PER SERVING: 150 calories, 1 g protein, 7 g carbohydrates, 14 g fat, 0 mg cholesterol, 2 mg sodium

PROSCIUTTO BUTTER

In a food processor or blender, whirl ½ cup (¼ lb.) room-temperature **unsalted butter** or margarine with ⅛ pound (about 4 thin slices) **prosciutto** and ¼ cup **parsley.** If made ahead, cover and chill up to 5 days. Transport in an insulated chest. Makes ½ cup.

PER TABLESPOON: 115 calories, 2 g protein, 0.1 g carbohydrates, 12 g fat, 35 mg cholesterol, 113 mg sodium

MUSTARD FLOWER VINAIGRETTE

In a small jar, combine ¼ cup **olive oil** or salad oil, 2 tablespoons **lemon juice,** and 1 teaspoon *each* **Dijon mustard** and **honey.** Cover tightly and transport to the picnic.

Mix with 4 to 6 cups **salad greens** (rinsed and drained miner's lettuce or butter lettuce) and ¼ cup freshly gathered, rinsed, and lightly packed **mustard flowers,** optional. Add **salt** to taste. Makes about ⅓ cup dressing, to dress salad for 2 to 4.

PER SERVING: 137 calories, 1 g protein, 4 g carbohydrates, 14 g fat, 0 mg cholesterol, 42 mg sodium

AROMATIC SPICE ALMOND TART

- 1¼ **cups** *each* **whipping cream and sugar**
- ¼ **teaspoon** *each* **ground cardamom and ground coriander**
- 2 **cups (about 11 oz.) whole blanched almonds**
- ¼ **teaspoon almond extract**
  Press-in pastry (directions follow)

In a 2- to 3-quart pan, combine cream, sugar, cardamom, and coriander. Stirring, bring to a boil over high heat. Reduce heat to medium and simmer, uncovered, for 5 minutes, stirring often. Remove from heat and stir in almonds and extract. At once, pour nut mixture into press-in pastry.

Bake in a 375° oven until a rich golden brown, 50 to 65 minutes. Set tart on a rack and let stand until just warm to touch. Remove pan rim and slide a long slender spatula between crust and pan bottom to free pastry from pan; replace pan rim and leave tart in pan to transport. Wrap airtight when cool; it keeps up to 2 days at room temperature. Cut into wedges. Carry extras home. Serves 6 to 9.

PER SERVING: 627 calories, 11 g protein, 54 g carbohydrates, 43 g fat, 134 mg cholesterol, 155 mg sodium

Press-in pastry. Combine 1½ cups **all-purpose flour,** 2 tablespoons **sugar,** and ⅔ cup (⅓ lb.) **butter** or margarine, cut into chunks. Whirl in a food processor or rub with fingers until fine crumbs form. Whirl in (or stir in with a fork) 2 **large egg yolks** until dough holds together.

Press dough evenly over bottom and sides of a 10- to 11-inch fluted tart pan with removable bottom. Bake in a 325° oven for 10 minutes; color will be very pale. Use hot or cold.

(Continued on next page)

At Hanauma Bay in Hawaii, sushi and tropical fruits and beverages make quickly gathered ingredients for an outing. On the Mainland you have similar options.

You will encounter choices like succulent smoked swordfish bellies; firm-textured smoked mackerel, yellowtail, or albacore; and moist-smoked salmon. The ready-to-eat fish is often still warm from the smoker. Ask for a taste to decide what to buy.

Away from San Diego, widely available smoked fish include salmon and Alaskan cod (sable or butterfish), as well as canned smoked herring.

Check smoked fish for bones as you eat, or before putting it into sandwiches. For a serving, allow at least ¼ pound fish; buy extra servings to take home if you like—smoked fish freezes well.

You can make sandwiches in bagels, onion rolls, or dense pumpernickel bread, or make open-faced ones on big crackers. Allow at least 2 sandwiches for each person. Buy cream cheese (the whipped kind is easier to spread); 1 ounce makes 2 sandwiches.

Hardy alfalfa sprouts can get along for a few hours without chilling; allow 2 to 3 tablespoons for each sandwich. Also have a cucumber and a few tomatoes to slice, and lemon to squeeze onto the fish. Bring along a small knife to cut things up with.

SUSHI PICNIC

Sushi-to-go#
Marinated Vegetable Salad#
Kim Chee or Pickled Ginger#
Island Pineapple   Bananas
Japanese Sweet Crackers#
Guava or Passion Fruit Drink
Tea in Individual Cartons

Even on the Mainland, you'll find these foods available in Asian markets and some supermarkets.

Sushi—tart-sweet seasoned cold rice—comes with many toppings and fillings. Some combinations are adventurous; to get what you want, ask, or read the ingredient list. Some kinds of sushi, such as *bara* sushi, are not shaped but are presented like salads and sold in individual bowls—in Hawaii, often quite fanciful ones. You will find perishable sushi in the refrigerator; or you might have some made to order. Keep sushi cold in an insulated chest until you eat it. Allow 6 to 8 pieces of sushi (each about 2-bite size) for a serving.

Allow ½ cup of a purchased vegetable (like broccoli or cauliflower) salad for each person. Kim chee and pickled ginger are sold packaged in containers of different sizes; they play the role of pickles. A medium-size (about 3 lb.) pineapple will serve 6; cut it into chunks, then bite fruit from the peel. Also buy 1 small banana per person.

HARBORSIDE PICNIC

Smoked Fish Platter#
Bread Basket#   Cream Cheese
Alfalfa Sprouts   Cucumber Slices
Lemon Wedges
Roma-style Tomatoes
Black Ripe Olives
Pickled Cherry Peppers
Pears   Seedless Grapes
Mineral Waters, Plain & Flavored
Apple Juice

In San Diego fish markets, especially those in Seaport Village, you'll find several kinds of smoked fish not often prepared this way. A waterfront picnic is a great way to try them.

Smoked fish from harborside markets in San Diego is base of buy-serve menu.

Macaroon Valentines

IF YOUR LOVE ADORES *intense chocolate and coconut, these macaroon valentines are sure to win you favor.*

Mix a simple dough loaded with coconut, shape it, and bake. Then dunk the macaroons in melted chocolate, coating them halfway for semi-indulgent cookies, or enveloping them completely for a really rich confection. Offer the sweets as a special treat or serve them for a simple Valentine's Day dessert.

Older children can make the macaroons easily with a little adult supervision.

CHOCOLATE-DIPPED MACAROON VALENTINES

- 4 **large egg whites**
- 1½ **teaspoons vanilla**
- ⅔ **cup sugar**
- ¼ **cup all-purpose flour**
- 3½ **cups lightly packed sweetened flaked coconut**
- 8 **ounces semisweet chocolate, chopped**
- 3½ **tablespoons butter or margarine**

In a large bowl, beat egg whites with a mixer or whisk until frothy. Add vanilla, sugar, and flour; mix until smooth. Stir in coconut until evenly moistened.

On 2 well-greased 12- by 15-inch baking sheets, evenly space ¼-cup portions of dough. Pat each into a flat-topped heart about ½ inch thick and 3 inches long. Bake in a 325° oven until macaroons are golden and only slightly wet-looking, about 25 minutes. Switch positions of pans halfway through baking. Transfer macaroons to racks and let cool.

A kiss accompanies heart-shaped Valentine's Day gift for Mom.

When macaroons are cool, dip halfway in melted chocolate, tilting pan to pool coating.

Place chocolate and butter in a 1½- to 2-quart pan; set pan over a slightly larger pan filled with about ½ inch water. Bring water to simmering over medium heat, and warm just until chocolate and butter melt; stir occasionally. Remove pans from heat; keep chocolate mixture over water.

One at a time, dip half of each macaroon in chocolate, tipping top pan and scraping sides to collect chocolate. (Save leftover chocolate for other uses.) Set macaroons slightly apart on waxed paper placed on a 12- by 15-inch baking sheet. Chill, uncovered, until chocolate hardens, about 45 minutes. Serve, or wrap each airtight in plastic wrap, then chill up to 1 week. Makes 10.

PER COOKY: 279 calories, 3 g protein, 40 g carbohydrates, 14 g fat, 11 mg cholesterol, 133 mg sodium

CHOCOLATE-COVERED MACAROON VALENTINES

Follow directions for **chocolate-dipped macaroon valentines,** but increase chocolate to 1 pound and butter to 7 tablespoons. Holding by edges, dip macaroons completely in chocolate, turning to coat; set flat side down to chill.

PER COOKY: 430 calories, 4 g protein, 53 g carbohydrates, 26 g fat, 22 mg cholesterol, 174 mg sodium

Seafood Soup Potluck Supper

A DINNER PARTY MIDWEEK? *You work all day, have little spare time, but still want to entertain? Try this seafood soup potluck supper for 8.*

Planning ahead makes it run smoothly. Do your shopping early and make parsley sauce ahead (it's served as a dip for salad vegetables and to add to the soup). Invite your guests to bring some of the fish, shellfish, dessert, or wine. Divvy up light duties for everyone—helping out adds to the fun.

Add clams, scallops, lobster, crab, and other seafood to the hot broth.

If you have time in the morning, set out the dishes and equipment you'll need.

For the salad, choose easy-to-clean vegetables such as bell peppers, slender carrots, celery, cherry tomatoes, green onions, tender inner leaves of romaine lettuce, and fennel (buy 3 to 4 lb. total). Have a guest rinse, trim, and arrange them all on a tray.

Have another guest oversee toasting the bread; someone else can arrange the seafood on a platter, while you watch over the soup and tend the fire. In the fireplace, the fish steeps in the broth; the fire also keeps soup hot for second helpings.

POTLUCK SEAFOOD SOUP

- **2** large cans (49 oz. each) or 12 cups regular-strength chicken broth
- **24** small thin-skinned red potatoes (1½-in. diameter, about 2½ lb. total)
- **3** medium-size leeks, white and tender green part rinsed well and thinly sliced
- **10** to 12 clams suitable for steaming, scrubbed
- **1** lobster tail (about ¾ lb.), meat freed from shell and cut into 1-inch cubes (optional)
- **½** to 1 pound skinned, firm-texture, white-flesh fish fillets, such as halibut, white seabass, or swordfish, cut into 1-inch cubes (if lobster is omitted, use larger amount)
- **½** pound bay scallops, rinsed well
- **½** pound medium-size shrimp (43 to 50 per lb.), shelled and deveined
- **1** cooked Dungeness crab (about 1½ lb.), cleaned and cracked (or use another ½ lb. shrimp)
  Parsley sprigs
- **2** tablespoons minced parsley
  Lemon wedges, optional

In a 6- to 8-quart pan that flames won't damage, bring broth to boiling over high heat. Add potatoes and leeks; when boiling, cover and simmer until potatoes

are tender when pierced, about 20 minutes. Meanwhile, in the fireplace, ignite several logs for a steady flow of heat.

On a platter or tray, arrange clams, lobster meat piled back into its shell, fish cubes, scallops, shrimp, and crab. Garnish with parsley sprigs and lemon.

Bring hot soup to the fireplace in pan (or continue to cook on the stove). Push pan close to the fire; the broth should sizzle and bubble on the side closest to the flames. For more heat, kindle small pieces of wood and stack them against the fire-facing side of the pan.

Add clams to pan; cover and cook about 2 minutes. Gently drop in remaining seafood; cover. Adjust fire to keep broth sizzling on fire side of pan. Cook until clams open and chunks of fish are opaque in center (cut to test), 5 to 10 minutes. Sprinkle minced parsley into soup. Ladle soup into wide bowls; add lemon juice to taste. Makes 8 servings.

PER SERVING: 319 calories, 34 g protein, 33 g carbohydrates, 6 g fat, 82 mg cholesterol, 277 mg sodium

PARSLEY SAUCE

In a blender or food processor, whirl 2 **large eggs,** 1 cup firmly packed **parsley,** 2 **green onions,** ends trimmed and chopped, 3 tablespoons **lemon juice,** 2 teaspoons **dry basil leaves,** and ¼ teaspoon **pepper** until parsley is minced. With motor running, gradually add 1 cup **olive** or salad **oil;** sauce will thicken. Serve, or cover and chill up to 2 days. Serve with salad, or to add to soup to taste. Makes 2 cups.

PER TABLESPOON: 66 calories, 0.4 g protein, 0.4 g carbohydrates, 7 g fat, 17 mg cholesterol, 6 mg sodium

TOASTED BREADSTICKS & GARLIC BUTTER

Cut each of 4 **sourdough sandwich rolls** (each about 6 in. long) in quarters lengthwise. Lay wedges, slightly apart, on 2 baking pans, 10- by 15-inch size.

In a 1- to 1½-quart pan over medium heat, melt 1 cup (½ lb.) **butter** or margarine with 3 **garlic cloves.** Liberally brush cut surfaces of bread wedges with butter. Bake in a 400° oven until bread is golden brown, about 15 minutes. Offer remaining butter to dip bread into, or to add to soup to taste. Makes 16 pieces.

PER SERVING: 142 calories, 1 g protein, 8 g carbohydrates, 12 g fat, 31 mg cholesterol, 195 mg sodium

Snacking on vegetables (on mantel) and on toasted breadsticks, guests watch as soup is ladled from the pan into individual bowls.

Breadstick Rolls

HAVE THEY GROWN LEGS—*or petals? In Italy, these whimsical dinner rolls are dubbed* garofani, *or carnations. We call our modified version breadstick rolls. Their unruly appendages have the taste and crusty texture of breadsticks; their centers are soft and chewy.*

The dough—and the way you shape and bake it—gives these rolls their distinctive features. The dough resembles modeling clay; it's stiffer than what you may be accustomed to, because it contains more flour. That consistency, however, maintains shape and gives the bread a somewhat denser texture. You cut the firm dough to make a fringed strip, then roll it up. The cut surfaces open up and become crisply crusted when baked.

Cook these rolls at a high temperature and spray intermittently with water to obtain a hard, shiny surface. Since it takes a few minutes to shape each pan of rolls, you can bake pans in sequence if you have only one oven.

These rolls are best freshly baked. If made more than 8 hours ahead, freeze, then thaw and reheat later.

ITALIAN BREADSTICK ROLLS

- 1 **package active dry yeast**
- 2 **cups warm water (110°)**
- 6¼ **to 6½ cups all-purpose flour**
- ¼ **cup olive oil or salad oil**
- 2 **teaspoons salt, or to taste**

In a large bowl, sprinkle yeast over the water; let stand about 5 minutes. Add 3 cups of the flour, oil, and salt. Beat with a dough hook or a mixer on low speed until flour is incorporated, then beat on high speed until dough is shiny, satiny, and stretchy, 4 to 6 minutes.

Add 2 cups flour.

If using a dough hook, beat dough on low speed until flour is incorporated, then beat on high speed until dough is smooth, 3 to 5 minutes. Gradually add another 1¼ cups flour, beating until flour is incorporated (if dough becomes too heavy for the machine, scrape dough onto a board and knead in remaining flour). Turn dough onto a floured board, and knead, adding flour if required, until dough is smooth, dense, firm, and nonsticky, with a feel similar to modeling clay, about 5 minutes.

If using a mixer, now switch to a heavy spoon and stir in as much flour as possible. Scrape dough onto a floured board; knead smooth. Gradually knead in 1¼ to 1½ cups flour until dough is smooth, dense, firm, and nonsticky, and feels like modeling clay, about 10 minutes.

Return dough to bowl. Cover with clear plastic wrap and set in a warm place until dough softens and puffs slightly (not doubled), 45 minutes to 1 hour.

Shape dough into a 16-inch-long loaf and slice crosswise into 16 equal pieces; keep covered with plastic wrap while shaping each piece. Roll or pat each dough section into a 2- by 8-inch strip. Along 1 long side, make 1½-inch-deep slashes about ¾ inch apart. Starting at narrow side, roll up strip, then pinch uncut end to seal; set uncut side down on greased 12- by 15-inch baking sheets, letting cut ends open up over base. Repeat with remaining pieces, placing rolls about 1½ inches apart on pan. Cover lightly with plastic wrap and set in a warm place. Let rise until rolls puff slightly, 20 to 30 minutes.

Place rolls in a 425° oven, bake 3 to 4 minutes, then spray bread all over with a fine mist of water. Continue baking, spraying with water 2 more times, about 3 minutes apart. Bake until rolls are golden brown, 18 to 20 minutes total; if more than 1 pan is in the oven, switch pan positions halfway through baking.

Transfer the rolls to racks. Serve warm or cool. Store at room temperature up to 8 hours; freeze for longer storage. To reheat, place thawed rolls in a single layer on a 12- by 15-inch baking sheet. Bake in a 400° oven just until warm, 5 to 7 minutes. Makes 16 rolls.

PER ROLL: 213 calories, 5 g protein, 38 g carbohydrates, 4 g fat, 0 mg cholesterol, 276 mg sodium

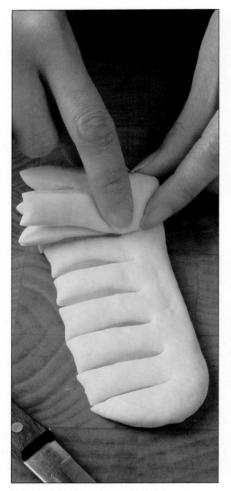

1 *Slash strip of dough at ¾-inch intervals, roll up, then pinch ends to seal.*

2 *Stand the fringed roll—uncut side down—on pan, letting cut dough open up over base.*

3 *Spray the rolls with water as they bake to give them glossy, crisp crusts.*

Alice Waters' Salmon Lunch

BARBECUED SALMON *seasoned with thyme and extra-virgin olive oil is the main feature of this luncheon menu from Berkeley restaurateur Alice Waters.*

Waters begins this menu with grilled baby corn and sweet cherry tomatoes. Then she serves the hot fish on a bed of lightly wilted chicory that is mixed with browned bits of mushrooms.

If these ingredients aren't available when you shop, choose the freshest offerings at the time. For the corn, you might substitute other more seasonal vegetables such as small onions to grill in their skins or sweet peas in the pod.

A specially constructed grill with wood burning pizza oven in her home kitchen is the center of preparation for this meal. If you don't have an indoor grill, use the broiler, or cook outdoors on the barbecue.

ALICE WATERS' SALMON LUNCH

Grilled Baby Corn   Cherry Tomatoes
Grilled Salmon on
Wilted Chicory Salad
Grilled Toast
Red Bananas   Grapes   Plums
White Bandol
or Dry White Zinfandel

If you plan to barbecue the meal, ignite the briquets about 35 to 45 minutes before cooking. Grill the corn in its husks (stripped of silks), make the salad, and then cook the fish. If there's room on the grill, toast the bread while the corn or fish cooks. Or toast bread after the fish is grilled.

Set hot, grilled salmon with thyme on wilted chicory salad.

GRILLED SALMON ON WILTED CHICORY SALAD

- **8** tablespoons extra-virgin olive oil
- **½** pound chanterelles or regular button mushrooms, cut into ½-inch cubes
- **¼** cup thinly sliced green onion
- **2** tablespoons red wine vinegar
- **4** cloves garlic, pressed or minced
- **⅓** cup minced fresh thyme leaves or 2 tablespoons dry thyme leaves
- **6** pieces salmon or rockfish, skinned fillets or steaks (6 to 8 oz. each)
- **9** cups bite-size pieces chicory (curly endive), washed and crisped
  Salt and pepper

In a 12-inch frying pan or 5- to 6-quart pan, combine 2 tablespoons olive oil and chanterelles; stir occasionally over high heat until mushrooms are lightly browned, 10 to 12 minutes. Meanwhile, stir together ¼ cup oil, green onion, vinegar, garlic, and ½ the thyme; set aside. Coat both sides of the fish with olive oil, using about 2 tablespoons total. Sprinkle both sides of fish with remaining thyme.

When mushrooms are browned, add oil-vinegar dressing. Remove from heat. Add chicory, half at a time if it doesn't all fit; turn and mix until greens are coated with dressing. At once, place salad on 6 dinner plates or 1 large platter.

Set the fish on a grill 4 to 6 inches above hot coals (you can hold your hand at grill level only 2 to 3 seconds), or on a rack in a 12- by 15-inch broiler pan 4 inches from the heat. Cook, turning once, until fish is no longer translucent in thickest part (cut to test), 8 to 10 minutes. Set fish on salad. Add salt and pepper to taste. Makes 6 servings.

PER SERVING: 469 calories, 37 g protein, 16 g carbohydrates, 30 g fat, 95 mg cholesterol, 195 mg sodium

GRILLED TOAST

- **1** large loaf (1½ lb.) round, crusty whole-wheat or sourdough bread
- **¼** cup extra-virgin olive oil

Cut the bread into slices ⅓ to ½ inch thick. Brush or drizzle slices lightly with oil. Place on a grill 4 to 6 inches above hot coals (you can hold your hand at grill level only 2 to 3 seconds), or on wire racks set on a 12- by 15-inch baking sheet 4 inches from the broiler. Toast lightly on both sides, 1 to 1½ minutes a side. Makes 6 to 8 servings.

PER SERVING: 266 calories, 10 g protein, 41 g carbohydrates, 9 mg fat, 3 mg cholesterol, 449 mg sodium

Turkey Pot Pie

LEFTOVERS ARE A BONUS *that you often plan for when you cook a turkey. And one good use for these extras is in turkey pot pie, with several options. Roast the carcass bones, then boil them to make a flavorful broth, or take the short-cut with canned chicken broth.*

In the broth, chunks of yams or sweet potatoes simmer to tenderness; then you add bright green kale and the turkey and pour it into a shallow casserole.

The neat trick is the crust. You shape and bake it separately. Then slide the crust onto the filling and serve.

TURKEY POT PIE

½ cup thinly sliced leeks, white part only
1 tablespoon butter or margarine
   Rich turkey broth or quick broth (recipes follow)
1 pound (about 2 large) yams or sweet potatoes, peeled and cut into ½-inch cubes
½ teaspoon rubbed sage
½ teaspoon dry thyme leaves
3 tablespoons *each* cornstarch and cold water, stirred together
½ pound kale, rinsed, stems discarded, and leaves chopped
3 cups bite-size chunks cooked turkey
   Parmesan-pepper pastry (recipe follows)

In a 5- to 6-quart pan over medium heat, stir leeks often in butter until limp, about 3 minutes. Add broth, yams, sage, and thyme; simmer, covered, until yams are tender when pierced, about 20 minutes. Stir cornstarch mixture into broth. Add kale and turkey; stir until mixture boils.

Pour turkey mixture into a shallow 2- to 2½-quart casserole. Loosen hot pastry from baking sheet and slide onto the top of the filling. To serve, break through pastry with a spoon, dipping out filling with the pastry. Makes 6 servings.

PER SERVING: 515 calories, 32 g protein, 48 g carbohydrates, 22 g fat, 106 mg cholesterol, 350 mg sodium

Rich turkey broth. Break a **turkey carcass** (from a 10- to 15-lb. cooked turkey) into large pieces in a 12- by 15-inch baking pan. Add 2 large **onions,** quartered; 1 large **carrot,** cut into 1-inch pieces; and 2 large stalks **celery,** cut into 1-inch

Gently slide hot baked pastry onto pie filling of turkey, yams, and kale.

pieces. Bake in a 375° oven, turning bones and vegetables occasionally, until bones are richly browned, 1½ to 2 hours.

Put the bones and vegetables in a 12- to 15-quart pan. Rinse roasting pan with **water** and scrape browned bits free; add to bones in pan. Add enough more water to cover bones. Bring to boiling over high heat; reduce heat and simmer, uncovered, adding more water as needed to keep bones covered, 4 to 6 hours.

Lift out and discard big bones. Pour broth through a fine strainer into a 5- to 6-quart pan. With a spoon, skim fat from surface and discard. Boil broth on high heat, uncovered, until reduced to 3 cups (if too much boils away, add water to make 3 cups). Use, or cool, cover, and chill up to 3 days.

Quick broth. Combine 2½ cups **regular-strength chicken broth** with ½ cup **Madeira** (or another ½ cup broth).

Parmesan-pepper pastry. In a food processor or a bowl, combine 1 cup **all-purpose flour,** ½ cup grated **parmesan cheese,** ½ teaspoon **pepper,** and 1 large package (8 oz.) **cream cheese,** cut into large chunks. Whirl until dough forms

a ball; or cut cheese into flour mixture with a pastry blender until evenly mixed. Then pat dough into a ball and knead on an unfloured board until mixture holds together, 1 to 2 minutes.

On a 12- by 15-inch sheet of foil, invert the casserole to be used for the turkey pie (preceding). With the tip of a knife, lightly trace around casserole's edge. Set casserole aside.

In the center of outline, pat pastry out until about ½ inch thick. Lightly dust pastry with **all-purpose flour.** Roll pastry out evenly until it extends about ¼ inch beyond the outline. Fold edge of pastry under ¼ inch; pinch or crimp edge. With a sharp knife or cooky cutters, cut a decorative design through pastry; take care not to tear foil underneath. With a fork, pierce the pastry every ½ inch just inside the pinched edge (to keep from puffing excessively as it bakes).

Slide pastry on foil onto a 12- by 15-inch baking sheet. Bake in a 350° oven until dark golden, 30 to 40 minutes. Use hot.

Gnocchi Roll

ITALY'S ANSWER *to the dumpling, gnocchi takes on a new form in this spinach- and pancetta-filled roll. Instead of shaping the potato-based dough into traditional little pillows, it's rolled out flat, spread with filling, then wrapped up like a jelly roll. Slice the cooked gnocchi, and serve with a rich, meat-enhanced tomato cream sauce.*

Clara Freschet Agnoli of Valle di Cadore, a quaint village tucked into the Italian Alps, shared this family dish with us.

GNOCCHI ROLL
(Rotolo di Spinaci)

½ ounce dried porcini or cèpes mushrooms
   Water
3 pounds beef short ribs
2 tablespoons olive oil
1 clove garlic, minced or pressed
1 large onion, chopped
¾ cup finely chopped celery
2 cups regular-strength beef broth
1 can (6 oz.) tomato paste
1 tablespoon minced fresh basil leaves or 1 teaspoon dry basil leaves
4 teaspoons sugar
   Salt and pepper
   Gnocchi dough (recipe follows)
   All-purpose flour
   Spinach-pancetta filling (recipe follows)
¾ cup whipping cream
2 tablespoons butter or margarine
   Fresh basil sprigs
1 cup freshly grated parmesan cheese

Soak mushrooms in ¾ cup warm water until soft, about 20 minutes. Squeeze and rub mushrooms to release any grit. Lift from water and squeeze dry; chop finely and set aside. Without disturbing sediment in bottom of the bowl, pour ½ cup of the water into a measuring cup; set aside. Discard remaining water.

Place short ribs in a 5- to 6-quart pan over medium-high heat; cook until well browned, 8 to 10 minutes on each side. Lift out ribs and set aside. To pan, add oil, garlic, onion, and celery. Scrape brown bits in pan free. Stir often until vegetables begin to brown, about 10 minutes.

Return short ribs to pan along with any accumulated juices. Add 1½ cups water, broth, tomato paste, basil, sugar, chopped mushrooms, and reserved

soaking liquid. Bring to a boil. Reduce heat and simmer very slowly, uncovered, until meat is very tender when pierced, 3½ to 4 hours; remove from heat. Lift out ribs and cool. Remove meat from bones and finely chop; discard bones, fat, and gristle. Skim fat from sauce; add meat. Add salt and pepper to taste. Use; or, if made ahead, cover and chill up to 3 days.

On a floured board, roll gnocchi dough out to make a rectangle slightly larger than 15 by 17 inches. To prevent sticking, lift edges of dough often and sprinkle board with flour. Trim edges to make a rectangle exactly 15 by 17 inches.

Distribute spinach filling evenly over dough to within 3 inches of 17-inch side nearest you and within about 1 inch of other sides. Starting with the nearest side, lift the edge over the filling, and slowly roll dough to form a smooth, compact cylinder. (If dough sticks, loosen with a spatula.) Seal roll by pressing dough firmly together at ends and along seam.

Wrap gnocchi roll snugly in a 17- by 22- inch piece of cheesecloth (or, if you don't have a large enough pan for cooking whole, cut roll in half crosswise with a sharp knife and wrap each half separately). Tie ends of cloth with string to enclose roll. To hold cloth in place, also tie string securely but not tightly around roll in 2 equidistant places.

You need a 20-inch-long fish poacher to cook the roll whole or 2 pans, each at least 10 inches in diameter and 4 inches deep, to cook halves simultaneously. Place whole roll on rack of fish poacher and lower into boiling water to cover. Or set halves in large pans and cover with boiling water. Return water to a boil over high heat, then reduce heat, cover, and simmer until roll feels firm when pressed with back of spoon, 20 to 25 minutes.

About 5 minutes before gnocchi roll is done, stir whipping cream into meat sauce; bring to a boil over high heat. Reduce heat to low and add butter, stirring constantly to incorporate. Keep hot; stir occasionally.

Drain most of the water from pan. Wearing oven mitts to protect your hands from heat, lift roll on rack from poacher. (If cooked in halves, grasp tied ends of half-rolls and remove from pan.) Let cool 5 minutes. Cut strings and remove cheesecloth. Use; or, if made ahead, wrap in foil and chill up to 24

A stunning presentation: gnocchi spirals top a bed of rich tomato cream sauce.

hours. (If chilled, let roll stand for 30 minutes at room temperature, then reheat, still wrapped in foil, in a 400° oven for 20 to 25 minutes.)

To serve, cut roll crosswise into ½-inch-thick slices. Spoon ¾ cup hot meat sauce onto each heated dinner plate; arrange 4 to 6 slices on top of sauce.

Sprinkle generously with parmesan cheese and garnish each plate with a basil sprig. (If preferred, slices can be presented on a large heated platter.) Offer remaining meat sauce and cheese to add to taste. Makes 6 to 9 servings.

PER SERVING: 635 calories, 27 g protein, 55 g carbohydrates, 35 g fat, 116 mg cholesterol, 894 mg sodium

Gnocchi dough. In a large bowl, combine 3 cups hot, finely mashed **russet potatoes,** 2 cups **all-purpose flour,** 1½ teaspoons **salt,** and 1 tablespoon **olive oil;** stir with a fork until coarse crumbs form. Add 1 **large egg** and stir until dough holds together. Scrape dough out onto a well-floured board and knead gently until smooth, 15 to 20 turns. If dough is too soft, add a little more flour. Use at once; dough softens rapidly if left standing.

Spinach-pancetta filling. Thaw 2 packages (10 oz. each) frozen chopped spinach. Put into a colander and, with your hands, squeeze as much liquid as possible from the spinach; put spinach into a bowl. In a 10- to 12-inch frying pan over medium heat, stir 1 large clove **garlic,** minced or pressed, and ⅓ pound sliced **pancetta** or bacon, finely chopped, until pancetta begins to brown. With slotted spoon, transfer meat to spinach and mix well. Add **salt** and **pepper** to taste. Use; or, if made ahead, cover and chill up to 2 days.

Adventures with Jalapeños

FAMOUS FOR THEIR FIERY FLAVOR, *jalapeño chilies (Capsicum annuum) are named for Jalapa in Veracruz, Mexico. Their heat depends on how much of a natural substance called* capsaicin *they contain. Judging the heat before you bite is always a gamble. Here's a clue: really hot chilies make you cough just by smelling them.*

These recipes dilute the chilies enough for you to taste their flavor. Use fewer chilies if you are leery of heat, more if you're bolder. Wear rubber gloves when preparing them; they can burn bare skin. Avoid rubbing or touching eyes, too.

FIRE & ICE SORBET

- ¾ cup sugar
- 1 cup water
- 2 to 4 fresh jalapeño chilies (2½ to 3 in. long), stemmed, seeded, and minced
- ½ cup lime juice
- 2 large egg whites

Combine ½ cup sugar, water, and chilies (use full amount for hottest flavor) in a 1½- to 2-quart pan. Bring to a boil over high heat, stirring until sugar dissolves. Continue boiling, uncovered, to blend flavors, about 2 minutes. Let cool. Add lime juice. Pour through a fine strainer into a metal 9- or 10-inch-square or 9- by 13-inch oblong pan. Cover and freeze until firm, at least 2 hours or up to 3 days.

At high speed, beat egg whites until foamy. While beating, sprinkle remaining ¼ cup sugar, 1 tablespoon at a time, into whites until they hold stiff peaks.

Break jalapeño ice into chunks and whirl in a food processor or with mixer just until slushy. Fold whites into the ice. Return to pan, cover, and freeze until firm, about 2 hours or up to 5 days. Makes 6 to 8 servings, about ½ cup each.

PER SERVING: 32 calories, 1 g protein, 20 g carbohydrates, 0 g fat, 0 mg cholesterol, 16 mg sodium

JALAPEÑO PUMPKIN SOUP

- 2 tablespoons butter or margarine
- 1 small onion, chopped
- 2 to 4 fresh jalapeño chilies (2½ to 3 in. long), stemmed, seeded, and minced
- ½ teaspoon *each* white pepper and curry powder
- 1 large (about 10 oz.) russet potato, peeled and cut into ½-inch cubes
- 2 medium-size carrots, peeled and chopped
- ⅓ cup chopped parsley
- 4 cups regular-strength chicken broth
- 1 can (16 oz.) pumpkin
- ¼ cup dry sherry

In a 4- to 5-quart pan over medium-high heat, melt butter and add onion, chilies (use full amount for hottest flavor), pepper, and curry powder; stir until onion is limp, about 4 minutes. Add potato, carrots, parsley, and 2 cups broth. Bring to a boil on high heat, cover, and simmer until vegetables are very tender when pierced, about 20 minutes.

In a blender or food processor, smoothly purée vegetable mixture; return to pan. Stir in pumpkin, remaining broth, and sherry. If made ahead, cover and chill up to 3 days. Stir over medium heat until hot. Makes 4 servings, 1¾ cups each. —*Linda Kranen, Palos Verdes Estates, Calif.*

PER SERVING: 207 calories, 6 g protein, 31 g carbohydrates, 8 g fat, 16 mg cholesterol, 138 mg sodium

SUPER JALAPEÑO JELLY

- About 1 cup stemmed, seeded, and minced fresh jalapeño chilies (about 10 chilies 2½ to 3 in. long)
- 1 medium-size green bell pepper, stemmed, seeded, and chopped
- 6½ cups sugar
- 1½ cups cider vinegar
- 2 pouches (3 oz. each) liquid pectin
  Green food coloring, optional

In a 4- to 5-quart pan, stir together chilies, bell pepper, sugar, and vinegar. Stirring over high heat, bring mixture to a rolling boil. Add pectin all at once, stirring constantly, and return to a boil that can't be stirred down. Stir while boiling for 1 minute. Immediately remove from heat and let stand until bubbling subsides; quickly skim off and discard any foam.

Pour hot jelly through a fine strainer into a 2-quart measuring cup. Stir and add a few drops food coloring to tint to the desired shade of green. Quickly pour hot jelly into hot ½-pint jars, filling to within about ¼ inch of tops. Wipe rims clean; put hot, clean lids on jars and screw bands on firmly. Let stand until cool. Press lids with your finger; if lids stay down, jars are sealed. Store in a cool, dark place. If lids pop back, jars are not sealed; chill up to 6 months, or about 1 month after opening. Makes 6 or 7 jars, ½-pint size.

PER TABLESPOON: 54 calories, 0 g protein, 14 g carbohydrates, 0 g fat, 0 mg cholesterol, 0.3 mg sodium

CHICKEN WITH JALAPEÑO JELLY

- 8 chicken thighs (about 2½ lb. total); remove and discard fat and skin
- 2 tablespoons butter or margarine
- ¾ cup jalapeño jelly (recipe precedes, or purchased)
- 1 tablespoon soy sauce
- 2 garlic cloves, minced or pressed
- 1 teaspoon ground ginger
  Salt

In a 10- to 12-inch frying pan over medium-high heat, brown chicken lightly in butter, about 10 minutes.

Meanwhile, mix together jelly, soy, garlic, and ginger; pour over chicken. Cover pan and simmer until chicken is white at bone (cut to test), about 25 minutes. Remove lid and turn heat to high; stir to prevent scorching and reduce until sauce thickens slightly, about 2 minutes. Remove pan from heat; lift chicken onto a serving plate and pour sauce over chicken. Makes 4 servings. —*Kristine L. Wilson, San Diego.*

PER SERVING: 411 calories, 32 g protein, 43 g carbohydrates, 12 g fat, 150 mg cholesterol, 457 mg sodium

Lentils, Rice, or Polenta for One

COOKING SOME GRAINS *and legumes for a single serving is hardly practical the conventional way. You often end up making more than you need, and sometimes half of it sticks to the cooking pan. But with a microwave oven, you can cook small amounts neatly with no leftovers.*

For a side dish, cook with water (or broth for polenta), then serve plain or with butter. The rice and barley can also be served for breakfast with light cream, brown sugar, and raisins or sliced bananas.

MICROWAVE POLENTA FOR 1

- 1 **cup water or regular-strength chicken broth**
- ¼ **cup polenta or yellow cornmeal**
- 1 **teaspoon butter or margarine**
  Grated parmesan cheese (optional)
  Salt

In a 1-quart glass measuring cup or bowl, stir together the water, polenta, and butter. Cook, uncovered, in a microwave oven at full power (100 percent), stirring once after 3 minutes, until polenta is tender and liquid is absorbed, 7 to 8 minutes. Spoon polenta onto plate and sprinkle with cheese and salt to taste. Makes ½ cup, 1 serving.

PER SERVING: 160 calories, 3 g protein, 27 g carbohydrates, 4 g fat, 10 mg cholesterol, 39 mg sodium

MICROWAVE RICE FOR 1

- 1 **or 1¼ cups water**
- ¼ **cup white or brown long-grain rice**
  Salt

In a 1-quart glass measuring cup or bowl, stir together 1 cup water with white rice (use 1¼ cups with brown rice). Cook, uncovered, in a microwave oven at full power (100 percent) until most of the water evaporates, 10 to 11 minutes (20 minutes for brown rice).

Cover with plastic wrap and continue cooking at half power (50 percent) until tender to bite, 2 to 5 minutes longer. Add salt to taste. Makes ¾ cup, 1 serving.

PER SERVING: 168 calories, 3 g protein, 37 g carbohydrates, 0.2 g fat, 0 mg cholesterol, 2 mg sodium

Single portion of lentils cooked in the microwave makes an easy grain dish for a small meal.

MICROWAVE BARLEY FOR 1

- ¼ **cup pearl barley**
- 1 **cup water**
  Salt

Sort through barley and discard any debris. Rinse and drain. In a 1-quart glass measuring cup or bowl, stir together water and barley. Cook, uncovered, in a microwave oven at full power (100 percent) until mixture boils, 3 to 4 minutes.

Cover with plastic wrap and cook at half power (50 percent) until barley is tender to bite, 18 to 20 minutes longer. Drain. Add salt to taste. Makes ¾ cup, 1 serving.

PER SERVING: 172 calories, 5 g protein, 36 g carbohydrates, 0.5 g fat, 0 mg cholesterol, 4 mg sodium

MICROWAVE LENTILS FOR 1

- ¼ **cup lentils**
- 1 **cup water**
  Salt

Sort through lentils and discard any debris. Rinse and drain. In a 1-quart glass measuring cup or bowl, stir together water and lentils. Cook, uncovered, in a microwave oven at full power (100 percent) until mixture boils, 3 to 4 minutes.

Cover with plastic wrap and cook at half power (50 percent) until lentils are tender to bite, 12 to 14 minutes longer. Add salt to taste. Makes ¾ cup, 1 serving.

PER SERVING: 162 calories, 13 g protein, 27 g carbohydrates, 0.5 g fat, 0 mg cholesterol, 5 mg sodium

Cooking with Canned Pears

WHEN COOKING WITH PEARS, *poaching the fruit is often the first step. But if you start with canned pears, you save not only a step, but time, too, as these three recipes illustrate.*

The first is a luxurious thick, smooth soup of puréed pears and parsnips; the balance of sweet with earthiness proves winning.

Pears make gelato to enjoy by itself, or as a more dramatic finale served with warm slices of the same fruit and doused with flaming anise-flavor Pernod.

PEAR & PARSNIP SOUP WITH TOAST

- ¼ cup (⅛ lb.) butter or margarine
- 1 large onion, chopped
- 3 medium-size (about 1¼ lb. total) parsnips, peeled and cut into chunks
- 4½ cups regular-strength chicken broth
  About ½ teaspoon *each* ground allspice and white pepper
- 2 cans (1 lb. each) pear halves in juice or light syrup, drained (reserve liquid for other uses)
  Herb-spice toast (recipe follows)
- ½ cup whipping cream, optional

Melt butter in a 4- to 5-quart pan over medium-high heat. Add onion and stir occasionally until lightly browned, 8 to 10 minutes. Add parsnips, broth, ½ teaspoon allspice, and pepper; cover and bring to a boil on high heat; reduce heat and boil gently until parsnips are tender when pierced, 15 to 20 minutes.

In a blender, whirl soup and pears a portion at a time. (If made ahead, cover and chill up to 2 days.) Return to pan and stir over medium heat until hot. Accompany with toast. Stir cream into individual portions and dust lightly with allspice. Serves 8.

PER SERVING: 266 calories, 4 g protein, 37 g carbohydrates, 12 g fat, 28 mg cholesterol, 232 mg sodium

Herb-spice toast. Mix 3 tablespoons **butter** or margarine with ½ teaspoon **dry thyme leaves**, ⅛ teaspoon **ground allspice**, and ¼ teaspoon **sugar**.

Trim crusts from 6 slices **sourdough bread** (each about 4 by 5 in., ½ in. thick); cut each slice into 3 triangles. Place in a 10- by 15-inch baking pan and broil 4 inches from heat until toasted. Turn over, spread with butter mixture, and broil until toasted. Serve hot. Makes 18.

PEAR & PERNOD GELATO

- 3 cups milk
- ½ cup sugar
- 3 thinly pared strips lemon peel (each 1½ in.), yellow part only
- 6 large egg yolks
- ½ teaspoon anise extract
- ¼ cup anise-flavor liquor (such as Pernod)
- 2 cans (1 lb. each) pear halves in juice or light syrup, drained (reserve liquid)

In a 3- to 4-quart pan, combine milk, sugar, and lemon peel. Stir over medium heat until milk is scalding. In a bowl, whisk 1 cup milk into yolks, then whisk egg mixture into pan. Stir over medium-low heat until custard coats back of a metal spoon in a smooth, thin layer, 10 to 12 minutes; discard peel. Stir in anise extract and liquor; cool, cover, chill.

In a blender or food processor, whirl pears with ⅓ cup of reserved liquid until smoothly puréed. Stir into chilled custard.

Pour mixture into container of an ice cream maker (self-refrigerated, or use 1 part salt to 8 parts ice) and freeze as manufacturer directs. When dasher will no longer rotate, remove lid and dasher, cover gelato with plastic wrap, top with lid, and freeze until firm, 6 hours to 3 weeks. Makes 1½ quarts, 6 to 8 servings.

PER SERVING: 231 calories, 6 g protein, 34 g carbohydrates, 7 g fat, 217 mg cholesterol, 56 mg sodium

WARM BUTTERED PEARS WITH GELATO

Drain 1 can (1 lb.) **pear halves in juice** or light syrup (reserve liquid for other uses) and cut lengthwise into ¾-inch-thick slices. Melt 1 tablespoon **butter** or margarine in an 8- to 10-inch frying pan over medium-high heat until it begins to brown. Add fruit; turn gently until hot.

Divide pears among 4 dessert plates. Scoop frozen **pear and Pernod gelato** (recipe precedes) to make 12 balls (each about ¼ cup); put 3 of the balls on each dessert plate.

Heat ½ cup anise-flavor liquor (such as Pernod) in a 1½- to 2-cup pan over medium-high heat. At the table, ignite liquor in pan and ladle it, flaming, with a long-handled spoon onto each dessert. Makes 4 servings.

PER SERVING: 349 calories, 6 g protein, 58 g carbohydrates, 10 g fat, 225 mg cholesterol, 90 mg sodium

Spoon flaming anise-flavor liquor over warm pear slices and frozen pear gelato— it's laced with the same spirit.

More February Recipes

OTHER FEBRUARY ARTICLES *include snack-size Dutch babies filled with cream cheese and tart chutney, a licorice-fragrant fennel salad, and a quick-to-prepare Reuben soup served with mustard- and cheese-topped toast.*

BABY DUTCH BABIES

Akin to egg-tender popovers, tiny Dutch babies bake in muffin cups with a filling of tart chutney and cream cheese. Serve as an appetizer or snack with a glass of wine or sparkling water.

- 2 tablespoons butter or margarine
- 2 large eggs
- ½ cup all-purpose flour
- ½ cup milk
- 1 small package (3 oz.) cream cheese
  About ¼ cup chutney, chopped if pieces are large

Use muffin pans with 1½- or 2½-inch cups; you need 24 small cups or 12 large ones. Divide butter equally among cups. Set pans in a 425° oven to melt butter, about 3 minutes.

As butter melts, combine in a food processor or blender the eggs, flour, and milk; whirl until blended. Cut cheese into cubes to equal the number of muffin cups.

Spoon about 1 tablespoon batter into each small cup or about 2 tablespoons into each large cup; use all the batter. Bake small cups 2 minutes, or large cups 5 minutes, to firm bottoms. Remove from oven and quickly add 1 piece cheese and ½ teaspoon (small cups) or 1 teaspoon (large cups) chutney to each cup. Continue to bake until puffed and browned on edges, 10 minutes longer for both sizes.

Slightly cool in pan, then scoop from pans with a large spoon. Serve warm or at room temperature. Makes 24 small or 12 large baby Dutch babies.

PER SERVING: 47 calories, 1 g protein, 4 g carbohydrates, 3 g fat, 30 mg cholesterol, 34 mg sodium

FRESH FENNEL & LEMON SALAD

In the cooler months, licorice-fragrant fennel (also called sweet anise or finocchio by Italians) is at its prime. You may find heads of fennel topped with woody stems and feathery green leaves, or the inedible stems may be trimmed off.

Here you use the crisp head sliced, lightly cooked, and served hot or cold in a salad.

- ½ cup pecan halves
- 3 tablespoons olive oil or salad oil
- ½ cup finely chopped onion
- 1 large head (about 1 lb. without stems) fennel, rinsed
- 3 tablespoons lemon juice
- 1 tablespoon finely shredded lemon peel, yellow part only
- 4 cups loosely packed butter lettuce leaves, washed, crisped, and torn into bite-size pieces
  Salt and pepper

In a 10- to 12-inch frying pan over medium heat, stir pecans in oil often until nuts are toasted, about 10 minutes. Lift out with a slotted spoon and set aside.

Add onion to pan; stir often over medium heat until limp, about 5 minutes.

Meanwhile, cut off and discard woody stems from fennel. Also cut off feathery leaves and save. Trim discoloration and bruises from fennel, then cut fennel in half lengthwise and thinly slice crosswise.

Add fennel, lemon juice, and lemon peel to onions. Stir often until fennel softens slightly, about 2 minutes. Remove from heat and use warm, or cover and chill at least 1 hour or until next day. Put lettuce in a bowl; add fennel mixture, pecans, and feathery leaves; mix with salt and pepper to taste. Makes 5 or 6 servings.

PER SERVING: 143 calories, 2 g protein, 6 g carbohydrates, 13 g fat, 0 mg cholesterol, 72 mg sodium

REUBEN SOUP WITH DIJON TOAST

Fans of the Reuben sandwich, take note: this popular combination can also become a fast soup. Corned beef and sauerkraut heat in broth; cheese and mustard flavor rye toast that's served on the side.

- 1 can (1 lb.) sauerkraut
- 6 cups regular-strength chicken broth
- 1 teaspoon caraway seed
- ½ pound thinly sliced corned beef or pastrami, fat trimmed and meat cut into thin strips
- 1 cup (4 oz.) shredded Swiss cheese
- ¼ cup thinly sliced green onions
  Dijon toast (recipe follows)

Sprinkle Swiss cheese into bowls of steaming soup; if you like, add sliced green onions as well.

Rinse sauerkraut in a strainer under running water; drain. Pour into a 5- to 6-quart pan. Add broth and caraway; bring to boiling. Add corned beef and heat through. Pour into 4 to 6 soup bowls, and add cheese and onions to taste. Accompany with toast. Serves 4 to 6.

PER SERVING: 354 calories, 23 g protein, 22 g carbohydrates, 20 g fat, 71 mg cholesterol, 1,318 mg sodium

Dijon toast. For each serving, use 1 or 2 slices of **rye** or pumpernickel **bread.** Arrange slightly apart on a 12- by 15-inch baking sheet. Broil 4 to 6 inches from heat, turning once, until lightly browned on both sides. Spread 1 side of each slice with 1½ to 2 teaspoons **Dijon mustard,** then evenly cover with 2 to 3 tablespoons shredded **Swiss cheese.** Sprinkle cheese lightly with **caraway seed.** Return to broiler until cheese melts. Serve hot.

CORNISH GAME HENS WITH MUSTARD CRUST

For Valentine's Day, serve butterflied bird roasted with mustard and rosemary.

¼ cup (⅛ lb.) butter or margarine, melted
¼ cup Dijon mustard
1 tablespoon minced fresh or crumbled dry rosemary leaves
2 cloves garlic, pressed or minced
4 Cornish game hens (1¼ to 1½ lb. each), thawed if frozen
Fresh rosemary sprigs (optional)
Salt and pepper

Mix butter, mustard, rosemary, and garlic; set aside.

Remove necks and giblets from game hens; reserve for other uses, if desired. With poultry shears or a knife, split hens lengthwise along 1 side of backbone. Pull hens open; place, skin side up, on a flat surface and press firmly, cracking bones slightly, until hens lie reasonably flat. Rinse hens and pat dry. Coat both sides with mustard mixture and set slightly apart in 2 baking pans, each 10 by 15 inches.

Bake in a 450° oven until meat is no longer pink at thigh bone (cut to test), 25 to 30 minutes. Transfer to a platter or dinner plates. Garnish with rosemary sprigs. Add salt and pepper to taste. Makes 4 servings. —*Kathy Donahue, Occidental, Calif.*

PER SERVING: 679 calories, 62 g protein, 3 g carbohydrates, 45 g fat, 226 mg cholesterol, 745 mg sodium

CHEESE BISCUIT STICKS

Cut wheat-flecked biscuit dough into sticks; bake. Cheese flavors the biscuits.

About 1 cup all-purpose flour
1 cup whole-wheat flour
1 tablespoon baking powder
1 teaspoon sugar
½ teaspoon salt
½ cup (¼ lb.) butter or margarine, cut into chunks
¾ cup shredded sharp cheddar cheese
½ cup milk

In a food processor or large bowl, mix 1 cup all-purpose flour, whole-wheat flour, baking powder, sugar, and salt. Add butter; whirl, or rub with your fingers until particles are the texture of coarse cornmeal. Stir in cheese. Add milk; whirl or stir with a fork just until evenly moistened. Scrape dough onto a board lightly dusted with all-purpose flour. Knead until dough holds together, 8 to 10 turns.

Form into a ball and set on a greased 12- by 15-inch baking sheet. Press into an even 8-inch round. Cut round into 1-inch-wide strips. Bake in a 425° oven until golden brown, 25 to 30 minutes. Transfer to rack. Cool about 15 minutes. Serve warm, cutting sticks apart at lines. Serves 8. —*Judy Taylor, Oakland, Calif.*

PER SERVING: 264 calories, 7 g protein, 24 g carbohydrates, 16 g fat, 44 mg cholesterol, 488 mg sodium

BUTTER BEAN & HAM CHOWDER

2 tablespoons butter or margarine
1½ cups thinly sliced green onion
2 large carrots, chopped
2 tablespoons all-purpose flour
3 cups regular-strength chicken broth
1 cup water
1 teaspoon dry marjoram leaves
6 ounces sliced cooked ham
2 cans (15 oz. each) butter beans, drained
1 package (10 oz.) frozen corn kernels, thawed
Salt and pepper

Vegetable chowder, laced with ham strips, makes a quick lunch or supper.

In a 3- to 4-quart pan, melt butter over medium-high heat. Add onion and carrots. Cook, stirring occasionally, until onion is limp, about 5 minutes. Stir in flour to coat vegetables.

Add broth, water, and marjoram. Bring to a boil. Cover and simmer until carrots are tender when pierced, about 10 minutes.

Meanwhile, cut ham into thin strips about 3 inches long. When carrots are tender, add ham, beans, and corn. Cover and simmer until soup is hot, about 5 minutes. Add salt and pepper to taste. Ladle into a tureen or bowls. Makes 6 servings. —*Janet Moore, Beulah, Colo.*

PER SERVING: 273 calories, 17 g protein, 36 g carbohydrates, 9 g fat, 27 mg cholesterol, 948 mg sodium

Beet & Apple Salad

    4 medium-size beets (about
       2 lb. total)
    ½ cup cider vinegar
    2 tablespoons honey
    1 small European-style cucumber,
       thinly sliced
    1 medium-size Red Delicious apple,
       cored and thinly sliced
       Horseradish cream
       (recipe follows)
       Salt

Trim tops off beets, leaving about 1 inch. Scrub beets. In a 5- to 6-quart pan, combine beets and 3 quarts water. Bring to a boil; cover and simmer until beets are tender when pierced, 30 to 35 minutes.

Drain and cool. Trim ends; rub off skin under running water. Quarter beets and thinly slice.

Mix vinegar and honey. Combine beets with ½ of the mixture. Mix remaining marinade with cucumber and apple. Cover and chill beet and apple mixtures at least 30 minutes or up to 4 hours. Pour beet mixture into a wide bowl. Spoon apple mixture over center of beets. Offer horseradish cream and salt to add to taste. Serves 6 to 8.—*Dorothea Kent, Port Angeles, Wash.*

PER SERVING: 128 calories, 2 g protein, 18 g carbohydrates, 6 g fat, 13 mg cholesterol, 74 mg sodium

Horseradish cream. Mix 1 cup **sour cream** with 2 tablespoons **prepared horseradish.**

Beets, apple, cucumber for marinating make refreshing, colorful winter salad.

Hot Pasta & Tuna Salad

   12 ounces dry large pasta shells
    1 tablespoon olive oil
    1 jar (7 oz.) roasted red peppers,
       drained and cut in thin strips
   ⅓ cup chopped parsley
    1 can (3½ oz.) pitted black ripe
       olives, drained
    1 can (12½ oz.) chunk-style tuna,
       drained
       Chili dressing (recipe follows)
       Salt and pepper

In a 5- to 6-quart pan, bring 3 quarts water to boil on high heat. Add pasta; cook, uncovered, until tender to bite, about 12 minutes.

Meanwhile, in a 10- to 12-inch frying pan over medium-high heat, combine oil, red peppers, parsley, olives, and tuna. Stir gently until hot, about 2 minutes. Stir in ½ of the chili dressing.

Drain cooked pasta and pour into a large bowl; mix with remaining chili dressing. Pour tuna mixture in center. Gently mix together. Add salt and pepper to taste. Makes 5 or 6 servings.—*Deborah Heath, Portland.*

PER SERVING: 467 calories, 23 g protein, 45 g carbohydrates, 23 g fat, 10 mg cholesterol, 396 mg sodium

Chili dressing. Mix ⅓ cup **olive oil,** 3 tablespoons **wine vinegar,** 2 tablespoons drained **capers,** ½ teaspoon **crushed dried hot red chilies,** and 2 cloves **garlic,** pressed or minced.

Main-dish hot pasta salad is mixed with tuna, olives, roasted peppers, and parsley.

Ginger Shortbread Wedges

    2 cups all-purpose flour
    1 cup firmly packed brown sugar
    1 tablespoon ground ginger
    1 cup (½ lb.) butter or margarine,
       cut into chunks

In a food processor or bowl, mix flour, brown sugar, and ginger. Add butter. Whirl, or rub with your fingers until mixture is the texture of coarse cornmeal. Press and squeeze mixture together, forming a large lump.

Put dough into a 9- or 10-inch-diameter cake pan (with removable bottom, if possible). With fingers, press dough into an even layer. With a fork, press tines around edge to form a decorative border and prick surface all over.

Bake in a 325° oven until golden brown, 1 hour to 1 hour and 10 minutes. Remove from oven and cut round into 12 to 16 wedges. Set on a rack and cool until warm, about 25 minutes. Cut around pan edge and remove pan rim, or invert cookies out of the pan. Serve cool. Store airtight up to 5 days, or freeze for longer storage. Makes 12 to 16 servings.—*Patt Hudler, Loleta, Calif.*

PER SERVING: 211 calories, 2 g protein, 25 g carbohydrates, 12 g fat, 31 mg cholesterol, 122 mg sodium

Present wedges of ginger shortbread with hot tea and tart, fresh kumquats.

IN SOUTHERN CALIFORNIA, *Jerry Garrity learned to love Mexican food. When he moved to Bend, Oregon, he did not find a land exactly flowing in salsa, so he started his own salsa-manufacturing firm. Naturally, this led to experiments in how best to use the product. One result is his splendid Mexican Chicken Lasagna, which brings new life to tired leftover chicken.*

The idea is broadly Italian, but a few salient details make the Mexican difference: mild salsa replaces tomato sauce, and canned green chilies flavor the filling.

MEXICAN CHICKEN LASAGNA

- 2 tablespoons salad oil
- 1 medium-size onion, chopped
- 2 cloves garlic, minced or pressed
- 1 medium-size red bell pepper, stemmed, seeded, and chopped
- 2 jars (16 oz. each) mild salsa
- ½ teaspoon pepper
- 2 tablespoons chili powder
- 1 teaspoon ground cumin
- 1 package (10 oz.) dry lasagna
  Cheese filling (recipe follows)

- 4 cups bite-size pieces cooked chicken
- 1 cup (¼ lb. *each*) shredded sharp cheddar cheese and jack cheese

Pour oil into a 4- to 5-quart pan over medium heat; when hot, add onion, garlic, and bell pepper. Cook, stirring often, until onion is limp, about 10 minutes. Add salsa, pepper, chili powder, and cumin; bring to a boil. Reduce heat and simmer, uncovered, stirring often, until sauce is reduced to 4 cups, about 10 minutes.

Meanwhile, in a 5- to 6-quart pan, cook lasagna, uncovered, in 3 quarts boiling water until tender to bite, about 10 minutes; drain well. Arrange ½ the cooked noodles in the bottom of a 9- by 13-inch baking dish; spread ½ of the cheese filling over the noodles, then top with ½ the cooked chicken. Spoon ½ the cooked sauce over the chicken, then sprinkle with ½ the shredded cheeses. Repeat layers, using remaining noodles,

cheese filling, chicken, sauce, and shredded cheeses.

If made ahead, cover and chill as long as 1 day. Bake, covered, in a 375° oven until mixture is hot throughout, 45 to 50 minutes (about 55 minutes if chilled). Let stand, uncovered, 5 to 10 minutes, then cut into rectangles; lift out with a spatula. Makes 8 or 9 servings.

PER SERVING: 469 calories, 36 g protein, 36 g carbohydrates, 20 g fat, 148 mg cholesterol, 1,139 mg sodium

Cheese filling. Combine 2 cups **small-curd cottage cheese, 2 large eggs,** ⅓ cup chopped **parsley,** and 1 can (4 oz.) canned **diced green chilies.**

Jerry Garrity
Bend, Ore.

WHEN SPENCER TRACY, *speaking of Katharine Hepburn in the movie* Pat and Mike, *said, "There ain't much meat there, but what's there is cherce," he could have been describing lamb shanks.*

When properly prepared, that is. Lamb shanks are tough enough to require slow,

"Our lasagna has a strong Mexican accent."

moist heat to bring the richly flavored meat to succulence and loosen it from the bones. Tony Martin bakes his lamb shanks for 4 hours in a fragrant steam of vermouth, onion, soy sauce, lemon juice, and garlic. The result is cherce indeed.

LAMB SHANKS À LA MARTIN

    4 large onions, thinly sliced
    4 lamb shanks, cracked (about
       3½ lb. total)
    ¾ cup dry vermouth
    ¼ cup soy sauce
    ¼ cup lemon juice
    4 large cloves garlic, minced or
       pressed
    ½ teaspoon pepper
       Hot cooked rice

Arrange onion slices in a 5- to 6-quart ovenproof pan, top with lamb shanks, then pour vermouth over meat and onions.

In a small bowl, stir together soy sauce, lemon juice, garlic, and pepper. Spoon over shanks. Cover meat and bake in a 350° oven for 3½ to 4 hours or until shanks are very tender when pierced and meat pulls from bone.

Serve lamb and onions on a platter with hot cooked rice; keep warm. Skim and discard fat from pan juices; boil juices on high heat until reduced to about ½ cup.

Serve the juices to spoon onto individual servings of lamb shanks and rice. Makes 4 servings.

PER SERVING: 347 calories, 23 g protein, 21 g carbohydrates, 19 g fat, 81 mg cholesterol, 1,111 mg sodium

South San Francisco

THE WORD MARMALADE *comes from the Portuguese* marmelo, *meaning quince; indeed, the earliest marmalades used this tart fruit instead of the familiar orange.*

In fact, many fruits can serve as the basic ingredient. J.W. (Steve) Stephenson's recipe—a paragon of simplicity—may call for an orange, but he says any citrus fruit will do.

Mr. Stephenson tells us that the classic marmalades of England and Scotland use the Seville orange (also called the sour orange), a fruit with sweet peel and sour juice. In the Spanish town of Seville, where orange trees line the streets, city employees

"The classic marmalades use the Seville orange, a fruit with sour juice."

harvest the fruit and ship it to Great Britain.

One obvious virtue of this marmalade is that it's possible to make a small amount at a time, so you don't have to face the tedious process of canning it or the discouragement of finding that unused portions have turned into chunks of sugar.

MICROWAVE MARMALADE

    1 large orange, 8 to 10 ounces
       Sugar

Rinse orange and cut into large pieces; pick out and discard seeds. Whirl the fruit in a food processor or blender until evenly chopped. Measure fruit and juices, then pour into a nonmetal 2- to 3-quart bowl. Measure sugar to equal fruit and juice; add to bowl. Stir to mix.

Cook, uncovered, in a microwave oven on high power (100 percent) until mixture is as thick as you like and clings to a metal spoon, 6 to 8 minutes; it thickens slightly as it cools. As marmalade cooks, stir well every 2 minutes. Let cool, then serve; or cover and chill up to 1 month. Makes about 1¼ cups.

PER TABLESPOON: 63 calories, 0.2 g protein, 17 g carbohydrates, 0 g fat, 0 mg cholesterol, 0.4 mg sodium

San Jose, Calif.

FROM SUBLIMITY, OREGON, *comes this super-cooky recipe. With becoming modesty, Chef Ronald Baribeau calls them simply Silver Creek Falls Brown Sugar Bars; he might, after all, have called them Sublimity Bars without missing the mark by much. These bars are not only delicious; they also contain enough fruits, nuts, and fiber to free the consumer from any feelings of guilt he or she might have over consuming sweets. Caloric they are; empty they are not.*

SILVER CREEK FALLS BROWN SUGAR BARS

    1   cup (½ lb.) butter or margarine
    1   cup *each* granulated and firmly
         packed brown sugar
    2   large eggs
    2   teaspoons vanilla
    1   tablespoon light molasses
    2   cups all-purpose flour
    1   cup regular or quick-cooking
         rolled oats
    1   teaspoon soda
    ½   teaspoon baking powder
    ½   cup *each* raisins and chopped nuts
    1½   cups sweetened shredded coconut

In a large bowl, beat together butter, granulated sugar, and brown sugar until creamy. Mix in the eggs, vanilla, and molasses.

In another bowl, combine flour, oats, soda, and baking powder. Add to butter mixture, blending well. Stir in raisins, nuts, and coconut.

Spread dough into a buttered 10- by 15-inch rimmed baking pan. Bake in a 350° oven until center feels firm when lightly touched, about 40 minutes. Cool on a rack for 10 minutes, then cut into bars and lift from pan.

Serve warm or cool. To store, package cool cookies airtight for up to 3 days; freeze to store longer. Makes 3½ dozen bars, each about 1 by 3½ inches.

PER BAR: 138 calories, 2 g protein, 19 g carbohydrates, 7 g fat, 25 mg cholesterol, 82 mg sodium

Sublimity, Ore.

February Menus

THE MERCURIAL MOOD of February may bring days dazzling enough for a picnic (see page 28), but more regularly it will display a harsher, chillier disposition.

Counter the wintry days with warming, hearty foods. One way to go is fast, with a light, quick-to-make soup to soothe your bones. Another option takes longer. Braise beef and bake potatoes slowly to tender perfection in the oven; their mouth-watering, savory aromas will entice those coming in from the cold. A third choice is to fuel up with sturdy muffins of bran and fruit before you take off on a frosty morn.

Floating in a sweet-sour broth, peas, mushrooms, and radishes add color and flavor to this main-dish soup. For dessert, offer cookies and fruit.

JAPANESE-INSPIRED SOUP FOR LUNCH OR SUPPER

Sushi Soup
Chinese Almond Cookies
Orange Wedges
Green Tea   Sauvignon Blanc

Light, faintly exotic, pretty, satisfying, and warm—all describe this soup that uses ingredients akin to some in sushi. The base is chicken broth, rice adds body, and rice vinegar gives a sweet-sour sushi tang. At the last moment, add colorful vegetables and tiny shrimp.

When the rice is done, the soup is almost ready. Bright shreds of carrots, peas, shrimp, and radish slices added last need only to heat before serving. A fruity Sauvignon Blanc goes particularly well with the soup. Buy the almond cookies, or bake a favorite; serve with the oranges and tea.

SUSHI SOUP

- 1 tablespoon olive oil or salad oil
- ¼ pound mushrooms, thinly sliced
- 2 teaspoons minced fresh ginger
- ⅓ cup long-grain white rice
- 6 cups regular-strength chicken broth
- 1 medium-size carrot, peeled and finely shredded
- 20 edible-pod peas, strings and ends removed, or 1 package (6 oz.) thawed frozen edible-pod peas
- ½ pound tiny cooked shelled shrimp
  About 2 tablespoons seasoned rice vinegar (or rice or distilled white vinegar with 1 teaspoon sugar)
  About 1 tablespoon soy sauce
- 4 medium-size red radishes (ends trimmed), thinly sliced
- ¼ cup chopped green onion
- 4 sheets (about 3 in. square) toasted or untoasted nori (seaweed), cut into ¼- by 1½-inch strips (optional)

To a 4- to 5-quart pan over medium-high heat, add oil and mushrooms. Cook, stirring often, until mushrooms are golden, about 5 minutes. Add ginger and rice; stir occasionally until rice is opaque. Add broth and bring mixture to a boil; cover and simmer until rice is tender to bite, about 20 minutes.

Add carrot and peas; simmer, uncovered, until vegetables are tender to bite, about 3 minutes. Stir in shrimp, 2 tablespoons rice vinegar, and 1 tablespoon soy sauce.

When hot, about 1 minute, add radishes and onion. Ladle soup into individual bowls. Add nori strips, seasoned rice vinegar, and soy sauce to taste. Makes 4 servings. —Cecelia A. Caso, Denver.

PER SERVING: 234 calories, 18 g protein, 24 g carbohydrates, 8 g fat, 111 mg cholesterol, 476 mg sodium

OVEN STEAK & POTATO DINNER

Baked Stuffed Flank Steak Roll
Baked Potatoes   Sour Cream
Zucchini & Citrus Salad
Vanilla Ice Cream   Hot Fudge Sauce
Milk   Zinfandel

Meat and potatoes seem right for a winter evening, but there's always room for variation on the familiar pairing. Here the steak is flank, rolled around a savory, sautéed mushroom filling and baked until very tender. The meat's juices form the flavorful sauce that enhances the meat and bake-alongside potatoes.

The steak bakes for several hours, but you don't have to watch it. You can marinate and stuff the meat the day before; first one home pops it in the oven for dinner. Sour cream may seem superfluous, but some baked potato lovers will disagree. A young, feisty Zinfandel goes well with the principal duo's solid flavors.

As the steak bakes, cook and quickly chill slender strips of zucchini; seasoned with mint and citrus, the squash makes a refreshing salad. Garnish each plate with some of the mint sprigs.

BAKED STUFFED FLANK STEAK ROLL

- ¼ cup *each* **lemon juice, soy sauce, and honey**
- 1 teaspoon **dry mustard**
- ½ teaspoon **pepper**
- 1 **flank steak** (about 2 lb.)
  Mushroom stuffing (recipe follows)
- 6 medium-size **russet potatoes** (3 lb. total), each scrubbed and pierced with a fork
- 2 cups regular-strength **beef broth**
- 2 tablespoons **cornstarch**
  Parsley or **mint sprigs**, optional

In a 9- by 13-inch baking pan, mix together lemon juice, soy sauce, honey, dry mustard, and pepper. Lay flank steak in sauce and turn over to coat all sides of meat. Cover with plastic wrap and refrigerate at least 1 hour or up until the next day; turn meat several times.

Lift steak from marinade. Brush excess sauce off meat into pan.

Lay steak flat. Spoon mushroom stuffing onto center of the steak and across its width. Fold steak ends over the stuffing to overlap completely. With cotton string, tie the rolled meat in the center and at each end to hold securely. Place rolled steak, seam down, in the pan with marinade; cover tightly with foil. If made ahead, chill until next day.

Bake in the center of a 350° oven until meat is very tender when pierced, about 3 hours. About 1 hour before steak is done, add potatoes to oven on rack above the meat; bake until tender when pierced.

Using 2 spoons, carefully lift rolled steak and place seam down on a platter; clip and remove strings. Drape meat with foil and keep warm.

Carefully skim and discard fat from pan drippings. Stir broth and cornstarch into the pan. Stirring, bring the mixture to a boil over high heat; pour into a sauceboat.

Cut rolled steak crosswise into 6 equal slices. Arrange meat and potatoes on plates, garnish with parsley, and add sauce to taste. Makes 6 servings. —*Martha Turner, Oregon City, Ore.*

PER SERVING: 642 calories, 37 g protein, 62 g carbohydrates, 28 g fat, 100 mg cholesterol, 854 mg sodium

Mushroom stuffing. Rinse 1 pound **mushrooms,** drain, and slice thin. Chop 1 medium-size **onion.** In a 10- to 12-inch frying pan over medium-high heat, melt ¼ cup (⅛ lb.) **butter** or margarine. Add vegetables and cook, stirring occasionally, until golden brown, about 25 minutes. Stir in ½ cup chopped **parsley.** Let cool. If made ahead, cover and chill up until next day.

ZUCCHINI & CITRUS SALAD

- 3 medium-size **zucchini** (about 1 lb. total, ends trimmed), cut into ¼-inch-thick sticks, each about 1½ inches long
- 1 medium-size **lemon,** thinly sliced
- 2 tablespoons minced fresh **mint leaves** or **parsley**
- 1 tablespoon **sugar**
- ¼ cup **olive oil** or salad oil
- 3 tablespoons **orange juice**
- 1 teaspoon grated **orange peel**

In a 5- to 6-quart pan over high heat, bring 2 inches of water to a boil. Add zucchini and cook, uncovered, just until tender to bite, about 2 minutes. Drain zucchini and at once immerse in ice water until cool; drain on paper towels.

Cut each lemon slice into 6 wedges. In a large bowl, combine lemon with mint, sugar, oil, orange juice, and peel. If made ahead, cover zucchini and dressing separately and chill up until next day. Combine zucchini with dressing and serve. Makes 6 servings. —*Roxanne E. Chan, Albany, Calif.*

PER SERVING: 106 calories, 1 g protein, 7 g carbohydrates, 9 g fat, 0 mg cholesterol, 3 mg sodium

(Continued on next page)

Spiraled slice of flank steak with mushroom filling goes with baked potato and pan juices; serve with tangy mint-citrus zucchini salad.

Muffins bake while you pull together the remaining items for this simple but wholesome start for the day.

Spread the dense, hearty muffins with butter and honey, or use yogurt combined with bananas and honey. Stir steaming mugs of your favorite herb tea with cinnamon sticks and enjoy the taste and aroma.

BRAN APPLE MUFFINS

- 1 cup *each* bran cereal and untoasted wheat germ
- 1½ cups whole-wheat flour
- ½ cup nonfat dry milk
- 3 teaspoons baking powder
- ¾ cup raisins
- ½ cup chopped walnuts
- 2 large eggs
- 12 ounces thawed frozen apple juice concentrate
- ¼ cup salad oil

In a large bowl, mix together bran cereal, wheat germ, flour, dry milk, baking powder, raisins, and walnuts; set aside.

Beat to blend eggs, apple juice concentrate, and oil. Add to dry ingredients and stir to mix well. Let batter stand until moisture is absorbed, about 5 minutes.

Spoon batter into paper-lined or greased muffin cups (2½ in. wide), filling each to top. Bake in a 375° oven until muffins are tinged a dark golden brown, about 30 minutes. Remove muffins from pan, cool slightly on rack, and serve warm. Or cool, wrap airtight, and store up until next day; freeze to store longer. Makes 12 muffins. —*Emilie N. Wanderer, Las Vegas.*

PER MUFFIN: 285 calories, 9 g protein, 45 g carbohydrates, 10 g fat, 46 mg cholesterol, 225 mg sodium

MARCH

Lobster with Roe Butter (page 53)

Fresh, easy, and make-ahead recipes highlight our March selections. Leading off are three simple, main-event entrées—fresh crab and lobster, and barbecued beef tenderloin—each handsomely presented with minimum fuss. Other recipes to prepare in advance span the menu from appetizer spreads to fruit desserts. If you have a wood-burning cookstove, check our guide and recipes. For a change of pace, we suggest pasta for breakfast. And, for the calorie conscious, we present a trio of mignonnette sauces and Turkey Jerky.

Main-Event Entrées

THE BEST ADVICE *when serving naturally glamorous entrées is to leave well enough alone. The chefs of these main-event entrées have wisely elected to follow this course: crab and lobster, boiled; beef tenderloin, barbecued or roasted. The sauces are simple and complementary.*

Serve the crab or lobster with sourdough bread, a butter lettuce or Belgian endive and watercress salad, and a dry Sauvignon Blanc or Merlot. With the beef, the chef serves a wholesome vegetable sauce and an aged Cabernet Sauvignon.

If you're hesitant about handling live shellfish and need to know how to clean them after cooking, see page 54.

DUNGENESS CRAB WITH A TRIO OF SAUCES

Serve with lemon mayonnaise, crab butter sauce, melted butter, or all three.

> 4 live Dungeness crab (each 1½ to 2 lb.)
> Lemon mayonnaise or crab butter sauce (recipes follow), or about ½ cup (¼ lb.) melted butter or margarine
> Lemon wedges

In a 10- to 12-quart pan over high heat, bring about 5 quarts water to a rapid boil. Pick up a crab, holding the body from rear, and plunge headfirst into water. Cook 2 crab at a time. Cover pan and cook 15 to 20 minutes; when boil resumes, reduce heat to maintain a gentle boil.

With tongs, lift out crab and immerse briefly in cold water to stop cooking and cool them enough to handle. To clean and crack, follow directions on page 54. If desired, reserve golden crab "butter" and cream-colored "fat" for sauce.

Pile crab onto a platter; serve with small dishes of mayonnaise, crab butter sauce, or melted butter, and lemon wedges. To eat, pluck meat from shell with a metal pick, a small fork, or the tip of a crab leg. Dip meat into 1 sauce. Serves 4. — *Art and Scott Hubbard, Los Altos, Calif.*

PER SERVING CRAB: 140 calories, 28 g protein, 1 g carbohydrates, 2 g fat, 96 mg cholesterol, 481 mg sodium

Lemon mayonnaise. In a blender or food processor, whirl 2 **large egg yolks,** 1½ tablespoons **lemon juice,** and 1 teaspoon **grated lemon peel** to blend. With motor running, add 1 cup **olive oil** or salad oil in a slow, steady stream; mixture thickens. Serve, or cover and chill up to 2 days. Makes 1½ cups.

PER TABLESPOON: 85 calories, .23 g protein, .07 g carbohydrates, 9 g fat, 23 mg cholesterol, 1 mg sodium

Crab butter sauce. Stir together ½ cup (¼ lb.) **melted butter** or margarine and reserved **crab butter** and **crab fat.** Serve warm. Makes about 1 cup.

Art presents Dungeness crab. His guests dip the tender crabmeat into homemade mayonnaise with a hint of lemon peel, or melted butter blended with golden crab "butter"; or squeeze lemon juice onto the meat.

Warren thinks lobsters are perfect. He simply cooks them in boiling water. Serve hot or chilled, in rimmed plates or bowls to catch good-tasting liquid.

Lobster with Roe Butter

Tanks of live lobsters in supermarkets make this shellfish readily available.

    4 **American lobsters (each about
       1½ lb.)**
       **About ½ cup (¼ lb.) butter or
       margarine, melted**

In a 10- to 12-quart pan over high heat, bring 5 quarts water to a rapid boil. Pick up a lobster, holding the body from the top (not tail), and plunge it headfirst into the water. Cook 2 lobsters at a time. Cover pan and cook 15 minutes; when boil resumes, reduce heat to maintain a gentle boil.

With tongs, lift out lobster and transfer each to a wide, shallow bowl or rimmed dinner plate. Serve each with a nutcracker and a small bowl of melted butter for dipping meat. To open lobster, break off tail, draining liquid into your bowl. Scrape red roe or green liver into melted butter, if you like.

With a fork (see picture on page 51 for correct angle of fork), pull tail meat out of shell. Break off legs and suck on them like straws to extract meat. Crack claws and pull out meat. Pull top shell away from body; scoop out any additional roe and liver to eat. Pull off and discard the finger-shape, spongy gills, then crack open body to pry out morsels of meat. Water that drains from lobster is good to drink. Makes 4 servings. — *Warren Epstein, San Francisco.*

PER SERVING: 350 calories, 31 g protein, 2 g carbohydrates, 24 g fat, 170 mg cholesterol, 803 mg sodium

Barbecued Beef Tenderloin with Bishop Vegetable Sauce

You may need to order ahead to get a whole beef tenderloin (or beef fillet). Expect to pay $40 to $50. You can barbecue or roast the meat.

    1 **whole beef tenderloin (about
       6½ lb.), trimmed of excess fat**
       Salt and coarsely ground pepper
       **Bishop vegetable sauce (recipe
       follows)**

To barbecue. Mound 50 charcoal briquets on firegrate of a barbecue with lid. Ignite coals; when they are just barely covered with gray ash, about 35 minutes, push ½ to each side of grate. Set a drip pan between coals. Place grill 4 to 6 inches above coals.

Fold thin end of fillet underneath to make meat as evenly thick as possible; tie securely with string. Sprinkle meat with salt and pepper; set on grill over pan. Put lid on barbecue and open vents. Cook until meat thermometer inserted in thickest part registers 130° for rare, about 50 minutes, or until desired doneness.

To oven-roast. Tie tenderloin as directed for the barbecue. Set meat on a rack in a 12- by 15-inch roasting pan. Bake in a 450° oven until meat thermometer inserted in thickest part registers 130° for rare, about 1 hour, or until desired doneness.

Let meat rest about 10 minutes, then cut across the grain in ½-inch-thick slices and serve with the vegetable sauce. Makes 12 servings. — *Jerry Bishop, San Diego.*

PER SERVING: 358 calories, 49 g protein, 0 g carbohydrates, 17 g fat, 145 mg cholesterol, 109 mg sodium

Bishop vegetable sauce. In a 10- to 12-inch frying pan over medium-high heat, melt ¼ cup (⅛ lb.) **butter** or margarine. Add 1 pound **mushrooms,** thinly sliced; 2 cloves **garlic,** minced or pressed; 2 medium-size **red onions,** thinly sliced; and 2 medium-size **green bell peppers,** cored, seeded, and thinly sliced.

Stir often until vegetables are tinged with brown, about 20 minutes. Add 1 bottle (6 oz. or ¾ cup) **diable meat sauce** (or a purchased steak sauce); stir until hot. (If made ahead, cool, cover, and chill until next day; reheat to serve.) Spoon into a bowl. Makes 3 cups.

PER TABLESPOON: 16 calories, .28 g protein, 2 g carbohydrates, 1 g fat, 3 mg cholesterol, 79 mg sodium

Jerry slices beef tenderloin. With the thick, tender slabs, he offers his signature chunky vegetable sauce to spoon on top, with rice pilaf and a green salad. Tenderloin was cooked unadorned in a covered barbecue.

How to Deal with a Live Crab or Lobster

FOR THE UNINITIATED, *a live lobster or crab can be intimidating. Here we show you how to handle these critters, and how to extract every wonderful sweet morsel from them (see recipes on pages 52 and 53).*

You find these shellfish in tanks or refrigerated at fish markets and some supermarkets. *They must be alive; make sure they can move. At home, keep up to 12 hours in the refrigerator, covered with a damp cloth. Check occasionally; cook at once if they won't move.*

Crab have pincers; so do lobsters, though theirs are generally banded. See below *for how to hold live crab and lobsters. To cook, plunge headfirst into boiling water to kill them instantly.*

Crab meat is in the legs and body cavity. In lobsters, most meat is in the tail and large claws. If you like, you can also suck the meat from the slender lobster legs.

How to Remove Meat from a Whole Lobster

1 *Hold live lobster by back; avoid tail, as lobster can flip fiercely enough to hurt. Once cooked, twist off claws and legs.*

2 *Twist tail off body. Add coral roe and green liver on tail to melted butter.*

3 *Push inverted fork deep into tail; pull out meat, following curve of shell.*

4 *Lift off top body shell. Scoop green liver and coral roe from shell and body; mix with melted butter.*

5 *Crack large claws along edge of shell, using a nutcracker.*

How to Clean & Crack a Whole Crab

1 *Grasp live crab from behind, around body. Once crab is cooked, pull off and discard triangular belly tab.*

2 *Lift off shell from rear; break off tiny front paddles on body. Scoop creamy mixtures from shell and save.*

3 *Pull off and discard red membrane with entrails on body. Also rinse back shell.*

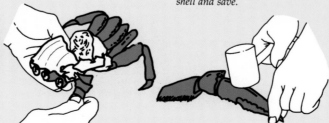

4 *Scoop and save gold butter from body; pull off soft gills. Rinse body well.*

5 *Twist legs from body. Then crack legs along shell edge, using a nutcracker or small wooden mallet.*

6 *Cut body into several pieces. Arrange pieces, legs, and back shell on platter.*

Pasta for Breakfast

START THE DAY *with pasta. It's a favorite in Elaine Holtzman's family. When her children were growing up, she often revitalized last night's spaghetti by cooking it with eggs and seasonings for a quick breakfast. Now her son, Tom Kaplan, carries on the tradition, with a few new twists. Tom serves his mother's specialty made with fresh taglierini, eggs, and cheese, as well as variations named after other family members.*

These pasta recipes, each making a single serving, are easy to tailor to individual preferences. Add more egg, cheese, and onion the way Mrs. Holtzman likes, or use less, as Mr. Kaplan prefers.

For a family, you might cook enough pasta for the group (use 3 to 4 quarts water for about 1 pound fresh or dry pasta), then season each serving to order. Choose from the basic pasta alla mama recipe; daughter-in-law Emily's version with avocado, tomato, and cilantro; grandson Max's with smoked salmon and green onion; or Papa's with hearty sausage and bacon.

You'll find these combinations easy to assemble for a nutritious breakfast or quick supper. If you use leftover pasta, allow 1½ to 2 cups cooked pasta for each serving. The noodles will warm quickly when stirred with the fat and seasonings in the frying pan.

PASTA ALLA MAMA

- ¼ **pound fresh or 3 ounces dry taglierini or spaghetti**
- 1 **tablespoon butter or margarine**
- 1 **clove garlic, minced or pressed**
- ½ **cup chopped red or yellow onion (optional)**
- 2 **or 3 large eggs, lightly beaten**
- 2 **to 4 tablespoons grated parmesan cheese**
- 3 **tablespoons chopped parsley**
  Salt and pepper

In a 3- to 4-quart pan over high heat, bring about 2 quarts water to a boil. Add noodles and cook, uncovered, until barely tender to bite, 2 to 3 minutes for fresh pasta, 8 to 9 minutes for dry. Drain well.

In a 10- to 12-inch frying pan, melt butter over medium-high heat. Add garlic

and onion; stir until garlic is limp, about 1 minute. Add pasta and mix well until hot and coated with butter. Add eggs, cheese, and 2 tablespoons parsley; mix just until eggs are softly set and cling to noodles, about 1 minute. Spoon onto a plate. Add salt and pepper to taste. Sprinkle noodles with remaining 1 tablespoon parsley. Makes 1 serving.

PER SERVING: 627 calories, 27 g protein, 67 g carbohydrates, 27 g fat, 587 mg cholesterol, 448 mg sodium

PASTA EMILY

Follow recipe for **pasta alla mama** (preceding); omit parsley. With cheese, add ½ cup diced **tomato**, ½ cup diced **avocado**, and 2 tablespoons chopped **fresh cilantro** (coriander). Garnish with 1 **avocado** or **tomato wedge** and additional chopped **cilantro**, if desired. Makes 1 serving.

PER SERVING: 762 calories, 30 g protein, 76 g carbohydrates, 38 g fat, 587 mg cholesterol, 459 mg sodium

PASTA MAXWELL

Follow recipe for **pasta alla mama** (preceding), adding 4 to 5 tablespoons chopped **smoked salmon** (about 1½ oz.) and 2 tablespoons thinly sliced **green onion** with the cheese. Garnish with 1 **green onion** (ends trimmed), if desired. Makes 1 serving.

PER SERVING: 680 calories, 35 g protein, 68 g carbohydrates, 29 g fat, 597 mg cholesterol, 782 mg sodium

PASTA PAPA

- ¼ **pound fresh capellini or 3 ounces dry capellini or dry coil vermicelli**
- 1 **hot or mild Italian sausage (4 oz.), casing removed**
- 2 **thick slices bacon, cut into ½-inch pieces**
- 1 **teaspoon minced garlic**
- 1 **tablespoon chopped green onion**
- 3 **large eggs, lightly beaten**
- 2 **tablespoons chopped parsley**
- 2 **to 3 tablespoons grated parmesan cheese**
  Salt and pepper

In a 3- to 4-quart pan over high heat, bring about 2 quarts water to a boil. Add noodles and cook, uncovered, until

Emily enjoys a favorite breakfast, a spin-off from Mama's recipe: noodles with avocado, tomatoes, and cilantro.

barely tender to bite, 1 to 2 minutes for fresh pasta, 3 to 4 minutes for dry. Drain well.

Crumble sausage into a 10- to 12-inch frying pan. Add bacon and stir often over medium-high heat until lightly browned. Drain off and discard all but 2 tablespoons fat.

Add garlic and green onions; stir often until onion is limp. Add cooked pasta and mix until hot and coated with fat. Add eggs, 1 tablespoon parsley, and parmesan cheese; stir until eggs are softly set. Spoon onto a plate. Add salt and pepper to taste. Sprinkle noodles with remaining 1 tablespoon parsley. Makes 1 generous or 2 smaller servings.

PER SERVING: 590 calories, 28 g protein, 35 g carbohydrates, 36 g fat, 465 mg cholesterol, 815 mg sodium

Two-Way Borscht

I N RUSSIA, *borscht is a favorite element of many meals. This popular beet soup comes in various forms and flavors. Here, we show two versions—one hot and hearty, the other cool and light—from Sonia Melnikova-Eichenwald, a recent Russian immigrant. Both can be made ahead.*

Mrs. Melnikova-Eichenwald loads her hot soup with vegetables and fresh herbs. She prefers an all-vegetable version, but you can add meat for a richer flavor.

The cold borscht uses spring beets with their tender tops. Add hard-cooked eggs, sour cream, cucumbers, and radishes to make a refreshing warm-weather meal.

SONIA'S COLD SPRING BORSCHT

- 12 or 13 small beets (about 3 lb. total) with tops
- 1 quart water
- 4 to 6 tablespoons red wine vinegar
- 2 quarts regular-strength chicken broth

Seasoning packet (recipe follows)
- 3 large russet potatoes (1½ lb. total), peeled and cut into ½-inch cubes
- 2 cloves garlic, pressed or minced
- 2 to 4 tablespoons sugar
  Salt
- 1 cup sour cream
- ½ cup thinly sliced chives or green onion
- 3 or 4 hard-cooked eggs, cut in half
- ½ cup chopped fresh dill or 2 tablespoons dry dill weed
- 1 small cucumber, thinly sliced
- 1 lemon, cut into wedges, optional
- 6 to 12 red radishes, whole or sliced

Trim tops off beets, leaving about 1 inch attached. Slice leaves crosswise into ¼-inch strips; rinse well, drain, and set aside. Scrub beets and rinse well.

In a 5- to 6-quart pan, combine beets, water, and ¼ cup vinegar. Cover, bring to a boil, then simmer until beets are tender when pierced, about 30 minutes. With a slotted spoon, lift beets out of pan and let cool. Pour cooking liquid into a bowl; reserve. Rinse pan.

To the pan add broth and seasoning packet; cover and bring to boiling. Add potatoes; cover and simmer until potatoes are tender when pierced, 15 to 20 minutes.

Meanwhile, remove stems, root ends, and peel from beets. Shred beets.

When potatoes are tender, add beet tops; simmer, uncovered, until tops wilt, 3 to 4 minutes. Add shredded beets, reserved beet cooking liquid, garlic, sugar, 1 to 2 tablespoons more vinegar, and salt to taste. Cool, cover, and chill until cold, at least 4 hours or up to next day.

Remove and discard seasoning packet. Pour into a tureen and offer sour cream, chives, eggs, dill, cucumber, and lemon to add to each serving. Serve radishes whole to eat with soup, or sliced to add to soup. Makes 8 entrée or 16 first-course servings.

PER ENTRÉE SERVING: 251 calories, 9 g protein, 33 g carbohydrates, 10 g fat, 115 mg cholesterol, 193 mg sodium

Seasoning packet. In a 15- by 24-inch piece of cheesecloth, tie up 1 large **onion,** quartered; 2 stalks **celery,** cut in half; 4 sprigs **fresh dill** or ½ teaspoon dry dill weed; and 3 sprigs **parsley.**

SONIA'S HOT WINTER BORSCHT

- 5 to 7 large beets (about 4 lb. total)
- 6 cups water
- 4 to 6 tablespoons red wine vinegar
- 3 tablespoons salad oil
- 2 large onions, chopped
- 3 large carrots, peeled and finely chopped
- 1 small yellow or red bell pepper, stemmed, seeded, and finely chopped
- 3 large Roma-type tomatoes, cored and coarsely chopped
- 3 to 3½ quarts regular-strength beef broth
  Seasoning packet (recipe follows)
- 4 pounds beef shanks (optional)
- 4 large russet potatoes (about 2½ lb. total), peeled and cut into ½-inch cubes
- 1 small head cabbage (¾ lb.), cored and finely chopped
- ⅓ cup chopped fresh basil leaves or 2 tablespoons dry basil leaves
- 4 cloves garlic, pressed or minced
  Salt
- 2 to 3 tablespoons sugar
- 2 tablespoons chopped parsley

Crunchy red radishes and thinly sliced cucumbers accompany fresh borscht. So do slices of hard-cooked egg, sour cream, minced chives, and dill sprigs.

1 cup sour cream
⅓ cup chopped fresh dill or 2
tablespoons dry dill weed
Lemon wedges (optional)
Small dried hot red chilies

Trim tops off beets, leaving about 1 inch of stems attached. Save tops for other uses or discard. Scrub and rinse beets well.

In a 10- to 12-quart pan, combine beets, water, and ¼ cup vinegar. Cover, bring to a boil, then simmer until beets are tender when pierced, about 45 minutes. With a slotted spoon, lift beets out of pan and let cool. Pour cooking liquid into a bowl and reserve. Rinse pan.

Add oil and onions to pan; stir often over medium-high heat until limp, about 5 minutes. Add carrots and bell pepper; stir often until vegetables are lightly browned, about 10 minutes. Stir in tomatoes and cook until soft, about 2 minutes.

Add broth (use 3½ quarts if you add meat) and seasoning packet to pan, and bring to boiling. (Add meat, if desired, and return to boiling. Cover and simmer until meat is very tender when pierced, about 2 hours. Lift out and let cool. Remove and discard fat and bones. Tear meat into bite-size pieces. Skim fat.)

Add potatoes. Cover and simmer until potatoes are tender when pierced, 15 to 20 minutes. Add cabbage, cover, and simmer until cabbage is limp, about 10 minutes. Discard seasoning packet.

Remove skin, stems, and root ends from beets. Cut beets into about 1-inch wedges, then cut crosswise into ¼-inch-thick slices. Set aside.

Add sliced beets, reserved beet cooking liquid, meat pieces, and chopped basil to pan. Bring to boiling. Stir in garlic; add salt, sugar, and 1 to 2 tablespoons more vinegar to taste. (If made ahead, cool, cover, and chill. Reheat to serve.) Ladle into a large tureen or individual bowls. Sprinkle with parsley. Offer sour cream, dill, lemon, and dried red chilies to add to each serving. Makes 10 entrée servings (16 if you've added meat), or 20 to 30 first-course servings. — *Sonia Melnikova-Eichenwald, San Francisco.*

PER ENTRÉE SERVING: 291 calories, 7 g protein, 46 g carbohydrates, 10 g fat, 10 mg cholesterol, 140 mg sodium

Seasoning packet. In a 15- by 24-inch piece of cheesecloth, tie up 2 stalks **celery,** cut in half; 4 sprigs **fresh dill** or ½ teaspoon dry dill weed; 3 sprigs **parsley;** 1 **bay leaf;** 8 **black peppercorns;** 8 **whole allspice;** and 1 **small dried hot red chili.**

Sonia serves her special hot borscht. Typical seasonings include dried chilies, sour cream, and chopped dill to taste. Offer garlic to rub onto pumpernickel bread and green onions to nibble.

Cooking on a Woodstove

THE WARMTH AND FRAGRANCE *of a fire in a wood-burning cookstove suggest times gone by, but cooking this way, even on a stove designed for heating your home or cabin, can be practical today.*

To support a pan safely, the stovetop must, of course, be flat. If your stove will hold a steady heat, chances are the surface temperature will often be between 300° and 500°, a good range for cooking. Why not use this heat for cooking as well as comfort?

HOW TO REGULATE HEAT ON A WOODSTOVE

Though woodstoves lack the precise heat controls of modern stoves, you can regulate cooking temperatures on them.

Stoking the fire is the first step. Heat output depends upon the amount and kind of wood burned, and how much air mixes with the fire. More fuel generates more heat. You need an open draft to get started, then less to hold the heat. With reduced draft, the stove radiates more heat. (With space-heating stoves, it may not be practical to build a hot fire just for cooking—if that would disrupt the basic function of warming the air.)

Woods burn differently. In general, pine burns quickly but doesn't give off much heat. Tamarack makes a hot fire that burns at a moderate rate. Birch and oak burn slowly, producing strong heat; they make good fuel for a fire that lasts. Experiment with fuel woods available to you to get the kind of heat you want.

A stove's temperature often jumps several hundred degrees as fresh fuel catches, then drops as it burns. By adding fuel frequently in smaller amounts, you can temper this cycle.

To test the surface temperature of stoves or ungreased pans, observe how a little water dropped on the surface behaves. If the water beads and rolls while sizzling, the surface is 450° to 650°; you can easily bring foods to a boil or pan-fry them on this heat. If the water drops spread out slightly and sizzle steadily, the stovetop is 300° to 400° and hot enough to simmer or bake foods. If the drops of water flatten and bubble, cooking will be slow, but perhaps adequate for long-term steaming. (Keep in mind that foods also may spatter as cooked.)

A helpful tool, especially for stovetop baking, is a surface thermometer available at hardware or woodstove stores for about $15. The thermometers usually register up to at least 800°.

Wood cookstoves have cooler and hotter areas—you just slide the pan around to find the heat you want. Smaller stoves designed for heating have fairly even surface temperatures.

PANS TO USE, FOODS TO COOK, MORE HEAT CONTROLS

Bottoms of pans used on a woodstove should be flat for maximum heat contact.

If foods are simmered (soups, rice), braised or stewed (spiced pork stew—following; chili, apples), or fried (potatoes, chicken), you need heavy pans for even heat. Use cast-iron, enameled cast-iron, or heavy-grade aluminum.

For baking such foods as cornbread (page 59) or biscuits, you need cast-iron pans *and* lids, because both must be heated before foods are added; their released heat helps cook the foods and creates the "oven."

If foods are boiled or simmered in a lot of water, as with pasta, potatoes, or green beans, you can use a thinner metal pan.

Or if the foods are steamed or cooked over hot water, as with rice pudding or a custard, the water pan can be a light metal.

For low, consistent heat, use a double boiler or a steamer, or fashion your own

For maximum heat to stir-fry, you need a stove with round, removable plates. Lift off a plate and nestle a wok in the opening over a hot fire.

To reduce heat, elevate pan ½ to 1½ inches on a metal trivet, wok ring, or metal rings (such as open-ended cans).

steamer. Put foods in a heatproof container that will fit inside the steamer on a rack. (You may need to fashion a string harness on the cooking container so you can remove it easily from the steamer.) Cover container if recipe directs. Add water in the steamer to bring level up to just below the rack.

Here are directions for cooking three dishes on a woodstove, each using a different technique. You will also find regular-stove alternatives.

SPICED PORK STEW

- **2 pounds boneless pork shoulder or butt, or leg, cut into 1-inch cubes**
- **1½ pounds tiny onions (½- to 1-in. diameter), peeled; or 1½ pounds small onions (1½- to 2-in. diameter), peeled and quartered**
- **1 cup dry red wine**
- **1 to 2 cups regular-strength chicken broth**
- **1 can (6 oz.) tomato paste**
- **¼ cup raisins**
- **¼ cup red wine vinegar**
- **2 tablespoons firmly packed brown sugar**
- **2 cloves garlic, pressed or minced**
- **2 teaspoons ground cumin**
- **1 whole dry bay leaf**
- **1 cinnamon stick, about 2 inches long**

To cook on a woodstove, set a cast-iron or other heavy 5- to 6-quart pan on stovetop heated to 300° to 500° until a drop of water splashed into the pan sizzles steadily, 10 to 15 minutes. Add meat, half the onions, and 2 tablespoons of the red wine; cover and simmer until liquid cooks out of meat and onions, about 20 minutes. Uncover and boil or simmer until almost all the liquid has evaporated, then stir often as drippings darken and turn a rich caramel color, 20 to 40 minutes.

Add remaining onions, remaining wine, 1 cup of the broth, tomato paste, raisins, vinegar, sugar, garlic, cumin, bay leaf, and cinnamon stick; stir to free browned bits in pan. Cover and bring mixture to a simmer. Simmer until meat is very tender when pierced, about 1½ hours, stirring occasionally; move pan to a cool or hotter area of stove, as needed, or elevate pan ½ to 1½ inches on a metal trivet to reduce rate of cooking. Add broth if stew begins to stick. When meat is tender; if you want a thicker consistency, cook, uncovered, until sauce reduces as you like.

To cook on a range, combine meat, half the onions, and 2 tablespoons of the wine in a 5- to 6-quart pan. Cover and cook on medium heat as directed for the woodstove. When the drippings are browned, continue as directed for the woodstove, cooking over medium-low heat.

Makes 5 or 6 servings. — *Steve Puffer and Janet Sturdevant, Sandpoint, Idaho.*

PER SERVING: 524 calories, 28 g protein, 24 g carbohydrates, 36 g fat, 109 mg cholesterol, 336 mg sodium

FRYING-PAN CORNBREAD

Baking on top of a woodstove is tricky until you get a feel for judging its temperature. To get started, we used a surface thermometer to measure the temperature of the stovetop; after practice, we could guess pretty accurately.

    1 cup yellow cornmeal
    1 cup all-purpose flour
    ¼ cup sugar
    1 tablespoon baking powder
    ½ teaspoon salt
    ⅛ teaspoon cayenne
       About ⅓ cup salad oil
    1 large egg
    1 cup milk
    1 can (8 oz.) corn, drained
    ½ cup sliced green onions (optional)
    ½ cup shredded cheddar cheese
       (optional)

To bake on a woodstove, you need a 10-inch cast-iron frying pan with a cast-iron lid. Side by side, set pan and lid, handle up, on stovetop until pan is hot enough to make a drop of water splashed into it sizzle steadily, 10 to 15 minutes. (The surface temperature of the stovetop should be between 350° and 400° and should stay between 300° and 400° as the bread bakes.)

If the drop of water bounces (if the surface temperature is 500° to 600° now and when the cornbread bakes), set the pan on a ½- to 1½-inch-high metal trivet.

Meanwhile, in a large bowl, combine cornmeal, flour, sugar, baking powder, salt, and cayenne; set aside. In another bowl, whisk together oil, egg, milk, corn, onions, and cheese; stir into cornmeal mixture just until blended.

When the frying pan is heated as directed, oil the inside of the pan. Pour batter into pan and cover with hot lid. Cook for 20 minutes; lift off lid and with a dry towel quickly wipe any condensation from inside of lid. Re-cover pan. If bread is browning around edges yet still moist in center, set pan on a ½- to 1½-inch-high metal trivet (or that much higher if already on a trivet) to continue baking.

Check and wipe any condensation from lid at 10-minute intervals until bread springs back when lightly pressed in the center and a slender wooden pick inserted in the center comes out clean, about 30 minutes total. If desired, sprinkle with cheese, cover, and cook until cheese melts, 3 to 4 minutes longer.

To bake in an oven, pour batter into a buttered 8- or 9-inch-square or round baking pan. Bake in a 400° oven until bread tests done (see preceding), about 25 minutes. If desired, sprinkle with cheese and bake until it melts, 1 to 2 minutes.

Cut into wedges, lift from pan, and serve warm. Makes 6 to 8 servings.

PER SERVING: 267 calories, 5 g protein, 37 g carbohydrates, 11 g fat, 39 mg cholesterol, 321 mg sodium

RICE PUDDING

You can cook this pudding in several hours in simmering water, or, with certain precautions, overnight with the same arrangement of pans on a stove that will keep a fire through the night.

       About 3 cups milk
    ⅓ cup short-grain rice, such as pearl
    ¼ cup sugar
    ½ teaspoon vanilla
    1 cinnamon stick (about 2 in. long)

To steam on a woodstove, first fashion a harness out of string for a 2- to 3-quart deep metal or heatproof bowl, so the bowl is easy to lift (or have wide tongs to lift the bowl). Mix together in the bowl 3 cups milk, rice, sugar, vanilla, and cinnamon stick. Cover securely with foil.

Choose a pan several inches deeper and wider than the bowl. Set a rack or trivet 1 to 3 inches above the pan bottom. Add water up to, not covering, the rack.

On a stovetop at 300° to 500°, bring water to simmering; lower bowl of pudding mixture onto rack. Cover water pan and simmer until pudding is thick and rice is creamy to bite, 3 to 4 hours. If

water boils, elevate pan on a ½- to 1½-inch metal trivet to maintain a simmer. Add hot water as needed to keep pan from boiling dry.

To cook on a woodstove overnight, you need a stove that can be fueled and closed down to keep the stovetop hot for 10 to 12 hours and the pudding hot enough to avoid spoiling.

Prepare pudding as directed for steaming; add boiling water to pan, and set pan on stovetop. Cook 6 to 8 hours. When you open the pan, water should be steaming and the pudding hot to touch. If temperature in center of pudding is below 120°, discard mixture, as harmful bacteria have developed.

To bake in an oven, stir 3 cups milk, rice, sugar, vanilla, and cinnamon stick together in a 9-inch-square baking dish or a 2- to 3-quart shallow casserole. Cover and bake in a 300° oven until thick and light golden color, about 3 hours. (Or you can bake the pudding uncovered; an amber, caramel-flavored skin will form on top.)

Stir pudding; serve warm. If thicker than you want, stir in more milk to desired consistency. Makes 4 cups, 4 to 6 servings.

PER SERVING: 149 calories, 5 g protein, 23 g carbohydrates, 4 g fat, 17 mg cholesterol, 60 mg sodium

Stew, cornbread, and pudding cook on wood-burning heater. To regulate heat, adjust pan positions, amount of fuel.

Chunky Spreads for Appetizers

SAVORY BLENDS *of vegetables, meat, or cheese can create delicious spreads for crisp toast. Serve the chunky mixes for party appetizers, luncheon entrées, or light snack-suppers.*

The first choice features baked vegetables—chopped, then lightly seasoned with vinegar—to eat on garlic toast. In the second recipe, watercress mayonnaise and chicken combine for a refreshing salad to scoop onto pumpernickel triangles. In the third recipe, you blend sweet cooked onions with prosciutto and creamy chèvre for a rye toast spread.

The mixtures can be made in advance. Serve Provençal vegetables at room temperature, chicken salad cold, and onions warm. The toast is best freshly made.

BAKED VEGETABLES PROVENÇAL WITH GARLIC TOAST

- ¼ cup olive oil
- 1 large eggplant (1¼ to 1½ lb.), cut in half lengthwise
- 1 large red bell pepper, cut in half
- 1 medium-size onion, cut in half
- 2 large Roma-type tomatoes, cored and cut in half
- 2 tablespoons wine vinegar
- ¼ cup chopped parsley
  Salt and pepper
  Niçoise olives (optional)
  Garlic toast (recipe follows)

Pour 2 tablespoons oil into a 10- by 15-inch pan. Lay eggplant, red pepper, and onion, cut sides down, in oil. Bake in a 350° oven until eggplant is very soft when pressed, 40 to 50 minutes.

Remove stems, skins, and seeds from baked vegetables (do not seed eggplant). Coarsely chop eggplant, pepper, onion, and tomato. Place vegetables in a strainer; gently press out excess liquid.

Pour vegetables into a bowl and add vinegar, parsley, remaining 2 tablespoons oil, and salt and pepper to taste. Mix to blend. (If made ahead, cover and chill up to overnight. Stir in any accumulated liquid before serving.)

Pour into a serving bowl and garnish with olives. Offer warm or at room temperature to spread on garlic toast. Makes about 4 cups, enough for 8 to 10 appetizer or 4 entrée servings.

PER APPETIZER SERVING: 190 calories, 3 g protein, 19 g carbohydrates, 12 g fat, 1 mg cholesterol, 138 mg sodium

Garlic toast. Mix 1 or 2 cloves **garlic**, minced or pressed, and ¼ cup **olive oil**. Cut 1 **baguette** (8 oz.) into ⅓-inch-thick diagonal slices.

Lay slices in a single layer on 2 baking sheets, 12- by 15-inch size. Broil about 4 inches from heat until golden, then turn over and brush tops with garlic oil. Broil until lightly browned, 1 to 2 minutes longer. Serve warm or cool.

CHICKEN SALAD WITH PUMPERNICKEL TRIANGLES

- 2 whole chicken breasts (1 lb. each), split
- ½ cup mayonnaise
- 2 tablespoons drained capers
- 1 tablespoon Dijon mustard
- 1 clove garlic, pressed or minced
- ½ cup lightly packed chopped watercress leaves
- ¾ cup thinly sliced celery
- 24 celery sticks (6 to 8 in.)
  Pumpernickel triangles (recipe follows)

In a 5- to 6-quart pan, bring 3 quarts water to boiling over high heat. Immerse chicken in water; return to boiling. Cover pan tightly; remove from heat. Let stand until chicken is white when cut in thickest part, 16 to 18 minutes. Lift out chicken and cool. Remove and discard skin and bones; tear meat into bite-size shreds.

In a bowl, mix mayonnaise, capers, mustard, garlic, and watercress. Add chicken and sliced celery; mix to coat. (If made ahead, cover and chill up to overnight.) Offer the chicken salad to spoon onto celery sticks and pumpernickel triangles. Makes 2½ cups salad, enough for 6 to 8 appetizer or 3 or 4 entrée servings.

PER APPETIZER SERVING: 329 calories, 22 g protein, 25 g carbohydrates, 16 g fat, 62 mg cholesterol, 548 mg sodium

Pumpernickel triangles. Cut 12 pieces **Westphalian pumpernickel** in half to make triangles. Lay slices in a single layer on 2 baking sheets, 12- by 15-inch size. Broil 4 inches from heat until lightly toasted, about 2 minutes. Turn slices over and brush with 2 tablespoons melted **butter** or margarine. Broil until lightly toasted, 1 to 2 minutes. Serve warm or cool.

SWEET ONIONS ON HERB TOAST

- 2 tablespoons butter or margarine
- 3 large onions, thinly sliced
- 2 ounces thinly sliced prosciutto, cut into thin shreds
- ¼ pound mild chèvre, such as Montrachet or bûcheron
  Herb toast (recipe follows)

In a 10- to 12-inch frying pan, combine butter and onions. Cook over medium-high heat, stirring often, until onions are golden and very limp, about 20 minutes; reduce heat if onions begin to brown. (If made ahead, cool, cover, and chill up to overnight. Stir over low heat until hot.)

Add prosciutto and chèvre to onions; stir until chèvre melts. Serve warm to spread on herb toast. Makes 2 cups, enough for 6 to 8 appetizer or 3 or 4 entrée servings.

PER APPETIZER SERVING: 177 calories, 6 g protein, 16 g carbohydrates, 10 g fat, 20 mg cholesterol, 410 mg sodium

Herb toast. Mix 2 tablespoons **butter** or margarine, melted, with 2 teaspoons minced **fresh thyme leaves** (or 1 teaspoon dry thyme leaves).

Place 24 **buffet rye bread slices** (2- to 3-in. size) in a single layer on 2 baking sheets, 12- by 15-inch size. Broil 4 inches from heat until golden, 1 to 2 minutes. Turn over. Brush with butter. Broil until golden, 1 to 2 minutes. Serve warm or cool.

Warm, slow-cooked onions and chèvre cheese mixture go with toasted rye bread.

Mignonnette Sauces

DISTINCTIVE FLAVOR *without a lot of calories—is it possible? Yes, if you use what the French call a mignonnette sauce. (Mignonnette is the French word for a coarsely ground pepper; it's not to be confused with the plant family mignonette.)*

The most familiar mignonnette is a thin, totally lean vinegar and ground pepper sauce that vies with horseradish as a way to bring out the wild side of oysters. Here we suggest three versions of our own.

It is the pairing of acid with some kind of heat that gives tangy impact to these sauces. You start with white wine vinegar or fresh lime juice, then add chilies or ginger to give the sauce some controlled fire. Tiny bits of vegetables or fruit add color and lend character and style to each mixture.

Besides being fat-free, these mignonnettes have the advantage of keeping well. You might make up a batch or two and keep some in the refrigerator to use freely. The sauces can last for at least a month, but quality drops if you keep them longer.

How do you serve a mignonnette sauce? With the same abandon as you might add a squeeze of lemon juice.

Ladle some onto any plainly cooked or raw vegetables that would taste good with a dash of lemon: carrots, broccoli, tomatoes, baked or boiled potatoes. Or mix with shrimp or crab to make a salad. Or spoon onto cold raw oysters served on the half-shell.

Because the sauces are thin, you might like to serve them in tiny individual dishes, so diners can dip in bites of simply cooked fish, poultry, or meat.

Give or take a few calories, 1 tablespoon of any of the sauces amounts to a mere 3 to 10 calories—and 1 or 2 tablespoons makes a serving.

Shrimp becomes salad when you add green apple mignonnette sauce; the sauce keeps well in refrigerator, has many uses.

GREEN APPLE MIGNONNETTE SAUCE

- 1½ cups lime juice
- ¾ cup finely diced peeled tart green apple
- 3 cloves garlic, minced or pressed
- 3 tablespoons *each* chopped tomato and sugar
- 1 tablespoon anchovy paste or 3 canned anchovy fillets, minced
- 1½ teaspoons crushed dried hot red chilies

In a 3- to 3½-cup jar, combine lime juice, apple, garlic, tomato, sugar, anchovy, and chilies. Use, or cover tightly and refrigerate; the sauce keeps, ready to use, up to 1 month. Makes about 2⅓ cups.

PER TABLESPOON: 9 calories, .12 g protein, 2 g carbohydrates, .06 g fat, .17 mg cholesterol, 14 mg sodium

CARROT MIGNONNETTE SAUCE

- 1½ cups white wine vinegar
- ⅓ cup peeled and finely diced carrots
- ⅓ cup *each* finely diced green bell pepper, minced shallots, and firmly packed brown sugar
- 2 tablespoons minced ginger
- 3 cloves garlic, minced or pressed

In a 3- to 3½-cup jar, combine vinegar, carrots, bell pepper, shallots, sugar, ginger, and garlic. Use, or cover tightly and refrigerate; the sauce keeps, ready to use, up to 1 month. Makes about 2⅔ cups.

PER TABLESPOON: 10 calories, .04 g protein, 2 g carbohydrates, 0 g fat, 0 mg cholesterol, 1 mg sodium

JALAPEÑO MIGNONNETTE SAUCE

To avoid skin irritation, wear rubber gloves when preparing the chilies—and take care not to touch your eyes.

- 2 cups white wine vinegar
- 6 small fresh green or red jalapeño chilies, stemmed, seeded, and finely diced
- 1 medium-size red or yellow bell pepper, stemmed, seeded, and finely diced
- 1 clove garlic, minced or pressed
- ¼ cup minced shallots
- ½ teaspoon coarsely ground black pepper

In a 3- to 3½-cup jar, combine vinegar, jalapeño chilies, bell pepper, garlic, shallots, and pepper. Use, or cover tightly and refrigerate; the sauce keeps, ready to use, up to 1 month. Makes about 2⅔ cups.

PER TABLESPOON: 4 calories, .08 g protein, 1 g carbohydrates, 0 g fat, 0 mg cholesterol, .38 mg sodium

Stuffed Chicken Breasts

F RESH, EASY, MAKE-AHEAD — *that's what busy cooks request. These recipes are just that; both use chicken breasts stuffed with a colorful filling: one with broccoli, the other with red peppers. Assemble a day ahead, then bake to serve.*

BROCCOLI & CHEESE-STUFFED CHICKEN BREASTS

  2 tablespoons butter or margarine
  1 small onion, chopped
  2 teaspoons dry tarragon leaves
  ¾ pound broccoli; or 1 package (10 oz.) frozen broccoli flowerets, thawed and drained
  2 tablespoons water
  1½ cups (6 oz.) shredded Swiss cheese or jack cheese
  6 chicken breast halves (about 1¾ lb. total), boned and skinned
   Chive-tarragon sauce (recipe follows)
   Salt

Melt butter in a 10- to 12-inch frying pan over medium heat. Add onion and tarragon. Cook, stirring occasionally, until onion is limp, about 5 minutes.

Cut tough stems from broccoli and discard. Trim off flowerets, coarsely chop, and set aside. Peel tender stems and chop; add to flowerets. Add broccoli and water to pan; cover, stirring occasionally, until stems are tender-crisp to bite, about 5 minutes. (If using frozen broccoli, coarsely chop and add to onion. Omit water; cook just until hot.) Remove from heat and stir in 1 cup of cheese; cool.

Place 1 chicken piece between 2 sheets of plastic wrap. Pound chicken with a smooth mallet until about ¼ inch thick. Repeat with each breast.

In the center of each breast half, mound equal amounts of the broccoli. Lift edges of chicken up and over filling to enclose. Set filled breasts, seam side

Bright green broccoli—along with onion and Swiss cheese—fills this tender chicken breast.

down, in a buttered 9- by 13-inch baking dish. Sprinkle remaining cheese evenly on top of each piece. At this point, you can cover and chill until the next day.

Bake, uncovered, in a 450° oven until meat turns white and filling is hot in center (cut to test), 15 to 18 minutes. Broil 4 to 6 inches from heat to brown cheese, about 2 minutes.

Transfer to a platter or plates. Offer chive-tarragon sauce and salt to add to taste. Serves 6.

PER SERVING: 253 calories, 29 g protein, 4 g carbohydrates, 13 g fat, 86 mg cholesterol, 181 mg sodium

Chive-tarragon sauce. In a bowl, stir together ⅓ cup **seasoned rice vinegar** or ⅓ cup rice wine vinegar, ½ teaspoon **sugar**, 1 tablespoon minced **fresh** or dry **chives,** and ½ teaspoon **dry tarragon leaves.**

ROASTED PEPPER & PARMESAN-STUFFED CHICKEN BREASTS

Follow directions for **broccoli and cheese-stuffed chicken breasts** but omit the broccoli, water, and Swiss cheese. After the onion is cooked, set aside. Drain and chop 2 jars (7 oz. each) **roasted red peppers.** Mix peppers with ¼ cup freshly shredded **parmesan cheese** and the onions.

Pound chicken pieces and fill as directed. Sprinkle about 2 teaspoons freshly shredded **parmesan cheese** (about ¼ cup total) on each piece and bake; don't broil. Make sauce, omitting tarragon. Serve with sauce and salt to taste. Serves 6.

PER SERVING: 163 calories, 22 g protein, 3 g carbohydrates, 6 g fat, 64 mg cholesterol, 173 mg sodium

A Light Hand with Seafood

LIGHT AND REFRESHING *describes these Southeast Asian dishes based on seafood. Crab claws and shrimp swim in broth for the Vietnamese soup; you add condiments to taste. Assertive seasonings—chili, ginger, and garlic—flavor the swordfish stir-fry, served hot over cool watercress.*

Bean paste, rice sticks, and fish sauce are available in Asian markets and some grocery stores; or use alternatives.

VIETNAMESE SUMMER SOUP

- 2 ounces rice sticks (*mai fun*)
  Water
- 6 cups regular-strength chicken broth
- 1 tablespoon finely chopped fresh ginger
- 1 tablespoon Vietnamese fish sauce (*nuoc nam*) or soy sauce
- ½ pound large shrimp (30 to 35 per lb.), shelled and deveined
- ½ pound cooked or thawed frozen crab claws (or large shrimp, shelled and deveined)

Seafood and rice sticks mingle in light soup. Enhance with lime, chilies, fried onions.

- ¼ cup sliced green onions
- 1 lime or lemon, cut into wedges
  Crisp-fried onions (directions follow)
  Crushed dried hot red chilies

Break rice sticks into 3-inch pieces. Cover with water and let stand until limp, about 20 minutes; stir to separate noodles.

Meanwhile, in a 5- to 6-quart pan over high heat, combine broth, ginger, and fish sauce; bring to boiling. Drain noodles and then add them to broth along with shrimp and crab; cover and remove from heat. Let stand until shrimp are opaque in center (cut 1 to test), about 10 minutes. Stir in green onions.

Pour soup into a tureen or ladle directly into individual bowls. Offer limes, crisp-fried onions, and chilies to season each portion. Makes 4 or 5 servings.

PER SERVING: 171 calories, 20 g protein, 13 g carbohydrates, 4 g fat, 102 mg cholesterol, 453 mg sodium

Crisp-fried onions. Peel and thinly slice 2 medium-size **onions**; separate rings. Pour ⅓ to ½ cup **all-purpose flour** into a bag. Add onions; shake to coat with flour.

In a deep 2½- to 3-quart pan, bring 1½ inches **salad oil** to 300° on a thermometer. Add onions, ¼ at a time. Cook, stirring often, until golden, about 5 minutes. Keep oil at 300°.

Lift out onions with a slotted spoon; drain on paper towels. If you've made them ahead, cool; store airtight up to 3 days. Makes 3½ cups.

PER ½ CUP: 78 calories, 1 g protein, 5 g carbohydrates, 6 g fat, 0 mg cholesterol, 1 mg sodium

THAI FISH & WATERCRESS SALAD

- 4 cups lightly packed watercress sprigs (tough stems removed), washed and crisped
- 1 pound boned and skinned swordfish or tuna steaks, ½ or 1 inch thick
- ¼ cup sliced almonds
- 3 tablespoons salad oil
- 2 tablespoons minced fresh ginger
- 3 cloves garlic, minced or pressed
- 2 or 3 fresh jalapeño chilies, stemmed, seeded, and thinly sliced crosswise

Stir-fried fish and shrimp top crisp watercress to make a hot-cold entrée salad.

- 1 tablespoon Oriental bean paste (optional)
- 1 tablespoon Oriental fish sauce or soy sauce
- ¼ pound large shrimp (31 to 35 per lb.), peeled, deveined, and halved lengthwise
  Lemon wedges

Arrange watercress equally on 4 salad plates; chill.

If fish is 1 inch thick, halve horizontally. Cut fish into strips about ½ inch wide and 3 inches long. Set aside.

In a wok or 12- to 14-inch frying pan over high heat, stir almonds until golden, 2 to 3 minutes. Pour out and set aside.

Mix oil, ginger, garlic, and chilies; add to wok and stir for 1 minute. Add bean paste, fish sauce, fish, and shrimp. Stir-fry gently until fish is opaque in center (cut to test), 2 to 3 minutes.

Evenly spoon fish over watercress; sprinkle with almonds. Offer with lemon wedges. Makes 4 servings. —*Yupa Holzner, Lake Arrowhead, Calif.*

PER SERVING: 325 calories, 31 g protein, 6 g carbohydrates, 20 g fat, 79 mg cholesterol, 668 mg sodium

Warm Fruit Desserts

OLD-FASHIONED, *but with a new twist, these two fruit desserts are both served warm from the oven. One combines familiar components for a new effect: shortbread base, apple filling, and crackly nut-and-meringue topping. The other pairs baked pineapple with berries and prunes.*

ROXIE'S APPLE SQUARES

- ½ cup (¼ lb.) butter or margarine
- 1¼ cups all-purpose flour
- 3 large tart green apples, such as Newtown Pippin
- 2 tablespoons lemon juice
- 2 large eggs
- 1 cup sugar
- ¼ teaspoon baking powder
- ½ teaspoon ground cinnamon
- ½ cup sliced almonds

In a bowl, beat butter and 1 cup of the flour until smooth. Press evenly into bottom of 7- by 11-inch or 9-inch-square baking pan. Bake in a 350° oven until golden, about 15 minutes.

Peel, core, and chop apples. Mix with lemon juice in a bowl. Arrange evenly over baked crust.

In the bowl, beat eggs until foamy. Gradually add sugar; continue beating until thick. Mix in baking powder, cinnamon, and remaining flour. Pour evenly over apples; sprinkle almonds on top.

Bake in a 350° oven until top is golden, 30 to 35 minutes. Cut into squares and serve warm. Or let cool and store, uncovered, up to 2 days (topping softens if covered). Makes 6 to 8 servings. — *Roxie Komian, Walnut Creek, Calif.*

PER SERVING: 369 calories, 5 g protein, 50 g carbohydrates, 17 g fat, 100 mg cholesterol, 150 mg sodium

Pineapple boats hold fruit cargo: warm prunes and pineapple, raspberries on top.

BAKED PINEAPPLE COMPOTE

- 1 large pineapple, about 5 pounds
- 8 ounces (1⅓ cups) pitted prunes
- ¼ cup firmly packed brown sugar
- 2 tablespoons butter or margarine
- 2 tablespoons lemon juice
- 1 cup fresh or thawed frozen unsweetened raspberries

Halve pineapple lengthwise through top. With a grapefruit knife, cut around edges of fruit, leaving ¾-inch-thick shells. Cut out core and discard. Cut across fruit (in shells) to make 1- to 1½-inch chunks. Slide knife beneath chunks to free from bottom of shells. Remove chunks. Pour pineapple juice out of shells into a 2- to 3-quart pan and set aside. Return pineapple chunks to shells. Place shells cut side up in a rimmed 12- by 15-inch baking pan. Bake in a 400° oven until chunks are hot to touch, 15 to 20 minutes.

Meanwhile, stir prunes, sugar, and butter into juice in pan; bring to a boil over high heat. Cover and simmer, stirring occasionally, until sauce is slightly thickened, 10 to 15 minutes. Mix in lemon juice. Spoon evenly over warm pineapple in shells, mix gently, then top with raspberries. Place shells on a platter and spoon fruit into bowls. Serves 6. — *Dorothea Kent, Port Angeles, Wash.*

PER SERVING: 266 calories, 2 g protein, 60 g carbohydrates, 5 g fat, 10 mg cholesterol, 46 mg sodium

Tangy Sweets from Goat's Milk

GOAT'S MILK has long had an appreciative, if rather limited, audience. But with the increasing popularity of goat cheeses—due largely to their fresh, sharp flavor from the milk—it's appropriate to investigate other ways to capture this tang.

Canned evaporated goat's milk, now widely available in markets (next to the canned milk), is a good place to start. In sweets, particularly, the milk's tartness proves refreshing. One classic use is in the Mexican confection cajeta (kah-hay-tah), a thick, liquid caramel made of goat's milk boiled with sugar. Eat by itself or dip dried fruit or cookies into it.

Norway's famous brown cheese or gjetöst (goat's and cow's milk) is the surprise addition in caramels. Tasters were mystified, then intrigued by the flavor.

CAJETA

- 1 can (12½ oz.) evaporated goat's milk
- 1 cup sugar
- 2 tablespoons butter or margarine

In a 3- to 4-quart pan, combine milk, sugar, and butter. Bring to a boil over high heat. Stir often for the first 10 minutes, then stir constantly (mixture scorches easily) as cajeta darkens to a medium caramel color and thickens but still flows readily from spoon, about 20 minutes total. Cajeta thickens as it cools.

Serve warm or cool in tiny bowls. To store, cover airtight and chill up to 3 months. To reheat in nonmetal container in a microwave oven, cook on full power (100 percent) until warm, 1 to 2 minutes;

Dip dried apricot into thick, golden cajeta, a traditional Mexican sweet; enjoy with tea and shortbread.

stir and serve. Makes about 1 cup; allow 3 tablespoons for a serving.

PER TABLESPOON: 55 calories, 1 g protein, 9 g carbohydrates, 2 g fat, 6 mg cholesterol, 21 mg sodium

GJETÖST CARAMELS

- 1 can (12½ oz.) evaporated goat's milk
- 1 cup sugar
- ½ cup (¼ lb.) butter or margarine, cut into pieces
- 1 package (8.8 oz.) gjetöst cheese, cut into ½-inch cubes
- 3 cups miniature marshmallows
- ½ teaspoon vanilla
- ½ cup chopped almonds

In a 5- to 6-quart pan, stir together milk, sugar, and butter. Over medium-high heat, stir constantly until mixture reaches 230° on a thermometer, about 25 minutes. Remove at once from heat and add cheese, marshmallows, vanilla, and nuts; stir until cheese and marshmallows are melted.

Pour into a buttered 8- or 9-inch-square pan. Chill until firm, about 1 hour. Cut into 1- to 1½-inch squares; wrap each in plastic wrap. Serve, or chill up to 1 month. Makes about 3 dozen pieces.

PER PIECE: 113 calories, 2 g protein, 13 g carbohydrates, 6 g fat, 9 mg cholesterol, 78 mg sodium

Stir marshmallows, gjetöst cheese, and almonds into goat's milk caramel for tangy candy.

More March Recipes

OTHER MARCH ARTICLES *featured directions for making turkey jerky, a satisfying brown rice & avocado salad, a streamlined method for preparing moussaka, a spicy golden sauce to dress up cooked vegetables, an intriguing dessert, and thick citrus marmalade.*

TURKEY JERKY

A modern twist on a very old American tradition—that's jerky made of turkey. Early pioneers, borrowing from the culinary lore of native Indians, preserved thin slices of salted game by drying meat in the sun or by the campfire. Game was followed by beef, and now turkey is the jerky for today's fitness conscious snacker.

Compared to jerky made with beef flank steak (when both meats are trimmed of all fat), turkey-breast jerky has only about a sixth as much fat by weight and is about a third lower in calories (1 oz. of turkey jerky has 88 calories). Its flavor is also milder, though not necessarily more delicate.

Start with a piece of boned, skinned turkey breast, or purchase the slender turkey fillets, called tenderloins, that lie parallel to the breastbone.

Cut turkey with the grain for a chewy-textured jerky, across the grain for a more brittle snack.

In addition to basic jerky seasonings, we include a teriyaki variation. For the liveliest flavor, let strips marinate the maximum time. Dry onion and garlic powders are options that give slightly more intense taste. If you want less saltiness, rinse the strips and pat them dry before drying.

It's the drying step—in a dehydrator or oven—that removes moisture, inhibits bacterial development, and preserves the turkey.

- 1 **pound boned and skinned turkey breast or tenderloins**
- 1 **tablespoon salt**
- ½ **cup water**
- 2 **tablespoons firmly packed brown sugar**
- 2 **cloves garlic, minced or pressed, or ¼ teaspoon garlic powder**
- ½ **small onion, minced, or ¼ teaspoon onion powder**
- 1 **teaspoon pepper**
- ½ **teaspoon liquid smoke**
  Nonstick cooking spray

Rinse meat and pat dry. Pull off and discard any fat and connective tissue. To make meat easier to slice, freeze it until it feels firm, but not hard. Cut turkey into ⅛- to ¼-inch-thick slices: cut breast piece with or across the grain, and tenderloins lengthwise.

In a bowl, stir together salt, water, brown sugar, garlic, onion, pepper, and liquid smoke. Add turkey and mix well. Cover and chill at least 1 hour or up to 24 hours; meat will absorb most of the liquid.

Depending upon drying method, evenly coat dehydrator racks (you need 3, each about 10 by 13 in.) or metal racks (to cover a 10- by 15-inch baking pan) with nonstick cooking spray.

Lift turkey strips from liquid, shaking off excess, and lay strips close together, but not overlapping, on racks.

In a dehydrator, arrange trays as manufacturer directs and dry at 140° until a cool piece of jerky (remove from the dehydrator and let stand about 5 minutes) cracks and breaks when bent, 4½ to 5 hours.

In an oven set at 150° to 200°, place pan on center rack; prop door open about 2 inches. Dry until a cool piece of jerky cracks and breaks when bent (see above), 3 to 5 hours.

Let jerky cool on racks, then remove. Serve, or store in airtight containers in a cool, dry place up to 3 weeks, in the refrigerator up to 4 months, or longer in the freezer. Makes about 7 ounces.

PER OUNCE: 88 calories, 15 g protein, 3 g carbohydrates, 1 g fat, 40 mg cholesterol, 751 mg sodium

TERIYAKI TURKEY JERKY

Prepare **turkey jerky** (recipe precedes), omitting salt and water. Add ¼ cup **soy sauce** and 2 teaspoons **Worcestershire.**

PER OUNCE: 94 calories, 16 g protein, 4 g carbohydrates, 1 g fat, 40 mg cholesterol, 498 mg sodium

BROWN RICE & AVOCADO SALAD

The sturdy flavor and texture of brown rice contrast pleasingly with smooth avocados in this salad. It satisfies as a main dish but also goes well with grilled meats.

- 1 **cup long-grain brown rice**
- 1 **tablespoon butter or margarine**
- 2½ **cups regular-strength chicken broth**
- 1½ **teaspoons dry marjoram leaves**
- 3 **medium-size (about 2 lb. total) firm-ripe avocados**
- ½ **cup minced parsley**
- 3 **green onions (ends trimmed), thinly sliced**
- 5 **tablespoons lemon juice**
- 3 **tablespoons olive or salad oil**
- 1 **teaspoon coarsely ground pepper**
  Salt

To a 10- to 12-inch pan, add brown rice and butter. Stir often over medium-high heat until rice turns opaque, about 3 minutes. Add broth and marjoram, mix, and bring to a boil on high heat. Reduce heat, cover, and simmer until rice is tender to bite, about 40 minutes. Let cool to room temperature or cover and chill at least 1 hour or up to 2 days; serve at room temperature or cold.

Cut 2 avocados in half and discard pits. Peel avocados and cut into ½-inch cubes; place in a large bowl. Add parsley, green onions, lemon juice, oil, and pepper; mix gently. If made ahead, cover and chill up to overnight.

Pour rice into a salad bowl and mix gently with diced avocados and dressing. Cut remaining avocado in half, pit, then peel. Cut each half into thin lengthwise slices and arrange slices, overlapping, over rice mixture. Spoon onto plates and add salt to taste. Makes 7 or 8 servings.

PER SERVING: 292 calories, 4 g protein, 26 g carbohydrates, 20 g fat, 4 mg cholesterol, 46 mg sodium

STOVETOP MOUSSAKA

One of the best-known casseroles of the Balkans and Middle East, moussaka features vegetables and meat combined in myriad ways. Eggplant is the most familiar, although potatoes, artichokes, squash, and other vegetables are enlisted as well, combined with seasoned lamb or beef.

Moussaka is usually layered and baked, but a quicker method is to cook this dish over direct heat. Here, we present a streamlined one-pan recipe.

Serve with hot cooked noodles or rice.

- 1 **large eggplant (about 2 lb.)**
- 1½ **teaspoons salt**
  Water
- 2 **tablespoons olive or salad oil**
- 1 **pound ground lean lamb**
- 1 **medium-size onion, chopped**
- 2 **garlic cloves, minced or pressed**
- 4 **medium-size firm-ripe Roma-type tomatoes (about ¾ lb. total), cored and seeded**

1 can (8 oz.) tomato sauce
3 tablespoons minced parsley
1½ teaspoons cumin seed
1 teaspoon crushed dried hot red chilies
1 package (10 oz.) thawed frozen pearl onions
Unflavored yogurt or sour cream, optional

Trim off and discard eggplant stem. Cut eggplant into 1-inch cubes and mix with salt; let drain in a colander for 30 minutes to 1 hour. Rinse eggplant well under cool, running water; drain and pat dry.

Pour oil into a 10- to 12-inch frying pan on medium-high heat. When hot, add eggplant; turn pieces often with a wide spatula and cook until cubes are lightly browned, 6 to 8 minutes.

Add 2 tablespoons water; stir and turn eggplant, then quickly cover pan. About every minute, add another 2 tablespoons water, turning pieces and replacing lid quickly; cook until eggplant is very soft when pressed, about 6 minutes longer. Scrape into a bowl and set aside.

Add lamb, onion, and garlic to frying pan, and turn heat to high. Stir to crumble lamb, then continue stirring until meat is very well browned, about 8 minutes. Stir in eggplant and any juices; also add tomatoes, tomato sauce, parsley, cumin seed, and chilies. Simmer, covered, on medium heat until flavors are well blended and tomatoes are soft, about 20 minutes longer. Gently stir in onions and cook until hot, 1 to 2 minutes more. Serve hot. If made ahead, cool, cover, and chill up to 2 days; to reheat, stir in frying pan over medium heat. Top portions with yogurt. Makes 6 servings.

PER SERVING: 339 calories, 15 g protein, 20 g carbohydrates, 23 g fat, 54 mg cholesterol, 468 mg sodium

SPICED YOGURT-CASHEW SAUCE FOR VEGETABLES

Infused with Indian flavors and sweet, slow-cooked onions, this richly seasoned sauce dresses plain vegetables with a delicious golden-tinged coating. It's especially good on potatoes, carrots, beans, and winter squash.

⅔ cup roasted salted cashews
2 tablespoons butter or margarine
2 large onions, thinly sliced
1 tablespoon minced fresh ginger
2 cloves garlic, pressed or minced
¼ teaspoon ground turmeric

⅛ to ¼ teaspoon cayenne
1 tablespoon all-purpose flour
1⅓ cups regular-strength chicken broth
1 cup unflavored yogurt
Salt and pepper

Whirl nuts in a blender until finely ground; set aside.

In a 10- to 12-inch frying pan, stir butter and onions frequently over medium-high heat until onions are very limp and light gold, 20 to 30 minutes; reduce heat to medium if onions begin to brown. Add ginger, garlic, and turmeric, and cayenne to taste; cook 1 minute. Stir in flour.

Add broth; stir over medium heat until boiling. Add ground nuts and yogurt; stir until sauce is hot. Add salt and pepper to taste. If made ahead, cool, cover, and chill up to 2 days; stir over medium heat until hot. Makes about 3⅓ cups.

PER ⅓ CUP: 104 calories, 3 g protein, 8 g carbohydrates, 7 g fat, 8 mg cholesterol, 102 mg sodium

AUSTRALIAN LAMINGTONS

They may look like fuzzy lambs, but tradition says these Australian cakes were named after Lord Lamington, governor of Queensland at the turn of the century. Aussies bake lamingtons for fund-raisers and serve them to deserving children; adults like them, too.

¾ cup sugar
½ cup (¼ lb.) butter or margarine
2 large eggs
1 teaspoon vanilla
¼ cup milk
1½ cups all-purpose flour
1 teaspoon baking powder
2½ cups sweetened flaked coconut
Cocoa icing (recipe follows)

In a large bowl, beat sugar and butter until creamy. Add eggs, 1 at a time, and beat well. Mix in vanilla and milk. Stir together flour and baking powder, then beat into egg mixture until blended.

Butter and flour-dust an 8-inch-square pan; spread batter evenly in bottom. Bake in a 350° oven until a slender wooden pick inserted in center comes out clean, about 25 minutes. Let cool in pan on a rack for 10 minutes, then turn out of pan onto rack and let cool.

Cut cake into 9 equal squares. Place coconut in a bowl. Dip cake pieces, 1 at a time, in icing, then turn in coconut to

coat. Place on a rack until icing is firm to touch, about 10 minutes. Serve, or store airtight up to 2 days. Makes 9 servings.

PER SERVING: 509 calories, 5 g protein, 74 g carbohydrates, 23 g fat, 100 mg cholesterol, 263 mg sodium

Cocoa icing. In a bowl, beat 3 tablespoons **butter** or margarine. Sift in ¼ cup **unsweetened cocoa** and 2¼ cups **powdered sugar.** Add 1 teaspoon **vanilla** and ⅓ cup **hot water.** Beat until smooth; use warm.

THREE-CITRUS MARMALADE

Striking a fine balance between bitter and sweet, this thick marmalade will liven up breakfast toast or muffins.

2 medium-size (about 2 lb. total) grapefruit
2 medium-size (about ¾ lb. total) thin-skinned oranges
2 large (about 10 oz. total) lemons
3 cups water
7 cups sugar

Quarter grapefruit; halve oranges and lemons lengthwise. Thinly slice fruit crosswise, saving juices; discard seeds and end pieces.

In an 8- to 10-quart pan, combine fruit, juices, and water; bring to a boil over high heat. Cover and simmer until peel is translucent, 25 to 30 minutes; stir often. Stir in sugar. Boil, uncovered, over medium-high heat until mixture is slightly thinner than you want for finished marmalade, 25 to 30 minutes; stir often. Cool and serve. To store, chill airtight up to 2 months; or seal, below. Makes 4 pints.—*Mrs. R. Noble, Idaho Falls, Idaho.*

PER TABLESPOON: 45 calories, .07 g protein, 12 g carbohydrates, 0 g fat, 0 mg cholesterol, .22 mg sodium

To seal. Pour hot marmalade into 4 clean, hot, pint-size canning jars to within ¼ inch of rim; wipe rims clean. Top with new lids heated as manufacturer directs, then tightly screw on bands; don't force.

Lower jars onto rack in an 8-quart or larger kettle of simmering water; if needed, add simmering water to cover jars by at least 1 inch. Bring water to 180° and hold at that temperature for 10 minutes. Lift out jars and set on a towel to cool completely.

Press centers of lids: if they stay down, jars are sealed; if they pop up, store jars in the refrigerator up to 2 months.

PETITE PEAR TEA CAKES

- ½ cup (¼ lb.) butter or margarine
- ¾ cup granulated sugar
- 2 large eggs
- 1 teaspoon vanilla
- ¼ cup unflavored yogurt or buttermilk
- 2 cups all-purpose flour
- 1 teaspoon baking powder
- ½ teaspoon baking soda
- ⅛ teaspoon ground nutmeg
- 1 can (1 lb.) sliced pears packed in juice or light syrup, drained (reserve liquid for other uses) and coarsely chopped
- 1 tablespoon powdered sugar

Tiny nutmeg-scented pear muffins go well with morning or afternoon tea.

In a large bowl, beat butter with granulated sugar until fluffy. Add eggs, vanilla, and yogurt; beat to mix well. Combine flour, baking powder, baking soda, and nutmeg; add to butter mixture and blend well. Stir in pears.

Spoon batter into buttered tiny muffin cups (about 1½-in. diameter). Bake in a 375° oven until golden brown and a slender wooden pick inserted in center comes out clean, about 20 minutes. Invert onto racks and cool 10 minutes; dust tops with powdered sugar. Serve warm or cool. If made ahead, store airtight up to next day. Makes 3 dozen. — *Susanne Staton, Wapato, Wash.*

PER CAKE: 77 calories, 1 g protein, 11 g carbohydrates, 3 g fat, 22 mg cholesterol, 55 mg sodium

---

Pour wine-egg mixture over bread slices, caramelized onions, and cheese; bake.

GRUYÈRE CHEESE PIE

- 2 tablespoons butter or margarine
- 2 large onions, thinly sliced
- 9 slices sourdough or French bread, each slice ½ inch thick and about 2½ by 4½ inches
- 1 teaspoon caraway seed
- 2½ cups (about ½ lb.) shredded gruyère or Swiss cheese
- 3 large eggs
- ⅓ cup all-purpose flour
- ¼ teaspoon ground nutmeg
- ¾ cup *each* milk and dry white wine

In a 10- to 12-inch frying pan, melt butter over medium heat. Add onions and cook, stirring occasionally, until very limp and golden, 20 to 25 minutes. Remove from heat; set aside.

Fit bread slices snugly together in a single layer over bottom of a buttered, shallow 2½-quart baking dish. Evenly distribute onions, caraway seed, and cheese over bread. In a bowl, whisk together eggs, flour, nutmeg, milk, and wine until well mixed; pour evenly over cheese.

Bake in a 375° oven until the top of the pie is golden brown and the center appears firm when dish is gently shaken, 25 to 30 minutes. Let stand 5 minutes before serving. Makes 6 to 8 servings. — *Fran Washko, Aurora, Colo.*

PER SERVING: 335 calories, 16 g protein, 30 g carbohydrates, 16 g fat, 146 mg cholesterol, 392 mg sodium

---

Combine vegetables, prosciutto, cheese in pasta salad; add raspberry vinaigrette.

ANTIPASTO PASTA SALAD

- 5 cups cold cooked pasta twists
  Cooked artichoke hearts (directions follow), or 1 can (8½ oz.) artichoke hearts packed in water, drained
- 1 cup pitted ripe olives
- 3 cups cooked broccoli flowerets
- ¼ pound mushrooms, thinly sliced
- 1 cup quartered cherry tomatoes
- ⅛ pound prosciutto or cooked ham, cut into thin strips
- 1 cup (¼ lb.) finely shredded asiago or parmesan cheese
  Vinaigrette (recipe follows)

In a bowl, mix pasta with artichokes (cut in quarters), olives, broccoli, mushrooms, tomatoes, prosciutto, cheese, and vinaigrette. Serve, or cover and chill up to overnight. Serves 8 to 10. — *Lee McGill, Lake Almanor Peninsula, Calif.*

PER SERVING: 323 calories, 11 g protein, 23 g carbohydrates, 22 g fat, 12 mg cholesterol, 425 mg sodium

Cooked artichoke hearts. Break tough outer leaves from 10 small **artichokes** (about 2-in. diameter); down to pale, edible inner leaves. Trim off thorny tips; peel bottoms. Cook in 2 quarts boiling water, uncovered, until tender when pierced, about 20 minutes. Drain; cool.

Vinaigrette. Combine ½ cup **raspberry vinegar**, ⅔ cup **olive oil**, 1½ teaspoons **dry basil leaves**, ¼ teaspoon **pepper**.

GREEN BEAN RAGOUT

1½ **pounds green beans, ends trimmed, cut into 2-inch lengths**
2 **tablespoons butter or margarine**
1 **clove garlic, minced or pressed**
1 **small onion, chopped**
1 **stalk celery, thinly sliced**
1 **large firm-ripe tomato, peeled, seeded, and cut into thin wedges; or 1 can (15 oz.) stewed tomatoes, drained**
1 **tablespoon chopped fresh basil leaves or ½ teaspoon dry basil leaves**
Salt and pepper

In a 10- to 12-inch frying pan, bring 1 inch water to boiling over high heat. Add beans and cook, uncovered, until barely tender when pierced, 7 to 8 minutes. Drain and set aside. (To keep the brightest green color, immerse beans in ice water until cool; drain.)

Return pan to medium heat. Add butter; when melted, stir in garlic, onion, and celery. Stir occasionally until vegetables just begin to brown, 10 to 12 minutes. Add tomato, basil, and green beans. Stir gently just until beans are hot. Season to taste with salt and pepper. Makes 5 or 6 servings. —*Rinda Fullmer, West Jordan, Utah.*

PER SERVING: 74 calories, 2 g protein, 9 g carbohydrates, 4 g fat, 10 mg cholesterol, 53 mg sodium

Cooked green beans warmed in tomato-basil sauce can keep their bright color.

CHICKEN WITH CURRANTS & JALAPEÑOS

1 **broiler-fryer chicken, cut up**
¾ **teaspoon paprika**
2 **tablespoons olive or salad oil**
5 **cloves garlic, pressed or minced**
2 **fresh jalapeño chilies, stemmed, seeded, and minced**
1 **large onion, chopped**
2 **medium-size carrots, sliced**
¼ **pound mushrooms, sliced**
1 **can (15 oz.) stewed tomatoes**
½ **teaspoon *each* ground cumin and fines herbes or dry thyme leaves**
¾ **cup dry white wine or regular-strength chicken broth**
½ **cup dried currants**

Rinse chicken and pat dry; sprinkle meat all over with paprika. In a 4- to 5-quart pan over medium-high heat, brown chicken in oil, a portion at a time; remove from pan and set aside.

Add garlic, chilies, onion, and carrots to pan. Cook until vegetables begin to lightly brown, 10 to 12 minutes; stir often. Add mushrooms, tomatoes with liquid, cumin, fines herbes, wine, currants, and chicken. Bring to a boil, then reduce heat and simmer, uncovered, until meat at thigh bone is no longer pink (cut to test), about 45 minutes. Serves 4. —*Barbara Jacque, Van Nuys, Calif.*

PER SERVING: 768 calories, 54 g protein, 31 g carbohydrates, 48 g fat, 203 mg cholesterol, 479 mg sodium

Brown the chicken, then simmer in sauce flavored with jalapeños and currants.

CHESTNUT TRUFFLE TORTE

¼ **cup (⅛ lb.) unsalted butter or margarine**
⅔ **cup sugar**
5 **large eggs, separated**
2 **cans (8¾ oz. each) chestnut spread (not purée)**
½ **cup all-purpose flour**
¼ **cup *each* brandy and whipping cream (or use ½ cup cream)**
16 **ounces melted, cool semisweet chocolate**
Icing (recipe follows)

In a bowl, beat butter, sugar, and yolks until fluffy. Beat in chestnut spread, flour, brandy, cream, and chocolate.

In another bowl, whip whites until they hold moist, stiff peaks. Fold together; pour into a buttered 9-inch cheesecake pan with removable bottom. Bake in a 325° oven until firm in center when lightly pressed, about 1¼ hours. Cool 10 minutes. Run a knife inside rim; remove rim. When cool, frost. Chill 2 hours, or, covered, up to 5 days. Serves 10 to 12. —*Dorothea Kent, Port Angeles, Wash.*

PER SERVING: 639 calories, 8 g protein, 79 g carbohydrates, 36 g fat, 149 mg cholesterol, 94 mg sodium

Icing. In a 1- to 1½-quart pan over low heat, stir until smooth ¾ cup **whipping cream,** 1 tablespoon **unsalted butter** or margarine, and 4 ounces **semisweet chocolate.** Chill until thick, 1 hour.

Moist torte includes chestnut spread, found in well-stocked supermarkets.

REGIONAL FOOD SPECIALTIES *give rise to a kind of fanaticism based on the concept of a supreme barbecue sauce, chowder, or chili recipe. As with cults, the disciples tend toward heretical opinions and sectarianism.*

Some chili fanciers (known in their own vernacular as chiliheads) blanch at the thought of beans in the bowl; others groan at the prospect of ground (as opposed to cubed) beef. Some curl their lips at the suggestion of using prepared chili powder, just as clam chowder purists (chowderheads, to some) vehemently reject the idea of celery in Boston chowder.

Chefs of the West, on the other hand, realize that in a pluralistic society there must be room for diversity. In this spirit of tolerance, we welcome the unorthodox efforts of Edward Tuit—who gives us not only beans, ground beef, and chili powder but throws in pork, green chilies, and white wine.

The result is spicy but not fiery.

EDWARD'S CHILI

- 1 **pound ground lean beef**
- ½ **pound chorizo sausage, casings removed (optional)**
- 1 **pound lean boneless pork shoulder or butt, cut into ½-inch cubes**
- 2 **medium-size firm-ripe tomatoes, cored and coarsely chopped**
- 1 **can (15 oz.) tomato sauce**
- 1 **can (about 1 lb.) kidney beans**
- 1 **can (7 oz.) diced green chilies**
- 2 **medium-size onions, chopped**
- 2 **cloves garlic, minced or pressed**
- ½ **cup dry white wine**
- 2 **beef bouillon cubes**
- 1 **tablespoon chili powder**
- 1 **teaspoon cumin seed**
  Salt and pepper
- 1 **medium-size red onion, chopped**
  About 2 cups (8 oz.) shredded sharp cheddar cheese

In a 5- to 6-quart pan over medium heat, crumble ground beef and chorizo with a spoon. Stir often until meats are well browned, 10 to 15 minutes. With a slotted spoon, lift out meats and set aside. Discard all but 1 tablespoon of the drippings, then add pork to pan and cook until browned on all sides.

Return beef and chorizo mixture to pan, then stir in tomatoes, tomato sauce, kidney beans and their liquid, chilies, the 2 chopped onions, garlic, wine, bouillon cubes, chili powder, and cumin. Bring to a boil over medium-high heat; cover and simmer until pork is very tender when pierced, 1½ to 2 hours. Stir as needed to prevent scorching. Skim and discard fat, season to taste with salt and pepper, then ladle into individual bowls.

Offer red onion and cheese to add to individual portions. Makes about 8 cups, 6 to 8 servings.

PER SERVING: 417 calories, 31 g protein, 19 g carbohydrates, 25 g fat, 99 mg cholesterol, 1,112 mg sodium

Santa Monica, Calif.

DESSERT WINES —*madeira, port, sweet sherry—alter the flavor of cream-based meat sauces in a remarkable way.*

"As with other cults, chiliheads tend to be a bit fanatical."

Behind a flavor best described as indescribable, toastiness and caramel play a part.

Such a sauce usually accompanies fowl, pork, or veal. But Michael Palumbo finds that Italian sausage, mild or hot, does not overpower it, and that pasta is the perfect vehicle for the resulting blend.

PASTA WITH SAUSAGE, MADEIRA & CREAM

- 1 pound mild or hot Italian sausage, casings removed
- ¼ pound mushrooms, sliced
- 2 large cloves garlic, minced or pressed
- ¼ cup madeira or dry sherry
- 1 cup whipping cream
- 1 teaspoon white pepper
- ¼ teaspoon ground nutmeg
  About 12 ounces (about 4¾ cups) dry spinach pasta twists
  Freshly grated parmesan cheese

In a 10- to 12-inch frying pan over medium-high heat, crumble sausage and stir often until meat is well browned, 10 to 15 minutes. With a slotted spoon, lift out sausage and set it aside. Discard all but 2 tablespoons of the drippings.

Add mushrooms and garlic to pan; cook, stirring often, until mushrooms are golden brown, 8 to 10 minutes. Add madeira, scraping brown bits free from pan. Add sausage, cream, pepper, and nutmeg. Boil on high heat until the sauce is slightly thickened and large, shiny bubbles form, 1 to 2 minutes.

Meanwhile, bring 3 quarts water to boil in a 5- to 6-quart pan on high heat. Add pasta and cook, uncovered, until tender to bite, about 10 minutes. Drain and pour into a bowl; top with sausage sauce and mix well. Offer cheese to spoon over individual portions. Makes 4 to 6 servings.

PER SERVING: 559 calories, 20 g protein, 45 g carbohydrates, 33 g fat, 144 mg cholesterol, 550 mg sodium

Foster City, Calif.

PERHAPS YOU HAVE WITNESSED *a pizza commercial that bases its appeal on* abbondanza—*abundance or lavishness. Compared with Gerald Knight's Ricotta Torta Milanese, any pizza would look like a prisoner's bread and water. The crust (if you can call anything so refined a crust) is puff pastry; the filling is verdant.*

Does all this sound like luxury? Keep in mind George Ade's description of down-on-the-farm dining: "There were no luxuries then; anything that could be et was a necessity."

RICOTTA TORTA MILANESE

- 1 carton (15 oz., about 2 cups) ricotta cheese
- 1 tablespoon dry Italian herb seasoning or 2 teaspoons dry basil leaves and 1 teaspoon dry oregano leaves
- 1 teaspoon ground sage
- 4 large eggs
- 2 packages (10 oz. each) frozen chopped spinach, thawed and squeezed dry
- ¼ teaspoon pepper
- 2 packages (17¼ oz. each) frozen puff pastry dough, thawed according to package directions
- 1 pound thinly sliced cooked ham
- 1 jar (7 oz.) roasted red peppers, drained and cut into strips
- 1 medium-size onion, very thinly sliced
- 2½ cups (about ¾ lb.) cold cooked Brussels sprouts, or 1 package (10 oz.) frozen Brussels sprouts, thawed
- 1 cup (4 oz.) shredded Swiss cheese

In a bowl, mix together the ricotta, Italian seasoning, sage, and 2 of the eggs; also combine spinach, pepper, 1 whole egg, and 1 egg yolk; set aside.

Use 1 sheet of the puff pastry to line the bottom of a greased 9-inch-diameter cheesecake pan with removable bottom; cut pastry to fit. Cut 2 more sheets of the dough in half and use to line the sides of the pan, extending the top edge of dough about ½ inch above rim of pan. Moisten edges where dough pieces come together with water; press to seal.

Arrange half of the ham slices evenly over bottom crust; top with half of the ricotta mixture, then half of the spinach mixture. Evenly top with half of the red pepper strips and half of the onion slices. Repeat layers using the remaining ham, ricotta mixture, spinach mixture, red peppers, and onions.

Cut Brussels sprouts in half lengthwise, pat dry with paper towels, and arrange over onions. Sprinkle with Swiss cheese. Cover with the remaining puff pastry dough, crimping edges together to seal; trim off excess dough. Cut a 1-inch hole in the center for steam

to escape. Lightly beat remaining egg white and brush over top crust.

Place pan in a shallow rimmed pan. Cover torta with a piece of greased foil. (If made ahead, chill up until next day.)

Bake on lowest rack in a 350° oven for 45 minutes. Remove foil and continue to bake until richly browned, about 45 minutes more. Let cool at least 45 minutes, remove pan rim, and cut into wedges. Makes 12 servings.

PER SERVING: 554 calories, 24 g protein, 38 g carbohydrates, 34 g fat, 133 mg cholesterol, 1,092 mg sodium

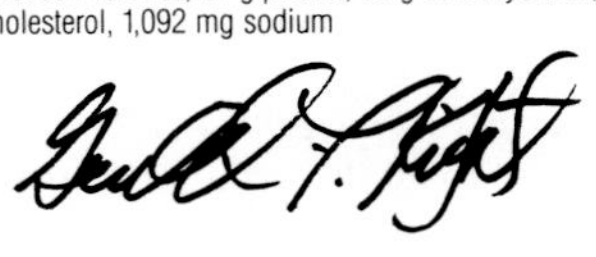

Eagle River, Alaska

BAKED PEARS *with a sweet sauce are a classic dessert. This sauce owes its name to brandy but gets its perfume from the cardamom and nutmeg that spice the "custard"—and from the amaretto the pears are cooked in.*

BAKED PEAR FOR TWO WITH BRANDY SAUCE

- 1 large ripe Bosc pear (about ¾ lb.), halved and cored
- 2 tablespoons almond-flavor liqueur (such as amaretto)
- 1 large egg yolk
- ¼ cup unflavored yogurt
- ⅛ teaspoon *each* ground nutmeg and ground cardamom
- 1 teaspoon *each* honey, lemon juice, and brandy

Place each pear half cut side up in an ovenproof ramekin (about 6 in. wide). Drizzle halves equally with liqueur. Bake, uncovered, in a 350° oven until pears are tender when pierced, about 45 minutes.

Meanwhile, in a 1- to 1½-quart pan, stir together egg yolk, yogurt, nutmeg, cardamom, honey, lemon juice, and brandy. Cook, stirring, over medium-low heat until mixture thickens, about 5 minutes.

Spoon warm sauce onto hot pear halves and serve at once. Makes 2 servings.

PER SERVING: 172 calories, 4 g protein, 33 g carbohydrates, 4 g fat, 138 mg cholesterol, 25 mg sodium

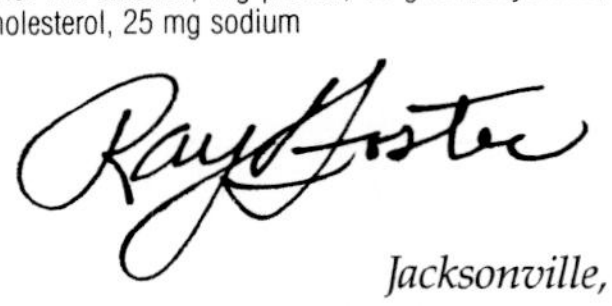

Jacksonville, Ore.

March Menus

Winning the cook's heart *every time are meals that require little effort to prepare, yet look and taste like labors of love. For March, here are three such meals. The first comes painlessly from the oven.*

A stir-fried salad is the basis for a quick supper (or maybe lunch) with a crisp surprise that also comes from the oven.

And to get breakfast going one morning, dress up some everyday breakfast foods with a fancy touch.

Stagger the time when you put foods in to bake so everything is ready at once.

The potatoes need to cook longest; put them into the oven, then make and apply the glaze for the roast. After meat has baked a while, add the apples to the same pan. Then rinse and chop kale, and have it ready to cook quickly over direct heat just as the baked foods finish cooking.

For dessert, ladle purchased caramel sauce over scoops of vanilla ice cream and sprinkle with pecan halves or chopped pecans.

Select a dry but fruity Gewürztraminer and serve it chilled; add lemon slices to glasses of sparkling water.

Carve honey-pepper pork loin to serve with bake-along apples (also seasoned with honey and pepper), golden brown roasted potato wedges, and buttered kale.

Honey-Pepper Pork Loin with Baked Apples

Trim fat to even thickness on a 2½- to 3-pound **center-cut pork loin roast;** set roast, bones down, in a 9- by 13-inch pan. Mix 3 tablespoons **honey** with 1 tablespoon **coarsely ground black pepper;** rub ⅔ of the mixture evenly over the fat on roast. Bake on the middle rack of a 350° oven until a thermometer inserted in the thickest part reads 155°, about 1½ hours.

Meanwhile, rinse and core 4 **red apples** (such as Winesap or Rome Beauty, each about 3-in. diameter). Spread remaining honey mixture evenly over tops of apples. After roast has cooked about 45 minutes, set apples, honey side up, in the pan alongside the roast. Bake apples until tender when pierced, about 45 minutes, or until roast is done. Add **salt** to taste. Makes 4 servings.

Per Serving: 461 calories, 39 g protein, 35 g carbohydrates, 18 g fat, 124 mg cholesterol, 95 mg sodium

Rosemary Roasted Potatoes

Scrub 3 large (about 2 lb. total) **russet potatoes.** Cut potatoes into 1-inch-wide wedges; arrange in a single layer, skin side down, in a 10- by 15-inch pan. In a small bowl, mix 4 teaspoons **olive oil** with 2 cloves **garlic,** pressed or minced, and 1½ teaspoons chopped **fresh rosemary leaves** or ¾ teaspoon dry rosemary leaves, crumbled. Brush cut surfaces of potato wedges with oil mixture; bake on the lowest rack in a 350° oven until potatoes are golden brown, about 1¾ hours. Add salt to taste. Makes 4 servings.

Per Serving: 222 calories, 5 g protein, 41 g carbohydrates, 5 g fat, 0 mg cholesterol, 14 mg sodium

Buttered Kale

Trim and discard stems and yellowed leaves from 1 pound **kale.** Rinse well, drain, then coarsely chop. Mound kale in a 5- to 6-quart pan; add 2 tablespoons **water** and 1 tablespoon **butter** or margarine. Cook, uncovered, over medium-high heat, stirring often, until kale wilts, about 3 minutes. Makes 4 servings.

Per Serving: 60 calories, 2 g protein, 7 g carbohydrates, 3 g fat, 8 mg cholesterol, 59 mg sodium

Instead of filling won ton wrappers, you slice, butter, and bake them to make the crisp crackers that are part of this main dish. Stir-fry a combination of vegetables, then chicken to make the hot salad that you can spoon onto the crackers and leaves of spinach or napa cabbage.

Bake the won ton wrappers while you prepare the salad ingredients, or bake them a few days ahead as they stay crisp when stored airtight.

Jasmine and chrysanthemum teas are both mild and slightly fragrant. You may find them in the supermarket, or you can buy them in Asian markets (along with the cookies) or tea shops. Serve the brewed tea hot or cold.

CRISP WON TON SALAD

- 4 **to 5 teaspoons salad oil**
- 1 **small onion, thinly sliced**
- ½ **cup thinly sliced celery**
- 1 **large carrot, cut into 1-inch-long matchstick pieces**
- 1 **tablespoon finely chopped fresh ginger**
- 2 **tablespoons water**
- 2 **boned and skinned chicken breast halves (about ¾ lb.), cut into ¼-inch-thick strips**
- 1 **can (5 oz.) sliced water chestnuts, drained**
- ½ **cup roasted, salted peanuts**
  Sesame dressing (recipe follows)
- ¾ **pound spinach (stems and yellow leaves discarded, leaves rinsed and drained) or napa cabbage leaves (rinsed, drained, and cut crosswise into ½-inch strips)**
  Crisp won ton strips (directions follow)
- ½ **cup sliced green onions**

Place a 10- to 12-inch frying pan or wok over medium heat. When hot, add 2 teaspoons of the oil and the thinly sliced onion; stir occasionally until light golden. Add celery, carrots, ginger, and

water; cover and cook, stirring occasionally, until carrots are tender-crisp to bite, 3 to 4 minutes. Pour into a bowl and set aside.

Add 2 teaspoons oil to pan and turn heat to high. When oil is hot enough to make a drop of water sizzle, add ½ the chicken. Cook until browned on bottom, then stir-fry until meat is white in center (cut to test). Add cooked chicken to vegetables. Add remaining oil to pan and cook remaining chicken the same way. When it is done, add to pan the chicken-vegetable mixture, water chestnuts, peanuts, and 3 tablespoons of the sesame dressing; stir-fry until hot, about 3 minutes.

Divide spinach among 4 or 5 dinner plates. Top spinach with crisp won ton strips. Spoon hot chicken mixture over won tons; sprinkle with green onions. Serve remaining dressing to spoon onto salads to taste. Makes 4 or 5 servings.

PER SERVING: 410 calories, 26 g protein, 39 g carbohydrates, 17 g fat, 80 mg cholesterol, 286 mg sodium

Sesame dressing. In a bowl, stir together ½ cup **seasoned rice vinegar** (or ½ cup rice vinegar or distilled white vinegar and 1½ teaspoons sugar); 2 tablespoons *each* **soy sauce** and **Oriental sesame oil,** 1 tablespoon **lemon juice;** and ⅛ teaspoon **chili oil** or cayenne.

PER SERVING: 24 calories, .14 g protein, 1 g carbohydrates, 2 g fat, 0 mg cholesterol, 159 mg sodium

Crisp won ton strips. Cut 1 package (7 oz., or half of a 14 oz. package) **won ton wrappers** into ½-inch-wide strips. Melt about 1 tablespoon **butter** or margarine; brush a 12- by 15-inch baking sheet lightly with butter. Lay won ton strips close together in a single layer on the baking sheet; brush tops of strips lightly with more butter.

Bake won ton strips in a 375° oven until light golden, about 6 minutes. Pour from pan onto a flat surface to cool. Repeat to bake remaining strips. If made ahead, package airtight and store in a cool place up to 2 days.

(Continued on next page)

Spoon stir-fried chicken and vegetables over crisp-baked won ton wrappers and spinach. Season with sesame dressing and sprinkle with green onions.

GRANOLA & YOGURT PARFAIT BREAKFAST

Granola Yogurt Parfaits
Honey   Strawberry Jam
Toasted English Muffins
Fruit Tray
Coffee   Tea

Granola and yogurt layered into tall, narrow parfait glasses, or even wine glasses, give breakfast a festive look.

Choose your favorite granola to make these parfaits; the lazy option is to serve bowls of yogurt and offer a selection of granolas to sprinkle on top.

Honey and jam can be added to the parfaits or spread on hot muffins.

For fruit, present a tray of kiwifruit wedges, tangerines, and grapes.

GRANOLA YOGURT PARFAITS

2 **cartons (8 oz. each) vanilla-flavored yogurt**
2 **cups purchased granola**

Spoon 2 tablespoons yogurt into the bottom of each of 4 parfait glasses (at least 8-oz. size). Top yogurt in each glass with about ⅛ of the granola. Evenly divide remaining yogurt among the glasses and top with remaining granola. Serves 4.

PER SERVING: 368 calories, 13 g protein, 51 g carbohydrates, 13 g fat, 6 mg cholesterol, 97 mg sodium

APRIL

Cross-Bridge Noodles (page 88)

Join us on a visit to China
as we meet regional cooks, shop with them in open-air
markets, watch as they prepare elaborate meals in
tiny kitchens, and sample many unusual dishes. Here we
share 23 of them with you to try at home—or even on a
picnic. Salute spring with an Easter brunch and seasonal
specialties: lamb, asparagus, and strawberries. Other
ideas include turkey breast on the barbecue, new ways to
use lentils, and nut-filled baklava pastries.

From China's Kitchens to Yours

FOR CENTURIES, *China has been famous for its foods—for the infinite variety and subtle complexity of its cuisine, and for the cultural importance of esthetic dining to its people. When Chinese people settle in different parts of the world, their culinary traditions usually come with them. Here in the West, where large numbers of Chinese have immigrated, restaurants reflecting various regional styles have sprung up in great numbers in the last few decades—and won devoted fans.*

But how does what we know here compare with the real thing?

To learn more about how food is prepared in China and to study regional differences in greater detail, Sunset sent an editorial research team directly to the kitchens of the People's Republic.

In August 1986, we proposed our project to the Chinese government. The Ministry of Commerce (which runs most of China's restaurants) offered to arrange the trip. Last May, our team spent 15 days in China, traveling through the four main areas where the best-known regional cuisines have developed. In the course of the trip, we sampled more than 300 dishes. We went to street markets, farming communes, restaurants, and private homes— to shop, study, taste, visit, and enjoy.

In the next 12 pages, we share the 23 best recipes we brought back from China—and tested in our editorial kitchens for use by Sunset readers.

Map names the five principal cities we visited.

OUR IMPRESSIONS: SOME BIG SURPRISES

What we found in private homes was absolutely amazing. In kitchens not much larger than a Western home's bedroom closet, Chinese families turned out meals with 10 or more dishes. Employing a large, detachable tabletop, a family with a small apartment could suddenly serve a dozen people. Some dishes were very simple, but others were rather complex, considering the facilities—usually just two gas burners and a water faucet. Most of the cooking was handled by one or two people, though sometimes extra helpers gave a hand with the preparation.

In restaurants, we were offered formal banquet meals. These usually began with a selection of cold appetizers— sometimes, as a centerpiece, artfully set out to resemble a bird, flower, or other symbolic figure. A succession of hot dishes would follow, often ending with soup, and then plain fresh fruit. Rice was offered but seldom eaten: we were too full.

The banquet-style presentations bore little resemblance to what most Westerners know from Chinese restaurants here. Though too elaborate for home kitchens, many banquet dishes were truly memorable. Among them: a beautifully presented meal at the Sichuan

On the Great Wall, Sunset food editor Linda Anusasananan (center) and photographer Glenn Christiansen join Chinese hosts.

Culinary Institute; hand-cut egg noodles served in broth at the Chengdu Restaurant; a charming teahouse lunch in Shanghai's picturesque Old Town; the "drunken shrimp" at the Banxi in Guangzhou.

In this large country, season and geography determine what you eat. Transportation systems are limited to mostly local service, so food generally stays close to where it is produced. Regions with warm climates and agricultural abundance have created the most interesting specialties.

BASIC FLAVORING INGREDIENTS

Many Chinese dishes are seasoned only with a little salt or soy sauce, some wine, and perhaps a bit of garlic or ginger. Other dishes require some special ingredients; you can find these at well-supplied supermarkets or Asian markets here.

Wine, made from rice, is used frequently; *shaoxing* is the most common kind. You can use dry sherry as a substitute.

Most Chinese vinegar is made from rice; it has a mellower, less acidic flavor than wine vinegar. Most often, the cooks use an aged black vinegar that has an aromatic, complex flavor much like that of an Italian balsamic vinegar. But use any unsweetened rice vinegar in these recipes.Or, as a substitute, use a wine vinegar tempered with sugar.

PLANNING A CHINESE MEAL

Chinese custom requires variety in a meal. Allow at least one dish per person. Add extra dishes for special occasions.

In our travels, tea was generally served before the meal. Beer, medium-dry Chinese white wine, shaoxing rice wine, orange soda, and mineral water accompanied meals. Gewürztraminer or dry Riesling would also be appropriate.

We have focused here on meals served at home. We've simplified menus and cooking techniques. Prepare a whole menu, or choose one or two new dishes to try along with familiar favorites.

At Beijing market, bok choy proves irresistible as local family takes editor shopping.

In Shanghai, tiny kitchen is like those in many apartments in big cities.

At family farm in Chengdu, selection of cold appetizers starts banquet; cold dishes ring plate of blossom-like tomatoes.

At Sichuan Culinary Institute in Chengdu, teacher shows class, reflected in mirrors, how to cook gong bao chicken.

From China's Kitchens: A Banquet in Sichuan

COLORFUL CHENGDU *is the capital of China's agriculturally richest province, Sichuan, in the southwest. With this region's abundance comes a complex cuisine. In addition to the fiery seasonings for which it is best known, the repertoire includes clean and refined—even medicinal—flavors. Sichuan banquets, which can consist of as many as two dozen dishes, often alternate spicy foods with light, natural flavors.*

To lend heat, many chili and pepper preparations are used and often combined.

The Qing family lives on a farm in Chengdu. When visitors come, the family offers its own specialty, a custard-like version of homemade tofu. They scoop the warm, soft tofu into bowls and serve a pungent black bean sauce over it for an entrée dish—or spoon warm honey over it and serve it as a dessert.

In their chicken dish, stir-fried chicken shreds get a complex kind of heat from aromatic Sichuan peppercorns and a paste of crushed chilies. A dozen whole cloves of garlic braised in broth with green beans become surprisingly mild.

The "four happy lions" are moist braised meatballs garnished with manes of stir-fried spinach. In the stir-fried pork, thin shreds of meat are quickly cooked with sliced mild chilies. The soup is served as a palate cleanser after the entrées.

The meatballs can be made up to a day ahead. Prepare ingredients for other dishes. Cook beans while the meatballs simmer, then stir-fry the chilies with pork. Heat the tofu and make the soup.

Qing family cooks country-style banquet in five-generation-old farm kitchen. Their specialty is homemade tofu (in wok at left). Straw and bamboo fuel their stove.

CHICKEN WITH CHILI PASTE

- ¾ **pound skinned boneless chicken breast**
- 1 **tablespoon cornstarch**
- 2 **tablespoons rice wine or dry sherry**
  About ¼ teaspoon salt (optional)
- 2 **tablespoons salad oil**
- 2 **tablespoons slivered fresh ginger**
- 1 **tablespoon minced garlic**
- 1½ **to 2 teaspoons chili paste**
- ½ **cup bamboo shoots, cut into thin slivers**
- 2 **stalks celery, cut into thin slivers about 2 inches long**
  Sauce (recipe follows)
  About ½ teaspoon ground Sichuan peppercorns (recipe follows)

Cut chicken into matchstick-size strips about 3 inches long. Mix with cornstarch, wine, and salt.

Place a wok or 10- to 12-inch frying pan over high heat. When hot add 1 tablespoon oil. Swirl oil to coat pan bottom. Add ginger and garlic; stir-fry until garlic is limp. Add chili paste, bamboo shoots, and celery; stir-fry 1 minute. Lift out of pan; add 1 tablespoon oil and chicken. Stir-fry until chicken turns white, about 2 minutes; return vegetables to pan and add sauce. Stir-fry until

sauce boils and thickens. Pour into a serving dish and sprinkle with Sichuan peppercorns. Serves 5 or 6 as part of a 5- or 6-course meal.

PER SERVING: 131 calories, 14 g protein, 5 g carbohydrates, 6 g fat, 33 mg cholesterol, 229 mg sodium

Sauce. Mix 2 tablespoons **rice wine** or dry sherry, 1 tablespoon **soy sauce,** 1 tablespoon **rice vinegar** or wine vinegar, 1 teaspoon **sugar,** 1 teaspoon **Oriental sesame oil,** and 1 teaspoon **cornstarch.**

Ground Sichuan peppercorns. Put 1 tablespoon **Sichuan peppercorns** into a 6- to 8-inch frying pan. Pick out and discard any debris. Cook over medium heat, shaking pan often, until peppercorns are fragrant and lightly toasted, 2 to 3 minutes. Finely crush with a mortar and pestle (or whirl in blender until finely ground). Makes 2 teaspoons.

FOUR HAPPY LIONS

- 3 **tablespoons salad oil**
  Meatball mixture (recipe follows)
- 1 **tablespoon minced fresh ginger**
- 1 **clove garlic, pressed or minced**
- 1 **cup regular-strength chicken broth**
- 1 **tablespoon soy sauce**
  Water
- 1 **tablespoon cornstarch**
- ¾ **pound spinach (stem ends trimmed and yellow leaves discarded), washed and drained**

Pour 2 tablespoons oil into a 10- to 12-inch frying pan and place over medium-high heat. When oil is hot, add meatballs and cook, turning, until browned on all sides, about 6 minutes. Spoon off and discard all but 1 tablespoon fat. (If made ahead, cover and chill until next day.)

Add ginger and garlic; cook, stirring, until garlic is golden. Add broth and soy sauce. Cover and simmer until meatballs are no longer pink in center (cut to test), 15 minutes (25 minutes, if cold). Lift out meatballs and place in a warm serving dish. Pour out pan juices and measure; add water if needed to make 1 cup. Mix cornstarch with 2 tablespoons water and stir into pan juices. Stir until sauce boils. Pour over meatballs.

Rinse pan and dry. Place over high heat. Add remaining 1 tablespoon oil and swirl oil over pan bottom. When oil is hot, add spinach and cook, turning, until wilted, about 2 minutes. Garnish base of meatballs with spinach. Serves 5 or 6 as part of a 5- or 6-course meal.

PER SERVING: 240 calories, 18 g protein, 8 g carbohydrates, 15 g fat, 97 mg cholesterol, 540 mg sodium

Meatball mixture. Soak 4 medium-size **dried shiitake mushrooms** in hot water until soft, about 20 minutes. Squeeze out excess water, trim off and discard stems, and finely chop mushrooms. Mix mushrooms; 1 pound **ground lean pork;** 1 **large egg;** ⅓ cup finely chopped **bamboo shoots;** ¼ cup chopped **green onions;** 2 tablespoons **rice wine** or dry sherry; 1 tablespoon *each* **cornstarch, soy sauce,** and minced **fresh ginger;** 1 clove **garlic,** pressed or minced; and about ¼ teaspoon **salt.** Shape into 4 equal-size balls.

GREEN BEANS & GARLIC

- 1 tablespoon salad oil
- 12 to 18 large cloves garlic, peeled
- 2 cups regular-strength chicken broth
- 1 pound green beans, ends trimmed
- 1 tablespoon cornstarch
- 2 tablespoons water

In a 10- to 12-inch frying pan, combine oil and garlic. Stir over medium heat until light gold, about 2 minutes. Add broth; cover and simmer until garlic is tender when pierced, about 5 minutes.

Bring broth to a boil and add beans. Cook, covered, just until beans are tender-crisp, 3 to 4 minutes. With tongs, lift out beans and arrange on a rimmed platter. Mix cornstarch and water and stir into broth. Bring to a boil, stirring, until thickened. Spoon sauce and garlic over beans. Serves 5 or 6 as part of a 5- or 6-course meal.

PER SERVING: 74 calories, 3 g protein, 11 g carbohydrates, 3 g fat, 0 mg cholesterol, 24 mg sodium

STIR-FRIED CHILIES & PORK

- ½ pound boneless pork, such as loin
- 1 tablespoon soy sauce
- 1 teaspoon cornstarch
- 2 tablespoons salad oil
- 3 large fresh Anaheim chilies, stemmed, seeded, and cut into thin rings (if you prefer a milder flavor, substitute 1 small green bell pepper, stemmed, seeded, and cut into thin slivers for 1 chili) Salt

Trim fat from pork. Cut pork into matchstick-size strips. Mix pork with soy and cornstarch.

Place a wok or 10- to 12-inch frying pan over high heat. When hot, add oil and swirl to coat pan. Add pork and stir-fry until lightly browned, about 3 minutes.

Add chilies and stir-fry until they turn bright green, about 2 minutes. Add salt to taste. Pour into a bowl. Serves 5 or 6 as part of a 5- or 6-course meal.

PER SERVING: 96 calories, 6 g protein, 3 g carbohydrates, 7 g fat, 17 mg cholesterol, 191 mg sodium

SOFT TOFU WITH BLACK BEAN SAUCE

- ¾ to 1 pound soft tofu
  Black bean sauce (recipe follows) or about ½ cup warm honey

Set tofu in a bowl that will fit in a steamer basket, wok, or deep wide pan; cover tofu. Place on a rack over about 1 inch boiling water in pan. Cover and steam until hot, about 10 minutes. (In a microwave, cover tofu with plastic wrap; cook at full power, 100 percent, until hot, about 4 minutes.)

Serve warm tofu topped with black bean sauce or honey. Serves 5 or 6 as part of a 5- or 6-course meal.

PER SERVING: 125 calories, 8 g protein, 3 g carbohydrates, 10 g fat, 0 mg cholesterol, 849 mg sodium

Black bean sauce. Rinse and drain ½ cup **salted fermented black beans;** coarsely chop beans. Chop ½ cup **canned salted mustard greens;** rinse and drain. In an 8- to 10-inch frying pan over high heat, stir 1 tablespoon **salad oil,** ½ cup thinly sliced **green onions,** beans, and mustard greens; cook until onion is limp, about 2 minutes. Remove from heat and stir in 1 tablespoon *each* **soy sauce** and **Oriental sesame oil** and 1 to 2 teaspoons **chili oil** or ¼ to ½ teaspoon **cayenne.**

Meal from Sichuan province features (clockwise from upper right) stir-fried chilies and pork, green beans and garlic, "happy lions" meatballs, and pickled vegetable soup.

PICKLED VEGETABLE SOUP

- ½ pound boneless pork, such as loin
- ½ cup canned salted mustard greens
- 3 cups regular-strength chicken broth
- 3 cups water
- 2 cups thinly shredded cabbage
- ½ teaspoon ground Sichuan peppercorns (see chicken with chili paste, page 78)

Trim excess fat from pork. Cut meat into matchstick-size strips. Cut mustard greens into same-size strips; rinse and drain. Pour broth and water into a 3- to 4-quart pan and bring to a boil. Add pork and mustard greens. Simmer, uncovered, until meat is no longer pink, 2 to 3 minutes. Skim off and discard fat. Stir in cabbage; cook just until limp, about 2 minutes. Pour into a tureen and sprinkle with ground peppercorns. Serves 5 or 6 as part of a 5- or 6-course meal.

PER SERVING: 127 calories, 9 g protein, 2 g carbohydrates, 9 g fat, 26 mg cholesterol, 144 mg sodium

From China's Kitchens: Family Gathering in Guangzhou

FORMERLY KNOWN *as Canton, the capital of the southern province of Guangdong is now called Guangzhou. Located in the fertile alluvial soil of the Zhujiang (Pearl River) delta, it has a productive agricultural base. The warm subtropical climate produces luscious fruits not found in the north, and the river yields a bounty of fish and seafood. This city teems with food, and with people who love to eat.*

Cantonese-style cooking is probably what first introduced most Westerners to Chinese food. Its interpretation is uneven in the West, but in China its reputation is unsurpassed. In a region that produces ingredients of such good quality, chefs often strive to preserve the natural flavors, enhancing them with only very simple seasonings. Stir-frying, steaming, and roasting are popular cooking techniques.

Lesser-known cooking styles from other parts of this province are readily found in Guangzhou. They include Hakka (more seasonings, liberal use of oyster sauce), Chiu Chow (spicier, often using bean paste), and Hainan (more tropical ingredients).

Cantonese-style meal consists of sweet potato soup, pork-filled chilies and bitter melons, crab with its butter, steamed chicken with greens.

HUANG FAMILY GATHERING

Sweet Potato & Carrot Soup
Steamed Chicken with Mustard Greens
Pork-filled Chilies & Bitter Melons
Steamed Crab
Braised Eggplant in Oyster Sauce
Rice
Medium-dry Chinese White Wine or Beer

Just about everyone in the Huang family cooks: husband, wife, father, and brother are career chefs. Mrs. Huang and her brother-in-law cooked this meal for us.

The soup, naturally sweet from vegetables, is served first in Guangzhou—unlike other regions, where it comes later.

The chicken is steamed just until barely done and served quite plainly to show off its tender smoothness.

For freshest, sweetest flavor, Mrs. Huang starts with a live crab. She kills it instantly with a heavy knife, giving it a sharp blow directly down the center. She cuts the back shell into small rounds to hold the creamy crab butter (and small pieces are easier to serve with chopsticks). Then she steams the crab just until barely done to serve with vinegar and slivers of fresh ginger. If you prefer, you might have a live crab cooked at the market. Then clean, crack, and reassemble with the crab butter cupped in its back shell (whole or cut into small rounds).

The filled bitter melons and braised eggplant show some Hakka influence.

Start the soup first, or make it ahead and reheat. Steam the chicken. While it cooks, fill chilies and bitter melons and brown (this can also be done ahead), then braise them. Also steam or boil the crab and braise the eggplant.

SWEET POTATO & CARROT SOUP

6 **cups regular-strength chicken broth**
6 **slices fresh ginger (each about the size of a quarter)**
2 **green onions, ends trimmed**
2 **cloves garlic, crushed**
2 **tablespoons soy sauce**
2 **tablespoons rice wine or dry sherry**
3 **large carrots, peeled and cut into 1-inch chunks**
1 **large sweet potato (about ¾ lb.), peeled and cut into 1-inch chunks**
1 **large russet potato (about ½ lb.), peeled and cut into 1-inch chunks**

In a 5- to 6-quart pan, combine broth, ginger, onions, garlic, soy, and wine. Cover and bring to a boil over high heat. Add carrots; cover and simmer for 15 minutes. Add sweet potato and potato;

cover and simmer until vegetables are very tender when pierced, 35 to 45 minutes longer. (If made ahead, cool, cover, and chill up to 2 days. Reheat to serve.) Pour into a tureen. Serves 5 as part of a 5-course meal.

PER SERVING: 150 calories, 5 g protein, 28 g carbohydrates, 2 g fat, 0 mg cholesterol, 506 mg sodium

STEAMED CHICKEN WITH MUSTARD GREENS

1 cup thinly sliced green onion
2 tablespoons minced fresh ginger
5 cloves garlic, pressed or minced
2 tablespoons rice wine or dry sherry
1 tablespoon cornstarch
2 whole star anise or ½ teaspoon anise seed, crushed
1 broiler-fryer chicken (3 to 3½ lb.), rinsed and patted dry
1 pound mustard greens, tough stems removed
2 tablespoons salad oil
    About ½ cup regular-strength chicken broth
    Salt

Mix onion, ginger, 4 cloves garlic, wine, 1 teaspoon cornstarch, and anise. Rub ⅓ mixture all over chicken, then fill it with remainder. Set chicken in a shallow bowl that will fit inside a steamer basket, wok, or deep, wide pan. Cover bowl and set in steamer basket or on a rack above about 1 inch boiling water in pan. Cover steamer basket or pan and steam until chicken is white at thigh bone (cut to test; Cantonese prefer it tinged with pink), 1 to 1¼ hours; add water to pan as needed.

Meanwhile, discard wilted and yellow leaves from mustard greens. Cut into 3-inch strips. Wash and drain; set aside.

When chicken is done, remove from pan and let cool about 10 minutes. With a cleaver, cut chicken into bite-size pieces through the bone; or leave whole to carve as desired. Arrange on a platter. Pour chicken juices into a measuring cup.

Set a wok or 12-inch frying pan over high heat. When pan is hot, add oil and swirl over pan bottom. Add about half of the greens and stir-fry until they wilt; stir in remaining greens. Add ¼ cup of the reserved chicken juices, cover, and cook until greens turn bright green, about 2 minutes. Lift out and arrange around chicken.

Pour pan juices into measuring cup with reserved chicken juices; if needed, add additional broth to make 1 cup. Mix with 2 teaspoons cornstarch. In the same pan used to cook greens, add 1 clove minced garlic and broth-cornstarch mixture. Cook, stirring, over high heat until boiling. Add salt to taste. Pour over chicken. Serves 5 as part of a 5-course meal.

PER SERVING: 522 calories, 40 g protein, 8 g carbohydrates, 36 g fat, 150 mg cholesterol, 169 mg sodium

PORK-FILLED CHILIES & BITTER MELONS

Wrinkled bitter melons have a definite bitterness; use all chilies if you prefer.

3 large straight Anaheim chilies or bitter melons (*fugua*), each about 8 inches long, or some of each
    Pork filling (recipe follows)
2 tablespoons salad oil
1 tablespoon salted fermented black beans, rinsed and chopped
1 tablespoon minced garlic
1 cup regular-strength chicken broth
1 tablespoon soy sauce
2 tablespoons rice wine or dry sherry
1 teaspoon sugar
1 tablespoon cornstarch

Cut chilies in half lengthwise and remove seeds. Trim ends off bitter melons and cut melons into ¾-inch-wide rounds; scrape out seeds. Fill cavities in both chilies and melons with pork filling.

Pour oil into a 10- to 12-inch frying pan; set over medium heat. Place chilies and melon, filling sides down, in pan. Cook until meat is browned, turning once, 3 to 5 minutes a side. (If made ahead, cool, cover, and chill until the next day.) Add black beans and garlic; stir until garlic is lightly browned. Add broth, soy, wine, and sugar. Cover and simmer over low heat until vegetables are tender when pierced, 5 to 7 minutes for chilies, 15 to 20 minutes for melons.

With a slotted spatula, lift out vegetables and set on a platter. Measure pan juices, skim fat, and add water to make 1 cup. Mix with cornstarch and stir into pan juices. Stir over high heat until it boils. Pour over vegetables. Serves 5 as part of a 5-course meal.

PER SERVING: 168 calories, 11 g protein, 9 g carbohydrates, 10 g fat, 31 mg cholesterol, 544 mg sodium

Pork filling. Mix ½ pound **ground lean pork,** 2 tablespoons minced **green onion,** 1 tablespoon **soy sauce,** 1 tablespoon **cornstarch,** 1 tablespoon minced **fresh ginger,** and 1 clove **garlic,** pressed or minced.

BRAISED EGGPLANT IN OYSTER SAUCE

2 tablespoons salad oil
5 Oriental eggplant (about 1 lb. total), stems removed, cut in half lengthwise; or 1 large eggplant (about 1 lb.), stem removed, cut lengthwise into 1½-inch wedges
¾ cup regular-strength chicken broth
1 tablespoon oyster sauce or soy sauce
1 teaspoon cornstarch
2 tablespoons water
2 tablespoons chopped fresh cilantro (coriander)

Place a 10- to 12-inch frying pan over medium heat. Add oil. When oil is hot, place eggplant, cut side down, in pan. Cook until browned, 2 to 3 minutes. Turn over and cook until skin is lightly browned, about 1 minute. Stir together broth and oyster sauce and add to eggplant. Cover and simmer until eggplant is very tender when pierced, 8 to 10 minutes.

Lift out eggplant with a slotted spatula and set on serving plate. Mix cornstarch and water and stir into pan juices. Cook, stirring, until mixture boils and thickens; pour over eggplant. Sprinkle with cilantro. Serves 5 as part of a 5-course meal.

PER SERVING: 82 calories, 2 g protein, 7 g carbohydrates, 6 g fat, 0 mg cholesterol, 155 mg sodium

From China's Kitchens: A Light Lunch in Shanghai

THE SOPHISTICATED CITY *of Shanghai, with a population of more than 11 million, lies in the center of the 20-mile-wide Changjiang (Yangtze) Delta, where the river opens toward the East China Sea. This water-oriented region is laced with rivers, lakes, and streams. The Chinese call it the land of fish and rice. Shanghai, with its bustling harbor, sits at the mouth of the Huangpu River.*

The Shanghainese like their dishes only lightly seasoned, preserving the foods' natural appearance and taste. They do, however, use oil, salt, and sugar rather generously. They cook foods thoroughly, preferring them on the well-done side. "Red cooking," a way of braising meats with soy and sugar to give a rich brownish red color, is a popular technique.

Shopping at outdoor market, Mrs. Xin buys bean sprouts to make lunch salad.

XIN LIGHT LUNCH

Shanghai Cucumber Salad
Bean Sprout Salad
Shrimp with Green Onions
Rice
Sparkling Water or Hot Tea

For a simple lunch, the Xin family enjoys serving two cool salads to eat with hot stir-fried shrimp. It's a refreshing light meal that goes together speedily.

Cook the rice. Make the cucumber and sprout salads. Then stir-fry the shrimp.

SHANGHAI CUCUMBER SALAD

1 small European cucumber
2 tablespoons rice vinegar (or wine vinegar plus ½ teaspoon sugar)
1 teaspoon salt
1 teaspoon sugar
¼ cup water

Cut cucumber into 2-inch lengths. Cut each piece lengthwise into 8 wedges. Mix cucumber with vinegar, salt, sugar, and water. Cover and chill at least 30 minutes or up to 2 hours. Lift out cucumber with a slotted spoon and place on a plate. Serves 3 as part of a 3-course meal.

PER SERVING: 17 calories, .01 g protein, 4 g carbohydrates, .07 g fat, 0 mg cholesterol, 736 mg sodium

BEAN SPROUT SALAD

1 pound bean sprouts
¼ cup rice vinegar (or wine vinegar plus 1 teaspoon sugar)
1 tablespoon sugar
1 tablespoon Oriental sesame oil
    About ½ teaspoon salt (optional)
1 small green bell pepper, stemmed, seeded, and cut into thin slivers about 3 inches long
4 ounces thinly sliced cooked ham, cut into thin strips about 2 inches long
    Egg shreds (recipe follows)

In a 5- to 6-quart pan, bring about 3 quarts water to a boil. Push bean sprouts into the water to immerse completely. Cook just until wilted, about 30 seconds. Drain and rinse with cold water until cool; drain well.

In a large bowl, mix vinegar, sugar, sesame oil, and ½ teaspoon salt. Add bean sprouts, pepper, ham, egg shreds, and more salt to taste. Mix and serve, or cover and chill up to 30 minutes. Serves 3 as part of a 3-course meal.

PER SERVING: 248 calories, 17 g protein, 17 g carbohydrates, 14 g fat, 205 mg cholesterol, 626 mg sodium

Egg shreds. Lightly beat together 2 **large eggs** and 1 tablespoon **water.** Place over medium heat a frying pan that measures 7 inches across bottom, or 7-inch crêpe pan. When pan is hot, brush lightly with **salad oil** and at once pour ¼ cup of the egg mixture into pan, tilting pan to spread egg over pan bottom. Cook just until edges begin to pull away from pan sides and egg feels set in middle. Turn out of pan and repeat with remaining egg. Cut egg into 3- to 4-inch-long thin strips.

SHRIMP WITH GREEN ONIONS

1 pound large shrimp (31 to 35 per lb.), shelled if desired
    Salt
1 tablespoon rice wine or dry sherry
1 tablespoon cornstarch
2 tablespoons salad oil
4 green onions (ends trimmed), thinly sliced

If shell is left on shrimp, devein by inserting a wooden pick in back of shrimp in several places and gently pulling vein out. Mix shrimp with about 1 tablespoon salt; let stand 5 minutes. Rinse well and drain. Mix shrimp with wine and cornstarch.

Set a wok or 10- to 12-inch frying pan over high heat. When pan is hot, add oil and swirl over pan bottom. Add shrimp and stir-fry until pink, 2 to 3 minutes. Add green onions and stir-fry until shrimp are opaque in thickest part (cut to test), about 1 minute longer. Add salt to taste. Serves 3 as part of a 3-course meal.

PER SERVING: 225 calories, 25 g protein, 5 g carbohydrates, 11 g fat, 186 mg cholesterol, 182 mg sodium

Light lunch from Shanghai combines hot stir-fried green-onion shrimp with cool cucumber and bean sprout salads.

From China's Kitchens: A Six-Course Dinner in Beijing

THE NATION'S CAPITAL *attracts chefs from all over the country. Originally, many came to cook for the imperial family. As a result, the term "mandarin" was applied to the best dishes of any region — those worthy to be eaten by royalty.*

But if you look at geography, this northern region loses some of its veneer of glamor. Beijing is located in the middle of flat, dry, dusty plains, where summers are hot and winters severely cold. The climate suits the growing of grains such as millet and wheat, and breads and noodles are eaten more frequently here than elsewhere. But fresh produce is in short supply, except during the prolific summer.

From the nearby province of Shandong, on the Gulf of Bo Hai and the Huang Hai (Yellow Sea), comes a bounty of seafood.

When Mongols invaded the north, they brought a fondness for lamb and for bold garlic flavors — a combination that's the mainstay of some popular dishes here.

What we sampled in Beijing was something of all of this: elaborate banquet-style dishes that originated elsewhere; precious imperial-style dishes using rare ingredients; cook-it-yourself Mongolian lamb; plump, crisp Peking ducks; and the subtle, light, wine-seasoned seafood and soups of Shandong.

ZHU FAMILY DINNER

Green Pea Starch Salad
Mr. Zhu's Steamed Fish
Boy Choy with Quail Eggs
Gingered Tomatoes & Eggs
Pork with Garlic Chives
Boiled Chicken with Soy Sauce
(optional)
Hot Cooked Rice
Beer   Orange Soda

In the Zhu household, Mr. Zhu prefers to do the cooking. His wife shops for vegetables at the neighborhood market, for meat at the government store. He makes a refreshing salad, boils a chicken, then cooks several simple dishes in rapid succession.

You can prepare all the ingredients for the dishes as early as the night before.

Up to 2 hours before serving, make the salad. If you include the chicken, simmer a whole 3½- to 4-pound broiler-fryer in water to cover just until it is no longer pink at the thigh bone, 45 to 60 minutes; serve it with soy sauce. Start the rice while chicken cooks. Then stir-fry remaining dishes in sequence. Serve dishes one at a time as they are cooked, or several at a time.

GREEN PEA STARCH SALAD

In China, vendors sell sheets of fresh pasta made from mung bean flour (it's called green pea starch). The sheets are cut into small pieces to make this salad. Here we use the more available dry bean threads — also made from mung beans.

- 8 ounces dry bean thread noodles (*saifun*)
- ⅓ cup rice vinegar (or wine vinegar plus 1 teaspoon sugar)
- 3 tablespoons soy sauce
- 2 tablespoons Oriental sesame oil
- ½ cup thinly sliced green onions
- ⅓ cup chopped fresh cilantro (coriander)
- 2 tablespoons minced fresh ginger
- 4 cloves garlic, minced
- 1 small cucumber, seeded and cut into thin, 3-inch-long slivers
  Salt
- 2 green onions, ends trimmed (optional)

In a 5- to 6-quart pan, bring about 2 quarts water to a boil. Add noodles; stir to separate noodles and let them soak off the heat until soft, 15 to 20 minutes. Drain well and cut noodles into 6- to 8-inch lengths. Place noodles in a large bowl.

Mix the vinegar, soy, oil, sliced onions, cilantro, ginger, and garlic. Add to noodles with cucumber; mix to blend. Add salt to taste. Garnish with whole onion. Serve, or cover and chill up to 2 hours. Serves 6 as part of a 6-course meal.

PER SERVING: 188 calories, 1 g protein, 35 g carbohydrates, 5 g fat, 0 mg cholesterol, 518 mg sodium

MR. ZHU'S STEAMED FISH

- 1 whole rockfish (1½ to 2½ lb.), dressed (remove head, if desired), or 1½ pounds rockfish fillets
  Salt
- 3 tablespoons fresh ginger slivers
- 3 green onions (ends trimmed), thinly sliced

Green Pea
Starch Salad

Bok Choy
with Quail Eggs

1 slice bacon, cut into ½-inch pieces
1 dried hot red chili (about 3 in. long)
1 tablespoon *each* rice vinegar (or wine vinegar) and soy sauce
Cilantro sprigs (coriander)

Rinse fish and pat dry. Make 3 diagonal slashes across body on each side of the whole fish. Place fish in a wide bowl or rimmed plate that will fit inside a steamer basket, wok, or deep, wide pan. (If fish is too long, cut it in half crosswise and set halves side by side.) Sprinkle fish lightly with salt, inside and out. Place half of the ginger, green onions, and bacon inside fish cavity; put remaining on top of fish (or put all on top of fillets). Set chili on fish. Pour vinegar and soy over top.

Drape a piece of foil over dish. Place dish in a steamer basket or on a rack set over about 1 inch boiling water in pan. Cover and steam until fish is opaque in thickest part (cut to test), 8 to 10 minutes for whole fish, about 5 minutes for fillets. Remove from steamer. If needed, reassemble halves and garnish with cilantro. Serves 6 as part of a 6-course meal.

Per Serving: 136 calories, 22 g protein, 2 g carbohydrates, 4 g fat, 42 mg cholesterol, 267 mg sodium

BOK CHOY WITH QUAIL EGGS

12 to 18 quail eggs
2 tablespoons salad oil
12 ounces baby bok choy heads, about 2-inch diameter at bases, ends trimmed
¼ cup water
Salt

In a 1½- to 2-quart pan, combine eggs and enough water to cover by 1 inch. Bring to a boil over high heat, then reduce heat and hold below simmering; cook, uncovered, 5 minutes. Drain and immerse eggs in cold water to cool. Peel.

Cut bok choy heads in half lengthwise. Rinse well and drain. Set a wok or 10- to 12-inch frying pan over high heat. When pan is hot, swirl 1 tablespoon oil over pan bottom. Add bok choy and stir to coat with oil. Add water, cover pan, and cook, turning often, until stems are barely tender when pierced and leaves are bright green, about 3 minutes. Lift out of pan and place on serving dish.

Pour any water out of pan. Add 1 tablespoon oil to pan and place over medium heat. Add eggs and cook, turning often, until eggs are golden, about 3 minutes. Place eggs on greens. Sprinkle with salt to taste. Serves 6 as part of a 6-course meal.

Per Serving (2 eggs): 76 calories, 3 g protein, 1 g carbohydrates, 7 g fat, 152 mg cholesterol, 37 mg sodium

GINGERED TOMATOES & EGGS

2 tablespoons salad oil
3 large eggs, lightly beaten
1 tablespoon fresh ginger slivers
2 green onions (ends trimmed), thinly sliced
2 large firm-ripe tomatoes, cored and cut into ½-inch wedges
Soy sauce or salt

Pour oil into a wok or 10- to 12-inch frying pan set over medium heat. When

oil is hot, add eggs and cook, lifting to let uncooked portion flow underneath. When set, break up eggs with spatula into bite-size pieces. Add ginger and onions and continue stir-frying until eggs are a darker gold color, about 2 minutes. Add tomatoes; stir-fry until hot. Add soy or salt to taste. Pour into bowl. Serves 6 as part of a 6-course meal.

Per Serving: 91 calories, 4 g protein, 3 g carbohydrates, 7 g fat, 137 mg cholesterol, 39 mg sodium

PORK WITH GARLIC CHIVES

Garlic stems were originally used in this recipe. They're rarely found here, so use garlic chives, available in Asian markets, or green onions and garlic.

½ pound boneless pork, such as loin, or shoulder or butt, cut into thin matchstick-size strips
1 tablespoon cornstarch
1 tablespoon rice wine or dry sherry
2 tablespoons salad oil
½ pound garlic chives, cut into 3-inch lengths (or green onions, cut into thin slivers, plus 3 cloves garlic, pressed or minced)
Salt and pepper

Mix pork with cornstarch and wine. Set a wok or 10- to 12-inch frying pan over high heat. When pan is hot, add oil and swirl to coat pan bottom. Add pork and stir-fry until lightly browned, 2 to 3 minutes. Add chives and stir-fry until bright green, 2 to 3 minutes. Add salt and pepper to taste. Pour into bowl. Serves 6 as part of a 6-course meal.

Per Serving: 161 calories, 8 g protein, 4 g carbohydrates, 13 g fat, 26 mg cholesterol, 23 mg sodium

Mr. Zhu's Steamed Fish

Gingered Tomatoes & Eggs

From China's Kitchens: Two Picnics

OUTINGS IN CHINA *often take advantage of spectacular settings, as in these picnics. One takes place on the fabled Great Wall, the other on a scenic lake in Hangzhou. You can try these dishes at home, or take them on a picnic, too.*

GREAT WALL PICNIC

Steamed Buns
Five Spice Fish
Soy-Chili Chicken Wings
Green Beans with Ginger
Golden Delicious Apples
Tangelos
Juice & Sparkling Water Blends

This picnic capped an exhilarating walk along the Great Wall. To create a Chinese-style sandwich, you stuff chunks of fragrant five spice fish into white steamed buns. Serve with chili-spiked chicken wings and marinated beans.

If time is short, you can substitute brown-and-serve dinner rolls for the buns.

STEAMED BUNS

1 package active dry yeast
1 cup warm water (110°)
⅓ cup sugar
2 tablespoons salad oil
1 teaspoon salt
3 to 3¼ cups all-purpose flour

In a large bowl, dissolve yeast in water; stir in sugar, oil, and salt. Let stand in a warm place 15 minutes. Add 3 cups flour and mix until dough holds together. Place on a lightly floured board; knead until smooth and elastic, 8 to 10 minutes, adding flour as required to prevent sticking.

Place in a greased bowl, cover with plastic wrap, and let rise in a warm place until doubled, 1¼ to 1½ hours.

Knead dough on a lightly floured board just to expel air. Cut into 8 equal pieces.

On a lightly floured board, knead each piece of dough into a smooth ball.

Set each bun on an oiled 3-inch square of waxed paper. Set, paper-side down, in a steamer basket or on a plate that will fit into a wok or deep, wide pan.

Cover lightly with plastic wrap and let rise in a warm place until puffy, about 30 minutes. Set steamer basket over boiling water or put plate on a rack set at least 1 inch above boiling water in a deep, wide pan. If using a metal lid, drape buns with a piece of foil, so condensation does not drip on them. Steam until buns spring back when lightly touched in center, 12 to 15 minutes. Remove from rack. Serve hot or at room temperature.

If made ahead, cool, wrap airtight, and store up to 12 hours. Freeze for longer storage; thaw and reheat over steam until hot, about 10 minutes, or covered with plastic wrap in a microwave oven at half-power (50 percent) until hot, about 2 minutes. Serve hot or at room temperature. Slash buns crosswise almost but not completely through. Makes 8.

PER SERVING: 242 calories, 5 g protein, 46 g carbohydrates, 4 g fat, 0 mg cholesterol, 277 mg sodium

FIVE SPICE FISH

1½ to 2 pounds firm white-flesh fish fillets, such as rockfish or halibut
3 green onions (ends trimmed), cut into 2-inch lengths and crushed
8 thin slices fresh ginger (each about the size of a quarter), crushed
⅓ cup soy sauce
2 tablespoons rice wine or dry sherry
2 tablespoons sugar
1 tablespoon Oriental sesame oil
½ teaspoon Chinese five spice (or ⅛ teaspoon *each* ground cinnamon, ground allspice, ground cloves, and crushed anise seed)

Cut fish into 1½-inch-wide slices about 1 inch thick and 2½ inches long. Mix fish with onions, ginger, soy, wine, sugar, sesame oil, and five spice. Cover and chill at least 4 hours or up to next day.

Lift fish from marinade and set slightly apart on a greased rack in a 10- by 15-inch broiler pan. Broil about 4 inches from heat, turning once, until opaque in thickest part (cut to test), about 10 minutes total. Serve warm or cool. (If made ahead, cool, cover, and chill until the next day.) Makes 8 servings.

PER SERVING: 130 calories, 19 g protein, 5 g carbohydrates, 3 g fat, 35 mg cholesterol, 739 mg sodium

SOY-CHILI CHICKEN WINGS

2 tablespoons salad oil
2 pounds chicken wing drumettes
¼ cup soy sauce
2 tablespoons rice wine or dry sherry
2 tablespoons sugar
1 teaspoon chili oil or 2 small dried hot red chilies
4 slices fresh ginger (each about the size of a quarter)
2 cloves garlic
2 whole green onions
1 cup water

Pour oil into a 10- to 12-inch frying pan and place over high heat. Add chicken and cook, turning, until browned on all sides, about 10 minutes. Add soy, wine, sugar, chili oil, ginger, garlic, onions, and water. Cover and simmer until chicken is white at the bone (cut to test), about 20 minutes. Uncover and boil, turning chicken often, until sauce reduces and thickens to coat wings, about 10 minutes.

Serve chicken warm or cool. (If made ahead, cool, cover, and chill until the next day.) Makes 8 appetizer servings.

PER SERVING: 191 calories, 12 g protein, 4 g carbohydrates, 14 g fat, 47 mg cholesterol, 560 mg sodium

GREEN BEANS WITH GINGER

1 pound Chinese long green beans or regular green beans, ends trimmed
¼ cup rice vinegar (or wine vinegar plus 1 teaspoon sugar)
2 tablespoons soy sauce
3 tablespoons fresh ginger shreds or 1 tablespoon minced garlic
Salt

Cut beans into 3-inch lengths. In a 5- to 6-quart pan, bring about 2 quarts water to a boil. Add beans and cook, uncovered, just until barely tender to bite, 4 to 5 minutes. Drain; immerse in ice water. Drain.

In a bowl, mix vinegar, soy, and ginger. Add beans and mix. Add salt to taste. Serve, or cover and chill up to 2 hours. Makes 8 appetizer servings.

PER SERVING: 22 calories, 1 g protein, 5 g carbohydrates, .06 g fat, 0 mg cholesterol, 262 mg sodium

HANGZHOU BOAT LUNCH

Shanghai Cucumber Salad
(see page 82)
Tang Bao
Chinese White Wine or Hot Tea
Asian Pears   Oranges

"Above there is heaven; below is Hang-zhou." This phrase is often used to describe the lovely resort south of Shanghai. Its colorful gardens, clean air, and fine food attract many tourists.

Here, as in neighboring Shanghai, people love to eat dumplings for lunch or a snack. Steamer baskets filled with dumplings are stacked tall in the centers of restaurant tables. We rushed just-steamed dumplings to a waiting boat for a picnic.

Our favorite dumpling was a pork- and shrimp-filled one, bursting with juices, to eat with vinegar and ginger shreds. Cold consommé is stirred into the filling; when the dumplings are cooked, the consommé melts to become a flavorful juice. In our simplified version, we use purchased wonton skins.

If you transport dumplings, bring a portable burner and steamer to reheat.

TANG BAO
(Soup dumplings)

- 6 small dried shiitake mushrooms
- ½ pound ground lean pork
- ¼ pound medium-size shrimp (43 to 50 a lb.), shelled, deveined, and finely chopped
- ¼ cup minced green onion
- 1½ tablespoons soy sauce
- 1 tablespoon minced fresh ginger
- 1 clove garlic, minced or pressed
- ⅓ cup canned consommé, chilled
  About 50 (about 1 lb.) wonton skins
- 1 large egg white
  Large cabbage leaves
  Rice vinegar or wine vinegar
- 1 piece fresh ginger (1 by 3 in.), peeled and cut into thin shreds

Soak mushrooms in hot water to cover until soft, about 20 minutes. Cut off and discard stems. Finely chop mushrooms. In a bowl, combine mushrooms, pork, shrimp, onion, soy, ginger, garlic, and consommé; stir until well blended.

Place 1 rounded teaspoon of pork filling in center of each wonton skin. Moisten center of each edge with egg

Boaters enjoy juicy dumplings on Hangzhou's West Lake. They dip the savory morsels in vinegar, then nibble them with a few shreds of fresh ginger.

white. Bring each pair of opposite edges of wonton skin to center and press to seal. Brush corners with egg white. Bring corners together to make 1 point in center; press and twist together to seal.

Set slightly apart in flour-dusted 10-by 15-inch pans; keep lightly covered. Repeat to fill remaining wrappers. (If made ahead, cover and chill up to 2 hours, or freeze; when solid, remove from pans and store airtight in freezer up to 1 month.)

Line a steamer basket with cabbage leaves (you may need to wilt them in boiling water to get them to lie flat), or use plates that will fit into a wok or deep, wide pan. Set cold or frozen unthawed dumplings about 1 inch apart on the steamer baskets or plates (cover plates loosely with foil). Set steamer baskets over a wok or plates on a rack over 1 to 1½ inches boiling water in pan. Cover steamer basket or pan; steam until filling is firm to touch, 10 minutes if cold, 15 minutes if frozen. Serve hot to dip in vinegar and eat with ginger shreds. Makes about 50, 4 entrée or 10 appetizer servings.

PER APPETIZER SERVING: 235 calories, 13 g protein, 35 g carbohydrates, 4 g fat, 72 mg cholesterol, 213 mg sodium

From China's Kitchens: A Classic Noodle Soup

IN BEIJING, *chef Chang Jing of the Kangle Restaurant served us this noodle classic. It was first created as a clever solution to a young man's academic problems.*

Many years ago, a youth from a wealthy Chinese family found himself unprepared to pass the Imperial exams. His father ordered him to remain confined in a cottage in the family's back garden to study. He was not to return to the house, even to eat. The house cook was to bring his food to him in his isolated quarters.

The cottage was quite far from the house, and surrounded by water. It was connected to the main residence only by a small bridge. Trying to provide the student with hot, nourishing food, the cook discovered that if he created a rich chicken broth, a layer of fat would rise to the surface and insulate the soup, allowing it to stay hot on the long walk to the cottage.

The chef also brought hot cooked noodles and thin slices of raw fish, shrimp, and chicken. At the cottage, he stirred the thin pieces of seafood into the hot soup; they cooked at once. Then the cook stirred in the hot noodles, and the student sat down to his meal.

Father and son were both pleased. The student was well fed, and he passed his examination.

These days, we need not ferry our meals across bridges. So if you like, skim the fat from the broth. Use a rich homemade broth—or canned broth, which will speed things up if you're in a hurry.

To complete the meal, serve with green beans and ginger (see page 86 for recipe) or stir-fried greens.

Raw seafood and chicken go into hot broth to cook. Noodles come next.

CROSS-BRIDGE NOODLES

1 **boned and skinned chicken breast half (about 3 oz.)**
1 **skinned white fish fillet (about 3 oz.), such as rockfish**
3 **ounces medium-size shrimp (43 to 50 per lb.), shelled and deveined**
2 **tablespoons minced fresh ginger**
2 **tablespoons rice wine or dry sherry**
1 **tablespoon soy sauce**
2 **tablespoons thinly sliced green onion**

12 **ounces fresh thin egg noodles, or 8 ounces dry thin egg noodles such as Chinese or capellini**
1 **small cucumber, at room temperature, cut in half lengthwise, seeded, and thinly sliced**
2½ **quarts regular-strength chicken broth**

Slice the chicken, fish, and shrimp into paper-thin pieces about ½ inch wide and 3 inches long (for easier slicing, first partly freeze poultry and seafood until firm, about 25 minutes). Arrange the slices on a plate. Press ginger, a portion at a time, through a garlic press to extract juice into wine. Add soy. Drizzle wine mixture over slices. Sprinkle with green onion.

In a 5- to 6-quart pan, bring about 3 quarts water to boiling. Add noodles.

Boil, uncovered, until noodles are barely tender to bite, 2 to 3 minutes for fresh, 5 to 7 minutes for dry. Drain noodles and garnish with cucumber. Cover and keep hot.

Meanwhile, in a 4- to 5-quart pan, bring broth to boiling over high heat. Skim and discard fat, if desired. Pour boiling broth into a warm tureen.

At the table, push raw seafood and poultry slices into the hot broth, stirring to cook slices evenly. Then stir in hot noodles. Ladle soup into bowls. Serves 4.

PER SERVING: 367 calories, 26 g protein, 47 g carbohydrates, 7 g fat, 99 mg cholesterol, 447 mg sodium

Devilish Bunnies

OVERWHELMED *by hard-cooked eggs from the Easter bunny? Take a devilish turn and make them into egg bunnies—appetizers that all ages can enjoy. Vegetables become ears, eyes, and tails.*

DEVILED BUNNIES

  8 hard-cooked large eggs
  6 tablespoons mayonnaise
  2 green onions (ends trimmed), thinly sliced
  1 tablespoon Dijon mustard
⅛ to ¼ teaspoon liquid hot pepper seasoning
    Salt and pepper
32 vegetable ears (choices follow)
32 eyes, such as drained capers, sliced ripe olives, or drained green peppercorns
16 vegetable tails (choices follow)

Crack shells and carefully peel from eggs. Cut eggs in half lengthwise. Scoop yolks onto a rimmed plate and set whites aside. Mash yolks finely, then mix with mayonnaise, green onion, mustard, liquid pepper, and salt and pepper to taste. If desired, spoon yolk mixture into a pastry bag with a wide (at least ½ in.) plain tip.

Squeeze or spoon yolk mixture equally into each cup of each white. To make each bunny, push 2 vegetables for ears

Easter eggs can go bunny-hopping when they sprout ears and tails.

Using a pastry bag, pipe seasoned yolk filling into egg white halves. Add vegetables, nuts, and capers to create the bunnies.

into yolk at 1 end of the egg and press in eyes in front of the ears. Stick a tail into yolk on the other end. If made ahead, cover loosely without touching ears and chill up to 4 hours. Makes 16. —*Elizabeth C. McConkie Brock, Sebastopol, Calif.*

PER BUNNY WITH CARROT EARS, CAPER EYES, AND BROCCOLI TAIL: 84 calories, 3 g protein, 2 g carbohydrates, 7 g fat, 140 mg cholesterol, 107 mg sodium

Vegetable ears. Choose slender **carrot** sticks, each about 2 inches long; tiny inner leaves of **Belgian endive;** raw or blanched **Chinese pea pods;** or blanched **green beans** (cut diagonally into 2-in. lengths). To blanch vegetables, see directions at right.

Vegetable tails. Choose **salted roasted whole almonds,** small blanched **broccoli flowerets** (directions follow), tiny **marinated mushrooms,** or **quartered cherry tomatoes.**

To blanch vegetables. In a 10- to 12-inch frying pan, bring 1 inch of water to a boil over high heat. Add vegetables and cook, uncovered, just until bright green and tender-crisp to pierce, 1 to 3 minutes. Drain and immerse vegetables in ice water until cool; drain. If made ahead, cover and chill up to next day.

Easter Brunch Dishes

EASTER MORNING ACTIVITIES may leave little time for cooking. But these festive egg dishes go together smoothly and quickly if you take advantage of the make-ahead steps we include in each recipe.

The crisp waffles are served with softly poached eggs and bacon on top; eggs presented fajita-style become a whole meal; and the last dish takes its inspiration from a Danish classic, replacing veal with eggs and adding croissants.

CORNMEAL WAFFLES WITH EGGS & BACON

 1 cup firmly packed (about ½ lb.)
   chopped bacon
   Cornmeal waffles (recipe follows)
   Poached eggs (directions follow)
 3 tablespoons chopped chives
   Chive spears (optional)
   Maple or maple-flavor syrup,
   warmed if desired

In a 10- to 12-inch frying pan over medium heat, stir bacon occasionally until crisp, about 10 minutes. Lift from pan with a slotted spoon and drain on paper towels. If made ahead, cover and chill until next day. Wrap loosely in foil and place in a 300° oven until warm, about 5 minutes. Or reheat on paper towels in a microwave oven at full power (100 percent) until warm, about 45 seconds.

Place 1 small or ½ large waffle on each plate. With a slotted spoon, transfer 1 egg at a time onto each waffle. Sprinkle each egg with ⅙ of the bacon and chopped chives. Garnish with chive spears. Offer syrup to add to taste. Makes 6 servings.

PER SERVING: 387 calories, 16 g protein, 23 g carbohydrates, 25 g fat, 444 mg cholesterol, 661 mg sodium

Cornmeal waffles. In a bowl, beat 3 **large egg whites** on high speed until they hold soft peaks; set aside. In another bowl, beat 3 **large egg yolks** and 2 tablespoons **sugar** until yolks are thick and light yellow. Beat in 1 cup **milk,** ¾ cup **all-purpose flour,** ¼ cup **cornmeal,** ¼ cup (⅛ lb.) **melted butter** or margarine, and ½ teaspoon *each* **salt, baking powder,** and **vanilla;** beat until smooth. Fold into egg whites.

Heat waffle iron, round or square, on medium-high heat (or 375° on an electric iron); when hot, brush grid with **salad oil.** Pour batter into the center of the grid (about ½ cup for 7-in. iron, about 1 cup for 9-in.). Close iron and bake until waffle browns, 3 to 5 minutes. Lift waffle from iron and serve; or, to keep warm, place directly on racks in a 200° oven for up to 30 minutes. Repeat to bake remaining batter. Makes 6 or 7 waffles, 7-inch size; 6 waffles, 9-inch size.

Poached eggs. To heat-set 6 **large eggs,** bring 3 inches water to boiling in a 4- to 5-quart pan. Immerse eggs in the boiling water for 8 to 10 seconds; lift from pan with slotted spoon and set aside.

Fill a 10- to 12-inch frying pan with 1½ inches water; heat until bubbles form on the pan bottom with an occasional bubble rising to the surface; adjust heat to maintain this temperature. Break each egg into the water, holding egg close to the surface. Cook eggs until set to your liking (poke white gently to check firmness), 3 to 5 minutes for soft yolks and firm whites. To serve eggs, lift from water, 1 at a time, with a slotted spoon and pat the back of the spoon with paper towels to dry egg (don't dry if making ahead).

To make ahead, immerse eggs at once in a bowl of ice water. Cover and chill up until next day. To reheat, transfer eggs with spoon to a large bowl of very hot-to-touch water (about 140°); let stand until eggs are hot to touch, about 10 minutes.

EASTER EGGS OSCAR

 6 croissants, each about 6 inches
   long, cut in half horizontally
 12 to 18 asparagus spears, tough
   ends trimmed and stems peeled
   (optional)
 ¾ pound shelled cooked crab
   Poached eggs (see directions,
   preceding)
   Hollandaise sauce (recipe follows)

Arrange croissants, cut sides together, on a 12- by 15-inch baking sheet. Heat in a 375° oven until croissants are crisp outside and warm inside, about 8 minutes.

Meanwhile, bring about 1 inch water to boiling in a 10- to 12-inch frying pan over high heat. Add asparagus; cook, uncovered, until stems are tender

Drizzle maple syrup over cornmeal waffle, poached egg, bacon, and chives. You can cook eggs the day before, chill, then reheat.

when pierced, 5 to 7 minutes. Drain and serve hot.

Or, if made ahead, immerse in ice water until cold. Drain, cover, and chill up until next day. To reheat, immerse in a large bowl of very hot-to-touch water (about 140°); let stand until warm, about 5 minutes; drain.

Set the bottom half of a croissant, cut side up, on each plate. Cover croissants equally with crab; put 2 or 3 asparagus spears atop crab on each plate. With a slotted spoon, place 1 egg on each croissant half. Pour sauce equally over eggs. Set a croissant top beside each portion. Serves 6.

PER SERVING: 539 calories, 22 g protein, 19 g carbohydrates, 41 g fat, 482 mg cholesterol, 771 mg sodium

Hollandaise sauce. In a blender or food processor, whirl 2 **large egg yolks,** 2 tablespoons **lemon juice,** and ⅟₁₆ teaspoon **cayenne** to mix. With motor running, slowly pour ¾ cup (⅜ lb.) hot **melted butter** or margarine into yolk mixture. Serve; or, if made ahead, pour into small metal bowl, cover, and chill up to 2 days. To reheat, set bowl in a larger bowl; pour hot-to-touch tap water into larger bowl to height of sauce in inner bowl; stir often until sauce is warm, about 5 minutes.

EGG FAJITAS

1½ **pounds jicama**
 1 **lime, cut into 6 wedges**
10 **to 12 flour tortillas, 7- to 8-inch size**
   Sausage and accompaniments (directions follow)
   About 1½ cups prepared salsa
   About 1 cup sour cream
   About 1 cup fresh cilantro (coriander) leaves
   Scrambled eggs (recipe follows)

Peel jicama; rinse and cut into sticks about ½ by 3 inches. Arrange in a dish with lime wedges; if made ahead, cover and chill up until next day. (Brush jicama with water to freshen, if needed.)

Stack tortillas and wrap in foil; place in a 300° oven until hot, about 10 minutes, or enclose in a plastic bag and heat in a microwave oven at full power (100 percent) until hot, about 1 minute.

Present tortillas, eggs, sausage and accompaniments, salsa, sour cream, and cilantro in separate bowls. To make each

To assemble egg fajitas, spoon browned sausage onto flour tortilla, then add sour cream, chilies, salsa, cilantro, and scrambled eggs. Serve with jicama and lime. To eat out of hand, fold tortilla edges over the filling.

fajita, put a tortilla on a plate and spoon ingredients onto tortilla. Eat with a knife and fork, or fold tortilla around filling and hold to eat. Squeeze lime over jicama and munch along with fajitas. Makes 5 or 6 servings, 2 fajitas each.

PER SERVING: 720 calories, 29 g protein, 54 g carbohydrates, 43 g fat, 442 mg cholesterol, 1,449 mg sodium

Scrambled eggs. Melt 1 tablespoon **butter** or margarine in a 10- to 12-inch frying pan over medium heat. In a bowl, beat to blend 8 **large eggs** and ½ cup sliced **green onions.** Pour into pan and cook, stirring occasionally, until eggs are softly set. Stir in ½ cup shredded **cheddar cheese;** cook to desired doneness, about 3 minutes for soft, moist eggs. Spoon scrambled eggs into bowl.

Sausage and accompaniments. Crumble 1½ pounds **bulk pork sausage** (or half chorizo sausage, casings removed) into a 10- to 12-inch frying pan. Cook over medium-high heat, stirring occasionally, until meat is brown, about 15 minutes. Transfer sausage to a bowl with a slotted spoon; discard fat. Serve, or cover and keep warm in a 300° oven up to 30 minutes. If made ahead, cool, cover, and chill up to overnight. Reheat, covered, in a 300° oven until hot, about 15 minutes.

Cut 1 can (4 oz.) **whole green chilies** into strips. Drain 1 can (2¼ oz.) **sliced black ripe olives;** arrange chilies and olives beside meat.

Lamb & Springtime Companions

LAMB AND SPRING *have a special affinity. They go together out of tradition, from the times when young lamb came only in spring. Here we propose ways to show off three fine cuts: a crown roast; a boned loin; and the leg. Each has companions to make a special menu.*

To make a crown, have three racks cracked and sewn together, bones out. Do it yourself or ask your meatman to assemble it. For the most dramatic look, trim meat from ribs down about 2 inches from tips.

CROWN ROAST OF LAMB WITH VEGETABLE RAGOUT & COUSCOUS

    Vegetable ragout mixture
    (directions follow)
 1 tablespoon fresh thyme leaves or
    1 teaspoon dry thyme leaves
 2 tablespoons olive oil
    Salt and pepper
 1 crown roast of lamb (3 racks tied
    together, bones out—5 to 6 lb.
    total), with surface fat trimmed
    Couscous (recipe follows)
 1½ cups regular-strength beef broth
 ½ cup *each* dry red wine and
    whipping cream
 ¼ cup (⅛ lb.) unsalted butter or
    margarine

Put vegetable ragout mixture in a 12- by 15-inch roasting pan and mix with half the thyme, olive oil, and salt and pepper to taste. Bake in a 475° oven for 30 minutes; remove from oven. Drain off and reserve vegetable juices, then continue baking vegetables until they are soft and edges are almost black, 20 to 25 minutes longer. In a food processor or with a knife, coarsely chop vegetables; keep warm.

About 30 minutes before vegetables are done, sprinkle lamb lightly with salt, pepper, and remaining thyme. Set roast, rib ends up, in a 12- by 15-inch roasting pan. Roast in a 475° oven until a thermometer inserted in thickest part of meat against the bone registers 140° for rare, 25 to 30 minutes, or 150° for medium, about 35 minutes. Put lamb on a platter; spoon couscous into center no higher than trimmed ribs. Spoon half the vegetables on top of couscous in roast; put remaining couscous and vegetables in separate bowls. Keep foods warm.

Tilt pan and skim off fat; discard. Add broth, wine, and reserved vegetable liquid to pan; bring to a boil over high heat, stirring to loosen browned bits. Boil, uncovered, until reduced by half, about 5 minutes. Drain any juices from lamb into pan. Add cream and boil until reduced to 1⅓ cups. Remove from heat and add butter, stirring to incorporate. Pour sauce into a small bowl. Slice roast into chops; offer sauce to add to lamb, couscous, and ragout. Serves 8 to 10.

PER SERVING: 886 calories, 37 g protein, 35 g carbohydrates, 65 g fat, 174 mg cholesterol, 111 mg sodium

Vegetable ragout mixture. Trim ends from 5 medium-size **zucchini** (about 1½ lb. total) and cut into 1½-inch-thick slices. Peel, core, and cut into wedges 2 medium-size firm-ripe **tomatoes.** Cut 1 large **onion** into eighths. Peel 3 large **carrots** (about ¾ lb. total), and cut into 1-inch-thick slices. Stem, seed, and cut 1 *each* medium-size **red** and **yellow bell pepper** (or 2 of either) into 1-inch pieces.

Couscous. In a 2- to 3-quart pan over high heat, bring 3 cups **regular-strength chicken broth** and 1 tablespoon **unsalted butter** or margarine to boiling. Stir in 2 cups **couscous;** remove from heat, cover, and let stand until liquid is absorbed, about 5 minutes. Stir with a fork to fluff. Makes 8 to 10 servings.

LAMB TOURNEDOS ON ARTICHOKE BOTTOMS WITH TARRAGON BEURRE BLANC

 1 boned lamb loin (about 1½ lb.),
    fat trimmed, rolled and tied
 ¼ teaspoon freshly ground pepper
 ⅔ cup *each* regular-strength chicken
    broth and dry white wine
 1 tablespoon Dijon mustard
 2 tablespoons minced shallots
 2 teaspoons minced fresh tarragon
    leaves or ½ teaspoon dry tarragon
    leaves
 ½ cup whipping cream
 ¼ cup (⅛ lb.) butter or margarine
    Cooked artichoke bottoms
    (directions follow)
    Black peppercorns

Sprinkle lamb with half the pepper; set on a rack in a 9- by 13-inch pan. Roast lamb in a 475° oven until a thermometer inserted in center of meat registers 140° for rare, 20 to 25 minutes, or 150° for medium, about 30 minutes. Transfer to a platter; keep warm.

In a 10- to 12-inch frying pan over high heat, combine broth, wine, mustard, shallots, tarragon, and remaining pepper. Boil, uncovered, until reduced by half, about 5 minutes; add cream and boil until reduced to 1 cup. Remove from heat and add butter; stir constantly to incorporate. Serve, or, to keep warm up to 2 hours, pour sauce into a warmed thermos and close. (Or pour sauce into a bowl and set in a container of hot water, changing water to keep sauce hot up to 2 hours.)

Cut lamb crosswise into 8 equal slices. Spoon half the sauce onto each of 4 heated dinner plates. Set 2 artichokes in sauce on each plate. Set lamb on artichokes. Pour remaining sauce over meat; garnish with a few peppercorns. Serves 4.

PER SERVING: 537 calories, 35 g protein, 34 g carbohydrates, 31 g fat, 159 mg cholesterol, 546 mg sodium

Cooked artichoke bottoms. In a 3- to 4-quart pan, combine 6 cups **water** with ¼ cup **vinegar;** set aside.

Pull off and discard tough outer leaves from 8 large **artichokes** (at least 3 in. across); trim stems flush with bottoms. Snap back larger leaves, then pull away, leaving fleshy base of each leaf attached; discard leaves. When you reach the pale inner leaves, trim off tops flush with top of artichoke base; discard leaves. Pare coarse fibers from artichoke sides; add artichokes to water as trimmed.

Bring water to a boil over high heat. Cover and simmer until artichokes are tender when pierced, about 30 minutes; drain. Scoop out and discard fuzzy centers; use artichokes hot, or cover and chill up to overnight. To reheat, place in an 8- or 9-inch-square pan, cover, and bake with lamb until hot, 10 to 12 minutes.

HERB-CRUSTED GRILLED LEG OF LAMB & TOMATOES WITH GARLIC POTATOES GRATIN

 1 leg of lamb, 5½ to 6 pounds
 3 cloves garlic, cut into quarters
 1 tablespoon *each* minced fresh
    leaves of thyme, rosemary,
    marjoram, sage, and mint (or
    1 teaspoon *each* of the dry herb
    leaves)
 ½ teaspoon salt
 1 teaspoon cracked pepper
 2 tablespoons olive oil
    Herbed tomatoes (recipe follows)
    Garlic potatoes gratin (recipe
    follows)

Trim excess fat from lamb and discard. Cut 12 gashes in leg and insert garlic. Combine thyme, rosemary, marjoram, sage, mint, salt, and pepper; rub lamb with oil, then herbs.

In a barbecue with lid, ignite 50 charcoal briquets on firegrate. When briquets are covered with gray ash (30 to 40 minutes), push half the coals to each side of grate and place a drip pan in center. Position grill 4 to 6 inches above coals. Set lamb on grill over pan. Add 5 briquets to each side of coal bed. Cover barbecue and open dampers. Every 30 minutes, add 5 more briquets to each side of coal bed.

Roast lamb until a thermometer inserted in thickest part of meat (against bone) registers 140° for rare, about 1¼ hours. Transfer meat to a platter and surround with herbed tomatoes; accompany with potatoes. To carve lamb, grasp narrow end of leg with a cloth and slice meat parallel to bone. Makes 6 to 8 servings.

PER SERVING: 391 calories, 47 g protein, 10 g carbohydrates, 17 g fat, 163 mg cholesterol, 304 mg sodium

Herbed tomatoes. Rinse 6 to 8 large (about 2 lb. total) firm-ripe **Roma-type tomatoes;** slice in half lengthwise. Set cut side up in a 10- by 15-inch baking pan. Combine 1½ teaspoons *each* minced **fresh leaves of thyme, rosemary, marjoram, sage,** and **mint** (or ½ teaspoon *each* of the dry herb leaves) with ¼ teaspoon **pepper** and ½ cup fine **dry bread crumbs;** sprinkle tomatoes with herb mixture. Drizzle 1 tablespoon **olive oil** over tomato halves. Bake in a 450° oven until tomatoes soften and crumbs are golden, 10 to 12 minutes. Season to taste with **salt.**

Garlic potatoes gratin. Butter a shallow 2½-quart pan or baking dish. Peel 6 large **russet potatoes** (about 5 lb. total) and thinly slice. Overlap slices in pan, making level. Sprinkle potatoes with 1 teaspoon **salt** (optional) and ½ teaspoon **pepper.** Combine 1½ cups **whipping cream** or half-and-half (light cream) with 2 tablespoons melted **butter** or margarine and 2 cloves **garlic,** minced or pressed; pour over potatoes.

Bake, uncovered, in a 450° oven until potatoes are brown and tender when pierced, about 45 minutes. Sprinkle 1½ cups (6 oz.) shredded **Swiss cheese** over potatoes; bake until cheese melts, 8 to 10 minutes longer.

PER SERVING: 417 calories, 12 g protein, 43 g carbohydrates, 23 g fat, 77 mg cholesterol, 114 mg sodium

Leg of lamb is carved French-style, parallel to bone; rarer meat comes with center slices. Baked tomatoes and gratin potatoes go with barbecued meat.

Wrap & Roll Desserts

MIDDLE EASTERN BAKLAVA *takes on some contemporary flavors and designs in these pastries. Traditionally, baklava is layers of fila with nut filling, cut into diamonds. Here, the thin flexible sheets of fila take different forms: a flamboyant-looking tart, sweet pinwheels, and crinkled, stuffed rolls. Two of the pastries use macadamia nuts; the other uses walnuts.*

Look for fila dough in the refrigerator or freezer section of supermarkets, Middle Eastern stores, and specialty food shops.

Offer baklava with morning coffee, or serve for dessert.

MACADAMIA BAKLAVA TART

- 1 cup (5 oz.) salted macadamia nuts, chopped
- 1 cup sweetened flaked coconut
- ¼ cup firmly packed brown sugar
- 1 teaspoon *each* ground cinnamon and ground nutmeg
- 1 package (1 lb.) fila dough
- 1 cup (½ lb.) melted butter or margarine
- Honey syrup (recipe follows)

Mix macadamias, coconut, sugar, cinnamon, and nutmeg; set aside.

To keep fila from drying when you're not working with it, cover it with plastic wrap.

Set aside 3 fila sheets; cover.

Lift off ¼ of the remaining fila sheets; cut in half across the narrow width; cover.

Lift off 1 whole fila sheet and lay flat. Working quickly, brush lightly with butter, then center 1 cut fila strip on top of the sheet. Brush strip lightly with butter. (Position each strip to cross in center, fanning out to create an overlapping round.) Make alternating layers on top of the strips with whole fila sheets (3 more) and strips (3 more), buttering each layer. Set the stack into a 10- to 11-inch tart pan with removable bottom; let edges hang over pan rim. Pushing gently, fit center of fila into pan.

Sprinkle ¼ of the nut mixture into pan. Cover with 1 whole fila sheet; brush lightly with butter. Repeat this step, adding 1 fila strip; brush lightly with butter. Repeat steps to use remaining nuts; as you add each strip, lay it across the strip beneath, fanning ends to create an overlapping round so the rim will be evenly thick. Layer remaining fila sheets (except the 3 that are reserved) and strips on top of filling, buttering each layer; finish with a whole sheet.

With your hand, roll the extended edge of fila sheets under to fit inside pan rim.

Cut partially through fila into the top nut layer, making diamonds about 1 inch wide and 1½ inches long.

Lay 1 of the 3 reserved fila sheets out flat. Brush lightly with butter, cut in half, and stack halves. Then cut the stack in quarters. Take hold of 1 quarter-stack, pinching in center to make a peak (see picture on facing page). Set peak on tart. Pinch remaining quarters and set on tart. Repeat this step with remaining 2

Golden baked fila encloses a sweet, nutty filling in a handsome tart (top left), in crisp pinwheels served with whipped cream (right), and in crunchy rolls (bottom).

fila sheets, pushing peaks together to make room for all of them.

Bake in a 350° oven until golden, 40 to 45 minutes. Remove from oven. At once pour honey syrup over top. Let cool to room temperature. Remove pan rim and set tart on plate. (If made ahead, cover and store at room temperature up to 3 days.) Cut into thin wedges to serve. Serves 12 to 16. — *Valerie Katagiri, Beaverton, Ore.*

PER SERVING: 346 calories, 4 g protein, 38 g carbohydrates, 21 g fat, 31 mg cholesterol, 173 mg sodium

Honey syrup. In a 2- to 3-quart pan, combine ¾ cup *each* **sugar** and **water** and 2 tablespoons **honey.** Boil on high heat, uncovered, until reduced to 1 cup, about 10 minutes. Stir in 1 teaspoon **lemon juice.**

Pinch each stack of buttered fila sheets in center and set on nut and fila layers in pan.

MACADAMIA PINWHEEL BAKLAVA

Use the same ingredients for **macadamia baklava tart,** preceding, but reduce the fila to ½ pound, the butter to ½ cup (¼ lb.), and make ½ recipe honey syrup.

Lay 1 sheet fila flat; lightly brush with butter. Repeat, stacking fila and using half the sheets. Sprinkle top sheet with ¼ of the nut mixture; cover with 1 sheet fila and brush lightly with butter. Repeat to use all the nut mixture. Lay remaining sheets of fila on top of nuts, buttering lightly between layers.

Starting on a long edge, roll fila layers into a log. With a sharp knife, cut log crosswise into 1-inch-thick slices. Place slices in a 10- by 15-inch baking pan.

Bake in a 350° oven until golden, 20 to 30 minutes. Pour syrup over hot slices. (If made ahead, cover and store at room temperature up to 3 days.) Serve slices warm or cool with **sweetened whipped cream,** sprinkled with **ground nutmeg** if desired. Serves 12.

PER SERVING: 285 calories, 3 g protein, 29 g carbohydrates, 18 g fat, 21 mg cholesterol, 143 mg sodium

Roll buttered fila around macadamia and coconut filling. Cut crosswise, then bake.

FILA CRINKLE WALNUT ROLLS

  2 **cups finely chopped walnuts**
  ¼ **cup sugar**
1½ **teaspoons ground cinnamon**
     About 1 pound fila dough
  1 **cup (½ lb.) butter or margarine, melted and cooled**
  1 **wooden dowel, ¼ inch in diameter and 16 to 18 inches long**
     Honey (optional)

Mix nuts, sugar, and cinnamon; set aside.

Keep fila covered with plastic wrap to prevent drying when you are not working with the dough. Lay 1 sheet of fila out flat; brush lightly with melted butter; fold in half crosswise and lightly butter top.

Leaving a 1-inch margin along folded fila edge, spoon 2 tablespoons nut mixture in an even band along length of sheet, allowing ½-inch margins at each end.

Lay dowel on nut mixture; fold narrow edge of fila over dowel, then roll fila onto dowel. With a hand on each end of dowel, push fila toward the center, making a crinkled roll about 7 inches long. Slide roll, seam down, into a 10- by 15-inch pan. Brush roll with butter; cover with plastic wrap. Repeat to make remaining rolls; space rolls about 1 inch apart on pans (you'll need 3 pans). Bake, uncovered, in a 350° oven until rolls are golden brown, about 15 minutes.

Cut rolls in half crosswise and transfer from pans with a spatula. Serve warm or cool, plain or drizzled with honey. If made ahead, store airtight up to 2 weeks; freeze to store longer. Makes about 3 dozen rolls. — *Marilyn Kezirian, Los Angeles.*

PER ROLL: 134 calories, 2 g protein, 11 g carbohydrates, 9 g fat, 14 mg cholesterol, 53 mg sodium

Gently push crinkled fila roll from the dowel into a baking pan, seam side down. Before baking, brush butter on top.

It's Guatemalan "Hide & Seek"

ESCONDIDAS, or "hide-and-seek," is the playful name for this quick and tasty dish from south of the border. Hiding beneath a puffy mantle of golden-fried egg batter is a flavorful, cheese- and ham-filled tortilla. At first glance, the dish looks like chilies rellenos (stuffed chilies): this trick is part of the reason for the name.

You brown the tortillas at the last moment, but other steps can be done ahead.

HAM & CHEDDAR ESCONDIDAS

8 corn tortillas (6- to 7-in. diameter)
8 slices cooked ham (each about ⅛ inch thick; about ½ lb. total)

1 can (7 oz.) whole green chilies, cut lengthwise into 8 equal portions
½ pound cheddar cheese, cut into strips about ⅜ inch thick and 3 inches long
½ cup thinly sliced green onions
Salad oil
Egg batter (recipe follows)
Mellow salsa (recipe follows)

In an ungreased 10- to 12-inch frying pan over medium-high heat, soften tortillas, 1 at a time. Heat each tortilla about 10 seconds on each side. Remove tortilla from pan and at once top with a slice of ham, then arrange down the center of the tortilla ⅛ of the chilies, ⅛ of the cheese (½ inch in from tortilla edge), and ⅛ of the green onions. Roll tortilla snugly around filling and pin shut with small wooden picks. Repeat to fill remaining tortillas. If made ahead, cover and chill up to 2 hours.

Pour about ¼ inch oil into the frying pan over medium-high heat; heat to 350° to 360°. Using 2 forks, immerse tortilla rolls, one at a time, in egg batter and coat generously. Lift out coated roll and set in hot oil. Cook until golden brown on bottom, then turn with the forks and brown remaining portion of roll (the browning takes about 1 minute per side). Lift roll from pan, drain briefly on paper towels, then set on an ovenproof platter. Keep warm, uncovered, in a 300° oven as you repeat steps to cook remaining rolls; do not stack. Spoon salsa to taste on individual portions. Makes 6 to 8 servings. — *Wanda Smith, Oakland.*

PER SERVING: 309 calories, 21 g protein, 18 g carbohydrates, 17 g fat, 252 mg cholesterol, 926 mg sodium

Egg batter. Separate 6 **large eggs.** In a large bowl, whip whites at high speed until they will hold moist, distinct peaks. In another bowl, use same beater to whip yolks with 3 tablespoons **all-purpose flour** and ¼ teaspoon **salt.** Gently fold yolks into whites and use at once.

Mellow salsa. In a 10- to 12-inch frying pan over medium-high heat, combine 1 tablespoon **olive** or salad **oil** and 1 medium-size **onion,** chopped. Stir often until onion begins to brown, 8 to 10 minutes. Stir in 1 can (14 oz.) **stewed tomatoes** with their liquid, 1 can (4 oz.) **diced green chilies,** ½ teaspoon *each* **dry oregano leaves** and **crushed dried hot red chilies,** and 1 cup **regular-strength chicken broth.** Boil, uncovered, until reduced to 2¼ cups, 15 to 20 minutes. Stir in ¼ cup minced **fresh cilantro** (coriander). Serve hot. If made ahead, cover and chill up to 3 days. Rewarm over low heat. Makes about 2¼ cups.

PER TABLESPOON: 9 calories, .20 g protein, 1 g carbohydrates, .42 g fat, 0 mg cholesterol, 49 mg sodium

TURKEY & JACK ESCONDIDAS

Follow directions for **ham and cheddar escondidas** (preceding), but instead of sliced ham use sliced cooked **turkey breast,** and instead of cheddar cheese use **jack cheese.**

PER SERVING: 294 calories, 23 g protein, 18 g carbohydrates, 15 g fat, 250 mg cholesterol, 495 mg sodium

Melted cheese oozes out of hot tortilla roll. Serve with cooked salsa; accompany with sliced avocado, cool sour cream, fresh cilantro.

Lentils—in Bread, Salad, a Side Dish

LENTILS PROVIDE *a mellow background for complex flavors, such as those characteristic of Indian cuisine. Inspired by these flavorings, here we use lentils in Western ways with bread, salad, and a side dish.*

You'll find common olive-green Chilean lentils in supermarkets, packaged in plastic bags and labeled simply as "lentils." Somewhat larger are the tan Red Chief lentils, often sold decorticated, *with the thin outer skin (or hull) removed to reveal the orange-red color inside. Look for the smaller and darker red-orange decorticated lentils, called Persians, in Indian and Mediterranean stores.*

Lentils with skins on cook in less than an hour. Decorticated ones cook much faster; watch closely or they'll get mushy. All types taste a lot alike.

Seed-speckled bread gets its golden hue from red decorticated lentils.

SEED-CRUSTED LENTIL BREAD

- ¾ **cup lentils, decorticated or with skins**
- 2 **tablespoons** *each* **mustard seed and sesame seed**
- ¼ **cup (⅛ lb.) melted butter or margarine**
- 1 **cup sugar**
- 2 **large eggs**
- 1½ **cups all-purpose flour**
- 1 **teaspoon baking soda**
- ½ **teaspoon salt**
- ½ **teaspoon curry powder**
- ¼ **teaspoon baking powder**
- ¾ **cup sweetened shredded coconut**

Sort lentils to remove any debris; rinse and drain. Put lentils in a 1½- to 2-quart pan; add 3 cups water and bring to boiling over high heat. Cover and simmer until lentils are tender to bite, about 15 minutes for decorticated, about 40 minutes for lentils with skins. Drain and cool.

In a 10- to 12-inch frying pan over medium heat, combine mustard seed and sesame seed. Shake pan frequently until sesame seed is lightly browned; set aside.

In a large bowl, mix together butter, sugar, and eggs. Stir in lentils. Mix together flour, soda, salt, curry powder, baking powder, coconut, and all but 2 teaspoons of the mustard–sesame seed mixture; stir into lentil mixture until well combined. Pour batter into a greased and floured 5- by 9-inch loaf pan and sprinkle remaining mustard–sesame seed mixture on top.

Bake in a 350° oven until loaf just begins to pull from sides of pan and top is tinged brown, about 1 hour. Cool 10 minutes and invert from pan. Serve warm, or cool and serve at room temperature. If made ahead, store airtight up to 1 week; freeze for longer storage. Cut into ½-inch slices. Makes 1 loaf, about 2 pounds.

PER SLICE (½" THICK): 166 calories, 5 g protein, 26 g carbohydrates, 5 g fat, 38 mg cholesterol, 155 mg sodium

LENTIL SALAD WITH GINGER VINAIGRETTE

- 2 **cups lentils, decorticated or with skins**
- 4 **cups regular-strength chicken broth**
- 1 **medium-size red or green bell pepper, stemmed, seeded, and thinly sliced**
- 1 **small red onion, chopped**
  Ginger vinaigrette (recipe follows)
  Salt (optional)

Sort lentils to remove any debris. Rinse and drain. In a 2- to 3-quart pan on high heat, bring broth to boiling. Add lentils, cover, and simmer until just tender to bite, about 8 minutes for decorticated, 30 minutes for lentils with skins. Drain, cool, cover, and chill until cold, about 2 hours, or up to overnight.

In a bowl, combine lentils, bell pepper, onion, and vinaigrette; mix well. Add salt to taste. Serves 6 or 7.

PER SERVING: 350 calories, 17 g protein, 34 g carbohydrates, 17 g fat, 0 mg cholesterol, 39 mg sodium

Ginger vinaigrette. Combine ½ cup **salad oil,** 3 tablespoons minced **fresh ginger,** ⅓ cup **lime juice,** and ½ teaspoon **pepper.**

BARLEY & LENTILS WITH MINT

- 1 **cup lentils, with skins or decorticated**
- 1 **cup pearl barley**
- 4 **cups regular-strength chicken broth**
- 1 **tablespoon butter or margarine**
- ¾ **cup whole blanched almonds**
- ¼ **cup raisins**
- ½ **cup minced fresh mint**
  Unflavored yogurt (optional)

Sort lentils to remove any debris. Rinse and drain lentils and barley. In a 2- to 3-quart pan, bring broth to boiling; add lentils (with skins) and barley, cover, and simmer until tender to bite, about 40 minutes; drain. (If using decorticated lentils, do not add until barley is almost tender, about 30 minutes. Then stir lentils into barley and cook just until tender to bite, about another 10 minutes.)

Meanwhile, in a 10- by 12-inch frying pan over medium-high heat, stir butter, almonds, and raisins often until almonds are golden and raisins are puffed, about 10 minutes; set aside. Stir minced mint into lentils and barley, then pour into a bowl and sprinkle with almonds and raisins. Offer yogurt to add to taste, if you like. Serves 6 to 7.

PER SERVING: 321 calories, 15 g protein, 44 g carbohydrates, 10 g fat, 4 mg cholesterol, 55 mg sodium

Cooking with Sorrel

IT LOOKS LIKE SPINACH, *but sorrel has a distinctive tang. In mild-climate gardens, this perennial grows year-round, providing kitchens with a steady supply. You can also find it in supermarkets that handle specialty produce.*

Use sorrel raw, like other leafy greens, in a salad. Or try it cooked, as we do here. Keep in mind that sorrel's bright green color fades almost instantly when heated.

Add the tart green shreds to eggs; their slightly acid flavor adds an interesting variation to a cheese omelet. Or steam salmon on a bed of the lively greens, then finish with a light mint-butter sauce. For a mild-hot contrast, stir-fry sorrel with chicken and chili. In soup, sorrel flavors ground turkey meatballs and delicately scents the light broth.

SORREL-CHEESE OMELET

  2 **large eggs**
  2 **tablespoons water**
  ¼ **cup lightly packed sorrel leaves, washed and stems removed; cut leaves into thin shreds**
     Salt and pepper
  1 **tablespoon butter or margarine**
  ¼ **cup lightly packed shredded Swiss cheese**
     Whole sorrel leaves (optional)

Shreds of sorrel lace this cheese omelet with color and tartness.

Lightly beat together eggs, water, sorrel, and salt and pepper to taste.

Add butter to a 6- to 7-inch frying pan over medium-high heat. When butter melts, add eggs. As eggs begin to set, lift edge up with a wide spatula, letting uncooked portion flow underneath. Continue cooking until eggs appear set but are still creamy on top. Sprinkle cheese over eggs. Fold about ⅓ of the omelet over center. Gently shake pan to slide unfolded edge of omelet just onto a warm plate. Flick pan downward so that the previously folded edge of omelet falls over omelet edge on plate. Garnish with whole sorrel leaves, if desired. Makes 1 serving.

PER SERVING: 368 calories, 20 g protein, 2 g carbohydrates, 30 g fat, 605 mg cholesterol, 329 mg sodium

SORREL-SCENTED BROTH WITH TURKEY

  ¾ **cup lightly packed sorrel leaves, washed and stems removed**
  2 **to 3 slices white bread**
  1 **pound ground turkey**
  1 **large egg**
  8 **cups regular-strength chicken broth**
  ⅛ **teaspoon ground white pepper**
     About ½ teaspoon salt, or to taste
  4 **strips pared lemon peel (yellow part only), each ½ by 4 inches**
  2 **medium-size carrots, peeled and cut into julienne strips**
  2 **to 3 tablespoons lemon juice**

Finely chop half the sorrel leaves. Cut remaining leaves into thin shreds.

Trim crusts off bread; discard crusts or save for another use. Tear bread into small pieces and whirl in a blender or food processor to make ¾ cup fine crumbs. Mix crumbs with turkey, egg, ¼ cup of the broth, chopped sorrel leaves, pepper, and salt to taste.

In a 5- to 6-quart pan, combine remaining broth and the lemon peel. Bring to boiling over high heat. Drop turkey mixture in tablespoon-size lumps into the boiling broth. Add carrots, then cover and simmer until meat is no longer pink in center (cut to test), about 5 minutes. Skim off and discard fat. Add lemon juice to taste. Ladle an equal portion of meatballs and soup into 6 wide soup bowls. Sprinkle an equal portion of sorrel shreds over each serving. Makes 9 cups, 6 servings.

PER SERVING: 220 calories, 19 g protein, 11 g carbohydrates, 12 g fat, 97 mg cholesterol, 394 mg sodium

STIR-FRIED CHICKEN WITH SORREL

  1 **pound boned and skinned chicken breasts**
  3 **tablespoons salad oil**
  3 **cloves garlic, pressed or minced**
  1 **small onion, chopped**
  ½ **teaspoon crushed dried hot red chilies**
  1 **can (3½ oz.) pitted ripe olives**
  5 **cups lightly packed sorrel leaves, washed and stems removed; cut leaves crosswise into 1-inch strips**
  ¼ **cup grated parmesan cheese**
     Salt

Cut chicken crosswise into ½-inch-wide strips. Place a wok or 10- to 12-inch frying pan over high heat. Add 2 tablespoons oil and chicken; stir-fry until lightly browned, 3 to 4 minutes. Lift out chicken and add to pan 1 more tablespoon oil, garlic, and onion; stir-fry until onion is lightly browned, 2 to 3 minutes. Add chilies, olives, and sorrel; stir-fry just until sorrel is wilted. Stir in chicken and 2 tablespoons cheese. Add salt to taste. Spoon onto plates. Sprinkle with remaining cheese. Makes 2 or 3 servings.

PER SERVING: 399 calories, 39 g protein, 6 g carbohydrates, 24 g fat, 93 mg cholesterol, 473 mg sodium

STEAMED SALMON WITH SORREL

  3 **cups lightly packed sorrel leaves, washed and stems removed**
  2 **salmon fillets (6 to 8 oz. each), ¾ to 1 inch thick, skinned**
     About ¼ cup regular-strength chicken broth
  2 **tablespoons butter or margarine**
  1 **tablespoon chopped fresh mint leaves or sorrel leaves**

Place whole sorrel leaves in an even layer in an 8- to 9-inch-diameter plate. Set fish on top; drape with foil. Set pan in a steaming basket or on a rack set in a wok or 12- to 14-inch frying pan above ½ to 1 inch of boiling water. Cover and cook over high heat until fish is opaque in center (cut to test), 10 to 15 minutes.

Hold fish on plate with a wide spatula; carefully pour juices into a measuring cup; keep fish warm. Add broth to juices to make ½ cup. Pour into a 6- to 8-inch frying pan. Boil, uncovered, over high heat, until reduced to ¼ cup. Turn heat to medium, add butter and mint. Stir until butter is melted and incorporated. Pour over fish. Makes 2 servings.

PER SERVING: 450 calories, 43 g protein, 2 g carbohydrates, 29 g fat, 154 mg cholesterol, 219 mg sodium

Salute to Umatilla County, Oregon

To **CELEBRATE** *their region's abundance*, members of a cooking club in Hermiston in northeastern Oregon put together this homespun meal featuring local foods.

Lamb, beef, barley, green beans, and peas—all grown in Hermiston's Umatilla County—go into the hearty stew. Yeast rolls made with bulgur play up the importance of the local wheat crop. The county also produces asparagus and strawberries.

SALUTE TO UMATILLA COUNTY

Umatilla Stew with Spring Vegetables
Asparagus with Tarragon Vinaigrette
Bulgur Wheat Rolls   **Strawberry Jam**
Pinot Noir or Merlot

You can prepare all the elements for this meal a day ahead.

Meat-and-vegetable stew goes well with bulgur-flecked rolls and cold asparagus salad.

UMATILLA STEW WITH SPRING VEGETABLES

- 1 **pound boned lamb shoulder**
- 1 **pound boned beef chuck**
- 2 **tablespoons salad oil**
- 3 **medium-size carrots, sliced**
- 1 **large onion, chopped**
- 1 **medium-size turnip, peeled and chopped**
- ½ **cup pearl barley, rinsed and drained**
- 5 **cups regular-strength beef broth**
- 2 **cups water**
- ½ **teaspoon pepper**
- ½ **pound green beans (ends trimmed), cut into 1-inch pieces**
- 1 **pound fresh peas, shelled, or 1½ cups frozen petite peas**
  Salt

Trim and discard fat from lamb and beef; cut meat into 1-inch pieces. In a 5- to 6-quart pan over high heat, brown meat in oil; lift out. Reduce heat to medium-high, add carrots, onion, and turnip; stir often until onion is limp, about 10 minutes.

Return meat to pan with barley, broth, water, and pepper. Bring to a boil over high heat, then cover and simmer until meat is very tender when pierced, about 1½ hours. (If made ahead, let cool, cover, and chill up to 2 days; lift fat off and dis-card. Reheat to simmering.) Skim and discard fat. Stir in beans and peas; cover and simmer until beans are tender to bite, 8 to 10 minutes. Salt to taste. Serves 6.—*Kathi Hendrix, Hermiston, Ore.*

PER SERVING: 354 calories, 29 g protein, 30 g carbohydrates, 13 g fat, 74 mg cholesterol, 111 mg sodium

BULGUR WHEAT ROLLS

- ½ **cup bulgur**
- ½ **cup water**
- 1 **package active dry yeast**
- 1 **cup warm milk (110°)**
- ¼ **cup sugar**
- ½ **teaspoon salt**
- 2 **tablespoons butter or margarine**
- 1 **large egg**
  About 3¾ cups all-purpose flour

Place bulgur and water in a small bowl. Let stand until water is absorbed, about 45 minutes. In a large bowl, soften yeast in milk. Add sugar, salt, butter, egg, and bulgur mixture. Stir in enough flour (about 3½ cups) to make a stiff dough.

Knead dough on a lightly floured board until smooth and elastic, 10 to 15 minutes; add flour as required to prevent sticking. Turn dough over in a greased bowl; cover with plastic wrap and let rise in a warm place until double, about 50 minutes.

Punch dough down and cut into 12 pieces. Shape each into a round and space evenly in a well-greased 9- by 13-inch pan. Drape with plastic wrap and let rise in a warm place until puffy, about 40 minutes. Bake in a 400° oven until well browned, 20 to 25 minutes. Remove from pan to a rack. Serve warm or cool. Makes 12.

PER ROLL: 222 calories, 6 g protein, 41 g carbohydrates, 4 g fat, 31 mg cholesterol, 128 mg sodium

ASPARAGUS WITH TARRAGON VINAIGRETTE

- 1½ **pounds asparagus, tough ends removed**
- ¼ **cup *each* white wine vinegar and olive oil or salad oil**
- 1 **tablespoon fresh or 1 teaspoon dry tarragon**
  Salt

In a 10- to 12-inch frying pan over medium-high heat, cook asparagus, uncovered, in ½-inch boiling water until tender-crisp to bite, about 7 minutes. Drain; plunge into ice water. When cool, drain. If made ahead, cover and chill up to 1 day. Place asparagus in a dish. Add vinegar, oil, tarragon, and salt to taste; turn to coat evenly. Serves 6.

PER SERVING: 97 calories, 2 g protein, 3 g carbohydrates, 9 g fat, 0 mg cholesterol, 2 mg sodium

An Easier Way with Coconut

THEY'RE TOUGH TO CRACK, *but if you know a few secrets, it's easy to penetrate the hard brown shell of a coconut and remove the crisp and mildly sweet white meat.*

One simple method is to bake the whole fruit first—the heat forces the coconut to expand, often cracking the shell. As it cools, the meat contracts from the shell, making it easier to pry free.

You can eat the fresh coconut plain, or try it in these three recipes—as an appetizer with orange-mint dip, a flavoring for flan, or a crust for chicken.

Fresh coconuts are generally available all year. When choosing one, shake it; you should hear lots of liquid sloshing around (the liquid is mildly sweet, and you can drink it if you like). The eyes of the coconut should show no sign of mold.

How to remove coconut meat from shell. With an ice pick or nail, pierce 2 or 3 of the coconut's eyes. Pour out liquid; reserve if desired. Place drained coconut on a 9-inch cake pan.

Bake in a 350° oven 25 to 30 minutes; shell may begin to crack. Let cool briefly, then place on a sturdy surface. To break into pieces, hit hard along cracks with a hammer. Pry white meat from shell with a sturdy, blunt-ended knife or screwdriver. Rinse and drain meat (a thin, brown skin will be left on the outside).

If shelled ahead, cool, cover, and chill as long as overnight.

COCONUT WITH ORANGE-MINT DIP

- 3 **large oranges**
- 1½ **teaspoons cornstarch**
- ¼ **to ½ teaspoon crushed dried hot red chilies**
- 3 **tablespoons chopped fresh mint**
- 2 **tablespoons white wine vinegar**
  Salt
  Coconut meat from 1 small coconut (about 1½ lb. in the shell); directions precede

Grate enough peel from 1 orange to make 1 teaspoon. Ream oranges to make 1 cup juice. In a 1- to 2-quart pan, mix orange juice, peel, cornstarch, and chilies. Stir over medium heat until sauce boils; let cool. Stir in mint, vinegar, and salt to taste; pour into a small bowl.

With a knife, cut coconut meat into ¼-inch-thick slices, 2 to 3 inches long. Mound coconut slices on a tray with cool

Dip slices of fresh coconut into cool orange-mint sauce for light appetizer.

sauce alongside; dip coconut into sauce to eat. Makes 12 to 14 appetizer servings.

PER SERVING: 99 calories, .90 g protein, 6 g carbohydrates, 9 g fat, 0 mg cholesterol, 5 mg sodium

COCONUT FLAN

- **Coconut meat from 1 small coconut (about 1½ lb. in the shell); directions precede**
- ⅔ **cup sugar**
- 2 **cups milk**
- 6 **large eggs**
- 1 **teaspoon coconut extract**
  Water

Coarsely shred enough of the coconut meat to make ¾ cup; set aside.

Pour ⅓ cup of the sugar in an 8- to 10-inch frying pan. Shake and tilt pan over low heat until sugar melts and turns an amber color; at once, pour into a 9-inch-diameter cake pan. Tilt pan quickly to let syrup flow over bottom (syrup does not have to cover pan completely); set aside.

Melt remaining ⅓ cup sugar in same frying pan, shaking pan over medium heat. When sugar turns amber color, add milk; stir over low heat until sugar melts and blends with milk (do not boil).

Meanwhile, cut remaining coconut into small chunks. In a blender or food processor, combine milk mixture and coconut; whirl until a thick pulpy mass. Let stand until cool enough to touch, about 15 minutes. Line a fine strainer with moistened cheesecloth; set in a

bowl. Pour mixture through cloth. Let drain, then squeeze cloth to remove all liquid; discard coconut. Whisk together eggs and coconut extract; stir into milk. Pour through fine strainer into sugar-coated cake pan.

Place cake pan in a larger pan and pour boiling water into larger pan so it comes about halfway up custard-filled pan. Bake in a 350° oven until center of custard jiggles only slightly when gently shaken, 20 to 25 minutes. Remove custard pan from hot water; let cool. Cover and chill at least 3 hours or as long as overnight.

Cut around pan sides with a knife, then cover flan with a rimmed serving plate. Holding plate in place, quickly invert. Leave pan in place a few minutes to allow flan to slip free and caramelized sugar to flow out. Sprinkle reserved coconut over top. Cut into wedges; serves 6 to 8.

PER SERVING: 318 calories, 8 g protein, 27 g carbohydrates, 21 g fat, 214 mg cholesterol, 91 mg sodium

COCONUT-CRUSTED CHICKEN

- 2 **large eggs**
- 1 **tablespoon cornstarch**
- 1 **teaspoon coconut extract**
  Coconut meat from 1 small coconut (about 1½ lb. in the shell); directions precede
- 2 **teaspoons curry powder**
- 2 **teaspoons sugar**
- ¼ **cup melted butter or margarine**
- 1 **cup salted roasted peanuts, finely chopped**
- 3½ **pounds chicken thighs, skin removed**

In a shallow pan, beat eggs, cornstarch, and coconut extract. Cut coconut meat into small chunks and chop finely in a food processor or with a knife. In another shallow pan, mix coconut, curry powder, sugar, butter, and peanuts.

Dip chicken in egg mixture to coat, then roll in coconut mixture to coat lightly, pressing coconut into chicken. Place chicken, slightly apart and meaty side up, in 2 greased 10- by 15-inch baking pans. Press remaining coconut mixture on top of chicken pieces to form an even layer.

Bake in a 375° oven until chicken is well browned and no longer pink at bone (cut to test), about 45 minutes. Serves 4.

PER SERVING: 477 calories, 30 g protein, 13 g carbohydrates, 35 g fat, 178 mg cholesterol, 260 mg sodium

A Spectacular Spring Cake

Tart-sweet berries, lemon, and pistachios combine to spectacular effect in this special spring cake. If you like, you can prepare the cake's components a day ahead. Assemble just before serving.

STRAWBERRY LEMON CRUNCH CAKE

Lemon-pistachio sponge cake (recipe follows)
Lemon cream (recipe follows)
Lemon crunch (recipe follows)
4 cups strawberries, rinsed, hulled, patted dry, halved lengthwise
Pistachios reserved from cake
Mint (optional)

Place cake on a platter and slip pieces of waxed paper under it to cover plate rim. Swirl all but 1 cup of the lemon cream on top and side of cake. Pat lemon crunch all over cake side and just over top edge; reserve any extra candy for other uses.

Arrange strawberries, either cut side down or up, on top of cake. If made ahead, loosely cover cake and remaining lemon cream; chill up to 2 hours. Offer pistachios and lemon cream to spoon over wedges of cake. Garnish with mint, if desired. Makes 8 to 10 servings.

PER SERVING: 463 calories, 9 g protein, 59 g carbohydrates, 23 g fat, 205 mg cholesterol, 174 mg sodium

Lemon-pistachio sponge cake. Place 1½ cups **shelled roasted pistachios** in an 8- or 9-inch-wide pan and bake in a 350° oven until deep golden in color, 10 to 12 minutes; cool completely. Reserve 1 cup. Finely chop remaining pistachios.

In large bowl of an electric mixer, beat 4 **large egg whites** at high speed until foamy. Beating, gradually add ¼ cup **sugar;** continue to beat until whites hold stiff, moist peaks. Set aside.

In another large bowl, beat at high speed 4 **large egg yolks** with ½ cup **sugar** and 1 teaspoon grated **lemon peel** until very thick. Add ¾ cup **all-purpose flour,** 3 tablespoons **water,** and chopped nuts; mix on low speed.

Stir a little egg white mixture into yolk mixture, then gently fold in remaining whites. Spread batter evenly in an ungreased 9- or 10-inch-diameter cheesecake pan with removable bottom.

Bake in a 325° oven until cake is golden and springs back when lightly touched in center, about 40 minutes. Let cake cool completely in pan on a rack. Run a spatula between cake and pan side, then remove side. Slide a spatula between

Strawberry sunburst crowns lemon-pistachio cake frosted with soft lemon cream and lemon crunch candy. Embellish servings with more lemon cream and whole pistachios.

cake and pan bottom and remove pan bottom. If made ahead, store cake airtight up to 1 day.

Lemon cream. In a 2- to 3-quart pan, mix 4 **large egg yolks,** ¾ cup **sugar,** ¼ cup **lemon juice,** 1 teaspoon **grated lemon peel,** and ½ cup (¼ lb.) **butter** or margarine, cut into pieces. Stir over medium-low heat until mixture thickens and heavily coats a metal spoon, 8 to 12 minutes. Cool, then cover and chill until cold, at least 1½ hours. Beat 1 cup **whipping cream** until stiff; fold into lemon mixture. If made ahead, cover and chill up to 1 day.

PER TABLESPOON: 59 calories, .41 g protein, 4 g carbohydrates, 5 g fat, 40 mg cholesterol, 27 mg sodium

Lemon crunch. Butter a 12-inch square of foil; set aside. In a 1- to 1½-quart pan, mix ¾ cup **sugar,** 3 tablespoons **water,** and 2 tablespoons **light corn syrup.** Boil over medium-high heat until syrup is 300° on a candy thermometer, 8 to 10 minutes; to check temperature, tilt pan to cover thermometer bulb.

Remove from heat; immediately stir in 1 teaspoon *each* **baking soda** and grated **lemon peel.** Pour foaming candy onto foil. Let cool. Enclose in a plastic bag; coarsely crush with a mallet. If made ahead, store airtight up to 1 week.

Turkey Breast on the Barbecue

TURKEY BREAST *is no longer simply the choice segment of a winter holiday bird. It's available year-round, and in forms that are suited to a great variety of treatments—including several that work well on the barbecue.*

Lean and light, turkey breasts are marketed whole, halved, or in chunks, with or without bone; as thin cross-grain pieces called cutlets or slices; and as fillets or tenderloins—the piece of the breast that lies alongside the breastbone. Usually reasonably priced, this meat is a good-value alternative to veal.

The secret for keeping turkey breast moist and juicy is to cook it quickly, just until it loses its pale pink color throughout; cooked more, it becomes firm and unpleasantly dry. Barbecuing is a good way to cook it quickly.

The barbecue is also a no-fat way to deal with two variations on classical sautéed veal dishes, piccata and saltimbocca, here made with sliced turkey breast. In a third dish, indirect heat evenly cooks a half-breast that goes with peaches and chutney. In a fourth, a sweet-sharp raspberry glaze gives color and flavor.

GRILLED TURKEY CUTLETS PICCATA

- 1½ tablespoons capers with liquid
- ¼ cup lemon juice
- 1 tablespoon olive oil
- ⅛ teaspoon pepper
- 1 pound boned, skinned turkey breast (cutlets or slices), cut cross-grain ¼ inch thick, rinsed and patted dry
  Lemon wedges
  Salt

Drain caper liquid into a shallow 8- or 9-inch-wide pan. Stir in lemon juice, oil, and pepper. Turn turkey in liquid to coat; cover and chill at least 30 minutes or up to 2 hours. Turn slices over once.

Place slices on a grill 4 to 6 inches above a solid bed of hot coals (you should be able to hold your hand at grill level for only 2 to 3 seconds). Cook, turning once, until meat turns white in center (cut to test), about 45 seconds per side; brush often with marinade. Transfer meat to a platter and sprinkle with capers; garnish with lemon wedges. Add salt to taste. Makes 2 or 3 servings.

PER SERVING: 217 calories, 35 g protein, 1 g carbohydrates, 7 g fat, 94 mg cholesterol, 216 mg sodium

BARBECUED TURKEY SALTIMBOCCA

- 1 turkey breast half (about 3 lb.), boned and skinned, rinsed, and patted dry (or 1¾ lb. boned, skinned turkey breast tenderloins)
- 1 large clove garlic, cut in half
- 2 teaspoons olive oil
- 16 to 20 large fresh sage leaves
- ¼ pound thinly sliced prosciutto
- 4 or 5 slices (about 1 oz. each) Swiss cheese

Cut meat diagonally across the grain into ½-inch-thick slices. Rub slices all over with cut garlic, then rub meat with olive oil. Press half the sage leaves equally onto 1 side of each piece of turkey. Cut prosciutto and cheese into same-size pieces to equal the number of turkey slices.

Place turkey, sage side up, on a grill 4 to 6 inches above a solid bed of hot coals (you should be able to hold your hand at grill level only 2 to 3 seconds). Cook 3 minutes, then turn slices over. Quickly top each piece with a slice of prosciutto, a slice of cheese, and remaining sage. Place lid on barbecue and open dampers; or tent a large sheet of foil over meat. Cook until meat is white in center (cut to test), about 3 minutes longer. Using a wide spatula, transfer pieces to a platter or plates. Makes 4 or 5 servings.

PER SERVING: 375 calories, 57 g protein, 2 g carbohydrates, 14 g fat, 156 mg cholesterol, 495 mg sodium

BARBECUED TURKEY BREAST WITH PEACHES & CHUTNEY

- ⅔ cup peach or Major Grey chutney
- 1 teaspoon minced fresh ginger
- 1 turkey breast half (about 3 lb.), boned and skinned, rinsed and patted dry
- 3 firm-ripe peaches, each about 2½ inches in diameter, or 6 canned peach halves
  Water
- 2 tablespoons lemon juice
- 6 to 8 green onions, ends trimmed
  Salt

In a barbecue with lid (uncovered), ignite 50 charcoal briquets on firegrate. When briquets are lightly covered with gray ash, about 30 minutes, push half the coals to each side of the grate. Position grill 4 to 6 inches above the coals.

In a blender, whirl ⅓ cup of the chutney with ginger until smoothly puréed. Coarsely chop remaining chutney and

set aside. Brush breast all over with some of the puréed chutney. Set breast on grill between (not over) coals. Cover barbecue and open dampers. Roast turkey until meat thermometer inserted in center registers 155°, 50 to 55 minutes. Brush meat occasionally with puréed chutney, quickly replacing lid.

Immerse fresh peaches in boiling water for about 30 seconds; lift from water and let cool for 1 minute. Pull off peel, cut fruit in half, pit, and coat flesh with lemon juice to prevent darkening. About 10 minutes before breast is done, lay fruit (fresh or canned, pit side down) and green onions on grill over coals. Cook, turning once, until peaches are hot and onion tops are wilted, about 10 minutes; brush several times with puréed chutney.

Arrange turkey on a platter and surround with peaches and onions. Slice meat across the grain, and serve with reserved chopped chutney. Add salt to taste. Makes 4 to 6 servings.

PER SERVING: 291 calories, 39 g protein, 27 g carbohydrates, 3 g fat, 100 mg cholesterol, 171 mg sodium

RASPBERRY-GLAZED TURKEY TENDERLOINS

- ½ cup seedless raspberry jam
- 6 tablespoons raspberry vinegar
- ¼ cup Dijon mustard
- 1 teaspoon grated orange peel
- ½ teaspoon dry or fresh thyme leaves
- 4 turkey breast tenderloins (about 1½ lb. total), rinsed and patted dry
  Salt

In a 1- to 1½-quart pan, whisk together jam, vinegar, mustard, orange peel, and thyme. Bring to a boil on high heat, stirring, until reduced by about a fourth and slightly thickened, 2 to 3 minutes. Reserve about ½ cup glaze to serve with the grilled meat.

Coat each turkey piece with some of the remaining raspberry glaze, then lay on a grill 4 to 6 inches above a solid bed of medium-hot coals (you should be able to hold your hand at grill level only 4 to 5 seconds).

Cook, turning for even browning and to avoid flares, until meat is white in center of thickest part (cut to test), 8 to 10 minutes; baste frequently with the glaze. Add salt to taste. Offer reserved glaze to spoon onto meat. Serves 4.

PER SERVING: 325 calories, 40 g protein, 32 g carbohydrates, 4 g fat, 106 mg cholesterol, 564 mg sodium

More April Recipes

OTHER APRIL ARTICLES *feature these entrées to brighten springtime meals: baked chicken breasts with a crunchy crumb coating and mustard sauce, tangy braised pork spareribs, and hot pasta with Swiss chard.*

DIJON CHICKEN WITH PANKO CRUST

Coarse, dried bread crumbs, known to the Japanese as panko, *give these baked chicken breasts an especially crunchy coating. You can make the crumbs yourself or buy them in Japanese markets.*

The flavors are Western; the lean, boned and skinned chicken breasts, oven-fried with a panko coating, go with a Dijon mustard sauce. However, the overall impression of this dish is not unlike that of a Japanese favorite, tonkatsu, *which is panko-coated pan-fried pork and a special sauce, also called tonkatsu.*

- ¼ cup (⅛ lb.) melted butter or margarine
- ¼ cup Dijon mustard
- 2 cloves garlic, minced or pressed
- ½ cup panko (Japanese-style bread crumbs), purchased or homemade (recipe follows)
- 2 tablespoons grated parmesan cheese
- 1½ tablespoons minced parsley
- 8 boned chicken breast halves (6 to 7 oz. *each*), skinned
  Dijon sauce (recipe follows)

In a large bowl, whisk together butter, mustard, and garlic. In another bowl, mix panko, parmesan, and parsley.

Turn chicken breast halves in butter mixture to coat completely. Lift out and dip rounded side of each breast into panko mixture. Place breasts, crumb side up, in a single layer in a 10- by 15-inch rimmed baking pan.

Bake in a 500° oven until crumbs are golden and chicken breasts are white in center of thickest part (cut to test), about 15 minutes. Place 1 or 2 breast halves on each dinner plate. Serve whole, or cut crosswise into thick slices. Accompany breasts with Dijon sauce. Makes 4 to 8 servings. —*Christie Williams Katona, Renton, Wash.*

PER SERVING: 276 calories, 40 g protein, 6 g carbohydrates, 9 g fat, 114 mg cholesterol, 460 mg sodium

Panko. Trim crusts from 2 slices of **firm-textured white bread.** Cut bread into cubes; whirl in a food processor or blender just until even, coarse crumbs form. Spread crumbs in a 9- to 10-inch pie pan. Bake in a 325° oven, stirring often, until the crumbs feel dry and crisp but are not brown, 8 to 10 minutes.

Dijon sauce. In a bowl, mix ½ cup **mayonnaise** with ¼ cup **Dijon mustard.**

PER TABLESPOON: 72 calories, .10 g protein, 1 g carbohydrates, 8 g fat, 5 mg cholesterol, 200 mg sodium

BRAISED PORK WITH VINEGAR

A generous dose of vinegar cuts the richness of pork in this simple braised meat and vegetable entrée. Garlic and ginger season the tart cooking liquid. Chunks of carrots and jicama add natural sweetness to the broth.

To complete the meal, serve hot cooked rice and stir-fried kale or spinach. If you like, add marinated cucumbers or radishes for a cool salad.

- 3 pounds country-style pork spareribs
- 2 tablespoons salad oil
- 6 to 8 cloves garlic
- 4 slices fresh ginger (each the size of a quarter)
- 1⅓ cups rice vinegar (or distilled white vinegar and 2 tablespoons sugar)
- 1⅓ cups water
- 2 tablespoons soy sauce
- 8 small carrots (about 1 lb. total), peeled
- 1 pound jicama, peeled and cut into ½-inch-thick wedges
  Parsley sprigs

Trim and discard surface fat from ribs.

Pour oil into a 5- to 6-quart pan; place over high heat. Add pork and cook, turning to brown all sides well; if pan is too crowded, cook a portion at a time.

Add garlic, ginger, vinegar, water, and soy sauce. Cover and simmer, turning meat occasionally to cook evenly, until meat is almost tender when pierced, 1¼ to 1½ hours.

With tongs, lift out meat and add carrots and jicama to broth. Set meat on vegetables; cover and simmer until carrots and meat are tender when pierced (jicama stays slightly crisp), 30 to 45 minutes longer.

Lift out meat and vegetables; set on a warm serving platter. Skim off fat from broth and discard. Pour broth into a small bowl; spoon over portions. Garnish with parsley. Makes 4 servings.

PER SERVING: 507 calories, 28 g protein, 25 g carbohydrates, 33 g fat, 102 mg cholesterol, 636 mg sodium

PASTA WITH SWISS CHARD

Popular with Italians, Swiss chard makes a light addition to this hot pasta entrée. Cook firm chard stems before the leaves.

- 1 pound Swiss chard or kale
- 1 cup pecan halves
- ¾ cup firmly packed chopped bacon
- 2½ cups dry short tube-shaped pasta
- 3 cloves garlic, pressed or minced
- ¼ to ½ teaspoon crushed dried hot red chilies
- 2 teaspoons Dijon mustard
- 2 tablespoons white wine vinegar
- 1½ cups (7 to 8 oz.) grated parmesan or romano cheese

Wash greens well and drain. Trim off tips of chard stems and discard; cut off stems flush with leaves. Finely slice stems and leaves, keeping separate. (Discard kale stems; chop greens.) Set greens aside.

In a 10- to 12-inch frying pan over medium heat, stir pecans frequently until they are a slightly darker brown, about 10 minutes. Pour out and set aside.

Add bacon to pan; stir often until brown and crisp, about 10 minutes. Lift from pan and drain on paper towels.

Meanwhile, bring water to boiling in a 5- to 6-quart pan. Add pasta; cook, uncovered, until tender to bite, about 15 minutes; drain. As pasta cooks, discard all but 3 tablespoons fat from frying pan. Add chard stems, garlic, and chilies (to taste) to pan; stir often until stems are limp, about 10 minutes. Add leaves and stir until tender to bite, about 5 minutes.

In a large bowl, mix pasta, mustard, and vinegar. Mix in cheese, then greens and bacon. Sprinkle with nuts. Serves 4 to 6.

PER SERVING: 569 calories, 26 g protein, 46 g carbohydrates, 32 g fat, 38 mg cholesterol, 997 mg sodium

Eggs make the golden sauce that holds this pasta and chicken dish together.

CHICKEN CARBONARA

- **4 slices bacon, chopped**
- **½ cup pine nuts or sunflower seed**
- **8 ounces dry linguine**
- **4 large eggs**
- **½ cup grated parmesan cheese**
- **⅓ cup whipping cream**
- **¼ cup chopped parsley**
- **¼ cup chopped fresh basil leaves or 2 tablespoons dry basil leaves**
- **3 cloves garlic, minced or pressed**
- **1½ cups diced cooked chicken**
- **1 to 2 tablespoons butter or margarine**

In a 10- to 12-inch frying pan, cook bacon and pine nuts over medium heat until golden (bacon takes about 7 minutes, pine nuts 5, sunflower seed 3).

In a 4- to 6-quart pan, cook linguine in 3 quarts boiling water, uncovered, until tender to bite, about 8 minutes. Drain. Meanwhile, with a slotted spoon, put bacon and nuts in a bowl. Add eggs, cheese, cream, parsley, basil, garlic, and chicken; beat until well mixed. Add enough butter to drippings to make ¼ cup; heat to melt.

Add hot linguine to frying pan, then add the egg mixture. Stir over medium heat just until eggs begin to set. Serves 4.—*Mrs. Barbara Keenan, Fort Morgan, Colo.*

PER SERVING: 669 calories, 40 g protein, 49 g carbohydrates, 36 g fat, 367 mg cholesterol, 457 mg sodium

PARMESAN ZUCCHINI STICKS

Easy, oven-fried zucchini sticks make a crisp snack; they're good for dinner, too.

- **⅔ cup grated parmesan cheese**
- **½ cup fine, dry, seasoned bread crumbs**
- **1 teaspoon *each* dry ground sage and dry rosemary leaves**
- **2 large eggs**
- **5 medium-size zucchini (about 1¾ lb. total), ends trimmed**
- **1 tablespoon olive or salad oil**
  Salt
  Parsley sprigs (optional)

In a bowl, mix cheese, bread crumbs, sage, and rosemary; set aside. In another bowl, beat eggs to blend.

Cut each zucchini in half cross-wise, then lengthwise into quarters. Add zucchini sticks to egg and mix gently. Lift out 1 stick, drain briefly, then roll stick in parmesan mixture to coat evenly. Repeat until all zucchini sticks are coated.

Lay sticks slightly apart in an oiled 10- by 15-inch baking pan. Drizzle olive oil over zucchini. Bake, uncovered, in a 450° oven until coating is well browned and crusty, about 25 minutes. Sprinkle zucchini sticks with salt to taste. Serve hot, garnished with parsley. Makes 6 servings as an appetizer or vegetable dish.—*B.L. Gonsalves, Sacramento.*

PER SERVING: 139 calories, 8 g protein, 11 g carbohydrates, 7 g fat, 99 mg cholesterol, 255 mg sodium

GAME HEN DINNER FOR TWO

One game hen, split for two, simmers with carrots, onions, spinach, and sauce.

- **1 Cornish game hen (about 1½ lb.), rinsed and patted dry**
- **6 small onions (1 to 1½ in. wide), peeled**
- **2 tablespoons butter or margarine**
- **1 cup regular-strength beef broth**
- **½ cup dry red wine**
- **1 tablespoon Dijon mustard**
- **½ teaspoon dry basil leaves**
- **3 slender carrots, peeled and cut in half crosswise**
- **½ pound spinach (stems and yellow leaves discarded), washed well and drained**

Cut game hen in half through back and breast. In a 12- to 14-inch frying pan on medium heat, brown game hen and onions well in butter, uncovered, about 15 minutes. Lift out bird and onions and set aside.

Stir broth into pan and boil on high heat until reduced to ⅓ cup. Blend in wine, mustard, and basil.

Return hen and onions to pan; add carrots. Simmer, covered, until thigh is no longer pink at bone (cut to test), about 15 minutes. Mound ingredients to 1 side of pan. Push spinach into broth and stir until wilted. Serve hen and vegetables with broth. Serves 2.—*Mary Lange, Fresno, Calif.*

PER SERVING: 701 calories, 47 g protein, 20 g carbohydrates, 48 g fat, 205 mg cholesterol, 612 mg sodium

Italian Pork Stew

2 pounds boneless pork shoulder or butt, cut into 1½-inch chunks
¾ pound mushrooms, halved
1 large onion, chopped
2 cloves garlic, minced or pressed
1 can (28 oz.) pear-shaped tomatoes
1 cup dry red wine
1 can (2 oz.) anchovy fillets, drained and minced
½ pound cooked ham, chopped
½ teaspoon *each* dry marjoram leaves, dry oregano leaves, dry rosemary leaves, and dry thyme leaves

In a 5- to 6-quart pan, cover pork and cook on medium-high heat to draw out juices, about 10 minutes. Uncover and boil on high heat until juices almost evaporate, then stir often until drippings are dark brown, about 8 minutes. Add mushrooms, onion, and garlic to pan; stir often on medium-high heat until onion is limp, about 5 minutes.

Add tomatoes and liquid, wine, anchovies, ham, marjoram, oregano, rosemary, and thyme; stir to break up tomatoes and free browned bits. Cover and simmer until pork is tender when pierced, about 1½ hours. Serves 6.— *Mrs. Scott Kemper, Sacramento.*

PER SERVING: 561 calories, 38 g protein, 11 g carbohydrates, 40 g fat, 137 mg cholesterol, 1,153 mg sodium

Ladle aromatic pork stew alongside polenta; a green salad completes meal.

Artichoke & Potato Salad

½ pound small artichokes (about 1½ in. wide)
6 medium-size (about 2 lb. total) thin-skinned potatoes, peeled
1 can (2¼ oz.) sliced ripe olives or ⅓ cup calamata olives
⅔ cup diced red bell pepper
Dressing (recipe follows)
Salt
2 tablespoons chopped fresh chives

Break off tough outer leaves from artichokes down to pale green edible leaves; cut off thorny tips. Trim stem ends.

In a 5- to 6-quart pan, bring about 1½ inches water to boiling on high heat. Add artichokes and potatoes. Cover and simmer until vegetables are tender when pierced, about 20 minutes for artichokes, 25 minutes for potatoes; lift out when cooked and set aside until just cool enough to touch. Quarter artichokes. Slice potatoes crosswise.

In a bowl, mix artichokes, potatoes, olives, bell pepper, dressing, and salt to taste. Serve warm or cool, topped with chives. Serves 4.— *Deborah Woodard Healy, Northridge, Calif.*

PER SERVING: 542 calories, 5 g protein, 43 g carbohydrates, 40 g fat, 0 mg cholesterol, 488 mg sodium

Dressing. Combine 3 tablespoons *each* **red wine vinegar** and **Dijon mustard,** and ⅔ cup **olive oil** or salad oil.

Tiny artichokes and potatoes cook together to make a warm vegetable salad.

Danielle's Chocolate Scrunch-ups

¾ cup (6-oz. package) semisweet chocolate baking chips
2 large egg whites
⅛ teaspoon cream of tartar
¼ cup granulated sugar
⅓ cup *each* chopped dates and chopped pecans
1 tablespoon powdered sugar
½ teaspoon unsweetened cocoa

Heat ½ cup of the chocolate chips in a bowl over hot water just until soft; stir until smooth, then set aside.

In a large bowl, beat whites and cream of tartar on high speed until frothy. Gradually beat in granulated sugar. Continue beating until whites hold stiff peaks. Fold in melted chocolate, remaining chips, dates, and pecans.

Drop batter in 2-teaspoon-size mounds 1 inch apart on ungreased 12- by 15-inch baking sheets. Bake in a 275° oven until mounds are dry to touch, about 15 minutes. Let stand 10 minutes, then loosen with metal spatula; leave on pan. With fingers, pinch top of each cooky to form a peak; cool.

Rub powdered sugar and cocoa through a fine strainer onto cookies. Makes about 2½ dozen.— *Danielle Lavery, Honolulu.*

PER COOKY: 43 calories, .51 g protein, 6 g carbohydrates, 2 g fat, 0 mg cholesterol, 3 mg sodium

Chocolate macaroons, with nuts and dates, have a powdered sugar–cocoa coat.

WHEN OVERCOOKED, *beef liver becomes beef leather; the trick is to keep it pink on the inside. Liver lovers usually take their favorite food with onions, but there are other ways to glorify it, as Langdon Sully shows in the following recipe.*

Mr. Sully's added ingredients are celery, bell pepper, tomato, and hot pepper seasoning. The result is a liver-and-onion dish as a Creole cook might do it.

BEEF LIVER, NEW ORLEANS-STYLE

1	pound thinly sliced beef liver
4	tablespoons all-purpose flour
2	tablespoons water
2	tablespoons salad oil
1	large onion, thinly sliced
½	cup diced celery
1	medium-size green or red bell pepper, stemmed, seeded, and cut into strips
1	can (about 15 oz.) tomatoes
	Salt
	Liquid hot pepper seasoning
	Hot cooked brown rice (optional)

Peel or trim membrane and tubes from liver and discard. Rinse liver and pat dry, then cut each slice into ½-inch-wide strips. Dust strips with 3 tablespoons of the flour; shake off excess. Smoothly blend remaining 1 tablespoon flour with water and set aside.

Add oil to a 10- to 12-inch frying pan over high heat; when oil is hot, add liver and cook quickly until browned but still pink in the center (cut to test). Lift from pan and set aside.

Add onion, celery, and bell pepper to pan and cook, stirring, for 2 minutes. Stir in tomatoes (break up with a spoon) and their liquid and boil rapidly 3 to 4 minutes to reduce slightly. Season to taste with salt and hot pepper seasoning. Stir flour-water mixture into pan and continue to stir until boiling vigorously.

Return liver to pan just until heated through, about 1 minute. Serve with rice. Makes 4 servings.

PER SERVING: 293 calories, 25 g protein, 22 g carbohydrates, 12 g fat, 402 mg cholesterol, 271 mg sodium

Langdon Sully

Vista, Calif.

THOUGH DANNY GRIFFITH'S *Potato Omelet is Spartan in the simplicity of its ingredients, there is something quite comforting about the dish—no doubt because of its very lack of complexity. The flavors of egg and potato are allowed to come through in straightforward fashion, with only the tiniest touch of green onion for enhancement.*

This omelet is a simplified version of the German bauernfrühstuck, *or farmer's breakfast—a scramble of eggs, potatoes, bacon, and onions designed to sustain anyone pitching hay from dawn to noon.*

NO-NONSENSE POTATO OMELET

1	large (about ½ lb.) russet potato
2	tablespoons butter or margarine
3	green onions, ends trimmed, thinly sliced
4	large eggs
2	tablespoons milk
	Salt and pepper

Scrub potato, dry, and slice very thinly.

Melt butter in an 8- to 10-inch frying pan over medium heat; add potato slices and cook, turning as needed, until tender when pierced, 12 to 15 minutes. Turn heat to medium-high and cook

"When overcooked, beef liver becomes beef leather."

"Designed to sustain anyone pitching hay from dawn to noon."

until lightly browned and crisp, about 5 minutes. Sprinkle with onions.

In a small bowl, beat eggs with milk. Pour egg mixture over vegetables and tilt pan to distribute evenly. Cook, lifting set portion so uncooked egg can flow underneath, until done to your liking. Slide out onto a warm platter. Add salt and pepper to taste. Makes 2 servings.

PER SERVING: 359 calories, 15 g protein, 22 g carbohydrates, 23 g fat, 581 mg cholesterol, 269 mg sodium

Danny Griffith

Eugene, Ore.

WHAT IS A BISQUE? *You might call it a chowder with a lorgnette. Certainly a soup containing sherry and whipping cream could not be called chowder. But neither would you call it cioppino, even though it contains tomatoes and garlic along with clams and other seafood.*

No, Rob Gischer's Puget Sound Tomato-Seafood Bisque is an original: more substantial than a purely broth-based soup, but lighter than the Manhattan-style chowder with its burden of vegetables. The addition of parsley at the end sets off the soup's coral color very prettily.

PUGET SOUND TOMATO-SEAFOOD BISQUE

> 2 cans (6 oz. each) chopped clams
> 1 can (10 oz.) condensed chicken broth
> 1½ cups tomato juice
> ½ cup dry white wine
> 2 tablespoons dry sherry
> ½ teaspoon dry oregano leaves
> 3 large firm-ripe tomatoes, peeled, seeded, and chopped
> 3 cloves garlic, minced or pressed
> 1 to 1½ cups (½ to ¾ lb. total) scallops, shrimp, or white-flesh fish fillets (or a combination), in bite-size pieces; rinse well
> 1 cup whipping cream
> 1 cup finely chopped parsley
> Liquid hot pepper seasoning
> Salt

In a 4- to 5-quart pan, combine clams and their liquid, broth, tomato juice, wine, sherry, oregano, tomatoes, and garlic. Bring to a boil over high heat; cover, reduce heat, and simmer until tomatoes are soft, about 5 minutes. Stir in scallops and cream, bring to a boil, and cook just until scallops are opaque throughout (cut to test), 2 to 3 minutes.

Remove from heat; stir in parsley and liquid hot pepper and salt to taste. Ladle soup into individual bowls. Makes about 4 servings, each 2-cup size.

PER SERVING: 372 calories, 29 g protein, 17 g carbohydrates, 21 g fat, 160 mg cholesterol, 1,407 mg sodium

Rob Gischer

Birch Bay, Wash.

"You might call it a chowder with a lorgnette."

EVERYONE IS AWARE *that pork should be adequately cooked, but no one need have qualms about Eric Sterbinsky's carnitas, which are made with pork that has been boiled for 3 to 3½ hours, then roasted for another hour or so. The result is meat of surpassing tenderness and crispness, supported by a spicy (but not aggressive) green sauce.*

Too bad carnitas *simply means "little meats"; the word is mellifluous enough to make a nice name for a child.*

STERBINSKY'S BOIL-AND-ROAST CARNITAS

> 1 pork shoulder or butt, 5 to 5½ pounds
> 3 large carrots, chopped
> 2 large onions, chopped
> ½ teaspoon *each* ground cumin, coriander, oregano leaves, and chili powder
> 6 cups water
> 1 jar (12 oz.) green chili salsa
> 1 can (7 oz.) diced green chilies
> ½ cup thinly sliced green onions, including tops
> 12 to 15 warm corn or flour tortillas (6- to 8-in. size)

Place pork in a 6- to 8-quart pan; add the carrots, onions, cumin, coriander, oregano, chili powder, and water. Bring to a boil over high heat; reduce heat, cover, and simmer until pork is very tender when pierced, 3 to 3½ hours.

Lift meat from broth (reserve broth for soup or other uses, if desired) and place in a 9- by 13-inch pan. Bake, uncovered, in a 350° oven until meat is well browned, 45 minutes to 1 hour. Drain off all fat, then shred meat, discarding bones and pieces of fat. Stir salsa, chilies, and green onions into meat; return to oven until hot, 10 to 15 minutes.

To serve, spoon meat mixture into soft tortillas, roll to enclose, and eat out of hand. Makes 12 to 15 servings, 2 to 3 filled tortillas each.

PER SERVING: 531 calories, 28 g protein, 19 g carbohydrates, 38 g fat, 114 mg cholesterol, 386 mg sodium

Eric R. Sterbinsky

Palmdale, Calif.

April Menus

OOKING PLANS, *just like the prover-bial April weather, can be varied this month. When the skies cooperate and you have a little time, pull out the barbecue for a Greek buffet. Cornbread, crisp vegetables, and broiled sand dabs taste light on a busy week-night. For a special occasion, a champagne brunch features potato pancakes and a mountain of strawberries.*

SOUVLAKI BARBECUE

Skewered Marinated Beef with Grilled Homemade Pita Wrappers
Tomatoes   Onion
Shredded Romaine
Souvlaki Sauce
Giardiniera   Calamata Olives
Yogurt with Honeyed Almonds
Ale   Limeade

This version of classic Greek souvlaki— *meat grilled on a skewer and then wrapped in pita bread—comes from the island of Thira (Santorin). A quart of yogurt works two ways: some goes into the herb sauce; some becomes dessert with honey and almonds. Frozen dough speeds the bread-making process.*

Allow an hour to marinate meat and roll out pita; you can do both steps ahead. The rest of the meal goes together in a hurry. For the souvlaki, you'll also need 2 medium-size tomatoes, cored and cut into thin wedges; 1 small onion, slivered; and 2 cups shredded romaine leaves. Buy a 16-ounce jar of pickled vegetables (giardiniera) and at least 8 ounces of olives.

SKEWERED MARINATED BEEF WITH GRILLED HOMEMADE PITA WRAPPERS

1½ **pounds boned beef sirloin (fat trimmed), cut into 1-inch chunks**
¼ **cup** *each* **olive oil and lemon juice**
2 **teaspoons ground cumin**
Grilled homemade pita wrappers (recipe follows)
Salt and pepper

In a bowl, mix beef, oil, lemon juice, and cumin. Cover and chill at least 1 hour or up to 1 day.

Meanwhile, prepare pita; set aside. Ignite about 60 charcoal briquets on fire-

To assemble souvlaki, top homemade bread wrappers with grilled meat, yogurt sauce, sliced onion, shredded lettuce, and tomato wedges; fold sides of bread over meat. Offer olives and pickled vegetables for nibbling.

grate of a barbecue; let burn until coals are just covered with gray ash, about 30 minutes. Spread coals into a solid, even layer; put grill in place 4 to 6 inches above them.

Lift beef from marinade and thread equal portions slightly apart on 8 slender 6- to 8-inch metal or wooden skewers.

Grease grill. For each souvlaki, place 1 meat skewer and 1 pita (remove plastic wrap) on grill. Cook meat, turning once, until done to your liking, 5 minutes total for rare. Cook bread until speckled gold on each side but still soft, about 4 minutes; turn with a wide spatula. Push

meat off skewer onto bread; add salt and pepper to taste. Makes 8 souvlaki, 4 servings.

PER SERVING: 597 calories, 41 g protein, 56 g carbohydrates, 22 g fat, 99 mg cholesterol, 619 mg sodium

Grilled homemade pita wrappers. Thaw 1 loaf (1 lb.) **frozen white bread dough.** Cut into 8 equal pieces. Dust each with **all-purpose flour** and roll into an 8-inch circle on a well-floured board; add flour to prevent sticking. Stack rolled pita between sheets of plastic wrap, sprinkling both sides of dough with more flour. If made ahead, cover airtight and chill up to 24 hours.

SOUVLAKI SAUCE

Mix 1 cup **unflavored yogurt** with 1 teaspoon **dry oregano leaves** and 1 tablespoon **water;** add **salt** and **pepper** to taste.

PER TABLESPOON: 9 calories, .75 g protein, 1 g carbohydrates, .21 g fat, .85 mg cholesterol, 10 mg sodium

YOGURT WITH HONEYED ALMONDS

In an 8- or 9-inch pan, bake 1 cup **whole blanched almonds** in a 350° oven until golden, 8 to 10 minutes. Pour hot nuts into a bowl and mix with ½ cup **honey.** Spoon nut mixture over 4 bowls of **unflavored yogurt** (you'll need 3 cups total). Makes 4 servings.

PER SERVING: 427 calories, 16 g protein, 53 g carbohydrates, 20 g fat, 10 mg cholesterol, 125 mg sodium

---

CELEBRATION BRUNCH

Potato Pancakes
Leek–Crème Fraîche Topping
Smoked Salmon   Lumpfish Caviar
Strawberry Mountain
Champagne   Papaya Nectar

You choose the occasion—it might be Easter, the start of spring, or a day with the family. To ease last-minute preparation, make the leek topping and potato pancakes a day ahead.

First prepare the berries and mound on a platter. Make the pancake topping (or bring to room temperature), and rinse ¼ cup black lumpfish caviar in a fine strainer until water runs clear; drain. Cook or reheat pancakes, then serve with leek mixture, caviar, and thinly sliced smoked salmon (you'll need ½ lb.).

Pause after eating the pancakes to melt sugar for the berry mountain. Equal portions of champagne and papaya nectar, mixed, go well with pancakes and dessert.

POTATO PANCAKES

   About 2½ pounds russet potatoes
 3 tablespoons all-purpose flour
½ teaspoon salt (optional)
½ teaspoon pepper
½ cup (¼ lb.) butter or margarine
   Fresh dill sprigs (optional)

Peel and shred potatoes. Immediately drop into a bowl of cold water. Drain; squeeze dry. Dry bowl; return potatoes to bowl and mix with flour, salt, and pepper.

Place 2 frying pans, each 10 to 12 inches wide, over medium heat. Melt 1 tablespoon butter in each, then add 2 tablespoons of the potato mixture for each pancake and spread into a thin 3- to 4-inch circle. Cook several pancakes at a time in each pan, turning once, until golden, 6 to 8 minutes total; add butter as needed to prevent sticking.

Lift cooked pancakes from pans and place in a single layer on 3 baking pans, each about 10 by 15 inches. (At this point, you can let cool, cover, and chill until next day.) Heat warm or cold pancakes, uncovered, in a 400° oven until crisp, about 10 minutes. Garnish with dill. Serves 4.

PER SERVING: 405 calories, 6 g protein, 45 g carbohydrates, 23 g fat, 62 mg cholesterol, 248 mg sodium

LEEK–CRÈME FRAÎCHE TOPPING

Trim roots and all but 2½ inches of green tops from ¾ pound **leeks.** Discard tough outer leaves. Split leeks lengthwise; rinse well. Thinly slice crosswise. Stir often in a 10- to 12-inch frying pan over medium heat with 3 tablespoons **butter** or margarine until limp, about 10 minutes. Remove from heat. Stir in ¾ cup **crème fraîche,** sour cream, or unflavored yogurt, and 3 tablespoons minced **fresh dill** or 1 tablespoon dry dill weed. Serve warm or at room temperature. If made ahead, cover and chill up to 2 days.

PER TABLESPOON: 39 calories, .42 g protein, 1 g carbohydrates, 4 g fat, 8 mg cholesterol, 24 mg sodium

STRAWBERRY MOUNTAIN

Rinse and hull 5 cups **strawberries,** pat dry, and mound on a heatproof platter. Place ½ cup **sugar** in an 8- to 10-inch frying pan over medium heat. Shake pan often until sugar melts and is deep amber, 6 to 8 minutes. Drizzle syrup from pan over strawberries. Let stand briefly for syrup to harden. Serve immediately, breaking apart with a fork.

PER SERVING: 153 calories, 1 g protein, 38 g carbohydrates, .70 g fat, 0 mg cholesterol, 2 mg sodium

(Continued on next page)

Potato pancakes go well with caviar, smoked salmon, dill, and creamy leek topping.

SAND DAB SUPPER

**Oven-fried Sand Dabs with
Basil-Chili Butter**
Sugar Snap Peas   Radishes
Spiced Cornbread
Raspberry Sherbet
Orange Juice or Dry Sauvignon Blanc

*Seasoned butter flavors fish, peas, and
cornbread in this quickly prepared menu.*

*While the cornbread bakes, trim roots off
radishes, pull strings and break ends off
peas (you'll need 1 lb. peas), and make
basil-chili butter. Then broil the fish and
steam the peas.*

OVEN-FRIED SAND DABS WITH BASIL-CHILI BUTTER

4   whole sand dabs (each about
    ½ lb.), gutted, heads removed if
    desired; or 1 pound sole fillets
    (each about ¼ in. thick)
    All-purpose flour
2   **tablespoons salad oil**
    Basil-chili butter (recipe follows)

Coat fish in flour; shake off excess. Heat
oil in a rimmed 10- by 15-inch baking pan
4 inches below broiler. Carefully turn
fish in hot oil, then broil until no longer
translucent in center (cut to test), about 4
minutes. Lift fish to plates with a spatula, and serve with basil-chili butter.
Serves 4.

PER SERVING: 178 calories, 22 g protein, 3 g carbohydrates, 8 g fat,
54 mg cholesterol, 92 mg sodium

Basil-chili butter. In a small bowl, stir ½
cup (¼ lb.) **butter** or margarine at room
temperature, 2 teaspoons **chili powder,**
and 2 tablespoons minced **fresh basil** (or
2 teaspoons dry basil).

PER SERVING: 105 calories, .24 g protein, .56 g carbohydrates, 12 g fat,
31 mg cholesterol, 124 mg sodium

SPICED CORNBREAD

1   cup yellow cornmeal
1   cup all-purpose flour
1   tablespoon baking powder
2   tablespoons sugar
½   teaspoon salt (optional)
1½ teaspoons *each* ground coriander
    and ground cumin
⅓   cup butter or margarine
1   large egg
1   cup milk
    Basil-chili butter (recipe precedes)

In a large bowl, mix cornmeal, flour,
baking powder, sugar, salt, coriander,
and cumin. Cut in butter until crumbly.
Add egg and milk; stir until evenly
moistened. Spread in a greased 8-inch-
square pan. Bake in a 400° oven until
deep golden, about 30 minutes. Serve
with basil-chili butter. Serves 4 to 8.

PER SERVING: 230 calories, 5 g protein, 30 g carbohydrates, 10 g fat,
59 mg cholesterol, 262 mg sodium

MAY

Chef's Salad of the Americas (page 119)

For Sunset's 90th anniversary issue, we take a fresh look at baking with sourdough, using a yogurt-based starter, and offer a varied selection of readers' favorite recipes. Foods native to the Americas are featured in a colorful chef's salad. Other articles suggest vegetable main dishes that focus on corn, converting garden snails into escargots, and ways to cook with Norwegian cheeses. We tempt readers with a sweet tooth with giant doughnuts from Italy and stunning strawberry desserts.

Sourdough—a Sunset Standby

SINCE GOLD MINING DAYS, *sourdough has been a Western staple, delighting generations with its tangy flavor in breads, pancakes, and other baked foods.*

Sourdough has been a standby at Sunset, too, from the first recipes published in 1933 to a longer discussion in 1961. A breakthrough story in 1973 gave directions for creating a dependable starter of flour, liquid, and beneficial bacteria that put the tang in sourdough baking; it was based on yogurt.

Two years ago, we asked you to write us about your sourdough experiences, especially with the yogurt-based starter. We received hundreds of responses—as well as many questions. To answer these and our own questions, we embarked on sourdough experiments. (Some most-asked questions are discussed on page 114.)

In brief, we found that starters are much more forgiving of neglect and variations in feeding than we had thought. You can change your technique to encourage more or less sour flavor, and you can use the starter in quick or more involved ways.*

Readers also sent many recipes; favorites begin on page 115.

YEASTS & BEASTS—
HOW A STARTER WORKS

No sourdough starter is exactly like another: each is a living organism with a different bacteria and yeast make-up. All starters ferment flour and liquid (usually milk or water): bacteria break down sugars in the flour and milk and produce acids, primarily lactic acid and some acetic acid (vinegar); these give sourdough its tang. Fermentation also produces some carbon dioxide bubbles.

Our 1973 recipe relies on bacteria in the yogurt to culture the starter. These bacteria may be different from ones in commercial starters, or in homemade ones that capture bacteria more haphazardly.

While bacteria create sourness, yeasts break down sugars in flour to form more carbon dioxide, which leavens the bread.

Yogurt-based starters typically don't have any yeast, although you may have the good fortune to capture some from flour.

Because starters vary so much in their leavening ability, our recipes contain another leavener as well. We don't think commercial yeast detracts from the sourdough taste; it just adds another flavor. And bread made with yeast rises faster than with starter alone—about 1½ hours versus 6 to 8 hours.

CARE & FEEDING OF YOUR
PET STARTER

To keep bacteria and yeasts healthy, a starter must be fed flour and liquid occasionally, then it must stand. (Chill between uses.) For food choices, see box on page 114.

Just What's This Thing Called Sourdough Starter?

THOUGH MYSTERIOUS to some, starter is just flour, water, and yogurt. After a few days' incubation, bacteria in the yogurt multiply to give typical sour smell and flavor, and the starter is ready to use.

SOURDOUGH STARTER 1988

For best results, use milk and yogurt that are freshly purchased and opened.

    1 cup skim or low-fat milk
    3 tablespoons unflavored yogurt
    1 cup all-purpose flour

In a 1-quart pan over medium heat, or in a nonmetal container in a microwave oven, heat milk to 90° to 100°. Remove from heat and stir in yogurt. Pour into a warm 3- to 6-cup glass, ceramic, plastic, or stainless steel container with a tight lid.

Cover and let stand in a warm place (80° to 90°) until mixture is the consistency of yogurt, a curd has formed, and mixture doesn't flow readily when container is tilted. (It may also form smaller curds suspended in clear liq-

Starter is ready to use when it's bubbly, and clear liquid forms on top.

uid.) Process takes 18 to 24 hours. If some clear liquid has risen to top of milk during this time, stir it back in. But if liquid has turned light pink, discard the batch and start again.

Once curd has formed, stir in flour until smooth. Cover tightly and let stand in a warm place (80° to 90°) until mixture is full of bubbles and has a good sour smell (2 to 5 days). Again, if clear liquid forms during this time, stir it back into starter. If liquid is pink, start over. To store, cover and refrigerate. Makes about 1⅓ cups.

To feed the starter and maintain a supply, first bring it to room temperature (you can put container in a bowl of warm—not hot—water to speed). Use, or feed and let stand as follows. Try to feed at least once a month for best results.

To feed, add warm **skim** or low-fat **milk** (90° to 100°) and **all-purpose flour** to starter in quantities equal to what you'll be using in the recipe. (For example, if it calls for 1 cup starter, add 1 cup milk and 1 cup flour.) Cover tightly and let stand in a warm place (80° to 90°) until bubbly, sour-smelling, and clear liquid has formed on top (picture above), 12 to 24 hours. Use, or cover and chill. Stir to use.

To increase the starter supply (for gift-giving or quantity baking), you can add up to 10 cups *each* of milk and flour to 1 cup of starter (use a large container). The mixture may need to stand up to 2 days before the clear liquid forms on top.

Great crust, chewy interior, and sour flavor are a sourdough baker's reward. Next to container of starter is classic French bread. Italian flour-dusted loaf in foreground is made with parmesan and pepper. Recipes begin on page 115.

Environment. When creating a starter, incubate it between 80° and 90°: higher, and bacteria may die; lower, the starter may develop mold. Place atop your water heater—or in an oven with the light on or warmed with pans of boiling water.

An established starter is stronger; after feeding, it can stand at room temperature if a warm spot isn't handy. If you feed the starter milk, as we suggest, you'll know it's ready to use or chill

when a clear liquid forms on top. This shows that the acid level has risen and is starting to break down milk protein. High acid means sour flavor.

Bacteria in starters grow best without oxygen, so store your starter in a tightly closed container. Air fosters mold, too.

Neglect or care? In our 1973 story, we suggested feeding the starter every two weeks. Some readers who ignored this wrote with revival tales worthy of Southern evangelists: after starters had nearly

died from international travel, natural disasters, and lack of food for up to two years, they revived. (Other readers guilty of such cavalier tactics lost their starters.)

For more on ignoring starters, see the question box on page 114.

A happy medium between neglect and slavish attention is to feed the starter at least once a month. If it has sat in the refrigerator longer, try reviving it.

(Continued on next page)

RESUSCITATE OR GIVE UP THE GHOST?

An "old" smell, no bubbles at room temperature, a top layer of dark brown liquid, and slight mold growth indicate your starter isn't feeling its best. First spoon off and discard any mold, then stir the starter. Feed it 1 cup *each* of flour and milk and let stand as directed in the recipe. After 24 hours, discard half the starter and repeat feeding and standing. Repeat a third time, if needed, until starter bubbles, has a "fresh" sour smell.

You can't bring a starter back from the dead. If, after repeated feedings, your starter still smells "off" and won't bubble, discard it. Also, if mold growth is heavy, begin a new starter.

GETTING THE MOST FLAVOR, BEST TEXTURE

Increasing the tang in your sourdough baked foods and getting chewy, light texture require surprisingly few acrobatics.

Sourness. The greatest trick for more sour flavor is patience: the longer dough stands in the "sponge" stage, the more sourness you'll get—up to a point. A sponge is a mixture of starter and part of the liquid and flour called for in a recipe. You let it stand 12 to 24 hours before adding other ingredients; as it stands, bacteria multiply and produce acidity, or sourness. After about 24 hours, the sponge won't get much more sour. Our recipes give you the option of a long sponge stage for flavor or a short one for speed.

Some readers reported their starters didn't get very sour until they were about a year old; with a long sponge stage, even our new starters produced good flavor.

A few readers wrote about starters that are *too* sour. To mellow, skip the sponge stage in our recipes, and after feeding the starter, let it stand only a few hours.

Texture. Discussions with professional bakers, and experiments in our test kitchens, point to the success of bread flour in achieving traditional chewy sourdough texture. Compared to all-purpose flour, bread flour is higher in

Sourdough Questions & Answers

WHY IS A YOGURT STARTER SO SUCCESSFUL? The bacteria you need to culture the starter are already present in the yogurt.

In testing, we reconfirmed that the brand of yogurt doesn't matter; new starters made with 10 different brands (and all fat levels—nonfat, low-fat, and regular) all "took," and produced similar flavor.

What should I feed my starter? Starters need periodic doses of flour and liquid to keep their bacteria active. We prefer feeding starters with all-purpose flour because of its versatility in baking, though you can use bread flour. Some people say bleached flour is less susceptible to mold invasion than unbleached. We've had good luck with both. Many readers mentioned trouble getting whole-wheat starters to work; ours was successful, but bran in the flour may inhibit fermentation.

To see if sourness changed, we varied the liquid fed to starter clones. Milk and water both produced sour bread, but milk offers the starter more food, so we prefer using it. The starchy water used to rinse chopped raw potatoes and water drained from cooked potatoes (both reader suggestions) gave us less sour results.

How frequently must I feed my starter? Many readers felt feeding the starter every two weeks, as we suggested in 1973, is a bother: "It's like a ball and chain to remember to keep the starter going." But another reader says, "The starter is no more demanding to maintain than any other house plant." This disparity led us to the next question.

What happens if I neglect it? In our test kitchen, we deliberately didn't feed a starter for 1½ years, then had it and a more pampered clone analyzed for yeast and bacteria content. The neglected starter was almost dead, but after two feedings tested as healthy again. Not all starters revive so easily. Luck, and a starter's initial health, seem to make the difference.

Why do starters "die"? The longer a starter stands without new food, the higher the acidity gets; too much acid, and beneficial bacteria can't survive. Yeasts are hardier, but not infinitely so. Mold infestations may also kill off good bacteria.

Can you use a starter too often? Overuse isn't a problem per se; if you bake several times a week or feed your starter a lot all at once (to increase quantity), it may take longer than usual to regain normal sourness.

After feeding, let it stand as directed in the recipe, page 112.

Can I freeze it when I'm not going to use it for a while? Starters generally freeze successfully up to a few months, but freezing does change the bacteria's cell structures. Longer freezing brings more changes and decreases the chance of success with the thawed starter.

How can I get really sour flavor? As explained above, a long "sponge" stage is the best insurance of sourness.

You can also increase sourness by letting a starter stand sufficiently after feeding.

Lack of food increases a starter's acidity (sourness), too, though bacteria may not be very healthy. In testing, we found that a pampered starter can produce a flavor just as sour as a neglected one. The reason: in a healthy starter, bacteria multiply and produce acidity very quickly.

How can I get chewy, San Francisco French bread texture? As discussed above, bread flour, in the right amount, makes yeast loaves springier. For slightly coarse, extra-chewy texture, try the Italian bread on page 116; the recipe's higher liquid level is responsible for its special texture.

the components that form gluten—the protein structure that develops when you knead dough; the dough is stronger and springier. For pancakes, muffins, and other breads that aren't kneaded and are softer in texture, all-purpose flour is a better choice.

For kneaded doughs, the correct amount of flour varies with weather and other factors. As you gain experience, you'll know when the dough feels right—it will still be tacky, but not sticky (not enough flour) or dry (too much).

Sufficient kneading is also important for good bread texture—dough should feel smooth and springy and have tiny bubbles just beneath the surface; under-kneaded dough will be heavy when baked.

Yeast-leavened doughs generally rise twice, punched between risings; this divides up air cells and makes lighter bread. For the first rise, dough should double in volume; poke a finger into dough—the impression should stay if dough has risen enough. After shaping, the dough rises again. When it's ready to bake, it will look puffy (but not yet be double), and will hold a slight impression when pressed.

Crust. Professional bakers of sourdough French bread use ovens with jets of steam to make the crust crisp. At home, you can spray bread with a mister during baking. We tried baking bread in terra cotta baking domes and on stones, which are meant to make bread crisp, but water spraying worked best.

AND A TIME-SAVING TIP

Sourdough bacteria multiply fastest between 80° and 90°, so recipes call for starter at room temperature. If skipping sponge stage, you can use the starter cold.

1988 SOURDOUGH FRENCH BREAD

¾ cup warm water (90°)
1 cup sourdough starter, at room temperature
3 to 3½ cups bread flour
1 package active dry yeast
1 teaspoon *each* salt and sugar
Cornmeal

In a large bowl, stir ½ cup water, starter, and 1 cup flour until smooth. For sourest flavor, cover and let stand in a warm place until bubbly and sour smelling, 12 to 24 hours. To speed, omit standing; proceed.

Soften yeast in remaining water; stir into sourdough mixture with salt and sugar.

According to 1 of the following ways, mix in remaining flour and knead.

By hand. Stir in enough flour to form a kneadable dough, about 2 cups. Turn dough out onto a lightly floured board and knead until smooth and elastic, 12 to 15 minutes; add as little flour as possible to keep dough from sticking. Place dough in a greased bowl; turn over.

With a dough hook. Mix in enough flour to form a somewhat stiff dough, about 2 cups. Beat on high speed until dough pulls cleanly from side of bowl, about 8 minutes. If dough still sticks or feels sticky, add flour 1 tablespoon at a time until dough pulls free and isn't sticky. Leave in bowl.

In a food processor. Place 2¼ cups flour in container (at least 8-cup capacity) with plastic or metal blade. With motor running, pour starter mixture into feed tube. Whirl until dough forms a ball and pulls from container, then whirl 45 seconds more. If dough feels sticky, add 1 more tablespoon flour at a time and mix in short bursts. Leave in bowl.

When kneaded, cover bowl with plastic wrap and let rise in a warm place until double, 1 to 2 hours. Gently punch down dough. Turn out onto a lightly floured board and knead gently just until smooth. Roll with hands into a 3½- by 12-inch log. Generously sprinkle a piece of stiff cardboard with cornmeal; set dough on cornmeal. Cover lightly with plastic wrap and let rise in a warm place until puffy, 10 to 30 minutes.

About 10 minutes before dough is ready, place a 12- by 15-inch baking sheet on lowest oven rack, then heat oven to 400°.

With a flour-dusted razor blade or sharp knife, cut several ¾-inch-deep diagonal slashes on loaf's top. Slip loaf off cardboard onto hot baking sheet, keeping slashed side up. Spray bread all over with water.

Bake for 5 minutes, then spray again with water. Repeat after 5 more minutes, then bake until deep golden, 25 to 30 minutes more. Let cool completely on rack. Makes 1 loaf, about 1½ pounds.

PER OUNCE: 74 calories, 3 g protein, 15 g carbohydrates, .2 g fat, .3 mg cholesterol, 89 mg sodium

FAVORITE RECIPES FROM READERS

"I am not convinced that eating sourdough bread and pancakes will contribute to longer life, but I am certain life will be more pleasant," wrote Fritz Bell from Hamilton, Montana. Many readers expressed similar affection for "this strange, capricious substance." Along with praise came questions, which led us to experiments (see page 112). Readers also sent recipes; favorites follow, and are pictured on page 113 and the back cover.

Choose here from rustic parmesan-pepper bread; whole-grain bread, in round or rectangular loaves; sesame bread made with sesame butter and seed; and braided rye with dill. Crisp waffles contain oats and part whole-wheat flour. Muffin fans have two choices: blueberry-bran and oat-corn. For dinner, try fennel biscuits. Sourdough extends to dessert, too—rich chocolate-cherry cake and apricot bread.

For recipes requiring kneading, knead by hand, with a dough hook, or with a food processor, as follows:

By hand. Stir in minimum amount of remaining flour called for in recipe to form a kneadable dough. Turn dough out onto a lightly floured board and knead until smooth and elastic, 10 to 15 minutes; add as little flour as possible to keep it from sticking. Place in greased bowl; turn over.

With a dough hook. Mix in the minimum amount of remaining flour called for in recipe to form a stiff but somewhat moist dough. Beat on high speed until dough pulls cleanly from side of bowl, 8 to 10 minutes. If it still sticks or feels sticky, add more flour until it pulls free and/or no longer feels sticky. If you've added too much flour, dough may pull almost immediately from bowl; add water a teaspoon at a time until it softens a little, then knead with hook. Leave it in bowl to rise.

In a food processor. Place minimum amount of remaining flour called for in recipe in container (at least 8-cup capacity) of a food processor with plastic or metal blade. Transfer starter mixture to a container with a spout. With motor running, pour this mixture into feed tube. Whirl until dough forms a ball and pulls from container side, then whirl 45 seconds longer. If dough feels sticky, add 1 more tablespoon of flour at a time; mix in short bursts. Leave dough in bowl to rise.

Except for waffles and pancakes, which are best freshly made, these baked foods will store up to 3 days at room temperature (chill the cake and blueberry muffins). Freeze airtight for longer storage.

SOURDOUGH ITALIAN CHEESE-PEPPER BREAD

1¼ cups warm water (90°)
1 cup sourdough starter, at room temperature
3 to 3½ cups bread flour
1 package active dry yeast
1 teaspoon *each* salt, sugar, and freshly ground pepper
⅔ cup grated parmesan cheese
  Cornmeal

In a large bowl, stir 1 cup water, starter, and 1½ cups flour until smooth. For sourest flavor, cover and let stand in a warm place until bubbly and sour smelling, 12 to 24 hours. To speed, omit standing; proceed.

Soften yeast in remaining water; stir into starter mixture with salt, sugar, pepper, and parmesan. According to 1 of the following ways, mix in remaining flour and knead. Dough will be very soft and sticky, even after kneading.

By hand. Add 1 cup flour. Beat steadily with a heavy spoon until dough is very stretchy, about 35 minutes. If your arm tires, let dough rest up to 15 minutes, then continue. With spoon, beat in ½ to 1 cup more flour to make a very soft, somewhat sticky dough. Leave in bowl.

With a dough hook. Mix in 1¼ cups more flour on low speed, then beat on high speed until dough is very stretchy when hook is lifted from it, about 10 minutes. Gradually beat in ¼ to ¾ cup more flour until dough pulls cleanly from bowl but still feels somewhat sticky. Leave in bowl.

With a food processor. Place 1¾ cups more flour in container (at least 8-cup capacity) with plastic or metal blade. With motor running, pour starter mixture into feed tube. Whirl until dough is very stretchy when pulled with a finger, about 1½ minutes; if motor starts to slow

down, let it rest briefly before completing mixing. Gradually add up to ¼ cup more flour to make a very soft, somewhat sticky dough. Scrape dough into a large bowl.

When dough is kneaded, cover bowl with plastic wrap. Let rise in a warm place until double, 2 to 3 hours. Do not punch or stir dough down. Grease a 12- by 15-inch baking sheet and generously sprinkle with cornmeal. Using a bowl scraper or stiff plastic spatula, gently ease dough out onto sheet. With floured fingers, gently tuck outer ½ inch of dough edge underneath itself to shape a round loaf.

Sprinkle dough with about 2 tablespoons flour; cover with a flour-dusted cloth. Let stand at room temperature until dough holds a slight impression when pressed with a finger, about 10 minutes.

Bake on bottom rack of a 400° oven until deep golden, about 30 minutes. Let cool on a rack at least 30 minutes. Serve warm or cool. Makes 1 loaf, about 2 pounds. —*Sam Hogander, Beaverton, Ore.*

PER OUNCE: 68 calories, 3 g protein, 12 g carbohydrates, .7 g fat, 2 mg cholesterol, 103 mg sodium

SOURDOUGH WHOLE-GRAIN LOAVES

1 cup sourdough starter, at room temperature
1½ cups warm milk (90°)
3¼ to 3¾ cups bread flour
1 package active dry yeast
¼ cup warm water (110°)
⅓ cup honey or firmly packed brown sugar
1½ teaspoons salt
1 large egg
2 tablespoons melted butter or margarine
½ cup *each* rolled oats, bulgur, cornmeal, and rye flour
1 cup unprocessed bran
1½ cups whole-wheat flour

In a large bowl, mix starter, milk, and 1½ cups bread flour. For sourest flavor, cover and let stand in a warm place until bubbly and sour smelling, 12 to 24 hours. To speed, omit standing; proceed.

In a bowl, soften yeast in water. Stir into starter mixture with honey, salt, egg, butter, oats, bulgur, cornmeal, rye flour, and bran. As directed at left for

recipes requiring kneading, add whole-wheat flour and more bread flour and knead.

Cover with plastic wrap and let rise in a warm place until double, 1½ to 2½ hours.

Punch dough down and knead briefly. Divide in half. Shape each half into a smooth round about 2 inches thick and 6 inches across. Place each in the center of a greased 12- by 15-inch baking sheet. Or shape each into a 3- by 8-inch log; place each in a greased 5- by 9-inch loaf pan.

Cover dough loosely with plastic wrap and let rise in a warm place until puffy, 25 to 45 minutes. For round loaves, use a floured razor blade to make slashes about ¼ inch deep. Bake in a 375° oven until well browned, about 35 minutes; switch positions of pans halfway through baking.

Remove from pans to racks and let cool completely. Makes 2 loaves, 1¾ pounds each. —*Janet Harms, Encino, Calif.*

PER OUNCE: 81 calories, 3 g protein, 15 g carbohydrates, 1 g fat, 7 mg cholesterol, 70 mg sodium

SESAME SOURDOUGH LOAVES

¾ cup sourdough starter, at room temperature
2¼ to 2¾ cups bread flour
1¼ cups warm water (90°)
1 cup sesame seed
1 package active dry yeast
1½ teaspoons salt
¼ cup *each* tahini (sesame butter), honey, and lemon juice
2 cups whole-wheat flour
1 large egg white, lightly beaten

In a large bowl, mix starter, 1 cup bread flour, and 1 cup water. For sourest flavor, cover and let stand in a warm place until bubbly and sour smelling, 12 to 24 hours. To speed, omit standing; proceed.

Place sesame seed in a 10- to 12-inch frying pan over medium heat; shake often until golden, about 8 minutes. Let cool; set aside ½ cup.

In a small bowl, soften yeast in remaining water. Stir into starter mixture with salt, tahini, honey, lemon juice, and remaining ½ cup sesame seed.

As directed for recipes requiring kneading, preceding, add whole-wheat flour and more bread flour and knead.

Cover and let rise in a warm place until double, 1½ to 2 hours.

Punch dough down and knead briefly. Divide in half. Shape each half into a flat round about 1 inch thick and 7 inches across; place each on a greased 12- by 15-inch baking sheet. Cover dough loosely with plastic wrap and let rise in a warm place until puffy, 30 to 45 minutes.

Brush loaves with egg white and sprinkle tops and sides evenly with reserved seed. Bake in a 375° oven until well browned, 25 to 30 minutes; switch positions of pans halfway through baking.

Transfer to racks and let cool. Makes 2 loaves, 1⅓ pounds each. —*Deborah Farriston, Malibu, Calif.*

PER OUNCE: 85 calories, 3 g protein, 13 g carbohydrates, 3 g fat, .1 mg cholesterol, 84 mg sodium

DOUBLE DILL SOURDOUGH RYE

Because of the proportion of rye flour, this dough isn't as springy as ones made only with wheat flour. It works best kneaded by hand.

- 1 cup sourdough starter, at room temperature
- ½ cup warm dill pickle brine (90°)
- 1½ cups rye flour
- 1 package active dry yeast
- ¼ cup warm water (110°)
- 1 tablespoon dry dill weed
- 2 teaspoons caraway seed
- 1 teaspoon salt
- 2 tablespoons unsweetened cocoa
- 2 tablespoons salad oil
- 3 tablespoons dark molasses
- 1 large egg
- 2¼ to 2½ cups bread flour
- 1 large egg yolk beaten with 1 teaspoon water

In a large bowl, mix starter with dill pickle brine and 1 cup rye flour. For sourest flavor, cover and let stand in a warm place until bubbly and sour smelling, 12 to 24 hours. To speed, omit standing; proceed.

In a bowl, soften yeast in water. Stir into starter mixture with remaining rye flour, dill, caraway, salt, cocoa, oil, molasses, and whole egg.

As directed for recipes requiring kneading, preceding, add bread flour and knead by hand. Cover with plastic wrap and let rise in a warm place until double, about 2¼ hours.

Punch dough down and knead briefly. Set aside ¾ cup of the dough.

Divide remaining dough into 3 equal pieces; with hands, roll each piece on a board into a 16-inch-long rope. Pinch ropes together at 1 end and place at 1 narrow end of a greased 12- by 15-inch baking sheet; tuck pinched portion under. Braid ropes; pinch at other end, and tuck pinched portion under.

Divide reserved dough into 3 equal pieces; roll each into a 10-inch-long rope, then braid as directed, preceding. Brush top of large braid with yolk mixture; center small braid on top.

Cover dough loosely with plastic wrap and let rise in a warm place until puffy, about 40 minutes.

Brush braids on tops and sides with yolk mixture. Bake in a 375° oven until well browned, 30 to 35 minutes.

Transfer bread to a rack and let cool. Makes 1 loaf, about 2 pounds. —*Marvin Zeisloft, Colfax, Calif.*

PER OUNCE: 85 calories, 2.7 g protein, 13 g carbohydrates, 2 g fat, 17 mg cholesterol, 214 mg sodium

OAT-WHEAT SOURDOUGH WAFFLES OR PANCAKES

- 1 cup sourdough starter, at room temperature
- 1 cup warm milk (90°)
- ½ cup all-purpose flour
- ⅓ cup melted butter or margarine
- 2 large eggs, separated
- ½ cup *each* whole-wheat flour and rolled oats
- ½ teaspoon baking soda
- ½ teaspoon salt, optional
- 1 teaspoon baking powder
  Salad oil

In a large bowl, stir starter with milk and all-purpose flour. For sourest flavor, cover and let stand in a warm place until bubbly and sour smelling, 12 to 24 hours. To speed, omit standing; proceed. Stir in butter and egg yolks until blended.

Mix whole-wheat flour, oats, soda, salt, and baking powder. Add to starter mixture; stir until evenly moistened. In another large bowl, whip whites until they hold stiff, moist peaks. Fold into batter.

To make waffles, heat a waffle iron to medium-hot (375° if electric). Brush grids with oil, fill ⅞ full with batter, close, and cook until waffles are crisp and deep golden brown, 5 to 8 minutes.

To make pancakes, heat an electric griddle to 400° (or heat a 10- to 12-inch frying pan on medium-high heat until a drop of water sizzles on it). Brush griddle lightly with oil. Spoon ¼ cup batter per pancake onto griddle; cook until most of bubbles on top of pancake pop and bottom is brown, about 3 minutes. Turn pancake over; cook until brown on bottom, about 1 minute more. Repeat.

Makes 11 waffles, each 4 inches square, or about 17 pancakes.

PER WAFFLE: 164 calories, 5 g protein, 18 g carbohydrates, 8 g fat, 68 mg cholesterol, 165 mg sodium

OAT-BUCKWHEAT SOURDOUGH WAFFLES OR PANCAKES

Follow directions for **oat-wheat sourdough waffles or pancakes,** omitting whole-wheat flour. Add ½ cup **buckwheat flour.**

SOURDOUGH BLUEBERRY-BRAN MUFFINS

- ½ cup sourdough starter, at room temperature
- 1 cup warm buttermilk (90°)
- ¾ cup all-purpose flour
- ⅓ cup sugar
- ¼ cup melted butter or margarine
- 1 large egg
- 1 cup fresh or frozen unsweetened blueberries
- ½ cup whole-wheat flour
- 2 cups bran flake cereal
- ¼ teaspoon salt
- ½ teaspoon baking soda
- 2 teaspoons baking powder
- ½ teaspoon ground cinnamon

In a large bowl, stir starter with buttermilk and all-purpose flour. For sourest flavor, cover and let stand in a warm place until bubbly and sour smelling, 12 to 24 hours. To speed, omit standing; proceed.

Add sugar, butter, and egg to starter mixture; stir well. Gently stir in berries.

In a bowl, stir whole-wheat flour, bran, salt, soda, baking powder, and cinnamon. Pour starter mixture over flour mixture. Stir gently until evenly moistened; batter will be lumpy. Heap into 10 greased 2¾-inch muffin cups.

(Continued on next page)

Bake in a 425° oven until a toothpick comes out clean, 25 to 30 minutes. Loosen with knife; invert on rack. Serve warm or cool. Makes 10. —*Stan Martin, Lake Oswego, Ore.*

PER MUFFIN: 191 calories, 5 g protein, 31 g carbohydrates, 6 g fat, 41 mg cholesterol, 339 mg sodium

OAT-CORN SOURDOUGH MUFFINS

½ cup sourdough starter, at room temperature
½ cup warm milk (90°)
1 cup all-purpose flour
½ cup *each* cornmeal and rolled oats
2 teaspoons baking powder
½ teaspoon *each* baking soda and salt
⅓ cup butter or margarine
1 large egg
½ cup firmly packed brown sugar

In a bowl, mix starter, milk, and ½ cup flour. For sourest flavor, cover and let stand in a warm place until bubbly and sour smelling, 12 to 24 hours. To speed, omit standing; proceed.

In a large bowl, stir remaining flour, cornmeal, oats, baking powder, soda, and salt. Cut in butter with a pastry blender or rub with your fingers until crumbly. In another bowl, beat egg and brown sugar until smooth; beat in starter mixture. Pour egg mixture into flour mixture and stir just until evenly moistened.

Fill 10 greased muffin cups, 2½-inch size, ⅞ full. Bake in a 425° oven until well browned and a toothpick inserted in center comes out clean, about 15 minutes. Loosen with a knife, then invert on rack. Serve warm or cool. Makes 10. —*Sylvia Rose, Santa Monica, Calif.*

PER MUFFIN: 216 calories, 4 g protein, 33 g carbohydrates, 8 g fat, 46 mg cholesterol, 319 mg sodium

SOURDOUGH FENNEL BISCUITS

1 cup sourdough starter, at room temperature
½ cup warm water (90°)
About 2¾ cups all-purpose flour
¼ cup olive oil
1½ teaspoons fennel seed
2 teaspoons baking powder
¾ teaspoon salt
½ teaspoon baking soda
1 egg white, lightly beaten

In a bowl, mix starter, water, and 1 cup flour. For sourest flavor, cover and let stand in a warm place until bubbly and sour smelling, 12 to 24 hours. To speed, omit standing; proceed. Stir in oil.

Crush ½ teaspoon of the fennel seed; set aside remaining seed. In a bowl, stir crushed fennel, baking powder, salt, baking soda, and 1¾ cups more flour. Add starter mixture; stir until dough cleans side of bowl.

Turn dough out onto a lightly floured board and knead for about 30 seconds; add flour if required to prevent sticking. Flour board, then roll out dough into a 6- by 14-inch rectangle.

Brush dough with egg white; sprinkle with reserved seed. Cut into 2- by 3-inch rectangles. Place biscuits about ½ inch apart on a 12- by 15-inch baking sheet.

Bake in a 450° oven until deep golden, about 15 minutes. Transfer to a rack and serve warm or cool. Makes 14 biscuits. —*Paige Langdon, Redwood City, Calif.*

PER BISCUIT: 153 calories, 4 g protein, 24 g carbohydrates, 4 g fat, .5 mg cholesterol, 219 mg sodium

SOURDOUGH CHOCOLATE-CHERRY CAKE

1 can (16 oz.) pitted sour pie cherries in water
About ¼ cup milk
½ cup sourdough starter, at room temperature
1½ cups all-purpose flour
1 cup sliced almonds
⅔ cup (⅓ lb.) butter or margarine
1 cup sugar
2 large eggs
¼ teaspoon *each* ground cinnamon, ground nutmeg, and almond extract
½ cup unsweetened cocoa
1½ teaspoons baking soda
½ cup semisweet chocolate baking chips
Powdered sugar (optional)

Drain cherries well, saving liquid; add milk to liquid to make 1 cup. In a bowl, mix starter, liquid mixture, and 1 cup of the flour. For sourest flavor, cover and let stand in a warm place until bubbly and sour smelling, 12 to 24 hours. (If doing this step, also cover and chill cherries.) To speed, omit standing and proceed.

Place almonds in an 8- or 9-inch wide pan. Bake in a 350° oven until golden, 8 to 10 minutes; set aside to cool.

In large bowl of a mixer, beat butter and sugar until well combined. Then beat in eggs, 1 at a time, with cinnamon, nutmeg, and almond extract. Sift remaining ½ cup flour, cocoa, and soda into butter mixture; beat until smooth. Add starter mixture; beat well. Stir in almonds, cherries, and chocolate chips.

Butter and cocoa-dust a 9- by 13-inch pan; spread batter evenly in pan. Bake in a 350° oven until cake pulls from sides of pan, about 45 minutes. Let cool in pan on a rack for at least 10 minutes. Serve warm or cool. If desired, sift powdered sugar on top of cool cake. If made ahead, chill airtight up to 3 days. Makes 12 servings. —*Sharon Donaldson, Reno.*

PER SERVING: 353 calories, 6 g protein, 43 g carbohydrates, 19 g fat, 75 mg cholesterol, 232 mg sodium

SOURDOUGH CALIFORNIA APRICOT BREAD

½ cup sourdough starter, at room temperature
½ cup warm milk (90°)
1½ cups all-purpose flour
1 large egg
½ cup *each* granulated sugar and firmly packed brown sugar
3 tablespoons salad oil or melted butter or margarine
1 teaspoon baking powder
½ teaspoon salt
¼ teaspoon baking soda
½ cup *each* chopped dried apricots and chopped walnuts

In a bowl, mix starter, milk, and ½ cup flour. For sourest flavor, cover and let stand in a warm place until bubbly and sour smelling, 12 to 24 hours. To speed, omit standing; proceed.

In a large bowl, beat egg, granulated and brown sugars, oil, and starter mixture until well blended. In another bowl, combine baking powder, salt, baking soda, remaining 1 cup flour, apricots, and nuts; add to egg mixture and stir until evenly moistened.

Pour batter into a greased 5- by 9-inch loaf pan. Bake in a 350° oven until bread pulls from sides of pan, 55 to 60 minutes. Let cool in pan on a rack for 5 minutes, then turn out onto rack and let cool completely. Makes 1 loaf, 1¾ pounds. —*Nell Rogers Lane, Novato, Calif.*

PER OUNCE: 97 calories, 2 g protein, 16 g carbohydrates, 3 g fat, 11 mg cholesterol, 70 mg sodium

Chef's Salad 1988

SALADS HAVE HIGHLIGHTED Sunset's food pages since our first recipes appeared in February 1929. Here, we feature a modern salad with brilliantly colorful ingredients; it focuses on foods native to the Americas, particularly to southern regions.

As more people come to the West from Central and South America, some of these less familiar items are appearing regularly in supermarkets and ethnic markets.

CHEF'S SALAD OF THE AMERICAS

Common and uncommon ingredients share a New World heritage in our chef's salad. Following are new world ingredients you can choose to tailor a salad to your taste.

2 large heads butter lettuce (about 3 lb. total), washed and crisped
2 pounds jicama
2 small firm-ripe avocados
1 tablespoon lemon juice
  Hominy (following)
  Roasted red peppers (following)
  Nopalitos (following)
  Blue potatoes (following)
  Tomatillos (following)
  Carnitas (following)
  Squash (following)
  Fried dried chilies (following)
½ cup cilantro (coriander) sprigs
  Orange-lime vinaigrette (following)

Arrange large lettuce leaves on 4 dinner plates. Chop the remaining lettuce and nest in leaves.

Rinse, peel, and shred jicama. Mound equal portions on lettuce.

Cut avocados in half lengthwise; pit and peel. Brush with lemon juice and lay cut side down. Starting about ½ inch from narrow end, make ¼-inch-wide lengthwise cuts through wide end of avocado halves. Fan out; brush with juice.

Arrange on each plate an avocado half and ¼ of the hominy, peppers, nopalitos, potatoes, tomatillos, carnitas, and squash. Garnish with chilies and cilantro; add dressing. Makes 4 main-course servings.

PER SERVING: 899 calories, 31 g protein, 81 g carbohydrates, 54 g fat, 82 mg cholesterol, 482 mg sodium

Hominy. Drain 1 can (15 oz.) **yellow** or white **hominy.** (Or you can use corn; the recipe is on page 120.)

(Continued on next page)

Make Choices to Create Your Own Salad

Tomatoes, cherry tomatoes, or tomatillos

Jicama and cilantro

Chilies— dry, fresh, or canned

White or blue (purple) potatoes, malanga, or yuca

Cactus: fresh or canned nopalitos

Roasted red peppers. Drain 1 jar (7 oz.) **roasted red peppers;** cut into ¼-inch strips. (Or roast bell peppers, recipe follows.)

Nopalitos. Rinse ¾ cup drained, canned **nopalitos** under running water to remove slipperiness; drain. (Or use fresh nopalitos, recipe follows.)

Blue potatoes. Scrub 4 medium-size (about 1 lb. total) **blue,** purple, or thin-skinned **potatoes** and put in a 4- to 5-quart pan; add **water** to cover by 1 inch. Bring to boiling on high heat. Simmer, covered, until potatoes are tender when pierced, about 20 minutes; drain. Let cool, peel, and cut into 1-inch chunks. If made ahead, cover and chill up to 1 day. (Or use yuca or malanga, recipe follows.)

Tomatillos. Husk and rinse 4 medium-size (about ¼ lb.) **tomatillos.** Cut into thin slices. (Or use tomatoes, recipe follows.)

Carnitas. Cut 1 pound **boneless pork shoulder** or butt into ¾-inch cubes. In an 8- or 9-inch-square pan, mix meat with 3 tablespoons **vinegar,** ¼ teaspoon *each* **ground cinnamon, ground cumin,** and **chili powder.** Cover and bake in a 350° oven for 45 minutes. Uncover and bake, stirring occasionally, until pork is well browned, about 1 hour longer. Serve hot; if made ahead, cool, cover, and chill up to 3 days. To reheat, cover and bake in a 350° oven until hot, about 10 minutes.

Squash. Wash and trim ends of 4 small (about 1 lb. total) **yellow crookneck squash** or zucchini. Cut squash in half lengthwise; brush with **salad oil.** Place cut side down in an 8- or 9-inch-square pan. Bake in a 450° oven until tender when pierced, 10 to 20 minutes. Serve hot or cool. If made ahead, cover and chill up to 1 day.

Fried dried chilies. Rinse and dry 1 large **dried California (Anaheim) chili.** Break off stem, shake out seeds and discard them. Cut chili crosswise into thin strips. In an 8- to 10-inch frying pan over low heat, stir chili in 2 tablespoons **salad oil** until strips begin to curl, 2 to 3 minutes (watch closely to avoid burning). Drain. If made ahead, store airtight up to 1 week.

Orange-lime vinaigrette. Stir together 1 cup **orange juice,** ½ cup **lime juice,** 3 tablespoons minced **fresh hot red chilies,** and 3 tablespoons minced **cilantro** (coriander). If desired, also offer chipotle mayonnaise, recipe follows.

OPTIONAL INGREDIENTS

Following are additional New World ingredients you can choose to tailor a salad to your taste.

At the supermarket, you're likely to find tomatillos, jicama, cilantro, some of the chilies, all the potatoes, and the canned nopalitos.

Surprisingly, yuca and malanga are found in many supermarkets as well as in Latin markets (along with fresh nopalitos). But these roots are not very showy and are easily overlooked.

Corn: the fresh form of hominy. Use 2 cups cooked **corn kernels,** cooled; or 1 package (10 oz.) frozen whole-kernel corn, thawed.

Roasted peppers: starting fresh. Cut 2 large **red** or yellow **bell peppers** in half; remove stems and seeds. Place peppers, cut side down, in a 10- by 15-inch rimmed pan. Bake, uncovered, in a 450° oven until charred, about 25 minutes. Let stand until cool enough to touch, then pull off skin and discard. Slice or tear peppers into narrow strips. If made ahead, cover and chill up to 2 days.

Fresh nopalitos: they taste like tart green beans. Select ½ pound tender-crisp **prickly pear cactus pads** (nopal cactus or nopalitos). If pads have spines, lay each pad flat and cut away about ⅛ inch around the perimeter. Hold knife blade parallel to pad, and shave off the spines, cutting from tip to base of pad. Rinse pads, drain, and cut into ¼-inch-wide strips.

Or buy ½ pound diced fresh nopalitos.

In a 2- to 3-quart pan, bring 1 quart **water** to boiling over high heat. Add nopalitos; boil, uncovered, until tender when pierced, 5 to 7 minutes. Drain; rinse with cold **water** until cool. Drain again. If made ahead, cover and chill up to 4 days.

Yuca: a potato alternative. Pronounced *yoo*-ka, this root is also known as cassava

or manioc (*Manihot esculenta*). It's a rough-looking root or tuber, native to Brazil, that is now cultivated throughout Central and South America, Africa, and Asian countries on the Pacific Rim.

Cooked yuca is bland, not too unlike boiled potatoes, but the texture is both mealier and wetter, and often fibrous.

Select odorless, firm yuca (if it has an odor, it's beginning to decay) that is well covered with a thin, bark-like peel (patches of white, pink, or tan skin will show through from underneath) and free of cracks that suggest dryness.

Sometimes the vegetable has been dipped in wax to preserve freshness; you cut off this coating when you peel yuca to cook it.

For salad, peel about 1¼ pounds **yuca;** cut in half lengthwise and pull out fibrous cord that runs down the center. Cut yuca into 1½-inch chunks and put into a 3- to 4-quart pan. Add **water** to cover by 1 inch. Bring water to a simmer on high heat. Reduce heat to maintain a very gentle simmer (yuca falls apart and gets mushy if boiled hard); cook, uncovered, until tender when pierced, 15 to 25 minutes. Check doneness frequently and lift out cooked pieces with a slotted spoon; drain. Let cool; if made ahead, cover and chill up until next day.

Malanga: another potato alternative. Malanga or yautia (*Xanthosoma*), a tuber native to the American tropics, is covered with a thin, brown, slightly shaggy peel with patches of yellow, tan, or red skin showing through. It has a nutty, earthy taste and a soft, mealy texture.

Select pieces that are very firm and free of cracks or soft spots. Malanga, like yuca, is often waxed to help preserve freshness; peel to use.

For salad, peel 1¼ pounds **malanga** and cut into 2-inch chunks (when cut, malanga is very slippery; hold with a towel to keep a firm grip while cutting).

Place chunks in a 3- to 4-quart pan; add **water** to cover chunks by 1 inch. Bring to boiling on high heat; simmer, uncovered, until just tender-crisp when pierced, 20 to 25 minutes (if cooked until tender, malanga falls apart); drain. Let cool and use, or cover and chill up until next day. Cut into 1-inch chunks.

Vivid native foods make a salad meal: potatoes (blue), tomatillos, red bell peppers, hominy, avocado, nopalitos, squash, chilies, jicama.

Tomatoes: big and small. Use 8 medium-size, firm-ripe **cherry tomatoes;** rinse and quarter. Or use 1 large firm-ripe tomato; rinse, core, and cut into ½-inch wedges.

Chipotle mayonnaise: another dressing choice. Chipotles are red jalapeño chilies that have been dried and smoked. Here you use the canned chili with its smoky-flavor sauce.

Stir together 1 cup **mayonnaise,** 1 tablespoon minced **canned chipotle chilies with sauce,** and 1 tablespoon **wine vinegar.**

Corn Takes Center Stage

ORN TAKES CENTER STAGE *in these three vegetable main dishes. Each combination features at least one form of corn: fresh or frozen in a filling; dry, ground in tortillas and polenta; and canned in a hominy stew. The results differ from each other, but all are more than adequate nutritionally. The foods accompanying each presentation not only add interest to the menus, but they also increase protein.*

All three entrées have helpful make-ahead steps and stylish presentations. The layered polenta torte can be assembled, then baked later; so can the cheese- and corn-filled tortillas. The savory hominy and bean stew also reheats well but needs some last-minute organization.

Polenta torte—baked with cheeses, chard, and tomato sauce—goes with grilled mushrooms, endive and watercress salad, and toasted walnuts. Raspberries in glass bowl are for dessert.

POLENTA TORTE WITH CHEESE & TOMATO SAUCE

- 4½ cups water
- 1½ cups polenta
- ½ teaspoon salt (optional)
- ½ pound fontina cheese, thinly sliced
- 1 package (10 oz.) frozen chopped chard, thawed, with liquid squeezed out
  Tomato sauce (recipe follows)
- ¼ pound gorgonzola cheese, crumbled
  Fresh marjoram leaves or chopped parsley (optional)

Mix 2 cups of water with the polenta. In a 4- to 5-quart pan over high heat, bring remaining water to a boil with salt; gradually stir in polenta mixture. Reduce heat and simmer gently, stirring with a long-handled spoon (the polenta spatters), until mixture is very thick and reduced to 4½ cups, 2 to 3 minutes.

Pour polenta into a 5- by 9-inch loaf pan; let cool. If made ahead, cover and chill up to 2 days. Run a knife around polenta; invert pan and shake gently to release. Pull a thread horizontally through polenta loaf to slice it into thirds.

Place largest slice of polenta on an oven-proof serving platter, at least 7 by 11 inches. Evenly distribute ⅓ of the fontina and ½ of the chard over the slice. Top with middle layer of polenta, half the remaining fontina, and all the remaining chard. Top with the last polenta slice; cover with remaining fontina. Spoon ⅓ cup of the tomato sauce on top of the polenta torte, then scatter gorgonzola over the sauce. If made ahead, cover and chill up to 6 hours.

Bake, uncovered, in a 350° oven until polenta is hot in center (cut to test) and cheese is browned at edges, about 35 minutes. Scatter marjoram leaves on torte; cut diagonally into 6 wedges; serve with hot tomato sauce. Makes 6 servings.

PER SERVING: 416 calories, 19 g protein, 41 g carbohydrates, 20 g fat, 58 mg cholesterol, 649 mg sodium

Tomato sauce. In a 10- to 12-inch frying pan, stir over medium heat ½ cup minced **onion** and 1 clove minced or pressed **garlic** in 1 tablespoon **olive oil** or salad oil until onion begins to brown on edges, about 5 minutes. Add 2 tablespoons chopped **fresh basil leaves** or 1 tablespoon dry basil leaves, 1 teaspoon chopped **fresh marjoram leaves** or ½ teaspoon dry marjoram leaves, 1 can (15 oz.) **tomato purée,** and 1½ cups **water.** Simmer, uncovered, until reduced to 2½ cups, about 15 minutes. Use hot or reheat; if made ahead, cool, cover, and chill up to 1 day.

CORN RISOTTO IN CORN TORTILLA CRÊPES

- 1 small head fennel (about 12 oz.) with lots of feathery leaves
- 1 large onion
- 5 tablespoons butter or margarine
- 4 cups corn kernels (cut from about 6 large ears), or 2 packages (10-oz. size) frozen whole-kernel corn, thawed
- 1 cup water
- 1 vegetable or chicken bouillon cube
- ¼ teaspoon fennel seed, crushed
- ½ pound havarti cheese, shredded
- 8 corn tortillas (6- to 7-in. size)

Remove feathery leaves from fennel and chill them in a plastic bag. Trim stalks and any discoloration from head, then finely chop the head along with onion.

Melt butter in a 10- to 12-inch frying pan. Remove 1 tablespoon and set aside. Add onion and fennel to pan and stir often over medium-high heat until onion is slightly browned, about 5 minutes.

Add corn, water, bouillon cube, and fennel seed. Stir on high heat until most of the liquid has boiled away, 8 to 10 minutes; remove from heat. Stir cheese into corn mixture and set aside.

If desired, cut half of each tortilla into a point. Immerse tortillas, one at a time, in simmering water just long enough to soften (if too wet, tortilla will tear); drain and place in lightly oiled 10- by 15-inch baking pan; spoon ⅛ of the corn mixture in a band over the uncut half (or half) of the tortilla; fold pointed half (or other half) over filling.

Repeat to fill remaining tortillas; place filled tortillas slightly apart in pan. Brush with reserved melted butter. If made ahead, keep airtight, at room temperature, up to 4 hours.

Bake tortillas, uncovered, in a 400° oven until filling is hot in center, 7 to 10 minutes. Garnish with reserved fennel sprigs. Makes 4 servings, 2 tortillas each.

PER SERVING: 642 calories, 25 g protein, 61 g carbohydrates, 36 g fat, 105 mg cholesterol, 583 mg sodium

PUEBLO STEW WITH TORTILLA LIDS

>   1 large onion, chopped
>   2 cloves garlic, minced or pressed
> 1½ tablespoons chili powder
>   2 teaspoons cumin seed
>   1 teaspoon dry oregano leaves
>   2 tablespoons olive oil or salad oil
>   1 *each* medium-size zucchini, pattypan, and crookneck squash, cut into 1-inch chunks
>   1 can (14½ oz.) golden hominy, drained
>   1 pound firm-ripe tomatoes, cored and chopped
>   ¼ pound green beans, ends trimmed, cut into 1-inch lengths
>   2 cans (1 lb. each) pinto beans
>   4 vegetable or chicken bouillon cubes
>   2 cups water
>   1 tablespoon minced fresh cilantro (coriander)
>   Warm tortillas (directions follow)
>   Cilantro sprigs
>   About 1 cup sour cream
>   About 1 cup (4 oz.) shredded jack cheese

In a 4- to 5-quart pan, cook onion, garlic, chili powder, cumin, and oregano in oil on medium-high heat until onion begins to brown, about 7 minutes; stir occasionally. Mix in squash, hominy, and tomatoes, and cook until tomatoes begin to fall apart, about 5 minutes. Add green beans, pinto beans, bouillon cubes, and water.

Simmer, uncovered, until green beans and squash are tender when pierced and mixture is the consistency of thick stew, about 30 minutes. If made ahead, cool, cover, and chill up to 1 day, then reheat. Add minced cilantro and ladle stew into 4 straight-sided bowls, at least 2-cup size.

Hominy and bean stew stays warm under flour tortilla lid; lid stays hot, too. Use tortilla as bread or wrapper for stew, adding cheese and sour cream to taste. Serve with grilled green onions.

Lay a warm tortilla over each bowl and, if desired, tie tortilla in place with raffia or string. Garnish with cilantro sprigs. Accompany each with sour cream and cheese to add to taste. Eat tortilla with stew, or spoon stew into tortilla to eat out of hand. Serves 4.

PER SERVING: 719 calories, 27 g protein, 81 g carbohydrates, 32 g fat, 50 mg cholesterol, 2,322 mg sodium

Warm tortillas. Stack 4 (7- to 8-in. size) **flour tortillas** and enclose in foil or plastic wrap. Bake foil-wrapped tortillas in a 350° oven until hot, about 10 minutes. Or microwave plastic-wrapped tortillas at full power (100 percent) until hot, about 40 seconds.

Garden Snails as Escargots

SLITHERING THROUGH *your garden, the common brown snail* (Helix aspersa) *is usually viewed with contempt. If you've thrown your hands up in despair of ridding your yard of these nibbling pests, it's time to take a stand. Arm yourself with a pot and the following savory recipes.*

For you have genuine escargot on the hoof. In France, this same snail is known as petit-gris.

STALKING THE SNAIL

Snails are strictly nocturnal. By day they hide in cool, moist places. At night they feed on your tender, succulent plants. You'll find them most easily in the gray light of morning.

For easiest collecting, create an area snails will like. Prop a wide board about 2 inches above the ground in a grassy area. Spray the board with water to keep it damp. Lightly water the lawn in the evening, after the sun has set. Snails will attach to the underside of the board to rest during the day—ready for you to pluck them away.

Snails smaller than 1 inch aren't worth the trouble to gather, clean, and cook.

Once you have your prey, proceed as follows—each step is important. You can have escargots on the table in about four days, or keep them for several weeks.

Or take the easy way out. Buy canned snails, and skip to the recipes.

A WORD ABOUT PESTICIDES

Gather snails from areas you know have not been treated with pesticides. Even so, snails travel, so it is essential to purge them (directions follow) to ensure your safety. If snails have ingested any toxic substances, they will die during the purging process; if they survive, any residue they contain is considered insignificant.

PURGING & FATTENING

To purge snails, first rinse them in a colander to clean off debris and soil, then put them in a large, clean container such as a bucket or dish pan. A gallon container is adequate for 2 dozen snails; the plastic dish tub (see below) will hold about 5 dozen. In the container, put a shallow dish with ¼ to ½ inch of water.

Cover the container securely with nylon netting (such as tulle or curtain fabric), several layers of cheesecloth, or a lid with plenty of tiny air holes. If there are any openings, the snails are apt to work their way out.

Keep the container out of direct sunlight and in a cool part of the room. At least every other day, rinse snails, change water, and clean the container; otherwise unpleasant odors will develop.

Check daily and discard any dead snails. Scratch the snail's foot to check; if it doesn't twitch, the snail is dead.

The snails' systems will be clear in about four days, but you can house them longer and fatten them as follows.

Clean the container, then put about 3 tablespoons cornmeal for each dozen snails. Return water dish and snails, and cover. Replace cornmeal each time you clean; increase or decrease the amount as necessary. Feed up to 2 weeks, then give water only for 2 days.

SHELLED SNAILS

Bring 1½ quarts **water** to boiling in a 3- to 4-quart pan over high heat. Rinse up to 4 cups **purged snails** (preceding) under cool running water to remove debris. Immediately pour snails into the boiling water; boil, uncovered, 2 to 3 minutes. Watch carefully, since a lot of foam develops.

Drain snails and rinse with cold water. With a slender wooden pick, pierce each snail and pull from shell. Cut off and discard gall (the coiled section that comes out of the shell last).

Favorite hiding places are the undersides of moist boards, leaves, and such; you can set up a lure like this. Best hunting is in A.M.

Purge snails for at least four days—keep in a securely covered, ventilated container; provide water. Rinse at least every other day.

Pull boiled snail from shell, using a small wooden pick or skewer.

Cut away the coiled section that was deep inside the shell. Continue cooking the snails until tender.

In a bowl, mix 1½ quarts cool **water** and ⅓ cup **vinegar.** Add snails and gently stir until water is cloudy, 2 to 3 minutes; drain and rinse snails. Repeat 2 or 3 times more, or until liquid remains clear.

COOKED SNAILS

In a 3- to 4-quart pan, mix freshly shelled or canned **snails** (up to 2 cups, about 12 oz., preceding); 3 cups **regular-strength beef broth;** 1 small **onion,** sliced; 1 **bay leaf;** and ½ teaspoon **dry thyme leaves.**

Bring mixture to boiling, uncovered, over high heat; reduce heat and simmer, uncovered, until snails are very tender when pierced, about 30 minutes if canned, 1 hour if fresh. Drain snails and use in one of the following recipes. If cooked ahead, cool, cover, and chill up to 2 days; or freeze up to 3 months.

CRISP-BAKED SNAILS IN HERB BUTTER

1 or 2 large heads Belgian endive (about 6 oz. each), leaves separated and rinsed
   About ⅓ cup soft unripened goat cheese or herb-flavor soft cheese spread
1 large egg
1½ cups (9 oz.) cooked snails (preceding)
¼ to ⅓ cup fine dry bread crumbs
   Garlic herb butter (recipe follows)
   Parsley sprigs

Select 16 or 20 perfect large endive leaves. Mound cheese equally in the stem end of each leaf; set aside.

In a small bowl, beat egg to blend. Add the cooked snails and mix with egg. Lift out snails, 1 at a time, and coat with bread crumbs. Place snails about 1 inch apart in a buttered 10- by 15-inch baking pan. Bake in a 400° oven, turning once with spatula, until crisp to touch and lightly browned, about 15 minutes.

Melt herb butter (in pan over low heat or in nonmetal container in microwave oven); keep warm.

Arrange an equal number of endive leaves on 4 dinner plates; cluster an equal number of the snails on each plate. Drizzle snails with butter and garnish with parsley. Makes 4 first-course servings.

PER SERVING: 278 calories, 19 g protein, 8 g carbohydrates, 19 g fat, 140 mg cholesterol, 423 mg sodium

Garlic herb butter. In a bowl, stir until blended ¼ cup (⅛ lb.) **butter** or margarine, at room temperature; 1 large clove **garlic,** pressed or minced; 1 tablespoon finely chopped **fresh chives;** 1 tablespoon **lemon juice;** and ⅛ teaspoon **cracked black pepper.** Makes ¼ cup.

SNAILS IN PASTRY SHELLS

1 sheet (½ of a 17¼-oz. package) frozen puff pastry, thawed
   About 1 cup (2 packages, each 4 oz.) garlic- and herb-flavor soft cheese spread
2¼ cups (13½ oz.) cooked snails (preceding)
1 large egg

On a lightly floured board, roll pastry into an 18-inch square. Cut into 36 pieces, each 3 inches square. Spoon a rounded teaspoon of cheese onto the center of each pastry and press an equal amount of snails into each mound of cheese. Beat egg to blend, then brush on pastry rims. On each pastry, bring edges together and press firmly to seal. Set pastries, sealed side down, in a 10- by 15-inch pan. (If made ahead, cover and chill up to next day.)

Brush pastries with egg. Bake in a 400° oven until golden brown, about 15 minutes. With a spatula, transfer pastries to a platter. Makes 12 appetizer servings.

PER SERVING: 195 calories, 9 g protein, 9 g carbohydrates, 13 g fat, 64 mg cholesterol, 186 mg sodium

SNAILS WITH BRUSSELS SPROUTS

3 tablespoons olive oil or salad oil
4 medium-size heads garlic
2 or 3 large Brussels sprouts
6 slices firm white bread (3¾- by 4¼- in. slices, ¼ inch thick)
1 cup regular-strength chicken broth
½ cup whipping cream
½ teaspoon fresh thyme leaves, chopped, or ¼ teaspoon dry thyme leaves
1½ cups (9 oz.) cooked snails (preceding)

Pour oil into an 8- to 9-inch-square pan. Cut garlic in half crosswise, handling gently to hold cloves in head.

Set garlic, cut side down, in pan. Bake in a 350° oven until garlic is richly browned on bottom (take care not to scorch), about 45 minutes.

Meanwhile, carefully remove large outer leaves from each sprout. Select

Brussels sprout leaves cradle snails; eat with roasted garlic.

24 of the largest, most perfect leaves; reserve remaining sprouts for other uses. In a 3- to 4-quart pan, bring about 3 inches of water to boiling on high heat. Drop leaves into boiling water and immediately lift out with a slotted spoon; immerse in ice water, then drain on paper towels.

If made ahead, garlic and leaves can sit at room temperature up to 4 hours.

Trim crusts from bread; cut slices in half diagonally. Lay bread triangles in a single layer in a 10- by 12-inch baking pan. Bake in a 350° oven until bread is toasted on top, about 3 minutes; turn pieces and continue baking until toasted on other side, about 2 minutes longer.

While bread toasts, boil broth, cream, and thyme leaves in a 2- to 3-quart pan, uncovered, on high heat, until reduced to ¾ cup, about 12 minutes. Add snails and slowly simmer until snails are hot, about 3 minutes.

Cluster 6 sprout leaves, cup up, on 1 side of each of 4 hot plates; quickly nestle an equal number of snails in each leaf. Spoon sauce around or over the snails. On each plate, place 2 garlic halves and 3 toast triangles. Spread baked garlic on toast to eat with the snails and sauce. Makes 4 first-course servings.

PER SERVING: 362 calories, 18 g protein, 25 g carbohydrates, 22 g fat, 74 mg cholesterol, 412 mg sodium

Cooking with Norwegian Cheese

FROM THE DAIRIES OF NORWAY *come three cheeses, each with special properties well suited to these dishes.*

Most familiar is jarlsberg, with its pale golden color and shiny holes. Similar to Swiss (emmenthal) cheese but milder in flavor, jarlsberg doesn't flow away when melted, yet tastes velvet smooth; it's particularly good for the grilled sandwich.

Widely available but less well known—and with a limited but devoted following—is gjetost (say yeah-toast), a firm brown cheese. You'll find it in ½-pound bricks or cut to order at the supermarket. With reason, Norwegians call it "brown cheese"; they start most days with paper-thin slices on buttered bread.

Gjetost is made of goat's milk, cow's milk, and whey, boiled until the mixture looks like caramel and tastes distinctively sweet. When melted and blended with sour cream to coat these meatballs, the cheese makes a complex-tasting sauce, delicious on the meat and baked potatoes that can accompany this entrée.

Look for the third, nokkelost, in your supermarket's specialty cheese section or in cheese shops. Its color and texture resemble jack cheese, but it's smoother and studded with a seasoning mix of allspice, cloves, and cumin. (A similar, less complex Scandinavian cheese is kuminost.)

This spicing makes nokkelost good for salads; here it's coated with crumbs, baked until crusty outside, creamy inside, then served with hot red cabbage.

Crumb-coated baked nokkelost tops hot cabbage salad; serve with dark rye triangles.

GRILLED JARLSBERG CHEESE SANDWICH

1 large onion, thinly sliced
About 2 tablespoons butter or margarine
4 slices firm white bread
4 to 6 ounces jarlsberg (or Swiss) cheese, thinly sliced

In a 10- to 12-inch frying pan on medium heat, stir often 1 tablespoon of the butter and onion until onion is very soft and golden, about 30 minutes.

Spread 1 side of bread slices with remaining butter. Mound onion equally on unbuttered side of 2 slices; top with cheese. Set bread, buttered side up, on cheese.

Place sandwiches in frying pan and cook, covered, on medium-low heat until cheese is soft and bread is browned, about 12 minutes total; turn sandwiches once. Remove from pan, cut in half diagonally, and serve hot. Makes 2 servings.

PER SERVING: 472 calories, 21 g protein, 32 g carbohydrates, 29 g fat, 85 mg cholesterol, 509 mg sodium

NORWEGIAN MEATBALLS WITH GJETOST SAUCE

1 pound ground lean pork or lean beef (or ½ of each)
1 large egg
¾ cup regular-strength chicken broth
¼ cup all-purpose flour
¼ cup half-and-half (light cream) or milk
½ cup shredded gjetost cheese
⅓ cup sour cream
1 tablespoon chopped fresh dill
Salt and pepper
Fresh dill sprigs

Mix pork, egg, ½ cup of the broth, and flour. Shape into 1-inch balls and place slightly apart in an ungreased 10- by 15-inch pan. Bake in a 450° oven until well browned, about 15 minutes. Loosen meatballs from pan with a spatula; keep them warm in pan.

In a 1½- to 2-quart pan on medium heat, bring remaining broth and the half-and-half to steaming; do not boil. Add gjetost and stir until melted. Turn heat to low and stir in sour cream and chopped dill. Add meatballs and drippings; stir to mix. Add salt and pepper to taste, then pour into a bowl. Garnish with dill sprigs. Makes 4 main-dish servings.

PER SERVING: 355 calories, 27 g protein, 14 g carbohydrates, 21 g fat, 158 mg cholesterol, 215 mg sodium

RED CABBAGE SALAD WITH BAKED NOKKELOST

1 medium-size crisp red apple such as Winesap or Red Delicious
1 small head (about 1 lb.) red cabbage
1 clove garlic, minced or pressed
¼ cup balsamic or red wine vinegar
¼ cup olive oil or salad oil
1 medium-size onion, quartered and thinly sliced crosswise
Walnuts, nokkelost, and toast (directions follow)
Salt and pepper

Core apple, cut into 6 wedges, then thinly slice wedges crosswise; put in a small bowl and cover with water.

Rinse cabbage and remove 4 large perfect leaves; finely shred head of cabbage.

In a 10- to 12-inch frying pan on medium-high heat, combine garlic, vinegar, and oil; when hot, add onion. Mix well. Add cabbage; cook and stir until just wilted, about 2 minutes. Drain apple and add with the walnuts to cabbage.

Put a cabbage leaf on each plate and mound salad into it; with spatula, top with cheese. Serve with toast and salt and pepper to taste. Makes 4 main-dish servings.

PER SERVING: 628 calories, 21 g protein, 41 g carbohydrates, 45 g fat, 106 mg cholesterol, 489 mg sodium

Walnuts, nokkelost, and toast. Pour ¾ cup **walnuts** into an 8- or 9-inch round or square baking pan. Bake in a 350° oven until nuts are lightly toasted, about 10 minutes; remove nuts and set aside.

Trim crusts from 5 slices **dark rye bread;** cut each into 4 triangles. Brush pieces lightly with **olive oil** (use about 2 teaspoons total); place in 10- by 15-inch pan.

Cut 6 ounces **nokkelost** (or kuminost or jack cheese) into 4 pieces, each ½ inch thick. In a small bowl, beat 1 **large egg** to blend; put ¼ cup **fine dry bread crumbs** in another small bowl. Mix cheese with egg. Lift out 1 piece at a time and coat with crumbs. Then, 1 piece at a time, recoat with egg, then crumbs. Place cheese pieces well apart in pan used for nuts.

Bake bread triangles and cheese in a 500° oven until they are slightly darker brown, about 5 minutes.

Giant Doughnuts from Italy

THESE GIANT DOUGHNUTS *from Italy were treats originally reserved for special festival days only. Now, though, street vendors hawk the nutmeg-fragrant pastries year-round. With the recipe given here, you don't even have to be in Rome to do as the Romans do.*

Made from cream-puff dough, the large rings are easily shaped: pipe the dough onto pieces of foil, then slip the dough and foil into hot oil to fry the pastry (the foil slides free). The rings are tender-crisp outside, moist and tender inside. While still warm, shake them with sugar and nutmeg; they're good warm, or saved until the next day.

PIAZZA GRANDE DOUGHNUTS

- 1 **cup water**
- ½ **cup (¼ lb.) butter or margarine**
- ½ **cup sugar**
- 1¼ **cups all-purpose flour**
- 4 **large eggs**
- 1 **teaspoon vanilla**
- 1 **teaspoon ground nutmeg**
  Salad oil

Cut 6 squares of foil, each about 7 inches. Butter 1 side of each.

In a 2½- to 3-quart pan, combine water, butter, and ¼ cup sugar. Bring to a rolling boil over medium heat, stirring until butter has melted. Add flour all at once, and beat vigorously with a spoon until dough is smooth and forms a ball; continue to cook, stirring, for 1 minute.

Remove from heat and add eggs, 1 at a time, beating until each is well mixed and dough is glossy (or whirl in a food processor, adding eggs 1 at a time). Beat in vanilla and ½ teaspoon nutmeg.

Spoon dough into a pastry bag fitted with a ¾-inch plain tip. Onto each sheet of foil, pipe dough to form rings that are about 5½ inches in diameter; use all the dough.

Pour 1 inch salad oil into a deep, 4- to 5-quart pan. On high heat, bring oil to 370° to 375°; adjust heat to maintain temperature. With a wide spatula, transfer a sheet of foil with dough on it to hot oil (foil floats free; lift out with tongs).

Cook until doughnut is richly browned, about 5 minutes; turn after each minute. Lift out doughnut and drain on paper towels. Repeat to cook remaining rings of dough.

In a plastic bag, combine remaining sugar and nutmeg. When doughnuts are almost cool, put into bag, 1 at a time, and shake to coat well with sugar mixture. Serve, or store airtight until next day. Makes 6.

PER DOUGHNUT: 432 calories, 7 g protein, 37 g carbohydrates, 29 g fat, 224 mg cholesterol, 203 mg sodium

Fragrant with nutmeg, super-size doughnut is best eaten warm (but extras will keep a day).

1 *Squeeze dough from a pastry bag onto a 7-inch square of foil; lap ends.*

2 *Immerse ring, on foil square, in hot oil. Ring will slip off once immersed; lift out foil with tongs. Fry pastry.*

3 *Gently shake doughnut in a bag filled with granulated sugar and nutmeg; coat well.*

Strawberry Stunners

WONDERFUL ON THEIR OWN, *strawberries are stunning with a little embellishment to spotlight their beauty and flavor.*

A cloud of soft meringue floats on a bed of warm, orange-flavored berries in the first simple dessert. Chocolate cages hold kirsch-flavored berries and cream in the second choice.

MERINGUE CLOUD WITH STRAWBERRIES

    2 tablespoons pine nuts or slivered
       almonds
    6 cups strawberries, rinsed, hulled,
       and sliced
       About ½ cup granulated sugar
    ¼ cup orange-flavor liqueur or
       orange juice
    3 large egg whites
    ¼ teaspoon cream of tartar
    1 tablespoon powdered sugar

Place nuts in an 8- or 9-inch pie or cake pan and bake in a 350° oven until golden, about 10 minutes. Remove nuts from oven. Turn oven temperature to 500°.

Meanwhile, mix strawberries with 1 to 2 tablespoons granulated sugar (to taste), and liqueur. Pour into a shallow 2- to 3-quart serving pan or ovenproof dish.

In a large bowl, combine egg whites and cream of tartar; beat with an electric mixer on high speed until foamy. Gradually add 6 tablespoons granulated sugar,

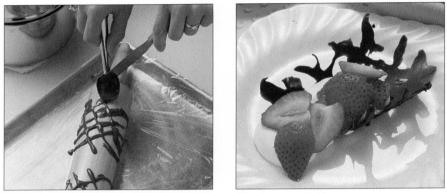

Drizzle melted chocolate over rolling pin to make see-through cages to hold cream and berries.

beating just until whites will hold stiff, moist peaks. Mound mixture over center of strawberries. Sprinkle with nuts. Sift powdered sugar on top of meringue.

Bake in a 500° oven just until top is golden, about 4 minutes. Serve at once. Makes 6 servings.

PER SERVING: 150 calories, 3 g protein, 32 g carbohydrates, 2 g fat, 0 mg cholesterol, 27 mg sodium

CHOCOLATE CAGES WITH STRAWBERRIES

    ½ cup semisweet chocolate baking
       chips
    2 teaspoons solid shortening
    3 cups strawberries, rinsed, hulled,
       and sliced

    2 tablespoons sugar
    2 tablespoons kirsch or light rum
    ½ cup whipping cream, softly
       whipped, or about 1½ cups
       vanilla ice cream

Smoothly wrap a rolling pin with a piece of plastic wrap; line a 10- by 15-inch pan with plastic wrap. Set the pin diagonally across pan.

Stir chocolate with shortening in the top of a double boiler over hot water just until melted. (Or heat in a nonmetal bowl in a microwave oven at half-power—50 percent—until melted, about 3 minutes; stir occasionally.) Place over hot water to keep fluid.

With a spoon, drizzle streaks of the melted chocolate diagonally over the curve of the rolling pin to make 4 or 5 lines (each 4 to 5 in. long) about ½ inch apart. Repeat in the opposite direction, crossing the first lines (the lines do not need to be perfectly straight: see picture above). Make another cage the same way. Chill until firm, about 10 minutes. Gently lift plastic wrap off rolling pin and peel wrap from chocolate. Repeat with remaining chocolate to make 2 more chocolate cages. If made ahead, store cages, covered, in refrigerator up to 2 days.

Mix strawberries with sugar and kirsch.

To serve, place 1 chocolate cage concave side up on a dessert plate. Spoon ¼ of the cream or small scoops of the ice cream into and spilling out of the cage. Spoon about ¼ of the strawberries onto the cream. Makes 4 servings.

PER SERVING: 293 calories, 2 g protein, 29 g carbohydrates, 19 g fat, 33 mg cholesterol, 12 mg sodium

Sugar- and nut-crusted cloud of meringue bakes briefly on a bed of orange-scented berries.

More May Recipes

OTHER MAY ARTICLES *suggested a terrine pairing lox and cream cheese, a pair of soups featuring artichokes and corn, biscuits made with crunchy polenta, sliced eggplant "crêpes" folded around a pesto filling, orange-flavored risotto with shrimp, and a papaya and tomatillo relish.*

LOX & CHEESE TERRINE

Stack the elements of that classic duo, lox and cream cheese, in this handsome terrine. It's simple and smashing.

  1 **large package (8 oz.) and 1 small package (3 oz.) cream cheese, at room temperature**
  2 **tablespoons chopped fresh dill**
  2 **tablespoons lemon juice**
  6 **ounces thinly sliced cured salmon (lox)**
     Crisp red onions (recipe follows)
 12 **small bagels, split and toasted**
     Fresh dill sprigs

Beat together until blended cream cheese, chopped dill, and lemon juice. Line a 3- by 6-inch loaf pan with plastic wrap. Line the bottom of the pan with ⅕ of the lox. Spread ¼ of the cheese mixture in an even layer over lox. Cover with ⅕ of the lox, and repeat layers, ending with lox. Gently press to even out layers. Cover and chill until firm, at least 3 hours or up to 2 days.

Lift terrine out of pan and remove plastic wrap. With a thin, sharp knife, cut terrine into ½-inch-thick slices and place on salad plates alongside crisp red onions and bagels. Garnish with dill sprigs. To eat, spread terrine on bagels and add onions. Makes 12 first-course servings.

Crisp red onions. Thinly slice 1 medium-size **red onion.** Immerse in a mixture of 2 cups **water,** ⅓ cup **vinegar,** and 2 cups **ice cubes.** Let stand until crisp, about 20 minutes. Drain and lift out onions.

PER SERVING: 188 calories, 8 g protein, 17 g carbohydrates, 10 g fat, 32 mg cholesterol, 364 mg sodium

ARTICHOKE SOUP WITH TOASTED HAZELNUTS

The distinct flavors of artichokes and hazelnuts team superbly to make this elegant, fine-textured soup. Large artichokes, abundant right now, should be a good buy.

Layered lox and cream cheese: spread on bagel and top with red onion slices.

  1 **cup hazelnuts**
  ¼ **cup lemon juice**
  6 **large (3 in. across) artichokes**
  2 **tablespoons butter or margarine**
  1 *each* **large carrot and large onion, chopped**
  ¼ **teaspoon white pepper**
  5 **cups regular-strength chicken broth**

Place nuts in an 8- or 9-inch-wide pan. Bake in a 350° oven until golden brown beneath skins, 18 to 20 minutes; shake pan occasionally. Pour nuts onto a towel and rub with cloth to remove most of the skins. Chop coarsely; set aside.

In a 6- to 8-quart pan, combine 4 quarts water with lemon juice; set aside.

Pull off and discard artichokes' tough outer leaves. Trim stem flush with bottom and pare any coarse fibers. Drop into water as trimmed. Cover and bring to a boil over high heat; simmer until bottoms are tender when pierced, 30 to 35 minutes. Drain and let cool. Scrape and reserve pulp from leaves; discard leaves. Scoop out and discard fuzzy centers; coarsely chop bottoms.

Melt butter in a 4- to 5-quart pan on medium heat. Add carrot and onion; stir often until lightly browned, 12 to 15 minutes. In a blender or food processor, whirl carrot, onion, pepper, ⅓ cup hazelnuts, and artichoke pulp and bottoms, adding enough broth to make a smooth purée. Return to pan; add remaining broth. Stir until hot, 5 to 10 minutes. Garnish servings with remaining nuts. Serves 6 to 8.

PER SERVING: 252 calories, 8 g protein, 21 g carbohydrates, 17 g fat, 10 mg cholesterol, 172 mg sodium

(Continued on next page)

Hearty broth-based soup is packed with chicken, vegetables, and cream-style corn.

CHICKEN CORN SOUP

Cream-style corn—from a can—gives this simple-to-prepare whole-meal soup its richness and body while adding a touch of subtle sweetness.

- 6 **cups regular-strength chicken broth**
- 1 **broiler-fryer chicken (3 to 3½ lb.), cut up**
- 1 **large onion, chopped**
- 2 **medium-size carrots, peeled and chopped**
- 1½ **cups chopped celery**
- 1 **large (about ½ lb.) russet potato, peeled and diced**
- 3 **tablespoons minced parsley**
- ¼ **cup canned tomato sauce**
- 2 **medium-size zucchini, ends trimmed and coarsely chopped**
- 1 **can (17 oz.) cream-style corn**
  Freshly ground pepper

In a 5- to 6-quart pan, combine broth, chicken except breast pieces, onion, carrots, celery, potato, parsley, and tomato sauce; bring to boiling over high heat. Cover and simmer for 20 minutes. Add breasts; cover, and continue simmering until breast pieces are no longer pink in thickest part (cut to test), 15 to 20 minutes longer. Lift out chicken and cool.

Continue simmering soup, covered, over low heat. When chicken is cool enough to handle (about 20 minutes), add zucchini to soup. Then quickly pull and discard skin and bones from chicken; tear meat into bite-size pieces. Skim off and discard fat from soup. Add chicken and corn; simmer, covered, until hot, about 3 minutes. Add pepper to taste. Makes about 3½ quarts, 6 to 8 servings. —*Georgianna Smith, Redwood City, Calif.*

PER SERVING: 239 calories, 23 g protein, 23 g carbohydrates, 7 g fat, 59 mg cholesterol, 344 mg sodium

SWEET POLENTA BUTTER BISCUITS

Dusted with a snow of powdered sugar, these rich, golden butter biscuits blend the texture of Italian-style polenta with the sweetness of Southern corn muffins.

What's the difference between polenta and cornmeal? Polenta tends to be more coarsely ground.

- ¾ **cup (⅜ lb.) butter or margarine, at room temperature**
  About ½ cup granulated sugar
- 2 **large egg yolks**
- ¼ **teaspoon almond extract**
- ⅓ **cup milk**
  About 2 cups all-purpose flour
- 1 **cup polenta or yellow cornmeal**
- 2 **teaspoons baking powder**
- ⅛ **teaspoon ground nutmeg**
- ¼ **cup powdered sugar**

In a large bowl, beat butter and ½ cup granulated sugar until fluffy. Add egg yolks, beat well, then mix in almond extract and ¼ cup milk. Stir together 2 cups flour, polenta, baking powder, and nutmeg. Add to butter mixture; blend well.

On a lightly floured board, shape dough into a 2½-inch-diameter log. Cut into 12 equal slices. Place each slice about 1½ inches apart on a greased 12- by 15-inch baking sheet. Pinch tops to taper sides slightly, creating little mounds.

Brush biscuits with remaining milk, then sprinkle with 1 tablespoon granulated sugar. Sift powdered sugar evenly over all. Bake in a 375° oven until tops look crackled and edges are golden, 16 to 18 minutes. Serve warm or at room temperature. Store airtight up to 2 days; freeze to store longer. Makes 12.

PER BISCUIT: 282 calories, 4 g protein, 37 g carbohydrates, 13 g fat, 78 mg cholesterol, 195 mg sodium

EGGPLANT PESTO CRÊPES

These uncommon "crêpes" begin with slender slices of baked eggplant, which you fold around pesto filling, then bake.

- 1 **large eggplant (1½ to 2 lb., 4 to 5 in. wide), stem cut off**
- ¼ **cup olive oil**
  Pesto filling (recipe follows)
- ⅓ **cup shredded jack cheese**

Cut eggplant lengthwise into even ¼-inch-thick slices. Lay 10 to 12 of the largest slices in a single layer in 2 or 3 baking pans, 10- by 15-inch size. Reserve small slices for another use. Brush all with oil. Bake in a 425° oven until soft when pressed and lightly browned on bottom, 14 to 18 minutes. Let cool, then loosen slices with a wide spatula.

Spoon 2 to 3 tablespoons pesto filling onto each eggplant slice; fold sides over

Golden polenta gives these sweet biscuits a pleasant crunch and nutty corn flavor.

filling. Place seam side down in a greased, shallow baking dish about 9 by 13 inches. Sprinkle cheese in a band across crêpes. If made ahead, cover and chill up to overnight (filling may darken slightly).

Bake in a 350° oven until hot in center, 15 to 20 minutes. Makes 10 to 12 crêpes, 5 or 6 first-course or 3 or 4 entrée servings. —*Sheryl Benesch, Guerneville, Calif.*

PER CRÊPE: 139 calories, 6 g protein, 6 g carbohydrates, 11 g fat, 34 mg cholesterol, 108 mg sodium

Pesto filling. In a food processor or blender, combine 2 cups lightly packed **fresh basil leaves** (coarsely chopped if using a blender), 2 tablespoons **olive oil,** 3 or 4 cloves **garlic,** ½ cup grated **parmesan cheese,** 1 cup **ricotta cheese,** 1 **large egg yolk,** ¼ teaspoon *each* **ground nutmeg** and **dry oregano,** and ⅛ teaspoon **ground white pepper.** Whirl until smoothly blended.

ORANGE RISOTTO WITH SHRIMP

The perfume and sweet tang of fresh orange penetrates rice in an elegant risotto that complements marsala and shrimp.

-   3   **tablespoons butter or margarine**
-   1   **medium-size onion, minced**
-   1½ **cups short-grain white rice (such as pearl)**
-   1   **teaspoon grated orange peel**
-   1   **cup** *each* **orange juice and dry white wine**
-   2   **cups regular-strength chicken broth**
        Shrimp with marsala (recipe follows)

In a 10-inch frying pan or 4- to 5-quart pan over medium heat, melt butter; add onion. Cook, stirring often, until onion is slightly golden, about 6 minutes. Add rice and orange peel; stir often until most of the rice is opaque, about 4 minutes.

Add orange juice, wine, and broth; bring to a boil over high heat. Reduce heat and simmer, uncovered, stirring occasionally at first and then more often to prevent scorching as liquid is absorbed, until rice is tender to bite, about 40 minutes. Spoon onto a warm platter; keep warm while preparing shrimp. Serves 4. —*Sergio Battistetti, Ilima Hotel, Honolulu.*

PER SERVING: 581 calories, 30 g protein, 73 g carbohydrates, 18 g fat, 211 mg cholesterol, 352 mg sodium

Shrimp in marsala sauce with thyme seasoning rest on mellow risotto; orange garnish echoes risotto's citrus flavor.

Shrimp with marsala. In the same pan used for risotto, combine 2 tablespoons **butter** or margarine, ¾ cup **dry white wine,** and 1¼ teaspoons **dry thyme leaves.** Bring to boiling, uncovered, on high heat. Add 1 pound shelled and deveined medium-large **shrimp** (36 to 42 per lb.). Cook, stirring often, until shrimp are opaque in center (cut to test), about 2 minutes. Using a slotted spoon, transfer shrimp onto warm risotto; keep warm. To pan juices, add 3 tablespoons **marsala,** madeira, or medium-dry sherry; boil on high heat, uncovered, until slightly syrupy and reduced to about ¼ cup. Pour sauce over shrimp.

PAPAYA & TOMATILLO RELISH

Sweet papayas and tart tomatillos combine to make an unusual fruit relish.

Serve this versatile condiment hot or cold to accompany grilled lamb, pork chops, hamburgers, or curries.

-   1   **tablespoon salad oil**
-   ½   **small onion, thinly sliced**
-   ¼   **teaspoon ground cinnamon**
-   ⅛   **teaspoon cayenne**
-   1   **pound fresh tomatillos, husked, rinsed, cored, and finely chopped**
-   1   **large (about ¾ lb.) ripe papaya, peeled, seeded, and cut into** ¼-inch chunks
-   ⅓   **cup cider vinegar**
-   ¼   **cup firmly packed brown sugar**
-   ¼   **cup currants**

In a 10- to 12-inch frying pan over medium heat, cook oil, onion, cinnamon, and cayenne; stir often until onion is limp, about 7 minutes. Add tomatillos, papaya, vinegar, sugar, and currants. Boil, uncovered, over high heat, stirring occasionally, until liquid has cooked away, about 12 minutes. Serve; or cool, cover, and chill up to 4 weeks. Makes about 2½ cups.

PER TABLESPOON: 16 calories, .22 g protein, 3.2 g carbohydrates, .4 g fat, 0 mg cholesterol, .7 mg sodium

Pineapple, papaya, jicama, and celery make a salad to season with curry powder, currants, and almonds.

TROPICAL JICAMA SALAD

- 1 medium (about 1¼ lb.) jicama, peeled and cut into ⅛-inch matchstick pieces
- 2 cups small chunks pineapple
- 1 medium-size (about ¾ lb.) firm-ripe papaya, peeled, seeded, and diced
- 1 cup thinly sliced celery
- ½ cup whole blanched almonds
- 2 teaspoons salad oil
- ½ cup currants or raisins
- 1 teaspoon curry powder
- 1 cup unflavored yogurt
  Salt

In a bowl, combine jicama, pineapple, papaya, and celery. If made ahead, cover and chill up to 4 hours.

Meanwhile, in a 10- to 12-inch frying pan over medium heat, stir almonds frequently until golden brown and toasted, about 5 minutes; set aside. Add oil, currants, and curry powder; stir until currants are puffed, about 2 minutes. Remove from heat and combine with almonds; let cool. Stir yogurt into fruit mixture and spoon nut mixture over the salad. Add salt to taste. Makes 6 servings. —*Joan MacDonald, Eugene, Ore.*

PER SERVING: 227 calories, 7 g protein, 34 g carbohydrates, 9 g fat, 2 mg cholesterol, 54 mg sodium

---

Brown small, whole mushrooms and onion slices; mix with a hot marinade of oil, vinegar, dry mustard, and tarragon.

MARINATED MUSHROOMS WITH TARRAGON

- 1½ pounds small mushrooms (about 1-in. diameter)
- ⅓ cup salad oil
- 1 medium-size onion, thinly sliced
- ⅔ cup red wine vinegar
- 2 teaspoons firmly packed brown sugar
- 2 teaspoons minced fresh tarragon leaves or ¾ teaspoon dry tarragon leaves
- 1 teaspoon dry mustard
- ¼ to ½ teaspoon salt

Rinse mushrooms, drain, and trim off soiled stem ends. In a 4- to 5-quart pan over medium-high heat, cook mushrooms with 1 tablespoon of the oil until lightly browned, about 5 minutes; stir often. Add onion and stir often until slightly limp, about 2 minutes. Spoon vegetables into a bowl; set aside.

To pan, add remaining oil, vinegar, brown sugar, tarragon, and mustard. Heat until mixture is hot to touch; pour over mushrooms and onion. Add salt to taste. Let stand until cool; lift vegetables from liquid with a slotted spoon to serve. Or, if made ahead, cover and chill up to 4 days. Use remaining marinade liquid to season salads. Makes 6 to 8 appetizer servings. —*Shannel Reiter, Park City, Mont.*

PER SERVING: 70 calories, 2 g protein, 6 g carbohydrates, 5 g fat, 0 mg cholesterol, 38 mg sodium

---

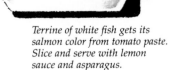

Terrine of white fish gets its salmon color from tomato paste. Slice and serve with lemon sauce and asparagus.

FAUX SALMON TERRINE

- 1¾ pounds boned and skinned firm, white-flesh fish fillets (halibut, sole, rockfish), cut into chunks
- 2 large eggs
- 1 small can (6 oz.) tomato paste
- ⅓ cup whipping cream
- 5 teaspoons drained green peppercorns
  Lemon sauce (recipe follows)

In a food processor, whirl fish, eggs, tomato paste, and cream until smoothly puréed. Mix in peppercorns. Spoon into a deep, straight-sided, 1-quart terrine or 4½- by 8½-inch loaf pan.

Cover terrine and set in a larger pan; put in a 350° oven. Pour about 1 inch boiling water into larger pan. Bake until fish mixture feels firm when lightly pressed in the center, about 30 minutes. Lift from pan, uncover, and cool. Then cover and chill until cold, at least 6 hours or until next day. Cut terrine into ½-inch slices; lift out with a wide spatula. Accompany with lemon sauce. Makes 8 to 10 servings. —*Anne Duffield, Flagstaff, Ariz.*

PER SERVING: 301 calories, 19 g protein, 5 g carbohydrates, 23 g fat, 102 mg cholesterol, 349 mg sodium

Lemon sauce. Combine 1 cup **mayonnaise**, 1 tablespoon *each* **lemon juice** and chopped **parsley,** and 2 teaspoons **Dijon mustard.**

LENTIL & BLACK BEAN SALAD

- 1½ cups (9 oz.) lentils
- 3 cups regular-strength chicken broth
- 3 tablespoons fermented Chinese black beans or drained capers
- 2 medium-size firm-ripe tomatoes Vinaigrette (recipe follows)
- ⅓ cup cilantro (coriander) leaves Salt and pepper

Sort lentils to remove debris. Rinse and drain. In a 2- to 3-quart pan, bring broth to boiling, add lentils, cover, and simmer until tender to bite, about 30 minutes; drain and cool.

Put fermented beans in fine strainer and thoroughly rinse with cool water; drain. Rinse and core tomatoes; cut a few thin slices and set aside. Chop remaining tomato and put into a bowl; add beans, lentils, and vinaigrette and mix. Top with cilantro and tomato slices. Add salt and pepper to taste. Serves 6 to 8.—*Mary Harvey, Huntington Beach, Calif.*

PER SERVING: 230 calories, 12 g protein, 24 g carbohydrates, 11 g fat, 0 mg cholesterol, 300 mg sodium

Vinaigrette. Combine ⅓ cup *each* **raspberry vinegar** and **olive oil; 2 cloves garlic,** minced or pressed; and 2 teaspoons *each* minced **fresh thyme leaves** and **fresh marjoram leaves** (or ¾ teaspoon of *each* dry herb).

Lentil salad is cosmopolitan blend of Chinese fermented black beans, raspberry vinaigrette, and tomatoes.

LEEK & GREEN ONION CHOWDER

- 3 pounds leeks
- 2 tablespoons butter or margarine
- 2 tablespoons all-purpose flour
- ½ teaspoon white pepper
- 6 cups regular-strength chicken broth
- 3 cups thinly sliced green onions, including tops
- ¼ cup lemon juice Thin lemon slices Sour cream Salt

Trim off and discard roots, tough leaves, and outer layer of leeks. Cut leeks in half lengthwise and rinse well under running water. Thinly slice the leeks; you should have about 10 cups.

In a 4- to 6-quart pan over medium-high heat, melt butter and add sliced leeks. Stir often until leeks are limp, about 10 minutes. Mix in flour and pepper, then stir in broth. On high heat, stir and bring leek mixture to a boil. Add green onions and cook just until onions turn bright green, about 4 minutes.

Stir in lemon juice, and ladle soup into 6 large bowls. Garnish each with lemon slices; add sour cream and salt to taste. Makes 6 servings.—*Betty Buckner, Port Angeles, Wash.*

PER SERVING: 150 calories, 5 g protein, 21 g carbohydrates, 6 g fat, 10 mg cholesterol, 117 mg sodium

The lily family contributes leeks and green onions as the base for a light soup. Lemon adds tang.

MACADAMIA BUTTER COOKIES

- About 6 ounces (about 1⅓ cups) salted macadamia nuts
- 1 cup (½ lb.) butter or margarine About 1¼ cups sugar
- 1 large egg
- 1 teaspoon vanilla
- 2½ cups all-purpose flour
- 1 teaspoon baking soda

Chop 1 cup of the nuts; set nuts aside.

With an electric mixer, beat butter and 1 cup sugar until fluffy. Add egg and vanilla; beat until well combined.

In another bowl, stir together flour, baking soda, and chopped nuts. Add to butter mixture, stir together, then beat to blend thoroughly.

Shape dough into 2 teaspoon–size balls. Place balls 1 inch apart on ungreased 12- by 15-inch baking sheets. With a flat-bottom glass (at least 2-in. diameter) dipped in remaining sugar, press balls ¼ inch thick. Press a whole nut or a chunk of nut into center of each cooky.

Bake in a 350° oven until cookies are golden brown, about 12 minutes. Transfer to racks to cool. Serve, or store airtight up to 4 days; freeze to store longer. Makes 4 dozen.—*Eleanor Kondo Ream, Salt Lake City.*

PER COOKY: 104 calories, 1 g protein, 11 g carbohydrates, 7 g fat, 16 mg cholesterol, 72 mg sodium

Crisp, buttery macadamia nut cookies wear whole-nut identification badge. Try with guava punch.

SOMEONE ONCE ASKED *Arthur Bryant, the Kansas City barbecue master,* for the secret to his sauce. His forthright answer: "The secret is, nobody else knows how to make it."

Professionals are often like that with their barbecue sauces, but not Chefs of the West. They are eager to let fellow chefs in on their secrets. In fact, barbecue sauces almost tie chowders and chilies as the most frequently submitted recipes since this column began, in 1940.

Some sauce entries have as bizarre a mixture of ingredients as the celebrated "eye of newt, toe of frog, wool of bat, and tongue of dog" cooked up by the witches in Macbeth. (Perhaps they were preparing for a barbecue when Macbeth encountered them on the heath.)

Sour mash bourbon is the unusual element in David Cohen's basting sauce. Since heat will evaporate the alcohol, why add bourbon? We like to think of it as the Spirit of the Corn bringing a blessing to the wedding of the other ingredients.

BOURBON BARBECUE BASTE

- 3 tablespoons butter or margarine
- 1 tablespoon olive oil
- 2 tablespoons minced onion
- 2 cloves garlic, minced or pressed
- 1 can (8 oz.) tomato sauce
- 1 can (6 oz.) tomato paste
- ½ cup bourbon whiskey
- ¼ cup firmly packed brown sugar
- 1 tablespoon Worcestershire
- 1 tablespoon soy sauce
- ¼ teaspoon *each* dry basil leaves, dry oregano leaves, and dry sage leaves
- 6 to 8 drops liquid hot pepper seasoning
  Pork spareribs, beef ribs, or broiler-fryer chicken halves

Melt 1 tablespoon butter with oil in a 3- to 4-quart pan over medium heat. Add onion and garlic and stir often until onion is limp, about 10 minutes. Mix in tomato sauce, tomato paste, bourbon, sugar, Worcestershire, soy, basil, oregano, sage, and hot pepper seasoning. Simmer, uncovered, for 10 to 15 minutes to blend flavors. Stir in the remaining 2 tablespoons butter.

Makes about 2 cups sauce, enough for 5 pounds spareribs, 8 pounds beef ribs, or 9 to 10 pounds chicken. Use generously to baste meats as they bake in the oven or cook on a grill. Covered and refrigerated, baste keeps for up to 2 weeks.

PER TABLESPOON SAUCE: 28 calories, .35 g protein, 3 g carbohydrates, 2 g fat, 3 mg cholesterol, 134 mg sodium

South Pasadena, Calif.

WHAT GOOD CAN COME *of a union between the delicate shrimp and the assertive cauliflower? Surprisingly, one result is a soup of great refinement; the effect is that of an exceptionally thick and creamy chowder with the flavor of shrimp.*

Cauliflower is a presence in the soup, but purged of any cabbagy flavor. It has been cooked just to tenderness in chicken broth (it's overcooking that brings out an uncharming aroma in this vegetable), then puréed. Serve the soup to guests, and ask them to guess the ingredients.

CAULIFLOWER-SHRIMP SOUP

- 1 head cauliflower, about 2 pounds
- 1¾ cups or 1 can (14½ oz.) regular-strength chicken broth
- 3 small leeks (about ¾ lb. total)

"Chefs of the West are eager to let fellow chefs in on their secret barbecue sauces."

¼ cup (⅛ lb.) butter or margarine
1 medium-size onion, chopped
1 clove garlic, minced or pressed
¼ cup all-purpose flour
2 cups half-and-half (light cream)
3 cups milk
2 tablespoons chopped fresh dill or
  2 teaspoons dry dill weed
1 pound tiny cooked shelled shrimp
  Salt and pepper

Discard cauliflower leaves and cut or break head into flowerets; rinse and drain.

In a 5- to 6-quart pan, combine cauliflowerets and broth; bring to a boil over high heat, then cover and simmer until cauliflower is very tender when pierced, 12 to 15 minutes. With a slotted spoon, ladle cauliflower into a blender or food processor and whirl until smoothly puréed; add a little broth, as required. Add remaining broth to the purée. Wipe pan clean and set it aside.

Trim ends and tops off leeks, leaving about 1½ inches of the dark green leaves. Peel off and discard coarse outer layer of each leek. Cut leeks in half lengthwise. Hold each half under cold running water, separating layers to rinse out dirt. Drain, then chop leeks.

In the pan, melt butter over medium heat. Add leeks, onion, and garlic and stir often until vegetables are limp, about 10 minutes. Stir in flour and cook until bubbly, then smoothly stir or whisk in cream and milk. Add dill and stir until boiling. Add cauliflower mixture and shrimp and heat through, 1 to 2 minutes. Season to taste with salt and pepper. Makes about 3 quarts, 6 to 8 servings.

PER SERVING: 288 calories, 19 g protein, 16 g carbohydrates, 17 g fat, 161 mg cholesterol, 278 mg sodium

Johnny La Newcomt

Avery, Idaho

CREAM CHEESE HARMONIZES *beautifully with any number of flavors, so naturally it has appeared on the cocktail table in the company of all sorts of salsas, chutneys, jellies, and other concoctions. At Howard Brown's house, you will find it awash in jalapeño jelly, that cool-looking green stuff whose sweetness does not quite mask its fire. On one occasion, Mr. Brown found some of this spread left over in the refrigerator. Because there was no other cheese in the house (and because it can be a long time between parties), he employed*

"Jalapeño jelly . . . that cool-looking green stuff whose sweetness does not quite mask its fire."

cream cheese with it for the Sunday omelet in place of the usual jack or cheddar.

The result was both a cheese and a jelly omelet, which Brown has named Omelet Picante-Dulce—hot and sweet omelet.

OMELET PICANTE-DULCE

8 large eggs
4 tablespoons water
  Salt and pepper
4 tablespoons (⅛ lb.) butter or margarine
1 small package (3 oz.) cream cheese, at room temperature and cut into chunks
4 tablespoons jalapeño jelly

To make each omelet, break 2 eggs into a small bowl and add 1 tablespoon of water; beat with a fork just enough to mix yolks and whites. Add salt and pepper to taste, or add to finished omelet.

Place a 7- to 8-inch omelet pan (or frying pan with curved sides) over medium-high heat; when hot, add 1 tablespoon of the butter and tilt pan to quickly coat bottom and sides with melting butter. Pour egg mixture into pan. When eggs are slightly opaque on pan bottom, push or lift the cooked portions with a spatula to allow liquid egg to flow underneath; repeat until omelet is set but top still looks moist and creamy. Shake pan occasionally to keep omelet from sticking.

Quickly distribute about a quarter of the cheese over half the omelet; top cheese with 2 teaspoons jelly. With the

spatula, fold plain half of omelet over filling and slide onto a warm plate. Top with 1 more teaspoon jelly. Repeat to make remaining 3 omelets; serve as made or keep warm until all are cooked. Makes 4 servings.

PER SERVING: 385 calories, 14 g protein, 15 g carbohydrates, 30 g fat, 602 mg cholesterol, 321 mg sodium

Howard Brown

Billings, Mont.

AHI (YELLOWFIN TUNA) *is a big fish that yields big steaks. When raw, the meat is red as beef, and soft—even flabby. When touched by heat, it firms up rapidly and colors to buff or tan. The currently fashionable way to deal with it is to char the steaks over barbecue coals and serve rare.*

If you prefer to cook your fish all the way, you may find ahi dry. Wayne Gordon has devised a way to keep the meat moist when well done. He flavors the steaks with bacon and briefly braises them with soy and white wine. The resulting dish was good enough to win grand prize in the Maui Seafood Spree Week recipe contest sponsored by the University of Hawaii.

AHI STEAK À LA GORDON

8 slices bacon
4 ahi (yellowfin tuna) fillets, each about 1 inch thick and 3½ inches across (about 2 lb. total)
4 teaspoons butter or margarine
2 tablespoons soy sauce
½ cup dry white wine

In a 10- to 12-inch frying pan over medium heat, cook bacon until crisp. Lift out, drain, and set aside. Discard all but 1 tablespoon of the drippings. Place pan over high heat; when hot, add fillets and brown on all sides. Evenly dot tops of fish with butter, then pour soy and wine over fish. Cover and cook over medium heat until fish is opaque in center (cut to test), 7 to 10 minutes. Lift out fish and put on a platter; keep warm. Boil wine mixture on high heat, uncovered, until reduced to about 3 tablespoons. Pour sauce over fish, and top each fillet with 2 slices bacon. Makes 4 servings.

PER SERVING: 463 calories, 57 g protein, 1 g carbohydrates, 24 g fat, 110 mg cholesterol, 862 mg sodium

Wayne Gordon

Lahaina, Hawaii

May Menus

M**AY IS FULL** *of occasions: May Day, Mother's Day, the Memorial Day holiday. Our menus adapt well to these special events.*

On Mother's Day, young cooks can put a special brunch together with little or no help. Our idea here is inspired by open-face Scandinavian sandwiches, which look attractive and are easy to assemble.

To celebrate a sunny weekend, whether early or late in the month, pack a picnic. This one's cool and refreshingly light.

For a hearty family supper, offer the braised chicken with vegetables. It's a meal in itself.

MOTHER'S DAY SMORREBROD

Open-face Ham & Egg Sandwiches
Grapes or Whole Radishes
Fresh-squeezed Orange Juice   Coffee

In Denmark, smorrebrod means buttered bread and refers to pretty open-face sandwiches eaten with knife and fork. Our very homey version pairs two breakfast favorites—ham and eggs.

Squeeze the oranges and wash the grapes or radishes. Assemble the sandwiches just before serving. With very young cooks, have an adult supervise the egg scrambling and coffee making.

OPEN-FACE HAM & EGG SANDWICHES

  Butter or margarine, at room
  temperature
4 slices Westphalian rye bread
12 or 16 thin slices (about 6 oz. total)
  cooked ham such as Westphalian
  or Black Forest
  Scrambled eggs (recipe follows)
1 tablespoon thinly sliced chives
  Salt and pepper

Spread butter on 1 side of each slice of bread. Ripple 3 or 4 slices of the ham over each slice of bread.

Place ¼ of the scrambled eggs over half of each sandwich. Sprinkle eggs

To start Mother's special day, daughters prepare open-face ham and egg sandwiches to serve with freshly squeezed orange juice.

with chives, and salt and pepper to taste. Eat with a knife and fork. Makes 4 sandwiches.—*Ulla Pironi, Belmont, Calif.*

PER SERVING: 275 calories, 18 g protein, 14 g carbohydrates, 16 g fat, 317 mg cholesterol, 915 mg sodium

Scrambled eggs. Lightly beat 4 **large eggs** with 2 tablespoons **water** until blended. Place a 6- to 8-inch frying pan

over medium-low heat and add 1 tablespoon **butter** or margarine. Pour in egg mixture. As it sets around edges, use a spatula to lift set portion and let uncooked egg flow underneath. Continue cooking until all egg is softly set.

Take this portable menu for a May Day outing or only as far as your patio. It's built around a light, refreshing pasta salad to eat with cold slices of turkey.

Roast a turkey breast the night before or—if you're in a hurry—purchase a 2- to 2½-pound cooked piece from the market or deli. The salad can also be made ahead, but add the lemon dressing not more than 2 hours before serving to preserve the green colors. For a picnic, pack turkey and salad in an ice chest to keep cold.

LEMON-MINT PEA & PASTINA SALAD

    8   ounces (about 1 cup) rice-shaped
        or other small pasta
    3   cups (1 lb.) petite frozen peas,
        thawed
    1   cup chopped celery
    ½   cup thinly sliced green onion
    ½   cup chopped fresh mint leaves
    ½   cup salad oil
    ¼   cup lemon juice
    2   teaspoons grated lemon peel
        Salt and pepper
        Romaine lettuce leaves, washed
        and crisped
        Fresh mint sprigs

In a 5- to 6-quart pan, bring about 3 quarts water to a boil on high heat. Stir in pasta and cook until just barely tender to bite, about 5 minutes. Drain and rinse with cold water; drain again.

In a large bowl, combine pasta, peas, celery, onion, and chopped mint; if made ahead, cover and chill until the next day.

Mix oil, lemon juice, and lemon peel. Add to pea mixture; mix and add salt and pepper to taste. Garnish with romaine and mint sprigs. Serve or, if made ahead, cover and chill up to 2 hours. Serves 8.

PER SERVING: 269 calories, 6 g protein, 29 g carbohydrates, 14 g fat, 0 mg cholesterol, 92 mg sodium

GIANT OATMEAL CHEWS

    1   cup (½ lb.) butter or margarine
    1½ cups firmly packed brown sugar
    2   large eggs
    ½   cup molasses
    2   teaspoons vanilla
    1½ cups all-purpose flour
    1   cup whole-wheat flour
    3   cups regular rolled oats
    1   teaspoon baking soda
    1   teaspoon baking powder
    1½ teaspoons ground cinnamon
    ½   teaspoon *each* ground allspice,
        ground cloves, and ground
        nutmeg
    1   cup raisins
    ¾   cup coarsely chopped walnuts

Beat together butter and sugar until creamy. Add eggs, molasses, and vanilla; beat until well blended. Mix flour, whole-wheat flour, oats, baking soda, baking powder, cinnamon, allspice, cloves, and nutmeg. Add to butter mixture; mix well. Stir in raisins and nuts.

On ungreased 12- by 15-inch baking sheets, place ⅓-cup portions of the dough about 3 inches apart. Flatten dough into 3-inch rounds.

Bake in a 375° oven just until light golden around the edges, about 12 minutes. Cool about 5 minutes on pans, then transfer to racks to cool. Serve warm or cool. Makes 20.—*Wendy Lagozzino, Seattle.*

PER COOKY: 326 calories, 5 g protein, 48 g carbohydrates, 14 g fat, 52 mg cholesterol, 172 mg sodium

(Continued on next page)

May Day picnic features turkey breast, salad of minted peas and pastina, cracker bread, melon, and oatmeal-molasses chews.

FRENCH COUNTRY CHICKEN SUPPER

Escarole with Zucchini Salad
Braised Chicken with Garlic,
    Tomatoes & Potatoes
Strawberries & Cream
Sauvignon Blanc   Milk

Braise chicken with a generous quantity of garlic, potatoes, and tomatoes. Serve with escarole and sliced zucchini dressed with a mustard vinaigrette.

While the chicken and vegetables cook, prepare the salad. Wash the berries and serve with cream—plain or whipped, as desired.

BRAISED CHICKEN WITH GARLIC, TOMATOES & POTATOES

2 tablespoons salad oil
1 broiler-fryer chicken (about 3½ lb.), cut into serving-size pieces
24 large cloves garlic, peeled
4 large (¾ lb. total) firm-ripe Roma-style tomatoes, cored and cut in half lengthwise
1 cup dry white wine
1 cup regular-strength chicken broth
4 small (2-in.-diameter) thin-skinned potatoes, scrubbed and cut in half
   Salt and pepper

Pour oil into a 12-inch frying pan or 5- to 6-quart pan over high heat. Add chicken pieces, a portion at a time (do not crowd pan). Cook, turning until well browned on all sides, 10 to 12 minutes. Reduce heat to medium and add garlic and tomato halves, cut side down; cook until tomatoes are lightly browned, about 2 minutes. Lift out tomatoes; set aside.

Return chicken to pan and add wine, broth, and potatoes. Cover and simmer until potatoes are tender when pierced, about 25 minutes. Set tomatoes on top of chicken and simmer, covered, until meat is no longer pink near thigh bone (cut to test), about 5 minutes longer. Lift out chicken, garlic, potatoes, and tomatoes and set on platter; keep warm. Boil pan juices, uncovered, on high heat until reduced to about 1 cup, about 5 minutes. Pour over chicken. Add salt and pepper to taste. Makes 4 servings.

PER SERVING: 771 calories, 55 g protein, 28 g carbohydrates, 48 g fat, 203 mg cholesterol, 226 mg sodium

Summer Fruit Cobbler (page 146)

Outdoor entertaining takes
over the summer spotlight in June. One idea is old-fashioned
fruit cobbler for a crowd, using the season's ripe berries,
peaches, or plums. Another is a Spanish-inspired tapas party,
where guests sample from an appealing array of dishes; we
offer both recipes and suggestions for organizing your party,
which you can expand to serve from 6 to 24 people.
For informal barbecues, use the grill to cook big wheels
of herb-seasoned Italian flat bread.

Tapas: Spanish Snacks

A MEAL OF LITTLE SNACKS, *Spanish tapas offer an appealing opportunity to sample from a wide variety of foods. As with Chinese dim sum, the spread can be modest or elaborate. To match your energy and party size, we present an expandable menu of make-ahead tapas for 6 to 24.*

Tapas have long been popular in Spain, where taverns offer them to fill the gap between lunch and very late dinner; sometimes they replace dinner entirely. It's a dining style that has caught on in our restaurants, often with twists that bear little resemblance to the tapas of Spain.

Peruvian-born Felipe Rojas-Lombardi, a New York chef, specializes in creating tapas; we include some of his best here. Like the Spanish, he uses garlic, olive oil, and balsamic vinegar to season many of his dishes. You can select familiar foods, such as grilled shrimp, or more unusual choices, like snails and hominy.

ORGANIZING THE PARTY

Depending on the size of your group, you can serve tapas from a buffet or at small tables a few steps apart. This station concept works especially well with big groups, helping to ease traffic flow.

As directed in the chart on page 145, you choose from knife-and-fork tapas (make-ahead dishes), tapas to grill (simply prepared meats and vegetables), tapas to go (ready-to-eat foods you buy), and drinks to go with tapas. As the party grows, rather than increasing the size of the recipe, increase the variety by adding more dishes from each category.

If you serve at stations, have small plates and forks on each table. For easy cleanup, consider disposable supplies.

TAPAS TO GRILL

Choose vegetables and sausage or shrimp as directed in the chart, page 145. You can assemble foods that cook on skewers the day before, then cover and chill them.

Arrange the hot coals in the barbecue to avoid flare-ups as you cook.

Flare-free barbecue. Ignite 70 charcoal briquets on firegrate in a barbecue with a lid. Let burn until coals are covered with gray ash, about 30 minutes. Push coals up against 1 side of firegrate in an even layer; they should cover only ¼ of the grate. Place grill 4 to 6 inches above coals.

Lay food on grill over empty part of grate (not above coals). Cover barbecue, open drafts, and cook each food as directed. If you'll be cooking for more than 45 minutes, add 5 briquets to fire every 30 minutes to maintain temperature.

Polish sausage. Thread 1 pound **Polish sausage links** or 3-inch sections of andouille sausage crosswise on a 12- to 16-inch metal or thin wooden skewer; space sausage slightly apart. Run another skewer through sausage, parallel to but slightly apart from the first, to hold meat flat. Barbecue as directed (preceding), until sausages are hot in center and lightly browned, about 4 minutes per side. Push off skewers; slice 1 inch thick.

PER OUNCE: 92 calories, 4 g protein, .46 g carbohydrates, 8 g fat, 20 mg cholesterol, 249 mg sodium

Shrimp. Allow at least 2 **large shrimp** (31 to 35 per lb.) for each person. Shell and devein shrimp. Thread shrimp crosswise through midsection on 12- to 16-inch metal or thin wooden skewers; space shrimp slightly apart. Run a second skewer through shrimp, parallel to but slightly apart from the first, to hold them flat. Barbecue as directed (preceding) until shrimp turn bright pink, about 4 minutes a side; brush several times with **garlic baste,** following.

PER SHRIMP: 32 calories, 2 g protein, .18 g carbohydrates, 2 g fat, 17 mg cholesterol, 16 mg sodium

Garlic baste. Mix 2 tablespoons **olive oil** with 1 clove **garlic,** minced or pressed, for *each* type of vegetable and for every 6 servings of shrimp.

Split leeks. Trim 6 slender **leeks** (about 1 lb. total), leaving about 3 inches green tops. Peel off tough outer layers. Trim ends of roots, but leave enough of the bottom so layers are attached. Split leeks in half lengthwise; rinse well. Barbecue as directed (preceding) until tops are limp and leeks are streaked light brown, about 5 minutes per side; brush several times with **garlic baste,** preceding.

PER HALF LEEK: 30 calories, .25 g protein, 2 g carbohydrates, 2 g fat, 0 mg cholesterol, 3 mg sodium

Multicolor bell pepper strips. Stem and seed 1 *each* large **green, red,** and **yellow bell peppers.** Cut lengthwise into 1½-inch-wide strips. Thread a third of the strips (alternating colors) crosswise on a 12- to 16-inch metal or thin wooden skewer; space slightly apart. Run another skewer through pepper strips, parallel to but slightly apart from the first, to hold strips flat. Repeat to skewer remaining peppers.

Barbecue as directed (preceding) until peppers are streaked light brown, 5 to 6 minutes per side; brush several times with **garlic baste,** preceding.

PER STRIP: 12 calories, .08 g protein, .5 g carbohydrates, 1 g fat, 0 mg cholesterol, .3 mg sodium

Mushrooms. Rinse and drain 1 pound **mushrooms** (about 1½ in. caps); trim ends. Thread the mushrooms through stems and caps onto 3 slender metal or wooden skewers, each 12 to 16 inches long. Barbecue as directed (preceding) until mushrooms are streaked light brown, about 4 minutes per side; brush several times with **garlic baste,** preceding.

PER MUSHROOM: 18 calories, .47 g protein, 1 g carbohydrates, 1 g fat, 0 mg cholesterol, .9 mg sodium

(Continued on next page)

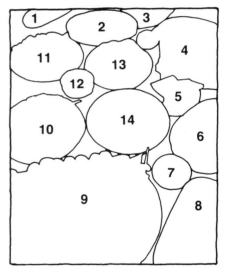

Choose foods to serve 6 to 24 people. Make some foods (*recipes start at left and continue on page 142), and purchase others ready to eat. 1 assorted breads; 2 snails and hominy*; 3 seasonal fruit; 4 selection of meats (with mustard) and cheeses; 5 quail eggs*; 6 pasta with cilantro sauce*; 7 black olives; 8 beets with oranges*; 9 skewered shrimp, sausages, bell peppers, and mushrooms to grill*; 10 smoked fish; 11 ham hocks in balsamic vinegar*; 12 green olives; 13 fish and chard pie*; 14 eggplant with cilantro pesto*. For other options, see menu planning chart on page 145.

Tapas to grill: Host barbecues skewered sausages, bell peppers, shrimp, and leeks over indirect heat (using banked coals in a covered barbecue) to prevent flare-ups.

not overlap), then brush slices with 1 tablespoon oil. Bake in a 450° oven for 10 minutes. Fan slices out further, then brush with 1 more tablespoon oil. Continue to bake until eggplants are lightly browned and very soft when pressed, 10 to 12 minutes longer. Let cool on pan. (If made ahead, cover and chill up to 2 days.)

Up to 2 hours before serving, purée the remaining oil, garlic, ginger, and chili in a blender or food processor. Add lemon juice, cumin, and about half the cilantro. Whirl until smooth; add remaining cilantro and purée. Scrape down container sides as needed. Add salt to taste.

Spread sauce on a rimmed platter and lay eggplants in sauce. Cut slices from stems as you serve. Makes 6 servings.

PER SERVING: 193 calories, 1.5 g protein, 8 g carbohydrates, 18 g fat, 0 mg cholesterol, 7.5 mg sodium

BEETS WITH ORANGES

- 2 **cans (16 oz. each) whole beets, drained**
  Raspberry vinaigrette (recipe follows)
- 2 **medium-size oranges, peeled and white membrane cut off**
  Salt

Place beets and vinaigrette in a small bowl, cover, and chill at least 6 hours or up to 2 days; stir occasionally.

Thinly slice oranges crosswise; arrange around the edge of a small rimmed platter. Lift beets from vinaigrette; place in center of platter. Spoon ¼ cup of vinaigrette over beets (discard remaining vinaigrette). Add salt to taste. Serves 6.

PER SERVING: 132 calories, 1 g protein, 13 g carbohydrates, 9 g fat, 0 mg cholesterol, 214 mg sodium

Raspberry vinaigrette. In a bowl, whisk 1 large clove **garlic,** minced; 1 tablespoon minced **fresh ginger;** 1 teaspoon minced **jalapeño chili;** ½ cup **raspberry vinegar** or red wine vinegar; and ¾ cup **olive oil.**

PASTA WITH CILANTRO SAUCE

- 1 **large egg yolk**
- 2 **tablespoons lemon juice**
- 1 **teaspoon minced fresh ginger**
- 1 **small clove garlic, minced or pressed (optional)**
- ⅛ **teaspoon cayenne**
- ¼ **cup** *each* **olive oil and salad oil**

Plantains. Peel 3 large, very ripe **plantains** (with black skins) or green-ripe bananas; cut each in half lengthwise. Barbecue as directed (preceding) until plantains are browned and soft when pressed, about 5 minutes per side; brush several times with **garlic baste,** preceding.

PER HALF PLANTAIN: 225 calories, 2 g protein, 48 g carbohydrates, 5 g fat, 0 mg cholesterol, 6 mg sodium

KNIFE & FORK TAPAS

Choose some vegetable dishes and some meat or fish entrées.

EGGPLANT WITH CILANTRO PESTO

- 1½ **pounds (8 to 12) Japanese eggplants**
- ½ **cup olive oil**
- 1 **teaspoon** *each* **minced garlic, minced fresh ginger, and minced fresh jalapeño chili**
- 1 **tablespoon lemon juice**
- 1 **teaspoon ground cumin**
- 2 **cups tightly packed fresh cilantro (coriander) sprigs**
  Salt

Starting near the stem, cut eggplants lengthwise into ⅓-inch-wide slices; leave stems attached. Place eggplants on 2 baking sheets, each 12 by 15 inches. Fan out slices of eggplant (vegetables should

2 cups firmly packed fresh cilantro
  (coriander) sprigs
12 ounces (5 cups) dry pasta spirals
¼ cup thinly sliced green onions
  Salt
  Cilantro sprigs

In a blender or food processor, whirl egg yolk, 1 tablespoon of the lemon juice, ginger, garlic, and cayenne. With motor running, add olive oil and salad oil in a slow stream; whirl until thick. A portion at a time, add remaining lemon juice, 2 tablespoons water, and the 2 cups cilantro; whirl until smooth. Set aside.

In a 5- to 6-quart pan, bring 2½ quarts water to a boil over high heat. Add pasta; boil until barely tender to bite, 4 to 5 minutes. Drain, rinse with cold water, and drain again. Put back in pan.

Mix pasta with cilantro dressing and onions; salt to taste. Place in a shallow serving dish. Serve at room temperature; if made ahead, cool, cover, and chill up to 2 days. Garnish with cilantro sprigs. Makes 6 servings.

PER SERVING: 383 calories, 8 g protein, 43 g carbohydrates, 20 g fat, 45 mg cholesterol, 5.5 mg sodium

HAM HOCKS IN BALSAMIC VINEGAR

3½ to 4 pounds ham hocks
  Ham seasonings (recipe follows)
  Balsamic vinaigrette (recipe follows)
2 tablespoons *each* minced parsley, minced red bell pepper, and thinly sliced green onion

Place ham hocks in pan with ham seasonings. Bring to a boil over high heat; simmer, covered, until meat pulls easily from bones, 2 to 2½ hours.

Gently lift hocks from pan (discard pan liquid) and let stand until cool enough to handle. Carefully remove and discard bones, keeping hocks whole. Place hocks slightly apart in a rimmed dish; gently press with fingers to reshape hocks into their original form. Cover and chill until firm, at least 4 hours or until next day.

Thinly slice hocks crosswise ¼ inch thick. Place slices in a single layer in 2 rimmed pans, each about 10 by 15 inches. Cut any uneven pieces into ½-inch chunks; place in a small bowl.

Drizzle ⅔ of the vinaigrette over sliced hocks and ⅓ over meat chunks. Let

stand at room temperature for 30 minutes, or cover and chill up to 2 days.

With a slotted spatula, lift meat slices from vinaigrette (reserve liquid) and arrange slightly overlapping on a rimmed platter. Lift meat chunks from vinaigrette (reserve liquid) and arrange in center of platter. Pour vinaigrette over meat. Sprinkle with parsley, bell pepper, and green onion. Makes 6 servings.

PER SERVING: 415 calories, 17 g protein, 4 g carbohydrates, 37 g fat, 54 mg cholesterol, 836 mg sodium

Ham seasonings. In an 8- to 10-quart pan, mix 4 quarts **water;** 1 medium-size **onion,** quartered; 6 **dry juniper berries;** 1 head **garlic,** cut in half horizontally; a 1-inch piece **fresh ginger,** cut in half; 1 **bay leaf;** 1 small **dried hot red chili;** and 7 or 8 sprigs **fresh cilantro** (coriander).

Balsamic vinaigrette. In a bowl, whisk together ½ cup **balsamic vinegar;** 1 teaspoon minced **fresh ginger;** 4 cloves **garlic,** minced or pressed; 1 teaspoon minced **fresh jalapeño chili;** and ¾ cup **olive oil.**

SNAILS & HOMINY

6 cloves garlic, minced or pressed
1 medium-size onion, finely chopped
¼ cup olive oil
¼ teaspoon *each* ground cloves and cayenne
1 teaspoon paprika
3 tablespoons all-purpose flour
1¾ cups regular-strength beef broth
¼ cup dry white wine
2 cans (7½ oz. each; or 3 cans, 4½ oz. each) snails, drained and rinsed
2 cans (about 1 lb. each) hominy, drained
2 tablespoons balsamic vinegar or red wine vinegar
½ cup minced parsley
  Salt
  Parsley sprigs

In a 10- to 12-inch frying pan over medium heat, cook garlic and onion in oil until onion is limp, about 5 minutes; stir often.

Blend in cloves, cayenne, paprika, and flour; stir until bubbly. Mix in broth and wine. Stir until boiling and thickened, about 3 minutes. Mix in snails and hominy; bring to a simmer. Cover and cook until flavors are blended, about 5 minutes; stir often. Remove from heat; let cool.

Knife & fork tapas: Colorful salads of mussels, pasta with cilantro sauce, and beets with oranges are make-ahead choices to serve with grilled foods (on plate).

Mix vinegar and minced parsley into pan. Salt to taste; spoon into a bowl. If made ahead, cover, chill up to 2 days. Garnish with parsley sprigs. Makes 6 servings.

PER SERVING: 252 calories, 13 g protein, 25 g carbohydrates, 11 g fat, 33 mg cholesterol, 508 mg sodium

MUSSELS VINAIGRETTE

1 teaspoon dry thyme leaves
½ cup plus 2 tablespoons olive oil
½ cup dry white wine
5 pounds mussels in shells, scrubbed and beards pulled off
¾ pound cooked small (about 1½ in. wide) red thin-skinned potatoes, quartered
1½ pounds firm-ripe tomatoes, cored and cut into 1-inch chunks
1 small onion, thinly sliced
½ cup frozen peas, thawed
⅓ cup distilled white vinegar
⅓ cup minced parsley
  Salt

In a 5- to 6-quart pan, combine thyme with 2 tablespoons *each* of oil and wine. Add mussels. Cover tightly, bring to a boil over medium-high heat, and cook until shells open, about 8 minutes. Uncover; let stand until cool enough to handle. Discard liquid and any mussels that don't open.

Pull mussels from shells (reserve 12 whole shells; discard remaining) and place in a large, shallow serving dish. Stir in potatoes, tomatoes, onion, peas, vinegar, parsley, and remaining olive oil and wine. Season to taste with salt. Garnish with reserved shells. Serve at room temperature. If made ahead, cool, cover, and chill up to 4 hours. Makes 6 servings.

PER SERVING: 371 calories, 16 g protein, 23 g carbohydrates, 23 g fat, 31 mg cholesterol, 341 mg sodium

FISH & CHARD PIE

Black mustard seed is sold at spice stores and Middle Eastern markets.

  1 **package (2 sheets, each 9½ in. square; 17¾ oz. total) frozen puff pastry, thawed**
  1 **large egg yolk mixed with 1 tablespoon water**
    Swiss chard filling (recipe follows)
  1 **pound boned and skinned rockfish fillets**
  ¾ **teaspoon black or yellow mustard seed**

Place 1 pastry sheet on a flat surface; cut other sheet in thirds. Around 3 sides of uncut sheet, place cut pastry pieces (edges should slightly overlap). Roll and trim pastry into a 20-inch circle; discard scraps. Brush with some yolk mixture. Fold pastry into quarters, yolk side in.

Tapas to go: Store-bought, ready-to-eat foods include seasonal fruit, black olives, bread, and mild goat cheese. For larger groups, add more choices from list at right.

Nestle into a buttered 9-inch cheesecake pan with removable bottom, then unfold evenly into pan. Let extra pastry hang over rim.

Pat half of chard filling into pastry; lay fish on chard. Evenly pat remaining filling over fish. Gather pastry over center of pan to enclose filling; gently twist and pinch excess to form a topknot. Brush with remaining egg yolk mixture; sprinkle with mustard seed. Cut 6 slashes (each 1½ in. long) on top of pastry, 2 inches from rim. (If desired, cover and chill until next day.)

Set pie on a 12- by 15-inch baking sheet. Bake, uncovered, in a 375° oven until pastry is well browned, 60 to 70 minutes. Let cool on rack for 15 minutes; remove rim. Serve slightly warm or at room temperature. Cut into wedges. Serves 8 to 10.

PER SERVING: 343 calories, 14 g protein, 24 g carbohydrates, 21 g fat, 43 mg cholesterol, 535 mg sodium

Swiss chard filling. Rinse 3 pounds **Swiss chard** and trim ends. Coarsely chop. In a 12- to 14-inch frying pan, mix ¼ cup **olive oil;** 2 small **fresh jalapeño chilies,** seeded and minced; 2 tablespoons minced **fresh ginger;** 1 medium-size **onion,** chopped; and 1 teaspoon *each* **ground nutmeg, ground cumin,** and **dry thyme leaves.** Stir over medium-high heat until onion is limp, 5 minutes.

Add chard, a portion at a time, and cook, stirring often, until chard wilts and becomes very limp, 10 to 12 minutes. Remove from heat and mix in 2 tablespoons **lemon juice;** add **salt** to taste.

TAPAS TO GO

For any size party, serve bread and fruit.

Bread. For every 6 people, allow at least a 1 pound loaf of **crusty bread.** If you need more than 1 loaf, you might offer several different kinds of bread or rolls.

Fruit. Choose the season's best: **grapes,** peaches, melons, berries, or apricots; allow about ½ pound per person (more for decoration, if you like). Rinse, drain, and arrange fruit so guests can easily eat out of hand.

Cheese. Buy by the chunk to cut as you eat. Choose **asiago,** fontina, goat, jack, or jarlsberg: ¾ to 1 pound of each.

Hard-cooked quail eggs. If you serve **quail eggs,** allow at least 1 per guest. To hard-cook, place eggs in a pan large enough to hold them in a single layer. Add cold water to cover by 1 inch. Bring to a boil over high heat; simmer 5 minutes. Cool under cold running water. Serve, or chill up to 2 days. Serve in shells; to eat, shell and dip in **salt.**

Olives. Choose one or more kinds: **Spanish-style,** green or black ripe, salt-cured, seasoned, or other favorites. Offer 2 cups of each olive you pick.

Nuts. Choose one or more kinds of roasted, shelled nuts: **Spanish** or other type of **peanuts,** pistachios, almonds, walnuts, pecans, macadamias, sunflower seed. Allow 2 cups for each type you serve.

Cold cured meats. You need about ¾ pound of each type you choose: thinly sliced **cooked ham,** prosciutto, or other cold cured meats.

Smoked fish. You need about ¾ pound of any type: **salmon,** trout, or whitefish; or canned fish such as herring or sardines. Thinly slice salmon or whitefish; serve trout whole to break apart as you eat. Drain canned fish, if desired.

TO DRINK WITH TAPAS

Offer a variety of beverages including sherries, wines, and sparkling water.

In Spain, sherry is the traditional accompaniment to tapas, and part of the tapas experience is trying different sherries. Spanish and American sherries differ greatly in flavor and style; Spanish are generally considered more complex.

Spanish sherries vary by maker, but these are general guidelines. *Fino* is dry, crisp, light, and best chilled; its color is usually deep amber. *Manzanilla* looks and tastes quite similar but tends to be drier with subtler nuances; serve chilled.

Amontillado has medium-dry, nut-like flavor. It's darker than fino and has more taste and body. Offer it at room temperature. *Oloroso* may be dry or sweet, and medium- to full-bodied (your wine merchant can recommend drier brands best with tapas). Serve chilled.

American sherries good with tapas are *dry* and *cocktail* or *golden* (medium dry).

For wine, try a dry Sauvignon Blanc or lightly oaked Chardonnay, and a mature, smooth Cabernet Sauvignon.

How to Plan a Tapas Party for 6 to 24

VARIETY IS PART of the appeal of a tapas meal. For a party of any size, you choose a sampling of dishes from each category below. As you add guests, choose more dishes, rather than increase recipe size. (For example, if you need 3 *tapas to go* selections, you could pick 1 type of olive, quail eggs, and Spanish peanuts. Or you could buy 3 kinds of cheese.) Each recipe, except the fish and chard pie, makes 6 servings; it serves 8 to 10.

As you expand the meal, you also increase your time commitment, but nearly all the work can be done ahead in stages over several days.

Just before party time, set out the food and drinks.

KNIFE & FORK TAPAS

You can prepare most of these dishes 1 or 2 days ahead. All are served at room temperature. Choose a few vegetable dishes and some with meat or fish. Recipes begin on page 142.

Eggplant with Cilantro Pesto
Beets with Oranges
Pasta with Cilantro Sauce
Ham Hocks in Balsamic Vinegar
Snails & Hominy
Mussels Vinaigrette
Fish & Chard Pie

For 6 people: 1 vegetable dish and 1 meat or fish dish.

For 12: 2 vegetable dishes and 1 or 2 meat or fish dishes.

For 18: all the vegetable dishes and 3 meat or fish dishes.

For 24: all the items.

TAPAS TO GRILL

Make a colorful display of foods ready for the grill, then cook them during the party and serve hot. Choose some vegetables and either sausage or shrimp, or use both. Directions begin on page 140.

Polish or Andouille Sausage
Shrimp   Split Leeks
Multicolor Bell Pepper Strips
Mushrooms
Plantains or Green-ripe Bananas

For 6 people: 1 or 2 vegetables plus shrimp or sausage.

For 12: 2 vegetables plus shrimp and 1 kind of sausage.

For 18: all the items.

For 24: all the items.

TAPAS TO GO

You buy these fresh or prepared foods to eat out of hand (only the eggs need cooking). To create a bountiful look even if you need less, you may want to buy several cheeses by the chunk, a few loaves of bread, and a generous amount of fruit. Serve bread and fruit for a party of any size. Cut cheese and bread as you eat. See facing page for quantities.

Crusty Loaves of Bread
Fruits of the Season
Cheeses, such as Asiago, Fontina, Goat, Jack, or Jarlsberg
Hard-cooked Quail Eggs in the Shell
Spanish-style or other Olives
Spanish Peanuts or other Nuts
Thin-sliced Cooked Ham, Prosciutto, or other Cold Cured Meats
Smoked Fish, such as Salmon, Trout, or Whitefish

For 6 people: 2 or 3 items in addition to bread and fruit.

For 12: 4 to 6 items in addition to bread and fruit.

For 18: at least 6 items, in addition to bread and fruit.

For 24: at least 8 items, in addition to bread and fruit.

TO DRINK WITH TAPAS

Offer a variety of imported and domestic sherries or wines for sampling, or serve both. Accompany with sparkling water. For more details about sherry and wine selection, see facing page.

Spanish Sherries: Fino, Manzanilla, Amontillado, Oloroso
California Sherries: Dry or Medium-dry
Wines: Chardonnay or Dry Sauvignon Blanc, Cabernet Sauvignon
Sparkling Water   Ice

For 6 people: 3 bottles sherry or wine, 2 bottles sparkling water.

For 12: 6 bottles sherry or wine, 4 bottles sparkling water.

For 18: 9 bottles sherry or wine, 6 bottles sparkling water.

For 24: 12 bottles sherry or wine, 8 bottles sparkling water.

Cobbler for a Crowd

To PUT TOGETHER ROUGHLY—*that's one dictionary definition of "cobble." Does it mean that a fruit cobbler is put together roughly? We think so; if your touch is a bit slapdash or even rankly amateur, it merely adds to a cobbler's homey, old-fashioned appeal.*

Cobblers lend themselves to infinite variations. But we favor ones with top crust only, lots of good fruit beneath, and tender, clear beads of tapioca to thicken the juices. Because the approach is so simple, you have a lot of flexibility. Using the chart at right, you can make a family-size cobbler or one big enough for a picnic crowd; just pick the appropriate pan size and the amount of filling and pastry to suit your needs.

SUMMER FRUIT COBBLER

Using the chart at right, choose and prepare the **fruit** you want. Select a pan suited to the amount of fruit you are using; pour fruit into pan and crush about ¼ of it with a potato masher. Add the specified amounts of **sugar, quick-cooking tapioca,** and **lemon juice** (if called for). Mix gently and set aside at least 15 minutes or up to 1 hour. Stir occasionally; as fruit stands, juices form to soften tapioca.

Meanwhile, measure ingredients for **cream cheese pastry,** using amounts appropriate for pan size. Put **cream cheese, butter,** and **sugar** into a bowl or food processor and beat with an electric mixer or whirl until well mixed. Add **flour** and mix or whirl until thoroughly blended.

How Much to Use for Family-Size or Crowd-Size Summer Fruit Cobbler

FRUIT FILLING

Pan size	Fruit	Sugar	Quick-cooking tapioca	Lemon juice
BERRY (black, boysen, logan, olallie, rasp)—rinse and drain fruit				
8-inch square	5½ cups	1⅛ cups	3 tablespoons	
9- by 13-inch	2¾ quarts	2¼ cups	6½ tablespoons	
11- by 17-inch	5½ quarts	4½ cups	¾ cup	
BLUEBERRIES—rinse and drain fruit				
8-inch square	5½ cups	¾ cup	3 tablespoons	1 tablespoon
9- by 13-inch	2¾ quarts	1½ cups	6 tablespoons	2 tablespoons
11- by 17-inch	5½ quarts	3 cups	¾ cup	¼ cup
PEACH—peel, pit, and thinly slice firm-ripe to soft-ripe fruit				
8-inch square	5½ cups	⅓ cup	1½ tablespoons	1 tablespoon
9- by 13-inch	2¾ quarts	¾ cup	3 tablespoons	2 tablespoons
11- by 17-inch	5½ quarts	1½ cups	6 tablespoons	¼ cup
PLUM—rinse, pit, and thinly slice firm-ripe to soft-ripe fruit				
8-inch square	5½ cups	¾ cup	3 tablespoons	
9- by 13-inch	2¾ quarts	1½ cups	6 tablespoons	
11- by 17-inch	5½ quarts	3 cups	¾ cup	

CREAM CHEESE PASTRY

Pan size	Cream cheese	Butter or margarine	Sugar	All-purpose flour
8-inch square	1 small package (3 oz.)	2 tablespoons (⅛ lb.)	2 teaspoons	½ cup
9- by 13-inch	2 small packages (3 oz. each)	½ cup (¼ lb.)	2 tablespoons	1½ cups
11- by 17-inch	3 small packages (3 oz. each)	¾ cup (⅜ lb.)	3 tablespoons	2¼ cups

Fold rolled pastry in half and lay on top of partially crushed fruit, then gently unfold rest of pastry. Fold rim of pastry under so folded edge is flush with pan sides; crimp.

Pat dough out 1 inch thick; enclose in plastic wrap and chill until just firm enough to roll easily, about 30 minutes.

Shape dough into a square or rectangle on a lightly floured board. With a floured rolling pin, evenly roll dough to shape pastry that measures 1 inch longer and wider than pan. Fold pastry in half and lay on top of half of fruit, then gently unfold. Fold rim of pastry under so folded edge is flush against pan sides; crimp decoratively. Cut several slashes in top of pastry to allow steam to escape. Beat 1 **large egg white** to blend, then brush lightly on pastry.

Bake cobbler in a 350° oven (set the smaller pans on a larger rimmed pan to catch juice bubbles) until pastry is golden brown, 50 minutes to 1½ hours. Serve warm or cool. (The 11- by 17-inch cobbler takes about 8 hours to cool and thicken to the maximum.) If made ahead, cover and hold at room temperature up until next day; serve cool, or reheat, uncovered, in a 350° oven until warm in center, 15 to 25 minutes. An 8-inch-square cobbler serves 6; a 9- by 13-inch serves 12; an 11- by 17-inch serves 24.

PER SERVING: 353 calories, 3 g protein, 65 g carbohydrates, 10 g fat, 27 mg cholesterol, 91 mg sodium

A big scoop of raspberry cobbler with vanilla ice cream is a great summer treat. Vary the cobbler in flavor, choosing among seasonal fruits in chart on facing page.

Italian Flat Bread from the Barbecue

COOK THESE BIG WHEELS *of seasoned bread over hot coals. The thin rounds, flavored with fresh Italian herbs or pungent Indian spices, bake in minutes over the barbecue to yield fragrant, chewy bread.*

You can make the bread in about 3 hours, or stretch the process over 2 days. Or gain time by using purchased frozen bread dough for the base. Serve the rounds as a first course with cheese and salad. Or barbecue the meat, then follow with breads cooked on the same grill.

GRILLED ITALIAN HERB FLAT BREAD

2⅓ cups warm water (110°)
1 package active dry yeast
1⅔ cups whole-wheat flour
1 teaspoon regular salt
  About 1 cup olive oil
  About 4½ cups all-purpose flour
1 cup chopped fresh basil leaves or ¼ cup dry basil leaves
¾ cup chopped fresh oregano leaves

or 2 tablespoons dry oregano leaves
¾ cup minced parsley
  Kosher or regular salt

In a large bowl, mix 1⅔ cups of water and yeast; let stand until yeast softens, about 5 minutes. Stir in whole-wheat flour. Cover with plastic wrap and let stand at room temperature 4 hours or up to next day. (If desired, skip the standing and continue; flavor will be slightly milder.)

Serve rounds of herb-speckled flat bread wth cheese and salad for a first course. Or eat the bread with barbecued meats; both can cook on the grill.

Add remaining ⅔ cup water, 1 teaspoon regular salt, and 3 tablespoons oil.

If using an electric mixer, add 1½ cups of the all-purpose flour and stir or mix slowly until ingredients are moistened. Beat on high speed until dough is stretchy, about 2 minutes. Then add 3 cups all-purpose flour and stir with a heavy spoon until well moistened. Scrape dough onto a floured board and knead until smooth and not sticky, adding flour if required, 5 to 10 minutes. Place dough in a greased bowl; turn dough over.

If using a dough hook, add 4 cups all-purpose flour and mix at low speed until ingredients are moistened. Then beat at high speed until dough pulls cleanly from sides of bowl, about 3 minutes. If dough is sticky, add all-purpose flour, 1 tablespoon at a time, until dough releases from bowl.

Cover bowl with plastic wrap and let stand in a warm place until dough is about double, about 1 hour. Or chill overnight. Knead with dough hook or on a lightly floured board to expel air bubbles, and divide into 6 equal balls.

On a floured board, roll each ball (keep remaining pieces covered with plastic wrap) into about a 10-inch-diameter round. Drizzle 1 side with about 1 tablespoon olive oil. Sprinkle about 1½ tablespoons fresh basil (or 1 teaspoon dry basil), 1 tablespoon fresh oregano (or ½ teaspoon dry oregano leaves), 1 tablespoon parsley, and kosher salt to taste. Roll lightly to press seasonings in.

Turn round over onto a piece of floured foil; repeat seasoning and rolling process on second side. Place foil-supported round onto a 12- by 15-inch baking sheet. Shape and season remaining dough, stacking each piece on top of the first. (If made ahead, cover and chill up to 3 hours.)

About 45 minutes before cooking, cover the firegrate of a barbecue with a solid, single layer of charcoal briquets. Mound, ignite, and let burn until coals are just covered with gray ash, about 45 minutes. Spread into an even layer; put grill in place 4 to 6 inches above. Coals are ready when medium (you can hold

Flip breads onto grill, peel off foil, and cook until lightly browned on both sides; watch carefully to avoid scorching.

your hand at grill level only 4 to 5 seconds).

Lift a piece of foil supporting a bread round; flip dough onto the grill and peel off the foil. You can cook 2 pieces of dough at a time on a 22- to 23-inch grill. Cook, turning once, until bread is speckled gold on both sides, 5 to 7 minutes total. With a spatula, remove bread and cook remaining dough rounds. Serve hot or cool. Makes 6 rounds (10-in. diameter), 2 or 3 servings per round.

PER SERVING: 262 calories, 15 g protein, 40 g carbohydrates, 13 g fat, 0 mg cholesterol, 124 mg sodium

GRILLED INDIAN MINT FLAT BREAD

Make **grilled Italian herb flat bread** (recipe precedes), omitting basil, oregano, and parsley. Sprinkle each side of each round with ¼ cup chopped **fresh mint leaves,** ½ teaspoon **cumin seed,** ¼ teaspoon **ground coriander,** and lightly with **kosher** or regular **salt** and **cayenne** to taste. Makes 6 rounds, 2 or 3 servings each.

PER SERVING: 258 calories, 5 g protein, 32 g carbohydrates, 13 g fat, 0 mg cholesterol, 123 mg sodium

QUICK GRILLED FLAT BREADS

Instead of making the dough for **grilled Italian herb flat bread** (recipe precedes), use 3 loaves (1 lb. each) **frozen whole-wheat** or white **bread dough,** thawed. Cut each loaf in half. Shape, season (Italian or Indian), and bake as directed. Makes 6 rounds, 2 or 3 servings each.

PER SERVING: approximately the same as the homemade bread, depending upon seasonings

Skate: A Fish Market Surprise

FASCINATING . . . WHAT IS IT? *may be your first response when you see skate, a fish with cartilage but no bones. The cartilage gives the delicate, tender, slightly sweet flesh a curious ridged look.*

A skate (also called ray or sting ray) is an oddly shaped sea creature ranging in size from several inches to many feet across. The skinny body has a long, even skinnier tail. A broad, flat, and meaty triangular wing (the part we eat) lies on each side of the body. Each wing has two layers of cream to deep red flesh separated by a layer of cartilage.

Straight from the water, a skate has a thick, slippery skin that's usually removed. (If you find bits of skin, just cut them off.) Markets usually sell wings whole or in pieces, either with cartilage or without (fillets). If desired, you can fillet the wings yourself. Both forms are easy to cook and eat.

Some stores carry skate regularly; other markets may be able to order it for you. Expect to pay $2.50 to $3.50 a pound.

Pan-frying, poaching, and broiling all work well with filleted and unfilleted skate. When dividing fish into portions, it's easiest to cut between ridges. If your pieces of skate are much thicker or thinner than noted in recipes, cooking times will vary.

To eat skate with cartilage, anchor fish with a fork, and scrape off cooked flesh.

PAN-FRIED SKATE

Cut 1 pound filleted or 1¼ pounds unfilleted **skate** into 4 equal pieces. Shake in a bag with ¼ cup **all-purpose flour;** shake off excess.

Pour 2 tablespoons **salad oil** into a 12- to 14-inch frying pan over medium-high heat. When hot, place fish in pan. Cook, turning several times, until well browned and no longer translucent in thickest part, 5 to 8 minutes for fillets ¼ to 1 inch thick, 8 to 12 minutes for unfilleted pieces ½ to 1¼ inches thick. Serves 4.

PER SERVING: 179 calories, 25 g protein, 2 g carbohydrates, 8 g fat, 62 mg cholesterol, 79 mg sodium

POACHED SKATE

Cut 1 pound filleted or 1¼ pounds unfilleted **skate** into 4 equal pieces. Fill a 5- to 6-quart pan ¾ full of water; bring to a boil over high heat. Add skate, cover, and simmer very gently until fish is no longer translucent in thickest part, 3 to 5 minutes for fillets ¼ to 1 inch thick, 5 to 9 minutes for unfilleted pieces ½ to 1¼ inches thick. Serves 4.

PER SERVING: 111 calories, 24 g protein, 0 g carbohydrates, .1 g fat, 62 mg cholesterol, 79 mg sodium

BROILED SKATE

Cut 1 pound filleted or 1¼ pounds unfilleted **skate** into 4 equal pieces. Place fish on a lightly greased rack in a 12- by 15-inch broiler pan.

Broil about 3 inches below heat, turning once, until no longer translucent in thickest part; this should take 3 to 5 minutes total for fillets ¼ to 1 inch thick, 6 to 10 minutes for unfilleted pieces ½ to 1¼ inches thick. Makes 4 servings.

PER SERVING: 111 calories, 24 g protein, 0 g carbohydrates, .1 g fat, 62 mg cholesterol, 79 mg sodium

COOL WATERCRESS, SKATE & COCONUT SALAD

> 1 **pound skate fillets or 1¼ pounds unfilleted skate, poached or broiled (directions precede)**
> 1 **quart lightly packed watercress sprigs, rinsed and crisped**
> ½ **cup diced red bell pepper**
> ¼ **cup *each* salad oil and lime juice**
> ¼ **teaspoon coconut extract**
>   **Salt and pepper**

Prepare skate; let cool. If made ahead, chill airtight up to 1 day. Use cold or at room temperature. Arrange equal portions of skate and watercress on 4 salad plates. In a bowl, stir bell pepper, oil, lime juice, and coconut extract. Spoon evenly over fish and greens. Add salt and pepper to taste. Makes 4 servings.

PER SERVING WITH POACHED SKATE: 242 calories, 25 g protein, 2 g carbohydrates, 15 g fat, 62 mg cholesterol, 96 mg sodium

SKATE WITH CUCUMBERS & CAPERS

> 1 **European-style cucumber (1 lb.)**
> 1 **pound skate fillets or 1¼ pounds unfilleted skate, broiled, poached, or pan-fried (directions precede)**
> 1 **tablespoon salad oil**
> ⅓ **cup minced Italian or regular parsley**
> 3 **tablespoons lemon juice**
> 2 **tablespoons drained capers**
>   **Italian or regular parsley sprigs**
>   **Salt and pepper**

Peel cucumber, halve lengthwise, and scoop out seeds. Slice crosswise about ⅓ inch thick; set aside.

Prepare skate; keep warm. In a 10- to 12-inch frying pan over medium-high heat, cook cucumber in oil until slightly limp, about 3 minutes; stir often. Remove from heat and stir in minced parsley, lemon juice, and capers. Spoon over skate; garnish with parsley sprigs. Season to taste with salt and pepper. Makes 4 servings.

PER SERVING WITH BROILED SKATE: 159 calories, 25 g protein, 4 g carbohydrates, 4 g fat, 62 mg cholesterol, 194 mg sodium

Tropical-style dressing of coconut, lime, and diced bell pepper seasons entrée salad of watercress and cool, deeply ridged skate fillet.

Nacho Nephews: Bean Dip Appetizers

TAKING A NOD *from nachos, here we use three different beans as bases for refreshing, satisfying appetizers. You use canned beans for a quick start, mash or purée them, and season well. Then you spread the mixture into a thick layer on a platter and top with more seasonings to make a colorful, flavorful presentation. Scoop onto vegetables or breads to eat.*

LAYERED BLACK BEAN DIP

    6 slices bacon, coarsely chopped
    1 small onion, chopped
    ½ teaspoon chili powder
    1 can (15 oz.) black beans, drained
       (reserve ⅓ cup liquid)
       Guacamole (recipe follows)
    1 cup (4 oz.) shredded jack cheese
    1 *each* small red and yellow bell
       pepper (or 2 of either), stemmed,
       seeded, and chopped
    ¼ cup thinly sliced green onion
       Sour cream
       Cilantro sprigs
       Jicama dippers (recipe follows)

In an 8- to 10-inch frying pan over medium heat, stir bacon, onion, and chili powder until bacon is crisp, 8 to 10 minutes. Drain off and discard fat. Let cool.

In a large bowl, coarsely mash beans; stir in reserved liquid and bacon mixture. Spread mixture into an 8-inch-diameter round on a large platter, and top evenly with guacamole. Sprinkle guacamole with cheese, then bell peppers and green onion. Garnish with a spoonful of sour cream and cilantro sprigs. Tuck jicama dippers, chili end out, around edge of beans. Scoop beans onto dippers to eat. Serves 6 to 8.

PER SERVING: 210 calories, 9.7 g protein, 18 g carbohydrates, 12 g fat, 16 mg cholesterol, 366 mg sodium

Guacamole. Cut 1 large ripe **avocado** in half; pit and scoop out pulp. Coarsely mash with a fork, adding 2 tablespoons **lemon juice**; 1 fresh **jalapeño chili**, stemmed, seeded, and minced; and **salt** and **pepper** to taste.

Jicama dippers. Peel and rinse 1 piece (about 1 lb.) **jicama**; cut into ¼-inch-thick slices, then cut crosswise into thirds. Dip tip of each piece in **chili powder**.

LAYERED GARBANZO BEAN DIP

    1 can (15½ oz.) garbanzos, drained
       (reserve ¼ cup liquid)
    ⅓ cup tahini (sesame seed paste)
    ¼ cup lemon juice
    ½ teaspoon ground cumin
    1 clove garlic, minced or pressed
       Salt and pepper
    ½ cup unflavored yogurt
    1 tablespoon minced fresh mint
       leaves or 1 teaspoon dry mint
    ½ cup diced cucumber
    ⅓ cup thinly sliced red radish
    ¼ cup crumbled feta cheese
    2 or 3 fresh mint sprigs
    6 pocket bread rounds (6-in.
       diameter), split, cut into triangles,
       and toasted

In a food processor or blender, whirl beans, liquid, tahini, lemon juice, cumin, and garlic until mixture is smooth; add salt and pepper to taste. Spread mixture into an 8-inch-diameter round on a large platter.

Stir together yogurt and minced mint; spread evenly over beans. Sprinkle cucumber, radish, and cheese over yogurt. Garnish with mint sprigs. Tuck pocket triangles around edge of beans. Scoop beans onto bread to eat. Serves 6 to 8.

PER SERVING: 279 calories, 10 g protein, 44 g carbohydrates, 7 g fat, 4.6 mg cholesterol, 508 mg sodium

LAYERED KIDNEY BEAN DIP

Look for the prepared antipasto in your market's fancy food or deli section.

    2 teaspoons olive oil
    1 clove garlic, minced or pressed
    2 ounces prosciutto or cooked ham,
       chopped
    1 tablespoon red wine vinegar
    1 can (15½ oz.) kidney beans,
       drained (reserve ¼ cup liquid)
    1 tablespoon minced fresh basil
       leaves
    ⅛ teaspoon pepper
    1 jar (about 7 oz.) prepared
       antipasto, drained
    1 cup (4 oz.) shredded provolone
       cheese
    ¼ small red onion, thinly sliced and
       separated into rings
    ½ cup fresh basil leaves, lightly
       packed, cut into thin shreds
    ½ pound purchased breadsticks or
       thinly sliced baguette

Pocket bread wedges go with garbanzos.

In a 6- to 8-inch frying pan over medium-high heat, combine oil, garlic, and prosciutto. Cook, stirring often, until prosciutto is crisp, 4 to 5 minutes; stir in vinegar. Let cool.

In a large bowl, coarsely mash beans; stir in liquid, prosciutto, minced basil, and pepper. Spread mixture into an 8-inch-diameter round on a large platter. Evenly distribute antipasto over beans, then scatter with cheese, onions, and basil shreds. Scoop onto a plate and eat with a fork; serve with breadsticks. Or spread beans on baguette slices. Serves 6 to 8.

PER SERVING: 254 calories, 12 g protein, 32 g carbohydrates, 9 g fat, 15 mg cholesterol, 708 mg sodium

Breadsticks go well with kidney beans.

Pan-grilled Risotto

ISOTTO, THE POPULAR ITALIAN *cooked rice, is not just a dish of infinite flavors, but one that can be varied in other ways. Here it is pan-grilled. Not only does risotto taste good this way; you make it ahead. Stirring risotto as it cooks develops its characteristic creamy texture.*

When risotto cools, it firms. Then you can cut it, brown in butter, and even reheat it in the oven after it's browned. Inside the slightly crusty exterior, the risotto retains its soft texture.

PAN-GRILLED RISOTTO WITH MOZZARELLA & BASIL

    About 6 tablespoons butter or
      margarine
  2 tablespoons olive oil
  2 medium-size onions, chopped
  1 clove garlic, minced or pressed
  1 cup arborio or short-grain white
      (pearl) rice
  1½ cups regular-strength chicken
      broth
  1½ cups water
  ¾ cup freshly grated parmesan
      cheese
  ½ pound mozzarella cheese, diced
  2 tablespoons minced fresh basil
      leaves or 2 teaspoons dry basil
      leaves

In a 3- to 4-quart pan over medium-high heat, melt 2 tablespoons of the butter with olive oil. Add onions and stir often until golden brown, 8 to 10 minutes. Add garlic and rice; stir until rice is opaque, about 3 minutes. Add broth and water; stir occasionally until boiling.

Reduce heat and simmer, uncovered, until rice is tender to bite and liquid has been absorbed, 25 to 30 minutes; stir

Crusty triangles of risotto complement simply cooked meats and vegetables.

often near end of cooking time to prevent sticking. Remove from heat and cool 25 to 30 minutes. Stir in ½ cup parmesan, mozzarella, and basil. Line a 9- by 13-inch dish or pan with foil. Scrape risotto into foil and spread smooth. Cover and chill until firm, at least 2 hours or up to 3 days.

Invert risotto onto a board; carefully peel off foil. With a sharp knife, cut risotto into 3-inch squares, then cut each square diagonally in half.

Melt 1 teaspoon butter in a 10- to 12-inch nonstick frying pan over medium-high heat. Cook triangles in pan (do not crowd) until golden brown, about 3 minutes on each side. As cooked, transfer in 1 layer to an ovenproof platter. Keep in a 300° oven. Cook remaining risotto; add butter as needed. (You can brown risotto up to 1 day ahead; to reheat, put in a 450° oven, uncovered, until sizzling, about 15 minutes.) Add remaining parmesan to taste. Serves 5 or 6.

PER SERVING: 409 calories, 16 g protein, 31 g carbohydrates, 25 g fat, 60 mg cholesterol, 462 mg sodium

GRILLED RISOTTO WITH ASPARAGUS

Make **pan-grilled risotto with mozzarella and basil** (preceding), but omit mozzarella and basil.

Snap off and discard tough ends from ½ pound **asparagus.** Cut stems into ⅛-inch slices. In a 10- to 12-inch frying pan over high heat, bring 1 inch **water** to boiling. Add asparagus; cook, uncovered, until just tender to bite, 1 to 2 minutes; drain. Let cool and add to risotto. Serves 5 or 6.

PER SERVING: 301 calories, 10 g protein, 31 g carbohydrates, 16 g fat, 30 mg cholesterol, 322 mg sodium

Scrape cooked, seasoned risotto into foil-lined pan. As risotto cools, it becomes firm enough to cut.

Carefully peel foil from cold risotto, inverted out of pan. With a sharp knife, cut risotto into squares, then triangles.

More June Recipes

OTHER JUNE ARTICLES *feature quick-to-make biscuits fragrant with fresh basil, and a mixed fruit jam combining berries, cherries, and apricots.*

BASIL BISCUITS

Hot and tender, with a crusty topping of cheese, these biscuits are richly fragrant with fresh basil. Quick to make, they're best warm from the oven.

- ⅔ **cup lightly packed grated parmesan cheese**
- 2 **cups all-purpose flour**
- 2 **teaspoons baking powder**
- ½ **teaspoon baking soda**
- ½ **cup (¼ lb.) cold butter or margarine**
- ⅓ **cup finely chopped fresh basil leaves**
- ¾ **cup unflavored yogurt**

Set aside 2 tablespoons of the cheese. In a large bowl, stir together the remaining cheese, flour, baking powder, and baking soda. Set aside 1 tablespoon butter; add remaining butter to flour mixture and rub mixture with your fingers (or cut with a pastry blender) until coarse crumbs form.

Stir basil into flour mixture. Add yogurt and stir until dough clings together in lumps. Pat dough into a ball, then knead on a board until the dough holds together, about 10 turns. Gently pat and roll dough to make a log about 7 inches long. With a sharp knife, cut crosswise into 7 equal pieces. If you want rounded biscuits, roll each piece of dough into a ball.

Set 1 piece in center of a buttered 8- or 9-inch-diameter cake pan; evenly space remaining pieces around center. Melt and brush reserved butter over tops; sprinkle with reserved cheese. Bake in a 400° oven until biscuits are dark golden on top, about 30 minutes. Remove from pan; serve hot. Makes 7.

PER BISCUIT: 298 calories, 8 g protein, 29 g carbohydrates, 17 g fat, 45 mg cholesterol, 469 mg sodium

SUMMER FRUIT JAM

Jams of mixed fruit are often invented on the spur of the moment to use up odds and ends. Sometimes the combinations bear repeating, as with this version.

- 2 **cups raspberries**
- 2 **cups blackberries or loganberries**
- 1 **cup sweet cherries**
- 1 **cup coarsely chopped apricots**
- 4½ **cups sugar**
- 1 **pouch (3 oz.) liquid pectin**

Rinse and drain raspberries and blackberries. Pour into a 6- to 8-quart pan and coarsely mash.

Rinse cherries, stem, pit, and cut in half. Add cherries, apricots, and sugar to pan. Set pan on high heat and, stirring constantly, bring mixture to a rolling boil that cannot be stirred down; boil exactly 1 minute. Remove from heat and at once stir in pectin, mixing for 2 to 3 minutes. Skim off any foam.

Ladle hot jam into hot, sterilized pint or half-pint jars, filling to within ¼ inch of rim. Wipe rims clean. Place hot, sterilized lids on jars and screw on bands snugly. Set jars on a rack in a deep 7- to 8-quart pan. Cover jars with at least 1 inch boiling water. Hold at simmering (180°) for 10 minutes. Lift jars from water (don't tilt, as this may loosen seal) and set on a towel to cool. Press lids; if they stay down, jars are sealed. Refrigerate unsealed jars up to 2 months. Makes about 2½ pints. —*Clara Dobberstein, Arcata, Calif.*

PER TABLESPOON: 49 calories, 1 g protein, 12 g carbohydrates, .03 g fat, 0 mg cholesterol, .14 mg sodium

Fresh basil, parmesan topping, and butter to spread on give biscuits lots of flavor.

Sherry, soy sauce, ginger, and garlic blend with mushrooms and onions to season fish fillets.

FISH FILLETS WITH SHERRY-MUSHROOM SAUCE

¼ **pound mushrooms, thinly sliced**
2 **tablespoons olive oil or butter**
1½ **pounds white-flesh fish fillets (each about ¾ in. thick) such as sea bass or rockfish**
1 **teaspoon cornstarch**
⅓ **cup water**
¼ **cup dry sherry**
1 **tablespoon soy sauce**
2 **cloves garlic, pressed or minced**
2 **teaspoons minced fresh ginger**
½ **cup sliced green onions**

In a 10- to 12-inch frying pan over medium heat, stir mushrooms in 1½ tablespoons of the oil until lightly browned, about 8 minutes; spoon mushrooms from pan and set aside.

Add remaining oil to pan over medium-high heat. When hot, add fish in a single layer. Cover and cook until fish is white in center (cut to test), about 8 minutes. With a wide spatula, lift fish from pan and keep warm.

Stir together cornstarch, water, sherry, soy sauce, garlic, and ginger. Pour mixture into pan; add mushrooms and stir to loosen brown bits. Still stirring, bring mixture to boiling on high heat. Add onions and pour sauce over fish. Makes 4 or 5 servings. —*Edith Beccaria, San Francisco.*

PER SERVING: 244 calories, 33 g protein, 5 g carbohydrates, 9.5 g fat, 60 mg cholesterol, 363 mg sodium

Sliced tomatoes and mozzarella sizzle on top of pizza; beneath cheese is a layer of garlicky pesto.

PESTO PIZZA

Pesto (recipe follows)
Crust (recipe follows)
½ **pound mozzarella cheese, shredded (2 cups)**
5 **large (about 1¼ lb.) firm-ripe Roma-type tomatoes**
Salt

Spread pesto evenly over crust. Sprinkle cheese evenly over pesto. Rinse and core tomatoes; slice thinly. Arrange tomatoes evenly over cheese. Bake pizza on lowest rack in a 450° oven until crust is brown on bottom (lift with spatula to check), 25 to 30 minutes. Add salt to taste. Makes 4 to 6 servings. —*Ann Smith, Portland.*

Pesto. In a blender or food processor, purée 4 large cloves **garlic,** 2 cups lightly packed fresh **basil leaves,** and ½ cup **olive oil** or salad oil.

Crust. In a bowl, mix 1½ cups **all-purpose flour,** 1 package **active dry yeast,** and ¼ teaspoon **salt.** Stir in ⅔ cup very warm **water** (130°) until dough forms. On lightly floured board, knead dough until smooth, 2 to 3 minutes. Brush a 14-inch-diameter pizza pan or a 10- by 15-inch rimmed pan with 2 teaspoons **olive oil** or salad oil. Press dough evenly over bottom and up pan sides, turning under to form rim.

PER SERVING: 332 calories, 6 g protein, 34 g carbohydrates, 20 g fat, 0 mg cholesterol, 97 mg sodium

International flavors for cauliflower include Mexican cilantro, Japanese shiitake mushrooms, Indian curry.

EAST-WEST CAULIFLOWER & MUSHROOMS

¼ **cup (⅛ lb.) butter or margarine**
1 **cup sliced regular mushrooms**
4 **fresh shiitake mushrooms (2½-in.-wide caps), stems discarded and caps thinly sliced; or 1 cup sliced regular mushrooms**
1 **large onion, sliced**
1 **teaspoon curry powder**
¼ **teaspoon crushed dried hot red chilies**
4 **cups cauliflowerets**
⅔ **cup water**
1 **large firm-ripe tomato, cored and diced**
¼ **cup chopped fresh cilantro (coriander)**

Melt butter in a 10- to 12-inch frying pan over medium-high heat; add regular and shiitake mushrooms, onion, curry powder, and chilies. Stir vegetables often until onion is limp, about 8 minutes.

Add cauliflowerets and water; stir to mix. Cover and cook until flowerets are tender when pierced, about 15 minutes. Stir in tomato and half the cilantro; cook until tomatoes are hot, then pour vegetables into a bowl and sprinkle with remaining cilantro. Serves 4 to 6. —*Grace Kirschenbaum, Los Angeles.*

PER SERVING: 106 calories, 2.5 g protein, 8 g carbohydrates, 8 g fat, 21 mg cholesterol, 93 mg sodium

OLIVE-PECAN CHICKEN SLAW

2 teaspoons butter or margarine
½ cup pecan halves
Dressing (recipe follows)
2 cups shredded cabbage
1½ cups ½-inch chunks cooked, boned, and skinned chicken breast
1 medium-size Red Delicious apple, cored and diced
1 jar (2 oz.) diced pimientos, drained
1 can (2¼ oz.) sliced black ripe olives, drained
¼ cup thinly sliced celery
Salt

Melt butter in an 8- to 10-inch frying pan over medium heat. Add pecans and stir occasionally until nuts are a darker brown, about 8 minutes. Drain on paper towels.

To dressing, add cabbage, chicken, apple, pimientos, olives, and celery; stir to blend. Sprinkle nuts onto salad; add salt to taste. Serves 6. —*Carole van Brocklin, Port Angeles, Wash.*

Dressing. In a salad bowl, stir together ½ cup **mayonnaise**, 2 tablespoons **lemon juice**, 1 teaspoon **Dijon mustard** or regular prepared mustard, ½ teaspoon **sugar**, and ¼ teaspoon **pepper.**

PER SERVING: 321 calories, 12 g protein, 10 g carbohydrates, 27 g fat, 45 mg cholesterol, 264 mg sodium

Cabbage leaves make bowl for entrée salad of chicken, shredded cabbage, apples, pecans, pimientos, and olives.

CHOCOLATE CHIP SCONES

2 cups all-purpose flour
¼ cup powdered sugar
1 tablespoon baking powder
6 tablespoons butter or margarine, cut into chunks
1 large egg
About ½ cup milk
½ cup semisweet chocolate baking chips
1 teaspoon granulated sugar

In a bowl, mix flour, powdered sugar, and baking powder. Cut butter into flour mixture with a pastry blender or rub with fingers until consistency of fine crumbs.

Break egg into a glass measuring cup and add milk to make ⅔ cup; stir to blend egg and milk. With a fork, stir milk mixture and chocolate into flour until fairly evenly moistened. Pat into a ball and knead on a lightly floured board until dough holds together, 6 to 8 turns. Pat dough into a 6- by 9-inch rectangle on a greased 12- by 15-inch baking sheet. Sprinkle with granulated sugar. Cut into 6 squares, then cut each square diagonally in half; separate wedges and space well apart.

Bake in a 450° oven until golden brown, 12 to 15 minutes. Makes 12. —*Donna Henderson, Monmouth, Ore.*

PER SCONE: 187 calories, 3 g protein, 23 g carbohydrates, 9 g fat, 40 mg cholesterol, 176 mg sodium

Bits of soft chocolate add a touch of sweetness to hot scones. They're perfect for breakfast or teatime.

FRESH PEACH PIE

7 medium-size (about 2½ lb.) ripe peaches
¾ cup orange juice
¾ cup sugar
3 tablespoons cornstarch
2 tablespoons lemon juice
1 baked 9- or 10-inch pie shell
2 to 3 teaspoons finely shredded orange peel (orange part only)
2 or 3 fresh mint sprigs

Peel, pit, and slice enough peaches to make 1 cup. Whirl slices in a food processor or blender until smoothly puréed; gradually add orange juice as fruit is being puréed.

In a 1- to 2-quart pan, stir sugar with cornstarch. Add peach purée; mix well. Stirring, bring mixture to a rolling boil on high heat. Cool purée quickly—set pan in cold or ice water and stir frequently until just slightly warm.

Meanwhile, peel, pit, and thinly slice remaining peaches; mix with lemon juice to help preserve color. Gently stir fruit slices and juice into purée, then pour mixture into the pie shell. Chill until cool, about 45 minutes or up to 4 hours (cover loosely when cool). Garnish pie with shredded orange peel and mint sprigs. Makes 8 or 9 servings. —*Gretchen Guard, Sun Valley, Idaho.*

PER SERVING: 222 calories, 2 g protein, 40 g carbohydrates, 7 g fat, 0 mg cholesterol, 123 mg sodium

Fresh peaches, sliced, will fill baked pie shell. Make cooked glaze of peaches and orange juices.

AN OLD ROMAN PROVERB *states that it takes four people to make a good salad dressing—a spendthrift for the oil, a miser for the vinegar, a judge for the salt, and a madman to mix them all up. This salad's dressing also requires the services of a pyromaniac, to ignite it.*

The refined salad has a peasant ancestry; people of Pennsylvania Dutch (or other north European) extraction used to make a similar one called "wilted lettuce."

Oil might be scarce, but bacon dripping was always around, the byproduct of traditionally heavy breakfasts. In spite of its seemingly incongruous blend of materials, it was a good dressing—but not as good as this one.

SPINACH WITH HOT BACON DRESSING FLAMBÉ

    About 1½ pounds spinach
½ **pound sliced bacon, cut into ½-inch pieces**
2 **tablespoons sugar**
¼ **cup cider vinegar**
1 **tablespoon dry mustard**
¼ **cup brandy**
2 **large hard-cooked eggs, chopped**
    Salt and pepper

Discard tough stems and yellowed leaves from spinach; rinse leaves well and pat dry. If made ahead, wrap in paper towels, seal in a plastic bag, and chill up until next day.

Break spinach leaves into bite-size pieces and place in a large salad bowl; cover and return to the refrigerator while making the dressing.

In a 10- to 12-inch frying pan over medium heat, stir bacon often until crisp, 5 to 8 minutes.

To bacon, add sugar, vinegar, and mustard; stir until mixture boils. Heat brandy until hot in a 2- to 4-cup pan; ignite and pour into vinegar mixture (not beneath a fan or flammable objects). Shake pan until the flames die.

Pour hot dressing over spinach and mix well. Sprinkle egg onto salad; add salt and pepper to taste. Serves 8 to 10.

PER SERVING: 166 calories, 5 g protein, 5 g carbohydrates, 14 g fat, 70 mg cholesterol, 208 mg sodium

Scotts Valley, Calif.

IT'S NOT EASY *to be both delicate and assertive, but Raoul Berke's Shrimp Cilantro manages to do so with style.*

Delicacy is inherent in the shrimp, with celery, cilantro, green onions, and olives adding their own subtle flavors. Assertiveness comes from red chili mayonnaise. Use more or less of the concoction—let your love of (or tolerance for) hot chilies be your guide. Extra chili mayonnaise goes well with hamburgers.

SHRIMP CILANTRO

1 **pound tiny cooked shelled shrimp**
1½ **cups diced celery**
½ **cup thinly sliced green onions, including tops**
¼ **cup lightly packed fresh cilantro (coriander), chopped**
¼ **cup chopped Spanish-style pimiento-stuffed green olives**
½ **cup mayonnaise**
    Red chili mayonnaise (recipe follows)
1 **large firm-ripe avocado**
    Butter lettuce leaves or 8 slices toasted thinly sliced white or whole-wheat bread

In a large bowl, combine shrimp, celery, green onions, cilantro, and olives. Blend the mayonnaise and ½ cup of the red chili mayonnaise; stir into shrimp mixture and mix gently until combined. Serve, or cover and chill as long as 6 hours.

"This salad dressing requires the services of a pyromaniac to ignite it."

To serve as a salad, peel, pit, and thinly slice the avocado. Arrange lettuce leaves on 4 plates, top with shrimp mixture, and garnish with avocado.

To serve as an open-faced sandwich, peel, pit, and mash the avocado; spread equally on toast. Spoon shrimp mixture on top.

Accompany portions with red chili mayonnaise to add as desired. Serves 4.

PER SALAD SERVING: 632 calories, 27 g protein, 9 g carbohydrates, 56 g fat, 306 mg cholesterol, 664 mg sodium

Red chili mayonnaise. Discard stems and shake seeds from 6 **small dried hot red chilies.** Coarsely crumble chilies into a blender; whirl until pulverized. Add 3 tablespoons **white wine vinegar** and 1 clove **garlic;** whirl until minced. Add 2 **large egg yolks;** whirl until mixed. With motor running on high speed, add ¾ cup **salad oil** in a very slow, steady stream; mixture will thicken. Season to taste with **salt.** Use, or cover and chill up to 2 weeks. Makes about 1 cup.

O. Beal, M.D.

Albuquerque

MYSTERIOUSLY NAMED BOTH *Picnic Stew and Soup to Warm Your Bones, Richard Heyman's creation is thick enough to justify the former name, sturdy enough to fulfill the promise of the latter. One thing is certain: take this stew on your picnic and you won't miss any of the other things you may have forgotten.*

PICNIC STEW

2   tablespoons salad oil
1½ pounds boned, lean beef chuck, cut into 1-inch cubes
2   large onions, chopped
2   cloves garlic, minced or pressed
2   cans (about 14 oz. *each*) tomatoes
1   can (14½ oz.) regular-strength beef broth
1   cup water
¾   teaspoon *each* dry thyme leaves and dry marjoram leaves
2   cups 1-inch-long pieces celery
2   cups ½-inch-thick pieces carrot
½   cup diced red or green bell pepper
¼   cup chopped parsley
¼   cup purchased green chili salsa
½   cup elbow macaroni

"Take this on your picnic and you won't miss any of the other things you may have forgotten."

2   medium-size ears of corn, husked, silks removed, and each broken into 1½-inch pieces; or 1 can (15 oz.) baby corn on the cob, drained
Salt and pepper

Pour oil into a 5- to 6-quart pan over medium-high heat. Add meat, a portion at a time, and cook until well browned on all sides. Add onions and garlic and stir often until onions are limp, about 10 minutes. Add tomatoes (break in with a spoon) and their liquid, broth, water, thyme, and marjoram. Bring to a boil; cover, and simmer until meat is very tender when pierced, about 2 hours.

Stir in celery, carrot, bell pepper, and parsley. Cover and continue to simmer for 15 minutes. Stir in salsa, macaroni, and corn. Cover and cook until carrots are tender when pierced and macaroni is just tender to bite, about 10 minutes longer. Season to taste with salt and pepper. Makes 5 or 6 servings.

PER SERVING: 344 calories, 30 g protein, 31 g carbohydrates, 12 g fat, 68 mg cholesterol, 661 mg sodium

Richard A. Heyman

Sunnyvale, Calif.

MOST PEOPLE THINK *of gazpacho as a light first course to a summer meal. Serious eaters may prefer a more substantial version, such as Roger Colatorti's. His hearty gazpacho is based on chicken broth rather than tomato juice, and it's further fortified by the addition of a coarse purée of bell pepper, cucumber, garlic, onion, and canned tomato.*

Many additional herbs and seasonings enrich the flavor, and diners are encouraged to add toppings from a smörgåsbord of chopped or sliced condiments. Serve with crusty bread for a notable lunch.

GAZPACHO COLATORTI

1   can (about 14 oz.) tomatoes
1¾ cups or 1 can (14½ oz.) regular-strength chicken broth
3   cloves garlic, halved
1   small onion, quartered
1   medium-size cucumber, peeled and cut into chunks
3   tablespoons *each* rice vinegar and olive oil
1   teaspoon *each* dry tarragon leaves and dry basil leaves
¼   teaspoon *each* ground cumin, chili powder, and liquid hot pepper seasoning
¼   cup coarsely chopped parsley
1   small red or green bell pepper, seeded and cut into chunks
3   green onions (ends trimmed), including tops, coarsely chopped
1   large can (15 oz.) tomato sauce
    About 3 tablespoons lime or lemon juice
    Condiments (suggestions follow)

In a blender, combine tomatoes and their liquid, and about half the broth. Add garlic, onion, cucumber, vinegar, oil, tarragon, basil, cumin, chili powder, liquid pepper, parsley, bell pepper, and green onions. Whirl until coarsely puréed. Pour into a large bowl and stir in the tomato sauce, remaining broth, and lime juice to taste. Cover and chill at least 2 hours or as long as overnight.

Ladle into individual bowls and offer condiments to add to taste. Makes 6 servings, each about 1⅓ cups.

PER SERVING, INCLUDING GREEN ONIONS, CUCUMBERS, AND TOMATOES: 134 calories, 3.5 g protein, 15 g carbohydrates, 8 g fat, 0 mg cholesterol, 569 mg sodium

Condiments. Select 3 or 4 of the following and present each in a small bowl: about ¾ cup thinly sliced **green onions,** including tops; about ¾ cup peeled, seeded, and diced **cucumber;** about ¾ cup stemmed, seeded, and diced red or green **bell pepper;** about ¾ cup peeled and diced firm-ripe **tomatoes;** 3 diced hard-cooked **large eggs;** about ¾ cup **unflavored yogurt.**

Roger Colatorti

Portland

June Menus

A S WEATHER WARMS *and days grow longer, we spend more time outdoors. These easy menus reflect the change of season.*

Plan a back-yard lunch party for children to celebrate the end of school. Treat guests to a casual dinner from the barbecue, or relax on the deck with brunch.

This is a no-utensils menu, ideal for the exciting first day of summer holidays.

As the pizza sauce cooks, rinse and cut the raw vegetables.

PEPPERONI PIZZA LOAF

- 1   **pound ground lean beef**
- 1   **large onion, chopped**
- 1   **clove garlic, minced or pressed**
- 1   **can (8 oz.) tomato sauce**
- 1   **can (4 oz.) chopped ripe olives**
- 1   **teaspoon *each* dry basil leaves and oregano leaves**
- ¼   **teaspoon pepper**
- ¾   **cup grated parmesan cheese**
- 1   **loaf (about 1 lb.) French bread**
- ¾   **pound cheddar cheese, shredded**
- 3   **to 5 ounces pepperoni sausage, thinly sliced**

Cook beef and onion in a 10- to 12-inch frying pan over medium-high heat, stirring frequently, until meat begins to brown, 15 to 20 minutes. Drain off and discard fat. Add the garlic, tomato sauce, olives, basil, oregano, pepper, and parmesan. Cook, stirring often, until all liquid has evaporated, 10 to 12 minutes. Set aside. If made ahead, cool, cover, and chill up until next day; reheat to continue.

Cut bread in half lengthwise. Set halves, cut sides up, in a 10- by 15-inch baking pan. Broil 5 inches from heat until toasted, 1 to 2 minutes; remove from oven. Spoon equal portions of cooked meat sauce evenly onto halves. Broil until edges of bread are brown and meat is sizzling, 3 to 5 minutes. Remove from oven and sprinkle bread evenly with cheddar cheese; top with pepperoni. Return to broiler and cook until cheese melts, about 3 minutes. Slice loaf halves diagonally across into 10 wedges. Serves 8 to 10 children, 5 or 6 adults. — *Georgianna Smith, Redwood City, Calif.*

PER WEDGE: 289 calories, 16 g protein, 18 g carbohydrates, 17 g fat, 47 mg cholesterol, 630 mg sodium

A marinade of balsamic vinegar and thyme flavors several parts of the meal.

Ignite the briquets for the barbecue about 1½ hours before time to serve dinner. For adult desserts, pour orange-flavor liqueur over strawberries and pineapple.

Pepperoni pizza, made with French bread, is popular fare at "no-more-teachers" party for youngsters.

GRILLED GAME HENS & VEGETABLES IN BALSAMIC MARINADE

- 4 **Rock Cornish game hens** (1¼ lb. each)
- 2 medium-size **zucchini** (about ¾ lb. total), ends trimmed and cut into ½-inch-thick diagonal slices
- 2 medium-size **crookneck squash** (about ½ lb. total), ends trimmed, and cut into ½-inch-thick diagonal slices
- 1 large **red bell pepper**, cut into 1½-inch-square pieces
- 8 large **mushrooms** (about ¾ lb. total), rinsed and stems trimmed
- 8 large **shallots** (about ½ lb. total), peeled
  Balsamic marinade (recipe follows)
  Salt

Rinse hens and pat dry. With poultry or kitchen shears, cut birds open lengthwise through breastbones. Open hens; press, skin up, to crack bones so birds lie flat. Place hens in a large, heavy plastic bag; put zucchini, crookneck, bell pepper, mushrooms, and shallots in another. Pour ⅓ of the marinade into each bag; seal bags and rotate. Set bags in a large pan. Chill for 1 hour or up to next day; turn occasionally.

Using long metal skewers (each 12 to 15 in.), thread 2 hens from wing to wing and from thigh to thigh to hold them flat. Repeat to skewer remaining 2 birds. Thread each type of vegetable separately on 5 additional skewers (9 skewers in all). Place birds and vegetables on a grill 4 to 6 inches over a solid bed of medium coals (you should be able to hold your hand at grill level only 4 to 5 seconds). Turn as needed for even browning; brush often with marinade from bags. If flare-ups occur, lift hens off grill until flames subside, or turn. Cook until meat at thigh bone is no longer pink (cut to test) and vegetables are soft when pressed, 30 to 35 minutes. To serve, push foods off skewers. Add salt to taste. Serves 4 to 6.

PER SERVING: 463 calories, 49 g protein, 11 g carbohydrates, 23 g fat, 146 mg cholesterol, 250 mg sodium

Balsamic marinade. Whisk together 1 cup **balsamic** or red wine **vinegar**, 2 tablespoons **Dijon mustard**, 1 tablespoon *each* minced **parsley** and **fresh thyme leaves** (or 1 teaspoon dry thyme leaves), and ¼ teaspoon **pepper**. Reserve

Flattened and skewered, game hens in balsamic marinade are easy to handle on the grill. Skewered vegetables cook alongside birds.

⅓ cup marinade for spaghetti salad (recipe follows).

COOL SPAGHETTI SALAD

Cook 12 ounces dry **spaghetti** in 4 quarts boiling **water**, uncovered, until just tender to bite, 10 to 12 minutes. Drain and put in a large bowl; stir in ¾ cup

thinly sliced **green onions.** Whisk ⅔ cup **extra-virgin** or regular **olive** or salad **oil** into reserved ⅓ cup **balsamic marinade** (recipe precedes). Pour over pasta and mix well. Serve, or cover and chill up to next day. Serves 6.

PER SERVING: 389 calories, 8 g protein, 44 g carbohydrates, 20 g fat, 0 mg cholesterol, 46 mg sodium

(Continued on next page)

NO-FUSS SUMMER BRUNCH

Quick Orange Coffee Cake Ring
Scrambled Eggs
Honeydew Melon Wedges
Hot Coffee

A quick coffee cake is the focus of this easy-to-fix brunch. You can serve melon wedges to go with the meal, or whirl the fruit with enough orange juice to make a sipping beverage.

While the cake bakes, cook the eggs. Offer oranges (left from cake) with melon.

QUICK ORANGE COFFEE CAKE RING

In a 3- to 4-cup pan, combine ½ cup (¼ lb.) **butter** or margarine, ⅔ cup **sugar,** and 3 tablespoons finely shredded **orange peel** (you need 2 medium-size oranges). Stir over medium heat until sugar dissolves. Remove from heat.

Remove dough from 2 packages (10 oz. each) **refrigerator biscuits;** separate biscuits. Coat each dough round with butter mixture and place, vertically side by side, in a greased 9- to 10-inch plain or decorative tube pan (about 3-qt. size). Drizzle any remaining butter over biscuits. Bake in a 375° oven until top is golden brown, 30 to 35 minutes. Run a knife around edge of pan, place a plate on top of pan, then invert to turn cake out. Serve hot. Makes 6 to 8 servings. — *Annette Meade, Nevada City, Calif.*

PER SERVING: 365 calories, 5 g protein, 50 g carbohydrates, 16 g fat, 51 mg cholesterol, 732 mg sodium

JULY

Giant Stacked Sandwich (page 166)

Easy meals for casual
summer living sparkle in our July issue. Dazzle your
friends with a Giant Stacked Sandwich at a Fourth of July
party. Or let your guests participate in the cooking at an
open-air Mongolian barbecue featuring thinly sliced lamb
in Chinese sesame buns. Salad and wine lovers will find fresh
inspiration in our colorful summer combinations. For camp
cooks we suggest menus and recipes for a weekend outing
free of last-minute surprises. Whimsical carved watermelons
or frozen desserts provide a festive finish.

161

Chopstick Barbecue

WHEN THE MONGOLS *invaded China, they brought with them their love of lamb. Today, this culinary legacy is still widely enjoyed in northern China. Thin slices of marinated lamb are stir-fried over a special cast-iron grill with broad, closely set slats. Then the meat is pushed into a sesame bun and eaten as a sandwich.*

MONGOLIAN BARBECUE

Marinated Radishes & Cucumbers

Mongolian Barbecued Lamb Sandwiches

Asian Pears   Almond Cookies

Chinese Beer   Iced Tea

For our Mongolian grill, we use a griddle or frying pans on a barbecue. The meal goes together very easily, since guests do the cooking. The buns can be made ahead and baked shortly before serving.

MONGOLIAN BARBECUED LAMB SANDWICHES

1½ to 2 pounds boneless lamb leg or shoulder, trimmed of excess fat and cut in thin strips (about 1 by 3 in.)

¼ cup soy sauce

3 tablespoons rice wine or dry sherry

3 tablespoons minced fresh ginger

2 cloves garlic, pressed or minced

2 tablespoons Oriental sesame oil

1½ cups thin shreds green onions or leeks

1½ cups lightly packed fresh cilantro (coriander) leaves

6 or 12 large eggs

   About 6 tablespoons salad oil
   Pickled garlic (recipe follows)
   Sesame buns (recipe follows)

Mix the lamb with soy, wine, ginger, pressed garlic, and oil. Cover and chill at least 4 hours or up to the next day. Place in 1 or 2 bowls. Arrange onions, cilantro, and eggs in separate containers. Pour salad oil into a small pitcher. Arrange the lamb, onion, cilantro, eggs, pickled garlic, and oil near the barbecue. Also have a pair of long cooking chopsticks or a spatula and potholders to use.

Set a griddle, 10- to 12-inch frying pan, paella pan, or wok on a grill 2 to 4 inches above a solid bed of hot coals (you should be able to hold your hand at grill level only 2 to 3 seconds). If barbecue is wide enough, you can set 2 pans on the grill so 2 people can cook at the same time. When griddle or pan is hot, pour in about 1 tablespoon oil; spread over surface or tilt pan to coat bottom. Add about ⅓ cup meat and cook, stirring and turning, to brown lightly, about 2 minutes. Then crack egg over meat, if desired. Stir-fry mixture just until egg is softly set. Sprinkle with onion and cilantro to taste and stir to mix. Scoop mixture onto a plate.

Put meat mixture into split bun. Add pickled garlic to taste.

Scrape pan with a spatula to remove residue; repeat to cook more. Makes 6 servings, 2 sandwiches each.

PER SERVING: 775 calories, 39 g protein, 82 g carbohydrates, 31 g fat, 354 mg cholesterol, 1,389 mg sodium

Pickled garlic. Peel 24 small cloves **garlic** (if thicker than ½ inch, cut in half lengthwise). In a 1- to 1½ quart pan, mix ½ cup **rice vinegar** or distilled vinegar, 3 tablespoons **sugar,** and 1 teaspoon **salt;** bring to a boil. Add garlic and cook 1 minute. Cool, cover, and chill at least 1 day or up to 2 weeks.

Sesame buns. To a wok or 10- to 12-inch frying pan, add 6 tablespoons **salad oil;** set over medium-high heat. When hot, stir in ½ cup **all-purpose flour** until smooth. Cook, stirring often, until roux turns deep gold, 6 to 9 minutes. Let cool.

In a large bowl, mix 3¾ cups **all-purpose flour** and ½ teaspoon **salt.** Make a well in the center and pour in 1½ cups **boiling water.** Stir with a fork to moisten flour. Knead on a lightly floured board until smooth and elastic, 15 to 20 minutes. Cover and let stand 20 to 30 minutes.

On a floured board, roll dough into a 12- by 15-inch rectangle. Spread roux over dough. Cut crosswise into thirds.

Stack pieces with roux-coated surfaces facing inside stack (some roux may ooze out). Cut to make 12 squares.

Roll each square into a 4- by 6-inch rectangle ⅛ inch thick. Fold 2 opposite long sides toward center, overlapping sides completely. With seam-side up, roll half of each folded piece to ⅛-inch thickness. Starting with thick end, fold dough over twice, in thirds, to cover thin end.

With thin end on top, dip bottom surface in sesame seed. With seed side up, roll out each bun to form a 3- by 5-inch rectangle about ¼ inch thick. Place slightly apart, seed side up, on ungreased 12- by 15-inch baking sheets. (If made ahead, cover and chill until the next day.)

Bake on the bottom rack of a 400° oven until golden brown and puffy, 15 to 20 minutes if at room temperature, 25 minutes if cold. With a sharp knife or scissors, slit 1 long and 1 short side of each bun, if needed, to open. Serve warm or cool. Makes 12.

Four Steps to Chinese Sesame Buns

1 *Cut roux-coated dough rectangle into thirds and stack, roux sides facing in.*

2 *Cut stack into 12 squares. Roll each into a thin rectangle.*

3 *Fold in sides to overlap. Roll ½ of the strip to ⅛-inch thickness. Starting at thick end, fold over in thirds.*

4 *Dip smooth side of bun into sesame seed. Roll into a rectangle, seed side up.*

In China, diners use long chopsticks to turn lamb on big griddle-grill at Beijing's 130-year-old Kaorouji Restaurant.

In the West, use a large griddle or frying pan over hot coals on a grill. Diners can take turns stir-frying small portions of marinated lamb with egg, onion, and cilantro.

Put savory filling into a crisp, flaky sesame bun. Slip sweet-tart pickled garlic into bun to taste; or eat it alongside, as a relish.

Surprising Summer Salads

SUMMER SPELLS SALAD to many people. A salad's light, fresh simplicity seems naturally suited to warm-weather dining. Serve salad before, with, or after the main course; or make it your whole meal, accompanied by some good bread and butter, and perhaps a wedge of cheese.

These three summer salad selections, designed by consultant Beverly Anderson of Mill Valley, California, taste especially good with wine. In each of them, the greens are balanced with a touch of sweet from fruit, honey, or sugar, or glossed with a bit of fat as found in cheese or oil to make them more compatible with wine.

In the first recipe, the traditional green salad is sparked with fresh herbs and crisp buttery croutons. It's a safe all-round offering with dry table wines, but it's exceptionally compatible with a toasty, creamy Chardonnay that has good fruit and body. Adding a little wine to the salad dressing makes the balance all the more agreeable.

The spinach salad picks up Asian flavors. It gets sweetness from Chinese sausage, red bell peppers, and Asian pears; smoothness from sesame oil and a mellow rice vinegar. These qualities make it blend well with a medium-dry fruity Gewürztraminer, White (Johannisberg) Riesling, or Chenin Blanc.

In the last recipe, notably compatible salad partners—nuggets of blue cheese and red grapes—harmonize well with a soft Merlot or Pinot Noir.

If you serve these salads with a beverage other than wine, you might like to increase the tartness of the dressings slightly to suit your taste.

CHARDONNAY WITH GREENS

- 10 cups washed, crisped, bite-size pieces red- or green-leaf, butter, or romaine lettuce (1 to 1¼ lb., untrimmed; use 1 or more kinds)
- 1 cup washed, crisped, bite-size pieces sorrel (tough stems removed) or arugula leaves (optional)
- 1 tablespoon minced fresh tarragon leaves, fresh oregano leaves, or

A plate brimming with greens, paired with Chardonnay, makes a light lunch. Buttery croutons, wine, and honey in dressing balance fruit acid in wine.

fresh thyme leaves (use 1 or a mixture of 3); or 1 teaspoon total of the dry herbs
- 3 tablespoons olive oil
- 1 tablespoon Chardonnay (or wine to be served with salad)
- 1 tablespoon champagne vinegar or wine vinegar
- 1½ teaspoons Dijon mustard
- 1½ teaspoons honey
  Buttered croutons (recipe follows)
  Salt and pepper

In a large bowl, combine lettuce, sorrel, and tarragon. Add oil and mix to coat leaves. Mix together Chardonnay, vinegar, mustard, and honey. Add to lettuce; mix to coat. Sprinkle with all the croutons. Add salt and pepper to taste. Makes 4 to 6 servings.

PER SERVING: 211 calories, 3 g protein, 15 g carbohydrates, 16 g fat, 23 mg cholesterol, 262 mg sodium

Buttered croutons. Cut ¼ pound day-old **French bread** into ½-inch cubes. Place in a 10- by 15-inch baking pan. Bake in a 300° oven until dry and firm, 12 to 15 minutes.

Remove from oven. Add ¼ cup melted **butter** or margarine and 2 tablespoons grated **parmesan cheese.** Mix to coat, then spread into an even layer in pan.

Return to oven and bake until lightly browned, 20 to 25 minutes more. Let cool. Serve, or store airtight up to 1 week. Makes 2½ cups.

Slivers of sweet peppers, juicy pear, Chinese sausage, and spinach with a low-acid dressing taste fine with a medium-dry Chenin Blanc or Riesling.

Spinach & Chinese Sausage Salad

4 Chinese sausages (about 6 oz. total), thinly sliced, or 6 ounces sliced dry salami, cut into thin slivers

½ cup minced shallot

½ cup sliced oyster or button mushrooms

1 large Asian pear (8 to 12 oz.) or Golden Delicious apple, cored and cut into matchstick-size strips

1 small red or yellow bell pepper (or half of each), stemmed, seeded, and cut into julienne strips

8 cups washed, crisped, bite-size pieces spinach leaves (about 12 oz., untrimmed)

1½ tablespoons *each* Oriental sesame oil and salad oil

2 tablespoons rice or cider vinegar Salt and pepper

In a 6- to 8-inch frying pan, stir sausage over medium-high heat until lightly browned, 5 to 7 minutes. Lift out sausage. Discard all but 2 tablespoons of the fat. Add shallots and mushrooms to pan; stir until shallots are limp, 2 to 3 minutes. Let cool. Stir in sausage, pear, and pepper.

In a large bowl, mix spinach with sesame oil and salad oil. Add pear mixture and vinegar; mix. Add salt and pepper to taste. Makes 3 or 4 entrée or 6 to 8 first-course servings.

Per Entrée Serving: 452 calories, 16 g protein, 24 g carbohydrates, 34 g fat, 45 mg cholesterol, 1,123 mg sodium

Grape & Blue Cheese Salad

9 cups washed, crisped, bite-size pieces butter lettuce leaves (about 1¼ lb., untrimmed)

3 cups washed, crisped, bite-size pieces radicchio or red-leaf lettuce leaves (6 to 8 oz., untrimmed)

1 cup small red seedless grapes

½ cup thinly sliced red onion

⅓ cup fruity extra-virgin olive oil

2 tablespoons berry vinegar (or wine vinegar plus ¼ teaspoon sugar)

2 tablespoons lemon juice

2 teaspoons Dijon mustard

2 teaspoons honey or sugar

½ teaspoon pepper

½ cup coarsely crumbled blue cheese Salt

Combine red grapes, blue-veined cheese, lettuce, radicchio, and red onion for a speedy summer salad. Accompany with a mellow Merlot.

In a large bowl, combine lettuce, radicchio, grapes, and onion. Add oil and mix to coat. Mix vinegar, lemon juice, mustard, honey, and pepper. Add to salad and mix well.

Spoon salad onto 4 to 6 salad or dinner plates. Sprinkle equally with cheese. Add salt to taste. Makes 4 to 6 servings.

Per Serving: 184 calories, 4 g protein, 9 g carbohydrates, 15 g fat, 8 mg cholesterol, 214 mg sodium

One Sandwich for a Crowd, Another for Your Pocket

SINGLE TO SUPER *is the size range of these two summer sandwiches. One is an individual packet to tuck in a backpack or pocket; the other serves a crowd. Both are based on thin, unleavened, flexible breads.*

For the group sandwich, you use the big rounds of cracker bread found in Middle Eastern markets and some supermarkets. The cracker's scale makes assembling an entrée for 10 to 12 pleasantly easy.

The crackers are crisp to begin with; you soften them by wetting them with water and letting them stand until some of the moisture is absorbed. Four cracker rounds get layered, cake-fashion, with seasoned cream cheese, chicken salad, and guacamole. You cut this "torte" into small rectangles to pick up and eat.

For the one-person sandwich, you roll flour tortillas around roast beef. Tortillas dry quickly in the air, so you use a wrapper to keep this sandwich fresh—and hold ingredients together as you eat.

For food safety, observe our directions for keeping the sandwiches cool if you want to carry them to a picnic.

GIANT STACKED SANDWICH

To make a half-sandwich that will serve 5 or 6, use only 2 pieces of cracker bread. First, soften crackers with water, then cut each in half to make 4 pieces. Use half of the remaining ingredients, assembling as directed.

4 rounds cracker bread (each about 14-in. diameter)
  Chicken salad (recipe follows)
1 package (6 oz. or 6 cups) alfalfa sprouts
  Guacamole (recipe follows)
1 pound (about 6 large) firm-ripe Roma-type tomatoes, cored, seeded, and chopped
  Cream cheese spread (recipe follows)
1 medium-size cucumber, thinly sliced
¾ pound shredded cheddar cheese
3 or 4 red radishes with leaves, rinsed and drained; or fresh dill sprigs, rinsed and drained

Gently run cool water over 1 cracker bread round, moistening evenly on both

Giant sandwich, cut into squares, serves crowd of hungry picnickers. Assemble it on a tray up to a day ahead. Wrap and chill; transport on tray. Rounds of cracker bread hold a meal's worth of chicken salad, alfalfa sprouts, guacamole, tomatoes, cucumbers, cheese. Garnish with radishes and fresh dill.

sides. Lay flat on a surface covered with plastic wrap. Cover cracker with plastic wrap. Wet a second cracker and stack on the first; cover with plastic wrap. Repeat to moisten and wrap remaining crackers. Pinch edges of plastic to make airtight. Let crackers stand to soften, about 45 minutes.

Reserve a perfect cracker for the top layer; if a cracker breaks or tears, you can patch it together for the sandwich's middle sections.

Lay 1 cracker on a flat platter or tray; spread cracker evenly with chicken salad. Arrange alfalfa sprouts on salad, making surface fairly level. Top with another cracker, aligning it with the first. Cover evenly with guacamole, then tomatoes.

Align a third cracker on the stack. Spread it with the cream cheese mixture. Arrange cucumber slices levelly on cream cheese, then scatter as evenly as possible with cheddar cheese. Cover stack with the reserved cracker. If made ahead, cover sandwich snugly with plastic wrap; chill as long as until the next day.

Break off all but a few of the radish leaves and trim off root ends. Wrap radishes in a damp paper towel, enclose in a plastic bag, and chill until ready to serve, up until the next day.

To transport sandwich and radishes, carry on platter to picnic site. Wrap in several layers of newspaper to help keep cool, and set in a cool place; plan to serve within 1 hour. Unwrap sandwich and garnish with radishes and/or dill.

With a sharp knife, cut the sandwich into pieces about 2 inches square. Pick up pieces to eat (see picture at left). Makes about 3 dozen 2-inch portions, plus corner pieces; 10- to 12-main dish servings or 3 dozen appetizers.

PER 2-INCH PORTION: 181 calories, 8.3 g protein, 15 g carbohydrates, 9.9 g fat, 24 mg cholesterol, 220 mg sodium

Cream cheese spread. In a bowl, stir together until blended (or whirl in a food processor) 1 large package (8 oz.) **cream cheese,** at room temperature; 1 cup **unflavored yogurt;** 1 cup chopped **green onions;** and 1 tablespoon chopped **fresh dill** or chopped fresh mint leaves.

Chicken salad. In a bowl, combine 2 cups finely diced **cooked chicken;** ½ of the **cream cheese spread** (preceding); and 2 cans (2¼ oz. each) **sliced black ripe olives,** drained. Add **salt** and **pepper** to taste.

Bicyclists peel back plastic wrap to eat beef-and-pepper hand rolls.

Guacamole. Pit, peel, and dice 2 large (about 1½ lb. total) ripe **avocados.** Coarsely mash in a bowl, mixing with 6 tablespoons **lemon juice** and ⅛ teaspoon **cayenne.** Add **salt** and **pepper** to taste.

BEEF & PEPPER HAND ROLLS

- 10 flour tortillas (about 10-in. diameter), at room temperature
  Dijon-pepper spread (recipe follows)
- 1 jar (7 oz.) Spanish-style green olives, drained and chopped
- 1 jar (7 oz.) roasted red peppers, drained and chopped
- 1 pound very thinly sliced cooked roast beef
- 10 medium-size lettuce leaves, washed and crisped
  Salt

Lay 1 tortilla flat; keep remaining ones covered with plastic wrap to prevent drying. Spread tortilla with ⅒ of the Dijon-pepper spread. Leaving ⅓ of surface plain, evenly cover rest with ⅒ of olives, peppers, roast beef, and 1 lettuce leaf.

Roll tortilla from filled side, so the sticky cheese section overlaps the tortilla and lightly seals the roll; wrap snugly in plastic wrap. Repeat for remaining rolls.

Serve, or chill up to 6 hours. Transport in an insulated container. To eat, pull plastic from 1 end of a roll, but leave sandwich partially wrapped as you eat to hold it together. Add salt to taste. Makes 10 rolls; allow 1 or 2 for a serving.

Dijon-pepper spread. In a bowl, stir until blended 1 large package (8 oz.) **cream cheese,** at room temperature; ½ cup **mayonnaise;** 1 tablespoon **Dijon mustard;** and 1 teaspoon **cracked black pepper.**

PER ROLL: 373 calories, 18 g protein, 20 g carbohydrates, 25 g fat, 68 mg cholesterol, 686 mg sodium

Easy on the Camp Cook: Menus for a Weekend Outing

WHEN YOU'RE CAMPING, *the food you cook outdoors just seems to taste better. But to the cook, the charm can wear thin if meals aren't well planned.*

These menus, designed for a weekend outing for four car-campers, help you assemble complete meals without last-minute surprises. They save time, too: each evening as you prepare dinner, you also cook some of the ingredients you'll need for the next morning's breakfast.

Most recipes make use of a campsite grill; you can substitute a portable barbecue. If you plan to leave early on the last day, cook that brunch on a campstove so you don't have to wait for coals to heat.

Check fire regulations for the area you plan to visit; some parks may have restrictions. And in this dry year, be especially careful when using fire.

At home, wash produce, measure ingredients (don't tote more than you need), and do as much preparation as possible.

To save space, repack noncrushable items, such as flank steak and sausages, in plastic bags.

Ice chests should provide ample refrigeration. Keep tightly closed, opening only when necessary. In your camp kit, include at least 4 slender metal or wooden skewers (12- to 15-in. length), a basting brush, heavy foil, long-handled tongs, and plenty of charcoal briquets and fire starter.

FRIDAY DINNER

**Sausage Supper Salad
with Grilled Toast**

Pineapple	Oatmeal Cookies
Beer	Grape Juice

Grill all the bread, but save half for French toast next morning.

Before you leave home, wash salad greens, wrap in paper towels, enclose in a plastic bag, and chill in ice chest to crisp. You can also make the dressing. For the cookies, bake a batch from a favorite recipe, or buy some.

Buy a peeled pineapple (about 1¾ lb.), or an unpeeled one (about 3 lb.) to peel and core in camp. Store half in a plastic bag in an ice chest until next morning.

SAUSAGE SUPPER SALAD WITH GRILLED TOAST

- 1 **pound Polish sausage, cut into ⅜-inch-thick diagonal slices**
- 1 **loaf (1 lb.) sourdough French bread, cut into ½-inch-thick slices**
- ¼ **cup (⅛ lb.) butter or margarine, melted**
- 8 **cups lightly packed bite-size pieces romaine lettuce, washed and crisped**
- 1 **large firm-ripe tomato, cored and cut into wedges**
- 6 **ounces Swiss cheese, cut into matchstick-size pieces**
- 1 **small red onion, thinly sliced and separated into rings
Sweet-and-sour mustard dressing (recipe follows)**

Thread equal portions of sausage slices slightly apart on 4 slender 12- to 15-inch metal or wooden skewers. Lay on a grill 4 to 6 inches above a solid bed of medium coals (you should be able to hold your hand at grill level only 4 to 5 seconds). Cook sausage, turning often, until hot and edges are well browned, about 5 minutes. Push skewers to a cool area of grill, or put on a platter, cover, and keep warm.

Meanwhile, brush half the bread slices on both sides with melted butter. Lay plain and buttered slices on grill and cook until toasted on each side, 2 to 2½ minutes total. When unbuttered toast is cool, store airtight.

Divide lettuce equally among 4 dinner plates. Scatter tomato, cheese, and onion over lettuce. Push equal portions of sausage off skewers onto salads; drizzle each with ¼ of the dressing. Serve with the buttered toast. Makes 4 servings.

PER SERVING: 963 calories, 36 g protein, 44 g carbohydrates, 72 g fat, 151 mg cholesterol, 1,578 mg sodium

Sweet-and-sour mustard dressing.
Whisk together ¼ cup **salad oil,** 3 tablespoons **red wine vinegar,** 1 tablespoon **sugar,** 1 teaspoon *each* **celery seed** and **Worcestershire,** 1 tablespoon **Dijon mustard,** and 1 clove **garlic,** minced or pressed.

SATURDAY BREAKFAST

**Twice-grilled French Toast
with Skewered Fruit
Canadian Bacon
Spiced Sour Cream Topping
Maple Syrup**

Coffee	Hot Chocolate

The toast stored for breakfast can soak overnight, or while you start the fire.

Out of heavy foil, fashion a griddle for the French toast and the bacon. You can save time by making the sour cream topping at home; store it in a leakproof container in an ice chest.

TWICE-GRILLED FRENCH TOAST WITH SKEWERED FRUIT

- 4 **large eggs**
- 1 **cup milk
Reserved grilled toast (from sausage supper salad, preceding)
Reserved ½ pineapple (from preceding menu), cut into ¾-inch-thick wedges**
- 2 **firm-ripe bananas, cut into ¾-inch-thick slices**
- ⅓ **cup butter or margarine, melted**
- 1 **package (6 oz.) sliced Canadian bacon
Spiced sour cream topping (recipe follows)
Maple syrup**

In a 9- by 13-inch rimmed pan, beat eggs and milk until blended. Lay toast slices in egg mixture (some may overlap); let stand about 1 minute, then turn slices over to absorb remaining liquid. Use, or cover tightly and keep cold up to overnight.

Thread pineapple and banana pieces alternately, and slightly apart, on 4 slender 12- to 15-inch metal or wooden skewers. Brush with 1 tablespoon melted butter.

Lay skewers on a grill 4 to 6 inches above a solid bed of hot coals (you should be able to hold your hand at grill level only 2 to 3 seconds). Cook, turning once, until fruit browns lightly, 3 to 4 minutes total. Move to a cool area on grill, or put on a platter, cover, and keep warm.

To fashion griddle for bacon and toast, cut 2 pieces of heavy foil slightly larger than grill. Stack sheets, then fold sides of foil up to make a 1-inch rim.

Place griddle on grill; brush with 1 tablespoon butter. Lay bacon slices on foil and cook, turning occasionally, until sizzling, about 2 minutes a side. Lift slices off and keep warm.

Brush griddle with remaining butter; set toast slices on foil. Cook, turning once, until golden brown, 2 to 3 minutes a side. Serve with grilled fruit and bacon, and spiced topping and maple syrup for diners to add to individual taste. Serves 4.

PER SERVING: 576 calories, 23 g protein, 59 g carbohydrates, 28 g fat, 346 mg cholesterol, 1,183 mg sodium

Spiced sour cream topping. Stir 1 teaspoon **ground cinnamon** and ⅛ teaspoon **ground nutmeg** into 1 cup (½ pt.) **sour cream.** Serve; or chill in leakproof container up to next day. Makes 1 cup.

PER TABLESPOON: 31 calories, 0.5 g protein, 0.7 g carbohydrates, 3 g fat, 6.3 mg cholesterol, 7.6 mg sodium

---

SATURDAY DINNER

**Grilled Flank Steak
with Chili-Lime Marinade
Barbecue-baked Potatoes with Salsa
Barbecued Corn on the Cob
Cherry Tomatoes
S'mores
Dry Red Jug Wine   Soft Drinks**

Portions of the steak, potatoes, and corn are reserved for brunch on Sunday morning. Keep these foods fresh by storing in an ice chest.

Start potatoes first. About 20 minutes before potatoes are done, set corn over coals; cook 5 minutes, then place flank steak beside corn and grill until meat is done to your liking.

GRILLED FLANK STEAK WITH CHILI-LIME MARINADE

¼ cup salad oil
½ teaspoon grated lime peel
⅓ cup lime juice
2 cloves garlic, minced or pressed
1 fresh jalapeño chili, stemmed, seeded, and minced
½ teaspoon cracked pepper
1 flank steak (1½ to 1¾ lb.), fat trimmed

In heavy plastic bag (1-gal. size), combine oil, lime peel and juice, garlic, chili, and pepper. Add steak, seal bag, and rotate to coat meat with marinade. Set bag in an ice chest and let stand 1 hour or up to next day; turn bag occasionally.

Place steak on a grill 4 to 6 inches above a solid bed of hot coals (you should be able to hold your hand at grill level only 2 to 3 seconds). Cook, turning once, until meat is done to your liking (cut to test), about 10 minutes for rare, about 14 minutes for medium-rare; brush often with marinade.

To serve, cut meat across the grain into thin, slanted slices. Set aside about ¼ of meat; when cool, enclose in a plastic bag and chill until next day for steak strips (recipe follows). Serves 4.

PER SERVING: 314 calories, 26 g protein, 2.2 g carbohydrates, 22 g fat, 64 mg cholesterol, 94 mg sodium

BARBECUE-BAKED POTATOES WITH SALSA

Scrub 6 medium-size (about 3 lb. total) **russet potatoes;** pat dry, then wrap each in a triple layer of heavy foil. Place potatoes around outer edge of a solid bed of hot coals (same used for steak—you should be able to hold your hand at grill level only 2 to 3 seconds). Turn potatoes often with long-handled tongs until tender when pierced, 45 to 55 minutes. Add 8 briquets at 15-minute intervals to maintain heat. Set aside 2 potatoes to make pan-fried breakfast potatoes (recipe follows). Unwrap remaining hot potatoes and add **prepared salsa** to taste. Serves 4.

PER SERVING: 167 calories, 4.9 g protein, 38 g carbohydrates, 0.2 g fat, 0 mg cholesterol, 16 mg sodium

---

SUNDAY BRUNCH

**Steak Strips &
Pan-fried Potatoes with Onion
Scrambled Eggs
with Jalapeño & Corn
Orange Juice   Coffee**

If you have to leave promptly after brunch, it's easier to cook this meal on the campstove. If you grill, be sure coals are completely extinguished before you go.

Use the same pan to cook each dish: start with the steak strips, then the potatoes; finally, scramble the eggs and serve.

STEAK STRIPS & PAN-FRIED POTATOES WITH ONION

3 tablespoons butter or margarine
1 clove garlic, minced or pressed
Reserved grilled flank steak in chili-lime marinade (recipe precedes)
¼ cup dry red or white wine (optional)
Reserved barbecue-baked potatoes (recipe precedes), cut into ¾-inch cubes
1 small onion, chopped
Salt and pepper

Melt 1 tablespoon butter in a 10- to 12-inch frying pan over medium-high heat. Add meat and stir occasionally until sizzling, 4 to 5 minutes. Pour in wine and cook until most of the liquid evaporates. Spoon out meat and set aside.

Melt remaining butter in pan. Add potatoes and onion; stir occasionally until potatoes are golden brown, about 15 minutes. Stir meat (and any juices) into potatoes. Season to taste with salt and pepper. (If using same pan to cook eggs, remove potatoes; keep warm.) Serves 4.

PER SERVING: 269 calories, 12 g protein, 21 g carbohydrates, 16 g fat, 45 mg cholesterol, 128 mg sodium

SCRAMBLED EGGS WITH JALAPEÑO & CORN

8 large eggs
1 cup milk
Reserved barbecued corn on the cob (recipe precedes), kernels cut off cob
1 to 2 fresh jalapeño chilies, stemmed, seeded, and minced
3 tablespoons butter or margarine
4 ounces cheddar cheese, cut into ½-inch cubes
Salt and pepper

In large bowl, combine eggs with milk, corn, and chilies to taste; beat to blend.

Melt butter in a 10- to 12-inch frying pan on medium heat. Pour egg mixture into pan and cook. Lift cooked egg to let uncooked egg flow underneath, until softly set. When almost set, stir in cheese. Add salt and pepper to taste. Serves 4.

PER SERVING: 436 calories, 23 g protein, 15 g carbohydrates, 32 g fat, 610 mg cholesterol, 440 mg sodium

Frozen Desserts from Ice Cream Cylinders

MAKING HOMEMADE ICE CREAM *is easier and neater these days; you use cylinder ice cream freezers instead of old-fashioned makers that require rock salt and ice. These recipes are scaled to the cylinders' smaller capacities.*

With cold fruit and yogurt, milk, or cream, you can make a frozen dessert in minutes. Just whirl the chilled ingredients together in a blender, then freeze.

For a richer dessert, make the vanilla or chocolate-orange gelato. Their smooth textures come from their cooked custard base. Make sure it is thoroughly chilled before freezing; allow at least 2 hours.

Each recipe makes 1 pint of frozen dessert. Double recipes for 1½-quart cylinders; halve for ½-pint freezers.

How Do Cylinders Work?

Replacing the ice and salt traditional makers use, these streamlined machines consist of aluminum cylinders with non-toxic refrigerant sandwiched between double walls.

You begin by placing the cylinder in a freezer set at 0° or below until frozen solid, about 8 hours, then set it in an outer case, fit it with a mixing blade, and fill with the dessert mixture for the 20- to 30-minute freezing process.

The key to success is a thoroughly frozen cylinder. If it isn't cold enough, the ice cream takes longer to freeze, and results may be slushy instead of firm.

Manufacturers suggest you turn your freezer to the coldest setting and place the clean, dry cylinder upright and un-covered in the chilliest spot. In frost-free freezers, this is generally next to the cold-air vent; in manual defrost freezers, the floor of the freezer is best. If you make ice cream often, keep the cylinder in the freezer between batches so it will always be ready.

Sizes & Costs

These freezers make up to 1 quart of frozen dessert; they're great for 1 or 2 servings or for small families.

Each cylinder is larger than the amount of dessert it's designed to make, allowing extra room for the mixture to move over the paddles and to expand slightly in volume. Some manufacturers label according to the cylinder's total volume, others according to the amount of the finished dessert. If you use more than the recommended amount, the dessert may overflow, be softer, or take longer to freeze.

Cylinder sizes range from ½ pint (makes ¾ cup and costs about $8) to 1½ quarts (makes 1 quart and ranges between $30 and $50). Some brands feature extra cylinders; some turn by electricity rather than by hand.

Turning Liquids Into Frozen Desserts

To freeze the dessert mixtures, set the frozen cylinder into the outer case, fit with mixing blade, and pour in the cold mixture. At once, secure lid and attach handle; slowly turn clockwise three or four times. (If you find it difficult to turn the handle, gently turn it counterclock-wise to free the blade; do not force. Or scrape sides with a rubber spatula.)

Freeze according to the manufacturer's directions, turning nonelectric models periodically, until mixture reaches desired consistency, 15 to 30 minutes for softly frozen texture. Remove lid and blade; serve or replace lid and let stand 20 to 30 minutes for firmer texture.

Because you turn the ice cream mixture only a few times, the finished product expands less and is denser than ice cream made by other methods.

Transfer any leftover ice cream to an-other container and store in freezer. To serve, let soften at room temperature to desired consistency.

Use only plastic or wood utensils in cylinders. Handle frozen containers with dry hands; wet hands will stick.

Frozen Berry Yogurt

- ⅔ **cup lightly packed fresh or thawed frozen raspberries, olallieberries, or blackberries**
- 5 **to 7 tablespoons sugar**
- 1 **teaspoon vanilla**
- 1⅓ **cups unflavored yogurt**

In a blender or food processor, combine berries, sugar to taste, vanilla, and yo-gurt; whirl until smooth and sugar dis-solves. If desired, press through a fine strainer to remove seeds; discard seeds.

Use, or cover and chill until the next day. Freeze as directed (preceding). Makes 1 pint, 2 or 3 servings.

PER SERVING: 162 calories, 5.5 g protein, 31.5 g carbohydrates, 1.7 g fat, 6 mg cholesterol, 70 mg sodium

Vanilla Ice Cream or Milk

If you have the ½-pint cylinder, use 1 large egg yolk for the half-recipe.

- 1 **large egg**
- 6 **tablespoons sugar**
- 1⅔ **cups half-and-half (light cream), milk, or whipping cream (or a combination)**
- 2 **teaspoons vanilla**

In a blender or food processor, combine egg, sugar, half-and-half, and vanilla; whirl until blended (if using all cream, do not overblend, because volume may expand beyond cylinder's capacity). Use, or cover and chill until the next day.

Freeze as directed (preceding). Makes 1 pint, 2 or 3 servings.

PER SERVING: 306 calories, 5.8 g protein, 32 g carbohydrates, 17 g fat, 141 mg cholesterol, 78 mg sodium

Peach Ice Cream or Milk

Follow recipe for **vanilla ice cream or milk** (preceding), but reduce half-and-half to 1 cup and add ¾ cup cold peeled and sliced ripe **peaches** and 2 teaspoons **lemon juice;** whirl until peaches are puréed.

Freeze as directed (preceding). Makes 1 pint, 2 or 3 servings.

PER SERVING: 246 calories, 4.7 g protein, 33 g carbohydrates, 11 g fat, 121 mg cholesterol, 57 mg sodium

Vanilla Gelato

- 1½ **cups milk**
- 6 **tablespoons sugar**
- 3 **large egg yolks**
- 1½ **teaspoons vanilla**

In a 1- to 2-quart pan, combine milk and sugar. Stir over medium heat just until sugar dissolves.

Place egg yolks in a bowl. Gradually whisk in 1 cup of the warm milk mixture, then pour egg mixture into pan, stirring. Continue to stir until liquid coats the back of a metal spoon in a thin, even, smooth layer, 6 to 8 minutes (do not scald or custard will curdle). Mix in vanilla. Cool, cover, and chill until cold, at least 2 hours or up to 2 days.

Freeze as directed (preceding). Makes 1 pint, 2 or 3 servings.

PER SERVING: 241 calories, 6.8 g protein, 31 g carbohydrates, 9.6 g fat, 289 mg cholesterol, 68 mg sodium

Watermelon Whatevers

WATERMELONS *take center stage with these whimsical carvings. Their broad surface and easy-to-cut rind make an ideal canvas for edible container centerpieces.*

Your tools include a spoon, knives (large chef's, small paring, and curved grapefruit), and nontoxic crayon. A melon baller and corer are optional.

First, draw your design on the melon with the crayon. Then cut along the lines, using a paring knife for straight edges, a

grapefruit knife for curves. Lift out cut pieces and scoop fruit from shell and trimmings. Cut fruit into bite-size pieces and return to cavity.

If you want a two-tone effect, cut through skin to the white of the rind, incising lines to outline a design, or scrape off skin with a paring knife to expose white rind.

Use your imagination to create your own work of art. Or try one of the three choices pictured here.

Carved tureen is inspired by Chinese melon carvings. Using a grapefruit knife to make a scalloped edge, cut about 3 inches off one end of melon. Cut fruit from melon rind and save. Next, trim round end of 3-inch dome so it sits flat; line inside with paper towels (to keep melon tureen from slipping), add a leafy garnish, and set on a plate. Carve designs if desired on melon tureen, then nest on base. Fill with fruit, including reserved melon.

Paws-in-air bear hugs a cache of juicy fruit. To create, first cut around design with a paring knife and a grapefruit knife (for curves). Next, punch out eyes with a corer, then turn melon pieces white side out and insert in holes; seeds form pupils. Cut a small slot to insert ear fashioned from melon rind trimmings.

Palm tree basket holds an ocean of red melon. Draw tree design over melon top. Following pattern, carve through shell; lift out cut pieces. Cut and scoop fruit from shell; cut fruit into chunks, return to cavity.

Traditional components of ratatouille fill cheese-topped frittata.

RATATOUILLE FRITTATA

- 1 **eggplant, about ¾ pound**
- 6 **tablespoons olive oil**
- 2 **cloves garlic, minced or pressed**
- 1 **medium-size red onion, sliced**
- 3 **small zucchini, thinly sliced**
- 1 **cup chopped red bell pepper**
- 4 **medium-size firm-ripe tomatoes, cored, peeled, seeded, and chopped**
- ¼ **cup minced fresh basil leaves**
- 6 **large eggs, lightly beaten**
- 1 **cup (about 4 oz.) shredded parmesan cheese**

Stem eggplant, quarter lengthwise, then slice thinly crosswise. In a 12-inch frying pan or 5- to 6-quart pan over medium heat, stir eggplant and ¼ cup oil. Cover and cook 10 minutes; stir once or twice. Add remaining oil, garlic, onion, zucchini, and bell pepper. Stir often, uncovered, over medium-high heat until zucchini is tender-crisp to bite, about 5 minutes. Add tomatoes and basil; stir until tomatoes are soft, about 2 minutes.

Reduce heat to medium. Pour eggs into pan, cover, and cook until eggs are set, about 5 minutes. Sprinkle cheese onto eggs. Cook, covered, until cheese melts, about 2 minutes. Serves 6. —*Carol Braswell, Fresno, Calif.*

PER SERVING: 335 calories, 16 g protein, 13 g carbohydrates, 25 g fat, 289 mg cholesterol, 433 mg sodium

---

Start the day on a healthy note with hearty cheddar-herb muffins.

WHOLE-GRAIN HERB-CHEESE MUFFINS

- ¼ **cup minced onion**
- ½ **cup diced green bell pepper**
- 3 **tablespoons salad oil**
- 2 **tablespoons honey**
- 1 **tablespoon Dijon mustard**
- 1 **cup milk**
- 2 **large eggs**
- ¾ **cup shredded cheddar cheese**
- 1½ **cups whole-wheat flour**
- ½ **cup yellow cornmeal**
- 2 **teaspoons baking powder**
- ½ **teaspoon *each* dry thyme leaves and dry tarragon leaves**
- ½ **teaspoon salt (optional)**

In a 7- to 8-inch frying pan over medium-high heat, cook onion and bell pepper in 1 tablespoon of the oil until limp, about 7 minutes; stir often.

In a large bowl, mix remaining oil, honey, mustard, milk, eggs, and cheese. In another bowl, stir together flour, cornmeal, baking powder, thyme, tarragon, and salt. Add egg mixture; stir until moistened. Spoon into 12 greased muffin cups, 2¼-inch size.

Bake in a 375° oven until muffins are well browned, 20 to 25 minutes. Makes 12. —*Doris Rogers, Port Orchard, Wash.*

PER MUFFIN: 170 calories, 6 g protein, 20 g carbohydrates, 7.8 g fat, 56 mg cholesterol, 175 mg sodium

---

Colorful mélange of zucchini, carrots, and peas cooks with lamb. Serve with bulgur, pan juices.

BRAISED LAMB & VEGETABLES WITH MINT

- 4 **shoulder lamb chops (about 2 lb. total), fat trimmed**
- 1 **tablespoon salad oil**
- 1 **large clove garlic, minced**
- 1 **medium-size onion, chopped**
- 1 **teaspoon ground cinnamon**
- ⅓ **cup minced fresh mint or 1½ tablespoons dry mint leaves**
- 1 **cup regular-strength beef broth**
- 2 ***each* medium-size carrots and medium-size zucchini, thinly sliced diagonally**
- 1 **cup fresh or frozen peas**
  Salt and pepper

In a 10- to 12-inch frying pan over medium-high heat, brown 2 chops at a time on both sides in oil. Lift lamb from pan and set aside. Add garlic and onion to pan. Stir often until onion is golden, about 10 minutes. Stir in cinnamon, mint, and broth.

Place chops on onion; cover and simmer until meat is very tender when pierced, 1 to 1¼ hours; turn over halfway through cooking. Add carrots and zucchini; simmer, covered, for 8 minutes. Add peas, cook, covered, until carrots are tender to bite, about 2 minutes. Add salt and pepper to taste. Serves 4. —*Roxanne Chan, Albany, Calif.*

PER SERVING: 356 calories, 35 g protein, 15 g carbohydrates, 17 g fat, 119 mg cholesterol, 129 mg sodium

BALLPARK SALAD

1 head (about 5 oz.) butter lettuce
1 pound frankfurters or cooked bockwurst sausage, sliced diagonally ¾ inch thick
1 cup (4 oz.) shredded Swiss cheese
4 large hard-cooked eggs, sliced
½ cup chopped dill pickles
½ cup sliced celery
¼ to ½ cup minced red onion
1½ cups stemmed and halved cherry tomatoes
Dressing (recipe follows)

Rinse lettuce, drain, wrap in paper towels, enclose in a plastic bag; chill until crisp. Line a platter with lettuce; arrange separate bands of frankfurters, cheese, eggs, pickles, celery, onion, and tomatoes on top. If made ahead, cover and chill up to 4 hours.

Spoon portions of each component with lettuce onto plates. Add dressing to taste. Makes 4 to 6 servings. —*Mrs. L.K. Ross, Elk Grove, Calif.*

PER SALAD SERVING: 379 calories, 19 g protein, 5.7 g carbohydrates, 31 g fat, 238 mg cholesterol, 1,139 mg sodium

Dressing. In a small bowl, stir 1 cup **mayonnaise** and 2 tablespoons *each* **catsup** and **Dijon mustard** until combined. If made ahead, cover and chill up to 1 day. Makes 1¼ cups.

PER TABLESPOON DRESSING: 82 calories, 0.2 g protein, 0.9 g carbohydrates, 8.8 g fat, 6.5 mg cholesterol, 125 mg sodium

All the trimmings go in frankfurter salad with mayonnaise-mustard-catsup dressing.

QUICK TART-SWEET PICKLED CARROTS

8 medium-size carrots (about 1¼ lb. total)
¾ cup cider vinegar
1 small dried hot red chili
1 cinnamon stick, about 3 inches long
1 vanilla bean, about 6 inches long, or 1 teaspoon vanilla
1½ cups orange juice

Cut carrots into sticks about 3½ inches long and ⅓ inch thick. Measure; you should have 1 quart (if not, adjust quantity to equal this amount).

In a 2- to 3-quart pan, bring vinegar, chili, cinnamon, and vanilla bean to a boil over high heat. Cover and simmer for 5 minutes. Add orange juice and carrots; return to a boil. Remove from heat. (If using vanilla, add now.)

Let carrots cool. Pour into a 1-quart jar or plastic container. Cover and chill at least 24 hours before serving. Discard cinnamon after 24 hours. Store carrots in the refrigerator up to 1 week. Makes about 75 sticks. —*Paulette Rossi, Portland, Ore.*

PER STICK: 4 calories, 0.1 g protein, 1 g carbohydrates, 0 g fat, 0 mg cholesterol, 2.7 mg sodium

Simmer vinegar, dried chili, cinnamon, and vanilla; add carrots and orange juice, then chill.

PLUM COFFEE CAKE

1 cup all-purpose flour
½ cup sugar
1 teaspoon baking powder
¼ teaspoon *each* ground nutmeg and ground cinnamon
2 large eggs
⅓ cup milk
3 tablespoons melted butter or margarine
5 medium-size firm-ripe Santa Rosa plums, halved, pitted
½ teaspoon ground cinnamon mixed with 2 tablespoons sugar

In a large bowl, stir together flour, sugar, baking powder, nutmeg, and cinnamon.

In a small bowl, stir together eggs, milk, and butter until blended; add to flour mixture and stir until well combined. Spread batter evenly in a greased 8- to 9-inch-diameter cake or quiche pan.

Evenly space plum halves, cut side up, on top of batter; press slightly into batter. Sprinkle batter and fruit with cinnamon-sugar mixture. Bake in a 375° oven until well browned, 40 to 45 minutes. Serve warm or cool. Leftovers can be covered and chilled up to 2 days. Makes 6 servings. —*Gretchen Berendt, Mesa, Ariz.*

PER SERVING: 273 calories, 5 g protein, 45 g carbohydrates, 8.6 g fat, 109 mg cholesterol, 160 mg sodium

Batter puffs up around plum halves during baking. Top with whipped cream.

AUSTRALIA IS A BIG, *empty country, and if Trevor Lowdell's Aussie Burger is typical of what goes on the barbie there, it must be inhabited by people with big, not-so-empty stomachs. This is food for heroes, especially heroes with sound arteries who have looked cholesterol in the face without flinching. (It might serve equally well as a snack for the average American teenager.)*

Each element of this super-burger is delicious in itself; together they can make you forget food, at least until the next meal. With apologies to Chef Lowdell, we've made the hamburger a trifle flatter than he recommends. Even so, our tasters recommend that you cut each hamburger in half

"This is food for heroes."

before tackling it; only the hinged and distensible jaws of a python could manage a bite of the original version. If you cook the eggs with soft yolks, there are bound to be drips; strip off your necktie, lean over your plate, and use lots of paper napkins.*

AUSSIE BURGER WITH THE LOT

- 1 **pound ground lean beef**
- 4 **slices (1 oz. each) sharp cheddar cheese**
- 2 **tablespoons butter or margarine**
- 4 **large eggs**
- 4 **hamburger buns, split, buttered, and toasted**
- 4 **thin slices red or white onion**
- 1 **can (8 oz.) sliced pickled beets, drained**
- 4 **thin slices firm-ripe tomato**
- 4 **medium-size butter lettuce leaves, washed and crisped**
  Salt and pepper

Shape beef into 4 patties, each ½ inch thick. Place a 10- to 12-inch frying pan over medium-high heat. When hot, add patties and cook until browned on the bottom. Turn patties over and cook until done to your liking (cut to test), about 4 minutes total for medium. About the last 2 minutes, top each patty with a cheese slice to warm.

Meanwhile, in another 10- to 12-inch frying pan, melt butter over medium heat. Add eggs and fry until whites are set but yolks are still runny. Leave "sunny side up" or turn and cook "over easy."

To serve, place a cheese-topped patty on each toasted bun bottom, top with an egg, then an onion slice, some pickled beets, a tomato slice, and a lettuce leaf. Add salt and pepper to taste, then cover filling with bun tops. Makes 4 servings.

PER SERVING: 632 calories, 37 g protein, 33 g carbohydrates, 39 g fat, 390 mg cholesterol, 720 mg sodium

Trevor Lowdell

Los Angeles

ALBERT SHAW'S FETTUCCINE *is doubly Italianate. It combines the bacon and egg of a carbonara sauce (or a good American breakfast) with the butter, cream, and parmesan cheese of fettuccine Alfredo. The redundance succeeds.*

FETTUCCINE ALBÉR

- ½ **cup (¼ lb.) unsalted butter or margarine**
- 3 **cloves garlic, minced or pressed**
- 5 **slices crisp cooked bacon, drained and crumbled**
- 1 **large egg**
- 1 **cup whipping cream**
- 1 **cup (5 oz.) freshly grated parmesan cheese**
- ¼ **teaspoon dry oregano leaves**
- 12 **ounces fresh fettuccine, homemade or purchased**
- 3 **tablespoons minced parsley**
  Salt and pepper

Melt butter in a 10- to 12-inch frying pan over medium heat; add garlic and stir often until garlic is soft but not brown, about 3 minutes. Remove from heat and add bacon.

In a small bowl, beat egg with cream, cheese, and oregano. Add egg mixture to pan and stir over medium heat until sauce is slightly thickened.

At the same time, add fettuccine to 3 to 4 quarts rapidly boiling water; cook, uncovered, just until barely tender to bite, 2 to 3 minutes. Drain fettuccine well and pour into a wide bowl; add sauce and parsley and mix well with 2 forks. Season to taste with salt and pepper. Serve at once. Makes 4 to 6 servings.

PER SERVING: 612 calories, 19 g protein, 44 g carbohydrates, 41 g fat, 205 mg cholesterol, 494 mg sodium

A. J. Shaw

Orinda, Calif.

JOHN KEATS OBSERVED *that poetry should surprise by a fine excess, not by singularity. Most Chefs of the West follow this dictum, blending good things with more good things until the cupboard is bare. Larry Brimner, on the other hand, surprises us by singularity. How? Listen.*

He sauces orange roughy, that delicate New Zealand ocean perch, with lemon yogurt. Strange, yes. Delicious? Most of our testers said that it was, although most also had to shout down an inner voice that urged caution (unflavored yogurt, however, was acclaimed as a tasty and less disquieting alternative).

CALIFORNIA ORANGE ROUGHY

- 1 pound orange roughy fillets, thawed if frozen
  Salt and pepper
- ½ cup low-fat unflavored or lemon-flavored yogurt
- 1 green onion (ends trimmed), thinly sliced
  Lemon wedges
  Salt

Rinse fish and pat dry. Arrange fillets in a single layer in a greased shallow 9- by 13-inch pan. Sprinkle lightly with salt and pepper, then evenly spread yogurt over fish. Sprinkle with the green onion. Bake, uncovered, in a 350° oven until fish is just opaque in center (cut to test), 12 to 18 minutes.

Transfer fish to dinner plates; accompany with lemon and salt to add to taste. Makes 3 or 4 servings.

PER SERVING: 162 calories, 18 g protein, 2 g carbohydrates, 8 g fat, 24 mg cholesterol, 91 mg sodium

Larry Dane Brimner

San Diego

IT SEEMS AT FIRST GLANCE *to be a bold move — blending the aristocratic shrimp with the plebeian coleslaw. But the results justify the bravado. First, cabbage is not necessarily the clownish vegetable some people think it to be; it's begun appearing on fancy menus. Second, the addition of red bell pepper, olives, caraway and celery seed, and dill weed lends a touch of exoticism. Third, there is enough shrimp in the mixture to make its own flavor statement. And finally, the dressing brings them all together in a fine ecumenical way. The lemon peel is a touch of genius.*

SHRIMP SLAW WITH CUCUMBER DRESSING

- 1 small head cabbage (about 1¼ lb.)
- 1 medium-size red bell pepper, stemmed, seeded, and diced
- 4 green onions (ends trimmed), thinly sliced, including tops
- 12 Spanish-style pimiento-stuffed olives, thinly sliced
- 1 pound tiny cooked and shelled shrimp

"Blending the aristocratic shrimp with the plebeian coleslaw...the results justify the bravado."

- ¼ teaspoon *each* caraway seed, celery seed, and dry dill weed
  Cucumber dressing (recipe follows)
  Salt and pepper
  Chopped chives (optional)

Finely shred enough cabbage to make 8 to 9 cups. In a large bowl, combine the cabbage with bell pepper, onions, olives, shrimp, caraway seed, celery seed, and dill weed; mix well. If made ahead, cover and chill up to overnight.

Combine cabbage mixture and dressing and mix gently. Season to taste with salt and pepper. Garnish with chives. Makes 6 or 7 main-dish servings.

PER SERVING: 320 calories, 15 g protein, 6 g carbohydrates, 26 g fat, 145 mg cholesterol, 456 mg sodium

Cucumber dressing. In a small bowl, stir together 1 cup **mayonnaise;** 1 cup peeled, seeded, and chopped **cucumber;** 1 tablespoon chopped **chives;** 2 tablespoons **rice vinegar;** 3 tablespoons chopped **parsley;** and ½ teaspoon grated **lemon peel.**

Lamar L. Parker

Tempe, Ariz.

IF AN ANCIENT GREEK *were to be set suddenly down in a modern Western community, he would marvel at the piety of our folk. Every summer evening, he would behold smoke from a thousand sacrifices drifting from a thousand shrines where officiants in ceremonial aprons were anointing the flesh of birds and animals with oil and herbs before entrusting it to their fires.*

He would not, however, be shocked to find that the celebrants proceeded to eat the flesh of these offerings: the Greeks did so, too, taking the view that the rising smoke was nutrition enough for the gods.

Ted Arnason's pineapple-glazed kebabs employ the traditional garlic and rosemary in their marinade, but add a surprise in the form of crushed pineapple. Many marinades promise more than they perform, perfuming meat without really flavoring it. But this one really penetrates, to confer an odd but delicious fruitiness.

PINEAPPLE-GLAZED KEBABS

- 1 can (about 8 oz.) crushed pineapple
- 1 teaspoon dry rosemary leaves
- ½ teaspoon dry dill weed
- ¼ cup dry white wine
- 3 tablespoons white wine vinegar
- ½ teaspoon pepper
- 2 tablespoons salad oil
- 1 large clove garlic, minced or pressed
- 1 leg of lamb (5 to 5½ lb.), boned, trimmed of excess fat, and cut into 1½-inch cubes
  Salt

In a bowl, combine pineapple and juice, rosemary, dill weed, wine, vinegar, pepper, oil, and garlic. Add lamb cubes and mix well. Cover and chill at least 30 minutes or up to overnight. Stir several times.

Lift meat from marinade, drain briefly, and thread on metal skewers. Whirl marinade in a blender or food processor to purée coarsely; then, with a brush, dab some of the mixture onto the meat.

Place skewers on a grill 4 to 6 inches above a solid bed of hot coals (you should be able to hold your hand at grill level for only 2 to 3 seconds). Cook, turning as needed, until browned on all sides but still pink in center (cut to test), 12 to 15 minutes total for medium-rare. With brush, dab marinade onto meat several times during cooking, using it all. Add salt to taste. Makes 6 to 8 servings.

PER SERVING: 307 calories, 40 g protein, 5 g carbohydrates, 13 g fat, 141 mg cholesterol, 98 mg sodium

Ted Arnason

Bellingham, Wash.

July Menus

CLIMBING TEMPERATURES *and lagging appetites make July a good month for simple meals that can be prepared quickly and enjoyed outdoors.*

Our first menu revolves around a roast chicken from the deli, made interesting with some unusual sidekicks.

The familiar favorites, tomato soup and grilled cheese sandwiches, get a new accent from a savory olive purée.

And for the Fourth of July, how about a hot dog barbecue where guests cook?

TORTILLA PANCAKE DINNER

Roasted Chicken   Tortilla Pancakes

Green Chili Mayonnaise

**Mixed Lettuces
with Herbs & Orange**

Carbonated Grapefruit Drink

**Vanilla Ice Cream with
Cayenne & Berries**

This meal features tender pancakes that taste like tortillas. Pancakes and chicken alike get dipped into chili mayonnaise.

Prepare mayonnaise and salad first; chill while you make pancakes and assemble the rest of the meal.

For the salad, choose from a variety of greens (red, butter, or romaine lettuce; arugula; or watercress). Wash and crisp 6 cups. Add 1 small orange, peeled and cut into wedges, and 1 teaspoon chopped fresh marjoram, thyme, or parsley. Mix the

Break tortilla pancakes into chunks to eat like bread—with roasted chicken, chili mayonnaise, and salad. Dessert is vanilla ice cream, dusted with a dash of cayenne, and fresh berries.

salad with about ¼ cup of oil-and-vinegar dressing, then dust with freshly ground pepper or Sichuan peppercorns.

To serve 4, buy 1 large roasted chicken or 2 small chickens (3 to 4 lb. total). Cut in halves or quarters.

For dessert, lightly sprinkle cayenne over vanilla ice cream and top with ripe berries.

TORTILLA PANCAKES

> 1 cup dehydrated masa flour (corn tortilla flour)
> ⅔ cup all-purpose flour
> 1 tablespoon baking powder
> ½ teaspoon salt
> 1 cup water
> 2 large eggs

In a bowl, mix together masa, flour, baking powder, and salt. In another bowl, mix water and eggs. Stir liquid into masa mixture just until blended.

Spoon batter, in ¼-cup portions, into a lightly greased 10- to 12-inch frying pan on medium heat. Spread batter out to make 4-inch-diameter rounds. Cook until tops look somewhat dry, about 5 minutes; turn tortillas with a wide spatula and brown the bottoms. Serve warm. Makes 8 pancakes, 4 servings.

PER PANCAKE: 110 calories, 3 g protein, 19 g carbohydrates, 2 g fat, 69 mg cholesterol, 315 mg sodium

GREEN CHILI MAYONNAISE

> 1 can (4 oz.) diced green chilies
> 1 tablespoon fresh cilantro (coriander) leaves
> ¼ teaspoon dry oregano leaves
> ⅛ teaspoon ground cumin
> ½ cup mayonnaise

In a blender, purée chilies, cilantro, oregano, and cumin. Pour into a bowl; stir in mayonnaise. Serve, or cover and chill up to 3 days; sauce thickens as it cools. Makes 1 cup, 4 servings.

PER TABLESPOON: 205 calories, 0.6 g protein, 2.5 g carbohydrates, 22 g fat, 16 mg cholesterol, 330 mg sodium

---

SOUP & SANDWICH LUNCH

Fresh Tomato Soup
Grilled Jack Cheese Sandwiches
Olive Purée
Crisp Summer Vegetable Sticks
Figs with Sour Cream & Brown Sugar
Iced Tea

Tomato soup, cheese sandwich with olive paste, vegetable strips make simple lunch.

For many, a comforting childhood food memory centers on grilled cheese sandwiches and tomato soup. Echoing this nostalgia is our homemade tomato soup with fresh basil, with grilled jack cheese sandwiches. The grownup touch is an olive purée to enjoy with the sandwiches.

Make soup first; keep warm while making purée and grilling sandwiches. Serve fresh, ripe figs topped with sour cream and brown sugar for dessert.

FRESH TOMATO SOUP

> 2 tablespoons butter or margarine
> 1 large onion, chopped
> 1 large carrot, peeled and chopped
> 5 large (2 lb. total) ripe tomatoes, cored, seeded, and quartered
> ¼ cup firmly packed fresh basil leaves
> ¾ teaspoon sugar
> ½ teaspoon white pepper
> 3 cups regular-strength chicken broth
> Salt

In a 3- to 4-quart pan on medium heat, cook butter, onion, and carrot, uncovered, until carrot is very tender when pierced, about 20 minutes; stir often.

Add tomatoes, basil, sugar, and pepper. Cover and simmer until tomatoes are very soft, about 15 minutes. Purée mixture in a food processor or blender; return to pan and stir in broth. Stir over high heat until hot. Makes about 6½ cups, 4 servings.

PER SERVING: 148 calories, 5 g protein, 18 g carbohydrates, 7.6 g fat, 16 mg cholesterol, 127 mg sodium

OLIVE PURÉE

> 1 can (2¼ oz.) black ripe olives, drained
> ¼ cup drained capers
> 2 teaspoons Dijon mustard
> 5 drained canned anchovy fillets
> ¼ teaspoon *each* cracked bay leaves and dry thyme leaves
> 1 large clove garlic
> 1 tablespoon olive oil or salad oil

In a blender or food processor, whirl olives, capers, mustard, anchovies, bay, thyme, garlic, and oil until smoothly puréed. Serve in a bowl at room temperature. Makes ½ cup.

PER TABLESPOON: 62 calories, 1 g protein, 1 g carbohydrates, 6.3 g fat, 1.4 mg cholesterol, 399 mg sodium

(Continued on next page)

FOURTH OF JULY HOT DOG BASH

Internationally Styled Hot Dogs
Condiments
Corn on the Coblet Salad
Watermelon
Sparkling Water   Bubble Floats

This meal for 8 offers the all-American hot dog plus dogs with international touches. You provide sausages, an assortment of breads and buns, and condiments; let guests cook and combine on their own—with some guidance from the chef.

You can make the salad up to a day ahead. Assemble frankfurters (1 or 2 per serving), the breads and buns (1 or 2 pieces for a serving), and condiments. Have watermelon ready to cut. Ignite coals about 45 minutes before cooking.

You might want to post these suggestions on a chalk board:

All-American dog: frankfurter plus bright yellow mustard, catsup, and piccalilli on a hot dog bun.

Parisian dog: frankfurter plus sliced cooked ham, mayonnaise, Dijon mustard, and brie cheese on a crusty roll.

Santa Fe dog: frankfurter wrapped in a warm flour tortilla with chopped tomatoes, chopped onion, fresh cilantro leaves, and shredded jack cheese.

Vienna dog: frankfurter in a rye bun with drained sauerkraut, sliced münster cheese, and German mustard.

To make the bubble floats, pour Italian spumante or ginger ale over fruit sorbet or ice cream in a tall glass. Serve with long spoons.

CORN ON THE COBLET SALAD

    6 medium-size ears of corn
  ⅔ cup salad oil
  ½ cup white wine vinegar
    4 teaspoons Dijon mustard
    2 teaspoons sugar
  ⅓ cup *each* finely chopped fresh
        mint leaves and fresh cilantro
        (coriander)
  ¼ cup finely chopped fresh dill
        Salt and pepper

Remove and discard husks and silks from corn. With a heavy, sharp knife, cut corn crosswise into 1- to 1½-inch rounds (if needed, use a hammer or mallet to help drive knife through cob). In a 4- to 6-quart pan over high heat, drop corn into boiling water to cover. Cover and cook corn until hot, about 3 minutes; drain.

In a large bowl, mix oil, vinegar, mustard, sugar, mint, cilantro, and dill. Mix in corn; season with salt and pepper to taste. Serve, or cover and chill up until next day. Pick up corn to eat. Serves 8.

PER SERVING: 227 calories, 2.3 g protein, 15 g carbohydrates, 19 g fat, 0 mg cholesterol, 11 mg sodium

AUGUST

Navajo Tacos (page 182)

Fresh ideas to inspire late summer meals brighten our August issue. For your enjoyment we offer leaf-wrapped sausage and seafood appetizers cooked on the grill; open-face Navajo tacos to eat with knife and fork; slivered salads prepared quickly using a food processor; and colorful, thirst-quenching beverages made with summer fruits. Amuse the youngsters with whimsical peanut butter concoctions and an outdoor display of your spun sugar showmanship.

Leaf-wrapped Appetizer Packets

ATTRACTIVE AND AROMATIC, *edible leaves wrap small pieces of meat and fish as they cook on the barbecue. The slightly charred leaves retain their flavors, complementing the foods they cover.*

Fresh shiso, also called beefsteak, is a leafy herb found in Japanese markets; use it or fresh mint to envelop prawns. Or wrap pork meatballs with basil leaves to surround morsels with fragrance as they turn crisp over hot coals.

Sturdy romaine leaves also make tidy packets. They keep their contents—fragile fish—moist and juicy.

Grill one or more of these make-ahead selections for an appetizer course. Larger portions can constitute an entrée.

SHRIMP IN SHISO LEAVES

24 large (31 to 35 per lb.) shrimp, about ¾ pound total
3   tablespoons lemon juice
¼   cup (⅛ lb.) melted butter or margarine
24 fresh shiso (beefsteak) leaves (each about 2 in. long) or large fresh mint leaves

Peel and devein shrimp; leave tails on. Mix shrimp with lemon juice and butter. Fold a shiso leaf around each shrimp, then run a slender wooden skewer through leaf-wrapped seafood, placing 2 on each skewer as shown below, pushing them close together. Brush with any remaining butter mixture. (If made ahead, cover and chill up to 4 hours.)

To cook, lay shrimp on a grill 2 to 4 inches above a solid bed of hot coals (you can hold hand at grill level only 2 to 3 seconds). Extinguish flares with spray of water. Cook, turning once, until shrimp

Start the party with appetizers from the grill. The aroma from the cooking leaves is sure to arouse appetites.

are opaque throughout (cut to test), about 4 minutes. Makes 6 to 12 appetizer servings, 3 entrée servings.

PER SKEWER: 61 calories, 4.9 g protein, 4.2 g carbohydrates, 8.5 g fat, 47 mg cholesterol, 76 mg sodium

MEATBALLS IN BASIL

- 1 pound bulk pork sausage
- ½ cup minced fresh basil leaves
- 1 teaspoon crushed fennel seed
- 20 to 25 whole fresh basil leaves (each about 2 in. long)

Mix sausage, minced basil, and fennel. Shape into 1-inch balls. Rinse whole basil leaves, drain, and pat dry. Wrap a basil leaf around each meatball, lightly pressing the leaf into the surface so it sticks; leaf doesn't have to cover meatball completely. Thread meatballs on long, slender wooden skewers—2 or 3 meatballs close together on each. (If made ahead, cover and chill up to overnight.)

To cook, lay skewers on a grill 2 to 4 inches above a solid bed of hot coals (you can hold hand at grill level only 2 to 3 seconds). Extinguish flares with spray of water. Cook, turning every 2 to 3 minutes, until no longer pink in center (cut to test), 10 to 15 minutes. Makes 20 to 25 meatballs, enough for 8 appetizer servings, 3 or 4 entrée servings.

PER SKEWER: 104 calories, 5.5 g protein, 1.3 g carbohydrates, 8.5 g fat, 22 mg cholesterol, 349 mg sodium

SESAME-GINGER-ROMAINE FISH BUNDLES

Water
- 16 green onions, at least 12 inches long, root ends trimmed
- 1½ pounds boned and skinned fillets of white fish, such as orange roughy or sole, about ½ inch thick
- 2 tablespoons minced fresh ginger
- 2 tablespoons lemon juice
- 2 tablespoons soy sauce
- 1 tablespoon Oriental sesame oil or salad oil
- 6 large romaine leaves
- 12 slices lemon, each ⅛ inch thick

In a 12- to 14-inch frying pan, bring about 1 inch water to boiling. Immerse 12 whole green onions in boiling water until limp, 15 to 30 seconds; drain. Immerse green onions in cold water until cool; drain.

Cut remaining 4 green onions into 3-inch lengths; split thick ends in half; set aside.

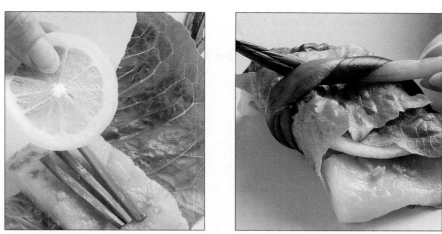

Marinated fish wrap: On a large romaine leaf, cut in half, place a piece of marinated fish topped with green onion and a thin slice of lemon. Wrap and secure bundle with a blanched green onion.

Sausage meatball: Wrap fresh basil leaf around sausage meatball laced with fennel and shredded basil. Grill on skewers.

Shrimp: Fold frilly Japanese shiso leaf around shrimp coated with lemon and butter. When grilled, the leaf gets crisp.

Cut fillets into 12 pieces, each about 3 by 3 inches. In a bowl, mix ginger, lemon juice, soy, sesame oil; add fish and coat with mixture.

Cut romaine leaves in half lengthwise along rib; remove rib. Lay 1 blanched onion out flat. Set lettuce leaf lengthwise down length of onion. Set 1 piece of fish 2 inches from root end of leaf. Top with 3 pieces cut green onion and 1 lemon slice. Fold end of leaf over top, then roll until leaf is completely wrapped around fish.

Center fish bundle, seam-side down, on onion, if needed. Lift onion ends and tie around bundle to secure. Wrap re-maining fish bundles. (If made ahead, cover and chill up to 4 hours.)

To cook, place bundles on a grill 2 to 4 inches above a solid bed of hot coals (you can hold hand at grill level only 2 to 3 seconds). Extinguish flares with spray of water. Cook until fish is opaque in thickest part, 8 to 12 minutes; turn when half-cooked. To test, cut into center of 1 bundle with tip of a knife. Makes 12 bundles, enough for 12 appetizer servings, 4 to 6 entrée servings.

PER BUNDLE: 93 calories, 9.2 g protein, 3.2 g carbohydrates, 5.2 g fat, 11 mg cholesterol, 210 mg sodium

Navajo Tacos

I**N THE 16TH CENTURY,** *the Spanish came to the Southwest and introduced their culture and foods to the region's natives. One of the most significant of these imports was wheat. The Indians used flour from the grain to make a new version of their corn flat bread—called a tortilla by the Spanish. A delicious bonus of the wheat flour tortilla was that when fried, it turned into a golden, billowy, tender pillow, dubbed "fry bread" by the Indians.*

Nowadays, warm fry bread is topped with chili made of beans and meat to create Indian or Navajo tacos. These popular, open-face tacos are sold at rodeos, fairs, and similar events throughout the West, as well as in trendy restaurants serving Southwestern cuisine.

This version comes from Navajo Maurice Begay, who learned it from his mother. Though brave folks may try tackling this generously scaled, meal-size taco out of hand, it's more practically ap-proached with a knife and fork. Each element—fry bread, chili, cheese, and salad toppings—can be made ahead. The fry bread and the chili reheat well.

NAVAJO TACOS

> 1 or 2 large firm-ripe tomatoes, cored
> Fry bread (recipe follows)
> Chili beans (recipe follows)
> ¾ pound mild cheddar cheese, shredded
> ½ pound iceberg lettuce, finely shredded (about 4 cups)
> 1¼ cups thinly sliced green onions
> About 1 cup purchased salsa
> About 1 cup sour cream (optional)

Slice a thin section off the top and bottom of each tomato. Then cut tomato crosswise into ⅛-inch-thick slices. On each slice, make a cut from the edge just to the center; set tomatoes aside.

Lay each piece of hot fry bread, cupped side up, on a plate. Spoon chili equally into each cup, then top with cheese, lettuce, and onions.

Arrange 1 or 2 tomato slices on top of each taco: hold each slice on opposite sides of the center cut, and fold the flaps in opposite directions to form a base so the uncut half of the slice sits upright; set on lettuce.

Top tacos with salsa and sour cream to taste. Makes 6 servings. —*Maurice Begay, Midvale, Utah*

PER SERVING: 775 calories, 43 g protein, 66 g carbohydrates, 38 g fat, 106 mg cholesterol, 1,106 mg sodium

Fry bread. Mix together 2 cups **all-purpose flour,** ½ cup **instant nonfat dry milk,** 1 tablespoon **baking powder,** and ½ teaspoon **salt.** Add 2 tablespoons **shortening.** Rub mixture with fingers

Pat fry bread dough into flat rounds; cover finished rounds with plastic wrap while you make remaining ones. Then cook rounds quickly in hot oil, one at a time. Leavened with baking powder, the bread puffs and bubbles dramatically.

until coarse crumbs form. Add ¾ cup **water** and stir with a fork until dough clings together.

Put dough on a lightly floured board. Knead until smooth, 2 to 3 minutes. Divide dough into 6 equal portions; keep covered with plastic wrap. Shape a portion of dough into a ball, then pat out on a floured board to make a 6- to 7-inch round. Cover with plastic wrap and repeat to shape remaining portions. You can stack the pieces of dough with plastic wrap between each.

In a pan about 9 inches wide and at least 2 inches deep, heat ¾ inch **salad oil** to 375°. Turning once, cook each round of dough in oil until puffy and golden brown, 1½ to 2 minutes. Line 2 baking sheets, 12- by 15-inch size, with several layers of paper towels; put bread in a single layer on towels, and keep warm in a 200° oven until all are cooked.

If made ahead, let bread cool as fried, then package airtight; chill up to next day. Warm in a single layer, uncovered, on baking sheets in a 375° oven until hot, about 5 minutes. Makes 6 pieces.

Chili beans. Sort and discard debris from 1 cup **dry Great Northern beans** or pinto beans; rinse well. Put beans in a 3- to 4-quart pan with 1 quart **water;** bring to boiling on high heat. Cook, uncovered, 10 minutes. Remove from heat, cover, and let stand 1 hour. Drain beans; set aside.

Rinse and dry pan and return to medium heat. Add 1 large **onion,** chopped, and 1 tablespoon **salad oil;** stir until onion is limp, 3 to 4 minutes. Add onions to beans. Crumble 1 pound **ground lean beef** or bulk pork sausage in pan; stirring occasionally, cook over high heat until well browned, about 10 minutes. Discard fat.

Add beans and onion to meat along with 3 cups **regular-strength chicken broth;** 1 tablespoon **chili powder;** 2 cloves **garlic,** pressed or minced; and 2 teaspoons *each* **ground cumin, dry oregano leaves,** and **dry basil leaves.** Bring to boiling over high heat; simmer, covered, until beans are tender to bite, 1½ to 2 hours. If you want to reduce liquid, uncover and boil chili, stirring often, until desired thickness. Use; or cool, cover, and chill up to 3 days. To reheat, stir often over medium-high heat until boiling. Makes 4 cups.

Top hot taco with cheese, lettuce, onions, tomato, salsa, and sour cream. For a picnic, transport hot foods in an insulated chest—or fry the bread on site.

Colorful Quenchers

THIRST-QUENCHING *and colorful, Mexican* agua fresca *features fruit juice or pulp, combined with a liberal amount of water. A hint of sugar sweetens the drink and stabilizes the flavor so the liquid stays fresh-tasting longer.*

You can make this light beverage with prime summer fruits. The high proportion of water makes the drink refreshing rather than filling.

SUMMER AGUA FRESCA

Using the chart at right, choose ripe **fruit** or fruits; kiwi fruit should feel firm (with soft fruit, color tends to fade).

In a blender, smoothly purée measured fruit pulp or juice (a portion at a time, if needed) with appropriate amount of **sugar** and **lime juice**. Where recommended amounts of sugar and lime juice are flexible, adjust to taste.

Add flavored fruit mixture to **water**, then rub through a fine strainer into a large jar or pitcher; discard pulp. If made ahead, cover and chill up to 1 week. As a decorative touch, add slices or chunks of matching fruit just before serving. Pour the agua fresca over **ice cubes** into tall glasses.

PER ½ CUP CANTALOUPE AGUA FRESCA: 32 calories, 0.5 g protein, 7.8 g carbohydrates, 0.1 g fat, 0 mg cholesterol, 5.4 mg sodium

Purée one or more ripe summer fruits in blender, add sugar and lime juice, then mix with water.

How to Make Drinks from 11 Summertime Fruits

Fruit	Sugar	Lime juice	Water	Yield
CANTALOUPE—seed, peel; coarsely chop fruit				
2⅔ cups	3 to 4 tablespoons	2 to 3 tablespoons	2 cups	About 1 qt.
5⅓ cups	⅓ to ½ cup	⅓ cup	4 cups	About 2 qt.
FEIJOA (pineapple guava)—peel; coarsely chop fruit				
1¼ cups	¼ to ⅓ cup	2 tablespoons	3½ cups	About 1 qt.
2½ cups	½ to ⅔ cup	¼ cup	7 cups	About 2 qt.
HONEYDEW MELON—seed, peel; coarsely chop fruit				
3 cups	2 to 3 tablespoons	3 tablespoons	2 cups	About 1 qt.
6 cups	¼ to ⅓ cup	6 tablespoons	1 qt.	About 2 qt.
KIWI FRUIT—peel; coarsely chop fruit				
1⅔ cups	2 to 3 tablespoons	1 tablespoon	2 cups	About 1 qt.
3⅓ cups	¼ to ⅓ cup	2 tablespoons	1 qt.	About 2 qt.
MANGO—peel, cut out seed; coarsely chop fruit				
1 cup	3 to 4 tablespoons	2 tablespoons	3½ cups	About 1 qt.
2 cups	⅓ to ½ cup	¼ cup	7 cups	About 2 qt.
ORANGE—juice				
1 cup juice	3 to 4 tablespoons	3 tablespoons	3 cups	About 1 qt.
2 cups juice	⅓ to ½ cup	6 tablespoons	6 cups	About 2 qt.
PAPAYA—peel, seed; coarsely chop fruit				
1¼ cups	3 to 4 tablespoons	2 to 3 tablespoons	2¾ cups	About 1 qt.
2½ cups	⅓ to ½ cup	5 tablespoons	5½ cups	About 2 qt.
PASSION FRUIT—cut in half, rub pulp through strainer, discard seeds				
½ cup juice	¼ to ⅓ cup	1 tablespoon	1 qt.	About 1 qt.
1 cup juice	½ to ⅔ cup	2 tablespoons	2 qt.	About 2 qt.
PINEAPPLE—peel and core; coarsely chop fruit				
1¼ cups	3 to 4 tablespoons	2 tablespoons	3 cups	About 1 qt.
2½ cups	⅓ to ½ cup	¼ cup	6 cups	About 2 qt.
STRAWBERRY—rinse and hull				
2¼ cups	3 to 4 tablespoons	1½ tablespoons	2½ cups	About 1 qt.
4½ cups	⅓ to ½ cup	3 tablespoons	5 cups	About 2 qt.
WATERMELON—peel, remove seeds; coarsely chop fruit				
2⅔ cups	3 to 4 tablespoons	2 to 3 tablespoons	2 cups	About 1 qt.
5⅓ cups	⅓ to ½ cup	5 tablespoons	4 cups	About 2 qt.

Serve these wholesome, thirst-quenching fruit drinks in vivid hues as refreshing beverages for family gatherings.

Spinning Sugar

GLISTENING, GOLDEN STRANDS of spun sugar, used to top many an elegant dessert, are surprisingly easy—if somewhat messy—to make. We suggest setting up a workspace outside on a sunny (not humid or windy) day, then gathering an audience to watch and taste the results.

You'll need two wooden dowels—each ½ inch in diameter and at least 3 feet long—and a means of supporting them at least 3 feet off the ground. A pair of rung-backed chairs, back to back, works well. Cover with plastic if they don't have an easy-to-wipe-off finish.

Set chairs on a large, clean cloth (such as an old tablecloth) or paper (such as wrapping paper). Rub dowels with salad oil, or coat with nonstick cooking spray. Set dowels about 8 inches apart on chairs.

To make the spinner, you'll need an inexpensive wire whisk. With wire cutters, snip each loop at its center. (Or substitute two metal dinner forks for the spinner.) You'll also need a pastry brush and candy thermometer. Check thermometer for accuracy ahead of time in boiling water; it should read 212° if you're at sea level.

Using a wire whisk with cut loops, she throws strands of hot caramel over oiled dowels supported on chairs.

SOME CAUTIONS BEFORE YOU START

The very hot sugar syrup can cause serious burns; let the youngsters watch you spin, but don't let them participate. Make sure they stay well out of reach of flying drops of hot syrup.

You may find it easiest to cook the syrup on a campstove set up where you're working, but if your kitchen is close by you could go back and forth.

SPUN SUGAR

  2 **cups sugar**
  ½ **cup water**
  ¼ **teaspoon cream of tartar**
      Ice cream cones or scoops of ice cream with fresh fruit

In a 1½- to 2-quart pan, combine sugar, water, and cream of tartar. Cook on high heat, stirring often until sugar dissolves, then boil until temperature of syrup reaches 320° on a candy thermometer; syrup will be caramel color. Occasionally wash sugar crystals off pan sides with a pastry brush dipped in water.

Remove pan from heat; let syrup cool slightly to thicken, about 4 minutes. Working quickly, dip end of a wire whisk with loops cut (see instructions, preced-

Quickly swirl a 4-inch-wide, golden skein of spun sugar around an ice cream cone.

Delighted audience watches her wind spun sugar for a sparkling confection.

ing), or tines of 2 dinner forks held with backs together, into syrup. **Do not touch hot syrup.** Standing in place and using an underhand motion, fling syrup quickly from whisk or forks over supported, oiled dowels (see instructions, preceding). Strands of syrup will fly off as thin, shimmering threads and drop over the dowels, hardening almost instantly. Repeat rapidly until no more strands fly from whisk. Dip whisk in syrup and repeat steps.

When you have a thin curtain of spun sugar, gently but quickly lift off a 4-inch-wide section. Quickly swirl it around the top of a cone, or set swirl on top of a bowl of ice cream and fruit. Strands melt when handled, so touch as little as possible.

When the syrup cools too much to spin easily, reheat to melt (up to 3 times). Serve spun sugar within an hour or so, before it gets sticky, collapses, and melts. Allow about a 4-inch-wide puff for a serving. Makes 10 to 12 servings.

PER SERVING, SPUN SUGAR ONLY: 128 calories, 0 g protein, 33 g carbohydrates, 0 g fat, 0 mg cholesterol, 0.3 mg sodium

Golden halo of filaments tops a cone or a bowl of ice cream and fruit.

Fast-melting strands disappear in your mouth.

Savory Herb Waffles

CRISP, GOLDEN WAFFLES *make an easy-to-prepare choice for a light supper or hearty brunch. Here, we've gone beyond the basic waffle, served with butter and syrup, to create more sophisticated herb waffles with nonsweet toppings.*

You accompany the first offering with basil, parmesan cheese, and melted butter. Variations include chili and cheese waffles to go with salsa and sour cream, and waffles with tarragon to go with mushrooms and ham. Fruit goes well at the start of the morning meal, or for dessert at dinner.

BASIL PARMESAN WAFFLES

4	large eggs
¾	cup buttermilk
	About ⅓ cup melted butter or margarine
1	cup all-purpose flour
¾	teaspoon baking soda
2¼	cups (about 6 oz.) freshly shredded parmesan cheese
¼	cup chopped fresh chives
3	tablespoons chopped fresh basil leaves
½	teaspoon pepper
	Fresh basil leaves

In a bowl, whisk eggs to blend; mix in buttermilk and melted butter. In another bowl, stir together flour, baking soda, ½ cup cheese, chives, chopped basil, and pepper; pour into egg mixture and stir until moistened but not smooth.

Heat a waffle iron to medium-high heat, or turn an electric waffle iron to medium-high or 375°. When iron is hot, open and brush grids lightly with salad oil. Pour ⅔ cup batter in the center of the grid; close and cook waffle until golden brown, about 3 minutes. Keep warm on racks in a 200° oven. Repeat to cook remaining batter.

Lay each waffle on a plate and sprinkle each with an equal amount of the remaining parmesan cheese. Garnish with basil leaves. Offer melted butter to add to taste. Makes 4 waffles.

PER WAFFLE: 554 calories, 30 g protein, 29 g carbohydrates, 35 g fat, 352 mg cholesterol, 1,265 mg sodium

CHILI CHEDDAR WAFFLES

Prepare **basil parmesan waffles,** preceding, but omit parmesan cheese and basil. Into the flour mixture, stir ¾ cup shredded **cheddar cheese,** 2 teaspoons chili powder, and ¾ teaspoon **ground cumin.** Offer **sour cream** and purchased **salsa** to add to taste. Makes 4 waffles.

PER WAFFLE: 437 calories, 17 g protein, 28 g carbohydrates, 29 g fat, 339 mg cholesterol, 309 mg sodium

MUSHROOM TARRAGON WAFFLES

Melt 2 tablespoons **butter** or margarine in a 10- to 12-inch frying pan over medium-high heat. Add 4 cups sliced **mushrooms** and 1 teaspoon chopped **fresh tarragon;** stir often until mushrooms are lightly browned, about 15 minutes. Add ½ cup very thinly slivered **cooked ham;** set aside.

Make **basil parmesan waffles,** preceding, but omit parmesan cheese and basil. To the flour mixture, add 2 tablespoons chopped **fresh tarragon leaves** and ¼ teaspoon **salt.**

While last waffle cooks, reheat the mushroom mixture, stirring, on medium heat. Spoon an equal portion of the mixture onto each waffle. Offer melted **butter** to add to taste. Makes 4 waffles.

PER WAFFLE: 449 calories, 17 g protein, 30 g carbohydrates, 29 g fat, 343 mg cholesterol, 343 mg sodium

Parmesan shreds and basil leaves top crisp waffles seasoned with basil, cheese, and melted butter.

Slivered Salads

I N ONLY SECONDS, *the slicing blade of a food processor can reduce a pile of vegetables or fruits to thin slivers—the base for each of these salads.*

To increase efficiency, cut ingredients into the processor bowl in sequence; moisten with dressing, then invert the salad onto a plate to serve.

The step that takes the most time is preparing the ingredients so they will slice well in the processor.

No processor? A sharp knife still works. Or use a hand-powered slicer—such as Japanese ones with attachments that let you finely slice and sliver vegetables.

THREE-PEPPER SALAD

- 1 tablespoon parsley leaves
- 1 clove garlic
- 3 medium-size bell peppers (1¼ to 1½ lb.)—in any combination of red, yellow, or green—stemmed, seeded, quartered lengthwise
- ¼ cup extra-virgin olive oil or salad oil
- 2 tablespoons lemon juice
- ¼ teaspoon dry thyme leaves
- 1 piece (about 5 oz.) parmesan or dry jack cheese
  Parsley sprigs
  Salt and pepper

In a food processor, use metal blade to whirl parsley leaves and garlic until finely chopped.

Remove blade and add slicer. Fit 2 pieces of bell pepper at a time into feed tube; slice, pushing through with plunger. Repeat to slice all the peppers. Remove lid and slicer. Mix oil, lemon juice, and thyme leaves; pour over peppers.

Invert a platter over bowl; holding them together securely, invert salad onto platter. To arrange the salad, pull peppers out a little around the base.

Pull a cheese-shaving slicer over the cheese to make thin strips, using about ⅓ of the cheese; lay cheese on salad. Garnish with parsley sprigs. Add salt and pepper to taste; offer remaining cheese to slice and add as desired. Makes 4 servings.

PER SERVING: 279 calories, 13 g protein, 6 g carbohydrates, 23 g fat, 24 mg cholesterol, 572 mg sodium

Crab, cucumber, and radish are dressed with black sesame seed and green onion strands.

CRAB SALAD WITH CUCUMBER & RADISH

- 1 green onion, ends trimmed
- 10 medium-size red radishes, ends trimmed
- 1 large (about 1½ lb.) European-style cucumber, ends trimmed
- ½ to 1 pound shelled cooked crab
- ⅓ to ½ cup seasoned rice vinegar (or white wine vinegar mixed with 4 teaspoons sugar)
- 1 teaspoon toasted black sesame seed (optional; sold in Asian markets)
  Salt

Pack white part of onion and as many radishes as possible into food processor feed tube; slice, pressing with plunger. Repeat to slice remaining radishes.

Cut cucumber crosswise in half, then lengthwise into quarters. Pack cucumber quarters into food processor feed tube and slice, pressing with plunger. Repeat to slice remaining cucumber. Remove lid; holding slicer in place, tip bowl to drain off any liquid. Push cucumber to make an even layer. Lay crab on cucumber.

Pour vinegar over crab. Invert a platter over bowl; hold them together and invert salad onto platter. To arrange salad, pull cucumber and crab out a little at base. If desired, use a knife to slice green portion of onion into thin strands. Garnish salad with onion and sprinkle with sesame seed. Add salt to taste. Makes 4 servings.

PER SERVING: 100 calories, 12 g protein, 10 g carbohydrates, 1 g fat, 57 mg cholesterol, 164 mg sodium

CANTALOUPE SALAD WITH LIME DRESSING

- 2 tablespoons fresh cilantro (coriander) or mint leaves
- 1 cup roasted salted peanuts
- 1 tablespoon tiny dried shrimp (optional; sold in Mexican and Asian markets)
- 2 small (about 2½ lb. each) cantaloupes, peeled, seeded, and flesh cut into 1½-inch-wide wedges
  Lime dressing (recipe follows)
  Salt

In a food processor, use metal blade to whirl cilantro until finely chopped. Add peanuts and shrimp; whirl until coarsely chopped.

Remove blade and add slicer. Fit cantaloupe wedges into feed tube; slice, pushing through with plunger. Remove lid and slicer. Pour lime dressing over salad. Invert a platter over bowl; holding them together securely, invert salad onto platter. To arrange the salad, pull out some of the fruit around the base. Add salt to taste. Makes 4 servings.

PER SERVING: 338 calories, 12 g protein, 38 g carbohydrates, 19 g fat, 0 mg cholesterol, 185 mg sodium

Lime dressing. Stir together ⅓ cup **lime juice,** 2 tablespoons **sugar,** and ½ teaspoon **crushed dried hot red chilies.**

Having Fun with Peanut Butter

WHIMSY DISTINGUISHES THESE *breakfast and lunch ideas for young cooks. Each recipe starts with homemade or purchased peanut butter—and each goes together quickly, so rewards are immediate.*

Children participate to the extent of their abilities—buzzing ingredients in the food processor or blender, spreading, shaping, or decorating. An adult should supervise use of electric appliances.

Choices include "moon rock" cookies that need no baking (wholesome for breakfast as well as for snacks), impressionistic lettuce monsters, personality sandwiches, and a peanut butter–banana shake.

MOON ROCKS

In a bowl, mix with hands or a spoon 1½ cups **granola-type cereal with raisins,** 1½ teaspoons **ground cinnamon,** ¼ cup *each* **nonfat dry milk** and **honey,** and ¾ cup **homemade** or purchased **peanut butter.** Squeeze into 1-inch balls. Eat, or chill airtight up to 1 week. Makes 28.— *Camille Ronzio, Eugene, Ore.*

PER PIECE: 80 calories, 2.6 g protein, 7.8 g carbohydrates, 4.7 g fat, 0.1 mg cholesterol, 6.1 mg sodium

For Moon Rocks, moisten granola cereal with peanut butter and squeeze into 1-inch balls.

Beady-eyed Lettuce Monster has raisin face, peanut butter, and pickle relish tucked into folded leaf.

LETTUCE MONSTER

Rinse a large **butter lettuce** leaf; pat dry. Spread inside with 1 tablespoon **homemade** or purchased **peanut butter;** sprinkle with about 1 teaspoon drained **sweet pickle relish.** Fold sides of lettuce over peanut butter; lay seam side down on plate. Attach **raisins** for eyes and nose, gluing with peanut butter.

PER PIECE: 107 calories, 4 g protein, 5.4 g carbohydrates, 8.5 g fat, 0 mg cholesterol, 38 mg sodium

BLOCKHEAD SANDWICH

On a piece of cool, toasted **whole-wheat** or white **bread,** spread about 1 tablespoon *each* **whipped cream cheese,** and **homemade** or purchased **peanut butter,** both at room temperature. For hair, use about 2 tablespoons **alfalfa sprouts** or grated carrot. Use **sliced ripe olives** or carrot pieces for eyes, nose, and mouth.

PER PIECE: 190 calories, 7 g protein, 14 g carbohydrates, 13 g fat, 10 mg cholesterol, 180 mg sodium

PEANUT BUTTER "QUAKE"

In a food processor or blender, whirl until smooth 1 medium-size **ripe banana,** 1 to 3 tablespoons **honey,** ¼ cup **homemade** or purchased **peanut butter,** and 1 cup *each* **vanilla-flavored yogurt** and **milk.** Makes 2½ to 3 cups.

PER CUP: 341 calories, 12 g protein, 44 g carbohydrates, 15 g fat, 15 mg cholesterol, 92 mg sodium

HOMEMADE PEANUT BUTTER

Whirl 2 tablespoons **salad oil** and 2 cups **roasted peanuts** in a food processor or blender until smooth; stop motor once to scrape mixture into blade. Use, or chill airtight. Makes 1¼ cups.

PER TABLESPOON: 96 calories, 3.8 g protein, 2.7 g carbohydrates, 8.5 g fat, 0 mg cholesterol, 0.9 mg sodium

Transform peanut butter snack into a Blockhead Sandwich with sliced olive features and alfalfa sprouts for hair. Peanut butter also flavors beverage.

More August Recipes

ENJOY THE FRESH FOODS *of summer in this boldly seasoned soup and in a colorful salad featuring ripe watermelon and fresh mint.*

FRESH CORN & SEAFOOD SOUP

Immigrants to Australia from Southeast Asia have popularized their traditional foods in this land of strong British culinary heritage. Such bold ingredients as garlic, ginger, fish sauce, chilies, cilantro, and coconut have taken a firm hold. Stephanie Alexander uses them well in a soup served at her restaurant, Stephanie's, near Melbourne; we present a version of the soup here.

You can serve the soup as the main attraction of a light meal. Or offer it preceding a simple main course, such as chicken and stir-fried vegetables.

Buy unsweetened, large-flaked coconut in health-food stores, fish sauce from Oriental markets. Or use alternatives available at the supermarket.

- 2 tablespoons salad oil
- 5 cloves garlic, thinly sliced
- 10 medium-size shallots (about ½ lb.), thinly sliced crosswise
- 2 tablespoons minced fresh ginger
- 8 cups regular-strength chicken broth
- 2 tablespoons fermented Asian fish sauce (*nam pla* or *nuoc nam*) or soy sauce
- 2 cups fresh corn kernels
- 1 or 2 fresh jalapeño or serrano chilies, stemmed, seeded, and cut into small slivers
- ¼ pound shelled cooked crab
- ¼ pound tiny cooked shelled shrimp
- 1 cup fresh cilantro (coriander) sprigs
  Curried coconut (recipe follows)

Pour oil into a 5- to 6-quart pan over medium heat. Add garlic, shallots, and ginger. Stir, cover, and cook, stirring once or twice, until shallots are slightly softened, about 5 minutes. Uncover and stir often until shallots are deep golden, about 5 minutes longer.

Add broth, fish sauce, corn, and chili to taste. Bring to a boil over high heat. Then cover and simmer until corn is tender to bite, 5 to 10 minutes.

Light broth contains tiny shrimp, crab, fresh corn, cilantro, and shallots.

Stir crab, shrimp, and ½ cup cilantro into soup. Offer remaining cilantro and the coconut to add to taste. Makes 11 cups, 5 or 6 servings.

PER CUP: 182 calories, 13 g protein, 16 g carbohydrates, 8 g fat, 56 mg cholesterol, 520 mg sodium

Curried coconut. Pour 1 tablespoon **salad oil** into a 10- to 12-inch frying pan over medium heat. All at once, add 1 teaspoon *each* **ground coriander** and **cumin seed,** and ½ teaspoon *each* **ground ginger** and **ground turmeric;** stir for 30 seconds. Add 1 cup **unsweetened, large-flaked** or shredded **dry coconut;** stir until coconut edges are golden, about 3 minutes. Makes 1 cup.

PER TABLESPOON: 35 calories, 0.3 g protein, 1 g carbohydrates, 3.5 g fat, 0 mg cholesterol, 2 mg sodium

WATERMELON-MINT SALAD

Sweet and crisp, ripe watermelon gains new character when mixed with mild onions, cool mint, and a mellow chili dressing. Serve this summer salad with grilled lamb chops, beef ribs, or perhaps barbecued hamburgers.

Because cut watermelon doesn't stay at its best for long, serve this mixture within 4 hours of preparation.

- 1 watermelon, about 6 pounds
- ¾ cup slivered mild white onion
- ½ cup minced fresh mint leaves
  Chili dressing (recipe follows)
  Salt

Slice the watermelon into 1-inch-thick rounds; cut rind from flesh and discard. Cut flesh into 1-inch cubes and remove visible seeds. Place cubes (you should have about 3 qt.) in a large bowl. Add onion and mint. If made ahead, cover and chill up to 4 hours.

Pour dressing over salad; mix gently. Add salt to taste. Makes 8 servings. — *Lydia Raymond, Oakland*

PER SERVING: 175 calories, 1.7 g protein, 19 g carbohydrates, 11 g fat, 0 mg cholesterol, 8.3 mg sodium

Chili dressing. Whisk together 3 tablespoons **cider vinegar,** 1 teaspoon **chili powder,** and 6 tablespoons **salad oil** or olive oil. Use, or cover and let stand up to 3 days. Makes ⅓ cup.

PUFF PANCAKE WITH MANGO

Sweet sliced mangoes and tart raspberries fill puffy oven pancake.

    4 large eggs
    1 cup milk
    1 cup all-purpose flour
    6 tablespoons butter or margarine
    2 firm-ripe mangoes (1½ lb. total)
    3 tablespoons orange marmalade
    1 tablespoon lemon juice
    1½ cups raspberries, rinsed and
       drained

Heat oven to 425°. In oven, warm a 12-inch frying pan with ovenproof handle or 3-quart shallow casserole.

Meanwhile, combine eggs, milk, and flour in a blender. Whirl until well blended. When oven reaches 425°, remove pan and add ¼ cup butter; tilt pan to coat with butter. Pour batter into pan; return to oven. Bake until brown and crisp around edges, 20 to 25 minutes.

Meanwhile, peel and pit mangoes. Cut fruit into ½-inch-thick slices. In a 10- to 12-inch frying pan, melt remaining 2 tablespoons butter over high heat. Stir in marmalade and lemon juice. Add mangoes; stir gently just until hot, about 5 minutes. Spoon mangoes into center of pancake. Sprinkle with raspberries. Cut into wedges. Makes 6 servings. —*Carole Van Brooklin, Port Angeles, Wash.*

PER SERVING: 347 calories, 8.4 g protein, 42 g carbohydrates, 17 g fat, 219 mg cholesterol, 187 mg sodium

ZUCCHINI APPLE BUTTER

Combine zucchini, apple, lemon, sugar, and spices to make fruit butter.

    3 zucchini (1 lb. total), peeled, with
       ends trimmed
    1 tart green apple (7 oz.)
    3 tablespoons lemon juice
    ⅓ cup maple or maple-flavor syrup
    1 cup firmly packed brown sugar
    2 teaspoons ground cinnamon
    ¾ teaspoon ground nutmeg
    ¼ teaspoon ground allspice
       Salt

Coarsely chop zucchini. Peel and core apple and coarsely chop. Put zucchini, apple, lemon juice, and syrup in a food processor or blender, and whirl until smoothly puréed. Transfer mixture to a 3- to 4-quart pan. Add sugar, cinnamon, nutmeg, and allspice; stir to mix.

Bring to a boil on high heat, then reduce heat and simmer, uncovered, stirring occasionally, until mixture thickens to a jam-like consistency (purée may splatter as it cooks), 20 to 25 minutes. Add salt to taste.

Serve; or cool, cover, and chill up to 2 weeks. Freeze for longer storage; thaw to serve. Makes 2¼ to 2½ cups. —*Barbara Keenan, Fort Morgan, Colo.*

PER TABLESPOON: 32 calories, 0.1 g protein, 8.1 g carbohydrates, 0 g fat, 0 mg cholesterol, 2.4 mg sodium

CHICKEN SALSA

Chicken with salsa makes easy entrée; eat with avocado, squash, tortillas.

    1 broiler-fryer chicken (3½ to
       4 lb.), cut up
    1 can (15 oz.) tomato sauce
    1 cup medium or mild prepared
       salsa
    1 clove garlic, pressed or minced
    1 small onion, thinly sliced
    2 teaspoons ground cumin
    1 teaspoon dry oregano leaves
    8 flour tortillas (7 to 8 in.)
       Salt

Rinse chicken; pat dry. Place on a rack in a 12- by 15-inch broiler pan. Broil 3 to 4 inches from heat, turning to brown both sides, 10 to 15 minutes total.

Transfer chicken to a shallow 3-quart casserole. In a bowl, mix tomato sauce, salsa, garlic, onion, cumin, and oregano. Pour sauce mixture over chicken. Cover dish tightly and bake in a 350° oven for 25 minutes.

Wrap tortillas in foil. After 25 minutes, uncover chicken and add tortillas to oven. Continue baking until chicken is no longer pink at thigh bone (cut to test) and tortillas are hot, 15 to 20 minutes longer. Remove chicken and tortillas from oven; salt chicken to taste. Serve tortillas alongside, to eat with sauce. Makes 4 servings. —*Lyn McNeel, Tularosa, N.M.*

PER SERVING: 517 calories, 48 g protein, 47 g carbohydrates, 15 g fat, 127 mg cholesterol, 1,128 mg sodium

Green Bean Salad with Yogurt-Dill Dressing

1½ pounds green beans, ends trimmed
1 can (3½ oz.) pitted ripe olives, drained
1 large firm-ripe tomato, cored and cut into wedges
⅓ cup chopped walnuts
Dill dressing (recipe follows)
Salt
Nasturtiums (pesticide-free and rinsed) or fresh dill sprigs

In a 5- to 6-quart pan, bring about 3 quarts water to a boil over high heat. Add beans and cook, uncovered, just until barely tender to bite, about 5 minutes. Drain and immerse in ice water. When cool, drain and cut diagonally into 3-inch lengths.

In a large bowl, combine beans, olives, tomato, walnuts, and dill dressing. Mix to coat vegetables. Add salt to taste. Garnish with nasturtiums or dill sprigs. Makes 6 to 8 servings. — *Karen Lohmann, Olympia, Wash.*

PER SERVING: 122 calories, 3.2 g protein, 0 g carbohydrates, 9.3 g fat, 0.9 mg cholesterol, 111 mg sodium

Dill dressing. Mix ½ cup **unflavored yogurt**, 2 tablespoons **olive oil** or salad oil, 3 tablespoons chopped **fresh dill weed** (or 1 tablespoon dry dill weed), 2 tablespoons **lemon juice**, and ½ teaspoon **pepper**.

Nasturtiums add bright color to green beans and tomatoes with dill dressing.

Walla Walla Salmon

¼ cup sliced almonds
¼ cup sweetened shredded dry coconut
1 tablespoon salad oil
2 large mild onions, thinly sliced
Teriyaki sauce (recipe follows)
4 pieces salmon fillet (6 oz. each)
Lemon wedges

In a 10- to 12-inch frying pan, stir almonds over medium-low heat until light gold, about 6 minutes. Add coconut; stir until toasted, 2 to 3 minutes. Remove from pan; set aside.

In the same pan, stir oil, onion, and 3 tablespoons of the teriyaki sauce over medium heat until onion is limp, 15 to 20 minutes.

Set fish, skin side up, on greased rack in a 12- by 15-inch broiler pan. Broil 3 to 4 inches from heat, brushing with remaining teriyaki sauce until fish is opaque in thickest part (cut to test), 6 to 8 minutes total; turn once. Transfer to serving dish and pile onion, coconut, and nuts on fish. Garnish with lemon. Serves 4. — *Sheryl Kindle Fullner, Everson, Wash.*

PER SERVING: 397 calories, 37 g protein, 12 g carbohydrates, 22 g fat, 94 mg cholesterol, 861 mg sodium

Teriyaki sauce. Mix 3 tablespoons **soy sauce**, 2 tablespoons **dry sherry** or water, 1 tablespoon **Oriental sesame oil**, and 1 tablespoon minced **fresh ginger**.

Salmon is embellished with teriyaki sauce, onions, nuts, and coconut.

Peach & Berry Bake

1 tablespoon cornstarch
1 teaspoon ground cinnamon
½ teaspoon ground nutmeg
½ cup sugar
1 quart sliced peeled peaches (about 2 lb.)
1 cup blueberries, rinsed
1 cup all-purpose flour
1 teaspoon baking powder
¼ cup (⅛ lb.) butter or margarine
1 large egg
¾ cup orange juice
2 tablespoons lemon juice

In a shallow 1½- to 2-quart baking dish, mix cornstarch, cinnamon, nutmeg, and ¼ cup of the sugar. Stir in peaches and blueberries.

In a food processor or a bowl, whirl or rub with your fingers the flour, baking powder, remaining ¼ cup sugar, and butter until it assumes the texture of coarse cornmeal. Add egg; whirl or stir to mix well. Sprinkle mixture evenly over fruit. Mix orange juice and lemon juice; pour evenly over fruit.

Bake in a 375° oven until bubbly in center and topping is golden brown, about 45 minutes. Scoop out portions and serve warm or cool. Makes 8 or 9 servings. — *Alice Kirkpatrick, Redding, Calif.*

PER SERVING: 204 calories, 2.9 g protein, 36 g carbohydrates, 6 g fat, 44 mg cholesterol, 109 mg sodium

Bake peaches and blueberries with biscuit topping and juice for homey dessert.

EGG-BASED BREAKFAST SANDWICHES *are no novelty, thanks to recent efforts on the part of several fast-food chains. But James Hensinger's breakfast sandwich, on the other hand, is genuinely novel—a hybrid between a BLT and a peanut butter sandwich. Don't condemn it without trying it; the combination is unexpectedly delicious, and the sandwich will sustain you until midday.*

It could, in fact, become a brown bag lunch if you carry the tomato separately and add it just before eating. Hensinger believes that the success of the sandwich depends upon having a really ripe, home-grown tomato.

WHAT, A BREAKFAST SANDWICH?

- 4 **thick-cut bacon slices**
- 2 **slices whole-wheat bread**
  About 3 tablespoons chunk-style peanut butter
- 1 **thick slice of a large, ripe beefsteak-type tomato**
  Salt

Cook bacon in a 10- to 12-inch frying pan over medium heat until crisp; drain well.

Meanwhile, toast bread; generously spread 1 slice with peanut butter. Top peanut butter with the cooked bacon and set tomato on bacon; add salt to taste. Top with remaining toast slice. Makes 1 hearty sandwich.

PER SERVING: 645 calories, 31 g protein, 29 g carbohydrates, 48 g fat, 37 mg cholesterol, 1,115 mg sodium

Aurora, Colo.

CHIPOTLES—SMOKED JALAPEÑO CHILIES *—are, like most other smoked foods, the offspring of necessity. Before canning was even dreamed of, our ancestors kept flies off their food by suspending it in the smoke of the campfire, the same smoke that kept mosquitoes off their relatively hairless hides. The accompanying heat also dried the victuals and helped preserve them from mold. Refinements in the process eventually led to such smoky delights as bacon, provolone cheese, lapsang souchong tea, and Virginia ham.*

"Build a breakfast sandwich that will sustain you until midday."

When Cortez landed in Mexico he found the natives employing a wide variety of chili peppers. If not consumed fresh, chilies with thin walls were (and still are) air-dried; those with thicker flesh (notably jalapeños) were suspended in smoke and heat to ensure drying before spoilage could occur. Smoked jalapeños are chipotles, *the essential flavoring element in Arthur Vinsel's Popotla's Chipotle Pork, a dish which incorporates the best elements of Mexican* carnitas *and Italian* risotto.

And what about Popotla? It is a tiny pottery-making town south of Tijuana.

POPOTLA'S CHIPOTLE PORK

- **About 1½ pounds boneless pork butt or shoulder**
- 2 **tablespoons butter or margarine**
- 1 **medium-size onion, chopped**
- ½ **cup chopped red bell pepper**
- ½ **cup chopped carrot**
- 1 **canned chipotle chili in adobo sauce and 1 tablespoon of the adobo sauce**
- 1 **cup dry sherry**
- 1 **cup water**
- 1 **cup long-grain white rice**
  Salt or garlic salt
- 1 **medium-size ripe avocado, pitted, peeled, and sliced**

Thinly sliced green onions, including tops
Fresh cilantro (coriander) sprigs

Trim and discard excess fat from pork; cut meat into 1½-inch cubes. Melt butter in a 5- to 6-quart pan over medium-high heat; add pork, a portion at a time, and cook until browned on all sides, then lift out and set aside. Add onion, bell pepper, and carrot to pan and stir occasionally until onion is limp, about 10 minutes.

Meanwhile, purée chipotle chili, adobo sauce, and sherry in a blender; add to the onion mixture. Also return pork to pan. Bring to a boil over high heat; cover, reduce heat, and simmer until pork is very tender when pierced, about 1½ to 2 hours. Add water and rice; stir to mix. Cover and continue to cook until rice is tender to bite and liquid is absorbed, 20 to 25 more minutes; stir once or twice. Season to taste with salt. Garnish with avocado, green onions, and cilantro. Makes 4 or 5 servings.

PER SERVING: 469 calories, 26 g protein, 42 g carbohydrates, 22 g fat, 91 mg cholesterol, 161 mg sodium

Newport Beach, Calif.

A POPULAR CULINARY *trend-spotter (a specialized journalist whose occupation permits—nay, requires—him to eat out a great deal on an expense account) has said that Cajun is out and Southwestern is in. Southwestern cuisine is noted for labeling each recipe with the magic words Santa Fe. Why should Chefs of the West try to row against the current?*

Thomas Stone's Chicken Santa Fe is more than trendy, though. It is delicious, spicy but not really hot, and attractively garnished and flavored by green chilies—those innocuous-looking vegetables whose mysterious flavor is practically addictive.

CHICKEN SANTA FE

1 **large can (7 oz.) whole green chilies**
2 **slices bacon**
1 **broiler-fryer chicken (about 3½ lb.), cut up**
1 **large onion, cut lengthwise into eighths**
2 **cloves garlic, minced or pressed**
½ **cup *each* dry white wine and regular-strength chicken broth**
1 **tablespoon prepared hot taco sauce**
¼ **teaspoon ground cumin**
  Salt and freshly ground black pepper

Dice half the chilies; cut the remaining ones lengthwise into thin strips. Set aside in separate containers. In a 12-inch frying pan or 5- to 6-quart pan, cook bacon over medium heat until crisp. Lift out and drain on paper towels.

Add chicken pieces to bacon drippings, without crowding. Cook over medium-high heat until browned on all sides; lift out pieces as browned and add remaining ones. Set browned chicken aside. Discard all but 2 tablespoons of the drippings.

Add onion and garlic to reserved drippings; stir often until onion is limp and layers are separated. Crumble bacon and add to onions, along with diced chilies, wine, broth, taco sauce, and cumin; mix well. Arrange chicken pieces, skin side up, in sauce. Spoon some of sauce onto the chicken, then lay chili strips on chicken.

Cover and simmer until meat at thigh bone is no longer pink (cut to test), about 30 minutes. With a slotted spoon, transfer chicken from pan to a platter; keep warm. Boil sauce, uncovered, on high heat until reduced by about half. Spoon

sauce around chicken. Add salt and pepper to taste. Makes 4 servings.

PER SERVING: 516 calories, 50 g protein, 7.3 g carbohydrates, 31 g fat, 162 mg cholesterol, 561 mg sodium

Thomas R Stone

Pleasanton, Calif.

V ERY SMALL CREATURES *must generate a lot of internal heat to balance the loss of heat from their surfaces, which are large compared to their volume. The hummingbird must eat almost constantly to survive, and to eat it must work; the work itself then uses up calories. You'll never see a fat hummingbird.*

We lumpish, earthbound creatures are in no position to imitate. If we overeat, we get fat. Yet there are exceptions: those who exercise very strenuously can utilize—indeed, actually need—large amounts of carbohydrates. Marathon runners "load" carbohydrates by stuffing themselves with pasta before a race. Long-distance bicyclists maintain their energy level by "power snacking."

Bill Patterson, who rediscovered the joy of 50- to 100-mile bike rides after a lapse of 45 years, developed his power bar in a search for the ideal fuel.

The odd ingredient in the bar, paraffin, is used in chocolate manufacture to improve smoothness and flowability, raise the melting point, and retard deterioration of texture and flavor. Butter can be used instead, but a butter-chocolate mixture doesn't cover as thinly or smoothly.

POWER BARS

1 **cup regular rolled oats**
½ **cup sesame seed**
1½ **cups dried apricots, finely chopped**
1½ **cups raisins**
1 **cup shredded unsweetened dry coconut**
1 **cup blanched almonds, chopped**
½ **cup nonfat dry milk**
½ **cup toasted wheat germ**
2 **teaspoons butter or margarine**
1 **cup light corn syrup**
¾ **cup sugar**
1¼ **cups chunk-style peanut butter**
1 **teaspoon orange extract**
2 **tablespoons grated orange peel**
1 **package (12 oz.) or 2 cups semisweet chocolate baking chips**
4 **ounces paraffin or ¾ cup (⅜ lb.) butter or margarine**

Spread oats in a 10- by 15-inch baking pan. Bake in a 300° oven until oats are toasted, about 25 minutes. Stir frequently to prevent scorching.

Meanwhile, place sesame seed in a 10- to 12-inch frying pan over medium heat. Shake often or stir until seeds are golden, about 7 minutes. Pour into a large bowl. Add apricots, raisins, coconut, almonds, dry milk, and wheat germ; mix well. Mix hot oats into dried fruit mixture. Butter the hot baking pan; set aside.

In the frying pan, combine corn syrup and sugar; bring to a rolling boil over medium-high heat, stirring frequently. Remove from heat and quickly stir in the peanut butter, orange extract, and orange peel. At once, pour over the oatmeal mixture and mix well. Quickly spread in buttered pan and press into an even layer. Then cover and chill until firm, at least 4 hours or until next day.

Cut into bars about 1¼ by 2½ inches. Combine chocolate chips and paraffin in the top of a double boiler. Place over simmering water until melted; stir often. Turn heat to low.

Using tongs, dip 1 bar at a time into chocolate, hold over pan until it stops dripping (with paraffin, the coating firms very quickly), then place on wire racks set over waxed paper. When firm and cool (bars with butter in the chocolate coating may need to be chilled), serve bars, or wrap individually in foil. Store in the refrigerator up to 4 weeks; freeze to store longer. Makes 4 dozen bars, about 1 ounce each.

PER PIECE: 188 calories, 4.4 g protein, 29 g carbohydrates, 9.8 g fat, 0.6 mg cholesterol, 40 mg sodium

Bill Patterson

Portland

"The long-distance bicyclist maintains his energy level by power snacking."

August Menus

THESE HOT-WEATHER MEALS, *inspired by torrid climates of other lands, are calculated to refresh body and soul—even those of the person in the kitchen.*

For dinner, go outdoors and serve a spicy Thai soup from the barbecue. Or, in the kitchen cook ahead, to make a cool Hawaiian fish salad with tropical touches; you might offer this for lunch or supper.

Less exotic, but infinitely practical for a summer meal, is a stacked, lean turkey enchilada you can bake or zap in the microwave oven.

The salad and the enchilada transport easily to the garden for alfresco dining—if your family is so inclined.

THAI BARBECUE SOUP

Green Onion–Yogurt Dip
Romaine Leaves & Cherry Tomatoes
Gingered Beef & Chili Potatoes
with Thai-seasoned Broth
Seedless Grapes   Peaches
Ginger Wafer Cookies
Sparkling Water   Beer

Meat and potatoes for a Thai family, this soup is easy enough for a week-night. You use the barbecue but cook in pans on the grill. Salad can serve as an appetizer, too.

Ignite the coals and let them build up heat while you organize ingredients. Gather them on a large tray to move out to the barbecue; don't forget hot pads.

GINGERED BEEF & CHILI POTATOES WITH THAI-SEASONED BROTH

¼ cup olive oil or salad oil

4 cups diced scrubbed thin-skinned red potatoes (about 1¼ lb.)

1 tablespoon chili powder
About 1 cup regular-strength beef broth

1 pound boneless sirloin beef steak, trimmed of fat and thinly sliced

2 garlic cloves, minced or pressed

2 tablespoons minced fresh ginger

⅓ cup fresh cilantro (coriander) leaves
Thai-seasoned broth (recipe follows)

Mound and ignite about 60 charcoal briquets on barbecue's firegrate; let burn until coals are just covered with gray ash, about 30 minutes. Spread coals into a solid single layer and position grill 4 to 6 inches above them.

To a 10- to 12-inch frying pan with a heatproof handle, add 3 tablespoons oil. Place on grill; coals should be hot enough that you can hold your hand at grill level only 2 to 3 seconds. When oil is hot, add potatoes. Stir often until potatoes are tender-crisp to bite, about 5 minutes.

Ladle hot broth into bowls of cooked potatoes and gingered beef and serve as main dish. Dunk lettuce and cherry tomatoes into onion-yogurt sauce.

Stir in chili powder, then 1 cup broth; cover and cook, adding more broth as needed, until potatoes are tender to bite and broth is absorbed, about 20 minutes. Scoop potatoes onto a platter. To pan, add remaining oil, beef, garlic, and ginger. Stirring often, cook just until meat is barely pink in center (cut to test), about 5 minutes. Stir potatoes and cilantro in with the beef.

To serve, spoon equal portions of meat and potato mixture into 4 large soup bowls, then ladle an equal amount of hot Thai-seasoned broth into each bowl. Makes 4 servings. —*J. Hill, Sacramento*

PER SERVING: 417 calories, 21 g protein, 35 g carbohydrates, 22 g fat, 49 mg cholesterol, 85 mg sodium

Thai-seasoned broth. In a 2- to 3-quart pan, mix together 5 cups **regular-strength beef broth;** ½ cup thinly sliced **green onion;** 4 **cardamom seeds,** husks removed and seeds crushed; 1 **cinnamon stick** (about 2½ in. long); ¼ teaspoon *each* **anise seed** and **cumin seed,** crushed. Cover and set over hot coals (beside potatoes); bring to a boil, then move the seasoned broth to a less hot area to keep warm until ready to serve.

GREEN ONION–YOGURT DIP

Mix together 1 cup **unflavored yogurt** or sour cream, ⅓ cup thinly sliced **green onions,** 2 tablespoons minced **fresh cilantro** (coriander), and 1 tablespoon **lime juice.** Makes about 1½ cups.

PER TABLESPOON: 7.3 calories, .57 g protein, .88 g carbohydrates, .16 g fat, .63 mg cholesterol, 7.7 mg sodium

---

TROPICAL ISLANDS SALAD

Hawaiian Fish & Mango Salad with Toasted Coconut Dressing
Hawaiian Sweet Bread   Butter
Chocolate-covered Macadamias
Iced Tea   Sauvignon Blanc

Serve at midday or in the evening. To carry out the island theme, buy Hawaiian or Portuguese sweet bread.

Starting as early as a day ahead, cook fish, crisp spinach, and toast coconut.

Cold fish fillet, topped with caviar, is fanned by mango slices and spinach.

HAWAIIAN FISH & MANGO SALAD WITH TOASTED COCONUT DRESSING

- **4 white-flesh fish fillets (3 to 4 oz. each), such as halibut, orange roughy, or mahi-mahi**
- **6 cups lightly packed spinach leaves, washed and crisped**
- **2 celery stalks, ends trimmed and thinly sliced**
- **1 small onion, thinly sliced**
- **2 ripe mangoes (about 1¼ lb. total)**
- **4 teaspoons lumpfish caviar (optional)**
  Toasted coconut dressing (recipe follows)

In a 3- to 4-quart pan over high heat, bring 2 quarts of water to a boil; add fish, remove from heat, and cover. Let stand until fish is opaque in center of thickest section (cut to test), about 4 minutes. With a slotted spatula, carefully lift out fish and let cool. If cooked ahead, cover and chill up until the next day. Serve at room temperature.

On side of each of 4 dinner plates, arrange ¼ of the spinach, celery, and onion. Place a fillet in center of each plate. With a sharp knife, peel mangoes. Cut parallel to pit on each side to slice fruit free. Cut fruit lengthwise into ¼-inch-thick slices. Fan mango slices equally on plates opposite spinach. In a fine strainer, rinse caviar under cold running water. Drain, then spoon caviar equally onto each fillet. Add coconut dressing to taste. Serves 4.—*Guy Banal, Bon Appetit Restaurant, Hawaii*

PER SERVING: 199 calories, 16 g protein, 22 g carbohydrates, 6.5 g fat, 17 mg cholesterol, 138 mg sodium

Toasted coconut dressing. In a 10- to 12-inch frying pan, stir 1 cup **sweetened shredded dry coconut** over medium-high heat until golden brown. If made ahead, package airtight up to 2 days.

In a small bowl, mix ¾ cup coconut with 1 cup **unflavored yogurt** and 2 tablespoons **lemon juice;** top with remaining coconut.

PER TABLESPOON: 16 calories, .45 g protein, 1.7 g carbohydrates, .85 g fat, .43 mg cholesterol, 11 mg sodium

(Continued on next page)

MEXICAN ENCHILADA STACK

**Cucumber & Melon
with Lemon & Mint
Layered Turkey Enchiladas
Milk   Pinot Grigio**

Stack, don't roll, to make these easy enchiladas; microwave or bake them.

For a cooling salad, dress peeled and seeded honeydew and cucumber wedges with lemon juice. Sweeten to taste with sugar, then sprinkle with chopped fresh mint.

LAYERED TURKEY ENCHILADAS

½ pound cheddar cheese, shredded
1 pound ground turkey
1 can (4 oz.) diced green chilies
1 small onion, chopped
1 cup purchased mild green salsa
¾ cup chopped Roma-type tomatoes
8 corn tortillas (6 to 7 in. diameter)

Set aside ½ cup cheese. Mix remaining cheese with turkey, chilies, onion, ½ cup salsa, and ½ cup tomatoes. Divide into 7 equal portions.

In a shallow 9- to 10-inch-diameter baking dish, lay 1 tortilla; top evenly with a portion of the turkey mixture. Continue to stack tortillas and top with turkey mixture, ending with a tortilla on top. Cover tortilla with remaining cheese and spoon remaining salsa and tomatoes on cheese.

To bake, cover enchiladas with foil. Bake in a 400° oven for 40 minutes. Uncover and bake until turkey is opaque in center (cut to test), about 40 minutes longer.

To cook in the microwave oven, cover stack loosely with plastic wrap. Microwave on full power (100 percent) for 6 minutes; rotate dish ¼ turn every 2 minutes. Uncover and continue to cook on full power until turkey is opaque in center (cut to test), about 12 minutes longer; rotate dish about every 2 minutes.

Let enchilada stand about 5 minutes, then cut into wedges. Serves 5 or 6. — *Mickey Strang, Ridgecrest, Calif.*

PER SERVING: 386 calories, 26 g protein, 23 g carbohydrates, 22 g fat, 90 mg cholesterol, 733 mg sodium

SEPTEMBER

Cooking in a Dutch Oven (page 200)

Dutch oven cooks share
their expertise with readers in September as they offer their
best techniques, tips, and recipes. The spirit of the Olympic
Games led us to gather the savory selection of Korean
specialties from Koreans who have settled in the West. For
warm-weather dining, we suggest chilled seafood
combinations and tempting salads featuring juicy, crunchy
Asian pears. Crisp autumn days demand heartier entrées; our
fitness-conscious lasagna variations include vegetables, tofu,
and ground turkey. Then, as a reward, try our blueberry
and peach shortcake with caramel custard.

Dutch Oven Miracles

DUTCH OVEN COOKING *has survived from the days of the open hearth, and flourishes still. When Lewis and Clark made their pioneering trek to the Northwest in 1805, they listed the Dutch oven as* one of their most valued pieces of equipment. Today, river-runners, wilderness campers, and even home cooks echo the sentiment. On the enthusiastic forefront of Dutch oven cookery are Juanita and Mike Kohler, Pat and Wally Kohler, and Pat and Dick Michaud. Not only do they teach the cooking technique; since 1985, they've also run the Great American Dutch Oven Cook-off, which takes place at the Festival of

Utah's Dutch oven experts cook a whole meal on elevated iron tables; you can use foil on the ground and make any or all of the dishes.

the American West at Utah State University in Logan.

Here the six cooks share their expertise and a half-dozen of their Dutch oven specialties.

HOW DID THE DUTCH GET INVOLVED?

Some say the name stuck when Dutch traders sold this pan door-to-door, along with other black cast-iron ware, to early American colonists.

The classic cast-iron Dutch oven is very heavy (an empty 12-in. pan with lid weighs about 20 lb.) and very durable. Many a pot has seen more than a generation of service, and there are people who still own and use Dutch ovens that made the trip West by covered wagon.

Although the name Dutch oven applies to several devices in which food can be cooked, here it refers to a heavy pan made of cast iron, with three short metal legs and a bail (wire handle) as well as a tight-fitting lid with a handle and a deep rim. The legs stand the pan over hot coals; the lipped lid holds more coals on top. Heat from both bottom and top creates an environment for baking or braising—as in a conventional oven.

Most Dutch ovens are 10 to 14 inches in diameter; smaller and larger ones exist.

HOW TO SET UP A DUTCH OVEN TO COOK

Use a double thickness of foil that is 3 to 4 inches wider than the Dutch oven's diameter (or use an old baking sheet you don't mind ruining with coals). Trace around lid in center of foil. (On baking sheet, draw outline with a felt-tip marker.)

Lay foil flat on a fire-safe, level surface in a draft-free spot. Or use a two- or three-sided wind barricade that is a little higher than the pan and 4 to 6 inches away from its sides. (A three-sided folding metal splashguard or windguard, sold at hardware stores, costs about $3.)

About 30 minutes before you start cooking, ignite the appropriate number of charcoal briquets for the first phase of cooking (directions follow; or check recipes on this page and on pages 202–203). If you will need to add more fuel later, ignite those briquets 30 minutes before you need them.

For bottom cooking (see illustration, page 202), arrange about ⅓ of the ignited

coals (or the number specified by a recipe) on the foil, spacing them evenly and keeping the outermost coals about ½ inch inside the ring you have traced. If you have more coals than the ring accommodates, arrange remaining coals evenly within the circle. When baking batters or doughs, do *not* set a coal

directly in the center or food may burn.

Set Dutch oven over coals.

For top cooking (see illustration, page 202), arrange remaining coals evenly over the lid.

(Continued on next page)

STUFFED CORNISH GAME HENS

Dutch oven diameter	10-inch	12-inch	14-inch
Charcoal briquets	30	36	52
Game hens, 1 to 1¼ pounds *each*	2	3	5
Stuffing (use a favorite recipe)	1½ cups	2 cups	4 cups
Salad oil	½ teaspoon	¾ teaspoon	1 teaspoon
Paprika	½ teaspoon	¾ teaspoon	1 teaspoon
Carrots, large, cut in 3-inch lengths	2	3	5
Ears of corn, medium-size, husks and silks removed, cut into chunks	1 or 2	2 or 3	3 or 4
Salt and pepper			
Servings	2	3	5

Rinse hens and pat dry; reserve giblets for other uses. Fill body and breast cavities equally with stuffing. Pour oil into Dutch oven and rub over the bottom. Place hens, breast up, in pan; dust birds evenly with paprika and surround with carrots. Put lid on pan.

Set up Dutch oven to cook (see at left). Beneath, use 10 freshly ignited coals for a 10-inch pan, 12 for a 12-inch pan, and 17 for a 14-inch pan. Ignite remaining coals.

Cook hens 25 minutes; lift lid off and add corn. Replace lid and arrange remaining ignited coals evenly over lid. Cook until meat at the thigh bone is no longer pink (cut to test), about 20 minutes longer. Add salt and pepper to taste.

PER SERVING WITHOUT STUFFING: 668 calories, 65 g protein, 27 g carbohydrates, 33 g fat, 198 mg cholesterol, 233 mg sodium

BRAISED SPARERIBS

Dutch oven diameter	10-inch	12-inch	14-inch
Charcoal briquets	46	56	62
Catsup	1 cup	1½ cups	2 cups
Tomato-based chili sauce	1¼ cups	1¾ cups	2½ cups
Onions, medium-size, finely chopped	1	2	3
Cider vinegar	½ cup	¾ cup	1 cup
Light molasses	¼ cup	⅓ cup	½ cup
Worcestershire	2 tablespoons	3 tablespoons	¼ cup
Pork spareribs, cut apart	4 pounds	6 pounds	8 pounds
Servings	4 to 6	6 to 8	8 to 10

In a Dutch oven, stir together catsup, chili sauce, onion, vinegar, molasses, and Worcestershire. Add spareribs and mix with sauce.

Set up Dutch oven to cook (see at left). Beneath, use 10 freshly ignited coals for a 10-inch pan, 12 for a 12-inch pan, 14 for a 14-inch pan. Put lid on pan; arrange 20 coals on lid of 10-inch pan, 24 on 12-inch pan, 28 on 14-inch pan.

Cook, stirring occasionally, until meat is very tender when pierced, 1½ to 2 hours. At two 30-minute intervals, add ½ remaining freshly ignited coals, ⅓ on bottom, ⅔ on top. With a baster, siphon fat from pan juices and discard.

PER SERVING: 623 calories, 37 g protein, 38 g carbohydrates, 36 g fat, 143 mg cholesterol, 1,403 mg sodium

Yeast Rolls

Dutch oven diameter	10-inch	12-inch	14-inch
Charcoal briquets	20	26	30
All-purpose flour, cups	About 4½	About 6	About 8½
Active dry yeast, packages	1	1	2
Sugar	5 teaspoons	2 tablespoons	3 tablespoons
Salt	½ teaspoon	¾ teaspoon	1 teaspoon
Butter or margarine, melted	2 tablespoons	3 tablespoons	¼ cup (⅛ lb.)
Milk, heated to scalding	1½ cups	2¼ cups	3 cups
Yield	18 rolls	24 rolls	36 rolls

In a large bowl, combine half the flour with yeast, sugar, and salt. Stir in melted butter and hot milk; beat with a heavy spoon until mixture is stretchy. Stir in remaining flour, 1 cup at a time, until a dough forms. Knead on a floured board until smooth and elastic, about 10 minutes. Add flour to prevent sticking.

Grease inside of Dutch oven. Divide dough into equal-size pieces to make number of rolls that fit pan size, then shape each piece into a ball. Set balls evenly apart in pan. Put lid on pan and let stand in a warm place until rolls are about double in size, about 1 hour. Set up Dutch oven to cook (see page 201), using ⅓ of the freshly ignited coals beneath and remaining coals on the lid.

Cook until rolls are browned on top, about 35 minutes. Lift off coals; remove lid. Run a knife around the edge of pan to loosen rolls. Serve from pan.

PER ROLL: 143 calories, 4.1 g protein, 26 g carbohydrates, 2.2 g fat, 6.2 mg cholesterol, 85 mg sodium

Pineapple Upside-down Cake

Dutch oven diameter	10-inch	12-inch	14-inch
Charcoal briquets	20	24	32
Pound cake mix (1-lb. package)	1	1½	2
Eggs, large	2	3	4
Milk	¾ cup	1¼ cups	1½ cups
Brown sugar, firmly packed	¾ cup	1 cup	1¼ cups
Butter or margarine	¼ cup (⅛ lb.)	6 tablespoons	½ cup (¼ lb.)
Canned pineapple slices, drained	7	9	11
Canned maraschino cherries, drained (optional)	7	9	11
Servings	8 to 10	12 to 16	18 to 20

In a bowl, combine cake mix, eggs, and milk; beat until smooth. Set batter aside.

Put brown sugar and butter in Dutch oven; put lid on pan.

Set up Dutch oven to cook (see page 201), using ⅓ of the freshly ignited coals underneath and remaining coals on the lid. Cook until sugar and butter melt, 3 to 4 minutes; stir to mix. Arrange pineapple slices in a single layer in the sugar mixture; place a cherry in the center of each slice. Pour batter over pineapple. Replace lid; cook until cake just begins to pull from sides of pan and a toothpick inserted in the center comes out clean, about 40 minutes.

Remove lid. Invert a shallow rimmed platter over pan; hold pan and platter together, using heatproof mitts, and quickly invert cake onto platter. Cut into wedges and serve with sauce on platter.

PER SERVING: 382 calories, 3.2 g protein, 57 g carbohydrates, 16 g fat, 70 mg cholesterol, 255 mg sodium

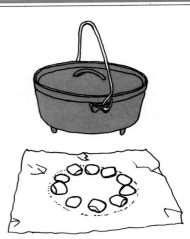

Set food-filled Dutch oven onto hot coals; arrange ring of coals on foil in a flat, draft-free place.

Lipped lid holds remaining hot coals, evenly spaced. Windguard shields pan from drafts.

If air moves in spite of the wind barrier, rotate the Dutch oven ¼ turn every 15 to 20 minutes so contents will cook evenly.

Check foods periodically to determine if cooking rate is appropriate. To reduce heat, remove a few coals in a symmetrical pattern (so cooking continues evenly), keeping the number of coals removed proportional to original numbers under and on top of the oven. To increase heat, add ignited coals in the same fashion.

For fuel flexibility, you need 10 to 12 additional ignited coals; start these coals with the measured batch. To maintain heat, add more ignited coals as directed in fuel section, following; push coals equally under pan or place evenly on lid.

Ash accumulates as coals burn, which tends to block air circulation. With a poker or a stick, gently push soft ash (not coals) aside, or scoop from lid.

If the coals are still hot when food is done, and you want to keep the food warm a bit longer, remove all but 4 or 5 coals.

Enclose cool ash in the foil for disposal.

HOW MUCH FUEL & HOW TO USE IT

Uneven lumps of glowing wood coals were the original fuel for Dutch ovens, but today's long-burning, uniformly shaped 2-inch charcoal briquets make heat regulation much more a science than an art.

First, count out the number of briquets you need for the kind of heat you want, and for the size of your Dutch oven.

You need moderate heat to simmer or bake foods, high heat to boil or sauté.

For moderate heat, multiply diameter of Dutch oven by 2, and use that many coals.

For high heat, multiply diameter by 3 and use this number of coals. In most cases, ⅓ of the coals go under the pan; the rest are placed on the lid.

To maintain even heat to cook 50 minutes or longer, you need more hot coals. After the first 30 minutes, add freshly ignited coals, then add more at 20- to 30-minute intervals. Do not add coals the last 30 minutes of cooking. For moderate heat, add 4 or 5 coals each time. For high heat, add 8 to 10. Use the maximum number for large pans. Put ⅓ of the coals (or at least 2) under pan, the rest on the lid.

If you want food to brown more on top as cooking nears completion, place freshly ignited coals on the lid.

DUTCH OVEN TIPS

You need a place to set the coal-filled lid when you check the foods; use a sheet of foil or a baking sheet. It's easier to steady the lid and coals without spilling ash on the food or burning yourself if you use a Dutch oven lid-lifting tool (for details, write to Dutch Oven Report, *Sunset Magazine*, 80 Willow Rd., Menlo Park, Calif. 94025). Or use a fireplace poker or long tongs that brace the lid as you lift it.

You also need potholders, and long tongs or a long-handled spoon to move coals.

Foods stick less if you season your Dutch oven. To do so, rub the clean, dry pan and lid all over with salad oil. Set pan and lid side by side in a 325° oven for 1 hour; let cool, then wipe clean with paper towels. After washing a Dutch oven, dry it thoroughly, coat lightly with salad oil, and wipe clean with a paper towel.

TRI-COLOR VEGETABLES WITH CHEESE

Dutch oven diameter	10-inch	12-inch	14-inch
Charcoal briquets	30	36	42
Water	¾ cup	1 cup	1¼ cups
Cauliflowerets	4 cups	6 cups	8 cups
Broccoli flowerets	4 cups	6 cups	8 cups
Crookneck squash, sliced ¼ inch thick	2 cups	3 cups	4 cups
Fresh tarragon, chopped	1 tablespoon	1½ tablespoons	2 tablespoons
Cheddar cheese, shredded	¼ to ½ pound	½ to ¾ pound	¾ to 1 pound
Green onions, chopped	¼ cup	⅓ cup	½ cup
Salt and pepper			
Servings	8 to 10	12 to 14	16 to 20

In a Dutch oven, mix together water, cauliflower, broccoli, squash, and tarragon. Put lid on pan.

Set up Dutch oven to cook (see page 201). Beneath, use 10 freshly ignited coals for a 10-inch pan, 12 for a 12-inch pan, 14 for a 14-inch pan. Arrange remaining coals evenly on lid. Cook until vegetables are tender-crisp when pierced, about 20 minutes. Sprinkle cheese and onions over vegetables; add salt and pepper to taste.

PER SERVING: 96 calories, 7.1 g protein, 7.8 g carbohydrates, 5 g fat, 15 mg cholesterol, 112 mg sodium

BACON, ONIONS & POTATOES

Dutch oven diameter	10-inch	12-inch	14-inch
Charcoal briquets	35	42	52
Bacon, chopped	½ pound	¾ pound	1 pound
Onions, medium-size, chopped	2	3	4
Thin-skinned potatoes, scrubbed and sliced ¼ inch thick	2 pounds	3 pounds	4 pounds
Salt and pepper			
Servings	6 to 8	8 to 10	12 to 16

Add bacon to Dutch oven and put on lid. Set up Dutch oven to cook (see page 201), using ⅓ of the freshly ignited coals beneath and remaining coals on the lid. Cook, stirring once, until bacon is crisp, 10 to 15 minutes. Add onions; cover and cook, stirring once, until onions are limp, about 10 minutes.

Mix potatoes with onions; cover pan and cook, stirring once, until potatoes are tender when pierced, about 25 minutes. Spoon out and discard fat. Add salt and pepper to taste.

PER SERVING: 357 calories, 8 g protein, 44 g carbohydrates, 17 g fat, 19 mg cholesterol, 210 mg sodium

Korean Specialties

To GET INTO THE SPIRIT of the 1988 Summer Olympics, we offered this selection of Korean specialties. Serve the dishes separately, or put them all together and present a rich ethnic eating experience.

To start, offer a classic Korean appetizer of nine elements. The traditional platter has sections for savory tidbits of vegetables, meat, and seafood. All get wrapped in tiny pancakes stacked in the tray's center; they're eaten plain, or spiced with fiery bean paste, a Korean favorite.

The paste, of chilies and fermented beans, is often used in robust Korean foods. In the following meal of salad, barbecued pork or squid, and noodles, the paste is part of each dish; for medium-hot results, use the lowest level noted in recipes.

Korean hot bean paste is sold in Korean and some Asian markets. If you can't find it, use Chinese or Japanese hot bean paste. Flavor varies with the brand, but the Korean paste is the most incendiary.

Our recipes come from Koreans who have settled in the West. The appetizer is from Booja Park of Irvine, California; the other dishes are from Young-Ran Hong, owner of the Sorabel Restaurant in Oakland.

KOREAN NINE-TREASURE DISH

Fillings (directions follow)
About 4 tablespoons Oriental sesame oil
Salt and pepper
Crêpes (recipe follows)
Hot bean paste (optional)

Prepare fillings in consecutive batches as follows. Keep warm or serve cool. If made ahead, cover and chill until next day. Let warm to room temperature to serve.

Place a 10- to 12-inch frying pan over high heat. When pan is hot, swirl 1 teaspoon sesame oil in it, then add cucumber. Stir-fry until hot and tender-crisp, 2 to 3 minutes. Lift from pan and set aside. Repeat for zucchini, bamboo shoots, and carrot. Cook fresh mushrooms the same way only slightly longer, stir-frying until lightly browned and liquid evaporates, 4 to 5 minutes. Repeat with shiitake mushrooms, cooking until lightly browned, about 2 minutes. Season each vegetable with salt and pepper to taste.

Add 1 tablespoon oil to the same pan over high heat. Stir-fry the shrimp mixture until shrimp are opaque in center (cut to test), about 3 minutes. Add salt and pepper to taste.

Add 1 more tablespoon oil to pan over high heat. Cook beef mixture until meat is lightly browned, 2 to 3 minutes.

On a platter, mound vegetables, shrimp, and beef individually around stack of crêpes. Put bean paste in a small bowl. Guests fill crêpes with choice of condiments, adding bean paste to taste; roll up to eat. Makes 36 crêpes, 9 to 12 appetizer servings.

PER SERVING: 42 calories, 2.3 g protein, 4.6 g carbohydrates, 1.4 g fat, 20 mg cholesterol, 121 mg sodium

Fillings. Keep each mixture separate.

Trim ends off 1 small cucumber and 1 large zucchini (½ lb. each). Cut vegetables in half lengthwise. Scrape out and discard seeds. Cut each vegetable into matchstick-size pieces 2 to 3 inches long. Mix each with ½ teaspoon salt; let stand about 15 minutes. Rinse, drain, and press out excess liquid.

Drain 1 can (7 oz.) bamboo shoots. Cut into matchstick-size pieces. Peel and trim ends from 1 large carrot (5 oz.). Cut into matchstick-size pieces. Thinly slice ½ pound fresh mushrooms.

Soak 10 medium-size (2-in.) dry shiitake mushrooms in hot water to cover until soft, about 20 minutes. Drain. Cut off and discard stems. Cut caps into thin slivers. Mix with 1 tablespoon soy sauce, 2 tablespoons dry sherry, and ½ teaspoon sugar.

Peel and devein ½ pound medium-size shrimp (43 to 50 per lb.). Add 1½ teaspoons wine vinegar and ½ teaspoon sugar. Trim fat from ⅓ pound boneless lean beef sirloin steak. Cut meat into thin slivers. Mix meat with 1 tablespoon soy sauce, 1 teaspoon sugar, 1 tablespoon thinly sliced green onion, 1 teaspoon minced garlic, 1 teaspoon minced fresh ginger, and 1 teaspoon Oriental sesame oil. Cover and chill at least 30 minutes or up to 2 hours.

Crêpes. In a blender, whirl until smooth 1½ cups water, 2 large eggs, 1⅓ cups all-purpose flour, and ¼ teaspoon salt.

Place a griddle or 10- to 12-inch frying pan with nonstick finish over medium-low heat. When pan is hot, brush lightly with salad oil. Drop batter, 1 tablespoon at a time, onto griddle, spreading it quickly and lightly with the back of a spoon into thin 4-inch rounds (be careful

not to scrape up cooked batter). Cook until dry on top, then turn and cook other side (1 to 1½ minutes total; crêpes should be pale white, not brown). Stack as done. Serve warm or cool. If made ahead, cover and chill up until next day. Warm to room temperature. Makes 36.

KOREAN RADISH SALAD

2 tablespoons distilled white vinegar
1 tablespoon Oriental sesame oil
1 clove garlic, minced
4 cups peeled, coarsely shredded, lightly packed daikon radish
Salt
2 to 3 tablespoons hot bean paste
2 tablespoons sliced green onion

In a bowl, mix vinegar, oil, garlic, radish, and salt and bean paste to taste. Garnish with onion. Serves 4 to 6.

PER SERVING: 41 calories, 1 g protein, 3.9 g carbohydrates, 2.6 g fat, 0 mg cholesterol, 53 mg sodium

KOREAN BARBECUED PORK

Have the pork sliced at the market.

1 to 1½ pounds boned pork shoulder or butt, sliced into ¼-inch-thick strips about 8 inches long and 2½ inches wide
Basic Korean hot sauce (recipe follows)
Sliced green onions

In a bowl, mix pork strips and hot sauce. Cover and chill 2 hours or until next day.

Lay strips on a greased grill 4 to 6 inches above a solid bed of medium-hot coals (you can hold your hand at grill level only 3 to 4 seconds). Turn often until no longer pink in center (cut to test), about 8 minutes. Sprinkle with onions. Serves 4 to 6.

PER SERVING: 224 calories, 13 g protein, 3.8 g carbohydrates, 17 g fat, 53 mg cholesterol, 422 mg sodium

Basic Korean hot sauce. Combine 1 tablespoon Oriental sesame oil; 1 tablespoon mirin (rice wine) or dry sherry; 2 to 3 tablespoons hot bean paste; 2 tablespoons soy sauce; 3 tablespoons water; 3 tablespoons sliced green onion; 1 clove garlic, minced; 1 teaspoon each sugar and pepper; and 2 teaspoons minced fresh ginger.

KOREAN NOODLES WITH HOT SAUCE

Buy the noodles in Asian food stores.

Prepare **basic Korean hot sauce** (recipe precedes), using only 1 to 2 tablespoons **hot bean paste.** Also, omit wine and water; add 3 tablespoons **distilled white vinegar;** set aside. Prepare **toasted sesame seed,** following; set aside.

In a 5- to 6-quart pan, bring 2½ quarts water to a boil over high heat. Add 12 ounces **dry thin buckwheat noodles** (or spaghetti) and boil, uncovered, until just tender to bite, 4 to 11 minutes. Drain; mix in pan with sauce and sesame. Garnish with thin **cucumber** slices. Serves 4 to 6.

PER SERVING: 260 calories, 8.3 g protein, 46 g carbohydrates, 4.6 g fat, 0 mg cholesterol, 365 mg sodium

Toasted sesame seed. In a 7- to 8-inch frying pan, toast 2 tablespoons **sesame seed** over medium heat, shaking pan often, until golden, 3 to 5 minutes.

SPICY STIR-FRIED SQUID

- 3 tablespoons soy sauce
- 2 to 3 tablespoons hot bean paste
- 1 teaspoon sugar
- 1 tablespoon sesame seed, toasted as directed, preceding
- 1 medium-size onion, slivered
- 3 tablespoons salad oil
- 1 medium-size carrot, shredded
- 1 pound cleaned squid mantles (tubes), cut into 1-inch rings

In a small bowl, mix soy sauce, bean paste, sugar, and sesame; set aside. In a 10- to 12-inch frying pan over medium-high heat, cook onion in 2 tablespoons oil until golden; stir often. Add carrot; stir until carrot is tender-crisp to bite, about 1 minute. Lift out vegetables and set aside.

Add remaining oil and squid to pan. Stir-fry until squid is opaque, about 2 minutes. Add bean paste and vegetables; stir until bubbling. Pour into a bowl. Serves 4.

PER SERVING: 244 calories, 20 g protein, 11 g carbohydrates, 13 g fat, 265 mg cholesterol, 890 mg sodium

Hot bean paste flavors three dishes in Korean dinner: barbecued pork (or stir-fried squid), buckwheat noodles, and radish salad. Include hot rice with meat or shellfish; offer purchased kim chee (top left).

Asian Pears in Quick Salads

THE JUICY CRUNCH *of Asian pears (also called apple pears) makes them especially appealing to eat raw.*

Here, thin, sweet-tart slices are prepared with tender greens, dry cheese, and succulent shrimp for quick-to-assemble salads and appetizer plates. Citrus juices, aromatic seeds, tart dressings, and herbs embellish the fruit's delicate flavor.

Round, with greenish yellow or russet skins, Asian pears are easy to use. With most types, the white flesh doesn't quickly discolor when cut. Coring is optional.

ASIAN PEARS WITH GINGER DRESSING

6 to 12 large butter or leaf lettuce leaves, washed and crisped
1 large or 2 medium-size Asian pears (1 lb. total)
Ginger dressing (recipe follows)
Fresh mint sprigs

Line each of 6 salad plates with 1 or 2 lettuce leaves. Core pears; cut lengthwise into thin slices. Arrange equal portions of the pear slices on lettuce. Drizzle ginger dressing evenly over fruit. Garnish with mint sprigs. Makes 6 salad servings.

PER SERVING: 186 calories, 0.4 g protein, 21 g carbohydrates, 12 g fat, 0 mg cholesterol, 6.9 mg sodium

Ginger dressing. Mix ⅓ cup **salad oil**, ⅓ cup **lemon juice**, 2 tablespoons minced **crystallized ginger**, 2 teaspoons thinly shredded **lemon peel** (yellow part only), and 1½ tablespoons **honey.**

ASIAN PEAR & CHEESE PLATE

4 ounces dry jack or parmesan cheese
2 medium-size Asian pears (12 to 16 oz. total), thinly sliced crosswise
1 cup watercress sprigs, washed and crisped
4 orange wedges
4 lemon wedges
1 teaspoon anise seed, crushed

With a cheese slicer or sharp knife, thinly slice the cheese. On 4 salad plates, arrange equal portions of cheese, pears, watercress, orange wedges, and lemon wedges. Sprinkle cheese and fruit evenly with anise seed. To eat, squeeze orange and lemon over cheese and fruit. Makes 4 first-course or dessert servings.

PER SERVING: 169 calories, 11 g protein, 16 g carbohydrates, 7.8 g fat, 19 mg cholesterol, 458 mg sodium

SHRIMP & ASIAN PEAR SALAD

4 to 8 large romaine lettuce leaves, washed and crisped
4 medium-size Asian pears (6 to 8 oz. each), thinly sliced crosswise
1 pound tiny cooked shelled shrimp
Mustard dressing (recipe follows)
Fresh tarragon sprigs (optional)
Salt and freshly ground pepper

Arrange 1 or 2 lettuce leaves on each of 4 dinner plates. Place ¼ of the pears and shrimp on each plate. Drizzle mustard dressing over shrimp and fruit. Garnish with tarragon sprigs. Add salt and pepper to taste. Makes 4 main-dish servings.

PER SERVING: 452 calories, 24 g protein, 25 g carbohydrates, 29 g fat, 221 mg cholesterol, 368 mg sodium

Mustard dressing. Mix together ½ cup **olive oil**, ¼ cup **white wine vinegar**, 1 tablespoon **Dijon mustard**, and 1 tablespoon minced **fresh tarragon** (or ½ teaspoon dry).

Thin, crisp Asian pear slices, drizzled with ginger and lemon dressing and topped with mint, make refreshing salad course.

Roses as Seasoning & Color

IN SHAKESPEARE'S DAY, *cooks commonly used roses for seasoning, but it's rather unusual today to find petals in your food. The petals' pleasing taste and fragrance warrant a try—as a dainty tidbit, in salad, or in vinegar.*

When selecting roses to eat, let your nose be your guide; aroma means flavor. Some specialty produce sections now offer roses for eating, or you can gather your own.

Do not use roses that have been treated with pesticides or fungicides.

CHEESE & PETAL TIDBITS

- 1 package (3 oz.) cream cheese
- 2 teaspoons raspberry- or orange-flavor liqueur
  Sugar
- ½ teaspoon rose extract or rose water (optional)
- 1 cup rose petals, rinsed and drained dry (from tight or loose buds)
  About ½ cup raspberries, rinsed and drained dry (optional)

Beat cheese until smooth with liqueur, sugar to taste, and extract. Spoon mixture into a pastry bag fitted with a ½-inch star tip. Pipe or spoon onto each rose petal. Top each with a berry, if desired. Makes about 20, 5 servings.

PER PIECE: 17 calories, 0.4 g protein, 0.4 g carbohydrates, 1.5 g fat, 4.7 mg cholesterol, 13 mg sodium

To make rose vinegar, pour wine vinegar over fragrant petals; let stand a few days, until petals bleach. Liquid picks up flavor.

Velvety petals cradle cream cheese rosettes for elegant after-dinner nibble with orange or nut liqueur.

ROSE GARDEN SALAD

- 2 cups spinach leaves, rinsed and crisped
- 1 cup arugula (or more spinach), rinsed and crisped
- 1 to 1½ cups rose petals, rinsed and drained dry
- ½ cup hulled, sliced strawberries
- ½ cup salted macadamias or shelled, salted pistachios
  Rose vinaigrette (recipe follows)
  Salt and pepper

In a salad bowl, gently mix spinach, arugula, rose petals, strawberries, and macadamias with vinaigrette. Add salt and pepper to taste. Makes 4 servings.

PER SERVING: 228 calories, 3 g protein, 6.2 g carbohydrates, 23 g fat, 0 mg cholesterol, 171 mg sodium

Rose vinaigrette. In a bowl, mix 3 tablespoons **rose vinegar** (recipe follows; or use raspberry or red wine vinegar), 3 tablespoons **salad oil,** ¼ teaspoon **dry tarragon leaves,** and 1 teaspoon **rose extract** or 1 tablespoon **rose water** (optional).

ROSE VINEGAR

- 2 cups lightly packed rose petals, rinsed and drained dry
- 3 cups white wine vinegar

Place petals in a 3- to 4-cup jar. Add vinegar; cover. Let stand at room temperature. After 1 day, push petals into vinegar. When petals are bleached and vinegar tastes of roses, about 3 days, strain vinegar and discard petals. Use, or store airtight up to 3 months. Makes 3 cups. —*Susan Kendall Nelson, Eaton, Colo.*

PER TABLESPOON: 2.4 calories, 0 g protein, 0.6 g carbohydrates, 0 g fat, 0 mg cholesterol, 0.2 mg sodium

Chilled Seafood

SERVED SIMPLY *with a few flavorful additions, chilled seafoods make ideal first-course dishes for warm-weather dining.*

The first combination is especially easy: it features rolls of sliced smoked salmon in a tart dill sauce. In the next dish, mussels steamed in wine are chilled, then served with toast seasoned with a concentrate of cooking juices, lemon, and garlic.

Last, large shrimp and avocado are presented on a gazpacho-flavored salsa.

SMOKED SALMON IN COOL DILL SAUCE

- ⅔ cup sour cream
- 1 tablespoon white wine vinegar
- 1 tablespoon *each* minced fresh dill (or 1 teaspoon dry dill weed) and chives
- ⅛ teaspoon liquid hot pepper seasoning
  Salt and pepper
- ⅓ pound thinly sliced smoked salmon
  Fresh dill sprigs or parsley sprigs

In a small bowl, stir together sour cream, vinegar, dill, chives, and liquid hot pepper; season to taste with salt and pepper. Use, or cover and chill until next day.

Divide salmon into 6 equal portions. Loosely roll each portion into a cylinder. Spoon equal amounts of dill sauce onto 6 salad plates. Lay 1 salmon roll in the sauce on each plate; garnish with a dill sprig. Makes 6 first-course servings.

PER SERVING: 85 calories, 5.4 g protein, 1.3 g carbohydrates, 6.5 g fat, 17 mg cholesterol, 212 mg sodium

MUSSELS ON LEMON-GARLIC TOAST

- 12 mussels in shells, scrubbed and beards pulled off
- 1 cup dry white wine
- ¾ teaspoon finely shredded lemon peel (yellow part only)
- 1 clove garlic, minced or pressed
- 1 tablespoon minced parsley
- 1 tablespoon extra-virgin olive oil
  Salt and pepper
  Toast (directions follow)
  Lemon wedges
  Parsley sprigs

Place mussels in a 10- to 12-inch frying pan, add wine, cover, and bring to a boil over high heat. Reduce heat to low and simmer until mussels open, about 5

Big, rosy shrimp and pale green avocado wedge in gazpacho salsa turn this version of the chilled Spanish soup into a first-course salad.

minutes. With a slotted spoon, lift out mussels and place in a bowl; cover and chill until cool, at least 30 minutes.

Boil wine on high heat, uncovered, until liquid is reduced to about 3 tablespoons, 5 to 6 minutes. Remove from heat, then stir in lemon peel, garlic, parsley, oil, and add salt and pepper to taste. Cover and chill until cool, at least 15 minutes.

Place 3 mussels on each of 4 salad plates. Lay 3 pieces of toast on each plate opposite mussels. Drizzle equal portions of lemon-garlic mixture evenly over toast. Garnish with lemon wedges and parsley sprigs. Pluck mussels from shells with a small fork and place on toast to eat. Makes 4 first-course servings.

PER SERVING: 226 calories, 9.2 g protein, 33 g carbohydrates, 5.8 g fat, 11 mg cholesterol, 426 mg sodium

Toast. Cut 1 **baguette** (8 oz.) into ½-inch-thick diagonal slices. Lay slices in a single layer in a 10- by 15-inch baking pan. Broil about 4 inches from heat until golden on both sides, turning once, about 2 minutes total. Let cool.

AVOCADO & SHRIMP IN GAZPACHO SALSA

- 18 extra-large shrimp (16 to 20 per lb.), shelled and deveined
- 1 tablespoon extra-virgin olive oil

- ⅓ pound (about 2 large) firm-ripe Roma-type tomatoes, cored, seeded, and finely chopped
- ¼ cup *each* finely diced cucumber and yellow bell pepper
- 1 tablespoon *each* minced green onion and chopped fresh cilantro (coriander)
- 1 clove garlic, minced or pressed
- 2 tablespoons lime juice
- 1 can (5½ oz.) chili-seasoned tomato cocktail
  Salt and pepper
- 1 large firm-ripe avocado
  Fresh cilantro sprigs

In a 10- to 12-inch frying pan, bring 1 inch water to boiling over high heat. Add shrimp and cook, uncovered, until bright pink, 2 to 3 minutes. Drain, then place in a bowl and mix with olive oil; cover and chill until cool, at least 1 hour.

Combine tomatoes, cucumber, bell pepper, onion, chopped cilantro, garlic, lime juice, and tomato cocktail; season to taste with salt and pepper. Use, or cover salsa and shrimp and chill until next day.

Cut avocado in half; pit and peel. Cut each half into thirds. Pour equal portions of salsa onto 6 salad plates. Lay 3 shrimp in salsa on each plate; set a wedge of avocado beside shrimp and garnish with a sprig of cilantro. Makes 6 first-course servings.

PER SERVING: 149 calories, 11 g protein, 6.5 g carbohydrates, 9.2 g fat, 70 mg cholesterol, 170 mg sodium

Leaner Lasagnas

A LONG-TIME FAMILY FAVORITE, *lasagna updates its profile to suit the leaner diet demanded by fitness-conscious diners.*

These versions have the hearty flavor of the original, but replace meat with vegetables. For added substance, include tofu, or lean ground turkey or veal.

VEGETABLE LASAGNA

- 1 package (8 oz.) dry lasagna noodles
- 4 carrots (about ¾ lb. total), ends trimmed, cut into ¼-inch-thick slices
- 3 zucchini (about 1 lb. total), ends trimmed, cut into ¼-inch-thick slices
- 2 tablespoons olive oil or salad oil
- 1 medium-size onion, chopped
- ½ pound mushrooms, thinly sliced
- 1 teaspoon *each* dry basil, dry thyme leaves, and dry oregano leaves
- 1 jar (32 oz.) marinara sauce
- 2 packages (10 oz. *each*) frozen chopped spinach, thawed
- ½ pound ricotta cheese
- ¾ pound mozzarella cheese, shredded
- ¼ cup grated parmesan cheese

In a 5- to 6-quart pan, bring 3 quarts water to a boil over high heat. Add noodles and carrots; cook 6 minutes. Add zucchini; cook until noodles are just tender to bite, 4 to 5 minutes longer. Drain well.

In the same pan, combine oil, onion, mushrooms, basil, thyme, and oregano. Cook over high heat, stirring often, until onion is limp and liquid evaporates, 5 to 8 minutes. Stir in marinara sauce; set aside.

Squeeze liquid out of spinach. Mix spinach and ricotta cheese; set aside.

In a shallow 2½- to 3-quart baking dish, spread ⅓ of the sauce. Arrange ½ of the noodles over sauce. Sprinkle evenly on top ½ *each* of the vegetables, spinach mixture, and mozzarella cheese. Repeat layers, ending with sauce. Sprinkle with parmesan cheese. (If made ahead, cover and chill up until the next day.)

Set baking dish on a 10- by 15-inch baking pan to catch any drips. Bake freshly assembled lasagna, uncovered, in a 400° oven until hot in center, about 25 minutes. Bake cold lasagna, uncovered, in a 350° oven, until hot in center, about 50 minutes. Let stand about 5 minutes before serving. Makes 6 servings. — *Emily Connery, Friday Harbor, Wash.*

PER SERVING: 580 calories, 29 g protein, 61 g carbohydrates, 27 g fat, 59 mg cholesterol, 1,365 mg sodium

TOFU LASAGNA

Follow recipe for **vegetable lasagna** (recipe precedes), but omit mushrooms. Coarsely break 1 pound **firm tofu** into chunks and drain in a colander. With paper towels, press tofu to remove excess liquid. Cook tofu with onion and herbs until liquid evaporates and onion is limp, about 5 minutes. — *Barbara Tuttle, Beaverton, Ore.*

PER SERVING: 680 calories, 40 g protein, 63 g carbohydrates, 34 g fat, 59 mg cholesterol, 1,374 mg sodium

GROUND TURKEY LASAGNA

Follow recipe for **vegetable lasagna** (recipe precedes), but omit mushrooms. Add ½ pound **ground lean turkey** or veal and cook, stirring, with onion and herbs until meat is crumbly, about 5 minutes.

PER SERVING: 631 calories, 35 g protein, 60 g carbohydrates, 31 g fat, 84 mg cholesterol, 1,398 mg sodium

Layer cooked zucchini and carrots with noodles, spinach-ricotta mixture, cheese, and mushroom-laced marinara sauce.

Warm Shortcakes with Caramel Custard

OLD-FASHIONED, *butter-rich shortcake is an ideal showcase for late summer's fruits. But instead of the predictable topping of whipped cream, we propose a caramel-flavored custard. This silky amber sauce complements the plump blueberries and sliced ripe peaches.*

The individual serving-size shortcakes are tender-sweet glazed biscuits scented with orange and nutmeg. They're best served warm from the oven. But to get a head start, you can make the custard several days ahead.

BLUEBERRY & PEACH SHORTCAKE WITH CARAMEL CUSTARD

- 2 **cups all-purpose flour**
- 6 **tablespoons sugar**
- 1 **tablespoon baking powder**
- 1 **teaspoon grated orange peel**
- ⅛ **teaspoon ground nutmeg**
- ½ **cup (¼ lb.) butter or margarine, cut into small pieces**
- 2 **large egg yolks**
- ¾ **cup half-and-half (light cream)**
  Sweetened blueberries and peaches (recipe follows)
  Caramel custard (recipe follows)
  Fresh mint sprigs

In a food processor or bowl, combine flour, ⅓ cup of the sugar, baking powder, peel, nutmeg, and butter. Whirl or rub mixture with your fingers until coarse crumbs form. Add egg yolks and ⅔ cup of the cream; whirl or mix with a fork just until dough is evenly moistened.

Pat dough into a ball and place on a lightly floured board. Flatten into a 1-inch-thick round. Using a 2½-inch-diameter cutter, cut dough into rounds. Place rounds on a greased 12- by 15-inch baking sheet, spacing them 1½ inches apart.

Pat scraps together, and form into another 1-inch-thick round. Cut as many more 2½-inch rounds as possible; put on pan (you should have at least 6 rounds in all). Brush tops with remaining cream and sprinkle evenly with remaining sugar.

Bake in a 400° oven until tops are golden brown, 14 to 16 minutes. Let cool on a rack until lukewarm. Split biscuits horizontally in half. Set the bottom of each biscuit on a dessert plate. Spoon equal portions of sweetened blueberries and peaches onto each biscuit; place top sections of biscuits on fruit. Pour 2 tablespoons custard around each serving; garnish each with a sprig of mint. Offer remaining custard in a pitcher to add to taste. Makes 6 servings.

PER SERVING: 472 calories, 7.6 g protein, 68 g carbohydrates, 21 g fat, 143 mg cholesterol, 387 mg sodium

Sweetened blueberries and peaches. Peel, pit, and slice 4 large (about 2 lb.) firm-ripe **peaches** into a bowl; mix with 1 tablespoon **lemon juice.** Rinse 1 cup **fresh blueberries** (or use thawed frozen berries); drain. Stir berries into peaches; sweeten to taste with **powdered sugar.** If made ahead, cover and let stand up to 1 hour.

Caramel custard. In a bowl, mix 3 **large egg yolks** with 2 tablespoons **sugar.** In a 1- to 1½-quart pan, warm 1¼ cups **milk** over medium heat until scalded, stirring often. Whisk about half the hot milk into yolks, then pour mixture back into pan. Stir on medium-low heat until custard thickly coats the back of a metal spoon, 10 to 15 minutes. Stir in 1 teaspoon **vanilla,** then remove from heat.

In a 3- to 4-cup pan, bring ½ cup **sugar** and 2½ tablespoons **water** to a boil over high heat; stir until sugar is dissolved. Boil, uncovered, just until liquid turns amber, 4 to 5 minutes. Immediately pour hot caramel into warm custard; caramel will harden. Stir the mixture until caramel is completely melted. Serve sauce warm or cool. If made ahead, cover and chill up to 2 days. Makes about 1½ cups.

PER TABLESPOON: 36 calories, 0.8 g protein, 5.8 g carbohydrates, 1.1 g fat, 36 mg cholesterol, 7.3 mg sodium

Warm, tender shortcake generously filled with sweet peach slices and fresh blueberries is served with caramel custard sauce.

More September Recipes

OTHER SEPTEMBER ARTICLES *feature some fresh combinations: thyme and lemon in cookies; soaked basil seeds to make a silky topping for ice cream; and flower or spice flavored caffeine-free teas to serve hot or chilled.*

THYME-LEMON COOKIES

Though often used in savory dishes, this versatile herb teams unexpectedly here with lemon peel to give crisp, sugar-dusted cookies an enticing fragrance and flavor.

- 1 **cup (½ lb.) butter or margarine**
- 1¾ **cups sugar**
- 2 **large eggs**
- 2¾ **cups all-purpose flour**
- 2 **teaspoons baking powder**
- 2 **tablespoons coarsely chopped fresh thyme leaves or 2 teaspoons dry thyme leaves**
- 1 **tablespoon grated lemon peel**

In a bowl, combine butter and 1½ cups sugar; beat with an electric mixer until thoroughly blended. Beat in eggs until mixture is smooth. Add flour, baking powder, thyme, and lemon peel; mix well.

Put remaining ¼ cup sugar into a small bowl. Shape dough into 1 tablespoon-size balls (if dough is hard to handle, chill at least 1 hour or up to 2 days); drop balls into sugar and roll to coat. Place balls 1 inch apart on ungreased 12- by 15-inch baking sheets. Bake in a 375° oven until edges are brown, 12 to 15 minutes (if using 1 oven, rotate sheets halfway through baking). With a spatula, transfer the cookies to racks to cool. Serve, or store airtight up

Tiny, fragrant thyme leaves lend exotic overtones to lemon cookies.

to 2 days. Freeze to store longer. Makes about 5 dozen cookies. —*Janet Moore, Beulah, Colo.*

PER COOKY: 73 calories, 0.8 g protein, 10 g carbohydrates, 3 g fat, 17 mg cholesterol, 48 mg sodium

SILKY BASIL SEEDS

Fish eyes? Frog eggs? What are these slippery little dots that look familiar, yet strangely out of context?

Rest easy—these textural delicacies are nothing more than wet basil seeds. When soaked in water, each tiny black seed develops a thin opalescent capsule around it, transforming it into a shimmery globe that resembles a tiny egg.

The neutral-tasting seeds are often used to add a silky texture to Thai dishes. Try spooning them over ice cream or into clear broths or soups.

Basil seeds are available in many Asian markets, Thai markets in particular, and in bulk through some garden shops and seed stores. (Seeds should be black. If a red or purple coloring covers seeds you buy at a garden shop or seed store, they have been treated with a pesticide and should not be eaten.)

Stir 1 tablespoon **basil seeds** into ¾ cup **water.** Let stand until soft capsules form around seeds, 15 to 30 minutes. If adding to savory foods, season to taste with **salt** and **lemon juice.** Makes about ¾ cup.

GINGER-CURRANT TEA

Brewed with fruits, spices, and dry flowers, these steeped tea-like beverages contain no caffeine. Serve them hot or cold.

- 1 **small orange**
- ¼ **cup chopped crystallized ginger**
- 2 **tablespoons currants**
- 8 **to 10 whole cardamom pods, hulls removed and seeds crushed**
- 1 **quart boiling water**
  Ice (optional)

With a vegetable peeler, pare peel (orange part only) from the orange; reserve remaining orange. In a 1½- to 2-quart teapot or pan, combine the orange peel, ginger, currants, cardamom, and water; cover and let steep about 5 minutes.

To serve hot, pour through a strainer, if needed, into cups. To serve cold, cool, strain, cover, and chill up to 2 days. Pour

Soaked in water, basil seeds swell into plump beads. On ice cream, they add an intriguing silken texture but almost no taste as you crunch them.

over ice. If desired, cut reserved orange into wedges to add to taste. Makes 4 servings, about 1-cup size.

PER SERVING: no accurate nutritional data available

SPICED HIBISCUS BREW

Look for dry jamaica (hibiscus) flowers in Mexican markets. They impart tartness and a vibrant fuchsia color.

- ¼ **cup dry jamaica (hibiscus) flowers**
- ¼ **cup raisins**
- 1 **cinnamon stick (3 in.), crushed**
- 4 **whole allspice, crushed**
- 1 **quart boiling water**
  Ice (optional)

In a 1½- to 2-quart teapot or pan, combine flowers, raisins, cinnamon, allspice, and water. Cover and steep 5 minutes.

To serve hot, pour through a strainer, if needed, into cups. To serve cold, cool, strain, cover, and chill up to 2 days. Pour over ice. Makes 4 servings, 1-cup size.

PER SERVING: no accurate nutritional data available

Begin the day with cornmeal crêpes filled and topped with blueberries and pistachios.

BLUEBERRY-PISTACHIO CORNMEAL CRÊPES

1¼ cups unflavored yogurt
¼ cup firmly packed brown sugar
¼ teaspoon ground cinnamon
2⅓ cups blueberries, rinsed and drained
½ cup minced salted pistachios
Crêpes (recipe follows)

In a bowl, combine 1 cup yogurt, sugar, cinnamon, 2 cups berries, and ⅓ cup nuts.

Lay 1 crêpe flat, speckled side up; spoon about ¼ cup berry filling down center. Roll to enclose filling. Repeat to fill all crêpes. Place 2 or 3 crêpes on each plate; top with remaining yogurt, berries, and nuts. Serves 4 or 5. — *Vicky Hay, Phoenix.*

PER FILLED CRÊPE: 194 calories, 5.6 g protein, 21 g carbohydrates, 10 g fat, 72 mg cholesterol, 147 mg sodium

Crêpes. In a blender, whirl 2 **large eggs,** ⅓ cup *each* **all-purpose flour** and **cornmeal,** and 1 cup **milk** until smooth.

Place a 6- to 7-inch crêpe pan or flat-bottom frying pan over medium-high heat. Brush with melted **butter** or margarine (use about 2 tablespoons total). Pour 3 tablespoons batter into pan, tilting to coat bottom. Cook until surface looks dry, about 1 minute. Turn, and cook until bottom is speckled, about 30 seconds. Stack as cooked. Stir batter frequently. Makes 10.

Shredded chicken, tarragon, and grapefruit go over avocado halves for entrée salad.

CHICKEN-GRAPEFRUIT SALAD ON AVOCADOS

2 cups bite-size chunks cooked chicken breast
½ cup thinly sliced celery
¼ cup thinly sliced green onion
Tarragon-pepper dressing (recipe follows)
3 large firm-ripe avocados
1 tablespoon lemon juice
Butter lettuce leaves, washed and crisped
2 large pink grapefruit

Mix chicken, celery, and onion with dressing. Peel, pit, and halve avocados; coat with lemon juice. Cut peel and white membrane from grapefruit. Cut parallel to membrane to free segments.

Arrange lettuce on 6 salad plates; set an avocado half on lettuce on each plate. Spoon equal portions of chicken salad over halves. Top each salad equally with grapefruit segments. Makes 6 servings.— *Dorothea Kent, Port Angeles, Wash.*

PER SERVING: 428 calories, 18 g protein, 18 g carbohydrates, 33 g fat, 53 mg cholesterol, 133 mg sodium

Tarragon-pepper dressing. Stir together ⅓ cup *each* **mayonnaise** and **sour cream,** 2 teaspoons **vinegar,** 1 tablespoon *each* chopped **fresh tarragon leaves** (or 1 teaspoon dry tarragon leaves) and minced **parsley,** ⅛ teaspoon **cayenne,** and ¼ teaspoon **pepper.**

Present couscous salad on a bed of spinach leaves; garnish with fresh dill sprigs.

COUSCOUS SALAD WITH DILL DRESSING

2¼ cups water
1½ cups couscous
⅓ cup pine nuts
½ cup *each* thawed frozen petite peas and chopped green onion
6 ounces Swiss cheese, cut into matchstick-size pieces
Dill dressing (recipe follows)
8 cups spinach leaves, washed and crisped
Salt and pepper

In a 3- to 4-quart pan over high heat, bring water to a boil. Stir in couscous; remove from heat, cover, and let stand until cool; stir with a fork.

Meanwhile, put nuts in an 8- or 9-inch-wide pan. Bake in a 350° oven until lightly toasted, about 10 minutes.

Add to couscous the nuts, peas, onions, cheese, and dressing; mix well. Line a platter with spinach; mound salad on leaves. Season with salt and pepper to taste. Makes 6 servings.— *Sally Vog, Springfield, Ore.*

PER SERVING: 497 calories, 18 g protein, 40 g carbohydrates, 30 g fat, 26 mg cholesterol, 232 mg sodium

Dill dressing. Mix 1 teaspoon grated **lemon peel** with ¼ cup **lemon juice;** ½ cup **olive oil;** 1 tablespoon **Dijon mustard;** 1 clove **garlic,** minced or pressed; and 2 tablespoons minced **fresh dill.**

GINGER-ZUCCHINI PANCAKES

2 large eggs
¼ cup milk
½ cup all-purpose flour
1 tablespoon minced fresh ginger
1 small red bell pepper, stemmed, seeded, and chopped
1 small onion, finely chopped
4 cups shredded zucchini
1 cup (4 oz.) shredded cheddar cheese
Salt and pepper
3 tablespoons butter or margarine

In a large bowl, beat eggs, milk, and flour until smoothly blended. Add ginger, bell pepper, onion, zucchini, and cheese; stir until well combined. Season to taste with salt and pepper.

Melt 1 tablespoon butter in a 10- to 12-inch nonstick frying pan over medium-high heat. Drop zucchini mixture, 1 heaping tablespoon at a time, into pan; spread to make each cake 3 inches across. Cook until golden brown on bottom, about 2 minutes; turn, and brown other side, about 1½ minutes longer. As cooked, transfer in 1 layer to ovenproof platter; keep warm in 200° oven. Repeat to cook remaining pancakes; add butter as needed. Makes 5 or 6 servings. — *Evelyn Tuller, Redwood City, Calif.*

PER SERVING: 217 calories, 9.3 g protein, 13 g carbohydrates, 15 g fat, 128 mg cholesterol, 207 mg sodium

Ever-abundant zucchini, bell pepper, onion combine in pancakes; ginger adds surprise.

GRILLED FISH PICANTE

4 shark or salmon steaks, each 6 to 8 ounces and 1 inch thick
2 tablespoons lime juice
½ cup purchased mild salsa
2 tablespoons butter or margarine, melted
Lime butter (recipe follows)
Lime wedges
Fresh cilantro (coriander) sprigs

Place shark steaks in a 9- by 13-inch pan. Drizzle evenly with lime juice and salsa. Cover and chill at least 30 minutes or up to 2 hours; turn over once.

Brush fish with melted butter. Place on grill 4 to 6 inches above a solid bed of medium coals (you should be able to hold your hand at grill level only 4 to 5 seconds). Cook, turning once, until fish is opaque in center (cut to test), 10 to 12 minutes total. Transfer to platter. Spoon 2 teaspoons lime butter onto each steak; garnish with lime and cilantro sprigs. Accompany with remaining lime butter. Serves 4. — *J. Hill, Sacramento.*

PER SERVING: 418 calories, 36 g protein, 3.1 g carbohydrates, 29 g fat, 143 mg cholesterol, 530 mg sodium

Lime butter. Beat together until fluffy ⅓ cup **butter** or margarine, ½ teaspoon grated **lime peel**, 2 tablespoons **lime juice**, 1 tablespoon minced **fresh cilantro** (coriander), and ¼ teaspoon **crushed dried hot red chilies.**

Hot grilled shark steaks get topped with pats of lime- and cilantro-seasoned butter.

SHERRY-PLUM CRISP

¼ teaspoon *each* ground allspice and ground nutmeg
¼ cup quick-cooking tapioca
¼ cup cream sherry
12 large firm-ripe plums, rinsed, pitted, and sliced
½ to ¾ cup firmly packed brown sugar
6 tablespoons butter or margarine
½ cup *each* all-purpose flour and granulated sugar
¾ cup crunchy unsweetened wheat and barley cereal
⅓ cup finely chopped walnuts

In a 9- by 13-inch pan, mix allspice, nutmeg, tapioca, sherry, plums, and brown sugar to taste. Let stand at least 15 minutes or up to 1 hour to soften tapioca; stir occasionally.

In a small bowl, combine butter, flour, and granulated sugar. Rub mixture with your fingers until fine crumbs form. Stir in cereal and walnuts. With your hands, squeeze mixture to form large lumps. Coarsely crumble lumps evenly over fruit.

Bake in a 350° oven until topping is golden brown, and fruit is bubbling vigorously, 45 to 50 minutes. Serve warm or cool. Makes 8 or 9 servings. —*Helen Littrell, Stockton, Calif.*

PER SERVING: 328 calories, 3.6 g protein, 57 g carbohydrates, 11 g fat, 21 mg cholesterol, 151 mg sodium

Chunks of streusel cover a rich, red, sherried plum filling; serve portions with scoops of ice cream.

THE NEW WORLD'S *most significant contributions to the world's food supply—peppers, potatoes, and tomatoes—are widely respected as such. The humble peanut, on the other hand, though rich in protein and calories, has always been the object of mild derision. A minor distraction at baseball games, an accompaniment to beverages of dubious nutritional value and social status, a child's lunch box sandwich staple (likely as not debased with grape or some other jelly), the peanut gets no respect. After all, how can you call anything a goober and take it seriously?*

Such is not the case in Indonesia, where the peanut is a nearly indispensable element of the cuisine. In vegetable sauces and salad dressings, it is often combined with hot chilies, ginger, and some of the less common herbs and seasonings of the Far East. Stephen Estvanik uses such an Indonesian-inspired marinade and baste for his spareribs.

"In Indonesia, the peanut is a nearly indispensable element of the cuisine."

INDONESIAN SPARERIBS

 4 **cloves garlic, quartered**
 1 **piece fresh ginger (1 in.), peeled and quartered**
 ¼ **cup peanut butter**
 1 **medium-size onion, quartered**
 ½ **cup soy sauce**
 ¼ **cup dry sherry**
 ¼ **cup orange-flavor liqueur**
 3 **tablespoons** *each* **prepared taco sauce or salsa, and lemon juice**
 1 **section pork spareribs, about 4 pounds**

In a blender, combine garlic, ginger, peanut butter, onion, soy sauce, sherry, liqueur, taco sauce, and lemon juice. Whirl until smoothly puréed.

Place spareribs in a 10- by 15-inch rimmed pan; pour soy mixture over ribs. Cover and refrigerate for 2 hours or up to overnight.

To barbecue ribs, mound 40 to 50 charcoal briquets on firegrate in a barbecue with a lid. Ignite and let burn until charcoal is covered with gray ash, about 30

minutes. Then bank half the charcoal on each side of the grate and place a drip pan in the center of the coals. Position grill 4 to 6 inches above coals. Add 10 briquets, half to each mound of coals now, and also every 30 minutes during cooking to maintain heat.

Lift ribs from marinade and shake gently to remove excess. Place ribs, meatiest side up, on grill directly above drip pan. Cover barbecue and open dampers. Cook until ribs are well browned all over and meat at bone in a thick section is no longer pink (cut to test), about 1¼ hours. Turn several times and baste ribs with marinade occasionally as they cook. Pour remaining marinade into a 2- to 4-cup pan and place over direct heat until boiling; stir to prevent scorching. Serve ribs with sauce to add to taste. Makes 4 or 5 servings.

PER SERVING OF RIBS: 588 calories, 42 g protein, 2.6 g carbohydrates, 44 g fat, 171 mg cholesterol, 496 mg sodium

PER TABLESPOON SAUCE: 24 calories, 1 g protein, 2.5 g carbohydrates, 1.3 g fat, 0 mg cholesterol, 342 mg sodium

Seattle

BOLOGNA, **THE CENTER** *of Italy's rich Emilia Romagna farming district and the site of an ancient and famous university, is known as* la grassa *(fat or abundant) and* la dottata *(learned).*

Being well fed and learned, it seems natural that the Bolognese should select tortellini in brodo *(tortellini in broth) as the city's favorite first course. They use an extra-strength but otherwise plain chicken broth as a bath for this filled pasta (which is sometimes referred to locally as Venus's navel). Paul Brooks complicates his broth with chicken breast, mushrooms, spinach, bell pepper, rice, and (for the flavor surprise) tarragon. The results are worth emulating.*

If you enjoy doing so and have all the time in the world, you might even try making your own tortellini. Chef Brooks prefers to buy his, and he favors green tortellini stuffed with cheese. You may, of course, experiment with other forms and flavors of pasta in the soup.

TORTELLINI SOUP

About ¾ pound spinach
4½ quarts or 3 cans (49½ oz. each) regular-strength chicken broth
1 package (8 oz.) fresh cheese-filled spinach tortellini
1 whole chicken breast (about 1 lb.), boned, skinned, and cut into ½-inch chunks
½ pound mushrooms, sliced
1 medium-size red bell pepper, stemmed, seeded, and diced
1 cup cooked rice
2 teaspoons dry tarragon leaves
Freshly ground pepper
Freshly grated Parmesan cheese
Salt

Discard tough spinach stems and yellowed leaves; rinse green leaves well, then coarsely chop and set aside.

Meanwhile, in an 8- to 10-quart pan, bring broth to boiling, covered, on high heat. Add tortellini and boil gently, uncovered, just until tender to bite, 6 to 8 minutes.

Add spinach, chicken, mushrooms, bell pepper, rice, and tarragon to broth; bring to a boil over high heat. Reduce heat to simmering, cover, and cook until chicken is no longer pink in center (cut to test), about 2 minutes.

Ladle soup into large bowls. Offer pepper, cheese, and salt to add to taste. Makes about 5 quarts, 10 to 12 main-dish servings.

PER SERVING: 159 calories, 13 g protein, 17 g carbohydrates, 3.9 g fat, 28 mg cholesterol, 123 mg sodium

Paul Brooks

Los Angeles

IN CASTING ABOUT *for an alternative to the ubiquitous green salad, Edward Tuit worked up this green, red, and yellow salad. Many of its elements reflect persistent tinkering, but his boldest contribution is the dill vinaigrette, which reverses the usual proportions of oil and vinegar. The result is a light dressing with a pronounced flavor.*

Another ingredient of note is fragrant balsamic vinegar; it's aged like a sherry or port and, like the best of these wines, tends to be expensive. You need not use much of it, though.

"Chef Tuit worked up this green, red, and yellow salad."

If your market has some of the relatively new orange, brown, or purple peppers at a reasonable price (or even an unreasonable one, if you feel sufficiently flush), you could add some of these for an even more colorful salad.

RED & YELLOW PEPPER SALAD

1 red onion, about ¾ pound
1 tablespoon balsamic vinegar or red wine vinegar
2 medium-size (about ¾ lb. total) red bell peppers
1 medium-size (about 6 oz.) yellow bell pepper (or use all red bells)
2 medium-size (about 1¼ lb. total) cucumbers, thinly sliced
Dill vinaigrette (recipe follows)
Salt

Thinly slice onion and separate into rings. Place in a 10- to 12-inch frying pan over medium heat. Add vinegar; stir for 2 minutes. Remove from heat and let cool. Stem, seed, and thinly slice the red peppers. Stem, seed, and cut yellow pepper into ½-inch squares. In a large bowl, combine onion, red peppers, yellow pepper, and cucumbers. Add dill vinaigrette and mix well. Serve; or cover and chill up to 4 hours, stirring several times. Add salt to taste. Makes 8 to 10 servings.

PER SERVING: 68 calories, 0.5 g protein, 4.7 g carbohydrates, 2.8 g fat, 0 mg cholesterol, 2 mg sodium

Dill vinaigrette. Mix together ⅓ cup **red wine vinegar;** 2 tablespoons **olive oil** or salad oil; 2 teaspoons **sugar;** 1 teaspoon **dry dill weed;** 1 clove **garlic,** minced or pressed; and ¼ teaspoon **pepper.**

Edward King

Santa Monica, Calif.

ACCORDING TO THE MOST RECENT *medical research, one thing is certain about beef: it either raises your cholesterol, lowers it, or has no effect on it.*

Whatever beef's current status, flank steak contains very little fat, and Jordan Paine trims off all that is visible before marinating and grilling the meat. Vegetable oil in the marinade helps the steak brown richly; the other ingredients are but pleasing embellishments to the natural good taste of this cut.

FLANK STEAK WITH CARRIAGE HOUSE SAUCE

1 flank steak (about 1½ lb.), trimmed of excess fat
¼ cup lemon juice
¼ cup firmly packed brown sugar
2 tablespoons Dijon mustard
2 tablespoons soy sauce
2 tablespoons olive oil or salad oil
1 clove garlic, minced or pressed
¼ teaspoon pepper

Score steak on both sides by cutting ¼-inch-deep diagonal slashes about 1 inch apart; set steak aside.

In a small bowl, whisk together lemon juice, sugar, mustard, soy sauce, oil, garlic, and pepper.

Brush steak all over with mustard mixture. Lay steak on a grill 4 to 6 inches above a solid bed of hot coals (you should be able to hold your hand at grill level only 2 to 3 seconds).

Cook, turning once and basting several times with mustard mixture, until done to your liking (cut to test), 10 to 12 minutes for medium-rare.

To serve, cut meat across the grain into thin slanting slices. Makes 4 to 6 servings.

PER SERVING: 288 calories, 22 g protein, 11 g carbohydrates, 17 g fat, 58 mg cholesterol, 567 mg sodium

Jordan Paine

Scottsdale, Ariz.

September Menus

HOT OR COLD, *these menus adapt to suit busy schedules and the last flash of summer's heat.*

Elements of each meal can be made ahead and served at room temperature. But all are equally appealing hot.

Before the day warms up, bake special breakfast biscuits to go with a light melon soup. Braise chicken or steam salmon for quick dinners.

COOL SOUP— HOT BISCUIT BREAKFAST

Cantaloupe-Tangerine Soup
Biscuit Twists
Parmesan or White Cheddar Cheese
Hard-cooked Eggs
Scottish or Irish Breakfast Tea

Cantaloupe gets whirled in a blender with tangerine concentrate to make a lively liquid that serves as a refreshing breakfast soup. Melon's popular partner, prosciutto, fills the biscuits, along with a pleasing sweet-hot combination of chilies, sugar, and cinnamon.

Chill soup in the refrigerator while you make the biscuits and cook the eggs. Serve the soup in bowls or mugs.

Breakfast soup, made from cantaloupe and topped with mint, accompanies cinnamon- and chili-seasoned biscuit twists. Serve meal with hot or cold tea, eggs, and cheese.

Look for slightly smoky-tasting Scottish breakfast tea in specialty tea and coffee shops or well-stocked grocery stores.

CANTALOUPE-TANGERINE SOUP

1 cantaloupe (about 3 lb.), chilled
1 can (6 oz.) frozen tangerine or orange juice concentrate, partially thawed
Mint sprigs

Cut cantaloupe in half; scoop out and discard seeds. Scoop flesh from shell. Whirl cantaloupe and tangerine concentrate in a blender until smoothly puréed. If desired, chill soup up to 24 hours; whirl again to blend. Pour soup into bowls; garnish with mint. Makes 4 cups, 4 servings.

PER CUP: 146 calories, 2.3 g protein, 35 g carbohydrates, 0.1 g fat, 0 mg cholesterol, 17 mg sodium

BISCUIT TWISTS

About 2 cups all-purpose flour
4 teaspoons baking powder
½ teaspoon salt (optional)
5 tablespoons cold butter or margarine
¾ cup milk
2 tablespoons melted butter or margarine
3 tablespoons sugar
½ teaspoon ground cinnamon
2 tablespoons minced fresh jalapeño chilies
⅓ cup (⅛ lb.) thinly sliced prosciutto or cooked ham, finely slivered
1 large egg white, lightly beaten

In food processor or a bowl, combine 2 cups flour, baking powder, salt, and cold butter. Whirl or rub with your fingers until fine crumbs form. With a fork, stir in milk until dough is moistened. Pat into a ball, then knead on a lightly floured board, making 10 to 12 turns.

On floured board, roll dough into a 12- by 15-inch rectangle. Brush with melted butter. Combine 2 tablespoons sugar, cinnamon, chilies, and prosciutto. Starting at a short side of the dough, sprinkle mixture evenly over half the rectangle. Fold dough in half over filling.

Cut dough through fold into 8 equal pieces; twist each 3 times. Space evenly on a 12- by 15-inch baking sheet. Brush twists with egg white, then sprinkle with remaining sugar. Bake in a 450° oven until deep golden, about 15 min-

Steamed salmon goes with vegetables, savory custard, Japanese sauce.

utes. If made ahead, chill airtight up to 1 day. Makes 8 pieces, 4 servings.

PER PIECE: 253 calories, 6.2 g protein, 30 g carbohydrates, 12 g fat, 35 mg cholesterol, 445 mg sodium

ORIENTAL STEAMED DINNER

Steamed Salmon Steaks with Potato Chawan Mushi
Sesame-Ginger Sauce   Watercress
Crisp Zucchini & Bell Pepper Sticks
Asian or Bartlett Pears
Iced Sake   Sparkling Water

The light Japanese version of custard—chawan mushi—is made of broth, eggs, and a little seasoning. Here, it encases tender potato slices. Add the sesame oil-based sauce to taste to the custard and salmon, and use as a dip for vegetables.

The salmon and individual servings of custard steam together in less than ½ hour. As they cook, mix the sauce. Also cut up 2 medium-size zucchini and 1 large bell pepper. Offer watercress sprigs to garnish custard and dip in sauce.

STEAMED SALMON STEAKS WITH POTATO CHAWAN MUSHI

1 small (¼ lb.) cooked thin-skinned potato, peeled and thinly sliced
4 paper-thin lemon slices, quartered
3 large eggs
1 cup regular-strength chicken broth
1 tablespoon soy sauce
1¾ to 2 pounds salmon steaks or fillets, ¾ inch thick

Place equal amounts of potato, then lemon, in 4 heatproof bowls (such as Oriental rice bowls, or custard cups), each about 1-cup size. In a bowl, whisk eggs, broth, and soy sauce until blended. Pour equally into small bowls; cover each tightly with foil.

Support a rack 1 inch above bottom of a deep 12-inch frying pan, or set rack in a wok. Add water to just below rack. Set covered bowls on rack. On a plate that fits into pan or wok, arrange salmon in a single layer. Set plate on bowls.

Bring water to a boil over high heat, then cover pan with a domed lid (use foil if lid is too shallow) and simmer until custard jiggles only slightly in center when dish is gently shaken (uncover and lift out to check), and fish is no longer translucent in thickest part (cut to test), about 15 minutes. Serve warm or at room temperature. If made ahead, let cool, then chill, covered, up to 1 day. Makes 4 servings.

PER SERVING: 376 calories, 45 g protein, 7.2 g carbohydrates, 17 g fat, 315 mg cholesterol, 411 mg sodium

SESAME-GINGER SAUCE

In a bowl, stir together ⅓ cup *each* **rice vinegar** and **mirin** (rice wine; or use dry sherry), 3 tablespoons *each* **soy sauce** and **Oriental sesame oil**, 2 tablespoons sliced **green onions**, and 1 tablespoon minced **fresh ginger**. Makes about 1 cup.

PER TABLESPOON: 39 calories, 0.2 g protein, 2.4 g carbohydrates, 2.6 g fat, 0 mg cholesterol, 194 mg sodium

(Continued on next page)

PIQUANT SPANISH CHICKEN

Escabèche of Chicken
Mixed Green Salad
Warm Hominy   Crusty Bread
Peaches with Red Wine & Sugar
Spanish Cariñena Wine or
Grapefruit Juice

A generous splash of vinegar gives chicken a Spanish touch. Mellow hominy is a fine foil for the lively sauce.

While the chicken simmers, make salad and heat canned hominy in its own liquid; drain before serving. Save a little dinner wine to pour over the peaches, adding sugar to taste. For youngsters, offer sugar or honey with fruit.

ESCABÈCHE OF CHICKEN

8 chicken thighs (about 2 lb.), skinned
2 tablespoons olive oil
   Escabèche sauce with onions (recipe follows)
   Salt

In a 10- to 12-inch frying pan over medium-high heat, brown chicken in oil, half at a time. As browned, lift meat from pan and set aside. Use pan with the oil to make escabèche sauce; add chicken and any juices. Bring to a boil over high heat, then cover and simmer, turning once, until thickest piece of meat is no longer pink in center (cut to test), about 20 minutes.

Lift meat and onions to a platter and keep warm. Boil sauce over high heat, uncovered, until reduced to 1 cup, about 3 minutes. Pour over meat. Add salt to taste. Serve warm or at room temperature. If made ahead, let cool, then chill, covered, up to 2 days. Makes 4 servings.

PER SERVING: 264 calories, 27 g protein, 11 g carbohydrates, 12 g fat, 35 mg cholesterol, 445 mg sodium

Escabèche sauce with onions. To pan used to brown chicken (preceding), add 2 or 3 cloves **garlic,** minced; 1 small **onion,** chopped; 1 **dry bay leaf;** 3 small **dried hot red chilies;** 6 **dry juniper berries;** 3-inch **cinnamon stick;** and ½ teaspoon *each* **ground coriander** and **dry thyme leaves.** Stir often until onion is golden, about 5 minutes.

To pan, add 1 tablespoon **tomato paste,** ⅔ cup **dry red wine,** ⅓ cup **regular-strength chicken broth,** ¼ cup **sherry vinegar** (or red wine vinegar), and 1 package (10 oz.) **frozen small whole onions;** mix well.

OCTOBER

Sweet & Sour Corn Relish Burger (page 224)

Our harvest of hearty
October dishes features a show-stopping buffet of colorful
Italian vegetable dishes, three bold seafood chowders, and
some lively ideas to add interest to the familiar hamburger. A
California winemaker shares recipes for an autumn luncheon
with dishes that complement white varietal wines. Chocolate
lovers discover an unusual giant puff pastry cake spread
with rich layers of velvety chocolate cream. For a change of
pace, we offer ways to cook with dry buttermilk, garnish
ideas using tiny grapes, and efficient techniques for
using a Chinese cleaver.

Contorni: Colorful, Cool Italian Buffet

IN ITALY, *menus often feature a series of* contorni—*vegetable dishes usually served at room temperature or only gently warm. Collectively, contorni are a colorful lot. They're simple but robust, lightly but flavorfully seasoned, and inevitably given an abundant splash of fruity extra-virgin olive oil.*

What is extra-virgin olive oil? It's the finest grade of olive oil. The oil's natural acidity (oleic acid) determines its rank. Extra-virgin, widely available here, is more costly and less acidic than other grades, but it is also more flavorful. If you like, however, you can substitute a milder, more neutral olive oil.

Try serving these vegetable dishes as a collection for a party of 8 or 9. Each dish has make-ahead steps. Add bread and a crisp, semidry to dry white wine such as Pinot Grigio or Sauvignon Blanc, and you have a fine meal. Or serve the dishes separately as first courses or salads.

TUSCAN BREAD SALAD

- ½ **loaf (1-lb. size) sourdough French bread, cut into 1-inch cubes**
- 6 **tablespoons extra-virgin olive oil**
- 1 **medium-size head (¾ to 1 lb.) fennel, tough stems trimmed off; reserve feathery green leaves**

- 2 **tablespoons balsamic or red wine vinegar**
- 1 **can (2 oz.) anchovy fillets, drained and minced**
- 1 **small red onion, thinly sliced**
- 1 **can (6 oz.) pitted large ripe olives, drained**
- 1 **jar (7 oz.) roasted red bell peppers, drained and cut into thin strips**
- ½ **cup lightly packed fresh basil leaves, cut into fine slivers**
  Pepper

In a 10- by 15-inch baking pan, mix bread cubes with 2 tablespoons of the oil. Bake in a 300° oven until crisp, about 30 minutes; stir occasionally. Let croutons cool.

Italian vegetable buffet includes (clockwise from left) Tuscan bread salad, green beans with porcini mushrooms, a mélange of roasted vegetables,

Trim base and any bruises from fennel; quarter head lengthwise. Sliver each quarter crosswise.

In a large bowl, whisk together remaining oil, vinegar, and anchovies. Add fennel, croutons, onion, olives, bell peppers, and basil. Mix salad until well combined, adding pepper to taste. Garnish with fennel leaves. Serves 8 or 9.

PER SERVING: 216 calories, 4.9 g protein, 18 g carbohydrates, 14 g fat, 3.5 mg cholesterol, 516 mg sodium

LEMON CHICKEN SALAD IN RADICCHIO

2 heads (each 3- to 4-in. diameter, or about 1 lb. total) radicchio

¼ cup pine nuts
1 large lemon, thinly sliced
2 cups minced cooked chicken breast
2 tablespoons extra-virgin olive oil
Salt and pepper

Remove 8 or 9 large radicchio leaves; rinse leaves and radicchio heads. Wrap in paper towels, enclose in a plastic bag, and chill until crisp, at least 1 hour or as long as 2 days.

Place pine nuts in an 8- or 9-inch-wide pan. Bake in a 350° oven until lightly toasted, 8 to 10 minutes, shaking pan occasionally. Set aside.

Discard lemon seeds; cut 2 slices into quarters and set aside. Cut each remaining slice into 10 wedges. In a large bowl, mix small lemon wedges with nuts, chicken, and oil. If made ahead, cover and chill up until the next day.

Finely shred heads of radicchio; discard cores. Mix with chicken salad. Add salt and pepper to taste.

Mound equal portions of chicken salad into the radicchio leaves, set on a large serving platter, and garnish salads with reserved lemon quarter-slices. Makes 8 or 9 servings.

PER SERVING: 111 calories, 12 g protein, 3.9 g carbohydrates, 6.3 g fat, 27 mg cholesterol, 28 mg sodium

(Continued on next page)

focaccia with fresh tomato-basil sauce, caramelized onions and dried tomatoes, radicchio leaves with lemon-chicken salad.

Sun-drenched colors and earthy flavors are captured in cook's palette of fresh vegetables, to season with green-gold extra-virgin olive oil.

GREEN BEANS WITH PORCINI-SHERRY VINAIGRETTE

- ½ ounce (about ⅓ cup) dried porcini mushrooms
- ¼ cup pine nuts
- 1 pound green beans, ends trimmed
- 2 tablespoons sherry vinegar or red wine vinegar
- ¼ cup extra-virgin olive oil
- ½ pound small regular (button) mushrooms (about 1-in. diameter), rinsed, ends trimmed, and cut in half
  Salt and pepper

Soak porcini mushrooms in ¾ cup warm water until soft, about 20 minutes. Squeeze and manipulate mushrooms to release any grit. Lift out and squeeze dry; discard water. Mince porcini; set aside.

Meanwhile, put pine nuts in an 8- or 9-inch-wide pan. Bake in a 350° oven until lightly toasted, 8 to 10 minutes; shake pan occasionally. Let cool.

At the same time, in a 10- to 12-inch frying pan, bring 1 inch water to boiling over high heat. Add beans and cook, uncovered, until barely tender when pierced, 7 to 8 minutes. Drain; immerse

beans in ice water until cool, then drain again.

In a large bowl, whisk together vinegar and oil with porcini mushrooms. Add mushroom halves, pine nuts, beans, and salt and pepper to taste. Mix ingredients together. Serves 8 or 9.

PER SERVING: 98 calories, 2.4 g protein, 6 g carbohydrates, 8.2 g fat, 0 mg cholesterol, 4.4 mg sodium

ROASTED VEGETABLE MÉLANGE

- ¼ cup extra-virgin olive oil
- 1 eggplant, about 1½ pounds (stem removed), cut into 1½-inch chunks
- 1 head garlic
- 1 *each* large green, red, and yellow bell peppers (or all of 1 color; about 1½ lb. total), stemmed, seeded, and cut into 1½-inch pieces
  Salt

Pour equal amounts of oil into 2 pans, each 10 by 15 inches. Place eggplant and garlic in 1 pan, bell peppers in the other. Turn vegetables to coat with oil. Bake in a 400° oven until eggplant is very soft when pressed and edges of vegetables begin to blacken, about 45 minutes; for even browning, switch pan positions halfway through baking.

Combine all vegetables in 1 of the pans; let cool. Separate garlic into cloves. Squeeze 4 or 5 cloves from peel to extract roasted garlic. Stir the very soft extracted garlic cloves gently with vegetables until evenly mixed.

If made ahead, cover and chill up until next day; bring to room temperature before serving.

Transfer vegetables to a serving dish. Offer the remaining roasted garlic to squeeze from cloves. Add garlic and salt to taste to individual portions. Makes 8 or 9 servings.

PER SERVING: 92 calories, 1.6 g protein, 9.1 g carbohydrates, 6.3 g fat, 0 mg cholesterol, 5.4 mg sodium

CARAMELIZED ONIONS WITH DRIED TOMATOES & HERBS

- 1½ pounds small onions (about 1-in. diameter), peeled
- 3 tablespoons oil from oil-packed dried tomatoes, or extra-virgin olive oil
- 1 tablespoon *each* fresh rosemary sprigs (about ½ in. long) and fresh sage leaves, or 1½ teaspoons *each* dry rosemary and dry sage leaves

- ¼ cup drained oil-packed dried tomatoes, cut into slivers
  Fresh rosemary sprigs

Place onions in a 9- by 13-inch baking dish or pan; drizzle with 2 tablespoons of the oil and sprinkle with the rosemary and sage. Bake, uncovered, in a 375° oven until onions are well browned and soft when pressed, about 45 minutes.

Stir in dried tomatoes and remaining oil; let cool. If made ahead, cover and let stand up until the next day.

Transfer to a serving dish and garnish with rosemary sprigs. Serves 8 or 9.

PER SERVING: 85 calories, 1 g protein, 5.9 g carbohydrates, 6.7 g fat, 0 mg cholesterol, 145 mg sodium

BRUSCHETTA

Look for focaccia in Italian bakeries, markets, and delicatessens.

- 4 large ripe Roma-type tomatoes (about ½ lb. total), cored and diced
- ½ cup finely diced celery
- 2 tablespoons *each* minced parsley and fresh basil leaves
- 2 teaspoons white wine vinegar
  About ½ cup extra-virgin olive oil
  Salt and pepper
- 1 sheet (1 lb., about 8 by 11 in.) plain focaccia (Italian flat yeast bread) or 1 loaf (1 lb.) sourdough French bread
  Fresh basil sprigs

In a bowl, combine tomatoes, celery, parsley, minced basil, vinegar, and 2 tablespoons of the olive oil; add salt and pepper to taste. Set aside; if made ahead, cover and chill up until next day.

Cut focaccia into 8 or 9 equal pieces; split each piece horizontally in half. (Or cut French bread into 16 to 18 slices, each ½ inch thick.) Lay focaccia (or bread) in a single layer in 2 baking pans, each 10 by 15 inches. Broil 5 inches from heat until lightly toasted, about 1 minute. Turn pieces over and broil until other side is lightly toasted, about 1 minute.

Set warm bread on a platter. Spoon equal portions of tomato mixture on bread; garnish with fresh basil sprigs. Serve warm. Offer remaining olive oil to pour generously over each serving. Makes 16 to 18 pieces, 8 or 9 servings. — *Dino Baglioni, Il Piccolino Trattoria, Los Angeles.*

PER SERVING: 259 calories, 4.9 g protein, 29 g carbohydrates, 14 g fat, 1.5 mg cholesterol, 300 mg sodium

Pride & Joy Potluck Recipes

THE POTLUCK, *a tradition in cooking that has adapted admirably to changing life styles, lets friends share in a meal's preparation, then bring dishes to a single location to be enjoyed. While economics was once the motivating factor behind potlucks, today a rival factor is time.*

Here are three intriguing recipes you'll be proud to bring to a party. The first is a boned pork roast, stuffed with two kinds of cheese, that goes with a wild rice salad; both are served cold. The third dish is a colorful Mexican fish salad.

PORK LOIN STUFFED WITH TWO CHEESES

- 4 ounces *each* cream cheese and ripened or unripened goat cheese, such as Montrachet or bûcheron
- 1 teaspoon ground dry sage
- ½ teaspoon dry thyme leaves
- 1 boned pork loin end roast (about 3 lb.)
- 12 to 15 large canned grape leaves, drained
- Lemon wedges (optional)
- Additional grape leaves (optional)

Thoroughly blend cream cheese, goat cheese, ½ teaspoon of the sage, and ¼ teaspoon of the thyme; set aside.

Open roast and place flat, fat side down, on a work surface. Cover the meat with plastic wrap and pound with flat side of a mallet until roast measures about 9 by 11 inches.

Using the 12 to 15 grape leaves, arrange in a double layer down center of meat, extending leaves beyond ends of roast. Next, spoon cheese mixture down center of leaves just to ends of roast (fill roast so you can reroll it to its original shape); fold ends of leaves over filling and then lay leaves over cheese to form a neat roll down center. Roll up meat, enclosing filling closely; securely tie with string at 2-inch intervals.

Place roast, fat side up, in a 9- by 13-inch pan. Rub remaining ½ teaspoon sage and ¼ teaspoon thyme over surface of roast. Insert a meat thermometer into thickest part of meat (not into filling). Roast in a 375° oven until thermometer reaches 155° to 160°, about 1¼ hours. Let cool; then cover and refrigerate for at least 3 hours or up to 1 day. Transport in a cooler.

To serve, garnish with lemon wedges and additional grape leaves, if desired. Slice meat ¾ to 1 inch thick. Makes 8 servings.

PER SERVING: 489 calories, 32 g protein, 3 g carbohydrates, 38 g fat, 112 mg cholesterol, 276 mg sodium

WILD RICE SALAD

- 1½ cups wild rice, rinsed and drained
- 3 cups regular-strength chicken broth
- ⅓ cup salad oil
- 2 tablespoons raspberry vinegar or wine vinegar
- 2 tablespoons finely chopped shallots or mild onion
- 2 teaspoons Dijon mustard
- ¼ teaspoon pepper

In a 2- to 3-quart pan, bring rice and broth to a boil over high heat. Reduce heat, cover, and simmer, stirring occasionally, until rice is tender to bite and most of the broth is absorbed, about 50 minutes. Let cool.

In a small bowl, blend oil, vinegar, shallots, mustard, and pepper. Pour the dressing over the cool wild rice and mix lightly. If made ahead, cover and refrigerate for up to 2 days. Serve at room temperature. Makes 8 servings.

PER SERVING: 202 calories, 5 g protein, 24 g carbohydrates, 10 g fat, 0 mg cholesterol, 417 mg sodium

VERACRUZ FISH SALAD

- 2½ pounds white-fleshed fish fillets, such as rockfish or orange roughy
- 3 large firm-ripe tomatoes, cored and coarsely diced
- ⅔ cup lime juice
- 3 cloves garlic, minced or pressed
- 1 cup sliced Spanish-style pimiento-stuffed olives
- ⅓ cup drained capers
- ½ cup thinly sliced green onions, including tops
- Salt and pepper
- About 8 large iceberg lettuce leaves, washed and crisped
- 1 or 2 limes, cut into wedges

Place fish in a 9- by 13-inch baking dish, overlapping fillets slightly. Cover the fish and bake in a 400° oven just until opaque in center of thickest part (cut to test), 12 to 15 minutes. Let cool; cover and refrigerate for at least 2 hours or up to 1 day.

Lift out fish, discarding pan juices. Pull out and discard any bones. Break fish into bite-size chunks. In a large bowl, combine tomatoes, lime juice, garlic, olives, capers, green onions, and fish; mix gently. Season to taste with salt and pepper. Line a serving bowl with lettuce and spoon in salad. Garnish with lime wedges. Transport in a cooler. Makes 6 to 8 servings.

PER SERVING: 179 calories, 28 g protein, 7 g carbohydrates, 5 g fat, 50 mg cholesterol, 648 mg sodium

Cold boned pork roast, stuffed with cheese, goes with artichokes and wild rice salad.

Building a Better Burger

A NOUVEAU TOUCH *for the familiar hamburger is a quick-to-make but out-of-the-ordinary relish. This small gesture gives fast family suppers an interesting twist, and can also pleasantly surprise guests.*

Our three choices are based on corn, zucchini, and pimiento with oranges. They're equally refreshing with other simply cooked meats, fish, or poultry.

SWEET & SOUR CORN RELISH BURGER

    2 cups lightly packed spinach
       leaves, rinsed well and crisped
       Toasted buns (recipe follows)
       Basic beef burgers (recipe follows)
    1 small onion, thinly sliced
       Corn relish (recipe follows)
       Salt and pepper

Lay spinach leaves equally on bottom section of buns; top each with a beef burger, onion slices, corn relish, and salt and pepper to taste. Cover with top sections of buns. Makes 4 servings.

PER SERVING WITHOUT RELISH: 508 calories, 34 g protein, 23 g carbohydrates, 30 g fat, 131 mg cholesterol, 373 mg sodium

Toasted buns. Cut 4 **hamburger buns** or Kaiser rolls (4 in. wide) in half horizontally. If desired, spread with **butter** or margarine (about 2 tablespoons total).

To toast on barbecue, lay buns cut side down on grill 4 to 6 inches above solid bed of hot coals (you should be able to hold your hand at grill level only 2 to 3 seconds). Cook until lightly browned, 2 to 4 minutes.

To toast in oven, lay buns cut side up in a 10- by 15-inch pan. Broil 3 to 4 inches from heat until lightly browned, 2 to 6 minutes.

Basic beef burgers. Divide 1½ pounds **ground lean beef** equally into quarters; shape into ½-inch-thick patties.

To barbecue hamburgers, place patties on a grill 4 to 6 inches above a solid bed of hot coals (you should be able to hold your hand at grill level for only 2 to 3 seconds). Cook until patties are browned and done to your liking; turn as needed. For rare—red in center (cut to test), about 5 minutes. For medium-rare—pink in center (cut to test), about 10 minutes.

To broil hamburgers, place patties on a rack in a 12- by 15-inch broiler pan. Broil 3 to 4 inches from heat until cooked to your liking, turning once. For rare—red in center (cut to test), about 5 minutes. For medium-rare—pink in center (cut to test), about 10 minutes.

Corn relish. Mix ½ cup cooked **corn;** 1 small firm-ripe **tomato,** cored and diced; ¼ cup diced **sweet pickle;** 1 tablespoon *each* **vinegar** and **salad oil;** ½ teaspoon **mustard seed;** and ¼ teaspoon **pepper.** Use, or cover and chill up to 5 days. Makes about 1⅔ cup.

PER TABLESPOON: 12 calories, 0.2 g protein, 1.8 g carbohydrates, 0.6 g fat, 0 mg cholesterol, 18 mg sodium

Sweet: corn, diced tomatoes and sweet pickles, and mustard seed make relish for hamburger on bed of spinach.

Zucchini Relish with Sweet Onion Burger

4 lettuce leaves, rinsed and crisped
    Toasted buns (recipe precedes)
    Basic beef burgers (recipe precedes)
    Zucchini relish (recipe follows)
    Salt and pepper

On bottom half of each bun put a lettuce leaf, a burger, relish, and salt and pepper to taste. Put bun tops on sandwiches. Makes 4 servings.

PER SERVING WITHOUT RELISH: 501 calories, 33 g protein, 22 g carbohydrates, 30 g fat, 131 mg cholesterol, 349 mg sodium

Zucchini relish. Trim ends from 2 medium-size **zucchini** (1¼ lb. total); cut in ⅛-inch-thick sticks; set aside.

In a 10- to 12-inch frying pan, combine 2 tablespoons **oil from dried tomatoes packed in oil** or olive oil; 1 tablespoon **butter** or margarine; and 1 small **onion,** thinly sliced. Cook, stir-ring often, over medium-high heat until onion is limp, about 5 minutes. Add zucchini and cook, stirring often, until vegetables just begin to brown, about 15 minutes. Stir in ¼ cup drained and chopped **dried tomatoes packed in oil.** Serve warm. If made ahead, let stand up to 3 hours. Or cover and chill up to 2 days. Makes 1½ cups.

PER TABLESPOON: 24 calories, 0.2 g protein, 0.8 g carbohydrates, 2.4 g fat, 1.3 mg cholesterol, 59 mg sodium

Pimiento-Citrus Relish Burger

⅓ cup mayonnaise
    Pimiento-orange relish (recipe follows)
    Toasted buns (recipe precedes)
2 cups lightly packed watercress, rinsed and crisped
    Basic beef burgers (recipe precedes)
    About ⅓ pound jicama, peeled, rinsed, and thinly sliced
    Salt and pepper
    Lime wedges

Mix mayonnaise with 1 tablespoon liquid from relish. Spread mixture on cut sides of bun bottoms; top with watercress and burgers. Arrange jicama on meat; add relish, salt and pepper, and squeezed lime juice to taste. Put bun tops on sandwiches. Makes 4 servings.

PER SERVING WITHOUT RELISH: 644 calories, 34 g protein, 25 g carbohydrates, 45 g fat, 141 mg cholesterol, 461 mg sodium

Pimiento-orange relish. With a knife, cut peel and white membrane from 2 medium-size **oranges.** Over a bowl, cut between membranes to remove segments. Mix together oranges, ⅓ cup sliced **canned pimiento,** and ½ teaspoon **crushed dried hot red chilies.** Serve, or cover and chill up until next day. Makes 1½ cups.

PER TABLESPOON: 6.6 calories, 0.1 g protein, 1.6 g carbohydrates, 0 g fat, 0 mg cholesterol, 0.6 mg sodium

Savory: sun-dried tomatoes and sautéed zucchini and onion top patty; green-leaf lettuce goes underneath.

Almost tropical: orange segments, jicama slices, red pimiento strips go on top; watercress goes below.

Giant Chocolate Napoleon

IT'S A PROJECT. *It's a commitment. But if you like chocolate, it's worth it.*

The giant-size puff pastry napoleon is unusual because the pastry, as well as the filling, is chocolate. For best results, follow the steps carefully, abiding by chilling times and oven temperatures.

This elegant dessert was inspired by chef Jean-Pierre Billoux of the restaurant at L'Hôtel de la Cloche, Dijon, France.

CHOCOLATE PUFF PASTRY CAKE WITH SPIRITED CANDIED ORANGES

- 2 cups sifted all-purpose flour
- ½ teaspoon salt
- 1 cup (½ lb.) cold unsalted butter or unsalted margarine
- 8 to 10 tablespoons ice water
- ⅔ cup unsweetened cocoa, sifted

Dot cocoa-butter mixture over ⅔ of dough, leaving a ½-inch border. Fold dough into thirds, pinch edges shut, and chill.

- Chocolate cream (recipe follows)
- 1 to 2 teaspoons powdered sugar
  Spirited candied oranges (recipe follows)
  About 1 pint vanilla bean ice cream

In a large bowl, mix flour with salt. Cut 3 tablespoons of the butter into cubes; add to flour. With a pastry blender or your fingers, cut or rub butter into flour mixture until fine crumbs form. Add enough water, stirring with a fork, to make dough cling together. Knead dough on an unfloured board until smooth, 3 to 5 minutes. Enclose dough in plastic wrap and chill until cold, about 45 minutes.

In a food processor or with an electric mixer, whirl or beat cocoa with remaining butter until well blended. Chill until firm but still spreadable, 10 to 15 minutes.

On a lightly floured board, roll dough into a 12- by 18-inch rectangle. Evenly distribute teaspoon-size pieces of the cocoa-butter mixture across ⅔ of the dough, to within ½ inch of edges. Fold the plain third of dough onto half of buttered section, then fold again onto the remaining buttered section. Pinch edges of dough securely to seal in butter. Enclose dough in plastic wrap and chill 30 minutes.

Stunning chocolate dessert, sliced, reveals paper-thin layers of buttery puff pastry. Accompany each serving with ice cream and candied oranges soaked in liqueur.

To "turn" dough, fold pastry rectangle into thirds, then in half; chill until firm. Repeat this step twice. Each time you roll pastry, butter layer spreads thinner.

Spread rich, velvety chocolate cream filling generously between layers of baked chocolate puff pastry. Assemble and chill at least 2 hours ahead so dessert slices well.

On a lightly floured board, roll dough into a 10- by 16-inch rectangle. Fold rectangle in thirds, then fold in half—like closing a book. This completes a "turn." Enclose in plastic wrap and chill 30 minutes. Give dough 2 more turns; chill for 30 minutes after each. After the last turn, wrap dough and chill at least 4 hours, or up to 5 days; or freeze up to 6 months.

Divide dough in half. On a lightly floured board, roll each piece to make a rectangle about ⅛ inch thick and slightly larger than 11 by 12 inches. To prevent sticking, lift dough often and sprinkle board lightly with flour. Dust 2 baking sheets, each 12 by 15 inches, lightly with flour. Put a piece of pastry on each. Chill, uncovered, until dough is firm, about 10 minutes.

With a sharp knife, cut each pastry piece into 2 rectangles, each 6 by 11 inches (cut straight down; if you pull knife through dough, pastry will not puff properly). Remove pastry scraps (bake to nibble); carefully lift rectangles and space 2 inches apart on baking sheets. Chill again until firm, about 10 minutes. With a fork, pierce the pastry every ½ inch.

Bake in a 400° oven for 10 minutes, switch pan positions, then reduce heat to 300° and continue baking until pastry

pieces have risen slightly and are darker brown, 15 to 20 minutes longer. With a wide spatula, carefully transfer pastry to racks; cool completely. At this point, you can wrap baked pastry airtight and freeze up to 2 weeks. To recrisp, place frozen baked pastry on baking sheets and heat in 400° oven until pastry feels dry, about 10 minutes. Let cool before assembling cake.

To assemble, set 1 pastry piece on a platter and gently spread with ⅓ of the chocolate cream. Top with another piece of pastry, aligning with the first; spread with half of the remaining chocolate cream. Top with another pastry piece and spread with remaining cream. Top with the last piece of pastry; dust with powdered sugar. Cover and chill at least 2 or up to 6 hours.

With a very sharp serrated knife, cut pastry cake crosswise into ½- to ¾-inch-thick slices. Lay slices of cake on dessert plates. Spoon 2 to 3 tablespoons spirited oranges and 1 or 2 scoops ice cream onto plates beside cake. Makes 10 to 12 servings.

PER SERVING: 636 calories, 7 g protein, 62 g carbohydrates, 45 g fat, 220 mg cholesterol, 126 mg sodium

Chocolate cream. In a 1- to 1½-quart pan over very low heat, stir 6 ounces **bittersweet chocolate** until melted; let stand until cool but still fluid. In a bowl,

beat 5 **large egg yolks** with ½ cup **sugar** on high speed until thick. Beat in cooled chocolate. Add ½ cup (¼ lb.) room-temperature **unsalted butter** or unsalted margarine, cut up, beating until blended.

In a deep bowl, beat 1⅓ cups **whipping cream** until soft peaks will hold; gently fold into chocolate mixture. Use, or cover and chill up to next day. Let stand at room temperature 1 hour before using.

Spirited candied oranges. Cut 3 unpeeled thin-skinned **oranges** (each about 3-in. diameter) crosswise into ⅛-inch-thick slices; remove seeds. In a 10- to 12-inch frying pan, bring 1 cup **sugar,** ½ cup **water,** and 1 **vanilla bean** (about 6 in.), split lengthwise, to boiling on high heat. Add oranges; simmer, uncovered, stirring often until peel is translucent, 25 to 30 minutes. With a slotted spoon, lift out oranges and bean (rinse bean, dry, save for reuse). Cool oranges; chop coarsely.

Measure syrup, adding any juice from oranges. If more than ¼ cup, boil, uncovered, until reduced to ¼ cup; if less, add water to make ¼ cup. Add oranges and 2 tablespoons **orange-flavor liqueur.** Use, or cover and chill up to 3 days.

Cooking with Dry Buttermilk

IF YOU ENJOY *foods cooked with butter-milk but don't like to drink it, dry but-termilk is a practical product to have on hand. It brings the same flavorful tang and lightness to dishes as its fresh counterpart — without the hassle of liquid leftovers.*

Dry buttermilk is made in much the same fashion as dry skim milk, has similar nutritional values and keeping qualities, and is found in the same location on super-market shelves. However, the dry butter-milk label may recommend refrigeration or cool storage to best preserve flavor and texture.

You can make more versatile use of dry buttermilk than of liquid. Use it generously to get flavor impact in a potato soup, in an oven-fried chicken coating, in buttermilk and cheese pie, pound cake, and streusel topping for baked apples.

Chunky potato soup gets subtle tang from dry buttermilk, which nicely balances its rich bacon flavor.

BUTTERMILK POTATO SOUP

    8   slices (about 6 oz.) bacon,
        chopped
    1   medium-size onion, chopped
  3½   cups regular-strength chicken
        broth
    2   large (about 1 lb. total) russet
        potatoes, peeled and cut into
        about ¼-inch cubes
  ½   cup dry buttermilk
  ⅔   cup finely chopped parsley
        Salt and pepper

In a 3- to 4-quart pan over medium-high heat, stir bacon and onion often until onion is limp, 10 to 12 minutes. Drain off excess bacon fat.

Add 3 cups broth, and potatoes. Bring to a boil over high heat. Cover and simmer until potatoes are soft when pierced, about 10 minutes.

In a small bowl, mix remaining broth and dry buttermilk until smooth. Stir into soup. Cook, uncovered, over low heat until hot (do not boil). If you want a thicker, smoother consistency, mash potatoes in soup. Stir in parsley. Ladle soup into bowls; add salt and pepper to taste. Makes 4 servings, 1½-cup size.

PER SERVING: 286 calories, 13 g protein, 26 g carbohydrates, 14 g fat, 27 mg cholesterol, 357 mg sodium

BUTTERMILK CHEESE PIE

  ⅓   cup all-purpose flour
  ¾   cup dry buttermilk
    2   cups (1 pt.) small-curd, low-fat
        cottage cheese
    2   small cans (4 oz. *each*) diced
        green chilies
  10   large eggs
  ½   cup (¼ lb.) melted butter or
        margarine
    1   pound jack cheese, shredded

In a large bowl, combine flour, dry but-termilk, cottage cheese, chilies, eggs, butter, and jack cheese. Beat with a mixer until well blended. Pour into a but-tered 9- by 13-inch pan; shake pan to make the filling level. If made ahead, cover and chill up until the next day.

Bake, uncovered, in a 350° oven until the casserole is lightly browned and feels firm in the center when lightly pressed, about 45 minutes. Let stand about 5 min-utes. Cut into rectangles and lift out with a spatula. Makes 8 to 10 servings. —*Sara Prickett, San Jose, Calif.*

PER SERVING: 418 calories, 27 g protein, 11 g carbohydrates, 30 g fat, 347 mg cholesterol, 775 mg sodium

BUTTERMILK, MUSHROOM & CHEESE PIE

In a 10- to 12-inch frying pan, melt 1 tablespoon **butter** or margarine. Add 1 medium-size chopped **onion** and 1 pound sliced **mushrooms.** Stir often on medium-high heat until liquid has cooked away, 15 to 25 minutes. Follow directions for **buttermilk cheese pie** (preceding), omitting chilies and adding mushroom mixture.

PER SERVING: 436 calories, 27 g protein, 12 g carbohydrates, 31 g fat, 350 mg cholesterol, 650 mg sodium

Sausage & Buttermilk Pie

In a 10- to 12-inch frying pan, stir 1½ pounds **bulk pork sausage** often over medium-high heat until well browned, 25 to 35 minutes. Drain meat; discard fat.

Follow directions for **buttermilk cheese pie** (preceding), omitting chilies and adding sausage.

PER SERVING: 531 calories, 33 g protein, 10 g carbohydrates, 40 g fat, 373 mg cholesterol, 1,054 mg sodium

Oven-fried Buttermilk Chicken Legs

- ½ cup fine dry bread crumbs
- ¼ cup dry buttermilk
- ½ teaspoon dry thyme leaves
- ½ teaspoon dry oregano leaves
- 6 whole chicken legs (drumsticks with thighs, 3½ lb. total)
- 3 tablespoons melted butter or margarine
  Salt and pepper

In a bag, combine crumbs, dry buttermilk, thyme, and oregano. Rinse chicken and shake off most moisture. Shake legs in bag to coat with crumbs.

Lay legs, skin up, slightly apart in a greased 10- by 15-inch baking pan. Drizzle legs with butter. Bake in a 400° oven until legs are brown and crisp and meat is no longer pink at bone (cut to test), 35 to 40 minutes. Add salt and pepper to taste. Serve hot or cool. Serves 6.

PER SERVING: 407 calories, 37 g protein, 9 g carbohydrates, 24 g fat, 137 mg cholesterol, 259 mg sodium

Baked Apples with Buttermilk Streusel

- 8 cups (about 2½ lb. total) Newtown Pippin or Golden Delicious apples
- ¾ cup all-purpose flour
- ½ cup dry buttermilk
- ½ cup firmly packed brown sugar
- 2 teaspoons ground cinnamon
- ¼ teaspoon ground ginger
- ½ cup (¼ lb.) butter or margarine

Peel, core, and thinly slice apples into a shallow 2½- to 3-quart baking dish.

In a bowl, stir together flour, dry buttermilk, sugar, cinnamon, and ginger. Rub butter with flour mixture until coarse crumbs form. Stir ⅓ cup crumb mixture into apples; spread fruit level.

Traditional pound cake contains no liquid, but dry buttermilk can be used to give it an intriguing tang.

Squeeze remaining flour mixture into lumps. Break into ¾-inch chunks over apples.

Bake, uncovered, in a 350° oven until apples are tender when pierced and streusel is lightly browned, 40 to 50 minutes. Serve warm or cool. Serves 6 to 8.

PER SERVING: 307 calories, 4.2 g protein, 47 g carbohydrates, 12 g fat, 36 mg cholesterol, 160 mg sodium

Buttermilk Pound Cake

- About 1¾ cups (⅞ lb.) butter or margarine, at room temperature
- 1 box (1 lb., 3½ cups) unsifted powdered sugar
- 6 large eggs
- 1 teaspoon vanilla
  About 2¾ cups sifted cake flour
- ¾ cup dry buttermilk
- ¼ cup sliced almonds (optional)

In a large bowl, beat 1¾ cups butter with an electric mixer until creamy. Mix powdered sugar into butter; beat until mixture is fluffy. Add eggs, 1 at a time, beating well after each. Add vanilla.

Stir together 2¾ cups flour and dry buttermilk. Stir into butter mixture, then beat until well mixed.

Heavily butter a 10-inch (12-cup) plain or decorative tube pan. Add almonds; tilt and rotate pan to attach almonds to the buttered surfaces. Or omit almonds and dust buttered pan with flour. Scrape batter into pan and smooth surface.

Bake in a 300° oven until cake just begins to pull from pan sides and a toothpick inserted in center comes out clean, 1¾ to 2 hours. Let cool in pan on a rack for 10 minutes. Cut around pan edges. Set a rack over cake in pan; hold pan and rack together and invert cake onto rack.

Serve cake warm or cool, thinly sliced. If made ahead, cool, wrap airtight, and hold at room temperature up to 2 days; freeze to store longer. Serves 12 to 16.

PER SERVING: 399 calories, 5.6 g protein, 44 g carbohydrates, 23 g fat, 160 mg cholesterol, 260 mg sodium

Bolder Chowders

TRADITIONALLY A POTAGE of seafood and vegetables, chowder takes on a bolder personality in these variations. Herbs, spices, and chilies give them verve.

Serve any one of the chowders as a one-bowl entrée for a family supper or an informal dinner with friends. Accompany with a green salad and a crusty loaf of bread or crisp breadsticks.

CURRIED FISH CHOWDER

- 2 tablespoons butter or margarine
- 1 large onion, chopped
- 2 tablespoons minced fresh ginger
- 1 clove garlic, pressed or minced
- 1½ tablespoons curry powder
- 6 cups regular-strength chicken broth
- 2 medium-size thin-skinned potatoes (about 1 lb. total), peeled and cut into ½-inch cubes
- 1 large carrot, peeled and cut into ½-inch cubes
- 3 strips (each ½ by 4 in.) pared lemon peel, yellow part only
- 2 small dried hot red chilies
- 1 pound skinned white-flesh fish fillets, such as rockfish or orange roughy, cut into ½-inch cubes
- ¼ cup thinly sliced green onions
- 1 cup unflavored yogurt
- 1 lemon, cut into wedges

In a 5- to 6-quart pan, combine butter, chopped onion, ginger, and garlic; stir often over medium-high heat until onion is limp, about 5 minutes. Add curry powder; stir 1 to 2 minutes. Add broth, potatoes, carrot, lemon peel, and chilies; bring to a boil over high heat. Cover and simmer until potatoes are tender when pierced, about 20 minutes.

Add fish, cover, and simmer until it is opaque in thickest part (cut to test), 2 to 3 minutes longer. If desired, remove and discard the chilies. Ladle into tureen; sprinkle with 1 tablespoon green onions. Add remaining green onions, yogurt, and lemon to taste. Makes 4 to 6 servings.

PER SERVING: 238 calories, 21 g protein, 23 g carbohydrates, 7.6 g fat, 39 mg cholesterol, 176 mg sodium

Curried Fish Chowder. Golden curry broth, spiced with dried chilies, is laden with white fish chunks, tender cubes of potatoes and carrots. Add yogurt to temper heat.

SHRIMP & RICE CHOWDER

- 2 fresh jalapeño chilies (about 3 in.)
- 2 tablespoons salad oil
- 1 large onion, chopped
- 2 cloves garlic, pressed or minced
- ½ teaspoon cumin seed
- 6 cups regular-strength chicken broth
- ⅔ cup medium-grain white rice
- 3 medium-size Roma-type tomatoes, cored and diced
- 1 package (10 oz.) frozen petite peas, thawed
- 1 pound tiny cooked shelled shrimp
- 1 large lime, cut into wedges

Cut 1 chili in half lengthwise. Thinly slice remaining chili and set aside. In a 5- to 6-quart pan, combine oil, onion, garlic, cumin seed, and 1 or 2 chili halves to taste. Stir over medium-high heat until onion is limp, about 5 minutes. Add broth and rice. Bring to a boil over high heat, cover, and simmer until rice is very tender to bite, 25 to 30 minutes.

Add tomatoes, peas, and ¾ of the shrimp. Simmer, uncovered, until hot. Remove and discard chili halves. Ladle chowder into wide soup bowls. Mound remaining shrimp equally in each bowl. Garnish with lime; sprinkle with sliced chili. Serves 6.

PER SERVING: 281 calories, 23 g protein, 30 g carbohydrates, 7.6 g fat, 148 mg cholesterol, 294 mg sodium

Shrimp & Rice Chowder. Pink shrimp, green peas, red tomatoes, and lime are colorful components of rice-thickened chowder. Fresh jalapeño chilies lend a hot edge.

Tarragon Wine Seafood Chowder. Clams steam open in tarragon- and wine-scented broth.

TARRAGON WINE SEAFOOD CHOWDER

¼ cup (⅛ lb.) butter or margarine
1 large onion, chopped
1 clove garlic, pressed or minced
¼ cup all-purpose flour
4 cups regular-strength chicken broth
1 cup dry white wine
1 cup water
¼ teaspoon dry tarragon leaves

2 medium-size thin-skinned potatoes (about 1 lb. total), peeled and cut into ½-inch cubes
12 to 18 clams in shells (suitable for steaming), scrubbed well
1 pound skinned white-flesh fish fillets, such as rockfish or orange roughy, cut into ½-inch cubes
½ cup whipping cream
¼ pound tiny cooked shelled shrimp or cooked shelled crab (optional)
2 tablespoons chopped parsley
Salt and pepper

In a 5- to 6-quart pan, melt butter over medium-high heat. Add onion and garlic; stir often until limp, about 5 minutes. Stir in flour, then broth, wine, water, and tarragon. Stir over high heat until boiling. Add potatoes, cover, and simmer until tender when pierced, about 20 minutes. Stir in clams. Cover and simmer until clams begin to open, 5 to 10 minutes.

Add fish, cover, and simmer until it is opaque in thickest part (cut to test), 2 to 3 minutes longer. Add cream and shrimp; cover and simmer until hot, 2 to 4 minutes. Ladle into a tureen or wide soup bowls. Sprinkle with parsley. Add salt and pepper to taste. Makes 6 servings.

PER SERVING: 318 calories, 22 g protein, 20 g carbohydrates, 17 g fat, 80 mg cholesterol, 189 mg sodium

The Indispensable Chinese Cleaver

THE CHINESE EQUIVALENT of the French chef's knife, this broad-bladed cleaver is rapidly gaining converts. The reasons for its popularity are simple—it's versatile and easy to use, and generally costs less than its European counterpart.

At first, the blocky design of the blade may seem awkward to handle. But with practice, you'll find it amazingly comfortable. In these pictures, master chef and cookbook author Martin Yan shows how many uses it has.

With the weight concentrated evenly into a relatively short length, the broad, rectangular blade offers several advantages. Good balance makes it easier to cut through dense food, such as winter squash or chicken bones, by hacking (see lower left picture, page 233). The

cleaver's short length requires less space for cutting, making it more maneuverable in a tight area. Turn the knife over, and the dull edge doubles as a mallet for tenderizing tough meats. Even the blade's *side* can be useful—as a convenient spatula to transfer cut food or smash garlic.

Cleavers are commonly graded by weight and size from 1 through 4—heavy to light. The most functional for the home cook is the medium-light-weight grade 3 blade, which can be used as an all-purpose knife to slice meats and vegetables. Grades 1 and 2—most commonly used by professional chefs—are larger and designed to chop through dense bones, such as spareribs.

All sizes are available in carbon, stainless, and high-carbon stainless steel. The

last choice combines the best of the other two—it has carbon steel's sharp edge and resists corrosion. Prices of cleavers vary and range from $6 to $17 for carbon blades, $10 to $27 for stainless, and $30 to $50 for good-quality high-carbon stainless (however, European-made Chinese-style cleavers can cost as much as $80). A top-of-the-line French chef's knife of comparable size and quality can cost $70.

Look for true Chinese cleavers in cutlery stores, department stores, and Asian food and hardware stores.

Maintain a cleaver as you would any knife: keep sharp by using a steel and stone, wipe dry after use, and protect the edge when you store it. To wash, don't soak the cleaver in water for a long time or put in a dishwasher.

Vertical slicing. *Hold food with fingers curved down and in. Slice straight down, pressing side of blade against knuckle of middle finger. Use knuckle as a cutting guide and move your hand back as you go. Don't raise sharp edge above knuckles.*

Horizontal slicing. *If needed, trim food to create a flat base. With palm flat and fingers straight, press down firmly and evenly on food. Slice blade back and forth horizontally through food, angling blade slightly downward.*

Cubing or dicing. *Slice food horizontally or vertically at even intervals. Stack slices (base piece should be flat), then slice through the stack at right angles to the first cuts; space the cuts the same distance apart to make even pieces.*

Slivers, matchsticks, julienne. *Thinly slice food horizontally or vertically. Stack slices (base pieces should be flat), then thinly cut vertically through stack.*

Roll cutting. *Use on long, slender vegetables, like carrots and zucchini. Trim end diagonally at a 45° angle. Roll food ¼ turn, cut again at same angle. Pieces are uniform in size, different in shape.*

Chopping or mincing. *Vertically slice food into small pieces. With one hand on blunt edge, hold down tip of blade as pivot; grip handle with other hand, and move knife in a rocking motion back and forth.*

Hacking. *Push blade into meat or vegetable; then, with your fist or mallet, drive knife through food. Don't forcefully slam down lighter-duty blade 3 or 4—or use on anything denser than chicken or hard squash; blade may chip.*

Tenderizing. *Turn the blade dull edge down. Evenly and rhythmically, swing the dull edge of knife up and down across surface of meat in a pounding motion. If meat needs more tenderizing, turn it over and repeat on the opposite side.*

Crushing. *Bang the width of the blade forcefully down on garlic. If you need extra strength, push down the blade with your fist as hard as you need. Crush lightly to remove just the garlic skin, harder to mash the entire clove.*

Winemaker's Lunch

THE PERFECT COMBINATION *of food and wine isn't limited to one right pairing. Some of the most open-minded suggestions are coming from winemakers themselves. Since varietal wines differ decidedly with each year and each winery, winemakers look to the character of each wine when choosing an edible partner for it.*

In this fall menu, a well-balanced, lightly oaked, and fruit-rich Chardonnay complements two of the courses. The dessert suits a fragrant, spicy Gewürztraminer.

The original meal came about when Rutherford Hill Winery asked culinary students to come up with dishes to enhance its wines. The menu begins with individual portions of a rosemary-scented potato and mushroom casserole. The broiled trout is flavored with a faintly sweet nut butter. Both dishes bring out a Chardonnay's fruity character.

Dessert is fruit with a lemon-ginger syrup. The Gewürztraminer needs to be on the sweet side; otherwise the contrast with the syrup will make the wine seem very sharp.

POTATO & MUSHROOM RAMEKINS

- 2 pounds russet potatoes, scrubbed
- 4 slices bacon, chopped
- ¾ pound mushrooms, thinly sliced
- 1 medium-size red onion, thinly sliced
- 3 cloves garlic, minced or pressed
- 1 tablespoon chopped fresh rosemary leaves or 1 teaspoon dry rosemary leaves
- 1 tablespoon minced parsley
- ¼ teaspoon paprika
  Pepper
- ¼ cup (⅛ lb.) butter or margarine, cut into ¼-inch cubes
- ½ pound gruyère or fontina cheese, shredded
- ¾ cup regular-strength chicken broth

Place potatoes in a 5- to 6-quart pan; cover with 1 inch water. Cover and bring to a boil over high heat; boil gently until tender when pierced, 25 to 30 minutes. Drain, let cool, then peel. Cut potatoes into ¼-inch-thick slices; set aside.

In a 10- to 12-inch frying pan over medium heat, cook bacon until crisp; stir often. With a slotted spoon, transfer bacon to paper towels to drain.

Discard all but 2 tablespoons bacon fat. To pan, add mushrooms, onion, garlic, rosemary, and parsley; stir occasionally until mushrooms are lightly brown, 10 to 12 minutes. Stir in bacon, paprika, and pepper to taste.

At this point, you can cover and chill ingredients up to 6 hours.

Butter 6 deep individual baking dishes (about 1½-cup size) or 1 shallow 2-quart baking dish. Make a layer with ½ of the potatoes, top with ½ the butter, ½ the mushroom mixture, and ½ the cheese. Repeat layers, ending with the cheese. Pour broth evenly over all.

Bake, uncovered, in a 425° oven until hot throughout and browned on top, 30 to 35 minutes. Makes 6 servings. — *Kristin Mathisen, San Francisco.*

PER SERVING: 427 calories, 17 g protein, 32 g carbohydrates, 26 g fat, 69 mg cholesterol, 316 mg sodium

BROILED TROUT WITH MACADAMIA NUT BUTTER

Serve the fish with hot cooked Chinese pea pods (you need about 1 lb.), and season them with the extra macadamia nut butter.

- 1½ teaspoons firmly packed brown sugar
- 1 jar (3½ oz.) salted macadamia nuts
- ¼ cup (⅛ lb.) butter or margarine, at room temperature
- 4 whole trout (about ¾ lb. *each*, dressed weight with head and tail), each in a single piece but filleted
  Freshly ground pepper
- 1 lemon, cut into 4 wedges

In a food processor or blender, whirl half the brown sugar with ½ cup macadamias and butter until nuts are finely ground.

Cut off trout heads and discard. Rinse fish and pat dry. Place fish, skin down, in a greased 10- by 15-inch baking pan; do not overlap. Evenly sprinkle remaining sugar on trout, then sprinkle with pepper.

Place about 2 teaspoons of the macadamia nut butter on each fish. Broil 5 inches from heat, about 1 minute to

soften butter. Quickly remove pan from oven and spread butter evenly over fillets. Return to broiler and cook until fish flakes in the thickest part when prodded with a fork, 3 to 4 minutes more.

With a wide spatula, gently transfer each fish to a warm dinner plate. Garnish with lemon wedges and sprinkle with remaining nuts. Accompany with remaining macadamia butter. Serves 4. — *Kelly Bennett, San Francisco.*

PER SERVING: 696 calories, 60 g protein, 7.9 g carbohydrates, 48 g fat, 191 mg cholesterol, 263 mg sodium

FRESH FRUIT IN LEMON-GINGER SYRUP

- 1 large lemon
- 1 piece fresh ginger, about 1½ inches thick and 3 inches long
- ½ cup sugar
- 1½ cups water
- ¼ cup lightly packed fresh mint leaves
- 3 to 4 cups fresh fruit, such as grapes, strawberries, or chunks of cantaloupe or honeydew melon
  Fresh mint sprigs

With a vegetable peeler, pare 8 strips of lemon peel (½ by 3 in., yellow part only). Cut 4 strips crosswise into very thin slivers. Place slivers and 4 remaining strips in a 3- to 4-quart pan.

Mince ½ of the ginger; thinly slice remainder and add all ginger to pan along with sugar, water, and mint leaves. Bring to a boil over high heat; stir often. Reduce heat and simmer, uncovered, until reduced to 1 cup, about 15 minutes. With a slotted spoon, remove lemon strips, ginger slices, and mint leaves.

Let syrup cool, about 1 hour. (If made ahead, cover and chill up to 5 days.) Place equal portions of fruit in each of 4 dessert bowls or glasses; spoon syrup equally over each serving. Garnish with mint sprigs. Makes 4 servings. — *Carolee Luper, St. Helena, Calif.*

PER SERVING: 165 calories, 1.4 g protein, 43 g carbohydrates, 0.6 g fat, 0 mg cholesterol, 9.9 mg sodium

Autumnal Popovers

PERFECT FOR COOL-WEATHER MEALS, *these popovers get their special character from wholesome grains, nuts, and cheese.*

You start with the basic smooth batter of eggs, flour, and milk, then add one of four seasoning combinations: wild rice and parmesan cheese, bran cereal and cheddar cheese, rolled oats and hazelnuts, or cornmeal and green onion.

The seasonings give more body to the popovers, which are not as thin and hollow as the plain ones. You can bake them in regular muffin pans, cast-iron popover pans, or in glass or ceramic custard cups.

HARVEST POPOVERS

> About 2 tablespoons butter or margarine, at room temperature
> 2 large eggs
> 1 cup all-purpose flour
> ¼ teaspoon salt
> 1 cup milk
> Harvest ingredients (choices follow)

Butter 8 muffin cups or heavy popover cups (each 2 to 2½ in. wide), or 6 to 8 custard cups (4- to 5-oz. size).

In a blender or with an electric mixer, whirl or beat eggs with flour, salt, and milk until very smoothly mixed. Stir in selected harvest ingredients. At once, ladle batter equally into buttered cups; fill to no more than ¼ inch below rims. If using individual cups, set them well apart in a 10- by 15-inch baking pan.

Bake in a 375° oven until popovers are puffed, very well browned, and firm to touch, about 50 minutes. Remove from oven and run a knife around the edge of each popover to loosen; invert from cups. Serve hot.

For extra-crisp popovers, return to baking cups, tilting popovers at an angle. Pierce sides with a thin skewer and return to turned-off oven for 5 to 10 minutes.

If made ahead, cool popovers on a rack; package airtight. Hold up to 24 hours. To reheat and recrisp, place popovers slightly apart in a 10- by 15-inch pan and bake in a 375° oven until warm, about 5 minutes. Makes 6 to 8.

Speckled with wild rice and cheese, these tall, crisp popovers are best hot.

Wild rice and parmesan. Rinse 3 tablespoons **wild rice** in a strainer under running water. In a 1- to 1½-quart pan, combine rice and 1 cup **water.** Bring to a boil on high heat; cover and simmer until tender to bite, about 45 minutes; stir occasionally. Drain well and let cool. Mix rice with ¼ cup grated **parmesan cheese** and 1 teaspoon grated **orange peel.**

PER POPOVER: 148 calories, 5.9 g protein, 16 g carbohydrates, 6.3 g fat, 83 mg cholesterol, 186 mg sodium

Bran and cheddar. Combine ⅓ cup **bran cereal flakes,** ¼ cup shredded **sharp cheddar cheese,** and ¾ teaspoon **dry rosemary leaves.** —*Lois Dowling, Tacoma.*

PER POPOVER: 141 calories, 5.3 g protein, 15 g carbohydrates, 6.6 g fat, 84 mg cholesterol, 166 mg sodium

Oats and hazelnuts. Place ¼ cup chopped **hazelnuts** or almonds in a 9-inch pie or cake pan. Bake in a 350° oven until golden, about 10 minutes. Combine nuts, ⅓ cup **quick-cooking rolled oats,** and ½ teaspoon **ground allspice.**

PER POPOVER: 156 calories, 5.2 g protein, 16 g carbohydrates, 7.9 g fat, 81 mg cholesterol, 130 mg sodium

Cornmeal and green onion. Combine ⅓ cup **yellow cornmeal,** ⅓ cup thinly sliced **green onion,** and 1 clove **garlic,** minced or pressed.

PER POPOVER: 156 calories, 5.2 g protein, 16 g carbohydrates, 7.9 g fat, 81 mg cholesterol, 130 mg sodium

Miniature Grapes

LILLIPUTIAN SIZE *distinguishes Black Corinth grapes, whose clusters are so small and artistically formed they seem to have been made by elves. These grapes are, nevertheless, a true seedless variety grown for many years in the West and dried to make Zante currants.*

Sometimes sold as "champagne grapes," flavorful Black Corinths are in season from mid-July to mid-October. Because you use one small cluster per serving, they add a bountiful look to fall dishes.

Here we capitalize on Black Corinths' decorative appeal. Balance a double cluster on the rim of a glass of fruity sparkling wine and pluck the tiny berries to enjoy as you drink—some people munch the most tender stems with the fruit.

You can grace a platter of cheese and crackers with these grapes. Or combine them with chicken to make an elegant variation on the classic véronique; briefly warm clusters in the sauce—to eat, push fruit from stems with your knife. For dessert, you can add sparkle to clusters with egg white and sugar, then freeze.

For an updated version of chicken véronique, accompany meat and sauce with tiny grape clusters.

SAUTÉED CHICKEN WITH CORINTH GRAPES

> 2 chicken legs with thighs attached (about 1 lb. total)
> ½ cup late-harvest sweet white wine, such as Johannisberg Riesling
> ½ cup whipping cream
> 2 clusters Black Corinth grapes (each about 1½ in. wide, 4 in. long)
> Salt and pepper

Frozen grapes echo sherbet's iciness. Sugar, egg white lend frosty appearance.

In a 10- to 12-inch frying pan over medium-high heat, cook chicken, turning occasionally until brown, about 12 minutes. Reduce heat to medium-low, cover, and cook until chicken is no longer pink at thigh bone (cut to test), about 15 minutes longer. Put chicken on plates; keep warm. Discard fat from pan.

To pan, add wine; boil, uncovered, on high heat until reduced to 2 tablespoons, about 3 minutes. Stir in cream. Place grapes in pan, reduce heat to medium; turn clusters several times until grapes are slightly softened and sauce is slightly thicker, about 3 minutes. Place clusters beside chicken, then pour sauce over both. Add salt and pepper to taste. Serves 2.

PER SERVING: 461 calories, 30 g protein, 9.2 g carbohydrates, 34 g fat, 169 mg cholesterol, 121 mg sodium

FROSTED CORINTH GRAPES

Make a few or many clusters. One large egg white and ¾ cup sugar will frost about 1½ pounds of grapes.

Lay clusters of rinsed, dry **Black Corinth grapes** flat (with stems, each should be about 1½ in. wide and 4 in. long). Lightly brush all over with slightly beaten **egg white,** turning fruit as you brush.

Have a helper hold each cluster horizontally by stem and fruit ends over a sheet of plastic wrap. Sprinkle evenly with **sugar,** turning each cluster as you work.

Holding stem, clip it with a clothespin to a freezer rack or cake rack taped on top of an empty can; be sure nothing touches grapes. Put plastic wrap beneath grapes to catch drips. Freeze until solid, about 3 hours. Nibble as is, or pair with **lemon sherbet,** sorbet, or ice cream. Store frozen grapes in plastic bags up to 2 months.

PER GRAPE CLUSTER: 64 calories, 0.5 g protein, 17 g carbohydrates, 0.1 g fat, 0 mg cholesterol, 4.1 mg sodium

Moscow (Idaho) Bar Cookies

FOR PROFESSIONAL *and home bakers, bar cookies have a special appeal: they are fast and easy because they require little individual handling. You make them by the slab, then cut them up to serve.*

These three recipes, by Joan Cunningham, are favorites of customers at the Main Street Deli in Moscow, Idaho. Each fills a standard baking pan.

Lemon cheesecake bars are layered; a cool-tasting cheese topping bakes on a thin nut crust. The second cooky—a firm, delicately flavored shortbread—gets its character from toasted almonds. And, finally, the chocolate-drizzled oat bars can be baked chewy or crisp.

LEMON CHEESECAKE BARS

> 3 tablespoons butter or margarine, at room temperature
> ¼ cup firmly packed brown sugar
> ½ cup all-purpose flour
> ½ cup chopped pecans or walnuts
> Cheesecake topping (recipe follows)
> 1 tablespoon finely shredded lemon peel (yellow part only), optional

In a food processor, whirl butter, sugar, flour, and nuts until a dough forms. Or rub mixture with your fingers until fine crumbs form, then pat firmly together. Press mixture evenly into an 8- to 9-inch-diameter baking pan with a removable bottom. Bake in a 350° oven until a medium brown color, about 20 minutes.

Spread cheesecake topping evenly over crust. Bake until topping is set in center when gently shaken, about 15 minutes. Cool, cover, and chill until firm, at least 1 hour or up to 2 days. Remove rim from pan and cut cooky into 12 wedges. Sprinkle with lemon peel; remove from pan with a spatula. Serve, or arrange in a single layer, cover, and chill up until the next day. Makes 1 dozen.

PER COOKY: 208 calories, 2.8 g protein, 21 g carbohydrates, 13 g fat, 51 mg cholesterol, 93 mg sodium

Cheesecake topping. In a food processor or with an electric mixer, mix until smooth 1 large package (8 oz.) **cream cheese,** at room temperature; ⅔ cup **sugar;** 1 **large egg;** 1 tablespoon **lemon juice;** 2 teaspoons grated **lemon peel** (yellow part only); and ½ teaspoon **vanilla.**

ALMOND SHORTBREAD

> 1 cup unblanched almonds
> 1¼ cups (⅝ lb.) butter or margarine, at room temperature
> ⅔ cup sugar
> ½ teaspoon almond extract
> 3 cups all-purpose flour

In a food processor or blender, coarsely chop almonds; set ½ cup of the large pieces aside. Whirl remaining almonds until very finely chopped. Add butter, sugar, and almond extract; whirl until well mixed. (Or, in a bowl, beat almonds with butter, sugar, and almond extract until creamy.) Whirl or stir in flour.

Press mixture evenly into a 10- by 15-inch baking pan; sprinkle with reserved nuts and press them lightly into dough. Bake in a 325° oven until a light golden color and firm in the center when gently pressed, about 25 minutes.

Immediately cut shortbread into about 3-inch squares, then cut each square diagonally in half. Leave cookies in pan and cool on a rack. Remove from pan with a wide spatula. Serve, or package airtight and store up to 3 days. Freeze to store longer. Makes 30.

PER COOKY: 156 calories, 2.3 g protein, 15 g carbohydrates, 10 g fat, 21 mg cholesterol, 79 mg sodium

PEANUT BUTTER OAT BARS

> 2 cups all-purpose flour
> 2 cups regular rolled oats
> 1½ cups firmly packed brown sugar
> ⅔ cup unsweetened shredded dry coconut
> ⅔ cup chopped walnuts or chopped unsalted roasted peanuts
> 1 cup (½ lb.) melted butter or margarine
> 1⅓ cups peanut butter
> ½ cup semisweet chocolate baking chips

In a food processor, whirl flour, oats, sugar, coconut, nuts, and butter until combined. (Or, in a bowl, stir together flour, oats, sugar, coconut, and walnuts; add butter and mix well.) Press mixture evenly into a 10- by 15-inch baking pan.

Bake in a 350° oven until edges brown lightly and cooky is firm when gently pressed in center, about 20 minutes. (Cooky will be chewy when cool; for a crisp cooky, bake until cooky is a darker golden color, about 5 minutes longer.) Cut into 3-inch squares. Leave cookies in pan and set on a rack; let cool. Spread peanut butter evenly over cookies.

Cut-in-the-pan cookies take shape with a knife stroke—(from top) lemon cheesecake, almond shortbread, peanut butter oat bars.

Melt chocolate over hot but not simmering water (or in nonmetal container in a microwave oven) just until soft; stir until smooth.

With a teaspoon or a pastry bag fitted with a ¹⁄₁₆-inch-diameter tip, drizzle chocolate in thin lines over peanut butter. With a wide spatula, lift cookies from pan. Serve, or store airtight in a single layer up to 3 days. Makes 15.

PER COOKY: 510 calories, 11 g protein, 50 g carbohydrates, 32 g fat, 33 mg cholesterol, 241 mg sodium

More October Recipes

OTHER OCTOBER ARTICLES *also take a healthy turn. Recipes feature a curry-seasoned soup, hearty pumpernickel bread, a make-ahead chicken salad you can serve hot or cold, cheese-and-apple sandwiches tucked into pocket bread, and a new version of granola with a hint of orange.*

ACORN CURRY SOUP

Baking is the first step for this richly flavored soup. Dry oven heat brings out the sweetness of acorn squash and onions; curry and chilies add zest.

- 2 **acorn squash (2¾ to 3 lb. total)**
- 2 **tablespoons butter or margarine**
- 1½ **teaspoons curry powder**
- ½ **to 1 teaspoon crushed dried hot red chilies**
- 1 **medium-size onion, chopped**
- 3 **cups regular-strength chicken broth**
- ¼ **cup sour cream**
  Watercress sprigs (optional)

Cut each squash in half lengthwise; scoop out and discard seeds.

Melt butter in a 9- by 13-inch baking dish in a 350° oven. Stir curry, chilies to taste, and onion into butter. Lay squash, hollow side down, in dish. Bake until tender when pierced, about 40 minutes.

Let squash stand until cool enough to touch. Scoop flesh from peel; discard peel. In a blender, whirl 1½ cups broth with half the squash and onion mixture until smoothly puréed; pour into a 3- to 4-quart pan. Repeat with remaining broth, squash, and onion mixture. (If made ahead, pour purée into a container, cover, and chill up to 1 week.)

Stir soup over medium-high heat until hot. Ladle into 4 to 6 shallow soup bowls. Stir sour cream until fluid; with a spoon, add a 2-inch strip to center of soup. Swirl cream with pointed tip of a paring knife to make a pretty pattern. Makes 6 cups, 4 to 6 servings.

PER SERVING: 146 calories, 3.1 g protein, 21 g carbohydrates, 6.9 g fat, 15 mg cholesterol, 77 mg sodium

RAISIN PUMPERNICKEL BREAD

Dense and dark, pumpernickel bread has considerable flavor and texture appeal if you like a hearty, peasant-style loaf. But this type of bread also packs a lot of nutrition, with its blend of rye flour, two forms of wheat flour (whole wheat and white), and plump raisins.

Cool swirl of sour cream adds final touch to soup made with squash and onions.

The dark color and intensity of flavor are contributed by molasses, cocoa, and instant coffee powder.

This is a one-loaf recipe; you can make it ahead and freeze all or part of the loaf. Try it warm, reheated, or toasted. It's equally appropriate for breakfast, or with a thick soup at lunch or supper.

- 2 **packages active dry yeast**
- 1¼ **cups warm water (about 110°)**
- 1 **cup** *each* **rye flour and whole-wheat flour**
- ¼ **cup dark molasses**
- 2 **tablespoons unsweetened cocoa**
- 1 **tablespoon instant coffee powder**
- ½ **teaspoon salt**
  About 1 cup all-purpose flour
- ½ **cup raisins**
- 1 **tablespoon salad oil**
- 2 **tablespoons cornmeal**
- 1 **large egg white**
- 1 **tablespoon water**

In a large bowl, combine yeast and warm water; let stand until softened, about 5 minutes. Add rye and whole-wheat flours, molasses, cocoa, coffee powder, and salt.

With a dough hook, electric mixer, or heavy spoon, beat dough until flour is moistened.

If using a dough hook, mix in 1 cup all-purpose flour. Beat at medium speed until dough is stretchy and pulls cleanly from bowl, about 3 minutes (if needed, add more all-purpose flour, 1 tablespoon at a time). Push raisins into dough.

If mixing by hand, stir in 1 cup all-purpose flour with a heavy spoon. Scrape dough onto a floured board. Knead, adding as little flour as possible, until dough is smooth and elastic, about 5 minutes. Pat raisins into dough, then

knead until well distributed. Place dough in an oiled bowl; turn to grease top. Cover bowl with plastic wrap, and let dough rise in a warm place until almost doubled, about 1 hour.

Sprinkle cornmeal in the center of a 12- by 15-inch baking sheet; set aside. Punch down dough. On a lightly floured board, knead dough to shape into a ball. Place dough on cornmeal and press to form a 6-inch round. Cover loaf lightly with plastic wrap; let rise in a warm place until puffy, about 30 minutes.

Beat together egg white and water; lightly brush loaf with egg mixture. Bake in a 350° oven until loaf is a rich, dark brown, about 30 minutes. Transfer to a rack. Serve warm or at room temperature. If made ahead, wrap airtight and store at room temperature up to overnight. Or freeze; unwrap to thaw. To reheat, place unwrapped loaf on rack in a 350° oven for about 20 minutes. Makes 1 loaf, about 2 pounds. —*Louise Galen, Los Angeles.*

PER OUNCE: 57 calories, 1.7 g protein, 12 g carbohydrates, 0.7 g fat, 0 mg cholesterol, 39 mg sodium

CURRIED COUSCOUS CHICKEN SALAD

Colorful, flavorful, easy. You can make it ahead, and it's good hot or cold. What is this paragon of culinary virtues? A well-seasoned couscous and chicken salad.

First, steep chicken breasts in broth; then use the broth—with curry lending character and currants adding sweetness—for the couscous.

Top salad with yogurt dressing.

- ¾ **pound (about 3 halves) boned and skinned chicken breasts**
- 2 **cups regular-strength chicken broth**
- 1 **cup couscous**
- ¼ **cup currants or raisins**
- 1 **tablespoon curry powder**
- ½ **teaspoon dry thyme leaves**
- ¼ **cup chopped parsley**
- 1 **small carrot, shredded**
- 1 **package (9 oz.) frozen artichoke hearts, thawed and drained**
- 1 **small red bell pepper, stemmed, seeded, and finely chopped**
- ¼ **cup chopped red onion**
- 4 **to 6 large lettuce leaves, rinsed and crisped**
- 2 **cups cherry tomatoes, rinsed**

1 medium-size cantaloupe (about 2 lb.), seeded and cut into wedges
Honey-yogurt dressing (recipe follows), optional
1 lemon, cut into 4 to 6 wedges

Put chicken and broth in a 5- to 6-quart pan over high heat. Bring to boiling; cover pan and remove from heat. Let stand until breasts are opaque in center of thickest part (cut to test), 16 to 18 minutes. Lift out chicken.

Bring broth to boiling over high heat. Add couscous, currants, curry powder, and thyme; stir and return to a boil. Cover, remove from heat, and let stand until couscous completely absorbs liquid, about 10 minutes.

Meanwhile, cut chicken diagonally into thin strips. With a fork, stir chicken, parsley, carrot, artichoke hearts, bell pepper, and onion into couscous. Serve; or cool, cover, and chill up to 2 days.

To serve, place a lettuce leaf on each of 4 to 6 dinner plates; scoop an equal amount of couscous mixture onto each leaf. Arrange tomatoes and melon wedges equally on plates. Accompany with honey-yogurt dressing and lemon wedges to flavor each portion. Makes 4 to 6 servings.

PER SERVING: 257 calories, 20 g protein, 41 g carbohydrates, 2 g fat, 33 mg cholesterol, 408 mg sodium

Honey-yogurt dressing. In a bowl, stir together ¾ cup **unflavored yogurt** and 1 tablespoon **honey**. Makes ¾ cup.

PER TABLESPOON: 14 calories, 0.5 g protein, 2 g carbohydrates, 0.5 g fat, 2 mg cholesterol, 7 mg sodium

CHEESE, CHUTNEY & APPLE SALAD POCKETS

Sometimes a sandwich doubles as a hand-held salad, as in this refreshing and colorful apple and cheese combination served in a pocket bread half.

The ingredients travel well, so if you want to go picnicking, store the freshly made apple salad in a rigid container; lay the walnuts and watercress on top, and cover. Place the salad and cheese in an insulated bag or carrier; serve within 4 hours.

2 tablespoons butter or margarine
1 cup walnut halves
2 medium-size (about 1 lb. total) Red or Golden Delicious or Granny Smith apples
2 tablespoons lemon juice

Tuck a chunk of brie cheese into this fresh salad of watercress, apple, nuts, and chutney nestled in pocket bread half.

½ cup Major Grey chutney, chopped
6 pocket bread rounds (each about 6-in. diameter), cut in half
6 cups watercress sprigs, washed and crisped
½ pound ripe brie cheese

Melt butter in a 10- to 12-inch frying pan over medium heat. Add nuts and stir often until they turn a darker brown, about 10 minutes. Drain nuts on paper towels.

Meanwhile, core apples and coarsely chop; mix with lemon juice and chutney. If made ahead, cover and chill apple mixture up to 8 hours.

Gently separate bread halves to form pockets. Mix nuts and watercress with apples. For each sandwich, spoon salad generously into a pocket bread half and add a bite-size chunk of brie. Makes 12 sandwiches, 6 servings.

PER SERVING: 475 calories, 16 g protein, 60 g carbohydrates, 20 g fat, 48 mg cholesterol, 701 mg sodium

FAVORITE GRANOLA

A popular breakfast cereal in many households, granola seems always to have one more variation. This one, enlivened with a fresh touch of orange and sweetened with honey, can be served with milk or eaten plain for snacking.

6 cups regular rolled oats
1½ cups sweetened flaked dry coconut
1 cup unroasted, unsalted sunflower seeds
¾ cup unroasted, unsalted cashews
¾ cup slivered almonds
⅔ cup lightly toasted wheat germ
1 tablespoon grated orange peel
½ cup honey
½ cup salad oil
1 teaspoon vanilla

In a large bowl, stir oats with coconut, sunflower seeds, cashews, almonds, wheat germ, and orange peel.

Combine honey and oil in a 1- to 2-quart pan; place over medium heat until hot. Stir in vanilla and pour liquid into oat mixture; stir to mix well.

Divide oat mixture evenly between 2 pans, each 9 by 13 inches. Bake, uncovered, in a 325° oven, stirring every 5 minutes, until granola is a dark golden color, 35 to 45 minutes total. If pans are in 1 oven, alternate positions halfway through baking. Let granola cool in pans; stir occasionally. Serve, or store airtight up to 4 weeks. Makes about 3 quarts. —*Toni Teineke, Seattle.*

PER SERVING: 262 calories, 7.3 g protein, 25 g carbohydrates, 16 g fat, 0 mg cholesterol, 4.1 mg sodium

Serve chocolate bread for breakfast or at tea. Powdered sugar decorates it.

CHOCOLATE BREAD

1½ cups warm water (110°)
1 package active dry yeast
2 tablespoons granulated sugar
4 cups all-purpose flour
⅓ cup unsweetened cocoa
2 tablespoons butter or margarine
1 large egg
¾ teaspoon salt
1 package (6 oz.) semisweet chocolate baking chips
Powdered sugar

In a bowl, mix water, yeast, and sugar; let stand about 5 minutes. Stir in 3 cups flour, cocoa, butter, egg, and salt. Beat with an electric mixer until dough is very stretchy, about 10 minutes. Stir in chocolate baking chips.

Sprinkle remaining flour on a board; scrape dough onto flour. Knead 5 or 6 turns to barely incorporate flour and make a smooth round, about 1 minute. Place dough in a greased 10- by 15-inch baking pan. Cover with plastic wrap; let rise until puffy, about 1 hour. Bake, uncovered, in a 350° oven until dark brown, about 50 minutes. On hot bread, set a paper stencil; rub powdered sugar through a fine strainer onto it; lift off. Serve hot or warm. Makes 1 loaf, about 2¼ pounds. — *Tenia Holland, Salt Lake City.*

PER OUNCE: 88 calories, 2.1 g protein, 14 g carbohydrates, 2.8 g fat, 9.3 mg cholesterol, 55 mg sodium

Blueberries and fruit jam make sauce for quick-to-cook chicken breasts.

CHICKEN BREASTS WITH BLUEBERRIES

2 tablespoons butter or margarine
2 whole chicken breasts (about 2 lb. total), cut in half, skinned if desired
⅓ cup peach or apricot jam
3 tablespoons Dijon mustard
⅓ cup frozen unsweetened blueberries
⅓ cup white wine vinegar
Watercress or parsley sprigs

In a 10- to 12-inch frying pan over medium-high heat, melt butter. Add chicken, meat side down; cook until brown, about 3 minutes, then turn chicken over.

Meanwhile, mix jam and mustard, mashing pieces of fruit. Spread jam mixture over meaty side of breasts; sprinkle with blueberries. Turn heat to medium-low and cook, covered, until breasts are no longer pink in center (cut to test), about 15 minutes. With a slotted spoon, lift chicken and blueberries onto a platter; keep warm.

Add vinegar to pan; scrape browned bits free. Boil on high heat until liquid, including juices drained from chicken platter, is reduced by ⅓ and thickened. Pour sauce over the chicken; garnish with watercress. Makes 4 servings. — *Sally Vog, Springfield, Ore.*

PER SERVING: 458 calories, 38 g protein, 22 g carbohydrates, 23 g fat, 132 mg cholesterol, 514 mg sodium

Pungent cilantro teams with basil in this refreshing variation on pesto.

BASIL-CILANTRO SAUCE FOR PASTA

1½ cups firmly packed fresh basil leaves
½ cup firmly packed fresh cilantro (coriander) leaves
3 cloves garlic
¾ cup grated parmesan cheese
½ cup olive oil
¼ cup *each* pine nuts and walnuts
½ cup half-and-half (light cream)
½ cup (¼ lb.) melted butter or margarine
Hot cooked pasta
Salt and pepper

In a food processor or blender, whirl basil, cilantro, garlic, parmesan, and oil until smoothly puréed. Add nuts and whirl until coarsely chopped. Add cream and butter and whirl just to mix.

If made ahead, cover, and chill up to 1 week. To serve, stir, then pour into a 1- to 2-quart pan and stir over medium heat until hot. Or place in a nonmetal bowl in a microwave on half power (50 percent) until warm, about 4 minutes; stir often. Makes about 2⅓ cups sauce; allow ⅓ cup for 1 cup pasta. Add salt and pepper to taste. — *Lynn Viale, Gilroy, Calif.*

PER TABLESPOON SAUCE: 73 calories, 1.3 g protein, 1.2 g carbohydrates, 7.3 g fat, 9.2 mg cholesterol, 57 mg sodium

Mazatlán Potato Salad

1 quart diced, cooked thin-skinned potatoes (1½ lb. uncooked)
1 can (10 to 12 oz.) corn kernels, drained
½ cup sliced celery
⅔ cup chopped red bell pepper
½ cup chopped red onion
⅓ cup salad oil
3 tablespoons cider vinegar
2 teaspoons chili powder
1 clove garlic, minced
½ teaspoon liquid hot pepper seasoning
Salt and pepper
Tortilla crisps (directions follow)

In a bowl, combine potatoes, corn, celery, bell pepper, and onion. Add oil, vinegar, chili powder, garlic, hot pepper seasoning, and salt and pepper to taste. Serve with crisps. Serves 6. — *Joyce Stetson, Angels Camp, Calif.*

PER SERVING: 277 calories, 4.3 g protein, 38 g carbohydrates, 13 g fat, 0 mg cholesterol, 69 mg sodium

Tortilla crisps. Dip 4 **corn tortillas** (6½- to 7-in. size) into water; drain. Stack tortillas and cut into shapes such as wide arrows or triangles. Lay pieces in a single layer in a 10- by 15-inch pan. Sprinkle lightly with **salt.** Bake in a 450° oven for 4 minutes; turn over, then bake until crisp, about 3 minutes longer. Serve warm or cool.

Crisp tortilla cutouts go with chili-flavored potato salad.

Dona Elena's Fish Soup

About 1¼ pounds thin-skinned potatoes, scrubbed and diced
1 large red bell pepper, stemmed, seeded, and diced
1 medium-size onion, diced
¾ cup chopped celery tops (including leaves)
¼ cup olive oil or salad oil
1 quart regular-strength chicken broth
1 can (14½ oz.) stewed tomatoes
½ cup Spanish-style olives
About 2 pounds lingcod fillets
2 tablespoons lime juice

1 tablespoon chopped fresh dill or 1 teaspoon dry dill weed
4 cloves garlic, minced or pressed

In a 5- to 6-quart pan on medium heat, cook potatoes, bell pepper, onion, and celery in oil until vegetables are lightly browned, 15 to 20 minutes; stir often.

Add broth, tomatoes and their liquid, and olives. Bring to a boil; cover and simmer gently until potatoes are tender when pierced, another 15 to 20 minutes.

Cut fillets in 6 to 8 equal pieces. Add to soup along with lime juice, dill, and garlic. Cover and simmer until fish flakes when prodded, about 5 minutes. Serves 6 to 8. — *Helen Kennedy, Albuquerque.*

PER SERVING: 262 calories, 24 g protein, 20 g carbohydrates, 10 g fat, 59 mg cholesterol, 444 mg sodium

Poached fish fillet rests on vegetables in broth; dill also flavors soup.

Vanilla Cheese Cloud with Berries

1 large package (8 oz.) cream cheese
½ cup sugar
1 vanilla bean (4 to 6 in.), or 1 teaspoon vanilla
2 cups sour cream or unflavored yogurt
8 cups berries (hulled strawberries, raspberries, blackberries), rinsed and drained; or partially thawed unsweetened berries
Mint sprigs

In the large bowl of an electric mixer, combine cream cheese and sugar. Slit vanilla bean lengthwise and, with the tip of a knife, scrape seeds from the bean into the bowl (or add vanilla). Beat mixture until smooth and fluffy. Beating on high speed, add sour cream by the spoonful, mixing until each addition is smoothly incorporated.

Mound berries onto 1 side of a wide bowl. Pour cheese mixture beside the fruit. Garnish with mint sprigs. Spoon portions of fruit and cream into individual bowls. Serves 8 to 10. — *Kim Hayworth, Brisbane, Calif.*

PER SERVING: 254 calories, 3.9 g protein, 21 g carbohydrates, 18 g fat, 45 mg cholesterol, 93 mg sodium

Cool mix of cream cheese, sour cream is banked against fresh or frozen berries.

THE SEED TRADE *uses the term "synthetic novelty" to describe an old flower or vegetable variety that is being reintroduced with a new name or a new promotional gimmick. Although most synthetic novelties slip quietly overboard during the night, a few survive to become staples. One such is the spaghetti squash.*

If you're over 50, you might remember a brief flurry of catalogs with badly printed images of the miraculous vegetable spaghetti. This wonder was represented as a gigantic watermelon-shaped object cut in half and spilling forth a river of spaghetti, apparently already cooked al dente *or beyond. Disappointment had to follow such promotion, and the vegetable spaghetti soon disappeared.*

A few years ago, it reappeared under a more accurate name, spaghetti squash, and this time it's sticking around. It is not spaghetti, but very good squash: though stringy in appearance, its flesh is tender-crisp and mild in flavor. And it takes well to a wide variety of sauces. Ted Kaye serves it with a turkey-tomato-chili sauce to make a low-fat, low-calorie alternative to spaghetti with meat sauce.

SPAGHETTI SQUASH WITH TURKEY SAUCE

- 1 spaghetti squash, about 3 pounds
- 1 pound ground turkey
- 1 medium-size red or green bell pepper, stemmed, seeded, and diced
- ¼ pound mushrooms, sliced
- 1 can (4 oz.) diced green chilies
- 1 jar (about 15 oz.) spaghetti sauce
- ½ teaspoon dry Italian seasoning mix
  Salt and cayenne
  About ¾ cup freshly grated parmesan cheese

To bake squash, rinse and pat dry. Pierce shell with tines of a fork in several places. Place in a baking pan (9 in. square or 9 by 13 in.). Bake, uncovered, in a 350° oven until shell gives when gently pressed, about 1½ hours. Halfway through baking, turn squash over.

Cut squash in half lengthwise; scoop out and discard seeds.

To microwave squash, cut in half lengthwise; scoop out and discard seeds. Place squash, hollow side up, in a 9- by 13-inch nonmetal container. Cover with plastic wrap. Cook on full power (100 percent) for 10 minutes. Rotate each piece; cover again and let stand 5 minutes. Continue to cook until shell gives when gently pressed, 10 to 15 minutes longer.

Keep squash warm until ready to serve.

While squash cooks, put a 10- to 12-inch frying pan over medium-high heat; add turkey and stir until crumbly. Add bell pepper and mushrooms and stir often until mushrooms are lightly browned, about 10 minutes. Stir in the chilies, spaghetti sauce, and Italian seasoning mix; scrape browned particles free in pan. Season to taste with salt and cayenne. Boil gently for 8 to 10 minutes to blend flavors.

To serve, pull squash from shell with a fork and place on a rimmed platter. Spoon sauce over squash. Offer cheese to spoon onto portions. Makes 5 or 6 servings.

PER SERVING: 322 calories, 22 g protein, 26 g carbohydrates, 16 g fat, 60 mg cholesterol, 794 mg sodium

Studio City, Calif.

THOSE WHO LOVE *Japanese food point to its esthetic appeal—the harmony of bowls, plates, and tea things, and the eye appeal of artfully cut and arranged fish,*

"Spaghetti squash was represented as a gigantic watermelon-shaped object cut in half and spilling forth a river of spaghetti."

"Some Japanese dishes are not only thoroughly cooked but are real rib-stickers."

meats, *and vegetables. Some praise the subtle flavors, ethereal yet earthy, of boiled rice, seaweed, raw fish, and soy. Those who do not care for this cuisine say that it is bland, that it leaves your appetite unassuaged, and that it wiggles on your fork or chopsticks.*

Some Japanese dishes are not only thoroughly cooked but are real rib-stickers as well. Take Kazuo Orimo's simmered pork and potatoes: as stout and sustaining as any Irish stew, it nevertheless has a flavor that can be described only as classically Japanese. Dr. Orimo uses soy, sake, mirin, and green onions to achieve this flavor. And the pork is definitely cooked: it won't wiggle.

JAPANESE COUNTRY-STYLE PORK & POTATOES

8 green onions, ends trimmed
1 tablespoon salad oil
1¼ to 1½ pounds lean, boneless pork shoulder or butt, cut into ½-inch cubes
2 medium-size onions, sliced
 About ¼ cup soy sauce
⅔ cup sake or dry vermouth
½ cup *each* water and mirin (rice wine) or sweet sherry
4 or 5 medium-size red thin-skinned potatoes (about 1½ lb. total), scrubbed and sliced ¼ inch thick
¼ teaspoon pepper
2 teaspoons sugar

Cut the green onions into 1-inch lengths, keeping green and white parts separate.

To a 5- to 6-quart pan over medium-high heat, add oil. When hot, add pork, a portion at a time. Stir often until meat is well browned; remove from pan as browned.

Add sliced onions to pan and stir often until limp, about 5 minutes. Return meat to pan and stir in ¼ cup soy sauce, sake, water, and mirin; bring to a boil on high heat. Cover and simmer gently for 25 minutes. Add potatoes, the white part of the green onions, pepper, and sugar. Increase heat to bring liquid to a boil, then cover and simmer gently until pork and potatoes are tender when pierced, about 25 minutes.

Stir in green onion tops, then ladle into individual wide soup bowls or rimmed plates. Add soy sauce to taste. Makes 4 to 6 servings.

PER SERVING: 304 calories, 22 g protein, 31 g carbohydrates, 10 g fat, 63 mg cholesterol, 770 mg sodium

Kazuo Orimo, M.D.

Stockton, Calif.

ALTHOUGH HUSH PUPPIES *are the traditional fish-fry accompaniment to catfish, their generally neutral flavor and rich crustiness help them blend with Cajun and all other styles of Southern cuisine.*

Badly made, as they often are, they might well be used as ballast, or even anchors. But as made by Johnny Lee Newcomb, they have the lightness, if not of balloons, at least of soufflés. Encasing the tender, light interior is a crisp crust. And their mixed grains make them healthful. With maple syrup, they're a substantial breakfast or brunch bread to share company with fruit (or juice) and coffee.

MULTI-GRAIN HUSH PUPPIES

¾ cup yellow cornmeal
¾ cup buckwheat flour
1½ cups whole-wheat flour
1 teaspoon baking powder
½ teaspoon baking soda
1 teaspoon salt
1 tablespoon sugar
1 tablespoon finely chopped alfalfa sprouts (optional)
½ cup finely chopped onion
½ cup buttermilk
¾ cup milk

½ cup (¼ lb.) butter or margarine, melted
1 large egg
 Salad oil
 Maple syrup (optional)

In a large bowl, stir together the cornmeal, buckwheat flour, whole-wheat flour, baking powder, baking soda, salt, and sugar. In another bowl, combine sprouts, onion, buttermilk, milk, butter, and egg; stir into flour mixture until evenly moistened.

In a 3- to 4-quart pan or a wok, heat 1½ inches salad oil to 365° (use a deep-frying thermometer); adjust heat to maintain this temperature. Drop batter, 1 tablespoon at a time, into oil; add as much batter as will fit into the pan without crowding. Cook until golden brown on all sides and dry in the centers (cut to test), about 2 minutes. Lift out; drain on paper towels. Place on a rimmed pan in a single layer and keep warm in a 200° oven until all are cooked.

If made ahead, let cool as cooked; cover airtight up to overnight. Bake, uncovered, in a 350° oven in a single layer in a 10- by 15-inch rimmed pan until sizzling, about 15 minutes.

Serve plain or with maple syrup to add to taste. Makes about 5 dozen.

PER PIECE: 43 calories, 0.8 g protein, 5 g carbohydrates, 2.2 g fat, 9.6 mg cholesterol, 71 mg sodium

Johnny Lee Newcomb

Avery, Idaho

"Light as balloons may be exaggerating."

October Menus

A SIMPLE HALLOWEEN SUPPER, *ideal for trick-or-treaters eager to depart, kicks off this month's menus. The plan comes from the Johns family in Salt Lake City.*

Boned pork loin is the roast for a Sunday dinner or other family occasions. And for a leisurely autumn brunch, try a savory cheese, apple, and onion tart; it's good hot or cool, as schedules demand.

Pack the meal in individual baskets. Use emptied baskets for trick-or-treating.

Split rolls for sandwiches, spread with mustard or mayonnaise, and fill with sliced turkey, jack cheese, and lettuce. Pick up potato salad and turkey at the delicatessen, or prepare your own salad. You can make and frost the cupcakes up to a day ahead; anise extract gives the icing a delicate licorice flavor.

PUMPKIN CUPCAKES WITH LICORICE ICING

        2   large eggs
        1   cup sugar
    $\frac{1}{3}$ cup salad oil
        1   cup canned pumpkin
    $1\frac{1}{4}$ cups all-purpose flour
    $\frac{1}{4}$ teaspoon salt
    $\frac{3}{4}$ teaspoon *each* baking soda, ground allspice, and ground cinnamon
        Licorice icing (recipe follows)

In a large bowl, beat eggs, sugar, oil, and pumpkin until thoroughly blended; set aside. Combine flour, salt, baking soda, allspice, and cinnamon; add to pumpkin mixture and stir just until blended.

Spoon batter equally into 8 or 9 buttered or paper-lined 2½-inch muffin cups. Bake in a 350° oven until cakes spring back when lightly touched in center, 20 to 25 minutes. Invert onto racks and cool completely. Spread tops with licorice icing. Serve, or cover and store at room temperature up until next day. Makes 8 or 9.

PER CUPCAKE: 345 calories, 4 g protein, 51 g carbohydrates, 15 g fat, 75 mg cholesterol, 199 mg sodium

Licorice icing. Beat together ¼ cup (⅛ lb.) **butter** or margarine at room temperature; 1 cup **powdered sugar**, sifted; ¼ teaspoon **anise extract** or ½ teaspoon vanilla; and 1 tablespoon **milk** until well blended and fluffy.

Hungry halloween mouse pulls crisp red apple out of basket packed for supper. Inside, she'll find a turkey and jack cheese sandwich, potato salad, and pumpkin cupcake.

ROAST PORK FOR SUNDAY

Roast Loin of Pork with
Dijon-Caper Sauce
Buttered Pastina
Stir-fried Greens &
Shiitake Mushrooms
Ripe Pears   Brie Cheese
Cabernet Sauvignon   Sparkling Water

Succulent boned loin is easy-to-carve. As meat roasts, wash and prepare vegetables to stir-fry. Then, while reducing liquids for roast sauce, cook the pasta.

For dessert, offer sweet, juicy Bartlett or winter pears with a wedge of ripe brie.

ROAST LOIN OF PORK WITH DIJON-CAPER SAUCE

1 boned, rolled, and tied center-cut pork loin, 3 to 3½ pounds
¼ teaspoon pepper
1 cup dry white wine
2 tablespoons Dijon mustard
1 cup whipping cream
2 tablespoons drained capers

Sprinkle pork with half the pepper; place, fat side up, on a rack in a 12- by 15-inch roasting pan. Roast in a 375° oven until a thermometer inserted in thickest part of meat registers 155°, 50 to 55 minutes. Put roast on a platter; keep warm.

Tilt pan to skim off and discard fat. Add wine, mustard, and remaining pepper to pan; bring to a boil over high heat, stirring to loosen brown bits. Boil, uncovered, until reduced by half, about 3 minutes. Drain any juices from pork into pan. Add cream and capers; boil until reduced to 1¼ cups, about 3 minutes. Pour sauce into a small bowl. Slice meat crosswise; offer sauce to add to taste. Serves 6 to 8.

PER SERVING: 460 calories, 31 g protein, 1.6 g carbohydrates, 35 g fat, 142 mg cholesterol, 256 mg sodium

BUTTERED PASTINA

In a 1- to 1½-quart pan over medium heat, combine ⅓ cup **butter** or margarine and 2 cloves **garlic,** minced or pressed. Stir until melted; remove from heat.

Pour golden Dijon-caper sauce over slices of roast pork loin; accompany with greens stir-fried with shiitake mushrooms, and buttered rice-shaped pasta.

Meanwhile, in a 5- to 6-quart pan, bring 4 quarts **water** to boiling over high heat. Stir in 12 ounces (about 1½ cups) **rice-shaped** or other small **pasta** and cook until just barely tender to bite, 5 to 8 minutes; drain. Pour pasta into a serving bowl and add garlic butter, ½ cup grated **parmesan cheese,** and **freshly ground pepper** to taste; mix well. Offer additional grated **parmesan cheese** to add to taste to individual portions. Serves 6.

PER SERVING: 337 calories, 10 g protein, 43 g carbohydrates, 13 g fat, 33 mg cholesterol, 256 mg sodium

STIR-FRIED GREENS & SHIITAKE MUSHROOMS

¼ pound fresh shiitake mushrooms (or 8 medium-size dried shiitake mushrooms, about ½ oz.)
1½ pounds kale, baby bok choy, or red Swiss chard (or use ½ lb. of each)
2 tablespoons olive oil
Salt

Trim tough stems from fresh shiitake mushrooms; rinse and drain. (If using dried shiitake mushrooms, soak in hot water to cover until soft, about 20 minutes. Squeeze out excess water, then cut off and discard tough stems.) Cut mushroom caps into thin strips.

Remove and discard wilted leaves from greens. Cut stems or stalks from leaves. Slice stems diagonally into ½-inch-wide pieces. Cut leaves crosswise into ½-inch-wide strips. Wash well and drain.

Place a wok or 12- to 14-inch frying pan over medium-high heat; add oil. When oil is hot, add mushrooms and stem pieces of greens; mix well. Cover and cook until stems are tender-crisp when pierced, 2 to 3 minutes. Add leaves and stir-fry just until wilted, about 2 minutes longer. Season to taste with salt. Serves 6.

PER SERVING: 59 calories, 2.1 g protein, 3.3 g carbohydrates, 4.8 g fat, 0 mg cholesterol, 74 mg sodium

(Continued on next page)

AUTUMN BRUNCH

Golden Apple-Onion Tart
Crisp Bacon
Pineapple, Grape & Kiwi Fruit Bowl
Tomato Juice   Hot Spiced Coffee

On a blustery morning, enjoy this warm tart with crisp bacon and fresh fruit.

If you like, make the tart early in the day and offer at room temperature. Brown bacon (about 1 lb.) and keep warm, or reheat in oven. For the fruit bowl, mix about 6 cups total of fresh pineapple, peeled and cored; red seedless grapes; and peeled slices of kiwi fruit.

Use this press-in pastry to line the pie pan for the quiche; you can make the dough the night before.

GOLDEN APPLE-ONION TART

	Press-in pastry (recipe follows)
¼	cup (⅛ lb.) butter or margarine
2	large onions, thinly sliced
2	large Golden Delicious apples, peeled, cored, and sliced
½	pound white cheddar cheese, shredded
3	large eggs
1	cup half-and-half (light cream) or milk
¼	teaspoon dry mustard
⅛	teaspoon pepper

Evenly press pastry over bottom and sides of a 10-inch pie pan or quiche pan. Bake in a 300° oven until pale golden brown, 25 to 30 minutes. Remove from oven.

Meanwhile, in a 12- to 14-inch frying pan, melt butter over medium heat. Add onions and stir occasionally until they are limp, about 15 minutes. Stir in apples; cook until onions are very limp and golden, about 10 minutes longer; turn often with a spatula. Evenly distribute onion mixture in pastry; sprinkle with cheese.

In a large bowl, whisk together eggs, half-and-half, mustard, and pepper until well blended; pour evenly over cheese. Bake in a 375° oven until tart is golden brown and center appears firm when pan is gently shaken, 25 to 30 minutes. Serve hot or at room temperature; cut into wedges. Serves 6 to 8.

PER SERVING: 466 calories, 14 g protein, 28 g carbohydrates, 33 g fat, 224 mg cholesterol, 399 mg sodium

Press-in pastry. In a food processor or with your fingers, whirl or rub 1½ cups **all-purpose flour** with ½ cup (¼ lb.) **butter** or margarine, cut into small pieces, until fine crumbs form. Add 1 **large egg**; process or stir with a fork until dough holds together when pressed.

Orange Zest Apple Pie (page 256)

T he festive season of
traditional family gatherings is ushered in with a pick-and-
choose Thanksgiving buffet, designed to please diners of
different generations and food preferences. Juicy apples from
the autumn harvest appear in a pair of hearty apple
pies. Patriotic paraphernalia add fun to our election night
buffet menu, but its make-ahead dishes work equally well
for an autumn dinner party. Among other featured ideas are
layered stratas for brunch or supper, an appetizer of brie
in a hot and flaky pastry package, and a selection of down-
to-earth vegetable dishes.

The Adjustable Thanksgiving

TRADITION TAILORED *to personal taste is the essence of this fine Thanksgiving dinner. Almost every dish offers pick-and-choose options designed to please all generations, with particular regard for finicky eaters, fancy eaters, and those with special dietary considerations.*

Turkey, of course, is the mainstay of the meal. But from the first nibble, you have choices to make. The appetizer tray includes raw vegetables and plain crackers for the cautious and those concerned with fat or cholesterol. For hearty appetites, there are cold cured meats, a mellow vegetable spread, and polenta flat bread. Dried tomatoes and fresh herbs should satisfy more cosmopolitan tastes.

Set up both the salad and main courses as buffets so people can make their selections easily. At the salad bar, offer separate bowls of mild lettuces and of more pungent-flavored leaves. Each person chooses the greens that suit his or her taste, then moistens the greens with lemon, a simple vinaigrette, or a creamy balsamic vinegar and chili dressing. Offer crisp toasted nuts and croutons—again to add to taste.

Once the salad is organized, people can go directly to the table, treating the salad

---

TAILOR-MADE THANKSGIVING DINNER

Appetizer Platter with Polenta Triangles
Mild & Bitter Greens Salad Buffet
Toasted Pine Nuts
Herb Cheese Croutons
Roast Turkey
Brown Turkey Gravy with White Wine
Wild & Tame Rice Stuffings
Roasted Red & Yellow Potatoes with Onions
Leek Bundles & Peas
Poached Cranberry & Citrus Relish
Caramelized Ginger Relish
Crisp Rolls   Butter Balls
Milk or Fruit Punch
Dry Sauvignon Blanc
Merlot
Orange Zest Apple Pie
Apple Pie with Satin Caramel Cream
Coffee

---

as a first course. Or they can deposit their salad at the table, then proceed to the turkey buffet to collect ingredients for the main course.

The plump turkey contains a wild rice stuffing with lots of seasonings; alongside bakes a simpler, lightly seasoned brown rice stuffing. Have guests choose the kind they prefer—or they can try some of both.

The giblet gravy is rich and dark. Enhance its flavor with a touch of white wine.

To solve the white versus sweet potato dilemma, roast both vegetables together with small onions, browning and glazing vegetables in a modest amount of olive oil. At the buffet, you can season them with salt and pepper or dot with sherry butter.

Hot or room-temperature peas flanked by tepid poached leeks can be enjoyed plain or enlivened with a tart caper sauce.

For relishes, there are a cooked cranberry classic and one with caramelized fresh ginger.

Dessert features more options, with homey and/or dressed-up apple pie. One pie has a double crust and orange sauce. The other is streusel covered with a cream topping (the pie recipes are on page 256).

Build-it-yourself First Course

From this colorful display of purchased and prepared elements, everyone is sure to find an item or combination that pleases.

APPETIZER PLATTER

- 2 ounces parmesan cheese
- ¼ cup dried tomatoes packed in oil, drained and slivered
- ¼ cup lightly packed fresh basil leaves
  Caramelized onion and roasted pepper spread (recipe follows)
- 1 can (6 oz.) pitted large black ripe olives, drained
- ¾ to 1 cup calamata olives or niçoise olives
- ⅓ pound *each* thinly sliced prosciutto and dry salami
- 2 large carrots, peeled and cut into thin sticks
- 1 *each* large red and yellow bell peppers, stemmed, seeded, and cut into wide strips

Polenta triangles (recipe follows) or unsalted or salted crackers

With a vegetable peeler, shave parmesan into very thin slices. If desired, mound in individual bowls on a large platter the cheese, tomatoes, basil, onion spread, ripe olives, and calamata olives. Or mound ingredients individually on the platter. Arrange alongside the prosciutto, salami, carrots, peppers, and crackers. To serve, let guests choose foods to nibble plain or on crackers or polenta triangles. Serves 12.

PER TABLESPOON: 16 calories, 0.2 g protein, 1.1 g carbohydrates, 1.3 g fat, 0 mg cholesterol, 6 mg sodium

Caramelized onion and roasted pepper spread. Combine 3 tablespoons **olive oil** and 3 large **onions,** thinly sliced, in a 10- to 12-inch frying pan over medium-high heat. Stir often until onions are golden and very limp, 20 to 25 minutes; reduce heat if onions begin to brown. Add 1 jar (7¼ oz.) **roasted red peppers,** 2 table-

spoons **tomato paste,** and 1 teaspoon **fresh thyme leaves** (or ¼ teaspoon dry thyme leaves); stir often to blend flavors, about 5 minutes longer. Let cool, then chop coarsely. If made ahead, cover and chill up until next day. Serve at room temperature. Makes 2 cups.

Polenta triangles. In food processor or a bowl, combine ⅔ cup **polenta,** 1 cup **flour,** ½ cup **butter,** and ½ cup grated **parmesan cheese.** Whirl or rub with your fingers until mixture forms fine crumbs. Add 1 **egg** and ¼ cup **milk;** whirl or stir just until moistened. Pat dough into a buttered 9- by 13-inch pan.

Bake in a 400° oven until surface is golden brown, 18 to 20 minutes; let cool. Cut into about 2-inch squares, then cut each square diagonally in half. If made ahead, cover and let stand up to overnight. Makes 48 pieces.

PER PIECE: 40 calories, 0.9 g protein, 3.6 g carbohydrates, 2.3 g fat, 12 mg cholesterol, 37 mg sodium

At the Salad Bar, Pick & Choose

These assorted greens and dressings cater to simple and complex tastes.

MILD & BITTER GREENS SALAD BUFFET

10 cups washed, crisped radicchio, Belgian endive, arugula, or escarole (1¼ to 1½ lb. total, untrimmed; use 2 or more kinds)

6 cups *each* washed, crisped romaine and butter lettuce (about 2 lb. total, untrimmed)

Lemon wedges

Balsamic vinegar and chili dressing (recipe follows)

Home vinaigrette (recipe follows)

Salt and pepper

Break greens into small pieces. Place bitter greens—radicchio, endive, arugula, escarole—in a bowl. Combine mild greens—romaine and butter lettuce—in another serving bowl. Have salad plates beside greens and accompany with lemon, balsamic dressing, vinaigrette, and salt and pepper to add individually. Makes 12 servings.

PER CUP OF GREENS: 18 calories, 1.5 g protein, 3.1 g carbohydrates, 0.3 g fat, 0 mg cholesterol, 8.4 mg sodium

Balsamic vinegar and chili dressing. In a blender or food processor, combine ¼ cup **balsamic vinegar** or red wine vinegar; 1 large **egg yolk;** 1 **fresh jalapeño chili,** stemmed, seeded, and chopped; 1 clove **garlic,** minced or pressed; whirl until chili and garlic are puréed. With motor running on high speed, gradually add 1 cup **extra-virgin olive oil** in a thin, steady stream until all is incorporated. If made ahead, cover and chill up to 1 week. Makes about 1⅓ cups.

PER TABLESPOON: 95 calories, 0 g protein, 0.2 g carbohydrates, 11 g fat, 13 mg cholesterol, 0.5 mg sodium

Home vinaigrette. Mix together ⅓ cup **red wine vinegar,** 1 cup **olive oil** or salad oil, 1 teaspoon **honey,** 2 tablespoons minced **shallots,** and ½ teaspoon **dry basil leaves.** If made ahead, cover and let stand until next day. Makes about 1½ cups.

PER TABLESPOON: 82 calories, 0 g protein, 0.5 g carbohydrates, 9 g fat, 0 mg cholesterol, 0.5 mg sodium

TOASTED PINE NUTS

Place 1 cup **pine nuts** in an 8- to 9-inch-wide pan. Bake in a 350° oven until lightly toasted, 8 to 10 minutes; stir occasionally. Let cool, then put in small bowl. If made ahead, cover and chill up to 1 week.

PER 1 TABLESPOON: 46 calories, 2.2 g protein, 1.3 g carbohydrates, 4.6 g fat, 0 mg cholesterol, 0.4 mg sodium

HERB-CHEESE CROUTONS

¼ cup (⅛ lb.) butter or margarine

¼ cup olive oil

1 teaspoon *each* dry basil leaves and dry oregano leaves

1 clove garlic, minced or pressed

½ pound (½ of a 1-lb. loaf) day-old French bread, cut into ¾-inch cubes

½ cup grated parmesan cheese

Melt butter with olive oil in a 12- to 14-inch frying pan over medium heat. Add basil, oregano, and garlic. Stir, then add bread cubes and mix well.

Pour cubes into a 10- by 15-inch pan and spread in an even layer. Bake in a 300° oven until very crisp and golden brown, 20 to 30 minutes. Remove croutons from oven and sprinkle with the parmesan cheese; mix gently. Let cool in pan, then pour into a serving bowl. If made ahead, store airtight up to 3 days. Makes about 3½ cups.

PER ¼ CUP: 145 calories, 3.1 g protein, 11 g carbohydrates, 9.9 g fat, 14 mg cholesterol, 211 mg sodium

(Continued on next page)

Pick and mix ingredients. Everyone can create a personal favorite.

First decision: white or dark meat. Then choose wild or tame rice stuffing, one or two kinds of roasted potatoes, leeks and peas, and accompanying sauces.

The Main Course: Still More Options

The stuffing recipe yields two kinds, with brown rice and several other ingredients shared. The basic brown rice stuffing bakes in a pan. The wild rice variation bakes in the turkey.

Stuffings, roasted vegetables, and leeks and peas all have make-ahead steps.

ROAST TURKEY WITH WILD & TAME RICE STUFFINGS & BROWN TURKEY GRAVY WITH WHITE WINE

 1 **turkey, 12 to 14 pounds**
    Brown turkey gravy with white wine (recipe follows)
    Wild and tame rice stuffings (recipe follows)
    About 3 tablespoons olive oil
    Fresh herb sprigs (parsley, rosemary, or thyme)

If turkey legs are trussed, release them; pull off and discard lumps of fat. Remove giblets, rinse, and start the gravy.

Rinse turkey inside and out and pat dry. Fill breast and body cavities of bird with portion of stuffing that contains the wild rice and Swiss chard. Skewer cavities shut. Rub bird all over with oil, then place breast down on a V-shaped rack set in a 12- by 15-inch roasting pan.

Roast in a 350° oven for 1 hour; remove from oven. Tip bird to drain juices into pan, then carefully turn it breast up. Insert a thermometer through thickest part of breast to bone. Roast until thermometer reads 160°, 2 to 2½ hours longer.

About 1 hour before turkey is done, place brown rice stuffing with spinach in a greased 2- to 2½-quart shallow baking dish. Cover tightly and bake until very hot in center, about 1 hour.

Remove skewers from bird; spoon stuffing into a wide, shallow bowl, mounding on 1 side. Mound spinach-flavored stuffing into bowl on the other side. Put turkey on a platter. Keep turkey and stuffing warm while you finish gravy. Garnish turkey and stuffings with herbs. Carve turkey and serve with your choice of stuffing, and gravy. Makes 12 to 14 servings.

PER 3-OUNCE SERVING TURKEY (WITHOUT SKIN OR BONE): 143 calories, 25 g protein, 0 g carbohydrates, 4 g fat, 65 mg cholesterol, 63 mg sodium

Brown turkey gravy with white wine. Wrap and chill remaining **turkey liver;** place remaining **giblets** in a 3- to 4-quart pan. Add 1 medium-size **onion,** quartered; 1 large stalk **celery,** chopped; 2 **dry bay leaves;** ½ teaspoon **dry thyme leaves;** 5 cups **water;** and **liquid from porcini mushrooms,** reserved from stuffing (recipe follows).

Bring to a boil over high heat, then cover and simmer until gizzard is very tender when pierced, about 2¼ hours. Add liver to pan; simmer 15 minutes more. Pour broth through a fine strainer into glass measuring cups; discard vegetables and giblets. You should have 5 cups broth; return to pan. If not, boil uncovered over high heat to reduce, or add **regular-strength chicken broth** to increase.

Pour fat and drippings from roasting pan into a glass measuring cup. Let stand for fat to rise, then ladle out and discard all but ¼ cup fat. Add this reserved fat and drippings to roasting pan. Add 1 cup broth to roasting pan; stir or whisk over medium-high heat until browned bits are free. Scrape mixture into pan of broth.

In a small bowl, stir ½ cup **cornstarch** with 1 cup **dry white wine** (or regular-strength chicken broth) until smooth; add to broth. Whisk or stir over high heat until boiling. Pour into a bowl or gravy boat. Makes 6 cups.

PER ¼ CUP: 41 calories, 0.5 g protein, 3.7 g carbohydrates, 2.6 g fat, 8 mg cholesterol, 3.5 mg sodium

WILD & TAME RICE STUFFINGS

Directions for how to cook the stuffings in and out of the turkey are at left.

 ½ **cup wild rice, rinsed and drained**
 1¾ **cups long-grain brown rice**
 1½ **ounces dried porcini (cêpes, boletus) mushrooms**
 ⅓ **pound *each* hot and mild Italian sausage, casings removed**
 ¼ **cup olive oil or salad oil**
 2 **medium-size onions, chopped**
 3 **cloves garlic, minced or pressed**
 ¼ **pound mushrooms, sliced**
 2½ **tablespoons minced fresh marjoram leaves or 1 tablespoon dry marjoram leaves**
 2½ **tablespoons minced fresh sage or 1 tablespoon rubbed sage**

 1¼ **cups sliced celery**
 ½ **pound Swiss chard, rinsed well, drained, and finely chopped**
 ¾ **pound spinach (stems and wilted leaves removed), rinsed well, drained, and finely chopped**
 1 **cup (4 oz.) grated parmesan cheese**
 ¾ **cup dry white wine**
 ½ **cup regular-strength chicken broth**
    Salt and pepper

In a 1- to 2-quart pan, put 1½ cups water. In a 3- to 4-quart pan, put 3 cups water. Bring water in both pans to a boil over high heat. Add wild rice to smaller pan and brown rice to the larger pan. Cover and simmer until both rices are tender to bite, about 45 minutes. Drain wild rice. (If made ahead, let rices cool; cover and chill up to 2 days. Stir rices with a fork.)

Meanwhile, place porcini mushrooms in a bowl and add 1⅓ cups hot water. Let stand until mushrooms are limp, about 20 minutes, then gently squeeze in the water to help release any grit.

Lift out mushrooms. Pour porcini soaking liquid into another container, taking care not to disturb residue in bottom of bowl. Save liquid for gravy (at left); discard residue. Chop soaked mushrooms and set aside.

Place 2 frying pans, each 10 to 12 inches, over medium-high heat. Add hot sausage to 1 pan; add mild sausage to the other pan. Stir often, breaking sausage into small bits, until meat is lightly browned, about 5 minutes. With a slotted spoon, transfer to paper towels to drain, then put each sausage in a separate large bowl.

To each frying pan, add 2 tablespoons olive oil and half the onions. To hot sausage pan, also add garlic, porcini mushrooms, regular mushrooms, and about ⅔ each of marjoram and sage. To other pan, add remaining herbs and celery. Stir often over medium heat until vegetables are very limp, about 10 minutes.

Add chard to pan with mushrooms, spinach to pan with celery. Stir contents of both pans often over medium-high heat until greens are wilted and liquid has evaporated, 4 to 6 minutes.

(Continued on next page)

To bowl with hot sausage, add chard mixture, wild rice, 2 cups of the brown rice, half the cheese, and ½ cup wine. To bowl with mild sausage, add spinach mixture, remaining brown rice, cheese, ¼ cup wine, and broth. Mix both mixtures, then season each to taste with salt and pepper. If made ahead, cover and chill up to 1 day. Makes 12 cups total, 12 servings.

PER ½-CUP SERVING OF STUFFING WITH SWISS CHARD: 153 calories, 5.6 g protein, 16 g carbohydrates, 7.5 g fat, 12 mg cholesterol, 196 mg sodium

PER ½-CUP SERVING OF STUFFING WITH SPINACH: 154 calories, 5.5 g protein, 16 g carbohydrates, 7.6 g fat, 12 mg cholesterol, 186 mg sodium

ROASTED RED & YELLOW POTATOES WITH ONIONS

- 3 pounds red thin-skinned potatoes (2 in. wide), scrubbed and cut in half
- 6 small sweet potatoes or yams (2½ lb. total), scrubbed and cut lengthwise into 1-inch wedges
- 1½ pounds onions (1½ in. wide), peeled and cut in half
- 6 tablespoons olive oil
  Salt and pepper
  Watercress or parsley sprigs (optional)
  Sherry butter (recipe follows)

In each of 2 baking pans, 10 by 15 inches, combine ½ of the red potatoes, sweet potatoes, onions, and oil. Mix to coat vegetables with oil, then spread out in an even layer. Bake in a 425° oven until vegetables are browned, about 55 minutes. If using 1 oven, switch pan positions halfway through baking.

(If made ahead, bake vegetables until tender when pierced, about 35 minutes. Remove from oven, cool, cover, and let stand at room temperature up to 6 hours. Reheat, uncovered, in a 425° oven until browned, 25 to 30 minutes.)

With a wide spatula, lift vegetables from pan into a serving bowl. Add salt and pepper to taste and garnish with watercress sprigs. Offer sherry butter to add to taste. Makes 12 servings.

PER SERVING WITHOUT BUTTER: 240 calories, 3.9 g protein, 41 g carbohydrates, 7.1 g fat, 0 mg cholesterol, 19 mg sodium

Sherry butter. Beat until creamy ¾ cup (⅜ lb.) **butter** or margarine (at room temperature). Add 3 tablespoons **sherry vinegar** or red wine vinegar; blend well. Serve at room temperature. If made ahead, cover and let stand up to 6 hours; or chill up to 3 days. Makes ¾ cup.

PER TABLESPOON: 102 calories, 0 g protein, 0 g carbohydrates, 11 g fat, 31 mg cholesterol, 117 mg sodium

LEEK BUNDLES & PEAS

- 12 medium-size leeks (about 5 lb. total)
- 2 pounds frozen petite peas, thawed
- 6 thin lemon slices, cut in half
  Salt and pepper
  Mustard caper dressing (recipe follows)

Trim root ends off leeks. Gently peel off 1 outer layer from each of 3 of the largest leeks and reserve. Cut remaining tough green stems off leeks and discard. Cut leeks lengthwise in half, almost but not quite through; rinse well.

In a 5- to 6-quart pan, bring 3 quarts of water to boiling. Push reserved outer layers into water and cook just until limp, about 1 minute; lift out with a slotted spoon. Immerse layers in cold water until cool; drain. Cut each piece lengthwise into 4 strips, each about ½ inch wide and 10 to 12 inches long.

Wrap a leek strip around center of each split leek to hold the sections together; tie a double knot to secure. Return water in pan to boiling on high heat. Immerse leeks in water and cook until tender when pierced, 7 to 10 minutes. Immerse in cold water until cool; drain.

Place leeks on a serving platter. If you want to serve peas at room temperature, arrange alongside leeks. Serve, or cover and hold at room temperature up to 6 hours or chill up to overnight and return to room temperature to serve.

If you want to serve peas warm, pour into pan used to cook leeks. Add about ¼ cup water and cook until steaming over high heat, stirring occasionally. Drain and add to platter with leeks.

Garnish with lemon slices. Add salt and pepper to taste. Offer mustard dressing to add to taste. Makes 12 servings.

PER LEEK WITHOUT DRESSING: 81 calories, 2 g protein, 19 g carbohydrates, 0.4 g fat, 0 mg cholesterol, 2.6 mg sodium

PER CUP PEAS WITHOUT DRESSING: 50 calories, 3.5 g protein, 8.6 g carbohydrates, 0.3 g fat, 0 mg cholesterol, 102 mg sodium

Mustard caper dressing. Mix ½ cup **olive oil**, ¼ cup **lemon juice**, 1 tablespoon **Dijon mustard,** and 2 tablespoons drained **capers.** Serve, or if made ahead, cover and chill up to 2 days. Makes about 1 cup.

PER TABLESPOON: 70 calories, 0 g protein, 0.4 g carbohydrates, 7.8 g fat, 0 mg cholesterol, 64 mg sodium

POACHED CRANBERRY & CITRUS RELISH

- ½ cup water
- ⅔ cup *each* sugar and orange juice
- 3 tablespoons lemon juice
- 1½ cups fresh or frozen cranberries
- 2 teaspoons *each* finely shredded orange peel and lemon peel (colored part only)
  Salt

In a 1½- to 2-quart pan, combine water, sugar, orange juice, lemon juice, and cranberries; bring to a boil on high heat, stirring often. Reduce heat to maintain a gentle boil and cook, uncovered, until reduced to 1½ cups; stir often. Mix in orange and lemon peels; add salt to taste. If made ahead, cover and chill up to 5 days. Serve at room temperature. Makes 1½ cups. —*Michael Otsuka, Berkeley.*

PER 1 TABLESPOON: 29 calories, 0 g protein, 2.4 g carbohydrates, 0 g fat, 0 mg cholesterol, 0.2 mg sodium

CARAMELIZED GINGER RELISH

- 1 piece (about 3 oz.) ginger, peeled
- 1 cup honey
- ½ cup apple juice or cider
- 3 tablespoons soy sauce

With a knife, cut enough ginger into fine slivers about 1½ inches long and ⅟₁₆ to ⅛ inch wide to make ½ cup.

In a 1½- to 2-quart pan, combine ginger, honey, and cider. Bring to a boil on high heat. Reduce heat to simmering and cook, uncovered, until reduced to 1 cup. Stir in soy sauce. If made ahead, cover and chill up to 5 days. Serve at room temperature. Makes about 1 cup.

PER 1 TABLESPOON: 73 calories, 0.1 g protein, 6.3 g carbohydrates, 0 g fat, 0 mg cholesterol, 64 mg sodium

Come to a Political Party

Y OU'VE CAST YOUR VOTE. *Did your candidates win? Why not have some friends over to follow the election returns as they come in? You can serve a buffet dinner that pokes a bit of fun at the political jargon we've all heard so much of these past few months.*

Going somewhere else election eve? You can use just the menu—without political trappings—and share a comfortable veal-shank dinner with your friends another fall night.

Fresh peaches are hard to find this time of year, but we couldn't resist using their name in our dessert. You can substitute frozen peach slices or small oranges.

ELECTION NIGHT SUPPER

Republican Punch with Grape Ideas
Ballot Bites   Assorted Nuts
Democratic Stew
**Liberal & Conservative
Vegetable Caucuses**
Lame Duck Salad   Roll Call Rolls
Party Platforms   Campaign Promises
Candidates   Acceptance Peaches
Chenin Blanc   Cabernet Sauvignon

The oven does most of the work for this meal. The stew, both vegetable dishes, and duck (if you use it) all bake.

If you have two ovens, all can cook at the same time; if not, you need to stagger cooking. Start the meat early, and chill; do the conservative carrots next and let stand at room temperature while you roast the liberal potatoes. Keep the potatoes warm as meat, then carrots, reheat. Or delegate: assign some dishes to kitchens other than your own.

REPUBLICAN PUNCH WITH GRAPE IDEAS

For each serving, thread 4 or 5 **seedless grapes** onto the pointed end of a slender wooden skewer (about 8 in. long); you can glue a small paper flag to the blunt end of each skewer, if you like.

Fill a tall flute glass with about ½ cup (4 oz.) **natural** or brut **champagne** or sparkling wine. Add a grape swizzle (if you pour the wine over the fruit, it fizzes excessively).

PER SERVING: 91 calories, 0.2 g protein, 3.6 g carbohydrates, 0.1 g fat, 0 mg cholesterol, 6.2 mg sodium

Newscasters keep guests informed at buffet; patriotic paraphernalia adds to the fun. Our menu takes liberties with election jargon—and takes advantage of make-ahead steps.

BALLOT BITES

Present a tray of your favorite nibbling foods, including crisp vegetables such as **radishes, fennel,** and little **carrots.**

DEMOCRATIC STEW

12 to 14 pounds veal shanks, cut about 1½ inches thick
¼ cup (⅛ lb.) butter or margarine
¼ cup minced fresh ginger

2 tablespoons grated lemon peel
1 teaspoon dry thyme leaves
½ teaspoon ground cinnamon
7 to 8 cups regular-strength chicken broth
3 tablespoons *each* cornstarch and water, mixed until smooth
Cover-ups (directions follow)

Rinse veal and pat dry.

(Continued on next page)

Make-ahead dishes minimize last-minute party effort. Just before serving, reheat veal shanks and vegetable dishes, assemble salad.

Put 2 tablespoons butter in each of 2 pans, each about 12 by 14 inches. Set in a 475° oven. When butter sizzles, lay shanks in a single layer in pans. Roast, uncovered, for 30 minutes, then turn shanks over and alternate pan positions. Continue roasting until juices around shanks begin to brown, about 30 minutes longer.

Mix together ginger, lemon peel, thyme, and cinnamon. Remove meat from oven and sprinkle ginger mixture over it. Add 3 cups broth to each pan. With a spoon, scrape and stir to release most of the browned bits in pans.

Cover tightly with foil. Return to oven and bake 1 hour; alternate pan positions. Continue baking until meat is tender enough to pull apart easily, about 1 hour.

With a slotted spoon, lift shanks gently from pans and set aside. Pour broth through a fine strainer into a 1½- to 2-quart pan; press any liquid from residue in strainer. Discard residue. Add enough remaining broth to pan to make 3 cups.

Rinse roasting pans and set shanks gently back in them in a single layer. At this point, you can cover meat and broth and chill until next day.

Cover shanks tightly with foil. Place in a 350° oven until hot, about 15 minutes if warm, about 45 minutes if chilled.

Bring broth to boiling on high heat; stirring constantly, add cornstarch mixture and return to boiling. Arrange shanks on a large rimmed platter, then pour sauce over them and sprinkle with cover-ups. Makes 12 to 14 servings.

PER SERVING: 462 calories, 53 g protein, 3.2 g carbohydrates, 25 g fat, 194 mg cholesterol, 241 mg sodium

Cover-ups. Combine ½ cup minced **parsley**, 3 cloves finely chopped **garlic**, and 1½ tablespoons grated **lemon peel**.

LIBERAL VEGETABLE CAUCUS

    4 **pounds red thin-skinned potatoes (about 2½-in. diameter), scrubbed and quartered**
    6 **tablespoons olive oil**
    1 **head garlic, peeled and coarsely diced**
       Watercress sprigs, rinsed and crisped
       Salt and pepper

Mix potatoes and oil in a roasting pan, about 12 by 14 inches. Bake, uncovered, in a 475° oven for 30 minutes, then add garlic and turn potatoes with a wide spatula. Continue baking, turning at intervals, until potatoes are well browned, about 20 to 25 minutes longer.

If made ahead, keep potatoes warm, uncovered, up to 4 hours; flavor is best if potatoes don't get cold. (You can use the turned-off oven; leave door ajar until temperature drops to about 200°, then close.) Reheat, uncovered, in a 350° oven until hot, 15 to 20 minutes. Pour into a bowl and garnish with watercress. Add salt and pepper to taste. Makes 12 to 14 servings.

PER SERVING: 164 calories, 2.8 g protein, 25 g carbohydrates, 6 g fat, 0 mg cholesterol, 11 mg sodium

CONSERVATIVE VEGETABLE CAUCUS

    4   **pounds carrots, peeled**
    1½   **pounds red or yellow bell peppers, stemmed, seeded, and chopped**
    1   **large onion, finely chopped**
    6   **tablespoons olive oil**
    2   **tablespoons balsamic or red wine vinegar**
         Parsley sprigs
         Salt and pepper

Using a food processor or hand-operated slicer, thinly slice carrots crosswise. Combine them with the peppers, onion, and oil in a roasting pan, about 12 by 14 inches.

Bake uncovered in a 475° oven until carrots begin to brown around edges, about 15 minutes. Then cook and turn frequently until carrots are glazed dark brown (they cook down a lot), about 1 hour longer. Add vinegar and mix well. If made ahead, let stand at room temperature (cover when cool) up to 8 hours. Reheat in a 350° oven, uncovered, until warm, 15 to 20 minutes. Pour into a bowl; garnish with parsley. Add salt and pepper to taste. Makes 12 to 14 servings.

PER SERVING: 115 calories, 1.6 g protein, 15 g carbohydrates, 6.2 g fat, 0 mg cholesterol, 42 mg sodium

LAME DUCK SALAD

    ½   **to ¾ pound green- or red-leaf lettuce**
         About ½ pound *each* escarole and curly chicory (or all escarole or chicory)
         About ½ pound radicchio
         Lame duck (optional, directions follow)
         House dressing (recipe follows)
         Salt and pepper

Wash and drain lettuce, escarole, chicory, and radicchio, separating leaves from cores and discarding bruised leaves. Wrap lettuce in paper towels, enclose in plastic bags, and chill 30 minutes or up to 2 days.

Line 1 large or 2 medium-size salad bowls with several large lettuce leaves. Tear remaining lettuce in small pieces; coarsely chop escarole and chicory and add to bowl. Add radicchio. Top greens with duck, add dressing, and mix well. Add salt and pepper to taste. Serves 12 to 14.

PER SERVING: 160 calories, 8.9 g protein, 4.4 g carbohydrates, 12 g fat, 29 mg cholesterol, 165 mg sodium

Lame duck. Buy a cooked **Chinese barbecued duck** (about 2¾ lb.). Or rinse and pat dry a 5- to 6-pound duck (thawed if frozen); reserve giblets for other uses. Wrap raw bird in foil, put in a 9- by 13-inch pan. Bake in a 350° oven until meat is tender enough to pull easily from bones, about 2½ hours. Unwrap and let cool.

Pull meat from duck, discarding skin and bones. Tear meat into fine shreds. Use at room temperature. If made ahead, cover and chill up until next day.

House dressing. Combine 1 teaspoon **dry tarragon leaves**, 1 tablespoon **mustard seed**, ¼ cup **Dijon mustard**, ½ cup **balsamic** or red wine **vinegar**, ½ cup **olive** or salad **oil**, and 1 small **red onion**, thinly slivered.

ROLL CALL ROLLS

Cut 12 **bagels** in half crosswise. Fit, cut side up, in 2 pans, about 10 by 15 inches each. Brush lightly with about ¼ cup (⅛ lb.) melted **butter** or margarine. Sprinkle with 2 to 3 tablespoons minced **parsley**. If made ahead, cover with plastic wrap and let stand up to 4 hours. Bake, uncovered, in a 350° oven 10 minutes. Reverse pan positions and bake until sizzling, about 10 minutes. Serves 12 to 14.

PER SERVING: 187 calories, 5.2 g protein, 26 g carbohydrates, 7.4 g fat, 18 mg cholesterol, 369 mg sodium

CAMPAIGN PROMISES

Buy **amaretti cookies** or another crunchy type; serve with the advice that they crumble as readily as campaign promises.

PARTY PLATFORMS

Buy **shortbread cookies** or make some from a favorite recipe; like party platforms, they will prove fragile.

CANDIDATES

Offer the large **Medjool** or other **dates.**

ACCEPTANCE PEACHES

 1½ **cups dry red wine**
 ½ **cup sugar**
 1 **vanilla bean, 5 to 6 inches long**
 6 **tablespoons lemon juice**
  Peaches or oranges (directions follow)
  Fresh candied orange peel (directions follow)
  Candied violets (optional)

In a 5- to 6-quart pan, mix wine, sugar, vanilla, and juice. Bring to a boil on high heat and stir until sugar dissolves. Reduce heat to simmering; add peaches or oranges. Gently turn fruit in syrup to heat—about 5 minutes for whole peaches, about 10 minutes for frozen slices, about 5 minutes for oranges. Lift out fruit with a slotted spoon and put in a bowl.

Boil syrup, uncovered, until reduced to 1 cup. Let cool. Pour over fruit. Also spoon orange peel with its syrup over fruit. Garnish with candied violets. Serve, or let stand up to 4 hours. Serves 12 to 14.

PER SERVING: 120 calories, 1.2 g protein, 30 g carbohydrates, 0.1 g fat, 0 mg cholesterol, 2.8 mg sodium

Peaches or oranges. Select 12 to 14 **peaches** (about 2¾-in. diameter), or use 5 pounds frozen unsweetened peach slices. Or select 12 to 14 **oranges** (2¾- to 3-in. diameter). Immerse fresh peaches in boiling water to cover for about 10 seconds; drain, then peel. Pare 4 oranges as directed for candied peel, following. Cut remaining peel and membrane from the oranges.

Fresh candied orange peel. With a vegetable peeler, pare orange part only from 4 **oranges** (2¾- to 3-in. diameter). Then cut peel into very fine strands.

Acceptance Peaches end evening's proceedings. Use peaches or oranges.

Put peel in a 2- to 3-quart pan and add 3 cups **water;** bring to boil over high heat, uncovered, then drain. Repeat this step.

Add ¼ cup **sugar** and 1 cup **water** to peel. Boil over high heat, uncovered, until syrup makes big bubbles and is almost evaporated, about 10 minutes. Watch closely toward the end of cooking to avoid scorching. Stir in 2 tablespoons **orange-flavor liqueur** and remove from heat. Let stand until cool; if made ahead, cover and chill until next day.

Pioneer Country Pies

Autumn apples *are the mainstay of these pies from two good Utah cooks. One has a traditional double crust and a fragrant hint of orange, the other a streusel topping. Both have festive embellishments.*

For either pie, choose Golden Delicious, Granny Smith, Jonathan, McIntosh, or Winesap apples. Newtown Pippins are also a good choice for the double-crust orange pie, but they don't get juicy enough to bake well in the tapioca-thickened, streusel-topped pie.

ORANGE ZEST APPLE PIE

2¾ to 3 pounds apples
2 teaspoons grated orange peel
¾ cup firmly packed brown sugar
⅓ cup all-purpose flour
1 teaspoon *each* ground cinnamon and ground nutmeg
  Pastry for a 2-crust 9-inch pie, rolled to fit pan
1 tablespoon butter or margarine
1 egg
  Orange sauce (recipe follows)

Peel, core, and thinly slice apples into a large bowl and mix with orange peel. Stir together brown sugar, flour, cinnamon, and nutmeg; add to apples and mix well.

Line a 9-inch pie pan with 1 round of the pastry. Pour apple mixture into pan, patting to compact slices and mound in

A sprinkle of caramelized almonds and a puff of whipped caramel cream adorn streusel-topped shredded-apple pie.

center. Dot fruit with butter, cut into small pieces. Lay remaining round of pastry over fruit. Trim pastry to within ½ inch of pan rim and fold edges under, flush to rim. Flute edges to seal; or press together, then scallop with the cupped side of a teaspoon.

Combine pastry scraps, roll out, and cut into decorative shapes. Beat egg to blend, brush lightly over top of pie, place decorative pastry pieces on pie, and brush them lightly with egg. Slash pastry in several places so steam can escape.

Bake pie in a 375° oven until crust is a rich golden brown, 45 to 55 minutes. Cool on a rack, then serve warm or at room temperature. If made ahead, cover loosely and let stand in a cool place until next day. Cut into wedges and top with orange sauce to taste. Makes 8 to 10 servings. —*Carol Whitecar, Bountiful, Utah.*

PER SERVING: 337 calories, 3.4 g protein, 51 g carbohydrates, 14 g fat, 31 mg cholesterol, 244 mg sodium

Orange sauce. In a 1- to 2-quart pan, stir 1 tablespoon **cornstarch** with 1 tablespoon **water.** Add 1 cup **orange juice** and ¼ cup **orange marmalade.** Bring to a boil, stirring, over high heat. Serve hot or at room temperature. If made ahead, cover and chill up until next day; let come to room temperature, or stir over medium-high heat until hot, about 2 minutes.

PER TABLESPOON: 17 calories, 0.1 g protein, 4.5 g carbohydrates, 0 g fat, 0 mg cholesterol, 0.7 mg sodium

APPLE PIE WITH SATIN CARAMEL CREAM

⅓ cup quick-cooking tapioca
⅓ cup sugar
1 tablespoon ground cinnamon
¼ teaspoon ground nutmeg
⅛ teaspoon ground cloves
  About 4 pounds apples
  Pastry for a 1-crust 9-inch pie, rolled to fit pan
  Streusel topping (recipe follows)
  Satin caramel cream (recipe follows)
  Caramelized almonds (recipe follows)

In a large bowl, stir together the tapioca, sugar, cinnamon, nutmeg, and cloves.

Rinse apples, quarter, and core. Shred fruit coarsely in a food processor or on a shredder; you should have about 10 cups (fruit will darken). Discard any large pieces.

Add apples to tapioca mixture and stir well. Let stand, stirring occasionally, to let tapioca soften, about 45 minutes.

Spoon apple mixture into pastry, mounding it in the center and pressing gently to compact fruit slightly.

Sprinkle streusel topping over apples. Bake in a 375° oven until streusel is golden brown, about 1¼ hours. Cool on a rack; serve warm or at room temperature. If made ahead, cover lightly and let stand at room temperature up until next day.

Serve cream to spoon over pie wedges to taste; or swirl cream onto cool pie, then cut and serve. Sprinkle almonds onto portions to taste. Makes 8 to 10 servings. —*Jane Osborne, Salt Lake City.*

PER SERVING: 269 calories, 1.6 g protein, 48 g carbohydrates, 8.9 g fat, 6.2 mg cholesterol, 134 mg sodium

Streusel topping. In a bowl, combine 2 tablespoons *each* **all-purpose flour, sugar,** and **butter** or margarine. With your fingers, rub mixture until coarse crumbs form. Use, or cover and chill up to 2 days.

Satin caramel cream. In a 10- to 12-inch frying pan over high heat, stir ⅔ cup **sugar** and ¼ cup **water** until sugar dissolves. Without stirring, boil syrup, uncovered, until it is golden caramel in color, about 10 minutes.

Add ½ cup **whipping cream** and ¼ cup **water;** stir until caramel dissolves (it may harden at first), about 10 minutes. Let cool. Stir in 1 cup **whipping cream** and 1 teaspoon **vanilla;** cover and chill until cold, 1 hour or up until next day.

Whip cream until it holds soft peaks. If made ahead, cover and chill up until next day; stir before serving.

PER TABLESPOON: 36 calories, 0.2 g protein, 3.3 g carbohydrates, 2.5 g fat, 9 mg cholesterol, 2.8 mg sodium

Caramelized almonds. In a 10- to 12-inch frying pan over medium heat, stir 1 cup **slivered almonds** until light golden brown, about 4 minutes. Sprinkle ¼ cup **sugar** over almonds; stir until sugar melts and coats nuts, about 3 minutes. Pour mixture onto a sheet of foil; when cool, serve, or store airtight up to 1 week.

PER TABLESPOON: 62 calories, 1.7 g protein, 4.8 g carbohydrates, 4.4 g fat, 0 mg cholesterol, 1 mg sodium

Classic double-crust apple pie is reminiscent of pioneer days, but updated with an orange sauce.

Cheese-Bread-Egg Casseroles

Wᴴᴀᴛ's ɪɴ ᴀ ɴᴀᴍᴇ? *These make-ahead (8 to 36 hours) breakfast, brunch, lunch, or supper casseroles may be called stratas, fondues, puffs, or overnight casseroles, but they are all essentially the same. You start by fitting layers (strata) of bread, cheese, and other ingredients snugly in a baking dish; saturating them with eggs and milk; and letting the dish stand so the liquid soaks in. Baked, the dishes are consistently moist and creamy.*

The combination is flexible, with many opportunities for variations that each create a new dish. The first variables are the bread and cheese. Here we make use of dark pumpernickel with jarlsberg, sourdough with mozzarella, rye with Swiss, and whole wheat with cheddar.

Like sandwich fillings, good-tasting elements such as sardines and dill, sausage and salsa, sauerkraut and corned beef, or a mixture of vegetables all pair quite readily with these specific bread-and-cheese combinations.

Mᴇxɪᴄᴀɴ Pɪᴢᴢᴀ Cᴀssᴇʀoʟᴇ

Use canned or bottled salsa, which is cooked, rather than refrigerated salsas.

  1 **pound bulk pork sausage**
     About 1 loaf (1-lb. size, cut into ½-inch-thick slices) sourdough bread, crusts trimmed
  1 **pound mozzarella cheese, shredded**
  2 **cups canned mild red salsa**
  6 **large eggs**
  3 **cups milk**
     Parsley sprigs

In a 10- to 12-inch frying pan, cook sausage over medium-high heat, stirring to crumble and brown meat evenly, about 8 minutes; drain off the fat and discard; set meat aside.

Butter a 9- by 13-inch baking dish. Line bottom snugly with a single layer of bread, cut to fit (edges can overlap slightly). Make another layer of bread to fit on top, then lift out and set aside.

Sprinkle bread with half the cheese, then pour 1 cup of salsa over cheese, and scatter half the sausage over salsa. Cover with the reserved bread slices; repeat to make top layer.

Beat eggs and milk until blended and pour over casserole, moistening top evenly. Cover with plastic wrap and chill 8 to 36 hours. Bake, uncovered, in a 350° oven until edges of casserole are browned and center is firm when gently touched, about 50 minutes. Cool 15 minutes on a rack. Top with parsley, and cut into rectangles. Makes 6 to 8 servings.

Pᴇʀ Sᴇʀᴠɪɴɢ: 512 calories, 28 g protein, 33 g carbohydrates, 29 g fat, 286 mg cholesterol, 1,246 mg sodium

Rᴇᴜʙᴇɴ Fᴏɴᴅᴜᴇ

To cut sodium content, rinse drained sauerkraut with cool running water, then drain again.

     About 1 loaf (1-lb. size, ½-inch-thick slices) rye bread, crusts trimmed
  ½ **pound thinly sliced corned beef**
  2 **cups canned sauerkraut, drained**
  ½ **cup minced dill pickles**
  ½ **teaspoon caraway seed**
  1 **pound Swiss cheese, shredded**
  6 **large eggs**
  3 **cups milk**
  2 **teaspoons dry mustard**

Butter a 9- by 13-inch baking dish. Line bottom snugly with a single layer of bread, cut to fit (edges can overlap slightly). Make another layer of bread to fit on top, then lift out and set aside.

Cover bread with half the corned beef slices. Mix together sauerkraut, dill pickles, and caraway seed and distribute half the mixture evenly over the corned beef. Sprinkle with half the cheese. Cover with the reserved bread slices; repeat to make top layer.

Beat eggs, milk, and dry mustard until blended; pour over casserole, moistening evenly. Cover with plastic wrap and chill 8 to 36 hours. Bake, uncovered, in a 350° oven until edges of casserole are lightly browned and center is firm when gently touched, about 40 minutes. Cool 15 minutes on a rack, then cut into rectangles. Makes 6 to 8 servings. —*Geneva Shaver, Claremont, Calif.*

Pᴇʀ Sᴇʀᴠɪɴɢ: 595 calories, 38 g protein, 39 g carbohydrates, 32 g fat, 316 mg cholesterol, 1,603 mg sodium

Bʀᴏᴄᴄᴏʟɪ-Pʟᴜs Cᴀssᴇʀoʟᴇ

Different kinds of whole-wheat breads can be used in this dish. Choose a standard whole-wheat, one with wheat berries, or try a multi-grain bread.

     About 1 loaf (1-lb. size, ½-inch-thick slices) whole-wheat bread, crusts trimmed
  ¼ **cup (⅛ lb.) butter or margarine**
  1 **large onion, diced**
  ½ **pound mushrooms, rinsed and sliced**
  3 **cups cooked broccoli flowerets, or 1 package (16 oz.) thawed frozen broccoli spears**
  2 **tablespoons dry basil leaves**
  1 **teaspoon pepper**
  1 **pound cheddar cheese, shredded**
  6 **large eggs**
  3 **cups milk**

Butter a 9- by 13-inch baking dish. Line bottom snugly with a single layer of bread, cut to fit (edges can overlap slightly). Make another layer of bread to fit on top, then lift out and set aside.

In a 10- to 12-inch frying pan over medium-high heat, melt 2 tablespoons butter and add onion and mushrooms. Stir often until liquid evaporates and mushrooms are lightly browned, about 15 minutes. Spoon into a bowl.

Chop broccoli. Melt remaining butter in the frying pan and add broccoli; stir often until broccoli is very dry. In the frying pan, stir together broccoli, basil, pepper, and onion mixture.

Distribute half the vegetable mixture over bread, then cover evenly with half the cheese. Cover with reserved bread; repeat to make top layer.

Beat eggs and milk until blended and pour over casserole, moistening evenly. Cover with plastic wrap and chill 8 to 36 hours. Bake, uncovered, in a 350° oven until edges of casserole are lightly browned and center is firm when gently touched, about 45 minutes. Cool for 15 minutes on a rack. Cut into rectangles. Makes 6 to 8 servings.

Pᴇʀ Sᴇʀᴠɪɴɢ: 539 calories, 29 g protein, 33 g carbohydrates, 37 g fat, 295 mg cholesterol, 762 mg sodium

Serve layered sardines, cheese, and bread casserole with red onion and sour cream.

NORWEGIAN STRATA

    About 1 loaf (1-lb. size) thinly sliced dense-textured dark pumpernickel bread

1 **pound jarlsberg cheese, shredded**

3 **cans (3¾ oz. each, 28 to 38 count) small sardines**

6 **large eggs**

2½ **cups milk**

1 **teaspoon *each* ground nutmeg and dry dill weed**

1 **medium-size red onion, minced**
    Sour cream (optional)

Butter a 9- by 13-inch baking dish. Line bottom snugly with a single layer of bread, cut to fit (edges can overlap slightly). Make another layer of bread to fit on top, then lift out and set aside.

Sprinkle half the cheese over the bread in the dish. Arrange half the sardines in 2 rows on top of the cheese. Cover with the reserved bread slices, sprinkle with remaining cheese, and arrange remaining sardines in 2 rows on top of it.

Beat eggs, milk, nutmeg, and dill weed until blended; pour over casserole,

moistening entire surface. Cover with plastic wrap and chill at least 8 or up to 36 hours. Bake, uncovered, in a 350° oven until edges of casserole are lightly browned and center is firm when gently touched, about 40 minutes. Cool 15 minutes on a rack. Sprinkle some onion onto strata. Cut into rectangles and offer with remaining onion and sour cream to add to taste. Makes 6 to 8 servings.

PER SERVING: 547 calories, 38 g protein, 37 g carbohydrates, 28 g fat, 326 mg cholesterol, 761 mg sodium

Warm Brie in Golden Puff Pastry

HOT AND FLAKY *outside, creamy in-side—the secret of this pastry appetizer begins with the brie. It must be firm and very cold or frozen when baked.*

BRIE PASTRY PACKAGE

- 1 **sheet (8 oz.) frozen puff pastry, thawed**
- 1 **round (8 oz.) cold, firm brie**
- 1 **egg, beaten**
  Mushroom filling (recipe follows)

Cut ⅓ off 1 side of the pastry and set aside. Roll remaining pastry ⅛ inch thick on a lightly floured board. Trim to an 11-inch-diameter round; reserve scraps.

Cut brie in half horizontally. Set 1 piece, rind down, in center of pastry. Top with ½ the filling. Set remaining cheese, rind up, on stack. Top with remaining filling.

Brush pastry rim with egg. Lay rim over cheese to enclose, pleating evenly to accommodate excess pastry; cut off pastry pleats. Press cut edges together to seal, then brush with egg. Save scraps.

Invert cheese pastry onto a 6-inch foil square. Roll scraps ⅛ inch thick and cut into fancy shapes (about 1½ in. wide).

Brush packet and pastry pieces with egg. Set several pieces onto packet. Put remaining pastries on a foil sheet about 12 by 15 inches; do not touch pastry edges.

Freeze packet, uncovered, until it feels firm when pressed, about 30 minutes. (If made ahead, freeze packet and pastries; wrap airtight and store up to 2 weeks; unwrap to continue.)

Slide foil with packet onto a 10- by 15-inch pan. Bake in a 425° oven until packet is golden brown, 30 to 35 minutes. With a spatula, transfer from foil to a platter and let cool 10 to 15 minutes; discard foil.

Meanwhile, reduce oven heat to 350°. Slide pastries on foil onto baking pan and bake pastries until golden brown, about 10 minutes. Surround packet with pastries. Cut into wedges; eat with knife and fork. Accompany with pastries. Makes 4 to 6 servings.

PER SERVING: 336 calories, 12 g protein, 18 g carbohydrates, 24 g fat, 89 mg cholesterol, 451 mg sodium

Mushroom filling. In a 10- to 12-inch frying pan over medium-high heat, combine 1 tablespoon **butter** or margarine; ½ cup chopped **onion;** and 1 **garlic** clove, minced or pressed. Stir until limp. Add ½ pound **mushrooms,** finely chopped; 3 tablespoons **port;** and ¼ teaspoon *each* **dry rosemary, dry thyme,** and **dry marjoram leaves.** Stir often until liquid evaporates.

Cut through golden pastry to melting brie layered with sautéed mushrooms. Eat with puff pastry crackers.

Ravioli with Pumpkin Filling

GOLDEN PUMPKIN, *spiced with ginger and curry, fill these tender ravioli. Cook them in broth for a soup, or simmer in water, then serve with a sherry cream. Either dish makes a first course or light lunch.*

Instead of making pasta as you would for traditional ravioli, take a short-cut with purchased won ton wrappers. The thin wrappers are deliciously silky and tender, but fragile; handle cooked ravioli gently.

You can make the ravioli ahead, then freeze them until time to cook.

PUMPKIN RAVIOLI SOUP

- 1 **pound spinach**
- 2 **tablespoons salad oil**
- 1 **large onion, sliced into thin slivers**
- 1 **clove garlic, pressed or minced**
- 4 **quarts regular-strength chicken broth**
- 2 **large carrots, peeled and cut into thin slivers**
  Pumpkin ravioli, freshly made or frozen (recipe follows)
  About ½ cup salted pumpkin seeds (optional)

Discard tough spinach stems and leaves. Cut leaves crosswise into ¼-inch strips; wash well and drain. Set aside.

In an 8- to 10-quart pan, combine oil, onion, and garlic; stir over medium-high heat until onion is limp. Add broth and carrots; bring to a boil. Reduce heat, cover, and simmer until carrots are tender to bite, about 5 minutes.

Add ravioli; simmer, covered, about 3 minutes. Add spinach and simmer, uncovered, until ravioli are heated through, 1 to 2 minutes longer (about 3 minutes if ravioli are frozen). Carefully lift out ravioli with a slotted spoon or skimmer and place in 6 to 12 wide soup bowls. Ladle soup over ravioli. Offer pumpkin seeds to sprinkle into soup. Makes 12 first-course servings, or 6 main-dish servings (with second helpings).

PER SERVING: 274 calories, 11 g protein, 32 g carbohydrates, 10 g fat, 83 mg cholesterol, 152 mg sodium

Pumpkin ravioli. In a 10- to 12-inch frying pan, combine 2 tablespoons **butter** or margarine; 2 medium-size **onions,** chopped; 1 tablespoon minced **fresh ginger;** and 1 clove **garlic,** pressed or minced. Stir often over medium heat until onion is limp, about 10 minutes.

Add 1 tablespoon **curry powder;** stir about 1 minute. Add 1 can (16 oz.) **pumpkin,** 1 cup (8 oz.) **ricotta cheese,** 1 large **egg,** and 1 large **egg yolk.** Mix well and add **salt** to taste. Makes 4 cups.

Cover with plastic wrap about 6 dozen **won ton wrappers,** each about 3 in. square (about 14 oz. total). Place 1 wrapper (keep remainder covered) on a board; place a scant tablespoon of pumpkin filling in center. Brush edges of wrapper with **egg white** (use 1 large white, slightly beaten). Fold wrapper over to make a triangle. Press edges together to seal.

Place ravioli on a flour-dusted baking sheet; cover with plastic wrap. Repeat to use remaining filling. Use more baking sheets as necessary to keep ravioli in a single layer. (If made ahead, chill ravioli up to 1 hour. Or freeze until firm; thaw 3 to 5 minutes, then remove from pan and package in airtight rigid containers up to 1 month.) Makes about 6 dozen.

PUMPKIN RAVIOLI IN SHERRY CREAM

- 2 **tablespoons butter or margarine**
- 1 **large onion, chopped**
- 1 **clove garlic, pressed or minced**
- 1½ **cups dry sherry**
- 1½ **cups regular-strength chicken broth**
- 1 **cup whipping cream**
  Pumpkin ravioli, freshly made or frozen (recipe precedes)
  Freshly grated or ground nutmeg

In a 10- to 12-inch frying pan, combine butter, onion, and garlic; stir often over medium-high heat until onion is limp, about 5 minutes. Add sherry and broth. Boil on high heat, uncovered, until reduced to 2 cups, about 8 minutes. Add cream; set aside.

Meanwhile, in 2 pans (each 5- to 6-qt. size), bring 3 quarts water to boiling over high heat. Add about ½ the ravioli to each pan. Cook ravioli, uncovered, over medium heat (water should simmer gently) just until heated through, 4 to 5 minutes (about 6 minutes if frozen).

When ravioli are almost cooked, reheat sherry sauce to simmering.

With a slotted spoon or skimmer, gently lift ravioli from water; drain briefly in spoon, then layer with sauce on 6 to 8 plates. Dust with nutmeg. Serves 6 to 8.

PER SERVING: 424 calories, 12 g protein, 47 g carbohydrates, 21 g fat, 166 mg cholesterol, 134 mg sodium

Halloween's staple makes an appearance as the filling in these triangular ravioli. Here, they float in broth with slivers of carrot, onion, and spinach.

Vietnamese *Pho:* A Meal in a Bowl

Soup with salad *is what you might call* pho, *a dish from Vietnam. Basically, it's a meal in a bowl.*

You pile slender rice noodles into the bowl, then top them with thin slices of raw beef. Pour a bubbling hot, fragrantly spicy broth over the beef to cook it lightly and warm the noodles. Then add the salad part—lots of bean sprouts and fresh herbs. Season with chili and hoisin. It's a light meal that's easy to assemble.

To keep the broth hot at the table, set it on a portable burner. Or bring the broth to boiling, put it in a tureen, cover, bring the tureen to the table, and serve at once. For less rare meat, cook it briefly in broth before serving.

You can make the dish with supermarket ingredients. Or try an Asian market for more authentic choices.

VIETNAMESE PHO

3½ quarts regular-strength beef broth
1 large white onion, thinly sliced into rings
6 slices fresh ginger (each about the size of a quarter)
1 stalk fresh lemon grass, ends and leaves trimmed; or peel from 1 small lemon (yellow part only)
1 cinnamon stick (3 in.)
1 teaspoon black peppercorns
1 pound boneless lean beef steak (such as sirloin, top round)
2 tablespoons thinly sliced green onions
⅓ pound bean sprouts
1 cup lightly packed fresh mint leaves
1 cup lightly packed fresh basil leaves
1 cup lightly packed fresh cilantro (coriander) leaves
2 or 3 fresh jalapeño chilies, thinly sliced in rings
2 large limes, cut into wedges
About ¼ cup hoisin sauce
About 2 tablespoons Asian red chili paste or sauce
¼ cup salad oil
1 pound dry rice noodles (*maifun* or rice sticks) or capellini
Fish sauce (*nuoc nam*) or soy sauce
¼ teaspoon ground black pepper

In a 5- to 6-quart pan, combine broth, about ¾ of the white onion (reserve remaining), ginger, lemon grass, cinnamon, and peppercorns. Cover and bring to a boil, then simmer about 1 hour.

Meanwhile, trim excess fat from beef. Slice meat across grain as thinly as possible into 1- by 3-inch strips. Arrange on a platter. Garnish with reserved white onion slices and green onions. If made ahead, cover and chill up to 4 hours.

Rinse and drain bean sprouts, mint, basil, and cilantro. Arrange on a platter with chilies and limes. Spoon hoisin sauce and chili paste into separate small bowls; if made ahead, cover and chill up to 4 hours.

In a 5- to 6-quart pan, bring about 3 quarts water and the oil to a boil, covered, on high heat. Add noodles; stir to separate and cook just until barely tender to bite, 2 to 4 minutes. Drain noodles and place equal portions into 6 large, deep soup bowls; or place all the noodles in 1 large serving bowl. Cover to keep warm.

Pour soup through a strainer into a serving pan or tureen. Discard cooked onion and seasonings. To broth, add fish sauce to taste. Sprinkle with ground pepper. (If you prefer beef well done, return strained broth to a boil, stir in meat, and cook to desired doneness; lift out meat with a slotted spoon and return to platter or put in individual bowls.)

At the table, place pan of soup on a portable heat source to keep hot; or set covered tureen directly on table. Offer meat, bean sprouts, herbs, noodles, hoisin sauce, and chili paste. Diners add meat with onion to each bowl, then ladle hot broth over meat, stirring to cook raw meat to rare (or to heat cooked meat). Add sprouts, mint, basil, cilantro, chilies, lime, hoisin, and chili paste to taste. Serves 6.

PER SERVING: 501 calories, 23 g protein, 84 g carbohydrates, 8 g fat, 45 mg cholesterol, 486 mg sodium

Add fresh herbs and bean sprouts to noodles and beef in broth for main dish.

Down-to-Earth Winter Salads

A SWEET EARTHINESS predominates in these winter vegetable salads. Steaming brings out the vegetables' flavors; the turn of your knife gives them geometric shapes.

For the first, serve rutabaga matchsticks, seasoned with a sweet and sour Oriental sauce, over sautéed kale. Cooked, puréed turnips and tahini make a mellow dip for raw carrot and turnip ovals. In the third recipe, sweet cubes of butternut squash balance a hot-tart dressing and slightly bitter greens.

ORIENTAL-STYLE RUTABAGAS & KALE

- 2 **rutabagas** (about 1¼ lb. total)
- ⅛ **pound Chinese link sausages** (*lop cheong*) **or pepperoni, thinly sliced crosswise**
- ¾ **pound kale** (tough stems removed), **cut into 2-inch pieces, rinsed and drained**
  Seasoning sauce (recipe follows)

Peel rutabagas, slice ¼ inch thick, then stack a few slices at a time and cut into ¼-inch-wide strips.

Pour about ½ inch water into a 3- to 4-quart pan. Place a steaming rack at least ¾ inch above bottom of pan, cover, and bring water to a boil over high heat. Add rutabagas; cover and steam until almost tender to bite, 6 to 8 minutes.

Meanwhile, place sausages in a 10- to 12-inch frying pan over medium-high heat. Cook, stirring often, until meat begins to brown, about 3 minutes. Transfer with a slotted spoon to paper towels.

Add kale and 2 tablespoons water to frying pan. Cover and cook until greens wilt, 2 to 3 minutes; stir once or twice. Lift greens onto a platter. Drain rutabagas; add to seasoning sauce with sausages and mix. Spoon sauce mixture over kale. Serve warm or cool. Makes 6 to 8 servings.

PER SERVING: 96 calories, 3.3 g protein, 9.3 g carbohydrates, 5.2 g fat, 5.8 mg cholesterol, 302 mg sodium

Seasoning sauce. In a large bowl, mix 2 tablespoons *each* chopped **fresh cilantro** (coriander) and **seasoned rice vinegar** or white wine vinegar; 1 tablespoon *each* **soy sauce, Oriental sesame oil,** minced **fresh ginger,** and **mirin** (sweet rice wine) or dry sherry; and 1 teaspoon **sugar.**

TURNIP-TAHINI DIP WITH CRISP VEGETABLES

- 4 **medium-size turnips** (about 1¾ lb. total)
- ¼ **cup canned tahini** (sesame butter)
- 2 **tablespoons lemon juice**
  Salt and pepper
- 2 **large carrots**
  Thin carrot shreds (optional)

Peel turnips. Cut 3 into 1-inch chunks. Pour about ½ inch water into a 3- to 4-quart pan. Place a steaming rack at least ¾ inch above pan bottom; cover pan and bring water to a boil over high heat. Add turnip chunks; cover and steam until turnips are very tender to bite, about 15 minutes.

Drain turnips, then place in a blender or food processor with tahini and lemon juice. Whirl until smoothly puréed, stopping motor several times to scrape mixture into blade. Season to taste with salt and pepper. Scrape into a bowl. If desired, cover and chill up until next day.

Cut remaining turnip in quarters, then cut into thin vertical slices. Cut carrots into thin, 2- to 3-inch-long diagonal slices. Arrange turnip and carrots on a platter. Serve with dip, garnished with carrot shreds. Makes 7 or 8 servings.

PER SERVING: 78 calories, 2.3 g protein, 9.4 g carbohydrates, 4.2 g fat, 0 mg cholesterol, 72 mg sodium

HOT & SOUR SQUASH WITH DANDELION GREENS

- ½ **cup slivered red onion**
- 2 **pounds butternut, kabocha** (Japanese), **or Hubbard squash**
- 1 **small red bell pepper, stemmed, cored, and cut lengthwise into thin slivers**
- 1 **teaspoon grated lime peel**
- ⅓ **cup** *each* **lime juice and salad oil**
- 1 **teaspoon crushed dried hot red chilies**
- ½ **pound dandelion greens** (tough ends trimmed), **rinsed and crisped**
  Salt and pepper

Place onion in a small bowl with ice water to cover; set aside. Peel squash and remove seeds. Cut flesh into ½- to ¾-inch cubes. Pour about ½ inch water into a 3- to 4-quart pan. Place a steaming rack at least ¾ inch above pan bottom; cover, then bring water to a boil over high heat.

Bold shapes belie the mellow tastes of (from top) rutabaga and kale salad, turnip and carrot slices with turnip-sesame dip, and cubed squash over dandelion greens.

Add squash; cover and steam until squash is tender to bite, about 10 minutes. Add bell pepper; steam, covered, just until limp, about 1 minute. Drain vegetables, immerse in cold water just until cool, and drain. Drain onion.

In a large bowl, gently mix squash and bell pepper with onion, lime peel and juice, oil, and chilies. Arrange a few dandelion leaves on a platter. Shred remaining greens; put on platter and top with squash mixture. Season to taste with salt and pepper. If made ahead, cover and hold up to 2 hours. Serves 6 to 8.

PER SERVING: 142 calories, 1.8 g protein, 15 g carbohydrates, 9.4 g fat, 0 mg cholesterol, 25 mg sodium

Skewered Surprise: Sweetbreads

To the uninitiated—*who expect a tender, sugary pastry*—sweetbreads (the thymus gland of a calf) may come as a bit of a surprise. Delicate in flavor and texture, however, they're a delicious organ meat—excellent plain or as a favored vehicle for elegant sauces.

Here, skewered and grilled, and served either as an appetizer or as a main dish, they pass muster with timid eaters and offer a refreshingly light change for sweetbread fans.

Sweetbreads are located at the base of the calf's throat. As the animal matures, the gland atrophies, changing flavor and texture. Sweetbreads are sold at the meat counter, usually packaged in plastic tubs, or ask for them frozen. You may need to order ahead.

When you want to remove the coarse membrane, poach the sweetbreads first, then pull off the membrane, separating the thymus segments as you work.

The basting sauce helps the pale meat brown appetizingly (as it cooks over hot coals).

GRILLED SWEETBREADS WITH FRAGRANT OILS

- 1 to 1¼ pounds sweetbreads
- 1 tablespoon *each* olive oil, soy sauce, and rice wine vinegar
- 2 teaspoons hot chili oil
- 1 teaspoon Oriental sesame oil
  Lemon wedges (optional)

Rinse sweetbreads. In a 3- to 4-quart pan over high heat, bring about 2 quarts water to a boil. Add sweetbreads. Reduce heat, cover, and simmer for 15 minutes; drain. When cool enough to handle (to speed cooling, immerse in cold water), separate sweetbreads into naturally divided segments about ¾ inch in diameter; pull off most of the thick, rubbery membrane. Also, pull out easily removed tubes (this is cosmetic; tubes are not tough).

Divide sweetbread segments into 8 portions; thread each portion onto a 10- to 12-inch slender metal skewer. If made ahead, cover and chill up until next day.

Stir together olive oil, soy, vinegar, chili oil, and sesame oil. If made ahead, cover and let stand up until next day.

Brush skewered sweetbreads generously with oil mixture. Lay skewers on a barbecue grill 4 to 6 inches above a solid bed of medium-hot coals (you should be able to hold your hand at grill level only 3 to 4 seconds). With tongs, turn skewers every 2 to 3 minutes, brushing frequently with oil mixture (if flare-ups occur, move sweetbreads away from flames at once). When sweetbreads are well browned in spots, about 15 minutes total, transfer to a platter.

Serve on skewers, or push from skewers onto dinner plates. As an appetizer, keep loose sweetbreads warm in a bowl on an electric warming tray; spear segments with toothpicks to eat. Offer lemon wedges to squeeze on to taste. Makes 4 entrée or 8 to 12 appetizer servings.

Per Entrée Serving: 169 calories, 20 g protein, 0.5 g carbohydrates, 9.1 g fat, 284 mg cholesterol, 367 mg sodium

Hot from the grill, skewered sweetbread segments were brushed with flavorful oils as they sizzled and browned.

Chipotle Chilies—without the Explosion

A CHIPOTLE CHILI *is not a variety of chili. It's a mature red jalapeño that is smoked as it dries, acquiring a pungent flavor and aroma that can be detected despite its assertive heat.*

How can you put this exceptional flavor to use without an explosion?

Here are three moderating ways. First, bake with beef short ribs. The ribs' sturdy, well-larded nature tames the heat, and the chilies' smoky flavor permeates the meat. Simmer a lone chipotle in chicken soup, then add fresh lime juice to smooth the hot edge. Try minced canned chipotles alone, or blend with mayonnaise, as a sauce with bite to go with fish, shellfish, meat, poultry, or hard-cooked eggs.

Chipotles are most widely available canned in a sauce (7-oz. size). The sauce, usually called adobo, is made with vinegar and spices. The chilies are also sold dried; you're most apt to find these in Mexican markets, particularly in Southern California. Dried chipotles keep indefinitely. If you use the canned ones, transfer the unused chilies and sauce to a small jar and refrigerate up to a week, or freeze to store longer. You can thaw and refreeze chilies until all are used. When cooking chipotles in liquid, the dried and canned forms can be used interchangeably.

Tuck canned or dried chipotle chilies in among short ribs and onions; add broth. Bake until meat is tender and saturated with chilies' smoky flavor.

BEEF SHORT RIBS WITH CHIPOTLE CHILIES

- 4 **lean beef short ribs (about 4 lb. total), cracked**
- 1 **large onion, chopped**
- 2 **dried chipotle chilies, or 2 canned chipotle chilies in sauce**
- 2½ **cups regular-strength beef or chicken broth**
- 1 **canned chipotle chili and 1 or 2 teaspoons of the sauce, minced together (optional)**
  About 3 cups hot, cooked rice
  Salt

In a deep 4- to 5-quart pan, arrange ribs and onion, tucking the 2 dried or canned chilies among the ribs. Add 1 cup broth and cover pan tightly with a lid or foil.

Bake ribs in a 400° oven until meat is tender enough to pull from bones, about 3½ hours. Uncover and bake until meat is brown, about 15 minutes. With a slotted spoon, put ribs and onions on a platter; keep warm. To pan, add remaining broth. With spoon, smash chilies and scrape browned bits from pan bottom. Skim and discard fat. Heat juices to boil-ing; pour into a bowl. Serve ribs with juice, minced chipotles, rice, and salt to taste. Serves 4.

PER SERVING: 572 calories, 43 g protein, 43 g carbohydrates, 24 g fat, 114 mg cholesterol, 106 mg sodium

CHICKEN & RICE SOUP WITH CHIPOTLE CHILIES

- 6 **chicken thighs (about 1½ lb.)**
- 6 **cups regular-strength chicken broth**
- 1 **dried chipotle chili, or 1 canned chipotle chili in sauce**
- 1 **small onion, diced**
- 1 **cup long-grain white rice**
- 2 **large carrots, peeled and thinly sliced**
  Lime wedges
  Salt

In a 4- to 5-quart pan, combine chicken, broth, chili, and onion. Over high heat, bring to a boil. Reduce heat, cover, and simmer until meat is no longer pink at bone (cut to test), about 25 minutes.

Lift chicken from pan and let cool. Stir rice and carrots into soup; cover and simmer until rice is tender to bite, about 20 minutes. Meanwhile, pull off and discard skin and bones from cool chick-en. Tear meat into shreds. When rice is cooked, return chicken to soup. If desired, remove chili. Add lime juice and salt to taste to each portion. Makes 4 to 6 servings.

PER SERVING: 239 calories, 18 g protein, 31 g carbohydrates, 4.4 g fat, 54 mg cholesterol, 123 mg sodium

CHIPOTLE CHILI MAYONNAISE

Cold, cooked shrimp, hard-cooked quail eggs, and purchased pâtés are enlivened by a touch of this mayonnaise. The same foods are also good with the canned chipotles, minced and mixed with some of the chilies' sauce.

- 1 **canned chipotle chili in sauce and 1 teaspoon of the sauce**
- ½ **cup mayonnaise**

Mince chili with sauce; mix with mayonnaise. Put into a small bowl. Serve as a dip. Makes about ½ cup.

PER TABLESPOON: 99 calories, 0.2 g protein, 0.5 g carbohydrates, 11 g fat, 8.1 mg cholesterol, 94 mg sodium

Adding Zip to Eggplant

ASIAN COOKS *often treat eggplant as a big, absorbent sponge, letting its soft, mild-tasting flesh soak up spicy sauces.*

In our first entrée, from Cambodia, eggplant is steamed, then bathed in a lemon-curry sauce. The second dish, from Sichuan, China, features eggplant slices filled with pork, fried until crisp, then served with a garlic-chili sauce.

In either recipe, you can use the slender Oriental eggplant or the plumper, egg-shaped globe type. Look for the chili paste and bean sauce in Asian markets, or use the alternatives suggested.

CAMBODIAN STEAMED EGGPLANT

- 1 to 1¼ pounds Oriental or globe eggplant, peeled and ends removed
- 1 large lemon
- 2 tablespoons salad oil
- 2 cloves garlic, pressed or minced
- 1 tablespoon minced fresh ginger
- ½ cup chopped shallots
- ¼ teaspoon ground turmeric
- ½ to ¾ teaspoon Asian red chili paste or sauce, or ¼ to ½ teaspoon crushed dried hot red chilies
- ¼ pound ground lean pork

Slivered lemon peel and mint garnish Cambodian Steamed Eggplant and accent its flavor.

- ¼ pound tiny shelled cooked shrimp
- 1 cup canned coconut milk
  Fish sauce (*nuoc nam*) or soy sauce
- 2 tablespoons slivered fresh mint leaves

Cut Oriental eggplant lengthwise in half if thicker than 2 inches; cut globe eggplant into 1½-inch-wide wedges. Set eggplant in a shallow bowl or rimmed plate that will fit inside a steamer. Place on a rack above 1 inch of boiling water. Cover and steam until eggplant is soft when pressed, about 30 minutes. (Or place on a nonmetal rimmed platter or plate, cover with plastic wrap, and cook in a microwave oven at full power—100 percent—until soft when pressed, 12 to 14 minutes.) Set the eggplant aside; keep warm.

Meanwhile, with a vegetable peeler, pare a few strips of peel (yellow part only) from lemon. Cut enough peel into thin shreds to make about 1 tablespoon. Then ream lemon to make 2 tablespoons juice; set aside.

Set a 10- to 12-inch frying pan over medium heat. Add oil, garlic, ginger, shallots, turmeric, and chili paste; stir until shallots are limp, about 2 minutes. Add pork; stir until lightly browned, about 5 minutes. Add shrimp and coconut milk; stir until hot. Add lemon juice and fish sauce to taste.

Transfer eggplant to a rimmed serving platter; if needed, drain off and discard accumulated liquid. Pour the coconut-meat sauce over eggplant. Sprinkle with lemon peel and mint slivers. Makes 3 or 4 main-dish servings.

PER SERVING: 298 calories, 14 g protein, 14 g carbohydrates, 22 g fat, 75 mg cholesterol, 108 mg sodium

SICHUAN EGGPLANT & PORK CAKES

- ¾ pound Oriental eggplant (about 1½-in. diameter), or 1 small globe eggplant, cut into 1½-inch-wide wedges; discard stems
  Pork filling (recipe follows)
  Salad oil
  Batter (recipe follows)
- 2 tablespoons minced fresh ginger
- ¼ cup thinly sliced green onion
- 1 tablespoon minced garlic
- 1 tablespoon bean sauce or soy sauce
- 1 to 1½ teaspoons Asian red chili paste or sauce, or ½ to ¾ teaspoon crushed dried hot red chilies
  Sauce mixture (recipe follows)

Cut Oriental eggplant crosswise into ⅛-inch-thick slices, but with every other cut do not slice all the way through—this forms ¼-inch-thick slices with pockets for filling. (With globe eggplant, cut from flesh side of wedge so skin side holds pocket together.) Fill each pocket with about 1 teaspoon pork filling.

Pour 1 to 1½ inches oil into a wok or 3- to 4-quart frying pan. Heat oil to 350° on a thermometer. Dip eggplant cakes in batter to coat, then carefully drop into oil. Fry about 6 at a time, turning occasionally, until eggplant is golden and tender when pierced, about 2 minutes. Lift out with a slotted spoon and drain on paper towels; keep warm. Repeat with remaining eggplant sandwiches. (If made ahead, cool, cover, and chill up to 2 days. Reheat in a single layer in a 10- by 15-inch baking pan in a 400° oven until hot and crisp, 10 to 15 minutes; drain on paper towels.)

Place wok or 8- to 10-inch frying pan over high heat. Add 1 tablespoon salad oil, ginger, onion, garlic, bean sauce, and chili paste. Stir-fry about 30 seconds. Add sauce mixture. Stir until it boils and thickens. Pour onto a serving platter. Arrange eggplant sandwiches in sauce. Makes 3 or 4 main-dish servings.

PER SERVING: 291 calories, 16 g protein, 30 g carbohydrates, 12 g fat, 38 mg cholesterol, 786 mg sodium

Pork filling. Mix ½ pound **ground lean pork** with 1 tablespoon **soy sauce,** 1 tablespoon **rice wine** or dry sherry, 1 tablespoon **cornstarch,** 1 tablespoon minced **fresh ginger,** and 1 clove **garlic,** pressed or minced.

Batter. Mix ½ cup **all-purpose flour,** 2 tablespoons **cornstarch,** ¾ teaspoon **baking powder,** and ⅔ cup **water.**

Sauce mixture. Mix ¾ cup **regular-strength chicken broth,** 2 teaspoons **soy sauce,** 1 tablespoon **rice** or cider **vinegar,** 2 teaspoons **sugar,** 1 teaspoon **Oriental sesame oil,** and 2 teaspoons **cornstarch.**

Three Starring Roles for the Carrot

THE ROOT OF THE PROBLEM *for carrots is abundance. Because they're so plentiful and nonseasonal, they often get overlooked. But carrots respond well to imaginative treatment that gives them stellar roles; here are three fine examples. The carrot torte with cardamom is a surprise dessert. The brilliant sorbet packs an extra punch of Vitamin A. And the mixed vegetable sauté is particularly colorful.*

CARROT-APPLE TORTE

2½ cups peeled and shredded carrots (about 1 lb.)
2 medium-size Golden Delicious apples (about 1 lb. total)
2 tablespoons lemon juice
1½ tablespoons *each* cornstarch and water
2 large eggs
1½ cups sour cream
2 tablespoons sugar
2 tablespoons minced crystallized ginger
½ teaspoon ground cardamom
  Whole-wheat pastry (recipe follows)

In a 2- to 3-quart pan, cook carrots in ¼ cup water, covered, over medium-high heat until tender to bite, about 4 minutes; stir often. Drain; pour into a large bowl. Peel, core, and cut apples into thin slices. Add apples and lemon juice to carrots; mix well.

In another bowl, stir together cornstarch and water. Add eggs, sour cream, sugar, ginger, and cardamom. Mix well. Add to apple mixture, and stir to blend.

Scrape mixture into pastry. Squeeze whole-wheat dough (left from pastry) together; coarsely crumble into peanut-size lumps, scattering evenly over filling. Place torte in a 10- by 15-inch pan. Bake in a 350° oven until edges and top are golden brown and center feels firm when lightly touched, about 1 hour and 10 minutes.

Let cool at least 30 minutes, then run a knife between torte and pan. Remove rim and set torte on a plate. Serve warm or at room temperature; if made ahead, cover and chill until next day. Makes 8 servings.

PER SERVING: 454 calories, 8 g protein, 57 g carbohydrates, 23 g fat, 153 mg cholesterol, 182 mg sodium

Whole-wheat pastry. In a food processor or with an electric mixer, mix ½ cup **sugar**, ½ cup (¼ lb.) plus 2 tablespoons **butter** or margarine, and 1 large **egg**

yolk. Add 2 cups **whole-wheat flour.** Whirl or stir until dough holds together. If made ahead, cover and chill up to 3 days.

Divide dough into thirds. Press ⅔ of dough evenly over bottom and 1 inch up sides of 9-inch cheesecake pan with removable bottom. Reserve any remaining dough.

CARROT & ORANGE SORBET

4 medium-size carrots (about 1 lb. total)
1 can (6 oz.) thawed frozen orange juice concentrate
1 cup water

Peel carrots and cut into 1-inch chunks. In a 2- to 3-quart pan, combine carrots, ⅓ cup orange juice concentrate, and water. Bring to boiling over high heat; cover and simmer until carrots are tender when pierced, about 15 minutes.

With a slotted spoon, put carrots in a blender or food processor. Whirl, adding liquid, until smoothly puréed; add remaining concentrate. Pour mixture into an 8- to 10-inch-square metal pan. Cover and freeze until hard, 4 hours or up to 1 month. Let stand at room temperature about 5 minutes to soften, then break into chunks with a heavy spoon.

Whirl chunks in a food processor or beat with a mixer until it becomes smooth slush. Serve at once, or cover and freeze up to 1 hour. Makes about 2 cups, 4 to 6 servings.

PER SERVING: 85 calories, 1.3 g protein, 20 g carbohydrates, 0.2 g fat, 0 mg cholesterol, 24 mg sodium

SAUTÉED CARROTS & PEPPERS

4 medium-size carrots (about 1 lb. total)
1 medium-size red bell pepper
1 medium-size fresh Anaheim (California) chili
2 tablespoons olive oil
2 teaspoons fresh rosemary leaves, or 1 teaspoon dried rosemary leaves
  Salt and pepper

Peel carrots; cut into matchstick-size pieces. Stem and seed bell pepper and chili; cut into matchstick-size pieces.

In a 10- to 12-inch frying pan over medium-high heat, stir-fry carrots in oil just until slightly browned, about 6 minutes. Add bell pepper, chili, and rosemary; stir-fry until pepper pieces are limp, about 2 minutes. Add salt and pepper to taste. Serves 6.

PER SERVING: 56 calories, 0.9 g protein, 8.3 g carbohydrates, 2.5 g fat, 0 mg cholesterol, 25 mg sodium

Wholesome whole-wheat crust surrounds tender carrot and apple torte.

Dried-Fruit Loaves for the Holidays

THE NATURAL SWEETNESS *in these two holiday loaves comes from dried fruit.*

The cake is generously packed with fruits and nuts and gently seasoned with ginger. Apples and prunes lend a moist sweetness to the oven-steamed brown bread. You can make both now, then store them for holiday gifts.

DRIED-FRUIT CAKE

- 1 cup chopped pitted dates
- 1 cup chopped dried apricots
- 1 cup golden raisins
- 1 cup chopped dried figs
- 1 tablespoon minced fresh ginger
- ¾ cup dry sherry
- ¾ cup all-purpose flour
- ¾ cup sugar
- ½ teaspoon baking powder
- 1 cup slivered almonds
- 1 cup chopped pecans
- 1 cup chopped salted pistachios
- ½ cup chopped crystallized ginger
- 3 large eggs
- ½ teaspoon almond extract or 1 teaspoon vanilla

Butter a 5- by 9-inch loaf pan. Line with parchment or waxed paper; butter paper. Set aside.

In a large bowl, combine dates, apricots, raisins, figs, fresh ginger, and ½ cup sherry. Mix well and let stand about 30 minutes. Meanwhile, stir together flour, sugar, baking powder, almonds, pecans, pistachios, and crystallized ginger. Beat together eggs and almond extract.

Add nut and egg mixtures to fruit mixture; stir to blend well. Spoon batter into prepared pan and spread evenly.

Bake in a 300° oven until the top is golden brown, about 1½ hours. Let cool in pan on a rack for 10 minutes, then turn out of pan. Peel off paper and let cake cool completely on rack. Wrap cake with cheesecloth or a dish towel. Drizzle remaining ¼ cup sherry all over cloth-wrapped cake. Overwrap cake with foil. Cover and chill at least 2 days or up to 2 months before serving. Makes 1 cake (about 3¾ lb.), about 20 servings. —*Roxanne Chan, Albany, Calif.*

PER OUNCE: 95 calories, 1.8 g protein, 15 g carbohydrates, 3.8 g fat, 14 mg cholesterol, 10 mg sodium

APPLE-PRUNE BROWN BREAD

- 1 cup *each* all-purpose flour, rye flour, and cornmeal
- 2 teaspoons baking powder
- 1 teaspoon baking soda
- ½ teaspoon salt (optional)
- 1 large egg
- 2 cups buttermilk
- ¾ cup dark molasses
- ½ cup chopped dried apples
- ¾ cup pitted, chopped dried prunes

In a large bowl, mix all-purpose and rye flours, cornmeal, baking powder, baking soda, and salt. In another bowl, beat egg to blend with buttermilk and molasses; stir in apples and prunes. Stir egg mixture into flour mixture until evenly moistened.

Scrape batter into 2 well-buttered loaf pans, each 4 by 8 inches. Cut 2 sheets of foil several inches larger than pan tops. Butter foil on 1 side; lay buttered side on top of pans; press foil snugly against pan sides. Bake in a 300° oven until bread pulls from sides of pan and springs back when lightly pressed in center (lift foil to check), 1¾ to 2 hours.

Run a knife around pan sides to loosen bread; turn out onto racks. Serve warm or cool, thinly sliced. If made ahead, wrap loaves airtight and chill up to 2 days, or freeze to store longer. Makes 2 loaves (1¼ lb. each).

PER OUNCE: 123 calories, 3 g protein, 27 g carbohydrates, 0.7 g fat, 15 mg cholesterol, 127 mg sodium

For an evening snack, offer mosaic-like slices of ginger-flavored fruitcake with a glass of sherry.

More November Recipes

OTHER NOVEMBER ARTICLES *feature hot fettucine liberally laced with colorful vegetables, a tart salsa using the season's ripe pomegranates, and ginger-flavored Italian cookies.*

FETTUCCINE WITH HARVEST VEGETABLES

This hot pasta entrée goes together quickly—it's especially fast when you chop the vegetables in a food processor.

- ½ **pound broccoli, tough ends trimmed off**
- 1 **large carrot, peeled and cut into chunks**
- 4 **cups lightly packed spinach leaves, rinsed and drained**
- 1 **small yellow bell pepper, stemmed, seeded, and quartered**
- 2 **large firm-ripe Roma-type tomatoes, cored and quartered**
- 2 **tablespoons butter or margarine**
- 1 **clove garlic, minced or pressed**
- 1 **cup half-and-half (light cream)**
- 9 **ounces fresh fettuccine**
- 1 **cup (4 oz.) grated parmesan cheese**
  Salt and pepper

Cut broccoli into large chunks. In a food processor or with a knife, finely chop separately the broccoli, carrot, spinach, bell pepper, and tomatoes.

Combine butter and garlic in a 10- to 12-inch frying pan on medium-high heat. Add vegetables; stir often until just tender to bite, 4 to 5 minutes. Add cream. On high heat, boil, uncovered, until sauce is reduced to 3½ cups, 8 to 10 minutes.

Meanwhile, in a 5- to 6-quart pan, cook pasta, uncovered, in 4 quarts boiling water until just tender to bite, about 5 minutes; drain. Add pasta to sauce; add ½ cup cheese and salt and pepper to taste, mixing well. Offer remaining cheese to add to taste. Serves 4.—*Dino Baglioni, Il Piccolino, Los Angeles.*

PER SERVING: 513 calories, 23 g protein, 55 g carbohydrates, 23 g fat, 110 mg cholesterol, 615 mg sodium

POMEGRANATE SALSA

Refreshingly tart pomegranate, fiery chili, and sweet orange go into this colorful salsa. Just stir the components together and serve the resulting sauce with simply cooked meat or fish.

The only tricky part is peeling the pomegranate without getting its staining, crimson juice all over. The secret is to work with the fruit under water.

- 1 **large or 2 medium-size pomegranates (about ¾ lb. total)**
- 1 **large orange**
- 1 **tablespoon chopped fresh cilantro (coriander)**
- 1 **green onion, ends trimmed and thinly sliced**
- 2 **teaspoons lime juice**
- ¼ **teaspoon ground cumin**
- 1 **to 3 teaspoons minced seeded fresh jalapeño chili**
  Salt

Break pomegranate into large chunks. Immerse chunks in a bowl of water and break apart to release seeds. Discard membrane and skin. Drain seeds; pat dry.

Cut peel and white membrane from orange. Holding fruit over a bowl, cut between inner membranes to free segments, adding them to bowl. Squeeze juice from membrane into bowl; discard membrane. Cut each segment into chunks.

To orange, add pomegranate, cilantro, onion, lime juice, cumin; add jalapeño and salt to taste. Serve, or cover and chill until next day. Makes 1 cup; serves 4 to 6.

PER TABLESPOON: 14 calories, 0.2 g protein, 3.5 g carbohydrates, 0 g fat, 0 mg cholesterol, 0.5 mg sodium

GINGERBREAD BISCOTTI

The spiciness of gingerbread distinguishes this version of biscotti, the classic twice-baked Italian cooky. First you bake ginger-flavored dough in flat loaves, then bake slices until crisp. Try the cookies with coffee, milk, or a sweet, rich wine.

- 1 **cup blanched almonds**
- ¾ **cup sugar**
- ½ **cup (¼ lb.) butter or margarine**
- ½ **cup dark molasses**
- ¼ **cup minced fresh ginger**
- 3 **large eggs**
- 3 **cups all-purpose flour**
- 1½ **teaspoons baking powder**
- 1 **tablespoon ground cinnamon**
- 1 **teaspoon ground nutmeg**
- ½ **teaspoon** *each* **ground cloves and ground allspice**

Place almonds in an 8- to 9-inch-square pan. Bake in a 350° oven until golden, 10 to 15 minutes. Let cool, coarsely chop, and set aside.

Juicy pomegranate seeds and orange chunks dot cool salsa. Spoon over broiled swordfish.

In large bowl of an electric mixer, beat sugar, butter, molasses, and ginger until smooth. Add eggs, 1 at a time, beating after each addition.

In a bowl, stir flour, baking powder, cinnamon, nutmeg, cloves, allspice, and almonds. Add to egg mixture; stir to blend.

On 2 greased 12- by 15-inch baking sheets, use well-floured hands to pat dough into 4 flat loaves, spacing them evenly on sheets; each loaf should be about ½ inch thick, 2 inches wide, and the length of the baking sheet. Bake in a 350° oven until browned at edges and springy to touch, about 25 minutes; switch positions of pans halfway through baking.

Let loaves stand on baking sheets until cool to touch, then cut into long, ½-inch-thick diagonal slices. On baking sheets, arrange slices close together with a cut side down. Return to oven and bake at 350° until cookies are brown, 15 to 18 minutes longer; switch positions of pans halfway through baking.

Transfer biscotti to racks and let cool completely. Serve, or store airtight up to 1 month; freeze for longer storage. Makes about 50.

PER COOKY: 85 calories, 1.8 g protein, 11 g carbohydrates, 3.7 g fat, 21 mg cholesterol, 39 mg sodium

Tender slices of pumpkin bread, studded with dates, apricots, and walnuts, go well with milk.

DATE & APRICOT PUMPKIN BREAD

2 large eggs
1 cup sugar
1 cup canned pumpkin
½ cup salad oil
½ cup orange juice
2 cups all-purpose flour
1 teaspoon baking soda
½ teaspoon *each* baking powder, ground cinnamon, ground cloves, ground nutmeg, and ground ginger
½ cup *each* chopped walnuts and chopped dates
¼ cup chopped dried apricots

In a large bowl, beat together eggs, sugar, pumpkin, oil, and orange juice. Stir flour with soda, baking powder, cinnamon, cloves, nutmeg, and ginger; add to egg mixture and beat to blend. Stir in nuts, dates, and apricots. Pour into a greased 5- by 9-inch loaf pan.

Bake in a 350° oven until a toothpick inserted in center comes out clean, about 1 hour. Cool 15 minutes; run a knife around pan edge, then invert bread onto a plate.

Serve bread warm or at room temperature. If made ahead, wrap and chill up to 5 days. Makes 1 loaf, about 2½ pounds. — *Jeanette Zimmerman, Van Nuys, Calif.*

PER OUNCE: 92 calories, 1.3 g protein, 13 g carbohydrates, 4 g fat, 14 mg cholesterol, 30 mg sodium

Hearty version of spinach and bacon salad has less conventional ingredients: cooked rice and toasted almonds.

ALMOND, RICE, SPINACH & BACON SALAD

⅔ cup sliced almonds
8 slices bacon
3 cups cool, cooked long-grain rice
6 cups packed spinach leaves, washed and crisped
½ cup slivered red onion
   Almond dressing (recipe follows)
   Salt and pepper

In a 10- to 12-inch frying pan over medium heat, stir almonds until golden, about 6 minutes; set nuts aside.

Add bacon to pan and cook until brown and crisp; drain on paper towels.

When cool, coarsely crumble bacon and set aside.

In a salad bowl, mix bacon, rice, spinach, onion, and dressing. Sprinkle almonds on salad; add salt and pepper to taste. Makes 6 to 8 servings. — *A. Hill, Sacramento.*

PER SERVING: 263 calories, 6.7 g protein, 20 g carbohydrates, 18 g fat, 5.4 mg cholesterol, 138 mg sodium

Almond dressing. Whisk together ⅓ cup **salad oil,** ¼ cup **red wine vinegar,** 1 tablespoon **sugar,** 1 teaspoon **dry mustard,** and ⅛ teaspoon **almond extract,** or to taste.

Corn chip topping adds novel twist to fish steaks baked in purchased salsa. Serve with avocado, sour cream, lime.

BAKED FISH, MEXICAN-STYLE

1½ pounds skinned and boned firm-textured fish steaks such as halibut, shark, or swordfish, cut ¾-inch thick
1 cup bottled tomato-based salsa
1 cup (¼ lb.) shredded sharp cheddar cheese
½ cup coarsely crushed corn chips
1 small firm-ripe avocado
   Sour cream (optional)
   Lime wedges

Rinse fish, pat dry, and lay side-by-side in an 8- by 12-inch baking dish. Pour salsa over fish. Evenly sprinkle cheese over salsa, then crushed chips over cheese. (If you want a crunchier topping, reserve chips and sprinkle over fish when you take it out of oven.)

Bake, uncovered, in a 400° oven until fish is opaque in thickest part (cut to test), about 15 minutes.

Meanwhile, peel, pit, and slice avocado. Serve fish and salsa with the avocado. Add sour cream and squeeze lime juice onto fish to taste. Serves 4. — *Jean Havens, Shelton, Wash.*

PER SERVING: 491 calories, 46 g protein, 26 g carbohydrates, 23 g fat, 84 mg cholesterol, 1,261 mg sodium

GOLDEN BAKED ACORN SQUASH

- 3 tablespoons butter or margarine
- 2 acorn squash (each about 1¼ lb.), cut in half lengthwise and seeded
- 3 tablespoons firmly packed brown sugar
- 3 tablespoons thawed frozen orange juice concentrate
- 3 tablespoons brandy or water
  Orange slices (optional)

In a 9- by 13-inch baking dish or pan, melt 1 tablespoon butter in a 350° oven; tilt pan to coat bottom with butter. Lay each squash half, cut side down, in dish. Bake, uncovered, in a 350° oven until squash is tender when pierced, about 35 minutes.

Meanwhile, in a 1- to 1½-quart pan, mix together remaining butter, brown sugar, orange juice concentrate, and brandy. Stir over high heat until boiling; set aside.

Turn squash cut side up; pour butter mixture evenly into each half. Bake until squash edges are browned, about 15 minutes. Transfer squash to a platter or plates, taking care not to spill sauce in center. Garnish with orange slices. Serves 4. —*P. M. Melliar-Smith, Menlo Park, Calif.*

PER SERVING: 222 calories, 2.1 g protein, 37 g carbohydrates, 8.8 g fat, 23 mg cholesterol, 98 mg sodium

Hot orange-flavored butter-sugar-brandy sauce fills baked acorn squash halves in this grand holiday dish.

CHICKEN WITH BARLEY & PECANS

- 3 tablespoons olive or salad oil
- ½ cup pecan halves
- 6 to 8 chicken thighs (about 1½ lb. total), skin removed
- 1 large onion, chopped
- 1 pound mushrooms, thinly sliced
- 1 cup pearl barley
- 2 cloves garlic, minced or pressed
- 3 cups regular-strength chicken broth
- 2 tablespoons minced parsley

Combine 1 tablespoon oil and pecans in a 10- to 12-inch frying pan over medium-low heat. Stir until nuts are golden in-side (break 1 to test), about 3 minutes; spoon out and set aside.

To pan, add 1 tablespoon oil and thighs; brown lightly, about 6 minutes. Lift out and set aside. Add remaining oil, onion, and mushrooms to pan. On high heat, stir often until golden, about 15 minutes. Add barley and garlic; stir until barley is toasted, about 2 minutes. Add broth; bring to a boil. Cover and simmer for 20 minutes. Add thighs; cover and simmer until barley is tender to bite, about 25 minutes. Top with nuts and parsley. Serves 4. —*Ann K. Shapleigh, Concord, Calif.*

PER SERVING: 749 calories, 38 g protein, 49 g carbohydrates, 45 g fat, 132 mg cholesterol, 170 mg sodium

One-dish supper features skinned chicken thighs cooked with onion, mushrooms, and barley.

CRANBERRY-PRUNE SQUARES

- 2 large eggs
- 1 cup sugar
- ¼ cup (⅛ lb.) butter or margarine, melted
- 1 cup all-purpose flour
- ½ teaspoon *each* ground allspice, ground cinnamon, and ground cloves
- ½ teaspoon baking powder
- 1 cup chopped almonds
- 1 cup chopped moist-pack prunes
- 1 cup fresh or frozen cranberries

In a large bowl, beat together eggs, sugar, and butter until well combined.

Mix together flour, allspice, cinnamon, cloves, and baking powder; stir into egg mixture, blending well. Stir in almonds, prunes, and cranberries.

Spread batter into a well-buttered 9-inch-square pan. Bake in a 350° oven until mixture feels firm when lightly touched in center and edges begin to pull from pan, about 45 minutes. Cut into 2¼-inch squares. Serve warm or at room temperature. If made ahead, cover and chill up to 3 days. Makes 16 pieces. —*Yvonne Visteen, Portland.*

PER PIECE: 188 calories, 3.5 g protein, 27 g carbohydrates, 7.9 g fat, 42 mg cholesterol, 53 mg sodium

Moderately sweet cranberry and prune squares can be served as a breakfast pastry or for dessert.

IN MEDIEVAL TIMES, *garlic was thought to ward off werewolves and vampires. Very likely. The trouble is that it also wards off your friends and relations. In spite of garlic's sometimes overwhelming fragrance, it remains a valuable flavoring ingredient. Heat can tame its acridity, as devotees of roasted garlic cloves will testify. In stews such as Fred Hill's, long and slow cooking will transform garlic into a scarcely identifiable, yet memorably warm and complex flavor.*

His veal stew has many of the ingredients of osso buco, but it leaves out the shin bone in favor of veal stew meat. Our taste panel loved the stew, and tasters were surprised to find that it contained 12 cloves of garlic. We would not have had the temerity to recommend such a dish otherwise. The garlic may, however, have lost its efficacy against vampires.

GARLIC VEAL STEW

- 2 to 3 tablespoons olive oil or salad oil
- 2 pounds boneless veal stew, cut into 1½- to 2-inch cubes
- 1 large onion, chopped
- 12 cloves garlic, halved
- 1½ pounds Roma-style tomatoes, peeled, cored, seeded, and coarsely chopped
- 1 cup tomato juice
- ¾ cup dry white wine
- ½ cup Spanish-style pimiento-stuffed olives, sliced
- 1 to 2 small dried hot red chilies
  Salt and pepper

Pour 2 tablespoons oil into a 5- to 6-quart pan over medium-high heat. When hot, add meat, a portion at a time, and turn pieces until browned. Lift meat out and set aside. Add onion, and more oil if needed, to pan; stir often until onion is limp and slightly browned, about 10 minutes. Stir in garlic, tomatoes, tomato juice, wine, olives, meat, and chilies to taste. Bring to a boil, cover, reduce heat, and simmer until meat is very tender when pierced, 1 to 1¼ hours; uncover and simmer until liquid is reduced to quantity desired.

Discard chilies, then skim and discard any fat from juices; season stew with salt and pepper to taste. Makes 4 to 6 servings.

PER SERVING: 361 calories, 31 g protein, 11 g carbohydrates, 21 g fat, 107 mg cholesterol, 533 mg sodium

Tucson

"In medieval times, garlic was thought to ward off werewolves and vampires."

THE CLASSIC WAY OF SERVING *mussels* is marinière—*steamed with white wine, butter, shallots, perhaps parsley or other herbs. From Edmonds, Washington, Eric Lie sends us an elegant Oriental variation. One essential ingredient of both preparations is the liquid given up by the mussels as they steam and open. The result should be a broth which has a strong savor of the sea. The ingredients listed below enhance this savor without overwhelming it.*

We entirely agree with Mr. Lie when he says that his recipe is a cut above the usual restaurant offering.

STEAMED MUSSELS, ORIENTAL-STYLE

2 to 2½ pounds mussels or clams suitable for steaming in their shells, well scrubbed
2 teaspoons soy sauce
1 tablespoon Oriental sesame oil
1 tablespoon minced fresh ginger
¼ cup rice vinegar
½ cup rice wine
1 cup thinly sliced green onions, including tops
2 cloves garlic, minced or pressed

Pull beards from mussels. In a 5- to 6-quart pan, combine soy sauce, sesame oil, ginger, vinegar, wine, onions, and garlic. Add the mussels and cover pan.

"Eric Lie sends us an elegant Oriental variation of steamed mussels."

Cook over medium-high heat until mussel shells open, 6 to 7 minutes. With a slotted spoon, transfer mussels to individual plates. Ladle cooking liquid equally into 4 small bowls. To eat, dip mussels into sauce, drain briefly, and enjoy. Makes 4 first-course servings.

PER SERVING: 115 calories, 8.6 g protein, 8.9 g carbohydrates, 4.9 g fat, 18 mg cholesterol, 452 mg sodium

Eric J. Lie
Edmonds, Wash.

MENTION IRISH CUISINE *and most people can think of nothing but corned beef and cabbage. Students of such matters usually say more about the high quality of Irish foodstuffs—the celebrated beef, bacon, and ham—than the skill in their preparation. Still, one Irish dish is well known: soda bread—a substantial bread with raisins—is a favorite accompaniment to tea, which, in Ireland, is likely to be a smoky Lapsang Souchong. The bread is similar to (if not merely a variant of) a tea cake that's known as barm brack.*

Some etymologists derive the latter from bairigen breac, *Gaelic for speckled cake. It seems equally likely that the first part is simply* barm, *an old-fashioned but respectable term for froth or foam, such as might come from the action of soda with buttermilk in some versions, or yeast with sugar in others—or all of the above, as in this loaf.*

BILL'S IRISH SODA BREAD

1 package active dry yeast
¼ cup warm water (110°)
About 2½ cups all-purpose flour
3 tablespoons sugar
½ teaspoon *each* salt and baking soda
1 tablespoon caraway seed
¾ cup buttermilk
2 tablespoons melted butter or margarine
½ cup raisins

In a small bowl, sprinkle yeast over water and let stand until softened, about 5 minutes. In a large bowl, stir together 1 cup flour, sugar, salt, soda, and caraway seed. Add yeast mixture, butter-

"In Ireland, soda bread is a favorite accompaniment to tea."

milk, and butter; beat to mix well. Add 1½ cups more flour and raisins; stir to moisten. Cover dough with plastic wrap and let stand in a warm place until doubled, about 1½ hours.

Scrape dough onto a lightly floured board and knead until smooth and elastic, about 10 minutes. Push raisins that pop out back into dough. Shape dough into a smooth ball. Set on a greased 12- by 15-inch baking sheet and pat dough into a 7-inch round. Cover lightly with plastic wrap and let stand in a warm place until puffy, 45 minutes to 1 hour.

With a floured razor blade or a very sharp knife, cut a cross about ¼ inch deep in center of loaf. Bake, uncovered, in a 350° oven until well browned, about 30 minutes. Let stand on a rack until just barely warm or cool. Makes 1 loaf, about 1¼ pounds.

PER OUNCE: 91 calories, 2.3 g protein, 17.4 g carbohydrates, 1.5 g fat, 3.5 mg cholesterol, 97 mg sodium

Bill Sandstrom
Bakersfield, Calif.

November Menus

A GATHERING OF GRAINS *gives menus this month a harvest flair. For breakfast, rice becomes a creamy risotto to eat with spiced sugar and milk. For lunch or supper, one meal features leftover turkey with a cool no-cook bulgur salad; the second combines wild rice and increasingly popular quinoa in a warm salad with nuts, apple, and tangerine.*

RISOTTO BREAKFAST

**Risotto Cereal with
Anise-Coriander Sugar
Milk or Light Cream
Persimmons, Bananas, Grapes
Coffee   Marsala**

This sweet, spicy cereal is a warm way to start a cool day.

This risotto has the same creamy texture as the famous Italian dish, but it's seasoned delicately for morning appetites. Offer extra milk and fruit to add to bowls.

To the coffee, add a touch of spiced sugar and marsala—another Italian inspiration.

RISOTTO CEREAL WITH ANISE-CORIANDER SUGAR

> About ¼ cup butter or margarine
> 1½ cups medium- or long-grain white rice
> Water
> 1½ cups milk
> Anise-coriander sugar (directions follow)
> Salt

In a 4- to 5-quart pan over medium heat, melt 2 tablespoons butter. Add rice and stir until opaque, about 2 minutes. Add water—3 cups for medium-grain rice, 4⅓ cups for long-grain rice. Add milk and bring to a boil over high heat.

Reduce heat and simmer, uncovered. Stir occasionally at first; then, as liquid is almost absorbed, stir frequently until rice is tender to bite and still creamy, 20

Ladle hot, smooth breakfast risotto into bowls; add spiced sugar and fruit.

to 30 minutes. Stir in ¼ cup anise-coriander sugar. Ladle into bowls and offer with remaining spiced sugar, butter, and salt to add to taste. Serve at once (risotto gets sticky if it stands). Makes 6 to 8 servings.

PER SERVING: 239 calories, 5.1 g protein, 40 g carbohydrates, 6 g fat, 19 mg cholesterol, 71 mg sodium

Anise-coriander sugar. Lightly crush 1 teaspoon **anise seed** with the back of a spoon or a mortar and pestle. Mix seed with ½ cup **sugar** and 1 teaspoon **ground coriander.** Makes ½ cup.

PER TEASPOON: 17 calories, 0 g protein, 0 g carbohydrates, 0 g fat, 0 mg cholesterol, 0.2 mg sodium

HARVEST GRAIN SALAD SUPPER

Hot Quinoa & Wild Rice Salad
Fresh Fennel & Celery Sticks
Eggnog Custard
Grapefruit Juice Spritzers

Quinoa, an ancient grain-like seed from South America, is becoming available in supermarkets. It has a delicious, wholesome flavor and a pleasant texture.

You can cook the quinoa and rice ahead, and also bake the custard.

HOT QUINOA & WILD RICE SALAD

> 1   cup wild rice
> ½   cup quinoa, or ⅓ cup long-grain white rice
>   Water
> ½   cup chopped hazelnuts
> 2   tablespoons olive oil or salad oil
> 1   medium-size onion, finely chopped
> 1   medium-size tart apple, cored and finely chopped
>   Tangerine dressing (recipe follows)
>   Salt and pepper
> 1   quart lightly packed watercress sprigs or curly endive leaves, rinsed and crisped

Pour each kind of grain into a fine strainer and rinse under running water; rub the quinoa with your hands to wash the surface of the grain well (it may have a slightly bitter natural residue on it).

In a 3- to 4-quart pan, bring 3½ cups water to boiling on high heat. Add wild rice; cover and simmer 30 minutes. Add quinoa. Cook, covered, until grains are barely tender to bite, 10 to 15 minutes longer; drain off any liquid. If made ahead, cover and chill until next day. Stir with a fork.

Meanwhile, put hazelnuts in a 10- to 12-inch frying pan over medium heat. Shake pan frequently until nuts are golden, about 8 minutes. Pour nuts from pan and set aside.

Turn heat to high; add oil to the pan. When oil is hot, add onion and apple; stir until browned, 2 to 4 minutes; add to nuts. Mix wild rice mixture in pan until warm. Remove from heat and mix in nuts, apples, onion, and the dressing; add salt and pepper to taste.

Mound watercress onto a platter. Spoon the warm salad onto the greens. Makes 4 to 6 servings.
PER SERVING: 411 calories, 8.2 g protein, 45 g carbohydrates, 23 g fat, 0 mg cholesterol, 24 mg sodium

Tangerine dressing. Mix together ½ cup **tangerine juice,** 2 tablespoons **lemon juice,** ⅓ cup *each* **currants** and **olive oil** or salad oil, and ½ teaspoon **fennel seed,** chopped.

EGGNOG CUSTARD

> 3   large eggs
> ⅓   cup sugar
> 1   teaspoon vanilla
> ¼   teaspoon ground nutmeg
> 2½ cups light cream (half-and-half) or milk

In a bowl, beat eggs just to blend with sugar, vanilla, and nutmeg; stir in half-and-half. Pour into a shallow 1½-quart baking dish or pan. Set in a larger pan in a 350° oven. Add boiling water to fill larger pan about ½ inch deep. Bake custard until center is set but still jiggles when dish is gently shaken, about 40 minutes. Lift from water and serve hot, warm, or cool. If made ahead, cover and chill up until next day. Makes 6 servings.
PER SERVING: 215 calories, 6 g protein, 16 g carbohydrates, 14 g fat, 174 mg cholesterol, 75 mg sodium

THANKSGIVING WIND-DOWN

Post-Thanksgiving Platter
Hot French Bread
Extra-virgin Olive Oil   Salt
Pumpkin Ice Cream
with Chopped White Chocolate
Spice Tea

Various elements from the Thanksgiving table get revamped here. The menu works well, however, at any time of year.

Make the tabbouleh just by soaking, then seasoning the bulgur; it's ready to eat in a few minutes but will hold for hours.

Instead of butter, try the Mediterranean method of offering flavorful olive oil from a small bowl as a dunking sauce for the bread, then sprinkle the bread lightly with salt as you eat it.

Scoop the pumpkin ice cream into plump balls, then roll quickly in chopped chocolate to make "frosted pumpkins" (they can go into the freezer if you want to make them a few hours before dinner), or simply put the ice cream in bowls and scatter with the chocolate.

(Continued on next page)

Cracked-wheat tabbouleh and leftover turkey embellished with lime juice vinaigrette make a hearty supper.

POST-THANKSGIVING PLATTER

Tabbouleh (recipe follows)
About 1 pound boned and skinned cooked turkey, thinly sliced
2 small oranges, cut in half or thirds
2 small, cooked sweet potatoes or yams, at room temperature, cut in half or thirds (optional)
2 medium-size firm-ripe avocados, cut in half or thirds and pitted
Cilantro sprigs or alfalfa sprouts
½ pound jicama, rinsed, peeled, and cut into thin sticks
¾ to 1 cup cranberry sauce or relish, purchased or homemade
Coarsely ground pepper

Pour tabbouleh into a large, fine strainer over a bowl; let stand until dressing drains into bowl, about 10 minutes.

On 4 or 6 dinner plates, mound equal amounts of the tabbouleh. Beside tabbouleh, arrange equal portions of the turkey, oranges, sweet potatoes, avocado, cilantro, jicama, and cranberry sauce. Ladle dressing drained from tabbouleh over the salads. Individually, add pepper to taste, and squeeze juice from oranges onto salads as you eat. Makes 4 or 6 servings.

PER SERVING: 673 calories, 28 g protein, 58 g carbohydrates, 39 g fat, 58 mg cholesterol, 79 mg sodium

Tabbouleh. In a bowl, combine 1¼ cups hot **water** and 1¼ cups **bulgur** (cracked wheat; use fine to medium texture); stir to moisten evenly. Let stand until bulgur is tender to bite, 10 to 20 minutes; drain well in a fine strainer.

In the bowl, combine bulgur, ⅔ cup **olive oil** or salad oil, 6 tablespoons **lime juice,** 3 tablespoons **red wine vinegar,** 2 teaspoons **sugar,** ½ teaspoon **ground cumin,** and **salt** and **pepper** to taste. Mix well. If made ahead, cover and chill up until next day.

Roast Loin of Pork with Cranberry-Chili Relish (page 287)

Join us in celebrating
the holiday season with family and friends. We offer two
menus for informal gatherings: a brunch for a crowd and a
portable barbecue buffet. For festive dinners at home we
feature a selection of boneless holiday roasts, each embellished
with a flavorful glaze of marinade. Treats to serve or give as
gifts include wine jellies, nut-laced caramel cookies, and
home-baked sourdough breads and cake.

Holiday Traditions: Big Outings for Family or Friends

BIG OUTINGS FOR FAMILY *or friends are holiday traditions for many Westerners. Two groups we joined also take advantage of fine scenery and winter weather, adding outdoor activity to the occasion.*

Though casual-seeming, these gatherings require some thoughtful coordination. At both parties we visited, planned potlucks resulted in wonderful meals.

BIG SKY BRUNCH FOR 16

Hot Ranch Egg Salad
Pan-browned Venison Sausages
Orange-Honey Butter
Assorted Breads:
Brown Bread, Muffins,
Sesame Sticks, Nut Bread,
Sourdough Biscuits
Sunshine Punch   Cowboy Coffee

At a Montana ranch, friends congregate in late morning, arriving with breads and pastries to contribute. But before everyone settles down to enjoy Claudette and Bill Pruitt's special egg dish, the group heads out for a brisk hike in the Beartooth Mountains—on cross-country skis, if there's snow. Along the trail, there's a campfire break with coffee or hot cider and a snack.

Back home, breads go into the oven to warm as the egg dish cooks and the Pruitt's homemade venison sausage browns (you can use regular pork links, allowing about ¼ lb. per serving).

Hot cider warms prebrunch hikers during a break in mountain walk.

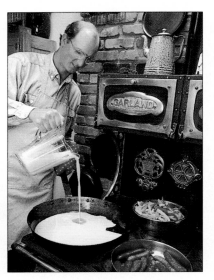

Back in the kitchen, Billy Pruitt cooks vegetables and scrambles eggs for quick but colorful entrée.

To go with the breads, the Pruitts whip butter with a little honey and grated orange peel.

To make sunshine punch, mix together frozen concentrates of orange, grapefruit, and pineapple juices, and dilute with sparkling water (to mellow, add canned apricot nectar). To make cowboy coffee, stir sweetened chocolate beverage mix to taste into individual mugs of coffee.

If you don't have a large frying pan, cook eggs in 2 batches in 8- to 10-inch pans.

HOT RANCH EGG SALAD

2   *each* **medium-size green bell peppers, red bell peppers, and yellow bell peppers**
3   **tablespoons butter or margarine**
1   **tablespoon** *each* **dry thyme leaves and dry basil leaves**
4   **garlic cloves, minced or pressed**
2   **medium-size onions, slivered**
1   **can (5 oz.) water chestnuts, drained and cut in half**
24   **large eggs**
¾   **cup milk**
     Parsley sprigs (optional)
     Salt and pepper

Rinse, stem, and seed peppers; cut them into ⅜-inch-wide strips and set aside.

In a 12- to 14-inch frying pan, combine 2 tablespoons butter, thyme, basil, and garlic. Cook, stirring often, over

medium heat until garlic is golden, about 5 minutes. Add pepper strips, onion, and water chestnuts. Continue cooking, stirring often, until vegetables are slightly limp, about 20 minutes. Pour mixture onto a large platter; keep warm.

In a bowl, beat eggs with milk. In frying pan, melt remaining butter over medium heat, tilting to coat bottom. Pour egg mixture into pan. Stir and lift cooked part of eggs, allowing uncooked egg to flow underneath, until eggs are softly set, about 20 minutes. Slip eggs from pan onto vegetables. Top with parsley. Add salt and pepper to taste. Makes 16 servings. —*The Pruitts, Big Timber, Mont.*

PER SERVING: 164 calories, 10 g protein, 5.6 g carbohydrates, 11 g fat, 418 mg cholesterol, 133 mg sodium

HOLIDAY BARBECUE BUFFET

Oysters with Tomatillo Salsa
Tortilla Chips   Jicama Sticks
Grilled Turkey Drumsticks, Breast &
Banana Squash with Cranberry Salsa
Skewered Sausage, Onions & Potatoes
with Mustard Cream
Mixed Skewered Vegetables
Christmas Cookies   Tangerines
Mulled Cider   Sparkling Water

Always ready to take advantage of glorious weather and an uncrowded winter beach, the families who gather for this holiday get-together in La Jolla, California, redefine the term "buffet."

It's a b.y.o.b. affair: bring your own barbecue. Lined up, the barbecues easily handle a cook-and-serve buffet.

Nice day, but no beach? Try a local park with picnic tables and barbecues.

In this festive menu, turkey and all the extras are transportable, and most of the foods are cooked at the site. It's a meal to satisfy 16 adults (with enough extra for about 6 small children).

A special feature of this meal is the cooky exchange. Each family brings a generous supply of one or more favorite kinds of cookies. Everyone eats some for dessert, then people swap extras to take home.

It's easy to divide duties, provisions, and supplies for this event. Some families can provide the barbecues; noncooks can bring raw foods to be cooked on the barbecues, and people who like to cook can bring finished dishes. A team of 2 or 3 chefs can easily oversee the grilling.

(Continued on next page)

Montana friends gather annually for a holiday brunch, preceded by an invigorating hike or cross-country ski trip. Buffet features eggs with sautéed vegetables, venison sausages, and assorted breads and biscuits.

For a holiday barbecue buffet at the beach, line up the grills to cook a feast of skewered vegetables, sausages, and turkey parts. Each family brings homemade Christmas cookies for dessert; extra cookies are swapped to take home.

Winter picnicking depends on flexibility, and this meal is designed to give you just that.

You cook on several barbecues, carried to the site of the gathering. But if you have access to a very large portable barbecue or are in a park with large stationary barbecues, take advantage of the more plentiful grill space. Everything cooks over medium coals, so grill space can be shared. You'll need tongs and insulated mitts or hot pads for moving foods as they cook.

All the small pieces of food (mostly vegetables) are threaded on skewers to be easy to handle. Our recipes suggest using 10- to 12-inch-long metal skewers; you need a total of about 3 dozen. If your grill is larger, use fewer but longer skewers.

Three different make-ahead sauces accompany various foods. Oysters with a tart green tomatillo salsa start the meal. In the main course, a tangy cranberry sauce is served with turkey and squash, and a smooth mustard cream accompanies sausages, potatoes, and onions. Or try the sauces interchangeably.

From the time the foods are ready for the grill and the coals are ready to use, it takes only 45 minutes to cook the meal.

Bring a scoop and a large metal can or bucket to hold hot ashes so you can clean out barbecues before departing.

OYSTERS WITH TOMATILLO SALSA

If you want raw oysters, have them shucked at the fish market—or do it at the picnic. Grilled oysters will pop open by themselves.

48 small Pacific oysters (2 to 3 in. wide)
Tomatillo salsa (recipe follows)

At home or at the picnic site, scrub oysters with a stiff brush under cool running water; transport in an insulated bag.

To shuck oysters, place 1 at a time on a solid surface, cupped sides down, with hinged end at your left (reverse if you are left-handed). Using a heavy potholder or glove to protect your hand, grasp oyster firmly at hinge end. Force an oyster knife between the shells at the opposite end, angling the knife down and sliding it across the shell's interior to cut the muscle free (you'll feel it give way).

Lift off top shell with oyster attached; cut oyster free and put in cupped shell with juices. (Or have this done at the fish market, then pack oysters on ice to keep them steady; serve within 24 hours.)

To barbecue oysters, set them, cupped sides down, on a barbecue grill 4 to 6 inches above hot coals (you can hold your hand at grill level only 2 to 3 seconds). When shells begin to open, remove carefully from grill; shells and juices are hot, so use tongs or hot pads. Cut oysters free from shells, discarding top shells.

As oysters are shucked or grilled, top with tomatillo salsa and eat from the shells. Makes 16 servings, 3 oysters each.

PER OYSTER: 31 calories, 3.5 g protein, 1.8 g carbohydrates, 0.8 g fat, 21 mg cholesterol, 40 mg sodium

Tomatillo salsa. Drain juice from 2 cans (13 oz. each) **tomatillos** and discard. Chop tomatillos and mix with 1 small can (4 oz.) **diced green chilies,** ½ cup minced **green onion,** ½ cup minced **fresh cilantro** (coriander), and 2 tablespoons **lime juice.** Add **salt** to taste. Serve; or, if made ahead, cover and chill up to 2 days. To transport, put in a tightly covered container and carry in an insulated chest. Makes 3 cups.

PER TABLESPOON: 3.4 calories, 0.2 g protein, 0.6 g carbohydrates, 0.1 g fat, 0 mg cholesterol, 15 mg sodium

GRILLED TURKEY DRUMSTICKS, BREAST & BANANA SQUASH WITH CRANBERRY SALSA

It takes a lot of space to grill these foods; you may need several barbecues.

2 boned and skinned turkey breast halves (about 2 lb. total)
6 turkey drumsticks (about 1½ lb. each)
3 pounds seeded banana squash, cut into about 1½- by 4-inch rectangles
Garlic oil (recipe follows)
Cranberry salsa (recipe follows)

Rinse breasts and drumsticks and pat dry. Cut turkey breasts across the grain into ⅜-inch-thick slices. If prepared ahead, cover and chill meat up until next day.

Thread 4 or 5 pieces of squash, perpendicular to wide sides, onto a 10- to 12-inch metal skewer. Thread another skewer through squash, parallel to the first and about 1½ inches from it. Repeat to skewer remaining squash. If prepared ahead, cover and chill up until next day.

To transport, carry turkey and skewered squash in an insulated chest.

On a barbecue (1 or more) with a lid, place grill 4 to 6 inches above a solid layer of medium coals (you can hold your hand at grill level only 4 to 5 seconds). Arrange drumsticks on grill and baste with garlic oil. Put lid on barbecue and open dampers. Cook drumsticks 15 minutes, turning every 5 minutes and basting with garlic oil. Lay skewered squash on grill and baste with garlic oil. Cover and cook until meat is no longer pink at bone (cut to test) and squash is tender when pierced, about 30 minutes. Every 10 minutes, turn meat and squash, basting with oil.

Scrape or brush grill quickly to clean. Baste turkey slices with oil. Lay on grill and cook uncovered, turning several times, just until no longer pink in center (cut to test) and lightly browned, 6 to 8 minutes. Arrange meat and squash (pushed off skewers) on a platter; accompany with cranberry salsa. If desired, slice some meat from drumsticks to share. Makes 16 servings.

PER 3 OUNCES BONED AND SKINNED TURKEY (WHITE AND DARK MEAT COMBINED): 230 calories, 21 g protein, 6.4 g carbohydrates, 13 g fat, 55 mg cholesterol, 59 mg sodium

Garlic oil. Mix together 1½ cups **olive oil** or salad oil and 6 **garlic cloves,** minced or pressed. Cover; let stand at least 4 hours, or up to 1 week. Use about ¾ cup for turkey and squash; reserve remainder for following recipes. Makes 1½ cups.

Cranberry salsa. In a food processor or with a large knife, finely chop 3 cups (12-oz. package) fresh or frozen **cranberries,** 1 small **onion,** ½ cup firmly packed **parsley,** and 1 teaspoon **crushed dried hot red chilies.** Mix with 2 teaspoons *each* grated **orange peel** and **lemon juice,** ¼ cup **orange juice,** and 3 tablespoons **honey.** Serve, or, if made ahead, put in a covered container and chill up to 2 days. To transport, carry in a covered container in an insulated chest. Makes 3 cups.

PER TABLESPOON: 8.8 calories, 0.1 g protein, 2.2 g carbohydrates, 0 g fat, 0 mg cholesterol, 0.5 mg sodium

(Continued on next page)

SKEWERED SAUSAGE, ONIONS & POTATOES WITH MUSTARD CREAM

For best flavor and appearance, cut up onions and potatoes at the picnic site. Bring a cutting board and knife. All the foods cook over the same heat, and can share grills.

> **10 russet potatoes (1½- to 2-in. diameter), scrubbed**
>
> **About 3 pounds knackwurst (garlic) or kielbasa (Polish) sausage**
>
> **6 onions (about 2½-in. diameter), each cut into 4 wedges**
>
> **¼ cup garlic oil (recipe precedes)**
>
> **Mustard cream (recipe follows)**

Scrub potatoes. Cut lengthwise into thirds. Thread 5 potato slices, perpendicular to sides, onto a 10- to 12-inch slender metal skewer (you need 12 skewers). Insert another skewer through slices parallel to the first skewer and about 1 inch from it. Repeat to skewer remaining potato slices.

Cut sausages into 12 equal pieces. Thread a 10- to 12-inch skewer (you need 6 skewers) perpendicularly through a piece of sausage, positioning skewer at least 1 inch in from an end. Thread an onion wedge onto skewer and push close to sausage. Run another skewer through sausage parallel to the first, at least 1 inch in from the other end of the sausage. Put an onion wedge on this skewer. Repeat process, filling each pair of skewers with 4 pieces of sausage, and ending with onion wedges (8 total).

Lay skewered potatoes on a barbecue grill (1 or more) 4 to 6 inches above a solid layer of medium coals (you can hold your hand at grill level only 4 to 5 seconds); don't overlap skewers. Brush potato tops lightly with garlic oil. Cook, turning to brown evenly, until tender when pierced, about 20 minutes. With each turn, brush tops with garlic oil.

As the potatoes cook, lay skewered sausages on top of them so they can start to heat (and so their drippings can also flavor potatoes). Have a heatproof tray handy; move sausages onto it as you turn the potatoes, or if sausages flare.

When potatoes are brown, place them at the sides of the barbecue and put sausages onto grill; brush onions lightly with garlic oil. Cook until sausages are hot in the center (cut to test), about 10 minutes.

Special sauces add zest. Creative combinations are encouraged.

Push potato slices, sausages, and onions from skewers onto a large platter. Serve mustard cream to spoon onto meat and vegetables. Serves 16.

PER SERVING WITHOUT MUSTARD CREAM: 371 calories, 12 g protein, 19 g carbohydrates, 27 g fat, 49 mg cholesterol, 866 mg sodium

Mustard cream. In the top of a double boiler, beat together 4 large **egg yolks,** 2 tablespoons **sugar,** ½ cup **Dijon mustard,** ¼ cup **white wine vinegar,** and 1 tablespoon **water.** Add 2 tablespoons **butter** or margarine. Cook over simmering water, stirring, until mixture is as thick as whipping cream, 5 to 8 minutes. Set top of the double boiler into ice water; stir often until sauce is cool.

Beat 1 cup **whipping cream** until it holds stiff peaks. Fold mustard mixture into cream. If made ahead, cover and chill up to 3 days. To transport, put in a covered container and carry in an insulated chest. Makes 3½ cups.

PER TABLESPOON: 25 calories, 0.2 g protein, 0.8 g carbohydrates, 2.3 g fat, 25 mg cholesterol, 70 mg sodium

SKEWERED MIXED VEGETABLES

> **About 4 pounds vegetables (choices follow; use 1 or several kinds)**
>
> **½ cup garlic oil (recipe precedes)**

Thread vegetables perpendicularly through widest part and closely together onto 10- to 12-inch metal skewers (you need about 6 total).

Place skewered vegetables on a barbecue grill (1 or more) 4 to 6 inches above a solid layer of medium coals (you can hold your hand at grill level only 4 to 5 seconds); don't overlap skewers. Brush vegetables on top lightly with garlic oil.

Cook, turning often, until vegetables are tinged with brown, 8 to 10 minutes. Brush tops with oil occasionally as vegetables are turned. Push vegetables from skewers onto a platter. Serves 16.

PER SERVING: 82 calories, 1.6 g protein, 4.3 g carbohydrates, 7 g fat, 0 mg cholesterol, 7 mg sodium

Vegetables to grill. Rinse, drain, and trim as directed.

Bell peppers—any color. Stem, core, and seed; cut into 1½- to 2-inch-wide strips, then cut in half crosswise.

Broccoli. Cut off tough ends and discard. Peel tender part of stalks. Cut lengthwise into sections no thicker than 2 inches.

Mushrooms (1½- to 2-in. diameter). Trim off discolored ends of stems.

Fennel. Cut off and discard woody stems. Cut bulb vertically into 2-inch-wide slices.

Zucchini (1½-in. thick). Cut off and discard ends; diagonally cut ¾-inch slices.

MULLED CIDER

If you use wine, offer pineapple juice or apple juice for the youngsters.

> **2 quarts apple juice or apple cider**
>
> **1 large can (12 oz.) thawed frozen pineapple juice concentrate**
>
> **2 medium-size oranges, cut into ½-inch slices, ends discarded**
>
> **5 cinnamon sticks (each about 3 in. long)**
>
> **12 whole cloves**
>
> **12 whole allspice**
>
> **3 quarts dry white jug wine (or 3 qt. apple juice and 1 can, 6-oz. size, thawed frozen pineapple juice concentrate)**

In an 8- to 10-quart pan, stir together apple juice, pineapple concentrate, orange slices, cinnamon sticks, cloves, and allspice. Cover and heat until simmering on medium to high heat (you can do this on a barbecue or a camp stove); simmer to blend flavors, about 15 minutes.

Add wine. If made at home, pour into a thermos to transport. Ladle into mugs. Makes 24 servings, 8-ounce size.

PER 8-OUNCE SERVING: 154 calories, 0.5 g protein, 21 g carbohydrates, 0.2 g fat, 0 mg cholesterol, 9.4 mg sodium

Stocking-Stuffers for Cooks of All Ages

IF YOU'RE LOOKING *for small, moderately priced gifts for stocking-stuffers, food and drink gadgets can often fill the bill.*

Here we've gathered three groups—one for young cooks, one for home cellar masters, and one for picnickers. Each gift costs $7 or less, with one $16 exception.

Tots and pans. Surprising numbers of cooking tools, even professional equipment, come in diminutive sizes. Choices include tart and loaf pans, spatulas, spoons, and whisks, all well suited to the small hands of young cooks, who often delight in the tools' authenticity.

Real corkers. The choice of useful wine gadgets (below left) is quite extensive. For example, tools that help preserve the quality of opened bottles range from a cork shaver to a pump that extracts air and also corks the bottle.

For the outdoors. Campers and picnickers can use the items pictured below right: containers to protect food from crushing, covers to keep bugs away from the food, clips to hold tablecloths in place on breezy days, and more.

To carry the gadget gift idea further, think about how food and beverage might be involved in a friend's hobbies—whether scuba diving, skiing, or needlepoint.

These really are for cooking! More than toys, small-size tools designed for specific jobs also fit small hands.

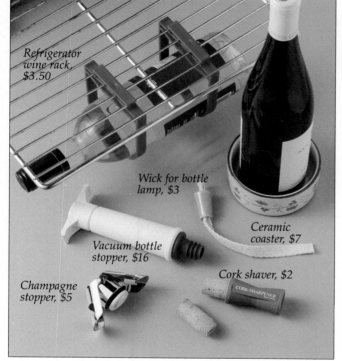

Wine gadgets make great gifts: clips and coasters to hold, stoppers to reclose, wick to turn bottle into a light.

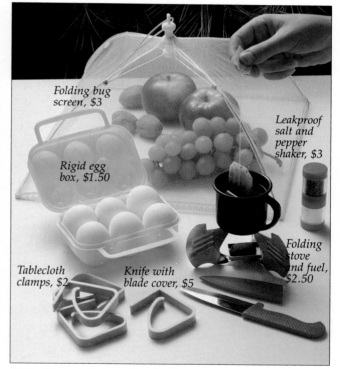

Lightweight tools that travel for picnicking, camping, and backpacking range from tablecloth clips to mini-stove.

A Christmas Cooky Masterpiece

LOOKING LIKE ROUGHHEWN *jewels*, Western-grown nuts are framed by these grand-scale caramel cookies. Thin, crisp, and shiny, they make striking desserts or impressive gifts.

Fragile to bite, the cookies are much easier to make and sturdier to handle than they look. The process is simple—but it requires some careful attention.

As the caramel around the nuts bakes, it spreads into a very thin layer 5 to 6 inches in diameter. You can bake only a few cookies at a time.

While hot, the caramel is soft. As it cools, the cookies become rigid. The trick is to get them off the pan after they harden enough not to stretch and tear, but before they get so brittle they break.

Stored airtight, these cookies stay crisp. If you want to make them more than a week ahead, they should be frozen for best flavor. If you're giving them away, hand-carry them—very carefully.

To create a striking visual effect and an easier-than-pie dessert, tuck a cooky vertically into a bowl of your favorite flavor of ice cream.

Push dough by the tablespoonful onto greased and floured baking sheets. As the cooky bakes, it spreads out dramatically.

NUT LACE COOKIES

- ¼ **cup (⅛ lb.) butter or margarine**
- ¼ **cup *each* light corn syrup and firmly packed brown sugar**
- ¼ **cup all-purpose flour**
- 1 **cup mixed whole or half almonds, hazelnuts, macadamias, pecans, pine nuts, pistachios, and walnuts, plain or salted (or any combination of these nuts)**

In a 1- to 2-quart pan, melt butter over low heat. Add corn syrup and brown sugar. Stir over high heat until boiling. Remove pan from heat and blend in flour and nuts.

Grease and flour 12- by 15-inch or 14- by 17-inch baking sheets (they must be flat, not warped). For each cooky, place 2 tablespoons of the nut mixture about 8 inches apart on the sheet—put only 2 cookies on a pan at a time.

With your fingers, push nuts apart into a 3- to 4-inch circle or oval. Bake in a 350° oven until cookies are a rich golden brown, about 10 minutes (if you have 2 pans in the oven, alternate positions at midpoint to ensure even browning).

Remove cookies from oven and let them cool on the pan until they firm up slightly, about 2 minutes; to test, slide a spatula under a corner. If the cooky is stretchy, wait just a few seconds longer. If it is hard, slide spatula under carefully and lift onto a rack. If cookies get too hard and stick to pan, return to oven to soften slightly.

When cool, serve, or immediately package airtight in rigid container. Cookies absorb moisture and lose their crispness quickly. If you stack the cookies in the containers, separate each layer with a sheet of waxed paper to protect them from breaking and sticking together. Hold at room temperature up to 1 week, or freeze up to 1 month. Makes 10.

PER COOKY (MADE WITH ½ SALTED NUTS): 178 calories, 1.9 g protein, 16 g carbohydrates, 12 g fat, 12 mg cholesterol, 118 mg sodium

Fragile, crisp caramel frames nuts harvested in the West: almonds, hazelnuts, macadamias, pine nuts, pistachios, and walnuts. Cooky is stunning accent for ice cream.

"Wild" to Traditional: Boneless Holiday Roasts

CARVING THE ROAST is a cinch with these boneless cuts from the loin or tenderloin. Embellished with a shiny glaze or flavorful marinade, they're simple, stunning entrées for your holiday dinner.

The loin is a muscle (sometimes called a strip loin) on each side of the backbone on the outside of the ribs; the tenderloin lies inside the ribs on each side. These little-used muscles are the tenderest part of the animal. Both, being long and slender, roast quickly at high temperatures, generally in less than an hour.

Conservative eaters might prefer beef or pork; the more adventurous can consider game, such as buffalo, caribou, or venison. Often labeled as wild, these three are actually ranch raised. Buffalo tastes much like beef. Caribou and venison have a more intense, faintly sweet flavor.

Loin and tenderloin roasts come at a premium. A boneless pork loin is the most reasonable—$15 to $20 for a 4-pound piece. A 4- to 5-pound beef tenderloin will range between $35 and $50. Beef tenderloin or boneless pork loin may be available at a

moment's notice, but during the holidays call a few days in advance.

For game, order as much as a month ahead (look in the yellow pages under Game or Meat). Game is often sold frozen, so you can buy it early and store it in your freezer. Some wholesalers will sell direct to the consumer and may offer the best price. There are also mail-order sources (for a list, send a stamped, self-addressed envelope to Wild Game, Sunset Magazine, 80 Willow Rd., Menlo Park, Calif. 94025). Prices are high and vary considerably—expect to pay

Glazed with a spicy cranberry, orange, and chili relish, pork loin makes handsome roast for holiday dinner. Serve extra relish with meat.

at least $50 to $75 for a 4-pound game roast—so ask about cost before placing an order.

ROAST LOIN OF PORK WITH CRANBERRY-CHILI RELISH

patty 3:30 27

- 3 cups fresh or frozen cranberries
- ¾ cup sugar
- 1 tablespoon finely shredded orange peel
- 1 cup orange juice
- 1 to 2 fresh jalapeño chilies, stemmed, seeded, and minced
- ¼ cup minced shallots
- 1 boned, rolled, and tied center-cut pork loin (3½ to 4 lb.)
  Orange wedges
  Salt

Set aside ¼ cup cranberries. In a food processor or with a knife, coarsely chop remaining cranberries. Put chopped fruit into a 2- to 3-quart pan. Add sugar, orange peel, orange juice, chili, and shallots. Bring to a boil over high heat. Reduce heat and boil gently, uncovered, stirring often until mixture thickens slightly, 8 to 10 minutes.

Place pork, fat side up, on a rack in a 12- by 15-inch roasting pan. Roast in a 375° oven until a thermometer inserted in center of thickest part of meat registers 155°, 55 to 65 minutes. Measure out ½ cup of the cranberry relish; brush it on the roast as it cooks, adding frequently and using it all. Transfer roast to a platter.

Garnish with reserved cranberries and orange wedges. Slice meat crosswise and accompany with remaining relish and salt to add to taste. Makes 8 to 10 servings.

PER FAT-TRIMMED SERVING: 368 calories, 34 g protein, 23 g carbohydrates, 15 g fat, 106 mg cholesterol, 82 mg sodium

SOY MUSTARD-GLAZED BEEF OR BUFFALO

You can usually have your meatman tie and roll the beef tenderloin. You may have to trim and tie the buffalo yourself.

- 1 whole beef tenderloin (4 to 5 lb.), rolled and tied, or 1 whole buffalo tenderloin (4 to 5 lb.)
- 1 cup Dijon mustard
- ⅓ cup firmly packed brown sugar

- 3 tablespoons dry sherry
- 3 tablespoons soy sauce
- 3 tablespoons minced fresh ginger
- 3 tablespoons Oriental sesame oil

Neatly trim any excess fat from roast, if needed. On the buffalo, trim off or scrape free all fibrous sinew and silvery membrane (if present); discard. Reserve any scraps of meat for other uses. To make an evenly shaped roast, tie snugly at 1½- to 2-inch intervals with a cotton string, tucking thin end of roast under, if needed.

Mix the mustard, sugar, sherry, soy sauce, ginger, and oil. Rub meat all over with ⅓ of the mixture; set the rest aside. Place meat on a rack in a 12- by 17-inch roasting pan. Roast in a 425° oven for 30 minutes. Brush to coat with some of the reserved mustard sauce. Continue roasting until a thermometer inserted in center of the thickest part registers 130° for rare (do not overcook buffalo or it will be very dry), 10 to 25 minutes longer.

Transfer roast to a platter and let rest in a warm place 10 to 15 minutes. Pour remaining mustard sauce into a small serving bowl. Slice meat crosswise and offer sauce to spoon over each portion. Makes 10 to 12 servings.

PER SERVING: 284 calories, 25 g protein, 9.5 g carbohydrates, 15 g fat, 78 mg cholesterol, 913 mg sodium

VENISON OR CARIBOU WITH WILD MUSHROOM & JUNIPER BERRY SAUCE

Venison, mainly imported from New Zealand, is relatively easy to get. Caribou and reindeer, which can be used interchangeably, generally come from Alaska, Canada, and northern Scandinavia; both are unpredictable and limited in availability. Also, you may have little choice in the size of the loin.

- 1 boned venison loin (4 to 6 lb.) or 1 boned caribou loin (4 to 6 lb.)
- ¼ cup salad oil
- 1¾ cups dry red wine, such as Merlot
- 1 small onion, minced
- 1 clove garlic, minced or pressed
- 1 dry bay leaf
- 2 tablespoons dry juniper berries
- ½ teaspoon dry thyme leaves
- ¼ teaspoon ground cloves
- 1 tablespoon coarse-ground pepper
- ¼ cup (⅛ lb.) butter or margarine

- ⅓ to ½ pound chanterelle or button mushrooms, rinsed, drained, and thinly sliced
- 2 cups regular-strength beef broth
- ¼ cup red currant jelly
- 1 cup whipping cream

From loin, trim off or scrape free and discard all fibrous sinew, silvery membrane, and tough bits of cartilage (if present). Reserve scraps of meat for other uses. To make an evenly shaped roast, tie loin snugly at 1½- to 2-inch intervals with cotton string, tucking thin end under roast, if needed.

In a heavy plastic bag (2-gal. size), combine oil, ¾ cup wine, onion, garlic, bay leaf, 2 teaspoons juniper berries, thyme, and cloves. Add loin, seal bag, and rotate to coat meat with marinade. Set bag in a pan and chill 2 hours or up until next day; turn meat over occasionally.

Lift meat from marinade; drain briefly. Place on a rack in a 12- by 17-inch roasting pan (if meat is too long, cut in half, and place pieces well apart on rack). Pat pepper all over meat. In a 475° oven, roast venison to rare, 135° on a thermometer inserted in the center of the thickest part, about 25 minutes (check after 15 minutes; thinner roasts cook faster). Roast caribou very rare, 125° to 127° on a thermometer inserted in center of the thickest part, 15 to 20 minutes (check after 15 minutes; thinner roasts cook faster). Put meat on a platter; keep warm.

Melt butter in roasting pan over medium-high heat. Add chanterelles and stir often until they are limp and just beginning to brown, 4 to 5 minutes. Add remaining wine and juniper berries, broth, and jelly; bring to a boil over high heat, stirring to loosen browned bits. Boil, uncovered, until reduced by half, about 10 minutes. Drain any juices from meat into pan. Add cream; boil until reduced to 2 cups, about 8 minutes longer. Pour sauce into a small bowl. Slice meat crosswise; offer sauce to add to taste. Serves 12 to 14.

PER SERVING: 302 calories, 28 g protein, 6.3 g carbohydrates, 18 g fat, 112 mg cholesterol, 160 mg sodium

Holiday Sourdough

HOLIDAY PLEASURES INCLUDE TREATS such as home-baked breads and cakes sweetened with fruit and spices. These three recipes add the tang and moistness of sourdough starter.

Choose from cardamom-flavored swirl bread, cranberry muffins with orange and apricots, and gingerbread cake. (Directions for sourdough starter are on page 112.)

SOURDOUGH HOLIDAY SWIRL BREAD

- ¾ cup sourdough starter, at room temperature
- ½ cup warm (90°) apple juice or milk
- 3¼ to 3½ cups all-purpose flour
- 1 package active dry yeast
- 5 tablespoons melted butter or margarine
- ¼ cup granulated sugar
- 1 teaspoon grated lemon peel
- ¾ teaspoon ground cardamom
- ½ teaspoon salt
- 1 large egg
- ⅓ cup *each* golden raisins and halved candied cherries
- ¼ cup chopped candied citron
- ⅓ cup firmly packed brown sugar mixed with ½ teaspoon ground cinnamon
    Lemon icing (recipe follows)

In a large bowl, stir starter, ¼ cup juice, and ½ cup flour until smooth. For sourest flavor, cover and let stand in a warm place (80° to 90°) until bubbly and sour smelling, 12 to 24 hours. To speed, omit standing; proceed.

Soften yeast in remaining apple juice; stir into starter mixture with 3 tablespoons butter, granulated sugar, lemon peel, cardamom, salt, and egg. Stir in enough flour to form a kneadable dough, about 2½ cups. Turn dough out onto a lightly floured board and knead until smooth and elastic, 8 to 12 minutes; add flour as required to keep dough from sticking.

Gently knead in raisins, cherries, and citron. Place dough in a large greased bowl, then turn dough over. Cover with plastic wrap and let rise in a warm place until double, 1½ to 2 hours.

Punch down dough. Turn out onto lightly floured board and knead gently to expel air. Roll into a 9- by 18-inch rectangle. Brush dough with remaining melted butter, and sprinkle with brown sugar mixture. Roll up dough, starting from long side; pinch seam closed.

On a greased 12- by 15-inch baking sheet, arrange roll seam down in a 9-inch-wide horseshoe. With scissors, make cuts at 1½-inch intervals from outside of horseshoe ⅔ of the way to center. Turn each section on its side, overlapping slightly.

Cover with plastic wrap and let rise in a warm place until puffy, about 1 hour. Bake in a 350° oven until deep golden, about 25 minutes. Loosen bread with a wide spatula, then slide onto a rack and let cool at least 10 minutes. Drizzle with icing. Serve warm or cool. Or let cool completely; store airtight up to 2 days, or freeze up to 2 months. (If freezing bread, ice after it has thawed.) Makes 12 servings. —*Marvin Zeisloft, Colfax, Calif.*

PER SERVING: 317 calories, 5.5 g protein, 61 g carbohydrates, 5.8 g fat, 36 mg cholesterol, 172 mg sodium

Lemon icing. In a bowl, beat until smooth 1 cup sifted **powdered sugar,** ½ teaspoon grated **lemon peel,** and 1½ tablespoons **lemon juice.**

SOURDOUGH CRANBERRY-APRICOT MUFFINS

- ½ cup sourdough starter, at room temperature
- ¾ cup sour cream, at room temperature
- 2 cups all-purpose flour
- ½ cup sugar
- ⅓ cup melted butter or margarine
- 1½ teaspoons grated orange peel
- 1 large egg
- ¼ cup chopped dried apricots
- 1 cup fresh or frozen cranberries
- 1 teaspoon *each* baking soda and baking powder
- ½ teaspoon salt (optional)
    Hazelnut streusel (recipe follows)

Fireside breakfast offers two sourdough treats: glazed, fruit-studded swirl bread, and cranberry-streusel muffins. Serve by the hearth with warming mugs of cocoa.

Sugar-dusted gingerbread cake, with whipped cream and dessert wine, winds up a meal with elegant simplicity.

In a bowl, stir starter, sour cream, and ½ cup flour until smooth. For sourest flavor, cover and let stand in a warm place (80° to 90°) until bubbly and sour smelling, 12 to 24 hours. To speed, omit standing; proceed.

To starter mixture, add sugar, butter, orange peel, and egg; stir until well blended. Mix in apricots and cranberries.

Combine remaining flour with baking soda, baking powder, and salt. Stir into starter mixture just to mix evenly. Spoon batter into 12 greased 2½- to 2¾-inch-wide muffin cups. Pat streusel on top.

Bake in a 425° oven until a toothpick inserted in center of a muffin comes out clean, 20 to 30 minutes. Loosen muffins with a knife and turn out onto a rack. Serve warm or cool. If desired, let cool completely; store airtight up to 1 day or freeze up to 2 months. Makes 12.

PER MUFFIN: 313 calories, 4.6 g protein, 43 g carbohydrates, 14 g fat, 53 mg cholesterol, 216 mg sodium

Hazelnut streusel. With your fingers, rub together until crumbly ½ cup firmly packed **brown sugar,** ⅓ cup **all-purpose flour,** ¼ cup (⅛ lb.) **butter** or margarine,

¼ cup chopped **hazelnuts,** and ½ teaspoon **ground cinnamon.**

SOURDOUGH GINGERBREAD CAKE

- ¾ cup sourdough starter, at room temperature
- 1 cup warm (90°) milk
- 3 cups all-purpose flour
- ¾ cup (⅜ lb.) butter or margarine
- 1 cup sugar
- 1 cup dark molasses
- 2 large eggs
- 2½ teaspoons baking powder
- 2 teaspoons ground cinnamon
- 1½ teaspoons *each* baking soda, ground nutmeg, and ground ginger
- ½ teaspoon salt (optional)
- ¼ teaspoon ground cloves
  Powdered sugar
  Whipped cream dusted with cinnamon (optional)

In bowl, stir starter, milk, and 1 cup flour until smooth. For sourest flavor, cover and let stand in warm place (80° to 90°) until bubbly and sour smelling, 12 to 24

hours. To speed, omit standing; proceed.

In large bowl of an electric mixer, beat butter and sugar until creamy. Add molasses; beat until combined. Mix in eggs, 1 at a time, then add starter mixture and beat until blended. Stir together remaining flour, baking powder, cinnamon, soda, nutmeg, ginger, salt, and cloves; add to starter mixture and beat to blend well.

Pour into a greased and floured plain or fluted 10-inch tube pan. Bake in 325° oven until a toothpick inserted in center comes out clean, about 1 hour.

Let cool in pan on a rack for 15 minutes. Run a knife between cake and pan sides, then invert cake onto rack. Serve warm or cool, dusted with powdered sugar and topped with whipped cream. If desired, let cake cool completely; store airtight up to 1 day or freeze up to 2 months. Serves 12. —*Anne Keenan, Nevada City, Calif.*

PER SERVING: 391 calories, 6.1 g protein, 62 g carbohydrates, 14 g fat, 80 mg cholesterol, 364 mg sodium

Lean But "High-Powered" Salads

LEAN SALADS ARE GOOD *for light and healthy eating, as long as the dressing doesn't destroy a well-laid foundation.*

Here, you're home free because the dressings are fat free; vivid seasonings provide the appetizing alternative.

The first is a vegetable salad of firm, waxy-textured potatoes coated with a dressing of tart lime, fresh ginger, and cilantro. Avocado, with its rich flavor, gives a smooth, unifying finish.

Skinned roast chicken and its fat-skimmed juices, aromatic seeds, and orange juice and peel are the basics of the main-dish salad. To it, add bright red onion, blanched briefly in vinegar water to intensify its color and add tang.

POTATO-AVOCADO SALAD WITH GINGER-LIME DRESSING

- 2 **pounds small (about 1½-in. diameter) red thin-skinned potatoes, scrubbed**
- ½ **cup thinly sliced green onion**
- 6 **tablespoons lime juice**
- 1 **to 2 fresh jalapeño chilies, stemmed, seeded, and minced**
- 2 **teaspoons minced fresh ginger**
- 1 **tablespoon chopped fresh cilantro (coriander)**
- ½ **teaspoon sugar**
- 1 **small firm-ripe avocado**
  Salt

In a 4- to 5-quart pan, bring 2 quarts water to boiling on high heat. Add potatoes; cover and simmer until tender when pierced, 15 to 20 minutes. Drain and let stand until cool enough to touch. Cut potatoes into quarters.

In a bowl, mix potatoes, onion, lime juice, chilies, ginger, cilantro, and sugar. If made ahead, cover and let stand (or chill) up to 3 hours. Peel, halve, and pit avocado; cut into ½-inch cubes. Add avocado to potatoes and stir gently until well mixed. Season to taste with salt. Serves 4 or 5.

PER SERVING: 205 calories, 4.4 g protein, 37 g carbohydrates, 5 g fat, 0 mg cholesterol, 21 mg sodium

ROASTED CHICKEN & PINK ONION SALAD WITH AROMATIC SPICES

- 1 **broiler-fryer chicken (3½ to 4 lb.)**
  Salt and pepper
- 2 **cloves garlic, minced or pressed**
- 3 **tablespoons red wine vinegar**

Shredded roast chicken and bright red onion are dressed leanly with orange juice, spices.

- 1 **medium-size red onion, thinly sliced into rings**
- 1 **tablespoon *each* coriander seed and cumin seed**
- 1 **cup orange juice**
- 1 **tablespoon *each* finely shredded orange peel and chopped fresh cilantro (coriander)**
  Butter lettuce leaves, washed and crisped

Remove giblets from chicken and reserve for other uses. Rinse chicken and pat dry; pull off and discard lumps of fat. Place bird, breast up, on a rack in a 9- by 13-inch pan. Lightly sprinkle chicken inside and out with salt, pepper, and garlic.

Bake in a 400° oven until chicken is browned and thigh is no longer pink at bone (cut to test), about 1 hour. Tip bird to drain juices from body cavity into pan. Let stand until cool enough to handle.

Meanwhile, in a 1- to 1½-quart pan, bring vinegar and 2 cups water to boiling over high heat. Add onion and cook, uncovered, just until slightly limp and brighter pink, about 10 seconds. Drain well and place in a large bowl.

Pull off chicken skin and discard. Pull chicken off bones and discard bones. Tear meat into bite-size pieces; add to onion.

Skim and discard fat from drippings in pan. Add coriander, cumin, orange juice, and orange peel to pan. Stir over medium-high heat until drippings boil and flavors blend, 2 to 3 minutes. Mix with chicken and onions. Add cilantro, and season to taste with salt and pepper. If made ahead, cover and chill up until next day.

Line 4 to 6 salad plates with lettuce leaves. Spoon equal portions of chicken-onion salad onto leaves. Serves 4 to 6.

PER SERVING: 213 calories, 28 g protein, 7.2 g carbohydrates, 7.4 g fat, 84 mg cholesterol, 84 mg sodium

Burmese Surprises

LESS KNOWN THAN THE CUISINES *of its Asian neighbors, the food of Burma deserves recognition. Here, we present a refreshing sampler menu inspired by the Burmese Nan Yang Restaurant in Oakland.*

If you're familiar with Indian, Thai, and Chinese cooking, you may recognize their influence on Burmese cuisine, but its flavor combinations are unique. Burmese food is less fiery than some Southeast Asian dishes; the primary seasonings used are dried shrimp, fish sauce, garlic, lemon, and ginger.

The ginger salad is an appealing combination of crunchy and sweet-hot ingredients. In rural Burma, it's a post-harvest, festival-season specialty.

Together, the cold noodle salad and spiced vegetable soup are a typical Burmese breakfast, but we suggest them for a Western supper with the first-course ginger salad to add substance.

All three recipes call for cabbage; red provides more color contrast for the salads, and green looks better in the soup, but you can use just one type. You'll find raw peanuts and flaked coconut in health-food stores. Look for the fish sauce, dried shrimp, and black fungus in Oriental markets or well-stocked grocery stores.

BURMESE GINGER SALAD

- ¾ **cup yellow or green split peas**
- ¾ **cup blanched (skinned) raw peanuts**
- ¾ **cup slivered fresh ginger (matchstick pieces ¹⁄₁₆ to ⅛ in. thick, 2 to 6 in. long)**
- ¾ **cup distilled white vinegar**
- ¾ **cup unsweetened flaked coconut**
- 2 **tablespoons sesame seed**
- ⅓ **cup salad oil**
- 2 **large cloves garlic, thinly sliced**
- 1½ **tablespoons fish sauce (*nam pla* or *nuoc nam*) or soy sauce**
- 1½ **cups finely shredded red or green cabbage**
- 1 **or 2 fresh jalapeño chilies, stemmed and thinly sliced crosswise**
- ⅓ **cup slivered onion**
- 3 **tablespoons small dried shrimp; whirl in a blender until powdered**
- 2 **limes or 1 lemon, cut into wedges**

Place peas and peanuts in separate small bowls and cover with warm water; let stand at least 3 hours or up to overnight. Drain well and pat dry. Also, place ginger and vinegar in a small bowl, then cover and chill at least 2 hours or up to 2 days; drain and discard vinegar.

In a 10- to 12-inch frying pan over medium heat, stir coconut often until golden, about 8 minutes; pour out and set aside. Repeat with sesame seed, 3 to 5 minutes.

Add oil to pan. When oil is hot, add split peas and stir often until deep golden, 12 to 15 minutes. Lift out with a slotted spoon and drain on paper towels. Repeat with peanuts, 4 to 5 minutes.

Add garlic to oil in pan and cook, stirring often, until golden, 1 to 3 minutes. Lift from pan with a slotted spoon and drain on paper towels. Let oil cool. Stir fish sauce into oil; set aside. (At this point, you can cover coconut, sesame, peas, peanuts, garlic, and oil mixture separately; store at room temperature up to 1 week.)

On a platter, arrange ginger, coconut, sesame, peas, peanuts, garlic, cabbage, chilies, onion, and shrimp in separate piles. At the table, pour oil mixture over salad, squeeze limes on top, and mix ingredients. Makes 6 first-course servings.

PER SERVING: 396 calories, 14 g protein, 27 g carbohydrates, 28 g fat, 7.2 mg cholesterol, 279 mg sodium

COLD NOODLE SALAD

- 8 **ounces dry vermicelli or linguini**
- 1 **clove garlic, minced or pressed**
- ¼ **cup salad oil**
- ½ **cup lemon juice**
- 1 **tablespoon fish sauce (*nam pla* or *nuoc nam*) or soy sauce**
- 1 **medium-size cucumber, thinly sliced**
- 3 **tablespoons small dried shrimp; whirl in a blender until powdered**
- 2 **cups finely shredded red or green cabbage**
- 2 **boiled medium-size thin-skinned potatoes, peeled and cut into ½-inch pieces**
  Fresh cilantro (coriander) sprigs

In a 5- to 6-quart pan, bring 3 quarts water to a boil over high heat. Add vermicelli and cook until barely tender to bite, 6 to 9 minutes. Drain, rinse with cold water, and drain again.

In a large bowl, mix garlic, oil, lemon juice, and fish sauce. Add vermicelli, cucumber, shrimp, cabbage, and potatoes; mix well. Spoon onto a platter and garnish with cilantro. Makes 6 servings.

PER SERVING: 280 calories, 7.3 g protein, 41 g carbohydrates, 9.8 g fat, 7.2 mg cholesterol, 189 mg sodium

Vegetable-prawn soup, cold noodle salad, and tea make up light Burmese supper.

SPICED VEGETABLE & PRAWN SOUP

- ½ **cup dry black fungus (cloud ears)**
- 7 **cups regular-strength chicken broth**
- 3 **cloves garlic, minced or pressed**
- 3 **tablespoons fish sauce (*nam pla* or *nuoc nam*) or soy sauce**
- 1 **teaspoon ground pepper**
- 2 **cups thinly sliced small pattypan squash**
- 2 **cups finely shredded green or red cabbage**
- 1 **pound large shrimp (31 to 35 per lb.), shelled and deveined**

In a small bowl, soak fungus in warm water to cover until soft and pliable, about 20 minutes. Work with fingers to loosen any grit, then lift from water (discard water). Cut out and discard hard knobby pieces. Slice fungus in ⅓-inch-wide strips.

Meanwhile, in a 5- to 6-quart pan, bring broth, garlic, fish sauce, and pepper to a boil over high heat. Cover and simmer for 10 minutes. Add fungus, squash, cabbage, and shrimp. Cook, covered, until squash is tender-crisp to bite, about 4 minutes. Makes 2 quarts, 6 servings.

PER SERVING: 133 calories, 17 g protein, 9.3 g carbohydrates, 3.8 g fat, 93 mg cholesterol, 674 mg sodium

Vintage Jellies

LIKE THE VARIETAL WINES *they're made from, these jellies have a vinous character, sparkling clarity, and color.*

Wine, sugar, and liquid pectin are the only ingredients. The process is fast, compared to fruit jellies—no fruit to cook, no juice to extract. Sugar reinforces the varietal character of the grape the wine is made from. Boiling cooks off alcohol.

But which wine to choose? The answer is easy: if you like to drink it, you'll enjoy eating it. We suggest, however, that you reserve costly wines for sipping and select moderately priced ones with a good level of fruit for jellies. Your wine merchant can suggest specific brands.

Here's a general overview to get you started. Sauvignon Blanc can be sweet or dry and austere, sometimes with vegetative overtones. Chardonnay, usually fuller and richer, often has a touch of vanilla from the aging barrels. Aromatic wines—Chenin Blanc, Gewürztraminer, Johannisberg Riesling—have delicate flavorings of flowers, fruit, or spices. Late-harvest versions of these wines, particularly those touched by botrytis, make intense jellies.

Blush wines like white Zinfandel, pale to brilliantly pink and rose, offer their lovely hues as a bonus.

Sugar softens tannin—or astringent roughness—in red wine, so even young, puckery reds make good jellies. Red wines vary dramatically, but generally Merlot is soft with a berry flavor while Cabernet Sauvignon, Pinot Noir, and Zinfandel tend to be more complex. All are good.

With jug wines, the same rule applies. If you like it, use it.

Serve jellies at occasions when wine is fitting. They go well with mild cheese and crackers, either before or after dinner.

You might want to make batches of jelly from different kinds of wine and assemble sampler packs—some for your own use, some for stocking-stuffers or hostess gifts.

If jellies will be stored at room temperature, you must process them in a water bath. Otherwise, omit this step and just refrigerate the jellies for several months.

VARIETAL WINE JELLY

2 **cups wine (see choices, preceding)**
3¼ **cups sugar**
1 **pouch (3 oz.) liquid pectin**

Wash and rinse 4 half-pint canning jars and metal rings; drain. Sterilize 4 new lids according to manufacturer's directions.

In a 5- to 6-quart pan, mix wine with sugar. Bring to a full rolling boil over high heat, stirring constantly. Stir in pectin. Return to a boil and cook for exactly 1 minute, stirring constantly.

Remove from heat and skim off any foam. Ladle mixture into jars, leaving ¼-inch headspace. Wipe rims clean. Put lids and bands on jars. Screw tightly; don't force.

At this point, process the jellies for storage at room temperature or else let them cool. To process the jellies, place jars on a rack in a canning or other deep kettle of water at 180° on a thermometer. If needed, add hot water to cover jars 1 to 2 inches. Return water to 180°; maintain temperature, uncovered, for 10 minutes.

Lift jars from water (do not tip) and set on a towel. Let stand until cool. Press center of lids to test seal; if lids stay down, jars are sealed. Serve jelly, or store sealed jars in a cool, dark place up to 2 years. Refrigerate unsealed or opened jars up to 3 months. Makes 4 half-pints.

PER TABLESPOON: 40 calories, 0 g protein, 10 g carbohydrates, 0 g fat, 0 mg cholesterol, 0.7 mg sodium

Wine jelly, cream cheese, and crackers make an elegant snack.

More December Recipes

OTHER DECEMBER ARTICLES *feature a sage-flavored, meat-and-vegetable pie and a cranberry tart in an almond crust.*

SAGE, SAUSAGE & SPINACH PIE

Simple, satisfying flavors distinguish this vegetable and meat pie, a warming choice for a cold evening.

        Pastry for a single-crust 9-inch pie
    8   pork link sausages, about ⅔
        pound total
    1   large onion, thinly sliced
    1   tablespoon all-purpose flour
    2   teaspoons rubbed sage
    1¼ cups regular-strength beef broth
    2   medium-size cooked thin-skinned
        potatoes, peeled and cut into ¼-
        by 1½-inch pieces
    1   package (10 oz.) frozen spinach,
        thawed, moisture squeezed out
        Salt and pepper

Line a 9-inch pie pan with pastry; set aside. In an 8- to 10-inch frying pan over medium-high heat, cook sausages, turning, until lightly browned, 10 to 12 minutes. Lift out sausages with a slotted spoon and let drain on paper towels.

Add onion to fat in pan; stir often until golden, 8 to 12 minutes. Add flour and sage; stir for 30 seconds, then add broth and stir until bubbling. Remove from heat; stir in potatoes and spinach. Season to taste with salt and pepper.

Spoon spinach mixture into pie pan. Arrange sausages on top in a sunburst pattern and push slightly into spinach. (At this point, you can cool, cover, and chill up to 1 day.) Bake in a 400° oven until bubbling, about 40 minutes. Let pie cool on a rack for 10 minutes, then serve warm. Serves 6.

PER SERVING: 436 calories, 11 g protein, 29 g carbohydrates, 31 g fat, 34 mg cholesterol, 562 mg sodium

CRANBERRY TART

Sugar-poached cranberries with an almond crust are a delicate combination of crunchy-crisp pastry and tangy glazed fruit.

    4   cups (1⅓ packages, 12-oz. size)
        fresh or frozen cranberries
    1½ cups sugar
    2   teaspoons cornstarch
    ½   cup raspberry jam
        Almond crust (recipe follows)
        Candied peel (recipe follows)
        Custard sauce (optional, recipe
        follows)

Shimmering cranberry tart, enhanced with raspberry jam, makes festive holiday treat.

In a 3- to 4-quart pan over low heat, cook cranberries and sugar until cranberries are translucent and begin to collapse, about 30 minutes (45 minutes if frozen); occasionally shake pan gently to mix.

Set a strainer over a bowl. Pour berries into strainer. Let stand until cool. Return juice to pan and blend with cornstarch. Stirring, bring to rolling boil on high heat. Add jam and stir until it melts. Mix in cranberries; pour into crust.

Mound candied peel in center of tart. Let stand at room temperature until filling is firm enough to hold its shape when cut, about 2 hours, or up until next day (cover loosely when cool). Offer custard sauce to pour over individual servings. Makes 10 to 12 servings.

PER SERVING: 405 calories, 3.6 g protein, 63 g carbohydrates, 17 g fat, 76 mg cholesterol, 122 mg sodium

Almond crust. In a food processor or blender, whirl ¾ cup **unblanched almonds** until finely ground. If using a blender, transfer ground nuts to a bowl. To almonds, add 1 cup **all-purpose flour,** ¾ cup (⅜ lb.) **butter** or margarine (at room temperature), ¾ cup **sugar,** 2 **large egg yolks,** 2 teaspoons **unsweetened cocoa,** and 1½ teaspoons **ground cinnamon.** Whirl or rub with fingers until dough holds together. Press dough firmly into a 12-inch tart pan with removable bottom, making bottom crust slightly thicker than rim.

Bake in a 350° oven until browned, 20 to 30 minutes. Remove from oven and gently remove pan sides, then gently slide a spatula or knife between pan and crust to loosen crust, keeping pastry in place on pan and being careful not to break the fragile rim. Let cool.

Candied peel. Thinly pare into 1 or several long, wide strips the peel (orange part only) from 1 medium-size **orange.**

In a pan, cover orange peel generously with water. Bring to boil over high heat. Drain. Repeat. Then add to peel ½ cup **sugar** and ½ cup **water.** Boil rapidly, uncovered, until all but about ½ cup liquid remains; shake pan frequently. Lift peel from syrup and drain. If made ahead, twirl peel into a loose mound, cover, and let stand at room temperature up until next day. Discard syrup.

Custard sauce. In a pan on medium heat, warm 1½ cups **milk** until steaming. In a bowl, whisk together 3 **large egg yolks** and ¼ cup **sugar.** Whisk ½ cup milk with yolk mixture; return to pan.

Cook on low heat, stirring, until mixture thickens and coats the back of a spoon in a thin layer, about 30 minutes. Stir in 1 teaspoon **vanilla** and 3 tablespoons **orange-flavor liqueur** (optional). Cover and chill until cold, at least 2 hours, or up to 2 days. Makes 1¼ cups.

PER TABLESPOON: 31 calories, 1 g protein, 3.4 g carbohydrates, 1.4 g fat, 43 mg cholesterol, 10 mg sodium

CHERRY–CREAM CHEESE COFFEE CAKE

Cherry-dotted cake squares, topped with sugar and cinnamon, go with milk.

2 large eggs
1 cup sour cream
¾ cup sugar
2 teaspoons grated lemon peel
1½ teaspoons baking powder
½ teaspoon baking soda
1¾ cups all-purpose flour
Filling (recipe follows)
1¾ cups frozen, unsweetened pitted cherries, thawed and drained
¼ cup sugar mixed with 1½ teaspoons ground cinnamon

In a bowl, beat eggs with sour cream, sugar, lemon peel, baking powder, and soda. Stir in flour to blend.

Spread ½ of batter in a greased 9-inch-square pan. Pour filling over batter, then sprinkle with half the cherries and half of sugar-cinnamon. Drop remaining batter in small mounds over cherries, smoothing to cover as much as possible. Sprinkle evenly with remaining cherries and sugar-cinnamon.

Bake in a 350° oven until cake pulls from pan sides, 50 minutes; serve warm or cool. Serves 8.—*Robin Hause, Fort Collins, Colo.*

PER SERVING: 355 calories, 7.2 g protein, 55 g carbohydrates, 12 g fat, 127 mg cholesterol, 204 mg sodium

Filling. In a bowl, beat 1 small package (3 oz.) **cream cheese** and 1 tablespoon **sugar.** Beat in 1 **large egg.**

CAULIFLOWER & PEA CURRY

Cook onion, then add curry seasonings, yogurt, peas, and steamed cauliflower.

1 head cauliflower (about 2 lb., cored, leaves removed), cut into flowerets
1 medium-size onion, chopped
3 tablespoons butter or margarine
1½ tablespoons poppy seed
1½ tablespoons curry powder
1½ teaspoons ground ginger
1 teaspoon cumin seed
¼ teaspoon crushed dried hot red chilies
1 cup unflavored yogurt
1 package (10 oz.) frozen peas, thawed

Pour ½ inch water into a 3- to 4-quart pan. Place a steaming rack ¾ inch above water. Bring to a boil over high heat, add cauliflower, then cover and steam until cauliflower is tender-crisp to bite, 8 to 10 minutes. Drain and keep warm.

Meanwhile, in a 10- to 12-inch frying pan over medium-high heat, stir onion often in butter until brown, about 8 minutes. Add poppy seed, curry powder, ginger, cumin, and chilies; stir often for 1 minute. Stir in yogurt, then peas and cauliflower. Serves 6.—*Sarah Kirwan, Crescent City, Calif.*

PER SERVING: 150 calories, 6.5 g protein, 15 g carbohydrates, 7.9 g fat, 18 mg cholesterol, 149 mg sodium

CHILI & CHEESE TOSTADAS

Serve oven-baked tostadas with sour cream, green onions, and salsa.

4 flour tortillas (7- to 8-in. size)
1 medium-size onion, chopped
1½ cups sliced mushrooms
1 cup chopped green bell pepper
1 can (4 oz.) diced green chilies
1 teaspoon dry oregano leaves
1 tablespoon salad oil
1½ cups *each* shredded cheddar and jack cheeses
12 thin slices large firm-ripe tomato
4 large eggs

Place tortillas on 2 greased rimmed baking pans, each 10 by 15 inches. Bake in a 450° oven until golden, 5 to 10 minutes; set aside. In a 10- to 12-inch frying pan over medium-high heat, stir onion, mushrooms, bell pepper, chilies, and oregano in oil until onion is brown, 15 minutes. Leaving an inch-wide circle uncovered in center of each tortilla, spread them with onion mixture, cheddar and jack cheeses.

Return to oven and bake until cheese is barely melted, about 3 minutes. Top evenly with tomatoes, leaving centers of tortillas open; break eggs into these spots. Continue to bake until eggs are set, about 10 minutes more. Serves 4.—*Harriet Barker, Meadview, Ariz.*

PER SERVING: 588 calories, 32 g protein, 33 g carbohydrates, 37 g fat, 356 mg cholesterol, 948 mg sodium

CHINESE PLUM CHICKEN

- 4 chicken breast halves or 8 thighs (2½ lb. total), skinned
- 1 cup Oriental plum sauce; or use 1 cup plum jam plus 1 tablespoon soy sauce
- ¼ cup minced onion
- 2 tablespoons lemon juice
- 1 tablespoon soy sauce
- 1 teaspoon grated lemon peel
- ½ teaspoon *each* dry mustard and ground ginger
- ¼ teaspoon *each* pepper, liquid hot pepper seasoning, and anise seed, crushed

Place chicken in a 9- by 13-inch baking pan or other 3-quart shallow baking dish. In a bowl, stir plum sauce, onion, lemon juice, soy sauce, lemon peel, mustard, ginger, pepper, liquid hot pepper seasoning, and anise seed. Pour over chicken.

Bake chicken, uncovered, in a 400° oven until meat is no longer pink in thickest part, about 25 minutes for breasts, 35 minutes for thighs; baste chicken halfway through baking. Lift meat to a platter; spoon sauce on top. Makes 4 servings. —*Diane McPherson, Kihei, Hawaii.*

PER SERVING: 434 calories, 44 g protein, 58 g carbohydrates, 2.5 g fat, 107 mg cholesterol, 654 mg sodium

Garnish glazed chicken breasts with green onions and offer with rice.

SPICED CREAM OF PUMPKIN SOUP

- 3 medium-size (1 lb.) leeks
- ½ cup dried currants
- 2 tablespoons olive or salad oil
- 1 large carrot, thinly sliced
- 3 cups regular-strength chicken broth
- 2 cups milk
- 1 can (16 oz.) pumpkin
- ¼ teaspoon ground nutmeg
  Toasted pumpkin seeds

Trim ends and all but 2 inches green tops from leeks; remove tough outer leaves. Split leeks lengthwise; rinse well, then thinly slice. Set aside.

In a 3- to 4-quart pan over medium heat, stir currants in oil until they puff, about 3 minutes. Lift from pan with a slotted spoon; set aside. Add leeks and carrot to pan; stir often until leeks are golden, about 15 minutes. Add 1 cup broth; cover and simmer until carrot is very tender to bite, 10 minutes.

In a blender or food processor, whirl leek mixture until smooth. Return to pan with remaining broth, milk, pumpkin, and nutmeg. Stir often over medium heat until soup is steaming, about 15 minutes. Stir in currants. Add pumpkin seeds to taste. Makes 2 quarts, 6 servings. —*Paulette Rossi, Portland.*

PER SERVING: 192 calories, 5.8 g protein, 26 g carbohydrates, 8.4 g fat, 11 mg cholesterol, 84 mg sodium

Pumpkin seeds enhance this soup's flavor; carrot heightens its orange color.

HAND-PAINTED CHRISTMAS COOKIES

- 1½ cups sugar
- 1 cup (½ lb.) butter or margarine
- 2 large eggs
- 1 teaspoon almond extract
- ½ teaspoon baking soda
- 3 cups all-purpose flour
  Frosting (recipe follows)
  Undiluted food coloring

Beat sugar and butter until fluffy. Beat in eggs and almond extract. Stir soda, then flour, into butter mixture until well blended. Cover; chill until firm, 2½ hours or up to 3 days.

On a floured board, roll ¼ of dough at a time ³⁄₁₆ inch thick. Cut with cooky cutters. Place 1 inch apart on 12- by 15-inch baking sheets. Chill and reroll scraps. Bake in 350° oven until golden, 12 minutes. Cool on racks.

Dip cooky tops in frosting; let dry, 1½ to 2 hours. Using fine paintbrushes, decorate cookies with food coloring. Let dry, 15 minutes. Serve, or store airtight up to 4 days. Makes about 5½ dozen, 2¼-inch size. —*Diane Boyer, Napa, Calif.*

PER COOKY: 87 calories, 0.9 g protein, 14 g carbohydrates, 3 g fat, 16 mg cholesterol, 39 mg sodium

Frosting. In a bowl, beat 3 **large egg whites** until foamy. Beat in 1½ teaspoons **almond extract** and 3½ cups sifted **powdered sugar** until smooth.

Paint frosted cookies with food coloring; rinse brush between colors.

ALTHOUGH THE NAME SUGGESTS *the very epitome of fast food, Dennis Dean's pizza burgers are carefully crafted, high-tech products. The seasonings are added to the meat rather than to the sauce, and their judicious blending makes a memorable sandwich, one that may even cure you of shaking catsup onto your hamburger.*

If you don't have English muffins in the house, you can make an equally tasty, if flabbier, version with split and toasted hamburger buns.

PIZZA BURGERS

    1   pound ground lean beef
    1   large egg
    ¾   cup grated parmesan cheese
    ¼   cup chopped parsley
    1   small onion, finely chopped
    ¾   teaspoon *each* dry oregano leaves
        and dry basil leaves
    ½   teaspoon ground cumin
    ¼   teaspoon *each* dry rosemary leaves
        and pepper
    ¼   teaspoon fennel seed
        Salt
    4   slices (about 6 oz. total) provolone
        cheese
    4   English muffins, split and toasted
    ¼   to ½ cup prepared pizza sauce or
        spaghetti sauce

"Dennis Dean's pizza burgers are carefully crafted, high-tech products."

In a bowl, combine meat, egg, parmesan, parsley, onion, oregano, basil, cumin, rosemary, pepper, and fennel. Mix well and divide into 4 equal portions; shape each portion into a patty ¾ inch thick.

Lightly sprinkle salt into a 10- to 12-inch frying pan over medium-high heat; when pan is hot, add meat patties and cook, turning once, until done to your liking (cut to test), 10 to 12 minutes for medium-rare. Top each patty with a slice of provolone cheese. When it begins to melt, transfer patties onto English muffin halves. Offer pizza sauce to spoon onto meat to taste, then top with remaining muffin halves. Makes 4 servings.

PER SERVING: 624 calories, 44 g protein, 30 g carbohydrates, 35 g fat, 181 mg cholesterol, 1,149 mg sodium

Dennis & Dean

Albuquerque

ALAS, SOME FASTIDIOUS DINERS *just will not soil their fingers with barbecue sauce. They miss half the fun, say those less finicky—licking their fingers to emphasize the point. William Geare, one of the latter, heats his crab in a barbecue sauce. He leaves it to the diner's ingenuity to fish out the crab meat and eat it with the sauce and sourdough bread for sopping. If you eat crab this way, we recommend wearing a bib, or at least a red necktie.*

For finicky diners, we suggest a less informal alternative: serve crab and sauce separately.

CRAB WITH BARBECUE SAUCE

    2   tablespoons butter or margarine
    1   medium-size onion, finely
        chopped
    3   cloves garlic, minced or pressed
    1¾ cups or 1 can (14½ oz.) regular-
        strength chicken broth
    1   can (8 oz.) tomato sauce
    1   cup catsup
    ½   cup *each* white wine vinegar and
        firmly packed brown sugar
    3   tablespoons Worcestershire
    1   tablespoon soy sauce
    1½ teaspoons dry mustard
    1   teaspoon *each* paprika and liquid
        hot pepper seasoning
    ½   teaspoon *each* celery seed, ground
        allspice, and dry thyme leaves
    2   dry bay leaves

"If you eat crab this way, we recommend wearing a bib."

    3   large Dungeness crab (5 to 6 lb.
        total), cooked and cracked
        Sourdough bread, sliced and
        toasted, if desired

Melt butter in a 5- to 6-quart pan over medium heat. Add onion and garlic and stir often until onion is limp, about 10 minutes. Stir in the broth, tomato sauce, catsup, vinegar, sugar, Worcestershire, soy, mustard, paprika, liquid hot pepper, celery seed, allspice, thyme, and bay. Bring to a boil over high heat; reduce heat and simmer, uncovered, until reduced to 3 cups, about 45 minutes.

If you want cold crab, serve sauce in individual bowls with crab to dip into sauce. Or add crab to sauce and let simmer until crab is heated through, 5 to 10 minutes, stirring gently several times. Serve bread with crab, and also dip it into the sauce. Makes about 3 cups sauce, 5 or 6 servings.

PER SERVING: 273 calories, 19 g protein, 38 g carbohydrates, 5.7 g fat, 64 mg cholesterol, 1,307 mg sodium

W.H. Geare

Salt Lake City

WHY DOES RALPH WALKER *call his recipe Country Chicken Livers? Perhaps it is because the livers are bedded around mustard greens, which have a down-home, country sound. Although they still grow down home, where they form a principal ingredient in the celebrated pot liquor, mustard greens have also acquired a touch of big-city class, especially in Oriental restaurants. Fancy produce* markets may offer several varieties, including a reddish-purple kind and the frilly, highly attractive mizuna mustard.

Mustard greens have a strong enough flavor to stand up to smoked meats and are good choices to serve with bacon, itself a natural accompaniment to liver.

COUNTRY CHICKEN LIVERS

About 1 pound mustard greens, coarse stems removed
8 thick-cut slices bacon, cut in half
1 pound chicken livers
1 large onion, sliced
½ pound mushrooms, sliced
1 tablespoon *each* dry white wine and Worcestershire

Rinse and drain mustard greens, then cut into wide strips; set aside.

In a 10- to 12-inch frying pan, cook bacon over medium heat until crisp; lift out and drain. Discard all but 3 table-spoons of the drippings, then put 1 tablespoon of the drippings into a 5- to 6-quart pan.

Meanwhile, rinse chicken livers, pat dry, and cut in half. Add livers to drip-pings in frying pan and cook on high heat, turning as needed, until slightly browned on all sides but still pink in cen-ter (cut to test). Lift out livers and set aside.

Add onion and mushrooms to frying pan, and pour in wine and Worcester-shire. Cover and cook for 15 minutes, then uncover and continue to cook until most of the liquid evaporates, about 10 minutes longer. Return livers to pan and stir just until livers are heated through.

While onions and mushrooms cook, place the 5- to 6-quart pan on medium-high heat. Add mustard greens and stir until wilted. Mound greens in the center of a platter and keep warm. Spoon liver mixture around greens, and garnish with bacon. Makes 4 servings.

PER SERVING: 393 calories, 32 g protein, 15 g carbohydrates, 23 g fat, 523 mg cholesterol, 548 mg sodium

Lacey, Wash.

OTHER COUNTRIES HAVE TAUGHT *us* much about cooking but little about breakfast. That remains our own specialty; even the vaunted full British breakfast is only a sketchy plan upon which we, with our rich and varied agriculture and our equally rich and varied ethnic back-grounds, have built a mighty structure.

Take Bob Kerr's scrambled eggs, for instance: the British can give you eggs and bacon, of course—and the bacon might even be leaner than our own. But cheddar cheese? Not until lunch, or possibly not even until after-dinner port. And salsa? Three thousand miles away, at least. And who would trade fresh orange juice for a grilled "tomahto," or hot biscuits for toast carefully chilled in a silver rack?

BOB'S SCRAMBLED EGGS

6 large eggs
2 tablespoons milk
4 slices crisply cooked bacon, crumbled
2 tablespoons butter or margarine
¼ cup thinly sliced green onion, including tops
1 cup (4 oz.) shredded sharp cheddar cheese
Prepared salsa

In a bowl, beat eggs until whites and yolks are well combined, then stir in milk and bacon. On medium heat, melt butter in an 8- to 10-inch frying pan with an oven-proof handle. Add egg mixture and cook until barely set; with a spatula, lift cooked egg from pan so uncooked portion can flow underneath. Remove from heat and sprinkle green onion and cheese evenly over eggs.

Place pan under a broiler, 3 to 4 inches from heat. Broil, watching carefully, just until cheese melts, 1 to 1½ minutes. Add salsa to taste. Serves 2 or 3.

PER SERVING: 435 calories, 25 g protein, 2.6 g carbohydrates, 36 g fat, 617 mg cholesterol, 590 mg sodium

Modesto, Calif.

"The Western breakfast was not built in a day."

December Menus

ACTIVITIES THIS MONTH *seem to demand more time than anyone ever has. Our menus work with hectic schedules—for nutritious meals in short amounts of time.*

When holiday activities beckon, draw the family together with chili served in cheese-draped bread boats. The hollowed-out bread acts as an edible container and takes only minutes to prepare.

Soup provides a one-bowl supper another night. It's a flavorful way to combine the basic elements of a good meal.

And for a relatively simple company dinner, cook vegetables and fish in sequence in the same pan.

Hot chili in crisp bread boats makes an appealing presentation. Try the simple homemade chili—or, if you're really pushed for time, use thick canned or deli chili (you'll need about 6 cups).

Dip fresh, raw vegetables into homemade or purchased guacamole for the appetizer salad. You'll need about 1½ pounds vegetables and 1 to 1½ cups guacamole.

While the bread boats crisp in the oven, make the chili, then fill the bread with chili and heat briefly to melt the cheese. If you like, heat your favorite version of sangria to serve hot, or offer it iced.

CHILI IN BREAD BOATS

1 pound ground lean beef
1 large onion, chopped
1 clove garlic, pressed or minced
3 tablespoons chili powder
1 teaspoon ground cumin
¼ teaspoon ground allspice
1 can (16 oz.) tomato sauce
1 can (7 oz.) diced green chilies
1 can (15¼ oz.) kidney beans, drained
   Salt and pepper
6 sourdough French rolls (each about 3 by 5 in.)
6 thin slices provolone cheese (about 6 oz. total)
½ cup sour cream (optional)

In a 5- to 6-quart pan, stir ground beef over high heat until crumbly, about 5 minutes. Add onion and garlic; stir until onion is limp, about 5 minutes. Reduce heat to medium and stir in chili powder, cumin, and allspice. Stir until spices are very fragrant, 1 to 2 minutes. Add tomato sauce, green chilies, and beans. Simmer, uncovered, stirring occasionally, until sauce is thick and beans are hot, 5 to 10 minutes. Add salt and pepper to taste. (If made ahead, cool, cover, and chill until the next day. Reheat to use.)

Slice through each roll, about ½ inch from top. Lift off cut portion and hollow

Chili in bread boats, served with guacamole, vegetables, and goblets of hot sangría, are in harmony with an evening of holiday music and caroling.

out insides of base to make a shell ¼ inch thick, then pull soft bread from top to make lid about ¼ inch thick; reserve scraps for another use.

Set rolls with lids alongside on a 12- by 15-inch baking sheet. Bake in a 400° oven until golden, 10 to 12 minutes. Spoon hot chili equally into rolls. Top with bread lids. Lay a cheese slice over top of each bread boat. Return to oven and bake just until cheese melts, 2 to 3 minutes. Serve hot. Add sour cream to taste. Break off pieces of bread and eat with chili. Makes 6 servings.

PER SERVING: 658 calories, 34 g protein, 70 g carbohydrates, 27 g fat, 79 mg cholesterol, 1,742 mg sodium*
*Analysis includes undrained beans

SPEEDY SOUP SUPPER

Olives   Celery Sticks
Kale-Sausage Soup
Cornbread   Butter
Tangerines   Ginger Cookies
Zinfandel   Milk

Spicy Portuguese sausage flavors this quick soup laden with bright vegetables.

Make the cornbread using your favorite recipe or mix. While it bakes, prepare the soup. Impatient diners can nibble on celery and olives while dinner cooks.

KALE-SAUSAGE SOUP

 1 **pound linguisa sausage, cut diagonally into ¼-inch slices**
 1 **large onion, chopped**
 2 **large carrots, peeled and chopped**
10 **cups regular-strength chicken broth**
 ¾ **pound kale, tough stems trimmed Salt and pepper**

In a 5- to 6-quart pan, stir sausage over high heat until browned, 8 to 10 minutes. Drain off all but 2 tablespoons of the fat. Add onion and carrots. Cook, stirring, until onion is limp, about 5 minutes. Add broth. Cover; bring to boil. Meanwhile, rinse and drain kale, then cut crosswise into ½-inch-wide strips. Add kale to boiling broth and stir until it is limp and turns bright green, 3 to 5 minutes. Add salt and pepper to taste. Makes 6 to 8 servings.

PER SERVING: 176 calories, 9.5 g protein, 8.8 g carbohydrates, 11 g fat, 23 mg cholesterol, 440 mg sodium

Bowls brimming with spicy linguisa sausage, kale, carrots, and hot broth quickly satisfy hungry appetites.

POACHED FISH & FENNEL DINNER

Spinach Salad with Orange & Capers
Fish & Fennel
Boiled Potatoes
Lime Sorbet & Vanilla Ice Cream
Kiwi Fruit
Sauvignon Blanc or Sparkling Water

Fennel and mild white fish fillets poach briefly, in sequence, in broth and wine. This cooking liquid then becomes a sauce that complements fennel, fish, and potatoes that are boiled separately.

First wash and crisp the spinach and slice oranges for salad. Make a basic vinaigrette, adding capers to taste. Next boil potatoes as you cook tomatoes, fennel, and fish.

For dessert, top lime sorbet and vanilla ice cream with kiwi slices. Add a splash of rum, if you like.

FISH & FENNEL

 2 **bulbs fresh fennel (about 1 lb. each)**
 2 **tablespoons olive oil**
 8 **cherry tomatoes, stemmed and cut in half**
 1 **cup regular-strength chicken broth**
 ½ **cup water**
 1 **cup dry white wine**
 4 **fish fillets (about 6 oz. each), such as orange roughy or white seabass**
 1 **tablespoon cornstarch**
 2 **tablespoons whipping cream Salt and pepper**

(Continued on next page)

Trim ends and tough stems off fennel. Reserve a few feathery sprigs for garnish and chop enough of remaining sprigs to make 1 tablespoon. Cut fennel bulbs in half lengthwise.

Pour oil into a 10- to 12-inch frying pan over medium-high heat. Add tomatoes. Stir occasionally until hot, about 2 minutes. Remove from pan with a slotted spoon and place on a serving platter.

Set fennel in oil, cut side down, and cook until lightly browned, about 2 minutes. Add broth and water; cover and simmer until fennel is very tender when pierced, 25 to 30 minutes. Lift out fennel with a slotted spoon or spatula and place on platter with tomatoes; keep warm.

Add wine to pan juices and bring to a boil. Lay fish in pan, cover, and simmer until opaque in thickest part (cut to test), 4 to 6 minutes. Lift fish out of pan with slotted spatula and set alongside fennel. Pour any accumulated juices from platter into pan. Keep platter warm.

Boil pan juices on high heat, uncovered, until reduced to 1⅓ cups, about 3 minutes. In separate bowl, mix cornstarch with cream. Add to pan juices; stir until boiling. Stir in reserved chopped fennel. Pour into a bowl; offer to spoon over individual servings.

Garnish platter with fennel sprigs. Add salt and pepper to taste. Makes 4 servings.

PER SERVING: 330 calories, 27 g protein, 6 g carbohydrates, 21 g fat, 42 mg cholesterol, 209 mg sodium

Recipe Notes

Articles Index

Index of Recipe Titles

General Index

Photographers

Glenn Christiansen: 32 (bottom), 61, 76, 77, 78, 79, 80, 82, 83, 84, 85, 87, 141, 163 (top left), 164 (right), 275. **Peter Christiansen:** 9, 16, 17, 24, 42, 52, 53 (right), 64, 75, 88, 89, 97, 99, 136, 137, 139, 146, 147, 148, 149, 152, 161, 162, 163 (bottom left), 166, 167, 176, 179, 182, 183, 184, 185, 188, 189, 190 (top left), 199, 200, 207, 209, 230, 231, 232, 233, 235, 238, 239, 244, 245, 247, 248, 249, 250, 256, 257, 261, 262, 265, 269, 278, 279, 280, 282, 288, 289, 298, 299. **David Franzen:** 32 (top). **Renee Lynn:** 125, 127 (bottom). **Norman A. Plate:** 4, 13, 14, 29, 33, 51, 53 (left), 56, 57, 59, 65, 101, 108, 109, 122, 123, 126, 127 (top), 130 (right), 151, 177, 196, 197, 205, 206, 208, 210, 211 (bottom left), 216, 217, 220, 221, 222, 253, 254, 255, 264, 267, 268, 274, 284, 285. **Bill Ross:** 28. **Chad Slattery:** 55. **David Stubbs:** 8, 27, 30, 94, 95, 260. **Darrow M. Watt:** 1, 7, 10, 11, 15, 18, 34, 35, 36, 37, 38, 39, 41, 43, 48, 49, 60, 62, 63, 72, 73, 90, 91, 93, 96, 98, 100, 111, 112, 113, 119, 121, 124, 128, 129, 130 (left), 131, 142, 143, 144, 150, 153, 158, 159, 164, 165, 171, 180, 181, 186, 187, 190 (bottom left), 190 (right), 191, 211 (top right), 219, 224, 225, 226, 227, 228, 229, 236, 237, 259, 263, 266, 277, 283, 286, 290, 291, 292, 293. **Tom Wyatt:** 223.